HENRY JAMES

LETTERS

Volume IV
1895–1916

Henry James with Molly Hooper Warner (Mrs. Roger S. Warner), a niece of Henry Adams, on the flats at Rye, 1906

HENRY JAMES

LETTERS

Edited by

Leon Edel

Volume IV

1895–1916

The Belknap Press
of
Harvard University Press
Cambridge, Massachusetts
London, England

1984

Library of Congress Cataloging in Publication Data
James, Henry, 1843–1916.
Letters.
Includes bibliographical references and indexes.
CONTENTS: v. 1.   1843–1875.—v. 2.   1875–1883.—[etc.]
—v. 4.   1895–1916.
1. James, Henry, 1843–1916—Correspondence.
2. Authors, American—19th century—Correspondence.
I. Edel, Leon, 1907–   . II. Title.
PS2123.A42   1974   813'.4   74–77181
ISBN 0–674–38780–5
ISBN 0–674–38783–X (v. 4)

Acknowledgments

The letters drawn from the last twenty years of Henry James's life come from a diversity of sources. As before, Ms stands for the holograph letter and Ts for typescript. "Ms Unknown" means that a copy of the letter exists but that I have not seen the original and may not know its whereabouts. Following are the institutions and collections whose documents I have used and to which I wish to express my thanks:

American Academy–Institute of Arts and Letters, New York
Archives of American Art, Washington
Barrett—C. Waller Barrett Collection, University of Virginia
Basel—University of Basel, Switzerland
Berg—Henry W. and Albert A. Berg Collection of English and American Literature, New York Public Library, Astor, Lenox, and Tilden Foundations
Bodleian—Bodleian Library, Oxford
British Library—formerly British Museum
Chester—Chester Public Records Office, U.K.
Chicago—Joseph Regenstein Library, University of Chicago
Colby—Colby College Library, Waterville, Maine
Columbia—Butler Library, Columbia University
Congress—Library of Congress
Countway—Francis A. Countway Library of Medicine, Boston
Dorset County Museum, Dorchester, U.K.
Duke—Duke University Library, Durham, N.C.
Gardner—Isabella Stewart Gardner Museum, Boston
Glasgow—University of Glasgow Library
Harvard—Houghton Library, Harvard University
Hillstead—Hillstead Museum, Farmington, Connecticut
Hopkins—Milton S. Eisenhower Library, Johns Hopkins University

Hove—Central Library, Hove, Brighton, U.K.
Huntington—Henry E. Huntington Library, San Marino,
 California
King's College Library, Cambridge, U.K.
Leeds—Brotherton Library, University of Leeds
Lubbock—Lubbock typescripts in Houghton Library, Harvard
Mass. Historical—Massachusetts Historical Society, Boston
Mellon—Mellon Gallery, Washington
Morgan—Pierpont Morgan Library, New York
NYPL—Manuscript Division, New York Public Library, Astor,
 Lenox, and Tilden Foundations
N.Y. Historical—New-York Historical Society
Penn. State—Pattee Library, Pennsylvania State University
Princeton—Firestone Library, Princeton University
Scotland—National Library of Scotland
Tate—Tate Gallery, London
Texas—Humanities Research Center, University of Texas at
 Austin
Vaux—Robertson James Archive, Berkeley, California
Yale—Beinecke Rare Book and Manuscript Library, Yale
 University

For manuscripts designated as private, I am indebted to General
Daille, Lady Buxton, Lady Iddesleigh, John James, Rev. H. P. Kingdon, Mrs. C. F. Kingdon, Frederica and Harold M. Landon, Dr. John
A. P. Millet, Anita Leslie, Edward J. Naumberg, Jr., J. M. and Dorothy De Navarro, Count Bernard Rucellai, the Marchesa Nannina
Fossi, and Dr. John Waterlow.
My thanks to the trustees and librarians of many of the institu-
tions have already been expressed in the earlier volumes. I wish to
thank once again the late John James and the present holder of the
copyrights, Alexander R. James. I had help with the Wharton and
Pinker letters from David E. Schoonover and Donald Gallup at the
Beinecke Library at Yale and from Aldo R. Cupo of the Yale Univer-
sity Library staff. I also wish to thank Robert Rosenthal of the
Joseph Regenstein Library, University of Chicago. The Bollingen
Foundation, during 1959–1961, generously provided a grant for the
copying of many of the letters.
G. Bernard Shaw and Harley Granville Barker long ago gave

me assistance that yielded some of the materials I have used. In Cambridge and in Paris I talked with Gaillard T. Lapsley and with Edith Wharton and W. Morton Fullerton, not knowing in the 1930s that our meetings would throw light on some of the materials published here.

Professor Lyall H. Powers of the University of Michigan read the manuscript and gave me valuable editorial assistance; Marjorie Edel helped with both the manuscript and the proofs; Professor Kathleen Falvey of the University of Hawaii clarified James's Italian. Dr. Malashri Lal of Jesus and Mary College in New Delhi, during a sojourn in Honolulu, assisted in the transcription of the letters to Edith Wharton and the annotation of these and other letters. I wish to thank also Henry James Vaux, who owns the Robertson James papers, to which I had access during the lifetime of his mother, Mary James Vaux; and Dr. Gordon N. Ray, with whom I collaborated in the editing of the James-Wells letters. I recall with pleasure the assistance of other scholars and collectors, among them Sir Rupert Hart-Davis, Louis S. Auchincloss, Adeline Tintner, the late Donald G. Brien, Mrs. John Hall Wheelock, Dr. Nathan G. Hale, Jr., James Gilvarry, Michael Millgate, Hugo R. Vickers, Francis Steegmuller, Ann L. McLaughlin, Victor Luftig, and Marc Simpson. Roger Warner generously supplied the unpublished photograph of his grandmother Molly Hooper Warner with Henry James at Rye, and the late Alvin Langdon Coburn (whose photographs provided frontispieces for the New York Edition) made available some of the illustrations used here as well as his reminiscences of the novelist.

L.E.

Contents

Illustrations

Introduction

The letters of Henry James's last twenty years reveal a considerable alteration in his personality. He is looser, less formal, less distant; he writes with greater candor and with more emotional freedom. He has at last opened himself up to the physical things of life—and has fallen in love. We perceive an artist who grows less rigid and more experimental in spite of his aging. And in his final letters he is face to face with the time of terminations.

I

Since letters offer only fragments of a life, the interstices in this gathering of Henry James's late correspondence need to be filled in. Anyone reading the letters would not know, for example, that James was deeply depressed after his failure in the theatre; and there is little evidence of this in his notebooks. He kept himself busy, and he kept writing; it is what he wrote that is most revelatory. He had rarely written about children in his earlier works; but now they become the subject of both novel and tale. To this period belongs his only murder novel, *The Other House*, in which a baby is the victim; and the celebrated "The Turn of the Screw," a drama of two children entrusted to a paranoid governess. The works reflect a period of inner nightmare in the life of the author. Corollary stories deal with writers who are "too good" for their public. Most significant of all, we find in these works a surfacing of sexuality, which James had kept so carefully submerged.

James had always been so straitlaced and puritanical about sex that some may be surprised to read, through his cautious verbalizations, a new consciousness of humans as physical beings. In his youth he had loved his cousin Minny Temple; but that love had seen her as ethereal, and when she died young he had turned her into an icon, a goddess of the mind. He tended to look away from women as physical entities. He grew to be one of the "poor sensitive gentlemen" about whom he wrote many tales. Passion was feared. Women were feared—unless they were safe and elderly, or safe and married. He was comfortable with young girls, like "Daisy Miller" from Schenectady, New York. Her dilemma as a flirt was told in the characteristic way in which James dealt with sex: through "manners" and societal taboos. Now, however, rendered vulnerable by aging, his failures in the theatre, and his depressed state, James began to explore psychologically disturbed young adults and tormented children and their sexual curiosity. In short, he turned back to his own childhood and adolescence. His stories are filled with an intense wish to know what goes on in adult bedrooms. Edmund Wilson, alone among critics, noticed these libidinal surfacings, and wrote: "Now sex *does* appear in his work—even becoming a kind of obsession—in a queer and left-handed way." It was in part queer and left-handed because James was trying to show the sexual curiosity of children—little Maisie, who is divided between her divorced parents and is in the very center of their new couplings; the unnamed adolescent girl of "In the Cage," who works as a postal clerk and tries to decipher, in the Mayfair telegrams she handles, the liaisons of her customers; the puzzled elderly man who watches young girls growing up in *The Awkward Age*; and the governess in "The Turn of the Screw," intent upon unraveling the past of her predecessors, a governess and a valet. The governess's imagination creates a frightening world for the little boy and girl entrusted to her care, and the little boy dies after one of her desperate cross-examinations. And finally, in *The Sacred Fount*, at the turn of the century, James places an obsessed adult in the midst of a weekend party; he is a psychological voyeur. Voyeurism, it is suggested, is honorable if one sticks to "psychological evidence." "What's ignoble," one character says, "is the detective and the keyhole." Rebecca West caricatured this novel long ago: "a week-end visitor spends more intellectual force than Kant can have used on *The Critique of Pure Reason* in an unsuccessful attempt to discover whether there exists between certain of his fellow-guests a relationship not more interesting among these vacuous people than it is among sparrows."

We see, in these writings of the transition period between James's plays and his late novels, an extraordinary artist, master of his craft, sophisticated, cosmopolitan, in every way a "man of the world," who yet is somehow deficient in sexual experience. From all appearances, James had never made love either to a woman or to a man. So much Victorian sex was underground that one wonders whether James had any knowledge of physical relations beyond what he had read in French novels and other works. His fiction of the late 1890s, however, breaks through the old discretions. Edmund Wilson remarks that "there are plenty of love affairs now and plenty of irregular relationships—illicit appetites, maleficent passions, now provide the chief interest"; but, he adds, "they are invariably seen from a distance."

James himself might have replied that he had to keep distance to make his adolescents credible. But there is his own distance as well: his vision is limited because of his limited experience, and therefore we have his continuing curiosity. The Oscar Wilde case had brought a sexual upheaval to British society; and beyond the homosexual underground there was considerably more freedom in the talk of the drawing rooms. This is indeed the subject of *The Awkward Age*—James's concern with "the liberal firesides beyond the wide glow of which, in comparative dimness, female adolescence hovered and waited." He was himself like his female adolescents, hovering and testing forbidden subjects, old drawing-room reticences. To be sure, he had read Maupassant, Flaubert, the Goncourts, and all the ribald French writings of an earlier time: he had a finely bound copy of the *Contes drôlatiques* in his library. But to know sex only in print is to know it entirely as verbal experience, dissociated from sensual realities. James's condition was common enough among a certain class of staid Victorians—whether in London or Boston. In adolescence he had been taken abroad: he had wandered in the Louvre with the other James children instead of playing with boys and girls of his own age and learning the boyhood language of sex. And when he returned to America it was to the gentility of Newport and the private school of a clergyman. He had ended up with a personal aloofness which probably shut him into auto-eroticism. He lived with his private sexual life as if he were an anchorite: he attained fame as one of the "monks" of literature who wrote about subjects other than sex—the struggle for power, the plight of the artist, the fate of innocent Americans emerging from a kind of Eden and finding themselves face to face with "wicked" Europeans. He wrote about his own innocence.

Certainly James is, as Edmund Wilson saw, "obsessed" by sex in these writings of his middle age; he is as curious as any young adult might be about the couplings going on around him. Max Beerbohm caught this aspect in one of his lively caricatures: the figure of the elderly novelist kneeling in a hotel corridor and studying two pairs of shoes, those of a woman and a man, beside a locked door. In *The Sacred Fount* James spoke of "a rage of wonderment." The wonderment was decidedly his. And the book showed he was trying at last to grow up sexually, to ripen that side of his nature, which had been retarded in the very midst of his maturities for more than five decades.

In this period, as the new century approaches, James seems to swim in a sea of erotic promise. Much later, however, he would write to a woman friend how happy he was to have left behind the period "of the Passions"—and he added, "the terrible passions." He would liken the calm he felt to "the great Atlantic liner alongside the wharf after the awful days out in the open."

It was in Italy, where James went in 1899 after finishing *The Awkward Age,* that his vulnerable self finally experienced the sensations of love, the body's insistence on active tenderness. He had taken no holiday for five years: his new habit of dictating directly to a typist had pinned him to his Garden Room in Rye. Italy had always been a land of sensual delight: in his youth he had characterized it as "a dishevelled nymph." In Rome, in the spring of 1899, the nymph materialized as a young American sculptor, of Norwegian descent, blond, strong, with vigorous hands that molded clay and carved statues—not very good statues, but that mattered little to Henry James. Hendrik Andersen reminded James of the time when he himself was young and had created a fictional sculptor in this very city whom he named Roderick Hudson; he had endowed Roderick with so many tantrums of passion that he destroyed himself after falling in love. James saw in Andersen a reflection of his own early inventions—a reflection of himself as creator in his own youth. Roderick had descanted on doing statues of Beauty, Wisdom, Power, Genius, Daring—and even a magnificent statue representing America! Andersen talked of all the great statues he was planning. James's letters to Andersen have survived. We do not have Andersen's, but what we know of the young man is that he was drawn to James not so much by affection as by the thought that the novelist might help him with his career. The drama of their encounter was that of an aging novelist who was living out certain submerged adolescent feelings and divesting himself of puritanical wrappings. The emotions are in his letters to Andersen, and they are the emotions of first love. James's copy of the English translation of Turgenev's novel *First Love* has a pencil mark opposite the sentence "Youth, youth, little dost thou care for anything!" We cannot know when he drew his pencil line, but the exclamation could have belonged to this time and to this new relationship. James purchased one of Andersen's lifeless busts—that of a charming young Italian noble, the Conte Bevilacqua—and invited the young sculptor to Lamb House. Andersen came: he thought James would publicize him and his work. They spent a weekend which the novelist long remembered. His letters tell of his subsequent anguish: the pain of absence, the ache of separation, the feeling that Andersen, who is always in Rome, is too aloof as he leads his own life in the imperial city. James owned a studio in Rye, which had come to him with Lamb House. He had a fantasy that Andersen might live and work in it; he urged him to come. But Andersen stayed away. And James did not write about him; he was not in the habit of advancing young careers. Gradually the love turned to bitterness. There is an underlying destructive rage some years later as James tells Andersen he sheds tears at his wasted efforts and grandiose dreams to build a "world city" filled with fountains and nudity. He deplores Andersen's failure to distinguish, in his heavy athletic statues, between the feminine and the masculine. James now pays close attention to the physical. He criticizes Andersen's statue of lovers kissing because the hands are not sufficiently "participant" in the lovemaking. He uses words hitherto absent from his epistolary vocabulary—phallus, penis, bottom, *derrière*. And between the lines of what he writes we read a sense of betrayal. There is too much megalomania in Andersen's dream city. James's object of affection has proved unworthy of him.

But his depression began to lift after the meeting in Rome. And presently the novelist, emerging from his gloom (and from behind the beard he has worn for a quarter of a century), reaches out to younger male friends: he wants to enlarge his newfound world of the affections, physical and emotional. He is more "easy" with himself and with his friends. He starts renewing old offers of hospitality to young Morton Fullerton, who lives among the flesh-pots of Paris; to Howard Sturgis, who lives at Qu'Acre near Windsor with his boyfriend known as "The Babe"; to the don of Eton and Cambridge, A. C. Benson; to young men arriving with letters of introduction, like Gaillard Lapsley, who brings a note from Mrs. Jack Gardner. James had known Morton Fullerton for a decade and had spent pleasant hours with him in Paris. He had been "my dear Fullerton" in the earlier letters. He is now "dearest boy." There are many notes of intimacy in James's letters to Sturgis, but he is more aloof with Benson—a deeply depressed individual and a son of the Archbishop of Canterbury. Later Logan Pearsall Smith will make overtures to James; but the novelist backs away from Smith's anecdotal personality. Shortly after his encounter with Andersen, when James was writing *The Sacred Fount*, he became friends with Stephen Crane and his mistress Cora. Cora had once kept a brothel called the "Hotel de Dream" in Florida. Ten years earlier James might have held back stiffly from her and her open ways. But now he is neighborly; he goes to their parties, munches Cora's doughnuts, and contributes money to help the illegitimate children of the American novelist Harold Frederic, recently dead of a coronary. This takes place in the context of the last of James's novels of bewilderment. He can now write *The Ambassadors*, with its theme of "live all you can," and *The Wings of the Dove*, in which Merton Densher, a recreation of Morton Fullerton, actually goes to bed with the woman he loves. Once his armor is breached, James can handle the sensuous and the physical, but he still wears the soft gloves of the genteel tradition and of his personal prudence.

Relations between man and woman in James's early stories were always depicted as draining one or the other partner. This familiar fantasy of sexual depletion may have been a part of James's fear of women. Relations with young men seem now to be rejuvenating. The letters to Andersen (pathetic and pleading), to thirty-year-old Jocelyn Persse (lively and eager), and to a very young Hugh Walpole (paternal and avuncular) were written during the Edwardian decade. They reflect an elderly hunger for experience. James is too old for frolics in London, but he wants his young friends to bring him social gossip so that he can frolic vicariously. They have become mirrors of his lost youth. "Believe it or not," Hugh Walpole told Rupert Hart-Davis about Persse, "Henry James was deeply in love with him." The Persse letters, however, are more cautious—the letters of two individuals who meet often and do not have to correspond about their relationship. We know that Persse, in his about-town life, was also busy with affairs of the heart, and in the end he married a woman to whom James, in the letters, coyly refers as "passionate Peebles." James described Persse as possessing "a constituted *aura* of fine gold and rose-colour." Hugh Walpole, who was a bit jealous and also found Persse rather boring, once asked James what "subjects in common" they shared in their talk. James replied, "one gets on with him in a way without them, and says to one's self, I think, that if he doesn't mind, why should one either?" Persse's spelling was faulty and James corrected him; he was not literary and read very little; he liked society and country visits, horse races, cigars and good claret. Thirty years after this time, when I corresponded with him, he described his visits with James to the Middlesex Music Hall and how much amusement they found there. "The primitive audience appealed to him," Persse wrote. And he remarked about himself, "Why he liked me so much I cannot say." James's phrase about the "aura of fine gold and rose-colour" provides an answer to this question.

Did James act out the physical promptings of sex? We know that in public he was always affectionate with both men and women— the pat on the back, the embracing hug, the firm grasp of the hand and arm, and the formal salon-kiss of accolade. James once astonished Bernard Shaw, who came to call on him in Lamb House, by throwing his arms about him and kissing him on each cheek, as if he were awarding him the legion of honor. Shaw told me this three decades later, his eyes twinkling and in his voice a mixture of wonder and I think ancient amazement, for he himself was a distancing man who put a wall of words between himself and people he met. Other reminiscences testify to James's natural affection. His nephew Billy James remembered that his uncle one day said to him, as he was taking leave of his brother Harry, "You must not be ashamed to express natural affection. I will look away and you can embrace and kiss your brother."

Somerset Maugham used to relate that Hugh Walpole once offered himself to the Master and James recoiled with "I can't, I can't, I *can't.*" That James was probably ambivalent about sex, even after he had recognized his libidinal feelings, seems clear from his novels. He had for too long made himself a master of reticences and avoidances and hidden certain emotions in the wrappings of "style." His narrator admits in *The Sacred Fount:* "It would have been almost as embarrassing to have had to tell them how little experience I had had in fact as to have had to tell them how much I had had in fancy." This confession is repeated in various ways in *The Ambassadors.* Middle-aged Lambert Strether talks of "too late, too late" and wonders why he has not allowed himself at least an "illusion of freedom." Throughout the novel Strether closes his eyes to what every other character knows—that Chad is having an affair with Madame de Vionnet. Like James, before his late awakening, Strether turns his eyes toward beauty, delicacies of behavior, the moods of Paris, with no awareness of the murmurs of sexual life—the libidinal content—within all that he cherishes, including the rich depths of Madame de Vionnet herself.

When Strether discovers that Chad and Madame de Vionnet do such common things as sleep together in country inns, he feels "sold." He has glorified the two as products of a high civilization, but in that civilization bedding seems not to exist for him. At the end he talks of his "New England conscience." It seems to tell him he cannot allow himself any liberties with his new discoveries. The conditioning of a lifetime can be powerful.

At this distance it is perhaps less important to know the exact form James's psychosexual life took than to know that he was open to feeling. He could now reach out to his younger friends, be loving and tender and embracing. Old inhibitions, old cautions had in part given way to what he himself called "the imagination of loving."

We may find, in the changes that occurred in James, the motivation for his undertaking to rewrite his early novels. There were words, there were formulations, that betrayed his younger innocence. Christopher Newman's heavy-handed love scenes in *The American* showed James's difficulty in demonstrating love for a woman. The old terms had to be altered, and so did Isabel Archer's feelings when she receives the kiss he could now call blinding at the end of *The Portrait of a Lady.* There were also pages about Osmond's bachelorhood that perhaps might be read wrongly in later years, and James struck them from the book. One sees that, over and above matters of style and "art," James wanted to delete his immaturities and emotional blurrings. All his revisions are in the service of new clarity; he finds more precise language and better imagery. The period he spent between 1905 and 1910 setting his works in order for the New York Edition suggests much more than a Flaubertian desire for literary perfection. He was inserting present modes of feeling into his past. With the changes in his life it was necessary to make changes in his art.

II

Edith Wharton and Henry James met in 1904 when he was finishing *The Golden Bowl* and planning his journey to the United States. Theirs was a friendship unique in the annals of American literature. We may read a part of that history in the 177 letters James wrote to her during the next eleven years, from which I have made a generous selection. As with most of his correspondents, he destroyed the letters she wrote him in the naive belief that others sought privacy as intensely as he did. But usually his letters were kept; thus he survives as master of his posthumous scene while the roles of his friends, and the exact terms of relationship, must be extrapolated from the Master's letters.

Mrs. Wharton had long seen James as an example of what an American artist could achieve when freed from provincialism and imbued with a gift of candor about his own people. James's literary inventions and techniques were of secondary interest to her. She was always a conventional writer and interested above all in the story she had to tell. Critics seeing resemblances between the two writers usually pointed to their having "Old New York" in common. But they belonged to two different periods of Manhattan's history: James knew it as a child in the forties and fifties and later in the seventies; Mrs. Wharton's New York was of the eighties and nineties, decades James had spent in Europe.

Edith Wharton, a woman of wealth, embodied for James the spirit and affluence of a new America that had not been his. He studied her and her world closely: she tied together many loose ends, she helped him bridge the gap of his expatriation. She especially threw open for James the doorway into the time of "big money." James's earlier men of wealth, like Christopher Newman, made their "pile" in various ways; Newman manufactured washtubs. The new men of wealth were in the modern sense "corporate." They dealt in coal mines and railways, cattle and furs and vast acreage, whole new

xxi

territories of the dissolving frontiers. The scale of wealth was beyond anything James had imagined. His final millionaire in *The Golden Bowl*, Adam Verver, is created out of the Whartonian world, which he was able to see at first hand during his 1904–1905 journey through the United States.

Like Henry James, Edith Wharton had passed through certain treacherous years during which she had to free herself from the shibboleths of her society. The two writers had first exchanged letters after she sent him her early work. James promptly urged her to "do the American subject" she seemed so in possession of, rather than to write factitious historical romances like the big novel with which she began her career. He was majestic, imperial, lawgiving. "Profit," he proclaimed, "by my awful example of exile and ignorance." The "ignorance" referred to his having lived abroad for twenty years, remote from the changing America. Mrs. Wharton took James's advice. She wrote *The House of Mirth* out of the direct experience of her New York and her own dilemma, and she became famous. She brought to James his missing decades. She also brought the example of herself, an accomplished and cultivated social being who wrote well, knew languages, and had deep roots in her society. She probably sharpened his growing desire to see the new America for himself. This was translated into action late in 1904. That autumn he stood on the Jersey shore and looked across the stretch of water at a new skyline, at buildings taller than any he had seen before.

Mrs. Wharton would say that James's friendship was "the pride and honour" of her life. During her last five years, when I had some talk with her, she said to me, "the man was greater than his works—and that's saying a great deal." I think she placed James among the few men who fulfilled a very particular role in her crowded life. She belonged to an age in which women, however free they felt (and even when they had a heritage of wealth as she did), still needed the approval and sanction, the encouragement and praise, of male friends. She moved usually in a masculine world. The role of adviser, even sometime lover, was accorded to her friend Walter Van Rensselaer Berry. Henry James played a similar, though more paternal, role. To other friends he described Mrs. Wharton as a "facilitated" and "pampered" woman. He was always candid; he mingled admiration with hesitation before her driving energies and the cleverness of her novels and stories. He saw that she had the blind spots of some who possess wealth; they simply are unaware of certain human needs, however much they may sympathize with the less privileged. Mrs. Wharton knew how ambivalent James felt about her. She could read his feelings in the stories he wrote about her—particularly in "The Velvet Glove" and "Crapy Cornelia," James's final tales, which describe women closely modeled on Edith Wharton.

And then, in one of those coincidences that we perhaps find more often in fiction than in life, Edith Wharton and James's friend of more than a dozen years, Morton Fullerton, had an affair. It was almost as if James had foretold it in *The Wings of the Dove,* in the love story of Kate Croy and Merton Densher. James had a way of inventing people before he met them. He had invented Hendrik Andersen in *Roderick Hudson,* and he invented in some degree this liaison between the powerful Edith and her passive-aggressive lover, the gallicized American. The latter's effect on Mrs. Wharton was sufficiently benign and even more liberating than the effect of the sculptor on James. The New York heiress had reached her forties a demivirgin. She and her Bostonian husband, Teddy Wharton, had slept in separate bedrooms almost from the first. (To sleep in the same room with her husband gave Mrs. Wharton allergies.) James when he first met Mrs. Wharton referred several times to her "dryness," as if he sensed that her passions and her capacity for love had been blocked at their source. She had suffered illnesses during her marriage, and she escaped into her writing from her dessicated life. Fullerton, who was very much a man of the world (as James knew), proved an ideal lover. He gave Edith Wharton a new interest, and with skill, tact, and gentleness opened her chaste eyes to the sensations of her body. It was a moment of exquisite discovery, one might say a moment of rebirth for the elegant and formidable lady. Her "love-diary" of this time tells us eloquently the confusions of feeling and the exhilarations she experienced. She had written and would write about what her society called "illicit love," but now she knew at first hand its deeper soundings.

Fullerton proved ardent and engaging. He had had long experience. He had flirted with homosexual love and had been an intimate of Lord Ronald Gower, the political and artistic British homosexual who, unlike his friend Oscar Wilde, had never been a subject of scandal; and had had a prolonged love affair with the aristocratic Margaret Brooke (also a friend of James's), the consort of the "white rajah" of Sarawak. He also had in his past an actress wife, who had borne him a daughter and from whom he was divorced; and an old-time Parisian mistress, who would blackmail him. This New England Don Juan had charm, suavity, and (like the Don) ease in sliding over principles of conduct and morality. Apparently both Mrs. Wharton and Fullerton had a sense of reality and an ability to take the measure of their liaison. It lasted for about three years, and they remained friends. A memory comes to me of my asking one day at the Pavillon Colombe whether Mrs. Wharton would show me the volumes Henry James had inscribed to her. She escorted me to a shelf full of Jamesian fiction in her library, and she pulled down volume after volume. Each was inscribed by James with great affection to Morton Fullerton. Mrs. Wharton smiled, I thought a bit sheepishly, and with a touch too of some bewilderment as if she was searching her memory. "My inscribed copies must be at Hyères" (her Mediterranean home). "You will have to come and see them there. I think Mr. Fullerton must have left these with me some time ago."

Edith Wharton's liberation from her old frame of life, as she began to take Europe in her stride, occurred at the same time that James was experiencing his own liberation; their separate discovery of the libido's life-giving force had in it, for both, a delayed fulfillment of adolescence—a release from a vestigial innocence. Mrs. Wharton was in her forties, James in his sixties.

James had met Fullerton as long ago as 1890 when, freshly graduated from Harvard, he came abroad and moved into London with the ease and assurance that were so much a part of his character. He had no trouble, though an American, in obtaining a position on the London *Times*, and his fluency in French soon got him dispatched to that paper's Paris bureau. Alice James noted in her diary on 19 April 1891 (apparently quoting her brother's gossip): "The ascendency of the American is emphasized by the fact that a young man from Cambridgeport, I believe named Fullerton, not more than twenty-five, was sub-editor of the *Times* and now is sent to Paris to undermine Blowitz." Henri de Blowitz was the head of the *Times* bureau in the French capital. Morton did not undermine him. Like Merton Densher, he was not capable of that kind of aggression. He worked conscientiously, wrote flowery Jamesian dispatches, and gave himself over to the pleasures of Paris. James was from the first much intrigued by him, and they met regularly whenever James crossed the channel.

In middle age Fullerton became an editorial writer for *Le Figaro* and that newspaper's specialist in American politics. It was at the *Figaro*, in the Rond Point des Champs Elysées, that I called on him late in 1929—I was to see him two more times, once during the second war, when he was 80. In 1929 he was a handsome, heavy man working in a comfortable office. He wore striped trousers and what looked like a frock coat; his large mustaches were waxed; a fresh flower reposed in his buttonhole. He had the air of a diplomat, not a journalist, and the manner of an old-time masher. He greeted me from behind his Empire desk, shook my hand warmly, talked of Henry James with a pleasant touch of nostalgia in his sophisticated voice. I had gone to see him about James's playwriting years. He was informed but imprecise. He remembered James at the Hotel Westminster when he was writing one of his plays; they had gone to boulevard theatres together and sat late into the night at boulevard cafes. He mentioned a letter James wrote to him after the failure of *Guy Domville* in which the Master had taken stock of his failure. He promised to find it for me—and did fifteen years later (see *Letters* III, 510). He had many lines of verse by heart, and liked to complete a statement with a poetic flourish: verse filled the same decorative purpose for him as the flower in his buttonhole. He played the role of an *homme de coeur* and played it to perfection. I had a feeling in his generalities and vaguenesses that he was throwing fine dust in my eyes, creating a haze out of his past in which nothing was sharp or clear; everything was soft and impressionistic.

The priapean New Englander, during his years abroad, developed many fanciful and delicate gestures. His very casualness, his air of romantic ease, the mask of the *bon viveur*, of yielding himself to the moods of life and love, must have fascinated and endeared him, especially in his younger years, to both Henry James and Edith Wharton. They knew how talented he was; they accepted his masks and his redundancies. What they deplored was the ease with which he slipped out of situations of his own making—that and his gift of indolence alongside his routine at the newspaper office. Almost every sentence James writes about Densher in *The Wings of the Dove* could be said to describe Fullerton, as, for example, "he was too credulous for diplomacy, or perhaps even for science, while he was perhaps at the same time too much in his mere senses for poetry and yet too little in them for art. You would have got fairly near him by making out in his eyes the potential recognition of ideas; but you would have quite fallen away again on the question of the ideas themselves. The difficulty with Densher was that he looked vague without looking weak—idle without looking empty." Fullerton must have recognized himself, for he asked James in his characteristically circuitous way whether a certain journalist named Cook had not been Densher's original. (James's offhand reply, dated 7 November 1902, appears in this volume.)

The Edwardian years were for James a time in which life offered new interests and varnished over the world he had painted in manners rather than in passions. And then, Mrs. Wharton introduced him into the early adventures of motoring. He discovered with delight how space and time could be telescoped while he sat motionless, wearing goggles, in Edith's open-top Panhard and looked at scenes that moved and vanished as in the newly invented cinematograph. Mrs. Wharton speeded up James's leisurely life in this way, gave it a new pulse as well as fresh materials for stories. She swept him around the eastern seaboard of the United States in late 1904 and early 1905; she took him on a new "little tour" of France. They motored also in England, for Mrs. Wharton took her car with her wherever she traveled, with her devoted chauffeur, Charles Cook, at the wheel. We find James continually reaching for hyperbole to describe the restless shuttle-woman, who crossed the Atlantic so often and had a "chariot of fire" on land. She becomes "the Angel of Devastation"—devastation of his time, his work, his elderly routines, his solitude. Sometimes he changes it to "Angel of Desolation." It depended on how he felt when she descended upon Lamb House. She became also Stravinsky's "Firebird," for she had some of the allegresse of a toe dancer and the ability to banish loneliness and endow James with a sense of her power. When she was distant, in America, she was simply "The Lady of Lenox" —where her chateau-like residence, The Mount, had been built. The Mount proved a harbor of refuge for Henry James when he wanted to escape the pavements and the new skyscrapers of New York and the importunities of his public. At The Mount he paced the carpet, smoked cigarettes, exchanged light talk with Walter Berry or Howard Sturgis, or read Walt Whitman aloud to them—for in his old age James had made his peace with Walt. By degrees he came to feel himself very much at home in this self-governing world of wealth and comfort—wealth on a scale he had never known, he who had always lived on a modest plane of bourgeois amenity. When he motored with Mrs. Wharton in France he complained in his letters that he had to stay at luxury hotels and mentioned that one's rich friends could be very costly. The gatherings at The Mount were duplicated in Sturgis's house, Qu'Acre. The new friends were joined by Gaillard (pronounced and sometimes spelled Gilliard) Lapsley, a young historian who had been elevated to a Fellowship at Trinity College in Cambridge. When I called on Lapsley at Trinity many years later, he lived in comfortable mahogany-furnished rooms. Large photographs of Edith Wharton and Henry James were placed discreetly among the furnishings. Lapsley tended to be formal, solemn, slow-paced in his talk, and he was very protective of Henry James. He disapproved of my saying that James had had "misadventures" in the theatre—doubtless my word was a bit clumsy, but what struck me was that it evoked so much caution. Lapsley was a historian and a don, used to handling young word-stumbling students. In still later years, Edith Wharton would telephone me at my apartment in Paris, usually at some early morning hour. Her old tired voice would come to life as she invited me to lunch (she would send her car)—on one occasion because Gilliard had just arrived "and we will spark each other for you about Henry James." She organized the lunch as if it was a great lark.

In this way I had a backward glimpse into James's expatriate world, the *grand monde* long after its old grandeur had passed—for we were in the era of Franklin Delano Roosevelt (of whom Mrs. Wharton and Lapsley strongly disapproved). Teddy Roosevelt had been Edith Wharton's friend, and she knew the ways of the old White House. I could see how happy she was to have the past revived by Lapsley's presence. She made Lapsley her literary executor, and he saw to it that her papers were locked away until 1968—well past her centenary. But long before, James's letters to Sturgis, to Fullerton, to Lapsley and others, had led us to the tales

James wrote about her. The letters complement these late tales in which the Master looks at Edith closely and evokes her vividly. She is an author in "The Velvet Glove," and her name, Amy Evans, suggests the plainness of Edith Jones, before she became Edith Wharton. Amy Evans has become a Princess, and rides in a chariot of fire, and James even entitles one of Amy's novels "The Top of the Tree," just after Mrs. Wharton has written *The Fruit of the Tree*. There is a certain amount of "fun and games" in James's Whartonian tales. Amy asks the famous writer to ride with her through Paris at night (one of James's vivid descriptive scenes) because she wants him to do a "log-rolling" preface to "The Top of the Tree." "We took that ride through Paris," Mrs. Wharton remembered when we talked, "but of course I would never have asked James to write a preface to any of my novels." She is also Mrs. Worthingham in one of the very last tales, "Crapy Cornelia," and the resemblance is very strong.

Mrs. Worthingham is described as a "polished and prosperous little person" with a capacity for smiling and twinkling. She wears more jewelry than Mrs. Wharton, but she has her pink-and-white quality and a suggestion of ruffles and ribbons. In the tale James likens her to a Dresden China shepherdess—he also uses a great deal of pastoral imagery to describe Edith Wharton and her surroundings. Mrs. Worthingham has the power to "please and amuse and serve"; she is "a little person of twenty superficial graces"; and he notices also her "secret pride." He admires "the attaching play of her iridescent surface, the shimmering interfusion of her various aspects; that of her youth with her independence—her pecuniary perhaps in particular, that of her vivacity with her beauty, that of her facility above all with her odd novelty; the high modernity, as people appeared to have come to call it, that made her so much more 'knowing' in some directions than even he, man of the world as he certainly was, could pretend to be, though all on a basis of the most unconscious and instinctive and luxurious assumption."

In his awareness of Mrs. Wharton's limitations James is led, in the second part of "Crapy Cornelia," to see the virtues of his own "Old New York." The story contrasts the polished, manicured and bejeweled Mrs. Worthingham with the gloomy-looking Cornelia, who belongs to James's old world, and to his generation. In the end he finds Cornelia much more amusing and feels more comfortable when he is with her. The shortcomings he begins to discern in Mrs. Worthingham lead James to his ultimate criticism of the new and rich America. His old society, with its timidities and its narrowness, its superficialities and failures, had been at bottom good-natured, and indeed "good" altogether.

This was clearly going to be the music of the future—that if people were but rich enough and furnished enough and fed enough, exercised and sanitated and manicured, and generally advised and advertised and made "knowing" enough, *avertis* enough, as the term appeared to be nowadays in Paris, all they had to do for civility was to take the amused ironic view of those who might be less initiated. In *his* time, when he was young or even when he was only but a little less middle-aged, the best manners had been the best kindness, and the best kindness had mostly been some art of not insisting on one's luxurious differences, of concealing rather, for common humanity, if not for common decency, a part at least of the intensity or the ferocity with which one might be "in the know."

In the later stages of their friendship James found he could not keep pace with Mrs. Wharton's driving energy. He could not always motor in tune with her timetable or her way of life. But he found her continually attractive, and his admiration grew rather than diminished. She on her side disapproved of James's frugality; she felt he was too permissive with his servants; she remarks in her memoirs, perhaps unfeelingly, out of her own prosperity, that James "denied himself (I believe quite needlessly) the pleasure and relaxation which a car of his own might have given him, but took advantage, to the last drop of petrol, of the travelling capacity of any visitor's car." She was not reckoning with the fact that James could never have driven a car himself and could not afford a chauffeur. Possession of his typewriter and a typist was technology enough for the Master.

III

The epistolary James is at his best in his late letters. The earlier letters are documentary and historical; the late ones contain a warmth and a faculty for affection which he tended to hold back in his younger years even when he wrote old friends like Grace Norton or W. D. Howells. Perhaps the distancings within his own family— the very elements of dissociation that contributed to his sister's illnesses—made James originally self-absorbed and intellectual in his personal relations. We must allow too for the fact that he wrote in an age of greater formality. It took a quarter of a century of European life to alter certain innate discretions, and he never got over some of his pomposities and euphemisms. His old justification for himself was that personal privacy and personal freedom demanded that he hold himself aloof and be noncommittal. He was always preserving himself for his art. And then he had to guard against the heavy importunities of "society" and the "Season" in London. He shrank always from what might be vulgar or common; that was the delicate and fastidious side of his character. Some of the earlier letters have the air of being written by a worldly and adventurous monk who always safeguards the avenues of retreat into his cell. James's tastes are patrician although he is fundamentally democratic. He cannot abide the pretensions of Paul Bourget; he scorns the snobbery and bad manners of the British upper classes. With his old friend Lady Ritchie, Thackeray's daughter, he believes in a democracy of social justice but insists that there cannot be equality beyond the ballot box—and wonders whether the ballot has any true meaning for the illiterate. There was no democracy of brains; there would always be an elite. He was very clear about the need for certain social values and for maintaining a sense of "reality." He had above all a great historical wisdom. He had long ago decided that overwhelming changes, as the world fashions and refashions itself, are rarely achieved in any one lifetime. And in each life, he felt, there had to be the freedom to choose. His choice was with Voltaire—one did best to cultivate one's own garden.

The war letters, of 1914–1915, the last great surge of energy and power, tell us of James's visits to hospitals; his admiration for the way Mrs. Wharton channeled her energy into war charities; his decision to become a British subject—and his clinging to the acts of life. His prose soars to the grandeur of great deeds, of lives laid down in their multitude in the limbo of a no-man's land, and he remembers from his youth and the Civil War the mourning widows and desolate children on the home front. The moment comes when he announces he can no longer endure "the wear and tear of discrimination." And he turns his face to the wall in the midst of the bloodletting, but not before dictating, during half-conscious hours, certain "final and fading words" (see Appendix V) in which he babbles of Napoleon and mints a few of his old fine phrases: "the Bonapartes have a kind of bronze distinction that extends to their fingertips and is a great source of charm in the women"; or, thinking of the battlefields, "they pluck in their terror handfuls of plumes from the Imperial eagle." James had always spoken against war and conquest, reserving for himself the conquests of words. Yet he could not conceal his admiration for one distinct quality in Napoleon—the side of him that challenged the impossible and the insoluble.

"I hate American simplicity," James once said to his niece Peggy, who wrote it down. "I glory in the piling up of complications of every sort. If I could pronounce the name James in any different or more elaborate way I should be in favour of doing it." And indeed, attempting to do the impossible, to discover the unsolvable within the scrutinies and adventures of his imagination, Henry James played a great game of living and creating during his half-century. When, in the end, he told Wells that "art makes life" he meant that he was on the side of civilized man's ability to comprehend and give shape to the great heaving ocean of existence—in which otherwise time and history drown. The shaping of chaos meant an aristocracy of art: for most individuals are inclined to let things be. We remember that James told Paul Bourget that "the great ones of the earth" lacked imagination. It was up to the artist to fill this void.

Brief Chronology

1895: After failure in the theatre, Henry James resumes writing of fiction but writes a one-act play, *Summersoft*, for Ellen Terry, which she never produces. Visits Ireland; spends autumn in Torquay turning old scenario into novel of violence, *The Other House*.

1896–1897: Two collections of tales, *Embarrassments* and *Terminations*, and *The Spoils of Poynton*. Begins search for a house in the country after spending summer at Playden, near Rye in Sussex.

1897: Purchases typewriter and starts dictating directly to his typist. Completes *What Maisie Knew*. Takes long lease of Lamb House in Rye.

1898–1899: Moves into Lamb House. Writes "The Turn of the Screw," "In the Cage," and *The Awkward Age*. Friendship with Conrad and H. G. Wells. During trip to Italy meets Hendrik Andersen, a young American sculptor to whom he writes intimate letters during next decade.

1900–1904: Friendship with Stephen Crane. Writes *The Sacred Fount, The Ambassadors, The Wings of the Dove*, and *The Golden Bowl*, and *William Wetmore Story and His Friends*. Friendship with Jocelyn Persse. Meets Edith Wharton.

1904–1905: Travels in United States. Revisits New England and stays with Mrs. Wharton in Lenox; travels to the South, then to the West Coast for first time; lectures on "The Lesson of Balzac."

1906–1907: Returns to England and writes *The American Scene* and "The Jolly Corner." Begins work on New York Edition of his novels and tales, revising some of his early novels. Assembles *English Hours* and *Italian Hours*. Friendship with Hugh Walpole. Visits Mrs. Wharton in Paris and travels in France in her "chariot of fire."

1908–1910: Pays second visit to Mrs. Wharton in Paris. Suffers long nervous illness. Journeys to America with ailing brother William, who dies of his heart ailment. Given honorary degrees by Harvard and Oxford.

1911–1912: Has shingles but begins work on *A Small Boy* and goes on to *Notes of a Son and Brother*, both dictated to Theodora Bosanquet. Moves to flat at 21 Carlyle Mansions in Chelsea, but keeps Lamb House for summers.

1913: Sargent paints his portrait for his seventieth birthday; it is presented to him by his friends together with a golden bowl.

1914: After outbreak of war, visits wounded in hospitals, aids refugees, and supports American Volunteer Ambulance Brigade.

1915: Becomes a British subject. Quarrels with H. G. Wells, who has satirized him. Has stroke in December; gives his last dictation.

1916: Receives British Order of Merit. Dies February 28. Ashes taken to America by Mrs. William James for burial in Cambridge, Massachusetts.

1
Withdrawal from London

1895–1900

1
Withdrawal from London

A note in HJ's pocket diary for 1914, dated July 30, tells us of his attempt to recall the events of 1895 and reaches over into ensuing years:

Rye.—Identified yesterday the date of sending Ellen Terry the little one-act play (afterwards *The High Bid*) from Osborne Crescent Torquay as August (toward end of) 1895—nearly 19 years ago. This gives me all the sequences:—

The note from Edward Warren from Point Hill, here, asking me to come to them—that August: (when it was impossible). The visit of Jon. Sturges to me at the Osborne [Crescent] in September and the return with him ill, gravely ill, to town (toward end of month or early in October I seem to make out). It was while there *then* that I conceived, under the effect of something he told me, the subject afterwards treated in *The Ambassadors*; what he said being indeed the mere germ. In that winter of 95–96 I saw at the Warren's in Cowley Street a little drawing in watercolours of the Lamb House gazebo-front that is down in the drawing-room here—Edward's gift to me afterwards. Went that autumn a great deal to see Jonathan at his nursing home in Upper Wimpole Street; made him in fact my constant attention. (Oh the old full De Vere Garden days of those years!)

In (and for) July 1896 [1897] went down to Bournemouth to escape the uproar in town. Had engaged W[illiam] MacAlpine as amanuensis that winter-spring and begun the practice of dictating. Went on with it over "In the Cage" and "What Maisie Knew." MacAlpine joined me at Bournemouth for a little—I gave him, I remember, first bicycle and lessons, and he at once became a great adept (I had myself begun the summer before at Torquay). Went down that August to be near Elly Hunter and her daughters at Dunwich in Suffolk (she had been the previous winter at Harrow, where I had been several times out to see her). Spent August at Dunwich save for coming up to town and going down thence to Torquay for short visit to W. E. Norris at Underbank. I have forgotten to note that the Paul Bourgets came to Osborne Crescent there (at Torquay) the previous summer August–September 1895 and made some stay—in great *late* (September) heat. Jon. S. came then *after* they had gone. September 1896 I came back from Underbank to Dunwich, and went thence to spend three days with . . .

These recollections are somewhat telescoped. After the failure of *Guy Domville,* Ellen Terry, largely as an act of sympathy, asked James to write a play for her. He visited Ireland and on his return saw through the press a collection of tales, *Terminations,* containing the much admired story "The Altar of the Dead." He then spent the summer and part of the autumn at Torquay, where he wrote the one-act *Summersoft* for Miss Terry and *The Other House* for the *Illustrated London News.* Jonathan Sturges visited him at Torquay in October and gave him the idea for *The Ambassadors.* Henry James made a long entry to this effect in his *Notebooks.*

It was in 1897 that he went to Bournemouth "to escape the uproar in town." The uproar was the preparations for Queen Victoria's Diamond Jubilee. He took with him William MacAlpine, the first of his typists. The summer of 1896 had been spent at Playden, a hilltop looking across a valley at Rye topped by its church near Lamb House. At Playden James wrote *The Spoils of Poynton* and read proofs of *The Other House.* In the autumn he moved to the Old Vicarage in Rye and saw Lamb House, which he would acquire two years later as his permanent home. The summer of 1897 was spent in Suffolk with his Emmet cousins, and by the summer of 1898 he was established in his Rye house after letting his De Vere Gardens flat. These were the stages of his withdrawal from London, where he had lived for twenty years.

Perhaps the most significant part of this diary note of 1914 refers to the typewriter. In 1896, when he was working on *What Maisie Knew,* James developed writer's cramp. He began then to dictate to MacAlpine, who was a shorthand reporter; finding that it took MacAlpine several days to transcribe his shorthand notes, James purchased a typewriter and practiced dictating directly to a typist. By the time he moved into Lamb House this had become his permanent way of work. His late novels were dictated to Mary Weld, who on leaving him to get married was replaced (after James's American trip) by the gifted Theodora Bosanquet, who in later life became herself a writer and editor. This method of writing changed

James's mode of life. Dictating to the typewriter pinned him down; he could no longer travel freely and write in hotels. The consequence was that he did not go abroad until 1899. It was during this trip that he met Hendrik Andersen.

One other change occurred that affected James's working life. After having handled his own business affairs for three decades, he put them into the hands of an eminent literary agent, James B. Pinker, who brought order into the novelist's copyrights, found publishers for his late novels, and relieved him of time-wasting business correspondence. Pinker also arranged for publication of the massive New York Edition of James's novels and tales.

To Mr. and Mrs. William James
Ms Harvard

34 De Vere Gardens W.
March 28*th* 1895

Dear Alice and dear William.

I have had within a few days a sweet letter from each of you. Yours, Alice, came to me the other day in Dublin; from which place I returned last night (after a stay of more than a fortnight), to find William's awaiting me here. I rejoice in the good news of your (Wm's) alleviated duties, easier work for the rest of the year. I hope the months will now ebb in a smooth current. I am much interested in your projected summer on the Cape and William's ulterior lectures in Colorado. How large your life swings compared to mine, and how much—beside the lone bachelor's—it takes in! I trust indeed, if these things depend upon it, that you may let the gentle Chocorua. I should think there would always be American families wanting such a "summer-home." But what I wish you most is comparative quiet—I mean immunity from the human deluge which seems to roll over you. But I fear that, with so many nets out and raking the waters, this is the boon that will be ever unattainable to you. Every glimpse you give me of your domestic life is a picture of heroic sacrifices, romantic charities, and acceptances of everyone else's burdens. It is magnificent—if it doesn't kill you. It almost kills *me* to think of it. My Irish episode,[1] thank heaven, is over, though the second phase of it, my visit to the sweet, really

5

angelic (as host and hostess) Wolseleys, was as delightful as any experience of wasteful and expensive social idleness *can* be to a preoccupied and hindered worker. My six days at the Castle were a gorgeous bore, and the little viceregal "court" a weariness alike to flesh and spirit. Young Lord Houghton, the Viceroy, "does it," as they say here, very handsomely and sumptuously (having inherited just in time his uncle, Lord Crewe's, great property); but he takes himself much too seriously as a representative of royalty, and his complete Home Rule—or rather hate–Home Rule boycotting by the whole landlord and "nobility and gentry" class (including all Trinity College, Dublin) leaves his materials for a "court," and for entertaining generally, in a beggarly condition. He had four balls in the six days I was there and a gorgeous banquet every night—but the bare official and military class peopled them, with the aid of a very dull and second-rate, though large, house-party from England. His English friends fail him—won't come because they know to what he is reduced; and altogether he is quite a pathetic and deso-late and impossible young man—from the constant standing—in a cloud of aide-de-camps—on one's hind-legs—to [from] whom I was devoutly thankful to retire. He means well—but he doesn't matter; and the sense of the lavish extravagance of the castle, with the beggary and squalor of Ireland at the very gates, was a most depress-ing, haunting discomfort.—On the other hand the Royal Hospital (Lord W.'s residence as Commander of the Forces) was a very de-lightful episode. *They* do, really, all that poor Lord H. fails to do, and the military *milieu* and types were very amusing and sug-gestive to me. Lord W. is a singularly and *studiously*, delightful Person and my acquaintance of seventeen years with them has made our relations of the easiest, as it has made their kindness, really, of the greatest. They *dragged* me to them, quite; but if they did so they most sweetly made it up to me. The Royal Hospital—a kind of Irish Chelsea ditto, or Invalides for 150 old Irish soldiers (founded by Charles II), is a most picturesque and stately thing—out of which the residence of the Commander has been liberally carved. It contains one of the finest great halls in the British islands, in which, on the 14th (while I was still at the Castle), Lady W. gave a remarkably beautiful fancy-ball. The ladies were each a special Gainsborough, Sir Joshua or Romney portrait, and the men (save H.J.) in uniform, court dress or (most picturesque) hunt evening dress—the prettiest of all the fopperies of the English foppish class. I was, by special license, the sole black coat. But it is a blessing to have returned to one's own little workaday world and to begin to hoe again one's little garden. This is the last of my social episodes, for months to come; and I positively pine and languish for a long stretch of operose *complete* detachment, such as I can only get by leaving London. I shall probably have to wait for this to the first of May—but then I shall go for several months. I have, thank heaven, absorbing and magnificent work cut out—the best I have ever done; and I have also my eye on the right little place (not Ramsgate!) whose name I won't yet reveal. I go down to see it, probably, next week—even as you two will have gone, fruitfully, I trust, to reconnoiter at Cape Cod. Is Harry[2] preparing to enter Harvard next autumn?—Something in your letter seemed to suggest it. My love and blessing to him if he is. Your anecdotes of Boott's[3] little tenacities and fidelities are very touching. I owe him a letter which he shall soon have. Your constant

Henry

1. HJ had visited Lord Houghton, the Lord Lieutenant of Ireland, son of his old friend Richard Monckton Milnes, first Lord Houghton. He had then stayed with his friends the Wolseleys. See *Letters* II, 130, 151.

2. WJ's oldest son, Henry (1879–1947), called Harry to distinguish him from his novelist-uncle.

3. Francis Boott (1813–1904), father of the late Elizabeth Boott Duveneck, now repatriated, was living in Cambridge.

To Theodora Sedgwick
Ms Harvard

34 De Vere Gardens W.
March 30*th* 1895

My dear Theodora.

I am very horrid indeed to have delayed so long to thank you for a most human and charming letter I had from you months and months ago. (I mean weeks and weeks—but months and months still more expresses my abjection and compunction.) I won't attempt to explain or to vindicate myself; but simply plead, once for all, that I long ago gave up the character of a correspondent, after having struggled too long to sustain it; and that I am now *really* lost to all shame, though I use some of the vocabulary of a penitent. In other words my correspondence went to pieces a good while ago—and the shattered fragments have never even—by *my* hand—been picked up. Please be affectionately thanked, all the same, for your graceful and friendly demonstration. I learned from William (who sends me a parcel by them) that Sally and Rupert are even now upon the waves; so that I shall presently, I trust, have soon intimate news of you. It will be delightful to see Sally—if fate shall prove not to have converted us into the alternative buckets in the well—I mean delaying her advent (in London) till my only annual flight shall have taken place. I shall hie me away the first days of May—for "parts" of which nothing would induce me to breathe the name—some hamlet of the plain in the British Islands. I am not going to Venice again this year—Lily[1] will tell you why. Nor am I going to St. Ives:[2] you know why, I think already. The Stephens indeed are trying hard to break their own connection with it—but no one grabs at their house, and they probably go back for this summer. They have been ravaged by influenza, Mrs. Stephen having had it severely, but having looked so intensely beautiful on her sofa in her longish convalescence that one felt it to be a sort of blessing in disguise. Leslie has wonders of work in him—lectures right and left—writes, still, half the Dictionary, and has just finished—in three or four months—the extremely difficult Life of his brother,[3] which he has achieved the feat of writing without materials and without sympathy. He has admirable working habits—and most enviable facility. I find twenty-five years of practice only make *me* write slower and slower; so that I am rapidly reaching a fine maximum of twenty-five words a day. I have just come back from seventeen days in Ireland—a wanton outbreak of three visits (in Dublin); one to poor young Lord Houghton (the Viceroy); one to the adorable Wolseleys (Lord W. the *pleasantest*—humanly, sweetly—host and *commensal* that ever was known—with an extraordinary charm in his unquenched youth, and rosy, blue-eyed freshness and bonhomie); and the other to the Herbert Jekylls (the Private Secretary of the Lord Lieutenant). The six days at the Castle were a Purgatorio—I was not made for viceregal "courts," especially in countries distraught with social hatreds: young Houghton seems to have centered his energies in trying to make up by a too-deadly correctness for the amiable désinvolture of his father—which I remember them both far enough back to recall that he hated and was humiliated by. He is very goodlooking, rich, gentle, well-meaning, widowed (with three girls), and grabbed at; but he is too conscious a representative of royalty to be even a tolerable host; and his "court" is moreover so deserted (he is *absolutely*, by the fine folks, boycotted) that it was grandeur terribly in the void. All the scarlet and gold at the Wolseleys, who live in a most picturesque old Charles II Commander-in-Chief Royal Hospital (an Irish Invalides, with a splendid great hall), made, in its pampered militarism, a very amusing *milieu*—for ten days—for a man of peace and lover of colour. But the *sight* of the Irish complication does nothing to make one think it less. The English are encamped there as in a foreign country—they *hold* it, for that requires no imagination. Will they ever have imagination to do more? I saw no signs of that. The simplicity of the soldiers! But they made me admire them like a housemaid. I love aide-de-camps: even the Lord Lieutenant's *eight*—who all dine in blue coats and brass buttons, with reverses of azure satin. I hope your solitary winter (I think I see you smile at the word I use) has had the repose of solitude without the sadness. Isn't Lily coming out? Please tell her to listen to that cry. I don't dare to send a message to Charles—my only message must be to write to him. I call you to witness I *will*. Yours, my dear Theodora, very gratefully and constantly

Henry James

1. Sally, Rupert, and Lily, children of Charles Eliot Norton.
2. Where Talland House, summer home of the Leslie Stephens, was situated.
3. *Sir Fitzgerald Stephen* by Leslie Stephen (1895).

To Edmund Gosse
Ms Leeds

34 De Vere Gardens W.
Monday [8 April] 1895

My dear Gosse.

Yes, I will come with pleasure to-morrow, Tuesday. Yes, too, it has been, it is, hideously, atrociously dramatic and really interesting—so far as one can say that of a thing of which the interest is qualified by such a sickening horribility.[1] It is the squalid gratuitousness of it all—of the mere exposure—that blurs the spectacle. But the *fall*—from nearly twenty years of a really unique kind of "brilliant" conspicuity (wit, "art," conversation—"one of our two or three dramatists, etc.") to that sordid prison-cell and this gulf of obscenity over which the ghoulish public hangs and gloats—it is beyond any utterance of irony or any pang of compassion! He was never in the smallest degree interesting to me—but this hideous human history has made him so—in a manner.[2] À demain—Yours ever,

Henry James

1. Oscar Wilde had been charged two days earlier with offenses under Section 11 of the Criminal Law Amendment Act of 1885 (homosexuality). Bail was refused, and Wilde went to Holloway Jail.

2. On the envelope flap HJ scrawled, after he sealed the letter, "Quel dommage—mais quel Bonheur—que J.A.S. ne soit plus de ce monde." The allusion was to Symonds. See *Letters* III, 398.

To Alphonse Daudet
Ms Harvard

34 De Vere Gardens W.
ce 22 avril [1895]

Mon cher ami.

À la bonne heure: Lundi 6, alors—c'est entendu. J'ai été à Brown's et on vous y promet pour ce jour l'appartement, c'est à dire les chambres, que vous m'énumérez. J'y retournerai aujourd'hui pour la question de la *dressing room*, communiquant avec la vôtre, qui ne présentera pas de difficulté—sans doute. On m'a dit seulement ceci: que du 5 au 9 les deux reines de Hollande seront à l'hôtel où elles occuperont (ça se dit-il?) beaucoup de chambres, et qu'après le dit 9 on pourra vous arranger mieux comme qualité de chambres que les premiers deux ou trois jours. En attendant on fera pour vous tout le possible.[1]—Bravo pour nôtre diner de Jeudi 9. Je compte donc religieusement sur vous deux. Vous vous seriez peut-être amusé au dîner du Literary Fund—le grand banquet annuel au profit d'une grosse charité—pour les gens de lettres infirmes et leurs veuves et leurs orphelins. Lord Houghton, qui y préside est un beau jeune homme (de 35 ans) actuellement Viceroi d'Ireland et fils du vieux bonhomme[2] que vous voyiez chez Flaubert; qui est mort il y a dix ans et à qui il ne ressemble guère. Avez vous absolument refusé?

Sinon, je vous conseillerais d'y aller—pour l'impression d'un grand *public dinner* anglais avec forcé *speeches:* c'est à dire si vous tenez—à cette impression.—Je reçois à l'instant où je vous écris un billet de George Meredith, nôtre vieux romancier glorieux, aimé du petit nombre (bien que depuis cinq ans on le cite à chaque instant sans le lire), qui m'engage fort à vous amener passer un après-midi dans son petit cottage, dans le ravissant Surrey.[3] Il souffre d'une maladie qui l'empêche de marcher—presque—autre part que dans son jardin et ne vient jamais à Londres. Mais ceci est une chose dont nous causerons en temps et lieu. Soignez-vous bien d'ici là—et reposez-vous bien d'avance. Tout à tous

Henry James

1. The Daudets had asked HJ to make the London arrangements for their visit.
2. See *Letters* II, 165.
3. Meredith, then 67, lived at Box Hill, Surrey.

To Ellen Terry
Ms Unknown

34 De Vere Gardens W.
April 23d 1895

My dear Miss Terry.

Our conversation of three months ago[1] has borne fruit that moves me to ask you if you could kindly give me ten minutes or even five (five would quite do), some morning—or afternoon—on Thursday, Friday or Saturday—or *any* day that suits you? The purpose of this will be [to] bring you with my own hand the (very full and detailed) sketch of the subject of a little one-act play—a comedy, in intention—and leave it with you to read at your convenience. It is a thing which must essentially—as a copious and minute scenario—for good or for ill speak for itself; but [there] are two or three things I should like to say *with* it (very brief ones), which it will be easier to utter than to write. In short I am at your service any time that you are so good as to mention, dear Miss Terry, to yours most truly

Henry James

1. After the failure of *Guy Domville* on 5 January 1895, Ellen Terry invited HJ to write a one- or two-act play for her. See HJ's *Notebooks*, ed. Matthiessen and Murdock (1947), 184–186. After their conversation about this on 5 February, HJ completed the scenario for the one-acter "Mrs. Gracedew," later called "Summersoft."

To Edmund Gosse
Ms Leeds

34 De Vere Gardens W.
Sunday [28 April 1895]

My dear Gosse.

Thanks—of a troubled kind, for your defense of my modesty in the *Realm*.[1] The article is brilliantly clever—but I have almost the same anguish (that is my modesty has) when defended as when violated. You have, however, doubtless done it great good, which I hereby formally recognise. These are days in which one's modesty is, in every direction, much exposed, and one should be thankful for every veil that one can hastily snatch up or that a friendly hand precipitately muffles one withal. It is strictly congruous with these remarks that I should mention that there go to you tomorrow A.M. in two registered envelopes, at 1 Whitehall, the fond outpourings of poor J.A.S.[2] I put them into two because I haven't one big enough to hold all—and it so happens that of that size I have only registered ones. I'm afraid I shan't see you—so preoccupied do the evenings seem—till the formidable 9th.[3] Our guest (you might have mentioned it in the *Realm*) has a malady of the bladder, which makes him desire strange precautions—and I see—I foresee singular complications—the flow of something more than either soul or champagne at dinner.—Did you see in last evening's ½d papers that the wretched O.W. seems to have a gleam of light before him (if it really counts for that), in the fearful exposure of his (of the prosecution's) little beasts of witnesses?[4] What a nest of almost infant blackmailers! Yours ever

Henry James

1. This article dealt with Alphonse Daudet's impending visit; it was later included in Gosse's *French Profiles* (1904).
2. Gosse had sent HJ some of Symonds's writings on homosexuality.
3. The date of HJ's dinner at the Reform Club in honor of Daudet.
4. An allusion to some of the Crown witnesses in the first trial of Oscar Wilde, one of whom was characterized by the judge as "a most reckless, unreliable, unscrupulous and untruthful witness." See *The Letters of Oscar Wilde*, ed. Hart-Davis (1962), 452.

To Leslie Stephen
Ms Berg

34 De Vere Gardens W.
May 6*th* 1895

My dear Stephen.

I feel unable to approach such a sorrow as yours[1]—and yet I can't forbear to hold out my hand to you. I think of you with inexpressible participation, and only take refuge from this sharp pain of sympathy in trying to call up the image of all the perfect happiness that you drew and that you gave. I pray for you that there are moments when the sense of that rushes over you like a possession that you still hold. There is no happiness in this horrible world but the happiness we have *had*—the very present is ever in the jaws of fate. *I* think, in the presence of the loss of so beautiful and noble and generous a friend, of the admirable picture of her perfect union with you, and that for her, at any rate, with all its fatigues and sacrifices, life didn't pass without the deep and clear felicity—the best it can give. She leaves no image but that of the high enjoyment of affections and devotions—the beauty and the good she wrought and the tenderness that came back to her. Unquenchable seems to me such a presence. But why do I presume to say these things to you, my dear Stephen? Only because I want you to hear in them the sound of the voice and feel the pressure of the hand of your affectionate old friend,

Henry James

1. The death of Mrs. Stephen, the former Julia (Jackson) Duckworth, mother of Virginia Woolf and Vanessa Bell.

To Mrs. Henry G. Woods
Ms Pennsylvania

34 De Vere Gardens W.
May 26*th* 1895

Dear Mrs. Woods.

I felt that I took rather a shabby farewell of you and the President[1] yesterday—but my benedictions were deep if they were not loud, and my appreciation of your kindness to our multitudinous party

13

insists on overflowing this morning into a definite assurance. We all felt, as we departed, and Daudet and his wife expressed it as soon as we got into the carriage, that we owed you a day of extraordinary beauty and of a really exquisite felicity. "C'est inoubliable—inoubliable!" Daudet kept repeating, and we recognized that it was largely so in consequence of the peculiarly successful turn your patience and prevision had given it. Let it be something of a reward to you that you helped to make an immense impression on that intensely sensitive and vibrating little Frenchman of genius, to relieve in that proportion his sense of suffering, and to bring out old England gloriously—with all her banners flying—to the foreign consciousness. The foreign consciousness is in some ways a strange affair, but it fully rose to the occasion yesterday. The boatrace was, as an impression, a pure gem: they returned to it again and again. Such emotions, moreover, in such cases—I mean in the case of genius or imagination and "literary position," count for more than simply themselves; they have a general, beneficent, and happy international effect. As for myself, I thought I loved Oxford enough already—but now the fatal sentiment is past all curing. I sincerely hope you haven't paid—are not paying too much today—for these fine things. But be both sustained and soothed even if you are—it is in a good cause. Believe me, dear Mrs. Woods, yours more than ever

Henry James

1. Margaret Louisa Woods (1856–1945), daughter of G. C. Bradley, then Dean of Westminster, wrote a number of volumes of prose and verse. Her husband was President of Trinity College, Oxford, at the time of the Daudet family's visit.

To William James
Ms Harvard

34 De Vere Gardens W.
June 1st 1895

My dear William.

I am very sorry to say I shall have to be brief today in spite of the fact that I have lately twice, and rather copiously, heard from you. I seem to find myself in a position in which everything presses upon me at once; and a great arrears of correspondence are piled up on the top of retarded problems of work. This is partly the result of a fortnight (in two different pieces), of gout and of three weeks of the Alphonse Daudets. The latter (seven persons—with the two Georges Hugos, the grandson of Victor and his wife) simply settled upon me—with that unspeakable French way of taking for granted, "for purposes," and to which *our* international behaviour has, I think, no equivalent. Don't be unhappy about the gout; it is the first episode for more than two years, and this second bout (a shoe on today for the first time) has been much the shorter of the two. The whole thing has been less violent than before; and if I didn't ever dine out I shouldn't have had even this. But it is difficult (for a lone man) to live in London and never dine out at all. What I *have* achieved is to do so much less than I did. Many thanks for the last Syracuse remittance,[1] though less than usual—that is than the slight occasional increase Bob's surrender has sometimes added. Many thanks also for your letter about your correspondence with Miss Mason. How right you did to write to her! Had she accepted, I would have halved with you. All's well that ends well; and her letter singularly honourable to her. I have been thinking of writing to her; but it is beaten down and crowded out by other multiplicities. I am still in town as you see, not at Midhurst, where I have even yet not had even a free day to go down and look at rooms. I have consequently, I fear, lost them; I mean the special ones recommended to me; but it doesn't much matter, as they have been described to me as very tiny, too tiny, and I always, in the end, like best to go to the sea. I shall go whenever I *must*, for I've no particular engagements ahead. London in itself is, each year, less bothersome to me—for time and trouble, all the general shrinkage, finally simplify: but the French and Americans are not a joke. However, there will be no more Daudets this year—save indeed for the importunity of their insistence that I shall devote some precious days, before the summer is over, to coming to see them at Champrosay.[2] I wish I could vivify this visit for you, but it would take me too far. Their visit was really *to* me (!!) strange as it may seem to you: that is they knew no soul here but me and Mrs. Tennant and Dolly Stanley.[3] I did what I could for them and what Daudet's dissociation from his legs permitted,[4] and everything went well. He is very appealing and pathetic in his advanced and yet combatted infirmity—wasted and worn, saturated with morphine and chloral ("depuis *dix* ans je n'ai que le sommeil artificiel"), and yet prevailing still by his meridional vitality and his intense superficial perceptiveness. His ignorance of England and the English is abysmal, and but scantily *comblée* by his visit. His elder son, Léon (27),[5] launched in literature ("Les Marticoles"), a *jeune féroce* ("un loup" his father calls him), has divorced, for horrors, Jeanne Hugo, to whom he was married, but Georges, Jeanne's brother, who has also repudiated her, is still his bosom friend. There are strange *dessous* in French literary circles; and I don't like Léon. I took them down (at his invitation), to see G. Meredith, and strange and grotesquely pathetic was the meeting between the French and English romancer—*coram populo*, on the railway platform—each staggering and stumbling, with the same uncontrollable paralysis, into the arms of the other, so that they almost rolled over together onto the line, beneath the wheels of a train! A.D., on his return to Paris, wrote me thus yesterday, as a preface to a terrible return to the charge about the visit to Champrosay: "Je ne veux vous dire aujourd'hui qu'une chose: avant d'aller à Londres j'avais pour votre talent subtil, la profondeur de votre esprit, une sympathie très-grande; maintenant, après ces trois semaines vécues en commun, pendant lesquelles je vous ai bien regardé, c'est toute mon amitié que je vous donne et toute la vôtre qui je vous demande. Ainsi, plus un mot là-dessus!" That is charming, and genuine, I think, and I am sincerely touched, but it is a rather formidable order to meet. However, he inspires great kindness. But as for "profondeur d'esprit," I told him *you* were the one. Look out; they are capable of disembarking in Cambridge. To finish—or rather to begin (his stay), I gave him and Léon a very elegant dinner of twelve at the Reform Club—twelve rather difficultly gathered on a basis of fluent French. He doesn't know a syllable of English. Basta.—Bob's letter, which you enclosed to me, made me ill; and so did your story of Carrie's instructions (for of course his conduct was based on that) to Mary not to come and see you. Carrie is really atrocious, and I can't pretend, now, to maintain my relation of correspondence with her. If she asks me why, I will plainly tell her. She is not worth doing anything at all to keep. I am sorry for her children—what an ass she is for them! As for Bob, the high, superior virtue of tone of his brutalities is a thing by itself.[6] I trust you are inured to them. He never gives me a sign of any kind at all: but Mary sometimes—very amicably—writes. Apropos of letters, your enclosure from Carrie Cranch stupefies me. I didn't know her mother was insane or that she (Carrie) was in an asylum. I haven't any "little things" of hers whatever, and never had in my life. What on earth does she mean? It is pure hallucination. But I go beyond my time-limit. I am writing a good deal; I mean workfully; and better than I have ever done. Pazienza. I hope your bonds are about to burst; and that Chocorua is let. Je vous embrasse.

Henry

1. Rents from HJ's share of the James family real estate in Syracuse, New York.
2. Daudet's country home near Draveil, a village on the Seine, not far from the Château de Vigneux.
3. Mrs. Tennant was the former Gertrude Collier, daughter of a naval attaché at the British embassy in France. During vacations at Trouville, she became a friend of Gustave Flaubert's. In 1877 Flaubert introduced her to Daudet. Lady Dorothy Stanley, formerly Tennant, was the wife of Sir Henry M. Stanley, the explorer.
4. Daudet suffered from creeping paralysis, a consequence of venereal disease.
5. Léon Daudet (1868–1942), French royalist and polemicist, a leading figure in *l'Action française*.
6. HJ is referring here to his youngest brother, Robertson, who was an alcoholic.

To Ellen Terry
Ms Unknown

34 De Vere Gardens W.
August 31*st* 1895

My dear Ellen Terry.

Your farewell note was very genial and graceful, and I thank you most kindly for your cheque for £100—to which, and its species, I make not the smallest pretension to be indifferent or superior for I shouldn't be able to keep it up.[1] "Teach" you, dear source of instruction?—yes, every scrap that your genius leaves a margin for. I fear that will be a narrow edge. Let this lucid and punctual acknowledgment, at any rate, fly after you in your flight. It's so hot and still and stagnant here that I feel the Atlantic will have no steeper an incline than the mere slope of the footlights. May you therefore sail grandly on—and may the same serenity float you through the whole business. It will seem a long year—but art *is* long, ah me! At all events, if the Americans are not to have the Gem, do excruciate them with a suspicion of what they lose. Save for that, be only a blessing and blest and come back fluent in the idiom of Mrs. G[racedew][2] and above all believe me yours, dear Ellen Terry, very devotedly

Henry James

17

1. See HJ to Ellen Terry, 23 April 1895. HJ delivered the one-act play to Miss Terry for her forthcoming tour of the United States. The £100 represented her option, but she never produced the play.

2. The leading role for Miss Terry.

To Horace E. Scudder
Ms Harvard

34 De Vere Gardens W.
September 3*d* 1895

Dear Mr. Scudder.

I let you know at the first possible moment of a difficulty which, though it will not, I think, prevent me from letting you have the first of my promised tales by October 15th, suggests to me that as I announced the thing to you by name I had better (lest there should be some advertising—) modify that precipitation. What I shall send you, then, will not be the thing I mentioned to you as "The House Beautiful,"[1] for the sad reason that that small fiction absolutely declines to be contained in 15,000 words, which is what I was trying for. It will make nearer 25,000 and after a mortal struggle I have to give up the effort to keep it down. It must go elsewhere, as of the major length, and I must try again for you on a tinier subject—though I thought this *was* tiny. It is, probably; but what I put into it isn't. The truth is I can't do the very little thing any more, and the process—the endeavour—is most expensive—it is so long and complicated. However, you *shall* have your three stories, and have them tiny. They are probably the last (*very* small ones), I shall ever do—so cherish them. I go back to the country tomorrow and shall put another attempt through by October 1st. It will probably be called—but I must, this time, hold my tongue about the name. I have written you thus partly because there may have been a small chance of your announcing *The House B.* and partly because I said I should perhaps also be able to let you have it *before* the date you fixed. This, alas, is now impossible. Yours most truly

Henry James

1. HJ's earlier letters to Horace Scudder are in *Letters* III, especially 307, 338–339. "The House Beautiful" eventually became *The Spoils of Poynton.*

18

To William James
Ms Harvard

Osborne Hotel, Torquay
September 30*th* '95

My dear William.

Your advice of having sent me £30.12.3., for which lively thanks, comes in plenty of time to make me feel humiliated by the recollection of favours still unacknowledged. Such for instance your so interesting letter in pencil from the mining camp at vertiginous heights—from (I have it here before me again) Divide and Cripple Creek; of date of August 15th.[1] It thrilled me, at the time, to get it, and my thrill would have re-echoed back to you, had it not been that, directly after getting it, I returned to this place (from a torrid, horrid three weeks in the midsummer London, necessitated by circumstances), to find my ubiquitous friends the P. Bourgets installed here for a month—the consequence of which was that all the time not given to pressing work was so gnawed round the edges by insidious conversation that the margin barely sufficed for the writing of inevitable day-to-day notes. The Bourgets have now departed (three days ago), and if complete silence, and pure conversational flatness has descended upon me, my margin is at any rate larger. To finish with *them*, they are a great intellectual and colloquial luxury and Bourget much chastened in some of his little forms (they are not, after all, very serious) of importunity and egoism. They cling to *moi qui vous parle* with a fidelity that touches me, and were delighted with this deliciously vacant and admirably blue-sea'd and densely-verdured and lovely-viewed warm corner of England. Bourget's mind is, in the real solitude in which I live, beneath what has been so much social chatter, a flowering oasis in conversational sands; and "Minnie" is a little person of remarkable gifts, perceptions and (to him) devotions. But he is more or less spoiled by a success that (in its extreme abundance) I don't wholly account for, and by the very agility of his cosmopolitan "play of mind." He is incurably restless and over-facilitated.[2] Basta. I shan't see them again till next summer. His plan is to go to Japan (for the *Revue dex Deux Mondes* and the N.Y. *Herald!*) this winter, after functioning as *Chancellier* of the Académie Française during the next three months. We have been having the most extraordinarily fine summer, full of warmth and dryness, and with the climax of a September tropical, without intermission, from beginning to end. The end is not yet—the heat is still excessive, with no symptom of a break in the long spell. It is a phenomenon unexampled in all the years I have lived in England, and the result of it has been—in this so gardeny place, with a great lawn and trees fringing, just beneath my window, the blue, perpetually audible water, to give me a sense of abundant summer that I haven't had since the time I spent, several years ago, at Vallombrosa. I expect to stay here till the first week in November. The from year-to-year deferred total renovation of my very dirty flat is at last underway—and complete repainting, repapering etc. to be effected; and I have succumbed to the opportunity to put in the electric light which is above, and below me, and all over the house—the landlord taking one half of the expense. The business will probably take the whole of October. Mrs. Stanley Clarke has just written me the news of Kitty Emmet's death[3]—a sad and startling incident. I had not ever heard she was ill, and her extinction seems to remind one closely of one's own limits: she was exactly my age. I had scarcely seen her for twenty-five years. Strange that her aged husband—aged even when she married him—should survive her. Her daughter Elizabeth, with the eldest son, Willie, whom I had already seen, were in London this June and lunched with me, and the youth confirmed my original very pleasant impression of him. The girl seemed full of hereditary naturalness. Poor Kitty—she scarce seemed to one a possible subject of any experience so ethereal as death premature and pathetic. Her husband is fortunately much children'd. But Elly will miss her as a caretaker of *her* progeny. I hope she doesn't look to *you* to succeed her. Another incident of my last days in London (last month) was a visit from Barrett Wendell,[4] whom I also went to see, and whose consciousness of a family party, and problems as to what to do with it, made him remind me of your and Alice's memorable peregrination. I thought he took it all more serenely than you, but didn't think his wife comparable to Alice. He has since then sent me his new book on Shakespeare, in which I have been (I had read some laudatory notice of it) much disappointed. Besides being critically very thin and even common, it is surely not written as the Prof. of "English" at Harvard should write. It has made me unhappy. But for God's sake don't tell him this—as I shall have to write him, with anguish, a mendacious letter of thanks. I rejoice much in what you tell me of your rejuvenescence in "Keane Valley" (where in the world is it?) and of the good omens with which you begin your winter—above all in the omen of "saving"—incomparable word. I am afraid that this year I shall not emulate you: one doesn't save much the year one has to pay bills for doing up one's habitation and especially for electrifying it. But I shall emulate and even surpass you as soon as I have completely worked free from the *funeste* effects of the almost completely unremunerated time I have given the last three or four years to vain experimentation with the theatre. During that time I made almost no money—it was a thing to bring one almost to the verge of bankruptcy, and it takes one some more time to catch up. This I am happy to say I am doing. I would give a great deal not to be going back to London for the Winter—I yearn to spend it in the so simplified country. But I must live part of the time at least in the house I have, and if I wish to keep my servants I mustn't abandon them for months—they simply *rot*. I have, thank God, quantities of work on hand and in prospect, and with better powers to do it than ever before. The "bike," I am sorry to say, here proves otherwise—I can't manage the steep hills. It's practically all steep hills.—You must feel greatly enriched by your western impressions—but your vivid picture of them gives me all the same no yearning for them, no sense of the need of them for myself. I sometimes feel as if I had already got all the impressions in life I can take in—and should concern myself now only with using them. Is Harry in college and is he happy? Does he live with you still? I wish you would ask him to try and find some moment of leisure for writing to me. Much love to Alice. Ever your

Henry

1. WJ was at Colorado Springs delivering a series of lectures on psychology for teachers.

2. HJ had known Bourget since 1884. See *Letters* II, 51.

3. Kitty Emmet (1843–1895), an elder sister of HJ's cousin Minny Temple. See *Letters* I, 218–222. Two of the Temple sisters married Emmets: Kitty's husband was Richard Stockton Emmet, and her younger sister, Ellen (Elly), had married Christopher Temple Emmet. See letter to Ellen Temple Hunter, 3 July 1897.

4. Barrett Wendell (1855–1921), professor of English at Harvard from 1880 to 1917, had just published a critical study of Shakespeare.

To Horace E. Scudder
Ms Harvard

Torquay
October 4*th* 1895

Dear Mr. Scudder.

I am in much humiliation and distress, for though I am sending you something by this post I am not sending you what will satisfy you. This is not, heaven knows, for want of time and labour—but because I *can't*, alas, even after renewed heroic effort, which has made the job the most consuming in all ways I've ever tackled, keep within your limits of space. It seems absurd, with a little twopenny subject, but so it is. I am not able today to send you the whole of the little story[1] of which I despatch all but some three thousand words—I can only send you, to catch this (tomorrow's) steamer as much as I am able to get back from the copyist. I have had it all copied once before and then cut into that as I had cut into my MS.; this is the second copy, and hence the delay: that is, in addition to *other* intrinsic causes. I will send you the final pages the hour they come back to me; but the melancholy truth is that they will transcend your measurement by two or three thousand words. As I wrote you the other day, I find, in my old age, that I have too much manner and style, too great and invincible an instinct of completeness and of seeing things in all their relations, so that *development*, however squeezed down, becomes inevitable—too much of all this to be able to turn round in the small corners I used to. I select very small ideas to help this—but even the very small ideas creep high up into the teens. This little subject—of an intense simplicity—was tiny at the start, but in spite of ferocious compression—it has taken me a month—it has become what you see. Of course, if it's absolutely too long for you—in spite of its high merit!—you will return it: I send it to make some decent—or indecent—semblance of keeping my promise. But my failure, with such a thing as this, makes me hopeless about the other two things as to which I have given you my assurance. I must candidly and cynically say that, rather than worry over them as I have worried over this, I shall have, if I find that worry inevitable (and culminating even then in a failure to meet your conditions), sadly to renounce the attempt. But I will *make* it, once more. Let me say that it would be simply fatal to this little "Glasses" to print it as two instalments—it wouldn't bear that at all; and if that is your alternative please, without hesitating, send it back to me. I am all the sorrier about my interminability, because I am obliged to say, in answer to your inquiry (of September 13th) on the subject of *The House Beautiful*[2] that that equally ill-starred fiction is disposed of—yet not even to a magazine. I have contracted with a publisher for a volume of tales which shall mainly not already have appeared; and it is settled that the *H.B.* shall form part of it. Thus is engulfed also another thing—*The Awkward Age*[3]—which I started, originally, to meet your invitation, but which it soon became obvious would fatally exceed that measure. I am very sorry, I repeat, for all this, and can only ask you to believe that the fault is not in my not having taken my problem seriously. I hope very much to make the final pages of "Glasses" reach you in time to be used conveniently in case you do find the thing usable. Believe me

Yours most truly

Henry James

1. The story was "Glasses," which Scudder accepted and printed in the *Atlantic* in a single installment in the February 1896 issue. It was reprinted by HJ in *Embarrassments* (1895).

2. See letter to Scudder, 3 September 1895.

3. *The Awkward Age*, begun as a short story, became the novel published in 1899.

To Francis Boott
Ms Harvard

Torquay

October 11*th* [1895]

My dear Francis.

This is but a p.s. of three lines to the letter I posted to you yesterday; after doing which I became aware that I hadn't alluded to poor W. W. Story's death, the news of which I had just seen in the *Times.*[1] I make up the omission rather on general grounds of aesthetic decorum than on that of supposing his departure affects you much—for I believe you didn't like him, or any feature of Casa Story. I feel a certain sense of historic mutation in the thought that Casa Story is no more: it had been for so long, and went back so far: it had seen so much and so many come and go. You it had seen go, hadn't it?—but not very often come! I saw poor W.W. in Rome sixteen months ago and he was the ghost, only, of his old clownship—very silent and vague and gentle. It was very sad and the Barberini very empty and shabby.[2] What will become of that great unsettled population of statues, which his children don't love nor covet? There were hundreds of them in his studio, and they will be loose upon the world. Well—he had had fifty years of Rome; and that is something.—I also forgot to mention to you that Mrs. Benedict[3] and her daughter lately passed through London on their way back to the U.S.—very futile and foolish, poor things, and exclusively taken up with a dog C.F.W. had acquired, in Venice, the last weeks of her life, and had scarcely lived with, as he was mainly in the hands of her gondoliers. He occupies the forefront of poor Mrs. B's existence and all her talk and—especially to those for whom he has no shadow of association with C.F.W.—he is a weariness to the spirit and a stumbling block to the feet. Mrs. B. is very considerably mad. But she is much better of her great prostration, and the little girl is gentleness incarnate. I receive the news of Kitty Emmet's death—I suppose you never retouched her. But you do retouch Tweedy? How it must improve them! How ghostly must Newport be! But I see ghosts everywhere. You are the only solid substance. Yours, my dear Francis, *da capo*,

Henry James

1. For HJ's earlier views on the American sculptor W. W. Story (1819–1895), see *Letters* I, 353–354.
2. During all the years of his Roman residence Story occupied a ducal apartment in the Palazzo Barberini.
3. Constance Fenimore Woolson's sister. See *Letters* III, 469–470.

To Alphonse Daudet
Ms Harvard

34 De Vere Gardens W.

ce 10 novembre 1895

Ah non, par exemple, mon très cher Daudet—pas le moins du monde *oublieux:* tout au contraire—vivant bien tendrement dans le souvenir et dans l'arrière-goût, et cela d'autant plus que je me sentais plus rivé à mon pieu. Il m'a été, croyez-le bien, je vous en supplie, materiellement impossible, tout l'été, de passer la Manche.

24

C'est une longue et lugubre histoire, que je ne vous infligerai pas, d'obligations accumulées devant lesquelles j'ai dû baisser la tête et plier le dos. Elles me tiennent encore—très sensiblement—jusqu'à me rendre douteux pendant bien des semaines à venir, la douce liberté d'aller vous voir. Je suis moins libre, hélas, que je ne vous le parais peut-être—et je suis certes beaucoup moins infidèle. Non, je suis tout simplement dans une période d'*arrièrages* comme je n'en ai jamais connue. Si vous me trouviez ou me croyiez mal disposé, rien ne manquerait à ma tristesse. Cette tristesse se dissipe à mesure que le travail se solidifie; et aussitôt que le trou sera comblé et le ciel balayé, vous m'entendrez frapper à votre porte. En attendant j'ai plus besoin de patience que vous—c'est à dire de cette égoïste espèce. Je suis depuis quelques jours à peine de retour de la campagne ou je suis allé m'interrer dans les premiers jours de juillet—pour n'en bouger qu'en rentrant, la semaine passée, dans la brume et la bousculade où je vis trop. J'ai passé presque quatre mois dans le midi de l'Angleterre, au fond de ce charmant Devonshire qui est un peu notre Provence, avec le doux Torquay pour lui servir de Cannes ou de Nice. J'y ai bien travaillé—sans voir presque personne—dans une station d'hiver complètement abandonnée l'été. Le 23 de ce mois je verrai Meredith—et aussi—j'espère-le 24, puisque je passe ces deux jours à la campagne chez sa fille—tout exprès pour me trouver près de lui. Je ne l'ai pas vu depuis le mois de juin et je crains bien que sa surdité ne l'ait complètement englouti. Son nouveau roman *Le Mariage Ahurissant*[1]—est sur le point de paraître, mais n'aura pas la fabuleuse fortune de la *Trilby* de Du Maurier, dont il s'est vendu dans ce pays et en Amérique, plus de 250 mille exemplaires—avec desseins de l'auteur—a 7 fr. 50 le volume. On vient d'en tirer une pièce, au théâtre du Haymarket et cette pièce s'annonce comme devant durer—"courir" comme nous disons ici—pendant deux ou trois ans! Ce que c'est que de "prendre mesure du pied"—comme nous disons encore—du bon gros public anglosaxon![2] Le rare Meredith n'est pas ce cordonnier-là—ni le pauvre James non plus.—J'ai reçu ce matin des nouvelles du pitoyable Wilde—par la visite d'un homme politique[3] qui dans le dernier gouvernement était membre (je crois même qu'il l'est encore) de la commission sur la question de la réforme des prisons—et qui a vu le malheureux, il y a quelques semaines, dans un état d'abattement complet, physique et moral—au point qu'on a dû beaucoup relâcher—lui alleger—la discipline et même le mettre à infirmerie—où probablement il fera le reste de son temps, dans des conditions relativement aisées. Il ne lui a trouvé (mon ami) aucune faculté résistante ni récuperative. S'il l'avait, seulement, cette faculté, quel chef d'oeuvre il pourrait faire encore! Mais je vous entretiens de trop tristes choses. J'ose à peine vous demander de vos nouvelles et celles de tous les vôtres, puisque c'est vous engager à m'écrire—et que je ne le mérite pas. Des nouvelles de cet "ahurissant" Léon, j'en ai et de remarquables, par le volume de lui que j'ai trouvé sur ma table en rentrant de la campagne, que je suis en train de lire, dont je suis très frappé et dont, d'ici à très peu de jours, je compte écrire le remercier. Rappelez moi, je vous prie, au souvenir très indulgent de Mme. Daudet, et croyez moi, mon cher ami, votre très affectueusement dévoué,

Henry James

1. HJ's rendering of Meredith's *The Amazing Marriage*, published that year.
2. HJ here translates a phrase he used in his notebooks during his theatrical failures: "to take the measure of the huge, flat foot of the public." See *Notebooks*, 180.
3. This may have been R. B. Haldane (1856–1928), who during the short-lived Rosebery government sat on the Commission for Penal Reform and visited Oscar Wilde at Pentonville jail. At the time of this letter, Wilde was in Wandsworth prison and about to be transferred to Reading Jail.

To W. E. Norris
Ms Yale

34 De Vere Gardens W.
February 4*th* [1896]

My dear Norris.[1]

Your letter is as good as the chair by your study-table (betwixt it, as it were, and the tea-stand) used to be; and as that luxurious piece of furniture shall (D.V.) be again. Your news, your hand, your voice sprinkle me—most refreshingly—with the deep calm of Torquay. It is in short in every way good to hear from you, so that, behold, for your sweet sake, I perpetrate that intensest of my favourite immoralities—I snatch the epistolary, the disinterested pen before (at 10 A.M.) squaring my poor old shoulders over the painful instrument that I fondly try to believe to be lucrative. It *isn't*—but one must keep up the foolish fable to the end. I am having in these difficult conditions a very decent winter. It is mild, and it isn't wet—not here and now; and it is—for me—thanks to more than Machiavellian cunning, more dinnerless than it has, really, ever been. My fireside really knows me on some evenings. I forsake it too often—but a little less and less. So you bloom and smack your lips while I shrivel and tighten my waistband. In spite of my gain of private quiet I have suffered acutely by my loss of public. The American outbreak[2] has darkened all my sky—and made me feel, among many things, how long I have lived away from my native land, how long I *shall* (D.V.!) live away from it and how little I understand it today. The explosion of jingoism there is the result of all sorts of more or less domestic and internal conditions—and what is *most* indicated, on the whole, as coming out of it, is a vast new split or cleavage in American national feeling—politics and parties—a split almost, roughly speaking, between the West and the East. There are really two civilisations there side by side—in one yoke; or rather one civilisation and a barbarism. All the expressions of feeling *I* have received from the U.S. (since this hideous row) have been, intensely, of course, from the former. It is, on the whole, the stronger force; but only on condition of its fighting hard. But I think it *will* fight hard. Meanwhile the whole thing sickens me. That unfortunately, however, is not a reason for its not being odiously there. It's there all the while. But let it not be any more *here:* I mean in this scribblement. My admiration of Smalley[3] is boundless, and my appreciation and comfort and gratitude. He has really *done* something—and will do more—for peace and decency.

I went yesterday to Leighton's[4] funeral—a wonderful and slightly curious public demonstration—the streets all cleared and lined with police, the day magnificent (his characteristic good fortune to the end); and St. Paul's very fine to the eye and crammed with the *whole* London world—everyone except Gosse, whom I went afterwards to see (and comfort!) at the B[oard] of T[rade]. The music was fine and severe, but I thought wanting in volume and force—thin and meagre for the vast space. But what do I know?—No, my dear Norris, I *don't* go abroad—I go on May 1st into the depths (somewhere) of old England. A response to that proposal I spoke to you of (from Rome) is utterly impossible to me now. It says very little to me at best, but I can't now, at all—this year—give up unremunerated months to a job I'm not at all keen to undertake and

27

for which I must desert work intensely pressing and unalterably promised.[5] I've two novels to write before I can *dream* of anything else; and to go abroad is to plunge into the fiery furnace of people. So either Devonshire or some other place will be my six months' lot. I must take a house, this time—a small and cheap one—and I must (deride me not) be somewhere where I can, without disaster, bicycle. Also I must be a little nearer town than last year. I'm afraid these things rather menace Torquay. But it's soon to say—I must wait. I shall decide in April—or by mid-March—only. Meanwhile things will clear up. I'm intensely, thank heaven, busy. I will, I think, send you the little magazine tale over which (I mean over whose number of words—infinite and awful) I struggled so, in September and October last, under your pitying eye and with your sane and helpful advice. It comes in to me this A.M.

I walk in Richmond Park on Saturday with the gallant Rhoda.[6] I have cut down Mrs. Henniker to almost nothing! I hope your daughter is laying up treasure corporeal in Ireland. I like *your* dinners—even I mean in the houses of the other hill-people; and I beg you to feel yourself clung to for ever by yours irrepressibly,

Henry James

1. William Edward Norris (1847–1925), a Victorian novelist who lived at Torquay and whom HJ described as "tremendously old-fashioned at 45." See *Letters* III, 486–487.

2. President Cleveland's reassertion of the Monroe Doctrine during the boundary dispute between Venezuela and British Guiana.

3. George W. Smalley (1833–1916), American journalist. See *Letters* II, 42–43.

4. Frederick Lord Leighton (1830–1896), the neoclassical painter. HJ described the funeral in *Harper's Weekly* XLI (20 February 1896), 183.

5. The family of W. W. Story had asked HJ to write a life of the sculptor. See letter to Boott, 11 October 1895.

6. Rhoda Broughton (1840–1920), the Victorian novelist.

To Edward Holton James
Ms Vaux

34 De Vere Gardens W.
February 15*th* 1896

My dear Edward.[1]

I have valuable gifts from you to acknowledge—the more shame to me that day after day has lately elapsed without my catching the

from its Tarpeian eminence—the terrace's, alas,—the prosy Vicarage receives me.[5] But I rejoice to have *any* immediate refuge. I'm afraid London has been deadly these last days. But this place has been deadly too, and I scarcely stir off the terrace.

Give me a sign before you leave, and believe me

Always your
Henry James

1. *Aphrodite: moeurs antiques,* a novel of courtesan life in Alexandria by Pierre Louÿs (1870–1925), had been recently published in France.

2. Edmond de Goncourt (1822–1896), whom HJ had met at Flaubert's, had just died.

3. M. Lucien Bergeret, a character created by Anatole France in his *L'Histoire contemporaine* (1896–1901), which consisted of four volumes of satiric commentary. The first volume, *L'Orme du mail,* had just been published. The word *désofilant* seems to be an HJ coinage; it might be translated "unflowering."

4. Zola had begun to show new interest during 1895–1896 in current political and social subjects which would lead two years later to his involvement in the Dreyfus affair. His novel *Rome,* published in 1896, was the second in his "Three Cities" series. It was preceded by *Lourdes* in 1894 and followed by *Paris* in 1898.

5. HJ spent the early part of the summer in Rye, Sussex, in the house of the architect Reginald Blomfield on Point Hill, Playden, and was about to move into the Vicarage at Rye.

To Edmund Gosse
Ms Harvard

The Vicarage, Rye
August 28*th* [1896]

My dear Edmund.

Don't think me a finished brute or a heartless fiend or a soulless ass, or any other unhappy thing with a happy name. I have pressed your letter to my bosom again and again, and if I've not sooner expressed to you how I've prized it, the reason has simply been that for the last month there has been no congruity between my nature and my manners—between my affections and my lame right hand. A crisis overtook me some three weeks ago from which I emerge only to hurl myself on this sheet of paper and consecrate it to *you.* I will reserve details—suffice it that in an evil hour I began to pay the penalty of having arranged to let a current serial begin[1] when I was too little ahead of it, and when it proved a much slower and more difficult job than I expected. The printers and illustrators overtook and denounced me, the fear of breaking down paralysed me, the combination of rheumatism and fatigue rendered my hand

and arm a torture—and the total situation made my existence a nightmare, in which I answered not a single note, letting correspondence go to smash in order barely to save my honour. I've finished (day before yesterday), but I fear my honour— with *you*—lies buried in the ruins of all the rest. You will soon be coming home, and this will meet or reach you God only knows where. Let it take you the assurance that the most lurid thing in my dreams has been the glitter of your sarcastic spectacles. It was charming of you to write to me from dear little old devastated Vevey—as to which indeed you made me feel, in a few vivid touches, a faint nostalgic pang. I don't want to think of you as still in your horrid ice-world (for it is cold even here and I scribble by a morning fire); and yet it's in my interest to suppose you still feeling so all abroad that these embarrassed lines will have for you some of the charm of the bloated English post. That makes me, at the same time, doubly conscious that I've nothing to tell you that you will most languish for—news of the world and the devil—no throbs nor thrills from the great beating heart of the thick of things. I went up to town for a week on the 15th, to be nearer the devouring maw into which I had to pour belated copy; but I spent the whole time shut up in De Vere Gardens with an inkpot and a charwoman. The only thing that befell me was that I dined one night at the Savoy with F. Ortmans[2] and the P. Bourgets—and that the said Bourgets—but two days in London—dined with me one night at the Grosvenor club. But these occasions were not as rich in incident and emotion as poetic justice demanded—and your veal-fed table d'hôte will have nourished your intelligence quite as much. The only other thing I did was to read in the *Revue de Paris* of the 15th August the wonderful article of A. Daudet on Goncourt's death—a little miracle of art, adroitness, demoniac tack and skill, and of taste so abysmal, judged by *our* fishlike sense, that there is no getting alongside of it at all. But I grieve to say I can't send you the magazine—I saw it only at a club. Doubtless you will have come across it. I have this ugly house till the end of September and don't expect to move from Rye even for a day till then. The date of your return is vague to me—but if it should be early in the month I wonder if you couldn't come down for another Sunday. I fear you will be too blasé, much. For comfort my Vicarage is distinctly superior to my eagle's nest—[3] but, alas, beauty isn't *in* it. The peace and prettiness of the whole land, here, however, has been good to me, and I stay on with unabated relish.

But I stay in solitude. I don't see a creature. That, too, dreadful to relate, I like. You will have been living in a crowd, and I expect you to return all garlanded and odorous with anecdote and reminiscence. Mrs. Nelly's will all bear, I trust, on miraculous healings and feelings. I feel far from all access to the French volume you recommend. Are you crawling over the Dorn, or only standing at the bottom to catch Philip and Lady Edmund[4] as they drop? Pardon my poverty and my paucity. It is your absence that makes them. Yours, my dear Edmund, not inconstantly

Henry James

1. *The Other House,* in *Illustrated London News.*
2. F. Ortmans, editor of *Cosmopolis,* an international journal which printed in its January and February 1896 issues HJ's tale "The Figure in the Carpet" and in January and February 1898 "John Delavoy."
3. Point Hill, in Rye, where he had stayed earlier.
4. Gosse's wife. Philip was his son.

To Mr. and Mrs. William James
Ms Harvard

The Vicarage, Rye
September 4 1896

My dear William and my dear Alice.

I have had a good letter from each of you, at three or four weeks' distance; and the infirmity of my organism compels me to *faire d'une pierre deux coups* and thank you *both* in this economical manner. Yours, dear Alice, was to send me, on William's behalf, a receipt of Brown Brothers, which he had asked you to forward; and a similar receipt, dear William, is contained in the pages addressed me by you from Cambridge on August 15th which reached me a few days ago. For the remittances attested on each of these occasions accept my constant gratitude. I think of you all this summer with a sympathy which I trust you won't find misplaced: your absence of a mountain home mingles with the impression of the ferocious heat and the ferocious politics; of the general want of amenity above and below, to represent you as exposed to the fury both of nature and of man. However, your last letter exhales courage and cheer—the one in which you tell me of having, together, outlasted the hot wave in good condition and good form at North Conway. May nothing more untoward have overtaken you since! But your adventurous lives and varied summers make me blush for my mouse-like existence. Save to move from Point Hill to this baser level on August 1st (a move of a quarter of an hour in distance) and to spend, the other day, a part of a week in London, I haven't, since May 1st here, tempted fortune in any manner, whatever. I have—on my nine weeks' lease—this house till the end of this month, which will have made five, then, that I shall have spent at Rye. I shall never have spent five quieter ones, nor of which I have liked and *gouté'd* more the quiet. Half a dozen times I've had a friend from Saturday to Monday—but nobody at all now, for a month, and not a creature to converse with, in general, but my fat and sleepy dog and, Crusoe-like, a charming, sociable canary-bird given me last Christmas by poor Mrs. Sands[1]—who was found dead on the floor of her room by her maid, occupied in dressing her for a dinner-party and coming back after having gone out only for two minutes, to get something. She had a weakness of the heart—that's all that's known. Three days before she had written to ask me to thank you for what you had sent her, and had said, at the end of a short note, written at the climax of the London rush: "Are you not coming up at all? I am sick of the whole thing." I went up to her funeral—a strange, shrunken concourse, at St. George's Hanover Square, of odds and ends of old "smart" friends and others. She was a pathetic, *ballottée* creature— with nothing small or mean and with a beauty that had once been of the greatest. One of the things that I spent, again last month, a few days in town for, was to give a Sunday to Wendell Holmes[2]—an episode that proved a very great pleasure. He spent a day with me at Point Hill, and was to have come down here for his penultimate Saturday to Monday. But I had to put him rudely off on account of a sudden press of work compelling me to sit at table from morning till eve—so I took the following Sunday with him in town to make it up, and went with him in the P.M. to Euston to see him off to Ireland and home. He was altogether delightful, more completely so than I have ever seen him, and happy with the immense "success" he had been having—he was, this year, in London, the social figure of the hour. I suppose it's I who have changed—not he; but he struck me as far *simpler* than he used to [be], and made me feel a hundred years old. Precious his faculty of uncritical enjoyment and seeing and imagining those he meets in no relation but their relation to himself—I wish I could—wish to heaven—have more of your, both of your, impressions and contacts: yours, Alice, with the expanding personalities of the children (so veiled in mystery to me—though their letters, some of which you have so kindly sent me, have illuminating gleams); and yours William, with all your scattered auditors and pupils, especially the soda-creamy thousands of "Chautauqua." I don't even know what or where or why Chautauqua is.[3] But I should think you would feel big with all you see and do. *I* do—all the time.—The Bourgets were in London with me—near me—for three days—those following O.W.H.'s departure. They were on their way back from a month in Ireland to furnish a little place they have bought at Hyères—which they offer me for the winter—as they expect to spend it in Japan! They are a strange spectacle, with their constant movement and restlessness and uncontrollability and want of peace and adjustment. His work goes to the deuce—but his success (the *reasons* of which are very incomplete to me) is so great that they abound in means, even with the work, and the ability too, I think, grazing, in their lurches, the rocks. Their career is, however, a lively spectacle to follow. I am so steeped here in solitude and so out of everything that I'm afraid I've no other news for you. Mary (Bob's, the younger—who has had a blighted summer here through having to spend most of it at the deadly Davos with a consumptive cousin)—Mary, I say, on the point of sailing, writes me that her father has been living in a studio in Boston all summer, "painting" and announcing that he will never again go to Concord.[4] Have you heard anything of him—or of his Catholicism? Mary says that she has heard from her mother that he thinks of coming abroad—a prospect that makes me tremble. But I scarcely expect it. I hope your worst trials and scatterings are over and that the autumn—in Cambridge, will close in round you kindly. I wish I had Peggy[5] to bike with me! My bike is my only companion—and this country—for miles and miles—very loveable and lovely. I embrace you both; and am ever, your

Henry

1. Mrs. Mahlon Sands, the American beauty and friend of the Prince of Wales. See *Letters* III, 358.

2. The younger Oliver Wendell Holmes.

3. Chautauqua: a system of adult education conducted from the 1870s to the 1920s in the United States and Canada through home studies and summer camps.

4. HJ's brother Robertson, whose family lived in Concord, had recently undergone what would be a brief conversion to Catholicism.

5. Margaret Mary James (1887–1952), William's daughter, later Mrs. Bruce Porter.

To Maurice Barrès
Ms Private

The Vicarage, Rye, Sussex
le 7 septembre 1896

Cher Monsieur Barrès et cher confrère.

Vous m'avez bien mieux traité que je ne méritais en me remerciant du petit signe expiatoire que je vous adressais l'autre jour sous forme d'un volume de contes—et plus encore en m'annonçant si gentiment—ce dont je remercie bien aussi Mme Barrès—la naissance de votre fils. J'étais trop honteux de ne vous avoir rien écrit au sujet de votre si aimable envoi de: *Du Sang, de la Volupté et de la Mort*,[1] pour me flatter d'espérer de vous le moindre bon souvenir. J'apprécie donc doublement vos amicales paroles et m'en sens tout soulagé. Loin de n'avoir rien à vous dire de votre livre, mon silence provenait essentiellement de la difficulté que je trouvais à vous en rendre un écho aussi plein que mon impression même. J'ai senti dans ce volume plus intensément encore que dans vos autres livres votre esprit et votre art si extraordinaires. Croyez bien que je les goûte et que j'y applaudis autant que personne. Je trouve de bonne hygiène, dans ce pays-ci, de vous prendre à larges doses. Plus encore que de tout cela je vous félicite de la belle simplicité d'être père. Je conserverai toujours un vif souvenir du jeune homme si intelligent, mais profond jusqu'au mystère, qui m'apparut à Florence il y a dix ans et qu'attendait la grande renommée.[2] A chaque pas qu'elle vous fera faire je verrai se fixer davantage cette ombre.

Reçevez je vous prie—et faites-en part à M. Pierre Philippe— toutes mes amitiés,

Henry James

1. HJ met Barrès (1862–1923) in Florence during the winter of 1887–1888 and intensely disliked his cult of the Self (*culte de moi*). See *Letters* III, 228. Barrès's Spanish travel impressions were published in 1894.
2. HJ is probably being ironic about Barrès's "mysterious profundity." In *Mes Cahiers* (Paris, 1963), 17, Barrès describes his meetings with HJ in Florence and says "Je lui expliquai la vie."

To Anton Capadose
Ms Unknown

34 De Vere Gardens W.
October 13*th* 1896

My dear Sir.[1]

You may be very sure that if I had ever had the pleasure of meeting a person of your striking name I wouldn't have used the name, especially for the purpose of the tale you allude to. It was exactly because I had no personal or private association with it that I felt free to do so. But I am afraid that (in answer to your amiable inquiry) it is late in the day for me to tell you how I came by it. "The Liar" was written (originally published in the *Century Magazine*)[2] ten years ago—and I simply don't remember. Fiction-mongers collect proper names, surnames, etc.—make notes and lists of any odd or unusual, as handsome or ugly ones they see or hear—in newspapers (columns of births, deaths, marriages, etc.) or in directories and signs of shops or elsewhere; fishing out of these memoranda in time of need the one that strikes them as good for a particular case. "Capadose" must be in one of my old note-books. I have a dim recollection of having found it originally in the first columns of *The Times,* where I find almost all the names I store up for my puppets.[3] It was picturesque and rare and so I took possession of it. I wish—if you care at all—that I had applied it to a more exemplary individual! But my romancing Colonel was a charming man, in spite of his little weakness. I congratulate you on bearing a name that is at once particularly individualizing and not ungraceful (as so many rare names are). I am, my dear Sir, yours very truly

Henry James

1. The text of this letter is printed in Isaac Da Costa's *Noble Families among the Sephardic Jews.*
2. "The Liar" was published in *Century Magazine,* May–June 1888, and reprinted in *A London Life* (1889). The tale deals with a Colonel Capadose, a genial mythomaniac, addicted to telling tall tales.
3. The name is not among the lists in HJ's extant notebooks.

To Jonathan Sturges
Ms Unknown

34 De Vere Gardens W.
Thursday [5 November 1896]

My dear Jonathan.[1]

I spill over, this A.M., in a certain amount of jubilation—all the more that I have your little letter of the other day to thank you for. One breathes, I suppose—the alarmed, anxious, prudent part of one. But I don't feel that McKinley[2] is the *end* of anything—least of all of big provincial iniquities and abuses and bloody billionaires. However he's more decent than the alternative—and your fortune will flow in, more regularly; and mine will permit me to say I'm delighted you "accept," and shall see that the cold mutton is not too much "snowed under" before you come. Only give me a few—three or four if possible—days' notice: then we will talk of many things—and among them of Rudyard Kipling's "Seven Seas,"[3] which he has just sent me and which I will send you tomorrow or next day (kindly guard it), on the assumption that you won't have seen it. I am laid low by the absolutely uncanny talent—the prodigious special faculty of it. It's all *violent*, without a dream of a *nuance* or a hint of "distinction"; all prose trumpets and castanets and such— with never a touch of the fiddle-string or a note of the nightingale. But it's magnificent and masterly in its way, and full of the most insidious art. He's a rum 'un—and one of the very few first *talents* of the time. There's a vilely idiotic reference to his "coarseness" in this A.M.'s *Chronicle*. The coarseness of the *The Mary Gloster* is absolutely one of the most triumphant "values" of that triumphant thing. How lovely, in these sweet days, your Haslemere hermitage must be! I hope you've still the society of your young friend—it eases the mind of your old one. What you said about Howells most true—he is very touching. And I feel so *remote* from him! The little red book is extremely charming. Write to me. Tout à vous,

Henry James

1. See *Letters* III, 435. Most of HJ's letters to Sturges were destroyed. This one was printed by Percy Lubbock.
2. William McKinley had just been elected President.
3. Kipling's collection of verse *The Seven Seas*, published in October. It contained a new group of army ballads, the "Song of the English," and the "Song of the Cities."

To James Abbott McNeill Whistler
Ms Glasgow

34 De Vere Gardens W.
February 18*th* [1897]

My dear Whistler.[1]

I take your present of the beautiful etching of the dear old house at the dear old Locker as a most benevolent and graceful act. It is a charming thing with a charming association—or, rather, with many more than one: since I hold it directly from your cunning and liberal hand, with the soft participation, too, as I fondly fancy, of Mrs. Whistler's sympathy. It is already swinging in glory on a poorly-populated wall, where a liberal space has been made for it, and where it is quite the fair high aristocrat of the collection. How much more *cachet* I now feel that I have! That I think better still of you goes without saying; but I also fancy even, more yours very gratefully

Henry James

1. HJ had known the American painter since his early London years. See *Letters* II, 167. He had lately renewed the friendship through Jonathan Sturges.

To W. Morton Fullerton
Dictated Ts Harvard

34 De Vere Gardens W.
25*th* February 1897

My dear Fullerton.

Forgive a communication, very shabby and superficial. It has come to this that I can address you only through an embroidered veil of sound. The sound is that of the admirable and expensive machine that I have just purchased for the purpose of bridging our silences. The hand that works it, however, is not the lame *patte* which, after inflicting on you for years its aberrations, I have now definitely relegated to the shelf, or at least to the hospital—that is, to permanent, bandaged, baffled, rheumatic, incompetent obscurity.[1] May you long retain, for yourself, the complete command that I judge you, that I almost see you, to possess, in perfection, of every one of your members. Your letter about my contribution to that flurry of old *romantique* dust[2] was as interesting to me as some of the sentiments it breathed couldn't fail to make it. All thanks for it—all thanks for everything; even for the unconscious stroke by which, in telling me how you have grown up since the day when her acquaintance (Mme. Sand's) was inevitable, you add to the burden of my years. Of course I knew you had; but I am cursed with a memory of my earlier time that beguiles me with associations at which I am able to see young friends, even the most "arrived," address a blank, uninfluenced stare. If I could wish you to be anything in any particular but what you are, I should wish you to have been young when *I* was. Then, don't you see, you would have known not only the mistress of *ces messieurs*,—you would almost, perhaps, have known *me*. And now you will never catch up! Neither shall I, however, my dear Fullerton—since it comes to that—if I give too much time to our gossip. I have so much less of that than you to do it in. Besides, it now begins to look definite that I *shall*, for a few days in April, have the pleasure of seeing you. I shall spend as many in Paris as possible—as many as the few—on my way then to three months in Italy.[3] Give me the benefit of your fine imagination to calculate exactly how few moments, with an eye to that, I can afford to take from the great business of arranging to be free. Let it answer your letter directly enough to assure you that no word of it was lost on yours, my dear Fullerton, always

Henry James

1. This letter to Fullerton (see *Letters* III, 269) is among the first HJ dictated. He began by using a shorthand stenographer, William MacAlpine; later he learned to dictate directly to a typist at the machine. HJ resorted to the typewriter at this time because of an acute attack of writer's cramp. See the chapter "A Fierce Legibility" in Edel, *The Treacherous Years* (1969).

2. An article in the *Yellow Book*, January 1897, on George Sand and Alfred de Musset, entitled "She and He: Recent Documents."

3. HJ abandoned this plan and did not visit the Continent until 1899.

To James Abbott McNeill Whistler
Dictated Ts Glasgow

34 De Vere Gardens W.
25*th* February 1897

My dear Whistler.

Yes, even though it be an outrage to a man with your touch to address him in accents condemned to click into his ear—thanks to interposing machinery—a positive negation of every delicacy; yet nevertheless I *must* thank you over my hand and seal, and with nothing less than documentary force, for making me the possessor of your delightful little document of Monday. To have pleased you,[1] to have touched you, to have given you something of the impression of the decent little thing one attempted to do—this is for me, my dear Whistler, a rare and peculiar pleasure. For the arts are one, and with the artist the artist communicates. Therefore your good words come to me as from one who knows. You know, above all, better than anyone, how dreadfully few are such. One writes for one's self alone—one has accepted, once for all, the worst; so that such a sign as your letter makes me has all the beautiful cheer and comfort of the happy windfall—the something more, so much more, than was included in the beggarly bond. You have done too much of the exquisite not to have earned more despair than anything else; but don't doubt that something vibrates back when that Exquisite takes the form of recognition of a not utterly indelicate brother. It was such a pleasure to see you again that I shall not neglect anything in the nature of the faintest further occasion. Yours, my dear Master, very constantly,

Henry James

1. HJ reciprocated Whistler's gift of an etching (see letter of 18 February) by sending him the just-published *The Spoils of Poynton.*

To Edward Parker Deacon
Dictated Ts Unknown

34 De Vere Gardens W.
6*th* June 1897

Dear Edward Deacon.[1]

It is base and scandalous that I have left your good letter of last winter so long unacknowledged. Please find, however, much of the explanation—most of it—in the machinery to which, like you, I am condemned. My hand, some time ago, went utterly to smash—but it has taken no longer than, clearly, it has taken you to learn to dictate. I have needed all these months to pick up the pieces of my correspondence, for I am only able to do so in the scraps of time, and odds and ends of moments, that I can help my amanuensis to spare from other work. Therefore continue to be as patient with me as you *have* been. Please believe that, in addition to my appreciation of the friendly things you say to me, my interest continues unabated in the varied drama of your life—the drama[2] that has restored you (for how long?) to your native land, and of which you give me an impression in your allusion to the part played in your existence by your daughters, by what you can do for them, and by all that they, I take for granted, are able to do for you. I feel as if I must give you the impression of a deadly monotony—for here have I lived ever since, ages ago, I left Bolton Street, where you saw me and where, one summer afternoon, just after your marriage, you made, not alone, that apparition that I never shall forget. There was nothing but beauty in it then. In all the years, at any rate, I have had in London but these two homes; and in the present one I have all the air of being destined to end my days and (all but) lay my bones. It would be interesting to talk with you of the terms a man in your situation—I mean so long an alien and so much Europeanised, finds himself able to make with New York conditions. They are better ones, I gather, than any that are possible for me. It is quite on the cards that I shall never again behold, I fear, the land of my birth. But I like to hear about it—therefore come back some day and tell me. London engulfs me more and more—by which I don't mean socially (heaven forbid!—I live more and more to myself and to my work); but by mere accumulations of time, habit and use. I go abroad less and less—though I suppose myself to be on the point of going, for

44

some weeks, to escape this dusty rush and crush of the Jubilee, which already, nearly a month beforehand, has converted the town by planking and partitions, hoardings and boardings of every description, into the likeness of a huge cattle-pen. I spend, after a day or two, the rest of this month in Paris—but Paris, alas, is rather dolefully changed. It is full of ghosts. You will be one of them. Meanwhile, however, I hope that in some place of cool Atlantic airs you are bearing the burden of flesh. Not that I shall ever think of you as too much overcharged with it. Do you still go to Newport? Some of your *ghosts* must be there. I gird my loins afresh at your *paroles de sympathie*. I wish I could see your girls. But I shall be sure to—the future is theirs and I shall hang on to it hard enough and long enough to be brushed by their wing. I give them meanwhile my blessing; and *je vous serre bien la main*—two lame ducks careful not to squeeze too hard. Forgive my mixed metaphor—and take my remembrance "neat." Yours, my dear Deacon, from ever so long ago and for—let us hope—ever so much longer,

Henry James

1. This letter is reproduced from a typed copy found among the papers of Gladys, Duchess of Marlborough (the former Gladys Parker, second wife of the ninth Duke). It was written to her father, whom HJ had met during his early days in London.
2. See HJ's remark of 28 February 1892 in *Notebooks* (1947) 116: "the dreadful E.D. 'tragedy' in the South of France." The tragedy consisted in Deacon's having shot and killed his wife's lover in a hotel in Cannes. See Hugo R. Vickers, *Gladys, Duchess of Marlborough* (1979).

To Frances Rollins Morse
Dictated Ts Harvard

34 De Vere Gardens W.
June 7*th* 1897

My dear Fanny.[1]

I have, as usual, endless unacknowledged benefits to thank you for after too many days. The last is your letter of the end of March, full of interesting substance as always and of things that no one else has the imagination or the inspiration to tell me. (My allusion to the imagination there is not, believe me, an imputation on your exactitude. The light of truth, of good, solid, vivid Boston truth, shines in each of your pages.) Especially are you interesting and

welcome, as I have told you before, I think, on the young generations and full-blown, though new, existences, that are in possession of a scene I knew as otherwise occupied. All the old
names—or most of them—appear to be represented by the remote
posterity of my old acquaintance. In this remote posterity,
however, I take an interest—and scraps and specimens of it, even
here, occasionally flash past me. The last two I can remember were
John Bancroft's[2] younger daughter, the other day, with her mother,
at Mary Beaumont's, where I went to see them; and Cabot Lodge's
big, ugly, pleasant son,[3] whom I dined with at the Hays'[4] and whom
I, somehow—perhaps too suddenly—figure as a possible suitor for,
or recipient of (let us hope they are identical!) the hand of the
charming little Muse. That sounds obscure, but look at the last
century. I don't mean—as my amanuensis is sure to have made me
ambiguous—the pre-Victorian, but the Union Square, New York,
perhaps I should say the Gilderian.[5] I can't swallow Senator Cabot
(though I am afraid he *is* cousin) but I much liked his clever and
civilized, and withal modest and manly, young son. On the Ban-
crofts, the graces have not been absolutely showered, but the little,
shy, yet talkative, contralto girl inspired me with confidence; and
Mrs. J. B. I have liked from ancient days. Mrs. Beaumont I see but
at the longest intervals—and rather with pain, or at least with pity.
She looks so deadly ill, and as if suffering were her portion. I mean
in that particular only; otherwise I judge her blissful, and she told
me her husband is about to become an admiral. Traces of her great
beauty still in some measure attend her. I tell you of these things,
in return for your own great abundance; though it's very small
change I give you back. I have had none but small change for a long
time—in spite of plotting a good deal for greater. I have stayed on
in town later than for some years past, and though I had, at the end
of March, all my plans made to go to Italy, have put it off till so late
that, in a few days, I shall have to be content with simply crossing
to Paris and seeing then what is to be further done. London is given
up to carpenters and seatmongers—being prepared, on an enormous
scale and a rather unsightly way, for the "circus" of the 22nd. The
circus is already, amid the bare benches and the mere *bousculade*
of the preparations, a thing to fly from—in spite of the good young
George Vanderbilt's[6] having offered me an ample share of a beautiful balcony in Pall Mall to see it from. I shall spend the next few

weeks in some place or places, north of the Alps, as yet utterly undefined, and be back in England before the summer is over. The voice of Venice, all this time, has called very loud. But it has been drowned a good deal in the click of the typewriter to which I dictate and which, some months ago, crept into my existence through the crevice of a lame hand and now occupies in it a place too big to be left vacant for long periods of hotel and railway life. All this time I am not coming to the great point, which is my hope, that you may have been able to be present (I believe with all my heart of course you were) at the revelation of the Shaw Memorial.[7] In charity, my dear Fanny, if this be the case, do write me a frank word about it. I heard from William and Alice more or less on the eve, but I fear they will have afterwards—just now be having—too much to do to be able to send me many echoes. I daresay that you will, for that matter, already have sent me one. I receive, as it happens, only this morning, a copy of *Harper's Weekly* with a big reproduction of St. Gaudens's bas-relief, which strikes me as extraordinarily beautiful and noble. How I rejoice that something really fine is to stand there forever for R.G.S.—and for all the rest of them. This thing of St. G.'s strikes me as a real perfection, and I have appealed to William to send me the finest and biggest photograph of it that can be found—for such surely have been taken. How your spiritual lungs must, over it all, have filled themselves with the air of the old war time. Even here—I mean simply in the depths of one's own being—I myself, for an hour, seem to breathe it again. But the strange thing is that however much, in memory and imagination, it may live for one again, with all its dim figures and ghosts and reverberations and emotions, it appears to belong yet to some far away *other* world and state of being. I talked of this the other day with Sara Darwin,[8] whose memories are so much identical with my own, and it was a relief to do so—in the absence of all other communications: that absence produced by the up-growth, since, of a whole generation, which began after the end and for which the whole history is as alien as the battles of Alexander. But I am writing you a long letter when I only meant to wave you a hand of greeting and gratitude. Correspondence is rather heavy to me, for I can tackle it only in the margin of time left over after the other matters that my machine has to grind. I hope your summer promises, and in the midst of a peculiar degree, at the present moment, of smoky London stuffiness, I envy you—for I see you in the mind's eye at Beverly—the element of wide verandah, cut peaches—I mean peaches and cream, you know—white frocks and Atlantic airs. You make me, my dear Fanny, in these high lights, quite incredibly homesick. Recall me, please, with every precaution, to your mother. How did William do it? Yours, very constantly

Henry James

1. Frances Rollins Morse (1850–1928), an old Boston friend of the James family.
2. John Bancroft, painter and friend of HJ's Newport years, son of the U.S. historian and diplomat George Bancroft.
3. The poet George Cabot ("Bay") Lodge (1873–1909), eldest son of Senator Henry Cabot Lodge (1850–1924) and the former Anna Cabot Mills Davis.
4. John Milton Hay (1838–1905), HJ's friend since the 1870s, was named ambassador to the United Kingdom by President McKinley.
5. HJ refers to Richard Watson Gilder's editorship of the *Century*.
6. George Washington Vanderbilt (1862–1914), youngest son of William Henry Vanderbilt and grandson of Cornelius Vanderbilt, was an agriculturist and forester who established the vast Biltmore estate near Asheville, North Carolina.
7. The Saint-Gaudens sculpture in memory of Colonel Robert Gould Shaw (1837–1863), who commanded the 54th Massachusetts regiment, the first black regiment of the Civil War, and who was killed during the assault on Fort Wagner in July 1863. WJ spoke at the inaugural. The younger James brother, Garth Wilkinson (1845–1883), was wounded in this charge.
8. The former Sara Sedgwick. See *Letters* II, 143, 150.

To Ellen Temple (Emmet) Hunter
Ms Harvard

Bath Hotel, Bournemouth
Saturday [3 July 1897]

Dearest Elly.[1]

It is an immense satisfaction to get your news—and no figure of speech to say that it has found me literally on the point of reaching out, for it, into the thick twilight of your whereabouts. I have had my general silence much on my conscience—and especially my dumbness and darkness to Rosina and Bay, for whom my movements must have been enveloped in a perfidious mystery that has caused me, I fear, to forfeit all their esteem. But let me tell you first of all how I rejoice in your good conditions and in your having found your feet. It was "borne in" upon me, on general grounds, that Southwold would never do for long, and it is charming that you have found so near and so nice a substitute. I especially delight (without wanting to sacrifice the rest of you) in such a letting-down-easy of the Art-Daughters. Please give them my tender love and tell them that, preposterous as it sounds, I have never, all this time and in spite of the rosiest asseverations, crossed the channel at all. The nearest I have come to it is to have, early last month, come down here to the edge of the sea and collapsed into the peace and obscurity of this convenient corner (long familiar to me) which, having a winter season, is practically empty at present. I will [tell] R. and B. when I see them just how it was that I happened to be so false—it is too long a story now. Suffice it that my reasons (for continuing to hug this fat country) were overwhelming, and my regrets (at not tasting of their brave Bohemia) of the sharpest. More-over all's well that ends well. If I *had* gone abroad I should be abroad now and the rest of the summer; and therefore unable to join you on your Suffolk shore—or at least alight upon you there—which is what I shall be enchanted to do. You describe a little Paradise—houris and all; and I beseech you to keep a divan for me there. The only thing is that I fear I shan't be able to come till toward the end—or *by* the end—of the month. I have more or less engaged myself (to a pair of friends who are coming down here next week for my—strange as it may seem—sweet sake) to remain on this spot till toward the 25th. But I will come *then,* and stay as long as you will let me. If you can *bespeak* any quarters for me at the inn, in ad-vance, I will take it very kindly of you. Can they give me a little *sitting room* as well as a bed room? If you can achieve any effective winking at them to do so I shall be very grateful. I always *need* some small literary bower other than the British bedroom—and in this case I would of course "meal" there; as that makes them always more zealous. I don't know the East Coast to speak of at all—and I can imagine no more winsome introduction to it. I quite yearn to commune with the young Parisians. Bravo, MacMonnies.[2] Bravo everybody—especially Grenville.[3] How I shall joy to frolic with him in the sand! Have they seen—the art-daughters—the image of the St. Gaudens' Shaw? It is altogether great. William's oration was a first-class success. I encircle you all and will write again!

Ever, my dear Elly, so constantly yours,
Henry James

P.S. The oddest trio of coincidences yesterday afternoon. I was reading the delightful *Letters* of that peculiarly Suffolk genius (of Woodbridge) Edward FitzGerald ("Omar Khayyam") and, just finishing a story in one of them about his relations with a boatman of Saxmundham (a name—seen for the first time—that struck me—by its strangeness and handsomeness), laid down the book and went a long walk—five miles along this coast, to where in a very pictur-esque and lonely spot, I met a sea-faring man with whom I fraternised.

"Do you belong to this place?"

"Oh no. I've been here five years; but I come from the Suffolk coast—Saxmundham."

"Did you know Mr. FitzGerald?"

"Know him? my brother was his boatman!"—and he tells me the story!—Then I walk home, and coming in, find your letter on my table. I tear it open and the first word I see in it—in your date—is *Saxmundham!*—Tableau!!! It never rains but it pours!—

1. Ellen James Temple (1850–1920), Minnie Temple's younger sister, married Christopher Temple Emmet (1822–1884) and after his death George Hunter (1847–1914). She was now in England with her daughters Ellen Gertrude (Bay) Emmet, a painter, Rosina Hubley Emmet, and Edith Leslie.

2. Frederick William MacMonnies (1863–1937), an American sculptor who was living in Paris.

3. George Grenville Hunter, five years old at the time of this letter, Ellen Hunter's only child of her second marriage.

To William Rothenstein
Dictated Ts Harvard

Bath Hotel, Bournemouth
July 13*th* 1897

Dear W. Rothenstein.

I am afraid I am condemned, in answer to your note, to inflict on your artistic sense more than one shock; therefore let the outrage of this ponderous machinery deaden you a little at the start perhaps to what may follow. I am sorry to say, crudely speaking, that I don't find myself able to promise you anything in the nature of a text for your characterisation of Sargent. Why shouldn't it, this character-isation, be complete in itself? I am sure nothing will be wanting to it. At any rate, the case, as it stands with me, is fairly simple and expressible: I have written so much and so hyperbolically and so often upon that great man that I scarce feel I have another word to say in public.[1] I must reserve my ecstasies for mere conversation, at the peril of finding myself convivially silent in the face of future examples. Only the other day, or the other month again, I sounded the silver trumpet in an American periodical—I mean on the occasion of his Academy picture. You painters are accustomed to such thunders of applause that the whole proportion for you is in these matters, I know, different. Yet I have thundered myself empty on the particular theme, and, with every appreciation of the confidence of which your invitation is a sign, I must ask you, this time, to excuse me.

After this, how shall I dare to say Yes to your still more flattering proposal that I shall lay my own head on the block? You can so easily chop it off to vent any little irritation my impracticability may have caused you. However, please take it as a proof of my complete trust in your magnanimity if I answer: With pleasure—do with me whatever you think I now deserve.[2] Only I fear I shall not be in town with any free day or hour to sit for a goodish while to come. Kindly let the matter stand over till we are gathered together again; but don't doubt meanwhile how delighted I shall be to see the copy of your series which you are so good as to promise me. Believe me yours most truly,

Henry James

1. William Rothenstein (1872–1945) sketched many writers and was a lively figure in the art world at the end of the century. HJ's writings on Sargent comprised an article in *Harper's New Monthly Magazine*, October 1887, reprinted in *Picture and Text* (1893); a "London Letter" in *Harper's Weekly*, 5 June 1897; and a further "London Letter" in the same journal, 26 June 1897. He also used Sargent as model for the painter-figures in some of his later stories.

2. HJ sat for a Rothenstein drawing later that year.

To William James
Dictated Ts Harvard

Dunwich, Saxmundham, Suffolk
August 7th 1897

My dear William.

Too long, too long, have I procrastinated. Benefits extreme have I received from you—two letters and the July advice from Brown Bros. Set it down, please—I mean my silence—to the chronic

On the beach near Dunwich, Suffolk, in 1897.

struggle for existence, rendered particularly acute of late by all this midsummer mixture of heat and motion, of getting out of town to places that one can in security only get back from by at once crossing it and dodging it: dodging because of all the traps that, in one way or another, it trips one up with at this time of the year. My last, so charming for the dog days, was having to serve, at the Court of Queen's Bench, on a long two-days British Jury[1]—for which, here, even the alien is impressed after ten years of residence. Complicated with that was a visit to Godkin and his wife,[2] who, with her mother, are settled for three months in a very comfortable and commodious, though hideous, country-house in the loveliest depths of Surrey. I enjoyed, however, as well as the sweetness of the land—albeit in Senegambian heat—the being, for a few days, with old E.L.G., whose humour and kindness and gossip and reflections on the state of the world in general and of the U.S. in particular all helped to pass the time. He is very low about the U.S.—I might even say very lowering. But as it seems that they can bear almost anything, they can bear, I suppose, even that. I never went abroad at all—as I must have written a goodish many weeks ago to Alice. The only thing I really care to do in that line is to go to Italy; and when that is crowded out, as it has been for three or four successive years and was overwhelmingly so, this time, till too late in the season for hot countries, I find it perfectly simple and easy to stick to British soil. My love of travel grows smaller and smaller—and that has a convenient side. I quitted London as early as possible in June, and spent the interval till the other day at the rather prosaic but also rather pretty and salubrious Bournemouth; which, as a place for the winter season, is in summer full of peace and emptiness. It was empty for me, that is, of almost everything but ghosts. Alice[3] passed there the greater part of her first winter in England—when I was some three months near her; and it was there that I saw almost all I did see of the great R.L.S.[4] I've come to this quiet corner in consequence of some pleasant little correspondence, a month ago, with the Emmet cousins, who, some weeks earlier, had dé-nichéd it for themselves, ingeniously, and gave me an account of it which, in the light of salubrity, economy, the picturesque and the chance to be a while with them, operated to make me take for the month of August some rather primitive but apparently (I arrived but yesterday) quite possible little quarters. The elder Cousin, with her three girls, the boy and two or three of their own Emmet and other kinsfolk, have quite appropriated the place—where it is pleasant to see them so much at peace and in conditions that happen so to fit. It's all very quiet and quaint and rustic and uncockneyfied; and Rosina and Bay, fresh from the great sensations of Paris, show, I think, a great deal of real "artistic" feeling in being able to taste so a quality—a charm of landscape and association—that profits to the utmost by the English ability to remain latent. I think it will be very pleasant to be a while near them—especially on the convenient basis of having planted one's Remington and begun to make it tick in one's tent. In addition to every other merit under heaven I find that a supreme "protection." Bay has brought back from Paris the most marked evidences of her really very great talent—and is now painting—riding three horses at once—the portraits, admirably well, of her mother, Rosina, Leslie and the boy respectively. If one ever teaches them to speak they will be all right: that, for intercourse, is their only defect. They tell me you have laboured on them much; but there is still much to do. Their mother has been an angel in arranging little matters for me here comfortably enough to risk it; and with Hunter taking a month's holiday on his native heath, the omens are favourable for her continued cheer. She is completely capable—and I find her constantly charming.

No, it wasn't in the least the sentiment of the Jubilee that made me drop going abroad. It was only arrears of occupation. Of the sentiment of the Jubilee I partook in the strictest moderation. You would know, had you been here, what I mean. It was hugely overdone—that is all I mean. And that is the great clumsy, ugly fate of everything to-day that's done at all. The machinery of insistence and reverberation—the newspaper deluge and uproar—deflowers and destroys and maddens. I saw not the tip of the tail of any part of the show. I had lent De Vere Gardens to the grateful and bedless Godkins, and spent the show-day at Bournemouth by a hot blue sea—the only person there not a departing excursionist. You are quite right about the perfect superfluity of writing to E. P. Deacon;[5] but I did the least and the worst I could, and had waited six months—indeed I think a good deal more—before noticing his letter. He is vacuous and vain but there is no harm in him—in spite of his *assassinat*. And he has a sort of fidelity to old memories.

Luckily, however, he doesn't trouble me with it—he had not written me since he was in prison. I rejoice in what you tell me of your children's growth and beauty: barmecide fare as it is to one so bare of such processes. I can only hope, as the days go on—by which I mean the years—to be clothed, as it were, at your expense—or even, in a kind of roundabout manner, at my own. Your letter—the last one—gave me the sense of all your variety and activity; especially as to the poetry of motion that you work with such energy into all the rest. It is very peaceful to sit here afar off and admire the whole thing. I shall sit here as long as I can. I have just heard from Howells, from Karlsbad; and as he is apparently to be here—that is in Europe, for months to come, I hope to manoeuvre some contact or communion with him. But there will be time to talk of that. There won't, however, my dear William, be time to do much else if I let myself, in letters, float too far on the swift Remington stream. (I don't, by the way, as you seem to suppose, dictate to shorthand, though my friend here is a master of it; I dictate straight to Remington.) I hope that by the time you get this you will have turned out of your summer schools all your summer scholars and be lying above them as a god—on some New Hampshire hill. May all the immortals surround you there—the divine wife and children. I send them my tender love. I was scorched by the hot wave I read of these last weeks in the American news. I hope you weren't too near the fire. We are in a long period here—just like last summer, as that was like the one before it. Only this one is more so—weeks and weeks without rain and almost without fresh air—or *fraîcheur*, which was what I meant to say. It's sweet to be out of town, and this low, quaint, uncockneyfied, old-world stretch of the East Anglian coast is much cooler than Bournemouth. The irrepressible Bourgets have been with me—but very briefly indeed, and now quite carried off to higher flights of every kind. They are in Scotland—under the wig wing—the wing, not the wig—of the young, amiable and "literary" Duchess of Sutherland. Excuse the transition[6] with which I am affectionately yours,

Henry

P.S. Doing British Juryman threw lights—and glooms!

1. HJ interrupted his stay in Bournemouth to do jury duty at the Court of Queen's Bench in London in a divorce hearing.
2. E. L. Godkin (1831–1902), HJ's former editor at the *Nation*. See *Letters* I, 81.

55

3. The reader must distinguish between this Alice, HJ's sister, who died in 1892, and the Alice referred to earlier, WJ's wife.

4. For HJ's friendship with Robert Louis Stevenson, see *Letters* III.

5. See letter to Deacon, 6 June 1897.

6. The "transition" was to the handwritten postscript and the penned correction of the typist's "wig" for "wing."

To Edward Warren
Dictated Ts Huntington

34 De Vere Gardens W.
15*th* September 1897

My dear Edward.[1]

Very kindly read, for me, the enclosed—which throws an odd coincidental light on the very house we talked of, day before yesterday (or was it yesterday?) as we bumped and bounced and vainly shifted sides. The place in question is none other than the mansion with the garden-house perched on the wall; and though to be fairly confronted with the possibility and so brought to the point is a little like a blow in the stomach, what I am minded to say to you is that perhaps you may have a chance to tell me, on Friday, that you will be able to take some day next week to give me the pleasure of going down there with me for a look. I feel as if I couldn't *think* on the subject at all without seeing it—the subject—again; and there would be no such seeing it as seeing it in your company. Perhaps I shall have speech of you long enough on Friday to enable us to settle a day. *I* should be capable of Monday. I hope you slid gently home and are fairly on all fours—that is on hands and feet—again. What a day we should have had again also—I mean this one—if we had kept it up! But *basta così!*—it does beautifully for your journey. A thousand friendships to Margaret. Always yours,

Henry James

1. Edward Prioleau Warren (1856–1937), HJ's architect friend, was helping him find a country house; the house in question here was seen by HJ during the summer he spent at Playden, Sussex, in 1896.

To Arthur Christopher Benson
Ms Bodleian

34 De Vere Gardens W.
September 25th 1897

My dear Arthur.

Send me by all means the Diary[1] to which you so kindly allude—nothing could give me greater pleasure than to feel I might freely—and yet so responsibly—handle it. I hope it contains a record of your Hawarden talk—of which you speak.—I shall be very glad indeed of a talk with you about W. Cory—my impression of whom, on the book, you deepen: whenever anything so utterly unlikely as articulate speech between us miraculously comes to pass.—I am just drawing a long breath from having signed—a few moments since—a most portentous parchment: the lease of a smallish, charming, cheap old house in the country—down at Rye—for *twenty-one* years! (One would think I was *your* age!) But it is exactly what I want and secretly and hopelessly coveted (since knowing it) without dreaming it would ever fall. But it *has* fallen—and has a beautiful room for *you* (the "King's Room"—George II's—who slept there); together with every promise of yielding me an indispensable retreat from May to October. I hope you are not more sorry to take up the load of life that awaits, these days, the hunch of one's shoulders than *I* am. You'll ask me what I mean by "life." Come down to Lamb House and I'll tell you. And open the private page, my dear Arthur, to yours very eagerly,

Henry James

1. Arthur Christopher Benson (1862–1925), an editor of Queen Victoria's selected letters and at this time a housemaster at Eton. He had begun to keep voluminous diaries, from which Percy Lubbock edited a selection in the 1920s.

57

To Arthur Christopher Benson
Dictated Ts Bodleian

34 De Vere Gardens W.
1*st* October 1897

My dear Arthur.

I return you with this—or rather separately—the charming Diary; which you will think perhaps I have kept too many days. But I have only been waiting, amid much occupation, for the right hour to give it the right sentiment. That is what—this last—I *have* finally given it. It has been, for me, a very friendly, happy, delightful contact; almost a tangible substitute for never, never seeing you. Give me more, in time; give me a great deal more; give me as much as you can. I like it enough for that. With my voracity for personal introspections, I find in your existence a great deal to feed upon. The fault of the record is of course that it's not really private enough; but that is the fault of all confidences. At any rate, I welcome it as a document, a series of data, on the life of a young Englishman of great endowments, character and position at the end of the nineteenth century. There is nothing I like better than that others should live *for* me, as it were—in case, of course, I can catch them *at* it. Therefore, in short, continue to live, and *do* continue to let me catch you. I will do anything—everything—munificently— to keep you going to this end. Bear that in mind, and put in all you can. I have read, of course, every word—and I think have had real inspirations in the way of making you out. There is absolutely not a word I have lost. Your episode at Hawarden[1] is a prodigy of *reportage:* how grand of you to be able to feel you have such a loaf upon the shelf in case the mothers, and even the sons, ever become too many for you! I would read the newspapers then.

I am much touched by your delightful friendliness about my little old house. Your taste in these things would not, I think, be afflicted by my little undertaking. I don't think it could be so exactly the right thing for me if it were not rather decent. But I won't willingly pander in this manner to any such sympathy (as you may benignantly drop upon me) as will help you in the least not to come down and see it for yourself the very first, or at most the very second or very third, time I try to make you. The merit of it is that it's such a place as I may, when pressed by the pinch of need, retire to with a certain shrunken decency and wither away—in a fairly cleanly and pleasantly melancholy manner—toward the tomb. It is really good enough to be a kind of little becoming, high-door'd, brass-knockered *façade* to one's life. This gives me an advantage, for I feel—after the Journal—as if I had got a little behind *your* knocker.—Why is the great interest of Mr. Gladstone somehow so awfully uninteresting? *Vale.* Yours always,

Henry James

1. Arthur Christopher Benson's father, Edward White Benson (1829–1896), Archbishop of Canterbury from 1882, had died while kneeling in prayer at Hawarden Church. Prime Minister Gladstone, a close friend of the Bensons, lived in Hawarden Castle.

To William Blackwood
Ms Scotland

34 De Vere Gardens W.
October 28*th* 1897

Dear Mr. Blackwood.

It gives me great pleasure to hear from you that you accept my proposal in regard to the volume on Mr. Story:—£250 "down" as before mentioned (as fee for the work) and £100 in case of its selling 7000—and again for any, or every, further 2000 sold. This to cover *all* rights, I shall not, as I was clear to the Waldo S.'s,[1] get at the business (be at all *able* to) immediately: but I shall attack it at my very first leisure and then with much concentration, and do, in fine, my very best for it. I shall live—with it—among many old friends and old ghosts. Believe me yours very truly

Henry James

1. Thomas Waldo Story was pressing HJ to write a life of his father, the sculptor W. W. Story (see letter to Francis Boott, 11 October 1895). HJ now signed a contract for this book but specified no date for delivery of the manuscript.

To William Dean Howells
Ms Harvard

34 De Vere Gardens W.
November 27th 1897

My dear Howells.

I have been more touched than I can say by the swift evidence I have received (from H. L. Nelson)[1] of the beneficent activity of the spirit in which you quitted me the other day in that deadly, dreary medium. I am sure you will be glad to know what your magic voice has wrought—a proposal, on Nelson's part, to which I have already lucidly responded. It seems therefore as if *The Awkward Age* were indeed to see the light, next year, in the amiable *Weekly*. You were wholly right as to the fee or guerdon—£600 ($3000) is exactly what would have been the form of *my* golden dream, and is what I have directly named. I am supposing that this applies to the *American* serial rights only, and that the English would be still *disponibles*; but as to them I should doubtless be still humbly subject to correction. I could probably get £250, or £300 for the English affair.—But enough of that element. What is more to the point is that you will never know at how psychological a moment you appeared to me the other day—but I almost *can* tell you, nevertheless, how beautiful a kind of poetic justice I find, and thank fortune, and yourself, for, in your so clearing up things for me (for you *have*, really, to a wondrous degree) in the fulness of these years that crown our long friendship. I wanted to say so to you *then*, much better than I did—but one is tongue-tied at all great moments. But one feels it not the less. Never forget, at all events, for *I* never shall, that it *was* a psychological moment.[2] I felt myself, somehow perishing in my pride or rotting ungathered, like an old maid against the wall and on her lonely bench. Well, I'm *not* an old maid (for the blessed trade) quite yet. And you *were* Don Quixote!

The proof of it is, my dear Howells, that you were so Quixotic as to return! And I'm sure Mrs. Howells plays Sancho to *that!* Yes, I desire to rub it in; you might perfectly be in Rome; and I might (more imperfectly) come down to see you there. Do *not*, at any rate, I beseech you, be afraid to come and see me next time. You have done it once for all, and I shall do nothing worse than embrace you. It was a joy to me to be reminded by your wife (please tell her so)

60

of a thousand tender things of the old sweet time. And I love your daughter—I break it to you thus. *Try my amanuensis!*—especially to tick it out to me loud and clear that you are coming again. Yours, my dear Howells, most affectionately,

Henry James

1. Henry Loomis Nelson was editor of *Harper's Weekly*, in which *The Awkward Age* was serialized from October 1898 to February 1899.

2. HJ was deeply depressed in spite of his continued creativity, and was disturbed by his inability to sell more fiction to American magazines. He needed money at this juncture to pay for his lease of Lamb House. Howells, as on earlier occasions, intervened to help his old friend.

To Mrs. William James
Dictated Ts Harvard

34 De Vere Gardens W.
1*st* December 1897

Dearest Alice.

It's too hideous and horrible, this long time that I have not written you and that your last beautiful letter, placed, for reminder, well within sight, has converted all my emotion on the subject into a constant, chronic blush. The reason has been that I have been driving very hard for another purpose this inestimable aid to expression, and that, as I have a greater loathing than ever for the mere manual act, I haven't, on the one side, seen my way to inflict on you a written letter, or on the other had the virtue to divert, till I should have finished my little book—to another stream—any of the valued and expensive industry of my amanuensis.[1] I *have*, at last, finished my little book—that is *a* little book, and so have two or three mornings of breathing-time before I begin another.[2] *Le plus clair* of this small interval "I consecrate to thee!"

I am settled in London these several weeks and making the most of that part of the London year—the mild, quiet, grey stretch from the mid-October to Christmas—that I always find the pleasantest, with the single defect of its only not being long enough. We are having, moreover, a most creditable autumn; no cold to speak of and almost no rain, and a morning-room window at which, this December 1st, I sit with my scribe, admitting a radiance as adequate as that in which you must be actually bathed and probably more mildly golden. I have no positive plan save that of just ticking the winter swiftly away on this most secure basis. There are, however, little doors ajar into a possible brief absence. I fear I have just closed one of them rather ungraciously indeed, in pleading a "non possumus" to a most genial invitation from John Hay to accompany him and his family, shortly after the new year, upon a run to Egypt and a month up the Nile; he having a boat for that same—I mean for the Nile part—in which he offers me the said month's entertainment. It is a very charming opportunity, and I almost blush at not coming up to the scratch; especially as I shall probably never have the like again. But it isn't so simple as it sounds; one has on one's hands the journey to Cairo and back, with whatever seeing and doing by the way two or three irresistible other things, to which one would feel one might never again be so near, would amount to. (I mean, of course, then or never, on the return, Athens, Corfu, Sicily the never-seen, etc., etc.) It would all "amount" to too much this year, by reason of a particular little complication—most pleasant in itself, I hasten to add—that I haven't, all this time, mentioned to you. Don't be scared—I haven't accepted an "offer."[3] I have only taken, a couple of months ago, a little old house in the country—for the rest of my days!—on which, this winter, though it is, for such a commodity, in exceptionally good condition, I shall have to spend money enough to make me quite concentrate my resources. The little old house you will at no distant day, I hope, see for yourself and inhabit and even, I trust, temporarily and gratuitously possess—for half the fun of it, in the coming years, will be occasionally to lend it to you. I marked it for my own two years ago at Rye—so perfectly did it, the first instant I beheld it, offer the solution of my long-unassuaged desire for a calm retreat between May and November. It is the very calmest and yet cheerfullest that I could have dreamed—*in* the little old, cobble-stoned, grass-grown, red-roofed town, on the summit of its mildly pyramidal hill and close to its noble old church—the chimes of which will sound sweet in my goodly old red-walled garden.

The little place is so rural and tranquil, and yet discreetly animated, that its being within the town is, for convenience and immediate accessibility, purely to the good; and the house itself, though modest and unelaborate, full of a charming little stamp and dignity of its period (about 1705) without as well as within. The next time I go down to see to its "doing up," I will try to have a photograph taken of the pleasant little old-world-town-angle into which its nice old red-bricked front, its high old Georgian doorway and a most delightful little old architectural garden-house, perched alongside of it on its high brick garden-wall—into which all these pleasant features together so happily "compose." Two years ago, after I had lost my heart to it—walking over from Point Hill to make sheep's eyes at it (the more so that it is called Lamb House!)—there was no appearance whatever that one could ever have it; either that its fond proprietor would give it up or that if he did it would come at all within one's means. So I simply sighed and renounced; tried to think no more about it; till at last, out of the blue, a note from the good local ironmonger, to whom I had whispered at the time my hopeless passion, informed me that by the sudden death of the owner and the preference (literal) of his son for Klondyke,[4] it might perhaps drop into my lap. Well, to make a long story short, it *did* immediately drop and, more miraculous still to say, on terms, for a long lease, well within one's means—terms quite deliciously moderate. The result of these is, naturally, that they will "do" nothing to it: but, on the other hand, it has been so well lived in and taken care of that the doing—off one's own bat—is reduced mainly to sanitation and furnishing—which latter includes the peeling off of old papers from several roomfuls of pleasant old top-to-toe wood panelling. There are two rooms of complete old oak—one of them a delightful little parlour, opening by one side into the little vista, church-ward, of the small old-world street, where not one of the half-dozen wheeled vehicles of Rye ever passes; and on the other straight into the garden and the approach, from that quarter, to the garden-house aforesaid, which is simply the making of a most commodious and picturesque detached study and workroom. Ten days ago Alfred Parsons,[5] best of men as well as best of landscape-painters-and-gardeners, went down with me and revealed to me the most charming possibilities for the treatment of the tiny out-of-door part—it amounts to about an acre of garden and lawn, all shut in by the peaceful old red wall aforesaid, on which the most flourishing old espaliers, apricots, pears, plums and figs, assiduously grow. It appears that it's a glorious little growing exposure, air, and soil—and all the things that were still flourishing out of doors (November 20th) were a joy to behold. There went with me also a good friend of mine, Edward Warren, a very *distingué* architect and loyal spirit, who is taking charge of whatever is to be done.

So I hope to get in, comfortably enough, early in May. In the meantime one must "pick up" a sufficient quantity of ancient mahogany-and-brass odds and ends—a task really the more amusing, here, where the resources are great, for having to be thriftily and cannily performed. The house is really quite charming enough in its particular character, and as to the stamp of its period, not to do violence to by rash modernities; and I am developing, under its influence and its inspiration, the most avid and gluttonous eye and most infernal watching patience, in respect of lurking "occasions" in not too-delusive Chippendale and Sheraton. The "King's Room" will be especially treated with a preoccupation of the comfort and aesthetic sense of cherished sisters-in-law; King's Room so-called by reason of George Second having passed a couple of nights there and so stamped it for ever. (He was forced ashore, at Rye, on a progress somewhere with some of his ships, by a tempest, and accommodated at Lamb House as at the place in the town then most consonant with his grandeur. It would, for that matter, quite correspond to this description still. Likewise the Mayors of Rye have usually lived there! Or the persons usually living there have usually *become* mayors! That was conspicuously the case with the late handsome old Mr. Bellingham whose son is my landlord. So you see the ineluctable dignity in store for me.) But enough of this swagger. I have been copious to copiously amuse you.

Your beautiful letter, which I have just read over again, is full of interest about you all; causing me special joy as to what it says of William's present and prospective easier conditions of work, relinquishment of laboratory, refusal of outside lectures, etc., and of the general fine performance, and promise, all round, of the children. What you say of each makes me want to see that particular one most. I rejoice with you, at any rate, over them all, and with William over what I hope *is* proving a simplified success. Most of all am I fondly *ému* in the prospect of the domestic relief that you are counting upon from your young German governess. May Peggy and Francis[6] twine about here even as the roses and jasmine clamber about the blushing walls of Lamb House! If she doesn't lift the labour you must just shunt the lot and come over here and live with *me.* I am delighted your sister Margaret gave you a good account of me. It was an immense pleasure to see her—and to see her so handsome and noble, and to find her such a complete *évocatrice.*

May she have taken up the redomesticated sense with many interwoven coloured threads of memory. I almost feel that what I have most to thank you for is the deeply interesting letter you so kindly enclose to me from the magnificent and mysterious Milwaukeeite. I don't in the least know who he is and can't even quite make out his name (unless it be Ilsley) but he is surely a charming creature, and does the handsome thing, all round, with a vengeance. It makes me really feel as if we *were* a family!—Not that there is the least doubt, however, that we are. There are, unmistakably, few such. At all events I quite voluptuously revel in Mr. Ilsley and should be immensely glad if it would come in William's way to mention it to him. I don't know about whom of us all he is best. In short he is a pearl, and I venture to keep his letter.—I had a very great pleasure the other day in a visit, far too short—only just six hours—from dear old Howells, who did me a lot of good in an illuminating professional (i.e., commercial) way, and came, in fact, at quite a psychological moment. I hope you may happen to see him soon enough to get from him also some echo of *me*—such as it may be. But, my dear Alice, I must be less interminable. Please tell William that I have two Syracuse "advices,"[7] as yet gracelessly unacknowledged—I mean to *him*—to thank him for. It's a joy to find these particular months less barren than they used to be. I embrace you tenderly all round and am yours very constantly

Henry James

P.S. It may interest you to know that (I didn't want to put my scribe into the Secret)[8] I get Lamb House (for twenty-one years, with *my* option of surrender the seventh or the fourteenth) for £70 per annum—four quarterly payments of less than £18. And *they* do all the outer repairs, etc.!

1. William MacAlpine was an experienced stenographer who had worked largely in the record-keeping of various scientific societies.
2. The long ghost story "The Turn of the Screw" was serialized in *Collier's Weekly* from 27 January to 26 April 1898.
3. HJ's longstanding joke—an "offer" of marriage.
4. The gold rush to the Klondike in the Yukon Territory had been in the news since the previous year.
5. Alfred William Parsons (1847–1920), landscape gardener and artist, who designed the sets for *Guy Domville*.
6. WJ's youngest children.
7. HJ's share of the rents from the family real estate in Syracuse.
8. The postscript is in HJ's hand.

To George P. Brett
Dictated Ts NYPL

34 De Vere Gardens W.
22*nd* December 1897

Dear Mr. Brett.

I should have thanked you for this—and my only excuse and my delay is "pressure"—for the very pretty little copyrighting volume, which duly and safely reached me.[1] This small fiction will form, in due course, part of a volume (tho' *not* be the first thing in it) which I shall be glad to see you publish when the rest of the material, I mean four or five other short tales, shall have accumulated. They will probably do so rather rapidly.[2]

Meanwhile the other matter I wrote you about has taken more definite shape. The tale I then alluded to, and which is too long to participate in such a collection as I just mentioned, appears serially in *Collier's Weekly* from some time about the beginning of the year and will be run, in shortish instalments, for about ten weeks. This is the publication—"The Turn of the Screw"—that I more particularly alluded to. My idea has been that I should like, for the book form, to make it only half a volume, accompanying it with another story of the same length and of a rather distinctly different type. It is possible, however, that that course may be something of a waste of opportunity—the thing's long enough to stand on its own feet. This reflection I have made in the light of the *Collier* people appearing to think the little work in question—for *their* purposes at any rate—much of a hit. At all events I had probably better let the question I here refer to stand over till the story has run something of its course: then I shall be able—from the impression it makes on me printed—more effectually to pronounce one way or the other; that is for a couple of longish things together or of shortish things apart. The *Turn of the Screw* is, as I think I mentioned, of about 40,000 words; which wouldn't, I suppose, be inadequate for a little volume if the other omens were propitious.[3] I hope the early part of the year is again bringing you over, and am yours very truly

Henry James

1. George P. Brett, manager of the New York branch of the publishing house of Macmillan and Company, printed up for HJ the tale of "John Delavoy" for American copyright deposit. Only two copies are known to exist. See Edel and Laurence, *A Bibliography of Henry James* (1961), p. 111.

2. "John Delavoy" was included in the collection *The Soft Side*, published in New York and London in 1900.

3. "The Turn of the Screw" was published in a volume called *The Two Magics* (1898) coupled with HJ's story version of his one-act play written for Ellen Terry (see letter to Ellen Terry, 31 August 1895) entitled in this form "Covering End."

To Grace Norton
Dictated Ts Harvard

34 De Vere Gardens W.
Christmas Day 1897

My dear Grace,

Is it really a year? I have been acutely conscious of its getting to be a horrible time, but it hadn't come home to me that it was taking on quite that insolence. Well, you see what the years—since years *il y a*, are making of me: I don't write to you for a hideous age, and then when at last I do, I take the romantic occasion of this particular day to write in this *un*sympathetic ink. But that is exactly what, as I say, the horrid time has made of me. The use of my hand, always difficult, has become impossible to me; and since I am reduced to dictation, this form of dictation is the best. May its distinctness make up for its indirectness. It's only if I wrote *your* hand that I should be inexcusable. Your beautiful last letter—by which I mean the one *before*, not the generous little note just received, and of which the magnanimity brings tears to my eyes—your beautiful other letter is embalmed in a fragrance as of faint rose leaves in a faint blue jar. From week to week, from month to month, have I been meaning to make you some sign. But, as you know, existence is mainly a business in which we are constantly throwing overboard the possible to keep the actual afloat, and it is only today that the possible really rides the waves. It is the dimmest, the greyest, the dreariest of all the gruesome London feasts. Life is all muffled and hushed and hindered by an intensity of fog, and one has literally a shipboard sense of huddling in the cabin and waiting for some resumption of the course. I am lying-to and feeling as if I were talking to you absolutely *through* the fog-horn; save that that is a warning and that this is a fond solicitation. I am to dine today, I believe, however, twice—which ought to contribute to cheer; once, early, with my brother Bob, who is staying with me, and once—at 8:30 with the American ambassador. And I try to think who is

67

dining with you, for I am sure you are dispensing and not engulfing turkey. Richard [Norton], and Mrs. Richard, I almost dare say. I take great pleasure in your mention, in this just-received note, of their representing something loveable and loving in your life, and endeavour, imagination aiding, to enter as much as possible into the detail of that. I send them, on it, my tender blessing. I dare say that, from time to time, you hear something of me from William; and you know, by that flickering light, that my life has had for a long time past a very jog-trot sort of rhythm. I have ceased completely to "travel." It is going on into four years since I have crossed the Channel; and the day is not yet. This will give you a ghastly sense of the insular object that I must have become; however, I shall break out yet, perhaps, and surprise you. Meanwhile, none the less, I was unable, these last days, to break the spell of immobility even to the extent of going over to Paris to poor Daudet's funeral.[1] I felt that, *là-bas*—by which I mean in the immediate house—a certain expectation rested on me, but I looked it straight in the face and cynically budged not. I dislike, more and more, the terrific organised exploitation, in Paris, on the occasion of death and burial, of every kind of personal privacy and every kind of personal hysterics. It is newspaperism and professionalism gone mad—in a way all its own; and I felt as if *I* should go mad if I even once more, let alone twenty times more, heard Daudet personally compared (more especially *facially* compared, eyeglass and all) to Jesus Christ. Not a French notice of him that I have seen but has plumped it coquettishly out. I had not seen him, thanks to my extreme recalcitrance, since the month he spent more than two years ago in London. His death was not unhappy—was indeed too long delayed, for all his later time had been sadly (by disease, borne with wonderful patience and subtlety) blighted and sterilised. Yet it is a wonderful proof of what a success his life had been that it had remained a success in spite of that. It was the most *worked* thing that ever was—I mean his whole career. His talent was so great that I feel, as to his work, that the best of it will quite intensely remain. But he was a queer combination of a great talent with an absence of the greater mind, as it were—the greater feeling. He is at the opposite pole, in this way, from our friend Bourget, who has so much the larger intelligence and larger initiation, and so much the smaller gift. À propos of the latter, I am still more perjured and perfidious.

These two winters have I been promising by all that's sacred to go and pay him a longish visit at a very sweet propriété that they have acquired at Hyères, and yet I still brazen out my falsity. They were both here much of last summer, but spent it mainly in Scotland and in the lap of duchesses, while I was, thank heaven, as unsocial (I don't mean to them, but to the like of their company) as I could possibly contrive. So I saw not much of them. But they are great successes, and one will still come in for more chances. Besides which, I *may* really, a short time hence, go toward them for a while. But what shall I tell you of any one nearer to you?—if such there be over here. I got a note from Miss Hogarth,[2] the other day, sending me poor little—good little, brave little, but uninspired little—Mary Angela Dickens, her eldest granddaughter, as I think, the eldest daughter, at any rate, (and one of seven!) of the late unfortunate younger Charles, whose widow is penniless save for a small Civil List pension finally obtained for her. The said little Mary Angela wants an American newspaper-correspondence on art and fashion, and appealed to me to help her to it. This is really quite out of my power—I am in no sort of touch with American newspapers; but the sight of Copperfield's child in a situation of penury, and clutching for life at flimsy straws, was all the more calculated to bring home to one the vanity of earthly glory and the grimness of earthly accidents. I really think that no Dickens off-shoot ought to be allowed to suffer much inconvenience! The State should care for them all. But meanwhile, as the State doesn't, I fear poor dear Miss Hogarth has, in her declining years, rather a melancholy environment. They must pull *her* leg, among them all—as "you Americans" say (I hear it echo through Kirkland Street).

Well, my dear Grace, I can't tell you the comfort and charm it is to be talking with you even by this horrid machinery and to squeeze the little round golden orange of your note dry of every testimony to your honoured tranquility that I can gouge out of it. My metaphors are mixed, but my fidelity is pure. How is the mighty Montaigne? I don't read him a millionth part as much as I ought, for of all the horrors of London almost the worst horror is the way it conspires against the evening book under the evening lamp. I don't "go out"—and yet, far too much of the time, I *am* out. The main part of the rest I devote to wondering how I got there. À propos of which, as much as of anything, do you read Maurice

Barrès? If you do, his last thing, *Les Déracinés*,[3] is very curious and serious, but a gruesome picture of young France. If it didn't sound British and Pharisaic I would almost risk saying that, on all the more and more showing, young and old France both seem to me to be in a strange state of moral and intellectual decomposition. But this isn't worth saying without going into the detail of the evidence—and that would take me too far. Then there is Leslie Stephen and the little Kiplings. Leslie seems to be outweathering his woes in the most extraordinary way. His health is literally better than it was in his wife's lifetime and is perhaps, more almost than anything else, a proof of what a life-preserver in even the wildest waves is the perfect possession of a *métier*. His admirable habit and knowledge of work have saved him. Poor pale, beautiful fatigued and exhausted Stella's death was a still more touching tragedy than her mother's;[4] but Vanessa has come to the front and become almost articulate and entirely handsome, and her aunt, Miss Duckworth,[5] assures me she will be a "great artist." Rudyard[6] and his wife and offspring depart presently for South Africa. They have settled upon a small propriété at Rottingdean near the Burne-Jones's, and the South Africa is but a parenthetic family picnic. It would do as well as anything else, perhaps, if one still felt, as one used to, that everything is grist to his mill. I don't, however, think that everything is, as the affair is turning out, at all; I mean as to the general complexity of life. His *Ballad* future may still be big. But my view of his prose future has much shrunken in the light of one's increasingly observing how little of life he can make use of. Almost nothing civilised save steam and patriotism—and the latter only in verse, where I *hate* it so, especially mixed up with God and goodness, that that half spoils my enjoyment of his great talent. Almost nothing of the complicated soul or of the female form or of any question of *shades*—which latter constitute, to my sense, the real formative literary discipline. In his earliest time I thought he perhaps contained the seeds of an English Balzac; but I have quite given that up in proportion as he has come steadily from the less simple in subject to the more simple,—from the Anglo-Indians to the natives, from the natives to the Tommies, from the Tommies to the quadrupeds, from the quadrupeds to the fish, and from the fish to the engines and screws. But he is a prodigious little success and an unqualified little happiness and a dear little chap. I prattle on, but my time is up. I haven't said half to you that I meant, but I have thirty more letters to write. Take this only as an instalment. *La suite prochainement.* As soon as I have posted the present I shall remember about five indispensable things that were at the very roots of my intention. I haven't even left myself time to tell you of the elegant apartment that I am preparing for your prolonged habitation in a little house I lately took a lease of down at Rye in Sussex. There, from next summer on, at any rate, I shall await you with calm confidence, and shall constantly be running up the fine old oaken stair to administer the last touches to your fine old oaken chamber. You have had excuses hitherto, but no excuse now will serve. For I *did* come to see you at East Molesley, and East Molesley, enchanting as it was, is not a patch on Lamb House. Goodbye, my dear Grace, believe that through all fallacious appearances of ebb and flow, of sound and silence, of presence and absence, I am always constantly yours,

Henry James

1. Alphonse Daudet died on 16 December 1897 in Paris.

2. Georgina Hogarth, sister of Charles Dickens's wife, who had lived with the Dickens family from the age of fifteen until the novelist's death.

3. *Les Déracinés* (1897) was the first volume of a trilogy by Barrès, insisting upon the mystique of French blood and the need to keep the young attached to the soil.

4. Stella Duckworth, daughter of the late Mrs. Stephen by her first marriage, had died the previous July of peritonitis, and Vanessa, Stephen's oldest daughter (1879–1961), had taken over the running of the house. She had already begun her study of painting.

5. Sarah Emily Duckworth, commonly referred to as "Aunt Minna."

6. Kipling, who had married the sister of HJ's friend Wolcott Balestier, had now returned to live in England after living in America from 1892 to 1896. See *Letters* III, 365, 371.

To Madame Alphonse Daudet
Ms Private

34 De Vere Gardens W.
Ce 31 décembre 1897

Madame.[1]

Je n'ai pas osé, jusqu'ici, vous troubler par de vaines paroles, mais je n'ai pas cessé de vous accompagner, dans ces jours de tristesse et de deuil d'une sympathie bien profonde et d'une pensée toute dévouée. Permettez, Madame, que je vous dise cela, et croyez bien qu'il n'y a aucune épreuve ni aucune douleur de votre existence si transformée et si assombrée auxquelles je ne me sente prendre une part respectueuse. Je songe en même temps à votre richesse de souvenirs, car les miens aussi—si restreints, hélas—me sont, et me seront toujours, bien précieux, et je me joins à vous tous pour entourer de toutes les tendresses de pensée—en ce sombre fin d'année—le cher et illustre absent. Croyez, Madame, à mon attachement très sincère.

Henry James

1. Madame Daudet, the former Julie Rosalie-Céleste Allard (1847–1940). She wrote under the pseudonyms Marguerite Tourney and Karl Steen.

To William James
Dictated Ts Harvard

34 De Vere Gardens W.
20 April 1898

My dear William.

There are all sorts of *intimes* and confidential things I want to say to you in acknowledgment of your so deeply interesting letter—of April 10th—received yesterday; but I must break the back of my response at least with this mechanical energy; not having much of any other—by which I mean simply too many odd moments—at my disposal just now. I do answer you, alas, almost to the foul music of the cannon.[1] It is this morning precisely that one feels the fat to be at last fairly in the fire. I confess that the blaze about to come leaves me woefully cold, thrilling with no glorious thrill or holy blood-thirst whatever. I see nothing but the madness, the passion, the hideous clumsiness of rage, or mechanical reverberation; and I echo with all my heart your denouncement of the foul criminality of the screeching newspapers. They have long since become, for me, the danger that overtops all others. That became clear to one, even here, two years ago, in the Venezuela time; when one felt that with a week of simple, enforced silence everything could be saved. If things *were* then saved without it, it is simply that they hadn't at that time got so bad as they are now in the U.S. My sympathy with you all is intense—the whole horror must so mix itself with all your consciousness. I am near enough to hate it, without being, as you are, near enough in some degree, perhaps, to understand. I am leading at present so quiet a life that I don't measure much the sentiment, the general attitude around me. Much of it can't possibly help being Spanish—and from the "European" standpoint in general Spain *must* appear savagely assaulted. She is so quiet—publicly and politically—so decent and picturesque and harmless a member of the European family that I am bound to say it argues an extraordinary illumination and a very predetermined radicalism not to admire her pluck and pride. But publicly, of course, England will do nothing whatever that is not more or less—negatively—for our benefit. I scarcely know what the newspapers say—beyond the *Times*, which I look at all for Smalley's cables:[2] so systematic is my moral and intellectual need of ignoring them. One must save one's life if one can. The next weeks will, however, in this particular, probably not a little break me down. I must at least read the Bombardment of Boston. May you but scantly suffer from it!

I have just come back from that monstrous rarity for *me*, a visit of three or four days in the country—to G. O. Trevelyan,[3] who is extraordinarily rich and much-housed, and spends Easter at his huge (or rather his wife's) modern mansion of Welcombe, near Stratford-on-Avon. The Eastertide has been lovely; that country was full of spring and of Shakespeare, besides its intrinsic sweetness; and I suppose I ought to have been happy. Fortunately I've got, through protracted and infernal cunning, almost altogether out of it. There was no one there—they live only in a furnished wing of the huge, hereditary white elephant of a house—but the Speaker and Speakeress of the House of Commons, who are very amiable folk. Also deadly commemorative Shakespeare trilogies at the Stratford theatre, to which we were haled for two nights. Basta!

I rejoice with intense rejoicing in everything you tell me of your own situation, plans, arrangements, honours, prospects—into all of which I enter with an intimacy of participation. Your election to the *Institut*[4] has, for me, a surpassing charm—I simply revel and, as it were, wallow in it. *Je m'y vautre.* But oh, if it could only have come soon enough for poor Alice to have known it—such a happy little nip as it would have given her; or for the dear old susceptible Dad! But things come as they can—and I am, in general, lost in the daily miracle of their coming at all: I mean so many of them—few as that many may be: and I speak above all for myself. I am lost, moreover, just now, in the wonder of what effect on American affairs, of every kind, the shock of battle will have. Luckily it's of my nature—though not of my pocket—always to be prepared for the worst and to expect the least. Like you, with all my heart, I have "finance on the brain." At least I try to have it—with a woeful lack of natural talent for the same. It is none too soon. But one arrives at dates, periods, corners of one's life: great changes, deep operations are begotten. This has more portée than I can fully go into. I shall certainly do my best to let my flat when I am ready to leave town; the difficulty, this year, however, will be that the time for "season" letting begins now, and that I can't depart for at least another month. Things are not ready at Rye, and won't be till then, with the limited local energy at work that I have very wisely contented myself with turning on there. It has been the right and much the best way in the long run, and for one's good little relations there; only the run has been a little longer. The remnant of the season here may be difficult to dispose of—to a sub-lessee; and my books—only a part of which I can house at Rye—are a complication. However, I shall do what I can this year; and for subsequent absences, so long as my present lease of De Vere Gardens runs I shall have the matter on a smooth, organised, working basis. I mean to arrange myself always to let—being, as such places go, distinctly lettable. And for my declining years I have already put my name down for one of the invaluable south-looking, Carlton-Gardens-sweeping bedrooms at the Reform Club, which are let by the year and are of admirable and convenient (with all the other resources of the place at one's elbow) *general* habitability. The only thing is they are so in demand that one has sometimes a long time to await one's turn. On the other hand there are accidents—"occasions."[5] Then—with this flat suppressed—I shall, with Lamb House but £70 a year and the Reform room but £50, I shall, in respect to *loyer,* have taken in a great deal of pecuniary sail. This business of making Lamb House sanitary and comfortable and very modestly furnishing is of course, as it came very suddenly, a considerable strain on my resources; but I shall securely outweather it—and this year, and next, thank heaven, my income will have been much larger than for any year of my existence.[6] My main drawback will be my sacrifice, on going to Rye, of my excellent Scotch amanuensis—whom I can't take with me, without too great an expense in making up to him the loss of his other—afternoon and evening—engagements here.

Moreover he is not a desireable inmate—I couldn't again, as I did for eight weeks last summer, undertake his living with me. My pressing want is some sound, sane, irreproachable young type-writing and bicycling "secretary-companion," the expense of whom would be practically a hundred-fold made up by increase and facilitation of paying work. But though I consider the post enviable it is difficult to fill. The young typists are mainly barbarians—and the civilized, here, are not typists. But patience. I don't go into the Bob-question more than to jubilate devoutly in your good news of him. I don't *understand*, I fear, very clearly, your inquiry as to my assent (that is the question itself) to your new Syracuse idea; but I *give*, that assent, freely to what you think best—judging it to be in the interest of conservatism and prudence. I hope War will make no difference in the advent of Harry and M.G. I shall be ready for H. by the mid-June. I embrace you all—Alice longer than the rest—and am, with much actuality of emotion, ever your

Henry

1. The Maine had blown up in Havana harbor in February, and the Spanish-American war had just begun. HJ had visions, fed by the war hysteria in the American press, of the bombardment of Boston, and was "mainly glad Harvard College isn't—nor Irving Street—the thing nearest Boston Bay" (letter to WJ, 22 April 1898). See also letter to Norris, 4 February 1896.

2. George W. Smalley. See letter to Norris, 4 February 1896.

3. Sir George Otto Trevelyan (1838–1928), author of a history of the American Revolution in six volumes (1899–1914).

4. William James had just been elected a corresponding member of the Institut de France, the French learned society created in 1795. HJ addressed the envelope "William James, Esq., *Membre correspondant de l'Institut (Académie des Sciences Morales et Politiques)."*

5. At this point HJ ceased dictating and completed the letter by hand.

6. Serialization of "The Turn of the Screw" and "The Awkward Age" and publication of a large number of tales and articles including regular contributions to the newly founded journal *Literature* gave HJ high earnings at this time.

To Antonio de Navarro
Ms Private

34 De Vere Gardens W.
June 15*th* 1898

My dear Tony.[1]

I am wondering what kind of a faithless monster you take me for. Well, strike, but hear me. I am unhappy, but not absolutely criminal. Your missive reached me the other day in the midst of a complication of *kinds* of pressure more overwhelming than any I have for a long time had to face—and the only thing was to pray hard and wait. I am still more or less under the mountain—but the tip of my nose is out and it is with the tip of my nose I write you—with the tip I have read your ms.—I have had:—

1*st*, finally and supremely to attend to every item of finishment and preparation for entrance of a remote and romantic little house in the country of which I am on the point of taking possession.

2*d*   To bear up under the overdue work retarded and ruined by that cataclysm.

3*d*   To recover from annihilation under a domestic crisis with a pair of servants who have lived with me for fifteen years.[2]

4*th*   To look for other servants and not find them.

5*th*   To instal in the country some American friends for whom I had taken a house and whom I have had to stay with and give *all* my time to.[3]

5*th*   To stay with the Henry Whites[4] and not do any of the things I planned to put in while there.

6*th*   To be all the time—and the same time—at Rye.

7*th*   To suffer unutterably from the sense of your surprise and contumely.—But at last!—Well, my dear Tony, I have read your ms. and I *can*, yes, put myself in the shoes of the editors.

The idea—isn't—interesting—enough. It hasn't enough to *give*. It is Hans Andersenesque—but no editor of an actual London magazine would look at a Hans Andersen tale to-day. They want either the intense real or the very cunning and human and suspense-creating romance. Your fantasy seems to them too slight and too—well, too *innocent*. The lay-figure doesn't lend himself. And the details are vague. The woman in the studio, the penny: it isn't localised tangible, special, something of life and observation. And they think your form, probably, and style, *vieux jeu*. I mean Florence, Dante, Beatrix, the long speech—love-speech—of the manikin.—These things haven't now a marketable value. There is the crude impression—*ex*pression—of a toiling brother, nursed in the secrets, the grim secrets, of the *métier*. *Il en faut plus*—more *métier*. It's a dog's trade, too. Try something *observed*, and observed only—the real "bloody" *facts* of some real bloody situation. I wish I could write to you—but I can't. I wish I could see you—but I can't.

I wish I could love you *de plus près* and greet Mrs. Tony too. But I love you better thus than this infamous scrawl represents. I hope you are all three in health and bloom and glory—so far as this poor mill-round knows it. Some day—*some*, only wait, wait, and trust me, I shall be with you. Yours, meanwhile, and the wondrous wife's and the blessed Babe's, most constantly

Henry James

1. Antonio Fernando de Navarro, son of a shipping magnate of Basque origin, married the American actress Mary Anderson (1859–1940), whom HJ had known during his early London years. A sportsman and antiquarian, an amateur of the arts, Navarro sent HJ from time to time various of his writings, which the novelist candidly and affectionately criticized.

2. HJ's butler and cook had both been drinking heavily. The crisis blew over, but recurred in more serious fashion in 1901. See letter to Mrs. WJ, 26 September 1901.

3. The friends were the elderly Godkins. See letter to WJ, 7 August 1897.

4. Henry White (1850–1927) served as diplomat under five American presidents. HJ became friends with him and his wife during the early phase of White's career in the American embassy in London.

To Mrs. J. T. Fields
Ms Huntington

Lamb House, Rye
September 5*th* [1898]

Dear Mrs. Fields.[1]

It is splendidly kind of you both to come so far for so bounded and curtailed an experience, and I beg you to assure Miss Jewett[2] how much I appreciate your generosity. I am sustained, only, in the effort not to be ashamed of the disproportions of the whole thing; by the sense that the charm of this little nook is, however modest, incontestable and that the journey is performed in rather exceptionally easy conditions. That is, the 11 A.M. from Charing Cross to Rye is a super-excellent train in spite of your having to change at *Ashford* at about 12.30, and have a wait there of twenty-five minutes. But the run, after that, down here, is of the briefest, and places you almost at my very door at about 1.30—excellent time for luncheon. I meet you at the station of course, and we are but five minutes from my house. The *4.53* back restores you to Charing Cross at 7.39. I proposed—I assented rather—to your alternative mention of Monday next, because tomorrow, Tuesday, a young nephew and a young cousin of mine,[3] who have been for some time with me, take leave in the middle of the P.M., to return to the U.S. and to France, and I feared the interference of that incident that I regret much, the delay I incur. I beseech you not to fail me and am, dear Mrs. Fields, very impatiently yours and Miss Jewett's

Henry James

1. This is one of the earliest of countless letters giving precise directions to HJ's friends how to reach Lamb House from London. Mrs. Fields (1834–1915), the former Annie Adams, was the widow of the editor and publisher J.T. Fields.
2. Sarah Orne Jewett (1849–1909), the American writer of short stories and a close friend of Mrs. Fields.
3. The nephew was WJ's oldest son, Harry; the cousin was Rosina Emmet (see letter to Ellen Temple Hunter, 3 July 1897).

To Paul Bourget
Ms Private

Lamb House, Rye
ce 26 septembre [1898]

Mon cher ami,

Votre lettre de Nauheim n'a de bien allègre que la nouvelle de l'amélioration de la santé de Mme Bourget, que je suis enchanté d'apprendre et qui doit pour vous et pour elle contrepeser bien des ennuis du siècle. J'espère que la voilà toute rétablie pour l'hiver: faites lui en, je vous prie, mes heartiest congratulations. Vous ne me faites part d'aucune observation recueillie à votre Bad Hessois—ce que je m'explique en vous supposant trop blasé, non pas pour en avoir—je vous défie d'y échapper, mais pour y trouver ce fait même (d'en avoir toujours) digne de remarque. Elles ont dû, du reste, porter presqu'uniquement sur ces malheureuses choses de France, dont vous me parlez si sombrement et au sujet desquelles je ne sais trouver, hélas, aucune parole le moins du monde comforting. Je ne les *comprends* pas, j'en suis trop éloigné par l'experience et par la façon de sentir; rien ici n'y correspond, ni le bon ménage que nous faisons avec les juifs,[1] et, en somme, les uns avec les autres, ni l'importance suprême que nous attachons à la justice civile, ni le "short work," que nous ferions de la militaire si elle prétendait s'y substituer. Je peux bien pourtant y prendre assez de part pour plaindre, jusqu'aux larmes presque, l'affolement du pays. Espérons que le

78

Lamb House, from the garden. The garden room, at right, was destroyed by bombing in 1941.

pays en sortira par la porte toute ouverte (ou qui le sera demain) de la révision. Je vous avoue que si la France se refus à cela je la trouverai *moins* à plaindre—a less interesting sufferer. Mais elle ne s'y refusera pas. Restent, sans doute, toutes les laideurs et les noirceurs de la situation—et tout ce qui doit en effet faire de Paris de ce moment un lieu de tourment digne de l'imagination du Dante. Je me réjouis de penser que vous avez le refuge de Costebelle[2] et que vous ne manquerez pas probablement, d'ici chercher bientôt la paix méditerranéane et le bruissement des sapins.—Je continue de bouger aussi peu que le fameux Sussex pig. (J'ai, par parenthèse, à la disposition de Madame Paul une boîte remplie d'échantillons de cette bête fabuleuse que je m'apprêtais à lui envoyer par parcel post à Londres au moment où j'appris votre départ pour l'Allemagne. Elle sortira tout d'abord de ma malle à mon arrivée au Plantier). J'ai eu tout le reste de l'été, trop de monde—en séjour—en même temps que trop de chaleur et de moustiques, mais le travail a marché toujours—grâce à Remington et compagnie—et j'approche de la fin d'un assez long roman, dont le commencement est sur le point—dreadful thought—de paraître, de *courir,* comme nous disons. À propos de quoi je vous remercie sans restriction de ce que vous m'écrivez sur la forme de *Maisie,*[3] etc. C'est parfaitement juste et je n'ai d'autre excuse que d'avoir dû *choisir* cette façon de faire par suite d'un embarras technique que l'évolution de mon sujet m'a infligé et que je ne puis ici vous rendre clair. Cela ne m'a nullement empêcher de bien voir le côté excessif de mon partipris de panorama et de premier plan. Et puis j'ai la *maladie* du détail—du détail fait et surfait.—Rappelez-vous bien aussi que j'écris pour un public (la malédiction de ma vie) que vous ne pouvez pas intellectuelement *pas concevoir.* Je dirais que j'aime encore mieux ce public de Dreyfus si *La Femme et Le Pantin,*[4] que je viens de lire sur votre conseil, ne m'avait trop attristé. Cette idée du pathétique, de se plaindre à ce point, d'avoir toujours à rouer de coups la sale négrillonne (car elle n'est que cela—et à moitié racoon! comme chez Ferdinand) qu'on a pris pour maîtresse, avant de la posséder—ne voilà-t-il pas ce qu'on a encore trouvé de plus compliqué comme "états d'âme"? Beaucoup de talent, un grand sens littéraire, oui, mais quelle aridité pittoyable et quelle ignorance crasse de la vie! Combinaison trop étrange!—Bien autrement beau le grand roman de la Serao,[5] dont je remercie Madame Paul encore mieux maintenant que je l'ai lu et admiré. Quelle oeuvre géniale et généreuse—so rich and so easy. Et quelle belle traduction intelligente, compétente, soignée! Voilà comme il faut être, comme il faut se voir traduit. J'ai bien envie d'en parler quelque part—et je n'y manquerai pas s'y l'occasion s'en présente. Bonne nuit. J'ai passé l'après-midi à Hastings—je tombe de fatigue et de sommeil—il est minuit trois-quarts. Je me recommande bien à l'amalgame de vos souvenirs et am yours, my dear Bourget, always,

Henry James

1. HJ refers to the latest developments in the Dreyfus case. Bourget was an anti-Dreyfusard and an anti-Semite.
2. Bourget's Riviera house at Costebelle, Hyères.
3. *What Maisie Knew*, published in September 1897.
4. *La Femme et le Pantin* (1898) a novel by Pierre Louys dealing with the breakdown of a man, the victim of a worthless woman.
5. Matilda Serao (1856–1927), the Italian novelist. HJ probably was reading at this time *Il Paese di Cuccagna* (1891). See his article on Serao in *Notes on Novelists* (1914).

To Edmund Gosse
Ms Leeds

Lamb House, Rye
Wednesday [12 October 1898]

My dear Gosse.

You make me cry—you make me cry bitterly. You have done it before, but it is worse this time. I thank you very sincerely—I am awfully pleased. But oh, I can do—I shall do still—so unspeakably better than that: which is only cleverness and ingenuity. To think of the good old Addington Archbishop (by a vague fragment of a tale he ineffectually tried to tell me) having given me the germ of anything so odious and hideous![1] I hope his family won't mind—I wrote, when the thing was serialized, to Arthur.—The difficulty, the problem was of course to add, organically, the element of beauty to a thing so foully ugly—and the success is in *trust* if I *have* done it. But I despise bogies, any way. The other thing has of course, like *The Other House*, its base origin[2] smeared all over it: being as it systematically shows itself but a one-act comedy completely worked-out and finished, but never acted; reclaimed a little for literature—and for my pocket—by being simply turned, on the

81

absolutely same Scenic lines, into narrative. And now if somebody will only *buy* them! You must come down here again! The autumn sun and feeling are as charming here as everything else and I shall remain late—on into December probably. It is admirable cycling weather, and I did twenty-two miles to-day with my irrepressible Scot between luncheon and (a late) tea. Name your day and join us. I shall be in town, of course, for a group of days (next month) before coming up to stay; if, even I do that at all. If I let De Vere Gardens I shall be an exile. I hope your house is safe and your burden adjustable; and I am, my dear Gosse, very gratefully yours

Henry James

P.S. I like more than I can tell you the things you say about things—in the T. of the S.—that you *felt*. I believe they *are* all there.

1. The late Archbishop of Canterbury had given HJ the original idea for "The Turn of the Screw."

2. "Covering End," the short-story version of the Ellen Terry one-acter. *The Other House* (1896) had originally been a three-act play.

To Elizabeth Cameron
Ms Mellon

Lamb House, Rye
October 15 1898

Dear Mrs. Cameron.[1]

I can't let this week's end roll by without doing what I have had it *all* the week at heart to do—wave a piece of grey paper from my high place, at you, in the guise of a white handkerchief. I haven't fluttered my scrap before, simply because I haven't wanted you to do anything but kindly *see* it—and this delay will deprive you, I trust, of every opportunity, every leisure, for waggling anything in return. You will get my note in the very act of your departure, and will pocket it to read in the train, as I remember the heroine of some French farce reads her love-letters—with complicated consequences. Let the consequence of *my* innocent friendship be only to remind you of the delightful nature (Laureate, Mrs. Laureate and all!) of my time at Surrenden.[2] I had a charming spin back, via Ashford—and first via Hothfield—in the October sunshine and over the just damp enough roads. Since then I've again been at it and wished the shorter days were not the price paid for the cooler ones—in which case I think I should have positively again stalled my steed in your ballroom. But I fondly count on seeing you, at no distant date, in Florence or Rome. Give my love please, to the Ambassador—while still I dare such familiarities. I eat and drink, I sleep and dream Dreyfus. The papers are too shockingly interesting, and I am yours, dear Mrs. Cameron, very constantly

Henry James

1. Elizabeth Sherman Cameron (1857–1944), wife of Senator James Donald Cameron (1833–1918), and friend for many years of Henry Adams.
2. Surrenden Dering, a large Elizabethan manor house in Kent, where the American Ambassador John Hay, Henry Adams, and the Camerons spent the summer of 1898.

To Guy Hoyer Millar
Ms Harvard

Rye [1898]

My dear Godson Guy.[1]

I learned from your mother, by pressing her hard, some time ago that it would be a convenience to you and a great help in your career to possess an Association football—whereupon, in my desire that you should receive the precious object from no hand but mine I cast about me for the proper place to procure it. But I am living for the present in a tiny, simpleminded country town, where luxuries are few and football shops unheard of, so I was a long time getting a clue that would set me on the right road. Here at last, however, is the result of my terribly belated endeavour. It goes to you by parcel post—not, naturally, in this letter. I am awfully afraid I haven't got one of the right size: if so, and you will let me know, you shall have a better one next time. I am afraid I don't *know* much about the sorts and sizes since they've all been invented since I was of football age. I'm an awful muff, too, at games—except at times I am not a bad cyclist, I think—and I fear I am only rather decent at playing at godfather. Some day you must come down and see me here and I'll do in every way the best I can for you. You shall have lots of breakfast and dinner and tea—not to speak of lunch and anything you like in between—and I won't ask you a single question about a single one of your studies, but if you think that is because I

83

can't—because I don't know enough—I *might* get up subjects on purpose.

Your most affectionate Godfather,

Henry James

1. Guy Millar was a grandson of George Du Maurier. HJ had known Guy's mother since her childhood.

To Dr. Louis Waldstein
Ms Unknown

Lamb House, Rye

October 21*st* 1898

Dear Sir.[1]

Forgive my neglect, under great pressure of occupation, of your so interesting letter of the 12th. I have since receiving it had complicated calls on my time. That the *Turn of the Screw* has been suggestive and significant to you—in any degree—it gives me great pleasure to hear; and I can only thank you very kindly for the impulse of sympathy that made you write. I am only afraid, perhaps, that my conscious intention strikes you as having been larger than I deserve it should be thought. It is the intention so primarily, with me, always, of the artist, the *painter*, that *that* is what I most, myself, feel in it—and the lesson, the idea—ever—conveyed is only the one that deeply lurks in any vision prompted by life. And as regards a presentation of things so fantastic as in that wanton little Tale, I can only rather blush to see real substance read into them—I mean for the generosity of the reader. *But*, of course, where there *is* life, there's truth, and the truth was at the back of my head. The poet is always justified when he is not a humbug; always grateful to the justifying commentator. My bogey-tale dealt with things so hideous that I felt that to save it at all it needed some infusion of beauty or prettiness, and the beauty of the pathetic was the only attainable—was indeed inevitable. But ah, the exposure indeed, the helpless plasticity of childhood that isn't dear or sacred to *some*body! That *was* my little tragedy—over which you show a wisdom for which I thank you again. Believe me, thus, my dear Sir, yours most truly,

Henry James

1. Louis Waldstein, M.D. (1853–1915), American physician, educated at Columbia University and abroad.

84

To James B. Pinker
Dictated Ts Yale

Lamb House, Rye
October 23 1898

Dear Mr. Pinker.[1]

By all means keep my three things if you do see any chance for them—or possibility of one—still: I couldn't suppose that you had any remaining faith. Moreover, the episode has been, for me, a horrible unexpected *scare*, the effect of which on my nerves, as it were, is—with the vision of my things declined on every side, unfavourable to work, and it seemed to me desirable to put an end to the suspense connected with the whole magazine question. I'm afraid I shouldn't be able to bear any much more of it. It comes to me late—one can take that in youth. But this is mainly a word to say that I shall be very glad indeed if you will come down to see me—I should like extremely to talk with you. *This* week would be rather bad for me, by reason of my happening to be taken up with some relations who are to be with [me] for several days; but *next* I hope you will come and I will in a few days write you again, giving you your choice of days and times. Believe me yours very truly

Henry James

1. Earlier this year HJ had confided his business affairs to the esteemed literary agent James Brand Pinker (1863–1922) and sent him three stories to be submitted to various journals. These were "The Given Case," "The Great Good Place," and "The Great Condition." Accustomed to handling his own market, HJ was worried by Pinker's long silence. But the tales were sold in due course and appeared ultimately in *The Soft Side* (1900).

To H. G. Wells
Ms Bodleian

Lamb House, Rye
December 9*th* 1898

My dear H. G. Wells,[1]

Your so liberal and graceful letter is to my head like coals of fire—so repeatedly for all these weeks have I had feebly to suffer frustrations in the matter of trundling over the marsh to ask for your news and wish for your continued amendment. The shortening days and the deepening mud have been at the bottom of this affair. I never get out of the house till 3 o'clock, when night is quickly at one's heels. I would have taken a regular day—I mean started in the A.M.—but have been so ridden, myself, by the black care of an unfinished and *running* (galloping, leaping and bounding) serial[2] that parting with a day has been like parting with a pound of flesh. I am still a neck ahead, however, and *this* week will see me through: I accordingly hope very much to be able to turn up on one of the ensuing days. I will sound a horn, so that you yourself be not absent on the chase. Then I will express more articulately my appreciation of your various signs of critical interest, as well as assure you of my sympathy in your own martyrdom. What will you have? It's all a grind and a bloody battle—as well as a considerable lark, and the difficulty itself is the refuge from the vulgarity. Bless your heart, I think I could easily say worse of the T. of the S., the young woman, the spooks, the style, the everything, than the worst any one else could manage. One knows the *most* damning things about one's self. Of course I had, about my young woman, to take a very sharp line. The grotesque business I had to make her picture and the childish psychology I had to make her trace and present, were, for me at least, a very difficult job, in which absolute lucidity and logic, a singleness of effect, were imperative. Therefore I had to rule out subjective complications of her own—play of tone etc.; and keep her impersonal save for the most obvious and indispensable little note of neatness, firmness and courage—without which she wouldn't have had her data.[3] But the thing is essentially a pot-boiler and a *jeu d'esprit*.

With the little play, the absolute creature of its conditions, I had simply to make up a deficit and take a small *revanche*. For three mortal years had the actress for whom it was written (utterly to try to *fit*) persistently failed to produce it, and I couldn't wholly waste my labour. The B[ritish] P[ublic] won't read a play with the mere names of the speakers—so I simply paraphrased these and added such indications as might be the equivalent of decent acting—a history and an evolution that seem to me moreover explicatively and sufficiently smeared all over the thing. The moral is of course Don't write one-act plays.[4]

But I didn't mean thus to sprawl. I envy your hand your needle-pointed fingers. As you don't say that you're *not* better I prepare

myself to be greatly struck with the same, and send kind regards to
your wife. Believe me yours ever,

Henry James

P.S. What's this about something in some newspaper? I read least
of all—from long and deep experience—what my friends write
about me, and haven't read the things you mention. I suppose it's
because they know I don't that they dare!

1. H. G. Wells (1866–1946) had met James earlier that year when he moved into
Spade House, across Romney Marsh from Rye. This was the beginning of their long and
troubled friendship. See Edel and Ray, *Henry James and H. G. Wells* (1958).

2. *The Awkward Age* had begun to appear in *Harper's Weekly* in the October 1
issue.

3. James is explaining in this letter how he kept his character of the governess in
"The Turn of the Screw" "impersonal"—so that she is not even named. In his preface
to this tale (New York Edition, IX, xiv–xxii) HJ may have been alluding to Wells's
inquiries when he wrote: "I recall . . . a reproach made me by a reader capable evidently,
for the time, of some attention, but not quite capable of enough, who complained that
I hadn't sufficiently 'characterised' my young woman engaged in her labyrinth; hadn't
endowed her with signs and marks, features and humours, hadn't in a word invited her
to deal with her own mystery as well as with that of Peter Quint, Miss Jessel and the
hapless children." To which James added: "We have surely as much of her own nature
as we can swallow in watching it reflect her anxieties and inductions." He further
remarks in his preface, in this same context, that it had been a question of "our young
woman's keeping crystalline her record of so many intense anomalies and obscu-
rities—by which I don't of course mean her explanation of them, a different matter."

4. "Covering End," with which "The Turn of the Screw" makes up the volume *The
Two Magics.*

To Frederic W. H. Myers
Ms Private

Lamb House, Rye
December 19th 1898

My dear Myers.[1]

I don't know what you will think of my unconscionable delay to
acknowledge your letter of so many, so very many days ago, nor
exactly how I can make vivid to you the nature of my hindrances
and excuses. I have, in truth, been (until some few days since)
intensely and anxiously busy, finishing, under pressure, a long job
that had from almost the first—I mean from long before I had
reached the end—begun to be (loathsome name and fact!) "serialized"—so that the printers were at my heels and I had to make a
sacrifice of my correspondence *utterly*—to keep the sort of cerebral

freshness required for not losing my head or otherwise collapsing. But I won't expatiate. Please believe my silence has been wholly involuntary. And yet, now that I *am* writing I scarce know what to say to you on the subject on which you wrote, especially as I'm afraid I don't quite *understand* the principal question you put to me about "The Turn of the Screw." However, that scantily matters; for in truth I am afraid I have on some former occasions rather awkwardly signified to you that I somehow can't pretend to give any coherent account of my small inventions "after the fact." There they are—the fruit, at best, of a very imperfect ingenuity and with all the imperfections thereof on their heads. The one thing and another that are questionable and ambiguous in them I mostly take to be conditions of their having got themselves pushed through at all. The *T. of the S.* is a very mechanical matter, I honestly think— an inferior, a merely *pictorial*, subject and rather a shameless potboiler. The thing that, as I recall it, I most wanted not to fail of doing, under penalty of extreme platitude, was to give the impression of the communication to the children of the most infernal imaginable evil and danger—the condition, on their part, of being as *exposed* as we can humanly conceive children to be. This was my artistic knot to untie, to put any sense or logic into the thing, and if I had known any way of producing *more* the image of their contact and condition I should assuredly have been proportionately eager to resort to it. I evoked the worst I could, and only feel tempted to say, as in French: "Excusez du peu!"

I am living so much down here that I fear I am losing hold of some of my few chances of occasionally seeing you. The charming old humble-minded "quaintness" and quietness of this little brown hill-top city lays a spell upon me. I send you and your wife and all your house all the greetings of the season and am, my dear Myers, yours very constantly

Henry James

1. Myers (1843–1901) was one of the founders of the Society for Psychical Research. See *Letters* III, 302.

To Paul Bourget
Dictated Ts Private

Lamb House, Rye
December 23 1898

Mon cher ami.

I appreciate immensely your deeply interesting letter and acknowledge it with only an hour's delay. You show me truly, great patience and kindness, and I am not in the least guilty of a professional fiction when I tell you that even had I not heard from you this morning I should very exactly have been engaged in my present epistolary act. I have your letter of many weeks ago still unacknowledged, and I assure you that I had no intention of adding another day, at this genial Christmastide, to my prolonged neglect of you. That neglect, cher confrère, has been the result, simply, of my latest manifestation of our confraternity. All my lucidity of mind—which does not at all mean that I answer for the quantity—has gone, day after day, since you were here, without an hour's intermission, to the production of about 135,000 words arranged as a fable of superior quality.[1] I ticked out the last only a few days ago, and have but just begun to look round me at the markedly inferior world of fact. One of the few things that I thus notice as in some degree redeeming the latter is your so admirably continued attitude of hospitality: to which, really this time, without possibility, I think, of perfidy, I count on being able personally to respond. Yes, at last, there seems every appearance that nothing can—absit omen!—prevent me from making good my vow. If I have stuck fast to Rye for nearly six months, I go up to town next week for only a few days. I have finally the unpleasant consciousness of appearing to have let, for six months, my apartment, which has stood empty this half-year and which I shall not desire to inhabit till some date now too distant to distinguish: so that, as soon as I have made it over to my tenant I shall be free to return here and start afresh—start for Folkestone, for Paris, for Costebelle, for Bogliasco, and for Rome. I hope to be on the Continent some twelve weeks and I will give you and Madame Paul, with the greatest pleasure, one of the very first of these. I will write you from Paris, where I shall have to spend ten days, a perfectly definite announcement. Kindly bear till then with my further protraction.

Yes, Lamb House has been a great comfort; with an autumn distinctly more charming—more nuancée—than the summer, and with lovely cloudless days, on this edge of Christmas, days of flooding sunshine and nights of an operatic moon. There are moments when I pronounce this little corner of Sussex almost a petite Provence. Don't fear, however, that I shall have been spoiled for enjoying la grande. We will talk of everything under your pines. You give me too bad an account of Paris—I can't afford not somewhat to differ from you. However, I shall by the time I see you have renewed my impression (I've not been there—songez donc—for five years!) and perhaps I shall have new perceptions of Paris itself, new teeth and claws.

Poor Ferdinand's[2] death also reminds me of many things. There have been other disparitions still—from the Waddesdon picture—than those you mention. I think, for myself, also of poor Maupassant, with whom I spent two or three days there.[3] It was almost my last sight of him. I saw Ferdinand about a year ago—but saw him, in general, as time went on, less and less. Yet I always had a lingering liking for him, and a feeling that we might have met more felicitously if he had been surrounded by conditions less inhuman. I ask myself what is to become of his great cold impossible palace—but of course the Rothschild abyss is big enough to reabsorb it to the very last racoon. What strikes me more than anything else, in connection with his death, is the difference marked between English and French nerves by the fact that the Crown Prince (by whom I mean of course the P. of W.) assisted yesterday, with every demonstration of sympathy, at his severely simple Jewish obsequies. And no one here grudges the Synagogue a single of its amusements—great as is the place which it and they occupy.[4]

I am very sorry to hear of Urbain Mengin's interruption[5]—for which, however, I had been mentally prepared; prepared with the preparedness of a man qui a pour principe an inalienable mistrust of the great ones of the earth and a thorough disbelief in any security of relation with them. How *should* there be such security with people who have no imagination? They are the objects, not the subjects, of imagination, and it is not in their compass to *conceive* of anything whatever. They can only live their hard functional lives. It is sad our young friend should have to pay for these truths. I will with pleasure bear his needs in mind should I be spoken to on the subject of some such requirement as you speak of. I only fear there are always more persons—many more—wanting such places than there are places turning up.

I'm very glad to hear you have opened the door again to the fairy Invention. She always passes and repasses a few times before she comes in, but come in she at last *does* if you only keep the threshold swept and put a chair to keep the door back. I am sure indeed that by this time she is comfortably seated with you. For myself, more than ever, our famous "Art" is the one refuge and sanatorium.

I send the heartiest greetings of the season to Madame Paul and am yours and hers very constantly,

Henry James

1. *The Awkward Age.*
2. Ferdinand de Rothschild (1839–1898), the collector and patron of the arts.
3. Maupassant had visited London in 1886, and HJ had entertained him and accompanied him to Waddesdon Manor, Rothschild's French chateau near Aylesbury.
4. HJ delicately reminds Bourget here of his (HJ's) pro-Dreyfus feelings.
5. Urbain Mengin (see *Letters* III, 223) had come to the end of his position as tutor of the Duke of Sutherland's son, who was now being sent to live in a *pension*.

To Grace Norton
Dictated Ts Harvard

Lamb House, Rye
Christmas Day 1898

My dear Grace.

Here goes again—I am letting my Remington loose at you. I find it is the only way. I am "that" demoralised and incapacitated that what I don't dictate I find I simply don't (excuse the apparent confusion) write. I *can* dictate, and I can't trace a letter. I never could; and you must always so have known it that only your admirable manners prevented your ever throwing it up at me. *My* admirable manners, as you see, lead to my acknowledging your beautiful— your very beautiful—last not much more than three months, I think, after the receipt of it. The weeks, somehow, have gone very fast, bringing me in a few large leaps and bounds to this amiable melancholy day, the choicest slice of which I sacrifice on your altar. I have been in this place almost every hour since the end of June. I have been what's called here very quiet—quite uncannily and mysteriously quiet: have scarce, that is, had a minute to myself, save so far as, in the mornings, I've closed the door for a good long job of work—a conclusion sharply terminated by luncheon and mostly by company, and intimately shared, throughout its brief course, by the sociable Remington. All of which, however, is peace ineffable compared with London. This is a little old brown and red and green and black hill-city, with which the autumn agrees even better than the summer, and there has scarce been an hour of it when I've not been under the charm of an undiscriminating resignation. Even this still, grey Christmas, mild and merciful, though not sunny and amusing as the beauty of the days just past promised felicitously to make it—even this dreary little festival gives another small twist to the spell. I am close to the fine old church that crowns the eminence and that is still "higher" inside than out, with a dear little all but Catholic Irish curate with whom I am on the best of terms; and I sit here, in a decent little old oak parlour which I wish you could see, and talk with you between the times I see the good folk go in to their righteousness and come out to their dinners. Mine won't be till much later on, with two friends to share it. One of these brags that he knows you and even that he has once shared *yours*. He has been with me here two months, delicate and *souffreteux*, but a mine of conversation and a little blaze of intelligence. Do you remember Jonathan Sturges,[1] of New York, who is lame and who never was at Harvard, but who was on some occasion eternally cherished by him, comforted and fed by you in company with his cousins, the "Will. Osbornes," friends of yours, as he professes, and at that time your neighbours? He thinks you the most gracious lady a wide experience of the world, since then especially, has ever revealed to him; and it is doubtless our being so much at one on your graciousness that has qualified him more than anything else for having been so long my constant inmate. I am learning the lesson that in a small country town where local society is nil, fate seeks to make the matter as broad as it's long by arranging compensations on strictly domestic lines. In other words, whereas in London the people you know are everywhere, in the country they are all in your own house! This is very ingenious of fate; and it is good for everything except reading, writing, arithmetic and the higher branches of solitude. Tonight at dinner, with the turkey, however, we shall be only four—and the turkey, for elegance, is to be a lady, a "splendid hen-bird." Sturges and I did indeed, only last night, dine out locally—and the local, here, is almost weird enough to deserve I should tell you more of it. But oh, it's so complicated! I don't really know where to begin—about the J. Symonds Vidlers of Mountsfield;[2] nor about good old little Mrs. Davies, straight out of *Cranford*,[3] whom her chariot having lost, under Christmas Eve influences, *both* its back wheels, we brought home with us in *ours* and committed, in the frosty moonlight and under her little archaically-sculptured wooden door-canopy of the last century, to the embrace of a rosy maidservant almost as fluttered as herself and quite as much out of *Cranford*. This is almost the first thing of the kind I have done since I've been here, the main exception being a dinner some weeks ago with the Brookfields of Leasam; he, Col. B., M.P., being the member for East Sussex and elder of the two sons of Thackeray's Mrs. Brookfield, lately defunct,[4] and she—his wife—all that there is of most from Buffalo, N.Y. I don't justify my hint at the weirdness, you see, quite as much as I might—though I do, I think, a little; but I will lay it on thick for you if you will only come over for three months and join, under my charming-coloured old roof, the domestic procession. I have just finished a piece of work that has for several months kept me sitting tight; but I go up to town a few days hence to see to the putting to rights of my apartment in De Vere Gardens, the effect on which of six months vacuity consoles me for arriving at the consciousness of apparently just having definitely let it, for the next half-year, to a rather high-sounding, but a thoroughly certified and secure, Scotch bachelor laird. I have insured against bagpipes and whisky, but not against a heartbreak. I find—by which I mean I am feeling—that it's odious to traffic thus in one's household gods. I am told, on the other hand, that it's only the first step that costs and the first tenant that smashes. After that one doesn't mind. The harm is done and the stain ineffaceable. You alone, my dear Grace, seem to me to have mastered the art of fine living. You sit close always, having blissfully, but the one seat. Well, if I had but one, I am aware by this time that it would certainly be this one—and to that favour shall I doubtless come at last. I don't ply you with questions, nor suppose, nor hope, nor pray, nor imagine, nor conjecture any of the many wrong things, for you, or about you, to which letters between those who so woefully don't meet, only too easily and vainly lend themselves. If I hope you are well, it unfortunately won't make you so; and if I suppose you are happy, it's not in the least because I'm not also perfectly capable of supposing you are miserable. What is much more to the point is that, with blatant egotism, I myself am quite decently firm on my feet, and quite decently *in*firm on everything else. I hope very much to be going abroad for a few weeks—by which I mean mainly to Rome—when I shall have swept and garnished my flat. It will be the first time for five years. Then I shall come back here for the spring and summer. I am really beginning to entertain premonitions of immortality through the vague stirrings of a comprehension of the charm of a garden. I have been doing, the autumn through, little things in mine—little potterings, mistaken helpless things; yet enjoying them as I couldn't enjoy, I'm sure, the Yellowstone Park. May your house be warm, my dear Grace, your head light, and your heart hard! How is Montaigne? But you needn't tell me—I see how you are getting *your* foregleams of immortality; and I am more than ever constantly yours

Henry James

1. See *Letters* III, 435.
2. John Symonds Vidler (1851–1912) and his wife, of an old Rye family, were neighbors of HJ's from the time he settled in Lamb House.
3. *Cranford,* by Elizabeth C. Gaskell (1810–1865) published in 1853, depicts life in a quiet Cheshire village in the early nineteenth century.
4. Colonel Arthur Montagu Brookfield (1853–1940) was Conservative M.P. for East Sussex from 1885. He was the son of Mrs. William Henry Brookfield (Jane Octavia Elton), the intimate friend of Thackeray; his wife was the former Olive Hamilton of Buffalo, New York. The Brookfields lived in Leasam House near Rye.

To Charles Eliot Norton
Dictated Ts Harvard

Lamb House, Rye
26th December 1898

My dear Charles,

I feel as if I required a great deal of courage to address you a letter—especially of this machine-made sort. But I have thought the matter well over—have trembled and sighed and almost wept all round about it; and the result is that, under the protection of this sunny, balmy south of England Christmastide, I take my life in my hand. What I mean, to put the case more simply, is that I know and feel only too well how in common courtesy—to put it *most* superficially—I ought long ago to have broken a silence consorting but too ill with my natural sentiments. Therefore I measure the coldness, and what in a vulgar mind I should think of as the resentment, due to my odious case, by all my own embarrassed, humiliated and generally contrite and grovelling sense of it. Let me say at once that a great part of the secret of my horrid prolonged dumbness has been just this ugly fact of my finding myself reduced, in my declining years, like a banker or a cabinet minister, altogether to *dictating* my letters. The effect of this, in turn, has been to give me a great shyness about them—which has indeed stricken me with silence just in proportion as the help so rendered has seemed to myself really to minister to speech. Many people, I find, in these conservative climes, take it extremely ill to be addressed in Remingtonese. They won't, in short, have a typewritten letter on any terms; and that very mature child of nature, my old friend Rhoda Broughton, assured me the other day that if I should presume to send *her* one, she would return it to me indignantly and unopened. The only result of that is that I send her nothing at all. Forgive, however, this long descant on my delays, my doubts and fears, my final jump, rendered thus clumsy by my nervousness. I don't even ask you to notice my letter in any way. I feel as if I had forfeited all right ever again to ask you for anything. I only beg you to let mercy slightly season your disgust. And then also to let Sally, Lily, and even Margaret—little, dear blessed being, as I have ever done for *her*—just plead for me a little. Perhaps Theodora will add a word. The last time she was in England I made a sort of compact with her to do anything that she ever could—easily, that is, and comfortably, in the common life-saving way—for me in Cambridge. Now is her chance. Let her make you read my letter—or if she can't, let her at least read it to you. With all this help it ought to pass.

The worst of such predicaments is, my dear Charles, that when one does write, everything one has, at a thousand scattered moments, previously wanted to say, seems to have dried up with desuetude and neglect. Oh, all the things that should have been said on the spot if they were ever to be said at all! This applies, you will immediately recognise—though it's a stern truth by which *I* suffer most—very poignantly to all the utterance I feel myself to have so odiously failed of at the time of the death of dear Burne-Jones.[1] I can only give you a very partially lucid account of why on *that* occasion at least no word from me reached you. I saw myself, heard myself, felt myself, not write—and yet even then knew perfectly both that I should be writing now and that I should now be sorrier than ever for my not writing then. It came, the miserable event, at the very moment I was achieving, very single-handed and unassisted, a complicated transfer of residence from London to this place, with all sorts of bewildering material detail (consequent on renovation, complete preparation of every kind, of old house and garden) adding its distraction to the acute sense of pressing work fatally retarded and blighted; so that a postponement which has finally grown to this monstrous length began with being a thing only of moments and hours. Then, moreover, it was simply so wretched and odious to feel him, by a turn of the wheel of Fate that had taken but an instant, gone for ever from sight and sound and touch. I was tenderly attached to him, with abundant reason for being, and there was something that choked and angered one, beyond what words could trust themselves to express, in the mere blind *bêtise* of the business. So the days and the weeks went. I went up from here to town, and thence to Rottingdean, for the committal of his ashes, there, to the earth of the little grey-towered churchyard, in sight of the sea, that was at the moment all smothered in lovely spring flowers. It was a day of extraordinary beauty, and in every way a quite indescribably sincere—I remember I could find at the time no other word for the impression—little funeral and demonstration. The people from London were those, almost all, in whose presence there was a kind of a harmony. I drove out from Brighton with good old Holman Hunt[2]—perfectly sincere *he*—and his wife, and I drove back with them. As for Burne-Jones's own folk, they were wonderful: his wife simply amazing; Mackail,[3] who altogether supported her, beautiful and admirable; and Margaret and Phil hospitable, hovering, almost radiant presences, each with its own and very different sort of grace. I had seen the dear man, to my great joy, only a few days before his death: meeting him out at a kind of blighted and abortive wedding-feast (that is a dinner before a marriage that was to take place on the morrow) from which we were both glad to disembroil ourselves: so that we drove together home, intimately moralising and talking nonsense, and he put me, in the grey London midnight, down at my corner to go on by himself to the Grange. It was the last time I saw him, and, as one always does, I have taken ever since a pale comfort in the thought that our parting was explicitly affectionate and such, almost, as one would have wished it even had one known. I miss him even here and now. He was one of the most loveable of men and most charming of friends—altogether and absolutely distinguished. I think his career, as an artistic one, and speaking quite apart from the degree of one's sympathy with his work, one of the greatest of boons to our most vulgar of ages. There was no false note in him, nothing to dilute the strain; he knew his direction and held it hard—wrought with passion and went as straight as he could. He was for all this always, to me, a great comfort. For the rest, death came to him, I think, at none so bad a moment. He had, essentially, to my vision, really *done*. And he was very tired, and his cup was, with all the mingled things, about as full as it would hold. It was so good a moment, in short, that I think his memory is already feeling the benefit of it in a sort of rounded, finished way. I was not at the sale of his pictures and drawings which took place after his death—I have not stirred from this spot since I came to it at the end of June; but, though I should immensely have cherished some small scrap, everything went at prices—magnificent for his estate—that made acquisition a vain dream. I saw Phil a couple of times—but Phil is a chapter by himself. His father's death had an immense immediate effect upon him, and will by this time have had another—of which I have been too absent, as yet, to judge. But I take a great interest in him—strange, incomplete, and yet with distinct gifts of his own, as he is. To know him is to watch his life with a curiosity almost inhuman, but not in the least to be the more qualified to say what may ever become of it.

But I am writing you a very long letter, when I only meant to make you a sign of contrition and remembrance. I feel really domesticated in this pleasant small corner. I have not renounced London, but I shall not, for a year, have been there to speak of. I am greatly hoping to go abroad next month for some twelve to fifteen weeks. Abroad means for me, only and always, Italy. Yet I've not been there for five years—nor, for that time, quitted England at all. You will, from the summit of your long and heroic privation, smile at such small sorrows. I greatly missed, last year, the intermission of Sally and Lily. It wasn't only that I lost *them*, but that, in so doing, I lost also something of you. I have had—and little wonder—scant news of you. I know you've renounced your professorship. I know you felt strongly on public events. But I am in a depressed twilight—of discrimination, I mean—that enables me to make less of these things than I should like to do. So much has come and gone, these six months, that how can I talk about it? It's strange the consciousness possible to an American here today, of being in a country in which the drift of desire—so far as it concerns itself with the matter—is that we *shall* swell and swell, and acquire and *re*quire, to the top of our opportunity. My own feeling, roughly stated, is that we have not been good enough for our opportunity—vulgar, in a manner, as that was and is; but that it may be the real message of the whole business to make us as much better as the great grabbed-up British Empire has, unmistakeably, made the English. But over these abysses—into them rather—I peer with averted eye. I fear I am too lost in the mere spectacle for any decent morality. Goodbye, my dear Charles, and forgive my mechanic volubility. Isn't it better to have ticked and shocked than never to have ticked at all? I send my love to all your house. You, I fear, are past praying for; but I pray, this summer, for Sally or Lily. Either may come first if the other will only come second. I have really, down here, a very genial nook to show any one of you who will only believe it enough to come and see your ever, my dear Charles, affectionate old friend,

Henry James

1. Edward Burne-Jones (1833–1898), the Pre-Raphaelite painter whose friendship HJ and Norton shared, had died on 16 June.
2. William Holman Hunt (1827–1910), one of the founders of the Pre-Raphaelite Brotherhood.
3. John William Mackail (1859–1945), poet and literary scholar.

To Edward Warren
Telegram Ms Huntington

[Rye, 9.38 A.M., February 27, 1899]

Am asking very great favour of your coming down for inside of day or for night if possible house took fire last night but only Green Room and Dining Room affected hot hearth in former igniting old

beam beneath with tiresome consequences but excellent local brigade's help am now helpless in face of reconstructions of injured
portions and will bless you mightily if you come departure of
course put off

Henry James

To Edmund Gosse
Ms Leeds

Lamb House, Rye

Tuesday night [28 February 1899]

All thanks, my dear Gosse, for your note. No, thank heaven; I've
escaped by a narrow squeak—but I've escaped with only two rooms
partially, very partially damaged—and only "structurally"—not as
to furniture, and not—rare fate—at all by supererogatory water—as
so easily might have been. By the "finger of providence" I was
sitting up to a very undue, (and for me) unusual hour—2 A.M.—
meaning at last, at last, to have "gone abroad" today, as ever is—and
thereby lingering late by my *foyer* to write a great many procrastinated letters that I knew I shouldn't have time for on the
morrow. *That* saved me—I sniffed the danger much sooner than if
I had been with my head under the bedclothes; and could quickly
summon the brave pumpers, who arrived promptly and showed
most laudable tact, sanity and competence—above all in not nervously and prematurely flooding me. They pumped most subtly—
and in short save for a scare and an absolutely strained and
sleepless—night—with the temporary loss of the use of two rooms
(insured completely), I am not the worse; and I am on the other
hand cheaply *warned*—old houses have insidious structural traps;
old recklessness and barbarities of fire-place-building and infamous
juxtapositions of *beam* and chimneys. It is all to be made again
better and saner and safer than it *ever* was—and I wait here a week
longer to see reparations started. Then I do at last go away for ten
weeks. Influenza, proofs, other things—above all the longing to
wait for spring—to really meet it—have kept me till now. I was for
a fortnight more or less down with the beastly blight—but am erect
and purged again. Only I don't *want* even *now* to go: this house is
so sustained a fit.—Don't you palpitate and gasp with poor great

little Rudyard—?[1] I pray for him tenderly, though with consistent pessimism. Good-bye and all thanks again. I seem to have innumerable letters to write. We shall gather ourselves together on my return. Love to your house. Ever your

H.J.

1. Kipling, who had traveled to the United States with his family during the midwinter, came down in New York with "inflammation" in one lung, probably a light case of pneumonia.

To William James
Ms Harvard

Le Plantier
Costebelle, Hyères
April 2*d*, 1899

Dearest William.

I greatly appreciate the lucidity and liberality of your so interesting letter of the 19th, telling me of your views and prospects for next summer etc.—of all of which I am now able to make the most intimate profit. I enter fully into your reasons for wanting to put in the summer quietly and concentratedly in Cambridge—so much that with work unfinished and a spacious house and library of your "very own" to contain you, I ask myself how you can be expected to do anything less. Only it all seems to mean that I shall see you all but scantly and remotely. However, I shall wring from it when the time comes every concession that can be snatched, and shall meanwhile watch your signs and symptoms with my biggest operaglass (the beautiful one, one of the treasures of my life: *que je vous dois*).

Nothing you tell me gives me greater pleasure than what you say of the arrangements made for Harry and Billy in the forest primeval—and the vision of their drawing therefrom experiences of a sort that I too miserably lacked (poor Father!) in my own too casual youth. What I most of all feel, and in the light of it conjure you to keep doing for them, is their being *à même* to contract local saturations and attachments in respect to their *own* great and glorious country, to learn, and strike roots into, its infinite beauty, as I suppose, and variety. Then they won't, as I do now, have to assimilate, but half-heartedly, the alien splendours—inferior ones too, as I believe—of the indigestible Midi of Bourget and the Vicomte Melchior de Vogüé,[1] kindest of hosts and most brilliant of *commensaux* as I am in the act of finding both these personages. The beauty here is, after my long stop-at-home, admirable and exquisite; but make the boys, none the less, stick fast and sink up to their necks in everything their *own* countries and climates can give *de pareil et de supérieur*. Its being that "own" will double their *use* of it.—I at last got away from home and spent sixteen days in Paris, where I was "very, very kind" (and easily and comfortably so) to Leslie and Rosina Emmet—Bay[2] being (then) still in England, where success will be eventually, I think, quite within her grasp. I breakfasted, dined, theatre'd, museumed, walked and talked them (*sans compter* constant tea and little cakes), and left them a souvenir on my departure (what I, for the moment, *could*). I've been here a week and depart tomorrow or next day. It has been rather a tension—so utterly inapt have I become for staying with any one for more than twenty-four hours; but my year-by-year defeated postponements, the preparations and (material) conciliations, the loveliness of the place etc. have made it the very least I could do. Both Bourget and his wife have been profusely kind and considerate. Their *train de vie* is a wondrous mark of prosperity and success (beyond even what I understand), and this little estate—(two houses—near together—in a twenty-five acre walled "parc" of dense pine and cedar, along a terraced mountain-side, with exquisite views inland and to the sea) is a precious and enviable acquisition. The walks are innumerable, the pleasant "wildness" of the land (universally accessible) only another form of sweetness, and the light, the air, the noble, graceful lines etc., all of the first order. It's classic—Claude—Virgil. Vogüé, the only other guest (working almost all day, however, for dear life, at the serial novel[3] he is running—almost ended—in the *Revue*) is an interesting and very "consummate" specimen of the *gentilhomme français* turned journalist novelist etc. All the same, they make me homesick. I treat the "Affaire" as none of my business (as it isn't), but *its* power to make one homesick in France and the French air, every hour and everywhere today, is not small. It *is* a country *en décadence*.[4] Once one *feels* that, nothing—on the spot—corrects the impression. However, I must glide—I can't go into details—and I seem to have spent all of every precious A.M. since I left Rye in writing letters. I all the more, again, bless *your* sacrifice of time as per your last.

I expect to get to Genoa on the 4th or 5th April and there to make up my mind as to how I can best spend the following eight weeks, in Italy, in evasion and seclusion. Unhappily I *must* go to Rome and Rome is infernal. But I shall make short work of it. My nostalgia for Lamb House is already such as to make me *capable de tout. Never* again will I leave it! I don't take you up on the Philippines—I admire you and agree with you too much. You have an admirable eloquence. But the age is *all* to the vulgar! Bob's letter is most curious, it [is] rather comforting, if it be not cynical to say so, as an indication of shrinkage (with the weakening mind) of his terrible "personality." Blessed is his long stay at Daneville. Farewell with a wide embrace. Ever your

Henry

1. Viscount Eugène Melchior de Vogüé (1848–1910), French novelist and man of letters, whose studies of Turgenev, Tolstoy, and Dostoevsky in *Le Roman Russe* (1886) played a significant part in making these writers known in the West.

2. "Bay" was Ellen Gertrude Emmet, later Rand. See letter to Ellen Temple Hunter, 3 July 1897.

3. This was *Les Morts qui parlent* (1899). A third guest at the Bourgets before HJ wrote this letter had been Urbain Mengin. In an unpublished memoir, Mengin recalls that during his brief visit he and HJ were able to have some private talk after lunch: "A young priest entered and Madame Paul Bourget went to meet him seemingly pleased by his coming. At this moment Henry James rose and asked me to take the air briefly with him. Once outside he told me that with this young priest and M. de Vogüé he found the atmosphere stifling. We took a short walk and HJ became light-hearted again. He spoke to me of my impending trip to Tuscany and hoped I would meet the charming Ouida (Marie Louise de la Ramée) whose novels interested him." Ouida (1839–1908) spent her later years in Florence.

4. The Dreyfus case had reached its revelations of the guilt of the forger who helped "frame" the Jewish officer. The forger committed suicide. Dreyfus would have a new trial that September.

To Minnie Bourget
Ms Private

Hotel de Gênes, Genoa
ce samedi [8 April 1899]

Dear Madame Paul.

I profit by the first moment of drawing breath in my Italiënische Reise to tell you more expressively than I could do by a mere message at the moment of leaving Le Plantier, how greatly I regretted during the last hours your temporary eclipse. Leaving you invisible and unwell was the only shadow on the delightful hours of that same afternoon and the charming day spent on the morrow at St. Raphael. The little *chemin de fer du Littoral* is a jewel and I urge your taking the run to Fréjus on the first occasion—even if you *don't*, in consequence, spend a day at the Grand Hôtel at St. Raphael (*not* Grand Hôtel des Bains) which is very good. I did everything—peregrinated to (almost) the far end of the Roman acqueduct at Fréjus and was affable to the British females on *both* sides of me at the (St. Raphael) table d'hôte. One of them, by the way (who had the longest chin in Europe and had bicycled over that afternoon from Costebelle!), has a villa near Le Plantier and succeeded in worrying out of me the shy confession of where—at Costebelle—I had been staying. "And where did you come from?" "Well—from Hyères." "Ah, you've been at Hyères? What part of Hyères?" "Well—properly, rather, the part near Costebelle." " 'Near' Costebelle—do you mean *at* Costebelle?" "Well, yes—it *was*, I suppose, 'at' Costebelle." "And at what hotel?" "I was not at a hotel." "Then where were you?" "I was staying at a villa." "Ah!—where was the villa?" "Well—up rather high; out of the way, thank heaven!" A silence. "Not La Luguette then?" "No." "And not Le Bocage either?" "No." Another silence. "But with some English friends at all events?" "No." "Then with some French?" "Well, yes—more or less French!" "Ah, the Léotauds?" "No." "Oh, I see—higher up?" "Yes—*much* higher up." "Ah, the P. Bourgets?" (breathlessly). "Well, yes—with M and Mme Bourget." Sensation—quick conversation of lady with other lady on her right and prosternation of both so great that I was really left in peace (on that side) for the rest of the dinner. Your name is a talisman. I came—on Thursday—from St. Raphael to Genoa, straight—if straight it can be called with that diabolical delay at Ventimiglia—nearly three hours of stuffy, dusty, pushing, scrambling, complaining, cosmopolitan crowd, enriched with a large affluence of Tedeschi; having on the way between St. Raphael and Menton found myself in the same carriage with an English friend whom I had not seen for eighteen years (Bullock-Hall) and who now turned up as proprietor of a villa at Vallescure and supreme authority on the Roman remains of the Riviera, of which he spared me not a single broken brick—any more

103

than he did a single aquarelle of the very large portfolio of his daughter who, with his French wife, was accompanying him on a visit to La Mortola, near Vintimille, the residence of another Briton—Hanbury—with famous gardens—where they were to spend the night and "meet" (for all the world as if in South Kensington!) the Grant Duffs![1] I give you these details as material for the notes to Bourget's *édition définitive* of *Cosmopolis*[2]—and aids to the comprehension of how much quiet reverie I achieved on my journey. I have in truth, ever since, been unable to achieve very much. I found awaiting me here a pressing invitation from an Italian friend—Captain Avignone,[3] who used formerly to be attached to the Arsenal at Venice and a very pleasant member of the old (of many years ago) Bronson-Curtis circle, and is now living at a delicious little villino near Recco—an hour from Genoa by train. I went out and lunched with him (the beauty of the spot, the sea, the view, the promontory of Porto Fino etc. divine) and on my way back stopped at Bogliasco and had tea with the Ranee[4] and her two sons (enjoying their Cambridge Easter holidays), with whom I also dine today. I spend tomorrow here and go probably on Tuesday to Venice (Palazzo Barbaro) and to Asolo—having found here, in letters, such formidable accounts of the still possible "social complications" in Rome, that I am putting off going there till toward the end of the month when these dangers may have diminished—in which case I shall spend, probably, all the month of May there. I also find here a note from Mrs. Wharton,[5] announcing to me that she is sending me a fruit of literary toil and that she further expects to be at "Claridge's"—London—the sojourn of kings—in May. "Nous vivons sous un prince ennemi"—du repos. Still—I found a little—of that luxury—though I fear I gave it but a little—at Le Plantier. I hope you have secured rather more for yourself since the departure of your anxious serialist[6]—and that you are full of convalescence and contentment. I am full, on my side, of grateful memories and blessed pictures. The beauty and harmony and nobleness of your eternal medium—that nothing can injure, diminish or disturb— had added a great stretch to my experience and a great fancy to my envy. You *are*, really, as I said to my neighbour, very "high up." I hope M. de Vogüé's fine gentlemanly tension sustained itself, without any sort of catastrophe—to the end. I have been reading *Jean d'Agrève* with a mixture of recognitions and reserves—but quel drôle de produit, un pareil livre, of an age—and of an individual mind—too conscious and too cultivated! However, I never knew a man *equally* "conscious" (with M. de V.) whom I liked as much! *Don't "acknowledge" or answer this in any way.* Only let Paul—in the fulness of his muscular superfluity—let me know, some day, when you move northward. Then I shall look for you in Paris.—The clatter, the chatter and *chiasso* of the Genoese street come into my room almost as a deafening—but it comes in with such sunny warmth of Italian air and shuffle of Italian feet and revival of Italian memories, that I am all for the joy of feeling myself here again— after the long interval and letting it give me once more as many as possible of the little old throbs and thrills of the great old super- stition. I greet you both *caramente* and am ever constantly yours,

Henry James

1. Sir Mountstuart E. Grant Duff (1829–1906). See *Letters* III, 442.
2. Bourget's 1893 novel.
3. Antonio Marcello Avignone, HJ's old Venetian friend, who had been widowed early. HJ had visited him in November 1888 when he stayed at Monte Carlo and again in March 1894 when he was in Genoa.
4. Margaret Alice Lilly (De Windt) Brooke (1850–1936), wife of Charles Vyner Brooke, the "white Rajah" of Sarawak. See her memoirs, *Good Morning and Good Night* (1934).
5. HJ had not yet met Edith Wharton, who was a friend of the Bourgets.
6. Melchior de Vogüé.

To Howard Sturgis
Ms Harvard

Hotel d'Europe, Rome
May 19, 1899

My dear Howard.[1]

It's a great pleasure to hear from you in this far country—though I greatly wish it weren't from the bed of anguish—or at any rate of delicacy: if delicacy may be connected, that is, with anything so indelicate as a bed! But I'm very glad to gather that it's the couch of convalescence. Only, if you have a Back, for heaven's sake take care of it. When I was about your age—in 1862!—I did a bad damage (by a strain subsequently—through crazy juvenility—neglected) to mine; the consequence of which is that, in spite of retarded atten- tion, and years, really, of recumbency, later, I've been saddled with it for life, and that even now, my dear Howard, I verily write you *with* it. I even wrote *The Awkward Age* with it: therefore look sharp![2]—I wanted especially to send you that volume—as an "acknowledgment" of princely hospitalities received, and formed the intention of so doing even in the too scant moments we stood face to face among the Rembrandts. That's right—*be* one of the few! I greatly applaud the tact with which you tell me that scarce a human being will understand a word, or an intention, or an artistic element or glimmer of any sort, of my book. I tell *myself*—and the "reviews" tell me—such truths in much cruder fashion. But it's an old, old story—and if I "minded" now as much as I once did, I should be well beneath the sod. Face to face I should be able to say a bit how I saw—and why I *so* saw—my subject. But that will keep.—I'm here in a warmish, quietish, emptyish, pleasantish (but not maddeningly so), altered and cockneyfied and scraped and all but annihilated Rome. I return to England some time next month (to the country—Lamb House, Rye—now my constant address—only). I see of course considerably Waldo and Mrs. W.[3] He is not at all well, and should take three months'—imperatively—rest and regimen. But his vast marble-shop! However, this is only to greet and warn you—and to be, my dear Howard, your affectionate old friend,

Henry James

1. Howard Overing Sturgis (1854–1920) was the youngest son of the expatriate American banker Russell Sturgis. Educated at Eton and Cambridge, Sturgis lived all his life in England in the family's Georgian villa, Queen's Acre (called Qu'Acre), on the edge of Windsor Great Park, with his friend William Haynes Smith, known as "the Babe." See the chapter "The Lessons of the Master," in Edel, *The Master* (1972). There are at Harvard 142 letters from HJ to Sturgis.
2. The account of HJ's "obscure hurt"—the source of his later backaches—is given in *Notes of a Son and Brother* (1914), chapter IX.
3. Waldo Story had married the former Maud Broadwood. See letter to Blackwood, 28 October 1897.

To Mrs. Waldo Story
Ms Texas

Villa Crawford
Sant' Agnello di Sorrento
Saturday [17 June 1899]

Dear Mrs. Waldo.

A word to report progress,[1] and to explain, also, a little, delay. I find this place prodigious, astonishing, and Crawford[2] himself—to whom I have fallen a helpless victim,—of the last magnificence. But the situation is that they are all so overwhelmingly kind, and their general complications of hospitality are so great, that I have succumbed to overwhelming pressure and promised to stay for the extremely festal celebration of Mrs. Crawford's birthday, which is to take place on *Thursday.* Such a point has [been] made of this that all my powers of collapse have been called into play, and I am therefore unable to see how I can get back to Rome before *Saturday* next—a whole week hence. I am sadly afraid it *may* entail my missing you, but if you don't depart till one of the following days I shall still catch you and we shall move northward perhaps at almost the same moment. I am writing to Mme Peruzzi to explain my delay—and to hope, even, that they may be going to Vallombrosa, where I shall be equally—or more—glad to spend a few days. This prolongation here is far from what I intended, though I somewhat feared the pressure; but I reckoned without too many things and all the elements of persuasion. I've not yet put in my promised twenty-four hours with Munthe,[3] but am to go to Capri tomorrow, till Monday, and to do some other excursions today and on Tuesday and Wednesday. The beauty and splendour of this place are *invraisemblables*—the comfort and luxury *ditto,* and the total impression most curious and interesting. If we can only have another drive together, you shall have it *all.* Mrs. Crawford is of a grace and kindness and charm—!—and Mrs. Berdan[4] keeps step. The children are delightful, even the governess and the secretary most interesting; all nature perpetually *performs* and Mrs. Fraser[5] and her son close up the rear while the Marchese Patrizzi (the pair) pop in and out. *À bientôt* at all events. I say everything to Waldo and am yours very constantly

Henry James

107

1. Progress on the life of W. W. Story.

2. Francis Marion Crawford (1854–1909), son of Thomas Crawford, the American sculptor, was the author of a series of popular novels. HJ had known him in Rome in 1869.

3. Axel Martin Fredrik Munthe (1857–1949), Swedish psychiatrist, whose memoirs, *The Story of San Michele* (1929), were widely read. He practiced medicine in Rome and Paris and had a villa on Capri. See *Italian Hours* (1910), the essay "The Saint's Afternoon."

4. Mrs. Berdan, wife of General Berdan (inventor of the Berdan rifle used in the American Civil War), was a well-known figure in American-European society.

5. Mimoli Crawford, a sister of the novelist, had married the British diplomat Hugh Fraser.

To Hendrik C. Andersen
Ms Barrett

Lamb House, Rye
July 19*th* 1899

My dear Hans Andersen.[1]

You must have wondered at not hearing from me—and I found your letter here on my arrival, from Italy some twelve days ago. But I thought it better to wait, to answer you, till your box and its precious contents had arrived—to give you news of it, and its condition; and this happy event has only *just* taken place. I have been for three or four days in London, and in my absence the box turned up; so that yesterday, on my return, I could have it carefully, tenderly unpacked and its burden, with every precaution, laid bare and lifted out. It is, the beautiful bust, I rejoice to tell you, in perfect condition (it was admirably packed), without a flaw or a nick—and is more charming and delightful to [see] even than it was in Rome. I heartily rejoice to possess it—and I am by this post writing to my bankers in London for a draft on Rome of the amount of $250—that is Fifty Pounds—which will immediately reach me and which I will instantly, on its arrival, transmit to you. I find the sum modest for the admirable and exquisite work. I have perched the latter on the chimney-piece of my dining room—the position I have that best lends itself, all things carefully considered—where he commands the scene and has a broad base to rest on` and the arch of a little niche to enshrine him, and where, moreover, as I sit at meat, I shall have him constantly before me, as a loved companion and friend. He is so living, so human, so sympathetic and sociable and curious, that I foresee it will be a lifelong attachment. Brave little Bevilacqua and braver still big Maestro Andersen! You will both make many friends here. So I thank you again, and give you a good and grateful *stratta di mano*, which I will repeat two or three days hence. I think very kindly of our too few but so interesting hours together, and I send you my benediction and my heartiest good wishes. Lift up your heart, keep up your head, and don't sacrifice your health. I hope you are not roasting before a slow fire or shivering in a clammy shade. Yours, my dear Andersen, most faithfully

Henry James

1. Hendrik Christian Andersen (1872–1940) was a remote relative of Hans Christian Andersen. Born in Norway, he was brought to the United States as a child and grew up in Newport. He studied painting in Paris and sculpture in Rome, where he lived for many years and had a studio. HJ had met him during his recent Italian journey, visited his studio, and purchased a bust of a young boy, Conte Alberto Bevilacqua.

To Mrs. Humphry Ward
Ms Barrett

Lamb House, Rye
July 26th 1899

Dear Mrs. Ward,[1]

I beg you not to believe that if you elicit a reply from me—to your so interesting letter just received—you do so at any cost to any extreme or uncomfortable pressure that I'm just now under. I am always behind with everything—and it's no worse than usual. Besides I shall be very brief.[2] But I *must* say two or three words—not only because these are the noblest speculations that can engage the human mind, but because—to a degree that distresses me—you labour under two or three mistakes as to what, the other day, I at all wanted to express. I don't myself, for that matter, recognise what you mean by any "old difference" between us on *any* score—and least of all when you appear to glance at it as an opinion of mine (if I understand you, that is) as to there being but *one general* "hard and fast rule of presentation." I protest that I have never had with you any difference—consciously—on any such point, and rather resent, frankly, your attributing to me a judgment so imbecile. I hold that there are five million such "rules" (or as many as there [are] subjects in all the world—I fear the subjects are *not* 5,000,000!) only each of them imposed, artistically, by the particular case—involved in the writer's responsibility to it; and each *then*—and then only—"hard and fast" with an immitigable hardness and fastness. I don't see, *without* this latter condition, where any work of art, any artistic *question* is, or any artistic probity. Of course, a thousand times, there are as many magnificent and imperative cases as you like of presenting a thing by "going behind" as many forms of consciousness as you like—all Dickens, Balzac, Thackeray, Tolstoi (save when they use the autobiographic dodge) are huge illustrations of it. But they are illustrations of extreme and calculated selection, or singleness, too, whenever that has been, by the case, imposed on them. My own immortal works, for that matter, if I may make bold, are recognizable instances of *all* the variation. I "go behind" right and left in "The Princess Casamassima," "The Bostonians," "The Tragic Muse," just as I do the same but singly in "The American" and "Maisie," and just as I do it consistently *never at all* (save for a false and limited *appearance*, here and there, of doing it a *little*, which I haven't time to explain) in "The Awkward Age." So far from not seeing what you mean in *Pêcheur d'Islande*,[3] I see it as a most beautiful example—a crystal-clear one. It's a picture of a *relation* (a *single* relation) and that relation isn't given at all unless given on both sides, because, practically, there are no other relations to make *other* feet for the situation to walk withal. The logic jumps at the eyes. Therefore acquit me, please, *please*, of anything so abject as putting forward anything at once specific and *a priori*. "Then why," I hear you ask, "do you pronounce for MY BOOK *a priori*?" Only because of a mistake, doubtless, for which I do here humble penance—that of assuming too precipitately, and with the freedom of an inevitably too-foreshortened letter, that I was dealing with it *a posteriori!*—and *that* on the evidence of only those few pages and of a somewhat confused recollection of what, in Rome, you told me of your elements. Or rather—more correctly—I was giving way to my irresistible need of wondering how, *given* the subject, one could best work one's self into the presence of it. And, lo and behold, the subject isn't (of course, in so scant a show and brief a piece) "given" at all—I have doubtless simply, with violence and mutilation, *stolen* it. It is of the nature of that violence that I'm a wretched person to *read* a novel—I begin so quickly and concomitantly, *for myself*, to write it rather—even

110

before I know clearly what it's about! The novel I can *only* read, I can't read at all! And I had, to be just with me, one attenuation—I thought I gathered from the pages already absorbed that your *parti pris* as to your process with *Eleanor*[4] was already defined—and defined as "dramatic"—and that was a kind of *lead:* the people all, as it were, phenomenal to a particular imagination (hers) and that imagination, with all its contents, phenomenal to the reader. I, in fine, just rudely and egotistically thrust forward the beastly way *I* should have done it. But there is too much to say about these things—and I am writing too much—and yet haven't said half I want to—*and,* above all, there *being* so much, it is doubtless better not to attempt to say pen in hand what one can say but so partially. And yet I *must* still add one or two things more. What I said above about the "rule" of presentation being, in each case, hard and fast, *that* I will go to the stake and burn with slow fire for—the slowest that will burn at all. I hold the artist must (infinitely!) know how he is doing it, or he is not doing it at all. I hold he must have a perception of the interests of his subject that grasps him as in a vise, and that (the subject being of course formulated in his mind) he sees *as* sharply the way that most presents it, and presents most of it, as against the ways that comparatively give it away. And he must there choose and stick and be consistent—and that is the hard-and-fastness and the vise. I am afraid I *do* differ with you if you mean that the picture can get any *objective* unity from any other source than that; can get it from, e.g., the "personality of the author." From the personality of the author (which, however enchanting, is a thing for the reader only, and not for the author himself, without hu-miliating abdications, to my sense, to count in at all) it can get nothing but a unity of execution and of tone. There is no short cut for the subject, in other words, out of the process, which, having made out most what it (the subject) is, *treats* it most, handles it, in that relation, with the most consistent economy. May I say, to exonerate myself a little, that when, e.g., I see you make Lucy "phe-nomenal" to Eleanor (one has to express it briefly and somehow), I find myself supposing completely that you "know how you're doing it," and enjoy, as critic, the sweet peace that comes with that sense. But I haven't the feeling that you "know how you're doing it" when, at the point you've reached, I see you make Lucy phenomenal, even for one attempted stroke, to the little secretary of embassy. And the reason of this is that Eleanor counts as presented, and thereby *is* something to go behind. The secretary *doesn't* count as presented (and isn't he moreover engaged, at the very moment—*your* moment—in being phenomenal himself, to Lucy?) and is therefore, practically, *nothing* to go behind. The promiscuous shiftings of standpoint and centre of Tolstoi and Balzac for instance (which come, to my eye, from their being not so much big dramatists as big *painters*—as Loti is a painter), are the inevitable result of the *quantity of presenting* their genius launches them in. With the complexity they pile up they *can* get no clearness without trying again and again for new centres. And they don't *always* get it. However, I don't mean to say they don't get enough. And I hasten to add that you have—I wholly recognise—every right to reply to me: "Cease your intolerable chatter and dry up your preposterous deluge. If you will have the decent civility to *wait,* you will see that *I* 'present' also—*anch'io!*—enough for *every* freedom I use with it!"—And with my full assent to that, and my profuse prostration in the dust for this extravagant discourse, with all faith, gratitude, appreciation and affection, I *do* cease, dear Mrs. Ward, I dry up! and am yours most breathlessly,

Henry James

1. Mary Augusta Ward (1851–1920), better known as Mrs. Humphry Ward. HJ had recently visited her in her rented villa near Rome. See *Letters* III, 60, 234–237.

2. HJ's own footnote here was "Later!!! Latest. Don't rejoin!—*don't!*"

3. The 1886 novel by Pierre Loti (pseudonym of Julien Viaud), which HJ admired. See his essay on Loti in *Essays in London and Elsewhere* (1893).

4. Mrs. Ward was completing this novel, which was published in 1900.

To Hendrik C. Andersen
Ms Barrett

Lamb House, Rye
July 27*th* 1899

My dear Boy!

I am very glad to hear from you of the safe arrival of my missive and of the good news of your escape from Rome being well in sight. I think of you with the liveliest sympathy and I have, even, when I do so, almost a bad conscience about my own happy exemptions (though it *can* roast a little here too); my little green garden where shade and breeze and grass keep their freshness and where a particular chair awaits you under a certain wide-spreading old mulberry-tree. I shall make you very welcome here when your right day comes. May nothing occur to delay or otherwise damage it. Only let me know as soon as you can before you *do* approach—that I may advise you properly about your best train from London, etc. And don't expect to find me "lovely" or anything but very homely and humble. My little old house is *in* a small—a very small—country-town and is on a very limited scale indeed. But it serves my turn and will serve yours. I've struck up a tremendous intimacy with dear little Conte Alberto, and we literally can't live without each other. He is the first object my eyes greet in the morning, and the last at night. But I'm afraid I said some thing (accidentally) that misguided you in leading you to suppose I have written in a journal about him. I haven't. What I meant was that sooner or later a great many persons will see, and be struck with him, *here. Pazienza*—and for God's sake keep yourself well. Good-bye—*à bientôt.* If you see the Elliotts[1] please tell them I have a very affectionate memory of them and wrote to them in fact after the vile earth-shock. As you don't mention that I gather it didn't shatter you, nor anything that is yours. Bravo for all the big things you feel stirring within you. Yours very heartily

Henry James

1. HJ had met Andersen in the Roman studio of John Elliott, an American sculptor, who was married to Maude, a daughter of Julia Ward Howe.

To Mr. and Mrs. William James
Ms Harvard

Lamb House, Rye
August 9th [1899]

Dearest William and dearest Alice.

I have your two excellent letters of successive days, and indeed *yours*, dear Alice, your beautiful *first*, with its noble offer of help etc., I haven't even yet properly acknowledged.[1] None the less I have still to ask you to let me make this poor scrawl serve for both of you, as I seem to flow over into considerable lengths and am, after my long and rather "reposeful" absence, and with time lost in London etc., since, very much pressed with work, now that I have got back to it. Thank heaven it is fully profitable. I am much affected by your gentle recognition of the elements of the situation here which I tried to sketch for you, and which if you had only *been* here, would make all sketching superfluous. I wish indeed you could only see Lamb House *now*—at the prettiest moment of the summer, with the garden in quite—its most—profuse "herbaceous" and other bloom and looking quite charming; the purple clusters of grapes heavy in the greenhouse, the splendid bignonia throwing out its rich red flowers all up and down the south (house) wall, the big purple clematis flushing *à l'envi,* and the wisteria heavily, or, rather lightly, draping the porch of my study. Peace (quite apart from the superficial influences) has come back to me—because it inevitably *had* to. My disposition in respect to the house has had these two full years (that is since September '97) to solidify—therefore it isn't a light matter. This place is of a singular and infallible lettability and saleability (I could sell it three days after completing purchase to Edward Warren, e.g., who knows his subject *à fond* and would pounce on it—or to three or four other persons happily known to me). But that has, thank God, NOTHING to do with the matter. It is exactly and intensely NOT as a "speculation"—bad or good—that I have accepted Mrs. Bellingham's offer—but because on the contrary the place is a haven of rest out of which I pray heaven I may never shift for all the rest of my days. *That* outlook is the very bribe of bribes—the relief and rest of the "last long home." The extraordinary congruity of the little place with all my needs, conveniences, tastes, limitations (and even extensions), with every sort of security, salubrity and economy—and a congruity not general and approximate, but stretching into every detail and ramification—this fact presented itself to me as making a kind of timorous epilepsy of the idea of *passing* her offer and committing myself afresh to the unrest of having everything thrown again into question, with my peace of mind at the mercy of every wind of rumour that blows in this gossipping little town—as to what they are doing—*going* to do, with L.H. (a perpetual worry and indignity) and with the enraging sense that everything I have done to it, and may yet inevitably do, is all done—and to *be* done—for mysterious, contingent, unpleasant and inferior parties other than myself. Mrs. B. is a fourth rate (though I believe very decent)

South African *theatrical* person, of a hand to mouth situation, and of in every way inferior contacts and possibilities—and it's no way in the interest of one's "dignity," of the decency of one's position or one's credit here, that one should positively *elect* to "keep on" with her when one has, on such uncommonly easy terms, a chance to keep on only with one's *self*. My whole being cries out aloud for something that I can call my own—and when I look round me at the splendour of so many of the "literary" fry my confrères (M. Crawfords, P. Bourgets, Humphry Wards, Hodgson Burnetts, W. D. Howellses etc.) and I feel that I may strike the world as still, at fifty-six, with my long labour and my genius, reckless, presumptious and unwarranted in curling up (for more assured peaceful production), in a poor little $10,000 shelter—once for all and for all time—*then* I do feel the bitterness of humiliation, the iron enters into my soul, and (I blush to confess it), I *weep!* But enough, enough, enough! I am on firm ground again, and back at work, and the way is clear. I thank you and Alice more than I can say for your offers of advances. There is not any appearance of probability *whatever* that I shall have to ask you for any of the Syracuse sinking fund. I have only to have five or six months of normal work to float comfortably over everything—and those I *shall* here. I am touched to tears (you will think me very lachrymose!) by *your*, dearest Alice, writing to your mother to keep some of your inheritance for me. *Do*, kindly, now, write to her *not* to—before she set me down as a sponge and a failure. But it was lovely of you to have this inspiration.—You will say, doubtless:—"Why the deuce then did you write to us in an—as it were—*appealing*, consultative way at *all?*" It was the impulse to *fraternize*—put it that way—with you, over the pleasure of my purchase, and to see you glow with pride in *my* pride of possession etc. I did so immediately—before I had seen Dawes or found out anything: which was idiotic, but gushing. And I reckoned, alas, without Baldwin.[2]—I have your pencil-note from Harry, in which his situation sounds rough, but his humour happy and his tone admirable. I had, lately, a very charming letter from him from Tacoma—which I shall answer before long, and when I have an address. But I hope *you*, Alice, are not worrying about him. They are evidently a very social community and paternally—not to say—maternally, governed.—I take joy in every hour of William's regimen and reaction. He must go back next year. His boxes have all safely come and are safely set apart. I subscribe tomorrow to the *Chronicle* for him. (This almost intolerable suspense of Dreyfus!)—I have Peggy's educatrix all drawn up for you—but I won't (it's too long) attempt to go in to details till I see you. Mademoiselle Souvestre,[3] a very good friend of mine, and a most distinguished and admirable woman (of sixty-five today)—daughter of the celebrated Émile—has had for many years a very highly esteemed school for girls at high, breezy Wimbledon, near London (an admirable situation)—where she has formed the daughters of many of the very good English *advanced Liberal* political and professional connection during these latter times. She is a very fine, interesting person, her school holds a very particular place (all Joe Chamberlain's[4] daughters were there and they adore her), and I must tell you more of her. She would be excellent for Peggy's French. The whole subject, in fact, demands *extreme* threshing out. She (Mlle. S.) is a special friend of the Ribots[5] in Paris—they form her *foyer* there. But good night again—it's past midnight, and I am your doubly affectionate

Henry

1. HJ's landlord, Arthur Bellingham, had just died in Canada (where he had gone to the Klondyke to take part in the Bonanza Creek gold rush), and HJ was in the process of purchasing the house from the estate, which was in the hands of Mrs. Francis Bellingham, the landlord's mother. He had written WJ and received from him a letter warning of the financial risks involved. HJ replied in an essay-length letter on 4 August 1899, calling WJ's letter "a colder blast than I could apprehend," and explaining that he had been cautious and had taken legal counsel. The purchase included not only the house but a studio in Watchbell Street nearby. HJ added: "At my age it should be something that one *wants*, simply, so much to do a thing—for I am not yet wholly senile." Mrs. WJ, apparently to calm the ruffled brothers, offered to lend HJ funds to make the purchase.

2. Dr. W. W. Baldwin (1850–1910), then in the United States, had told WJ he thought the price for the property was too high. HJ replied that Baldwin had no knowledge of Rye real estate. See *Letters* III, 177.

3. Marie Souvestre taught many children from many distinguished families at her school, including the Stracheys. Lytton Strachey learned his French from her, and for a time Eleanor Roosevelt was a student. WJ decided, however, that his daughter should live with an English family, and placed her with the Joseph Thatcher Clarkes, where Peggy suffered from the presence of too many Clarke boys and was extremely homesick.

4. Joseph Chamberlain (1836–1914), British statesman.

5. Théodule Ribot (1839–1916), French philosopher and like WJ a lecturer in experimental psychology.

To Cora Crane
Ms Columbia

Lamb House, Rye
Monday P.M. [4 September 1899]

Dear Mrs. Crane.

All thanks for the strange images[1]—which I never expected to behold. They form a precious memento of a romantic hour. But no, surely, it can't be any doughnut of *yours* that is making me make such a gruesome grimace. I look as if I had swallowed a wasp, or a penny toy. And I tried to look so beautiful. I tried too hard doubtless. But don't show it to any one as H.J. trying. My young lady, in the better one, is a great ornament.—I carried away a *scared* image of you, rather—that is of Brede Place and its latest arrivals. *Where* are the young Barbarians[2] all at play? Far, I hope, from Crane's laboratory. "H. Wynne"[3] goes to him, with this. Believe me yours most truly

Henry James

1. Stephen Crane (1871–1900), author of *The Red Badge of Courage,* had been living with Cora Taylor for some time, and she had taken his name. They found it easier to maintain the liaison in England than in the United States, and they had rented Brede Place, a large Elizabethan manor house eight miles from Rye, settling in it in 1899. HJ welcomed them as fellow Americans. The "strange images" were snapshots of Cora and HJ taken at a garden party at Brede Rectory on 23 August 1899, in one of which HJ was eating a doughnut.
2. The "young barbarians" were the illegitimate children of the American novelist Harold Frederic (1856–1898), who had died a few months earlier. Cora had taken charge of the orphans, and HJ contributed money to their upkeep.
3. HJ was apparently sending Crane a copy of S. Weir Mitchell's novel *Hugh Wynne, Free Quaker* (1897).

To Hendrik C. Andersen
Ms Barrett

Lamb House, Rye, Sussex
September 7th 1899

My dearest little Hans: without prejudice to your magnificent stature! Your note of this morning is exactly what I had been hoping for, and it gives me the liveliest pleasure. I hereby "ask" you, with all my heart. *Do,* unfailingly and delightfully, come back next sum-

With Cora Crane at a garden party at Brede Rectory, near Rye.

mer and let me put you up for as long as you can possibly stay.
There, mind you—it's an engagement. I was absurdly sorry to lose
you when, that afternoon of last month, we walked sadly to the
innocent and kindly little station together and our common fate
growled out the harsh false note of whirling you, untimely away.
Since then I have *missed* you out of all proportion to the three
meagre little days (for it seems strange they were only *that*) that we
had together. I have never (and I've done it three or four times)
passed the little corner where we came up Udimore hill (from Winchelsea) in the eventide on our bicycles, without thinking ever so

118

tenderly of our charming spin homeward in the twilight and feeling again the strange perversity it made of that sort of thing being so soon *over.* Never mind—we *shall* have more, lots more, of that sort of thing! If things go well with me I'm by no means without hope of having been able, meanwhile, to take the studio[1] so in hand that I shall be ready to put you into it comfortably for a little artistic habitation. Rye, alas, is not sculpturesque, nor of a sculpturesque inspiration—but what's good for the man is, in the long run, good for the artist—and we shall be good for each other; and the studio good for both of us. May the terrific U.S.A. be meanwhile not a brute to you. I feel in you a *confidence,* dear Boy—which to show is a joy to me. My hopes and desires and sympathies right heartily and most firmly, go with you. So keep up *your* heart, and tell me, as it shapes itself, your (inevitably, I imagine, more or less weird) American story. May, at any rate, *tutta quella gente* be good to you. Yours, my dear Hans, right constantly

Henry James

1. The Watchbell street studio that HJ acquired when he bought Lamb House.

To Rudyard Kipling
Ms Harvard

Lamb House, Rye
September 16th 1899

My dearest Rudyard.

I receive today from Rottingdean another volume[1] [of] your sustained—incomparably sustained—munificence, and it causes an overflow of my cup of preoccupation. This, behold, is the deluge, and the wave breaks at your feet. I've been, all summer, full of wonderments and uncontrolled and unenlightened imaginings about you, and to work them off at you a little will relieve me and not hurt you—as it is a part of their tender essence that they desire to impose upon you no manner of exertion; to permit you, in short, not so much as to wink at me in return a long Asiatic eyelash. I want only to set up a small stopgap till I can get round to see you. I see every little while in the papers how you are not—how you *can't* be; and that gives me a sort of basis for making out how you are. It seems to be borne in upon me more or less confidently that you are back from Scotland—and my knees ache with praying that you may have been buffeted there into all sorts of Highland hardihood. I do most cordially hope that you are out of the black shadow—or of some of it—of your last winter's nightmare.[2] But I grope toward you darkly, and so must it be. I commend myself very earnestly to the kind remembrance of Mrs. Carrie—I send her in fact, and to your children, my love and my blessing. I am here (back here—from four or five months of spring and early summer in Italy) these ten weeks, and very busy *buying* my little old house—as to which, by deaths and other convulsions, an apprehended pistol has been levelled at my head. But I am marching bravely to the altar—for that is what it seems like: the making an "honest woman" of a trusting thing whom I had publicly taken up with. I don't regret it. She wears well—but I have to make "settlements." Hence this crabbed hand—a plume from a broken or at least weary—wing.[3] Later on I should like much, for a day, to walk round to you and see with my eyes and hear with my ears and even feel with my hands. Every successive instalment of the Publication deepens my sense that these splendid specimens of postal delivery are the Handsomest Thing you've ever done—or I, at least have ever been made the subject of. And I don't speak of type or even of text.—I speak, hang it, of the spirit of the thing. They're more than literature: they're Furniture, and I am yours, both, and all, always constantly

Henry James

1. *Stalky and Company,* published in October 1899.
2. His illness in New York. See letter to Gosse, 28 February 1899.
3. HJ had just completed a short story, "Broken Wings," which he mailed to his agent the day after writing this letter.

To Charles Eliot Norton
Dictated Ts Harvard

Lamb House, Rye
24 November 1899

*Please read postscript first.

My dear Charles,

I heartily welcomed your typed letter of a couple of months ago, both for very obvious and for respectable subsidiary reasons. I am almost altogether reduced—I would much rather say promoted—to type myself, and to communicate with a friend who is in the same predicament only adds to the luxury of the business. I was never intended by nature to write—much less to be, without anguish, read; and I have recognised that perfectly patent law late in the day only, when I might so much better have recognised it early. It would have made a great difference in my life—made me a much more successful person. But "the New England conscience" interposed: suggesting that the sense of being so conveniently assisted could only proceed, somehow, from the abyss. So I floundered and fumbled and failed, through long years, for the mere want of the small dose of cynical courage required for recognising frankly my congenital inaptitude. Another proof, or presumption, surely of the immortality of the soul. It takes one whole life—for some persons, at least, *dont je suis*—to learn how to live at all; which is absurd if there is not to be another in which to apply the lesson. I feel that in *my* next career I shall start, in this particular, at least, from the first, straight. Thank heaven I don't write such a hand as you! Then where would my conscience be?

You wrote me from Ashfield, and I can give you more than country for country, as I am still, thank heaven, out of town—which is more and more my predominant and natural state. I am only reacting, I suppose, against many, many long years of London, which had ended by giving me a deep sense of the quantity of "cry" in all that life compared to the almost total absence of "wool." By which I mean, simply, that acquaintances and relations there have a way of seeming at last to end in smoke—while having consumed a great deal of fuel and taken a great deal of time. I dare say I shall some day re-establish the balance, and I have kept my habitation there, though I let it whenever I can; but at present I am as conscious of the advantage of the Sussex winter as of that of the Sussex summer. But I've just returned from three days in London, mainly taken up with seeing my brother William, as to whom your letter contained an anxious inquiry to which I ought before this to have done justice. The difficulty has been, these three months, that he has been working, with the most approved medical and "special" aid, for a change of condition, which one hoped would have been apparent by now—so that one might have good news to give. I am sorry to say the change remains, as yet, but imperfectly apparent—though I dare say it has, within the last month, really begun. His

German cure—Nauheim—was a great disappointment; but he is at present in the hands of the best London man, who professes himself entirely content with results actually reached. The misfortune is that the regimen and treatment—the "last new" one—are superficially depressing and weakening even when they are doing the right work; and from that, now, I take William to be suffering. *Ci vuol' pazienza!* He will probably spend the winter in England, whatever happens. Only, alas, his Edinburgh lectures are indefinitely postponed[1]—and other renouncements, of an unenlivening sort, have had, as indispensable precautions and prudences, to follow. They have placed their little girl very happily at school, near Windsor; they are in convenient occupation, at present, of my London apartment; and luckily the autumn has been, as London autumns go, quite cheerfully—distinguishably—crepuscular. I am two hours and a half from town; which is far enough, thank heaven, not to be near, and yet near enough, from the point of view of shillings, invasions and other complications, not to be far; they have been with me for a while, and I am looking for them again for longer. William is able, fortunately, more or less to read, and strikes me as so richly prepared, by an immense quantity of this—to speak of that feature alone—for the Edinburgh lectures—that the pity of the frustration comes home the more. A truce, however, to this darksome picture—which may very well yet improve.

I went, a month ago, during a day or two in town, down to Rottingdean to lunch with the Kiplings (these Brighton trains are wondrous!) but failed, to my regret, to see Lady Burne-Jones, their immediate neighbour, as of course you know; who was perversely, though most accidentally, from home. But they told me—and it was the first I knew—of her big project of publishing the dear beautiful man's correspondence: copious, it appears, in a degree of which I had not a conception. Living, in London, near him, though not seeing him, thanks to the same odious London, half so often as I desired, I seldom heard from him on paper, and hadn't, at all, in short, the measure of his being, as the Kiplings assured me he proves to have been, a "great letter-writer."

28*th* November

I was interrupted, my dear Charles, the other day; difficulties then multiplied, and I only now catch on again. I see, on reading over your letter, that you are quite *au courant* of Lady B. J.'s plan; and I of course easily take in that she must have asked you, as one of his closest correspondents, for valuable material. Yet I don't know that I wholly echo your deprecation of these givings to the world. The best letters seem to me the most delightful of all written things—and those that are not the best the most negligible. If a correspondence, in other words, has not the real charm, I wouldn't have it published even privately; if it has, on the other hand, I would give it all the glory of the greatest literature. Burne-Jones, I should say, must have it (the real charm)—since he did, as appears, surrender to it. Is this not so? At all events we shall indubitably see; though not, I trust, in the vulgar, ponderous form just given to the two stodgy volumes on Millais[2] perpetrated by his son. Even Millais, I think, was worthy of something better. As for B.J., I miss him not less, but more, as year adds itself to year; and the hole he has left in the London horizon, the eclipse of the West Kensington oasis, is a thing much to help one to turn one's back on town: and this in spite of the fact that his work, alas, had long ceased to interest me, with its element of painful, niggling embroidery—the stitch-by-stitch process that had come at last to beg the *painter* question altogether. Even the poetry—the kind of it—that he tried for appeared to me to have wandered away from the real thing; and yet the being himself grew only more loveable, natural and wise. Too late, too late! I gather, à propos of him, that you have read Mackail's Morris;[3] which seems to me quite beautifully and artistically done—wonderful to say for a contemporary English biography. It is really composed, the effect really produced—an effect not altogether, I think, happy, or even endurable, as regards Morris himself—for whom the formula strikes me as being—being at least largely—that he was a boisterous, boyish, British man of action and practical faculty, launched indeed by his imagination, but really floundering and romping and roaring through the arts, both literary and plastic, very much as a bull through a chinashop. I felt much moved, after reading the book, to try to write, with the aid of some of my own recollections and impressions, something possibly vivid about it; but we are in a moment of such excruciating vulgarity that nothing worth doing about anything or anyone seems to be wanted or welcomed anywhere. The great little Rudyard—à propos of Rottingdean—struck me as quite on his feet again, and very sane and sound and happy. Yet I am afraid you'll think me a very dis-gusted person if I show my reserves, again, over *his* recent incar-nations. I can't swallow his loud, brazen patriotic verse—an ex-ploitation of the patriotic idea, for that matter, which seems to me not really much other than the exploitation of the name of one's mother or one's wife. Two or three times a century—yes; but not every month. He is, however, such an embodied little talent, so economically constructed for all use and no waste, that he will get again upon a good road—leading *not* into mere multitudinous noise. His talent, I think, quite diabolically great; and this in spite—here I am at it again!—of the misguided, the unfortunate "Stalky." Stalky gives him away, aesthetically, as a man in his really now, as regards our roaring race, bardic condition, should not have allowed himself to be given. That is not a thing, however, that, in our paradise of criticism, appears to occur to so much as three persons, and meanwhile the sale, I believe, is tremendous. *Basta, basta.*

We are living, of course, under the very black shadow of South Africa,[4] where the nut is proving a terribly hard one to crack, and where, alas, things will probably be worse before they are better. One ranges one's self, on the whole, to the belief not only that they *will* be better, but that they really had to be taken in hand to be made so: they wouldn't and couldn't do at all as they were. But the job is immense, complicated as it is by distance, transport, and many preliminary illusions and stupidities; friends, moreover, right and left, have their young barbarians in the thick of it and are living so, from day to day, in suspense and darkness that, in certain cases, their images fairly haunt one. It reminds me strangely of some of the far-away phases and feelings of *our* big, dim war. What tremendously ancient history that now seems!—But I am launch-ing at you, my dear Charles, a composition of magnitude—when I meant only to encumber you with a good, affectionate note. I have presently to take on myself a care that may make you smile; noth-ing less than to proceed, a few moments hence, to Dover, to meet our celebrated friend (I think she can't *not* be yours) Mrs. Jack Gardner, who arrives from Brussels, charged with the spoils of the Flemish school, and kindly pays me a fleeting visit on her way up to town. I must rush off, help her to disembark, see all her Van Eycks and Rubenses through the Customs and bring her hither, where three water-colours and four photographs of the "Rye school" will let her down easily.[5] My little backwater is just off the highway from London to the Continent. I am really quite near Dover, and it's absurd how also quite near Italy that makes me feel. To get there without the interposition of the lumbering London, or even, if need be, of the bristling Paris, seems so to simplify the matter to the mind. And yet, I grieve to say that, in a residence here of a year and a half, I have only been to *patria nostra* once. I'm delighted to think that Richard and his wife have by this time got back to Rome, and I hope he has entered happily and smoothly on his new functions.[6] It seemed to me, last summer, an almost romantically interesting existence for them, and the work then started had promise of so many immediate and increasing thrills. Little Boni[7] alone was a joy to know, and I hope Richard is still keeping shoulder to shoulder with him. I wish I could be positive about the prospect of seeing them in the spring; but as yet I can only pray for it. Please commend me tenderly to Sally and Lily and Margaret—all abandoned and forsworn as they have lately been leaving me. I trust this means that the world about them really gives them "deeper moments" than those mostly confronting them, on their various visits, over here. Recall me genially, as well, please, to Theodora Sedgwick—while I watch to see if it makes her cold shoulder so much as wince. Good-bye, my dear Charles—I must catch my train. Fortunately I am but three minutes from the station. Fortunately, also, you are not to associate with this fact anything grimy or noisy or otherwise suggestive of fever and fret. At Rye even the railway is quaint—or at least its neighbours are. Yours always affectionately,

Henry James

January 13, 1900

P.S.—This should be a prescript rather than a postscript, my dear Charles, to prepare you properly for the monstrosity of my having dictated a letter to you so long ago and then kept it over unposted into the next century—if next century it be! (They are fighting like cats and dogs here as to where in our speck of time we are.) There has been a method in my madness—my delay has not quite been, not wholly been, an accident; though there *was* at first that intervention. What happened was that I had to dash off and catch a train before I had time to read this over and enclose it; and that on the close of that adventure, which lasted a couple of days and was full of distractions, I had in a still more belated and precipitate way to rush up to London. These sheets, meanwhile, languished in an unfrequented drawer into which, hurrying off, I had at random thrust them; and there they remained till my return from London— which was not for nearly a fortnight. When I came back here I brought down William and his wife, the former, at the time, so off his balance as to give me almost nothing but *him* to think about; and it thereby befell that some days more elapsed before I redis- covered my letter. Reading it over then, I had the feeling that it gave a somewhat unduly emphasised account of William; whereupon I said to myself: "Since it has waited so long, I will keep it a while longer; so as to be able to tell better things." That is just, then, what I have done; and I am very glad, in consequence, to be able to tell them. Only I am again (it seems a fate!—giving you a strangely false impression of my normally quiet life) on the point of catching a train. I go with William and Alice a short time hence, on—again!— to Dover—a very small and convenient journey from this—to see them so far on their way to the pursuit, for the rest of the winter, of southern sunshine. They will cross the Channel to-morrow or next day and proceed as they find convenient to Hyères—which, as he himself has written to you, you doubtless already know. I do, at any rate, feel much more at ease about him now. The sight of the good he can get even by sitting for a chance hour or two, all muffled and hot-watered, in such sun, pale and hindered sun, as a poor little English garden can give him in midwinter, quite makes me feel that a real climate, the real thing, will do much toward making him over. He needs it—though differently—even as a consumptive does. And moreover he has become, these last weeks, much more fit to go and find it. Q.E.D. But this *shall* be posted! Yours more even than before,

H.J.

1. WJ's Gifford Lectures, which became the book *The Varieties of Religious Experience* (1902). WJ had recently suffered a heart attack.
2. *The Life and Letters of Sir John Millais* (1899).
3. J. W. Mackail, *The Life of William Morris* (1899).
4. The Boer War.
5. HJ is as usual lightly mocking Mrs. Gardner. He had just written her: "How mysterious and complicated you are! You need really a few hours contact with my rustic simplicity."
6. Norton's son was director of the School of Classical Studies in Rome.
7. Giacomo Boni (1859–1925), Italian architect, author of a treatise on Dante studies in America.

To Isabella Stewart Gardner
Dictated Ts Gardner

Lamb House, Rye
November 27th 1899

Dear wild and wandering friend,[1]

Here again is an intensely legible statement of your needful proceeding at Dover on the arrival, at the nominal 2.30, of your boat from Calais. It will consist simply of your looking out for me, as hard as possible—if not as soft!—from the deck of the vessel. I shall be on the dock to meet you, penetrating with eagle eye the densest crowd: so that, after all, your looks won't so much matter. I shall try to have mine of my best. I shall await you, in other words—reach out the friendliest of hands to you as you step, *de votre pied léger*, from the plank. The rest is silence. You will have nothing whatever more to do but what I mildly but firmly bid you. If you only mind what I tell you, all will still be well. We shall combine convenient promptitude with convenient deliberation and reach Rye in time for tea and tartines. Be therefore at peace—and keep your powder dry. I wish you as smooth and swift and simple a business of it, all through, as may be possible to so complex an organism. The weather here is lovely now and the Channel a summer sea—which I trust we shall still profit by. *Thursday* then, I repeat, on the Dover Pier at 2.30. Yours more than ever impatiently,

Henry James

1. Mrs. Gardner was now embarked on the creation of a Venetian palace as her residence in Boston. With the aid of Bernard Berenson and others in Europe, she was assembling an extensive art collection to be housed in the palazzo. See *Letters* II, 266, and the preceding letter to Norton.

To Rhoda Broughton
Ms Chester

Lamb House, Rye
January 1st 1900

My dear Rhoda Broughton.

I am sadly afraid that my silence and absence, so ungracefully persisted in, have well nigh cost me your esteem—or at least ranked me, for you, with those who appear perversely to *desire* to be forgotten: in which case you will, no doubt, unstintedly have obliged me! But I really haven't desired anything but to find myself again so placed that I might sometimes knock at your door and succeed in winning you for one of those walks and talks of which I cherish the impression as occasions fondly planned and plotted for, and not less fondly remembered. This dreadful gruesome New Year, so monstrously numbered, makes me turn back to the warm and coloured past and away from the big black avenue that gapes in front of us. So turning, I find myself, not wholly without trepidation, yet also with a generous confidence, face to face with your distinguished figure—which please don't consider me, rude rustic and benighted alien as I've become, unworthy to greet. The country has swallowed me up, for the time, as you foretold me that it would, but I haven't quite burnt my ships behind me, and I'm counting the months till I can resume possession, for at least half the year in future, of my London habitation. I've let it, for a longish time, but I haven't renounced it, and I'm so homesick for the blessed Kensington fields that I gloat over the prospect of treading them, finally, afresh. Meanwhile I've felt remote and unfriended and have lacked courage to write to you almost only (as it might look) to say: "See—from the way I keep it up—how I get on without you!" I get on without you very badly—and worse and worse the *more* I keep it up. I've been the victim, among other things, of an economic crisis, and since I came down here to take possession in June '98, haven't spent, at any possible period for finding people, three continuous days in town. This means, as you may suppose, that I *have,* pretty solidly, taken possession. But it isn't what I wanted to write to tell you. I want to make you a sign of faithful friendship and fond remembrance, to assure you of how poor a business I find it to be so deprived of your society, and to give you my fervent wishes for the dim twelvemonth to come. It looks to me full of goblins, to be deprecated by prayer and sacrifice—and my incense rises for your immunity, of every kind, not less than for my own. I've nothing to amuse you withal, or you should have it—not even another heavy book. I've done a good deal of work; but it's scattered and obscured—not yet collected. As soon as some of it is, I shall lay a copy at your feet. But I succumb to the sense of what a torment it is to talk with you thus onesidedly and imperfectly. How much I should like to ask you and to say to you! Heaven speed my chance. Think of me, please, mean-while, as yours, dear Rhoda Broughton, always and always

Henry James

To Mrs. W. K. Clifford
Ts Lubbock

Lamb House, Rye
January 24*th* 1900

Dearest Lucy C.[1]

Immensely interesting and vivid your copious letter. (I think—I feel always as if—every written word from you is a drop of your blood, and I value it with a tragic appreciation—deprecating even while I devour.) You put her,[2] and the whole scene, before me—from the convulsions to the roast goose—and make me feel afresh (or at least I do feel) that she has still vitality enough for another mar-riage, another widowhood, another pension—another bloody war, bloody *anything!* How gallant your instant advance to her!—and how *exposed*, afresh, I can't but think, your humanity leaves you! However, heaven only knows what new incarnation will now catch her up! What a genius she has for picking up incomes and setting up afresh! Forgive my cynical tone—I feel with you, like one of the augurs behind the altar—winking at the other. But it's,I who do the winking—you are perfectly proper. And I *wholly* believe in her loss and the reality of her immediate woe. But the connection—for *him*—remains to me a document—*on* him—of the strangest character. He had probably, in fact, quite outlived it, and I think it an attenuation of one's view of her unhappiness (her loss and her injury) that he would probably have more and more got, and kept away from her;—practically (even though covertly) chucked and shunted her. Of course indeed she would still have had the gains and the credit. Yet, on the other hand, she is a born gambler! *What a woman!*—Writing to you in this ineffectual way makes me regret immensely these winter months of absence and eclipse. It would be so infinitely nicer to be sitting by your fire and tasting your charity—and your Benedictine! This second winter here has made me really homesick for town. Next year I shall, D.V., drink deep again. My brother reached Hyères ten days ago most safely and is doing already (through sun and the ability to *sit* out of doors—wrapped, and even hot-watered) so much better that my spirits have greatly risen. The dark month he spent here was a tension of the keenest—a strain of the sorest. But even here, at the last, he was better—and his feeling about himself has now evidently had a great lift. It is evident that the South (sun and air) is a distinct present *specific* for him. So I am much eased. But it has been a tormented stretch of months—and my work has, alas, suffered from it. But that too is coming round. A lively row (temporarily calmed) with Heinemann—over Pinker!—which, however, I must reserve for you.[3] There are many things I am reserving—and I hope you are doing the same. Alas, there is little prospect of my being in town, now—I have had a *haunted* three months, and I foresee the possibility of complications for the spring and summer: so I fear I must hug *these* weeks, make sure of quietness, make up for lost time here. (I mean in contradistinction to such a possible February and March perching in London as I lately told you of—as a small chance.) On some laughing spring day—early—when the bulbs are out, you *must* come down and see me here, for at least the "inside" of a day; as you did last year. And I will drive you to Winchelsea again—and we will infinitely converse. Goodness guard the Play and the Hawtrey![4] Goodness guard *you* and your house and your babes (everything that is yours—even the Christinas of woe), and keep you safe for the next good palaver with your affectionate old

Henry James

1. Mrs. W. K. Clifford, like Rhoda Broughton, was one of HJ's oldest London friends. Widow of a celebrated mathematician who died young, Mrs. Clifford supported her children by writing novels and plays, with which she made a distinct name for herself. HJ greatly admired her pluck and her humane responses, and he visited her often before he moved to Rye.

2. HJ refers here to an old friend, Christina Rogerson, who figured as one of Sir Charles Dilke's mistresses in the social scandal of the 1880s which abruptly ended Dilke's parliamentary career. After the scandal, and after the death of her alcoholic first husband, Mrs. Rogerson married the author and journalist G. W. Stevens. He was killed in the Boer War in 1899. On the day after writing this letter HJ wrote to Christina Rogerson Stevens, "there are kinds of wounds that make for our honour, and our patience, if not for our ease." HJ had been an admiring friend of Christina's mother, Mrs. Duncan Stewart.

3. Heinemann objected to HJ's having an agent: he preferred to deal directly with the authors he published.

4. Charles Henry Hawtrey (1858–1923), the London theatre manager, had just produced a play by Mrs. Clifford.

To Mrs. Everard Cotes
Ts Lubbock

Lamb House, Rye
January 26*th* 1900

Dear Mrs. Cotes.

I grovel in the dust—so ashamed am I to have made no response to your so generous bounty and to have left you unthanked and unhonoured. And all the while I was (at once) so admiring your consummately clever book,[1] and so blushing to the heels and groaning to the skies over the daily paralysis of my daily intention to make you some at least (if not adequate) commonly courteous and approximately intelligible sign. And I have absolutely no valid, no sound, excuse to make but that *I am like that!*—I mean I am an abandonedly bad writer of letters and acknowledger of kindnesses. I throw myself simply on my confirmed (in old age) hatred of the unremunerated pen—from which one would think I have a remunerated one!

Your book is extraordinarily keen and delicate and able. How can I tell if it's "like me"? I don't know what "me" is like. I can't *see* my own tricks and arts, my own effect, from outside at all. I can only say that if it *is* like me, then I'm much more of a *gros monsieur* than I ever dreamed. We are neither of us dying of simplicity or common addition; that's all I can make out; and we are both very intelligent and observant and conscious that a work of art must make some small effort to *be* one; must sacrifice somehow and somewhere to the exquisite, or be an asininity altogether. So we open the door to the Devil himself—who is nothing but the sense of beauty, of mystery, of relations, of appearances, of abysses of the whole—*and* of EXPRESSION! That's *all* he is; and if he is our common parent I'm delighted to welcome you as a sister and to be your brother. One or two things my acute critical intelligence murmured to me as I read. I think your drama lacks a little, *line*—bony structure and palpable, as it were, tense cord—on which to string the pearls of detail. It's the frequent fault of women's work—and *I* like a rope (the rope of the *direction and march of the subject,* the action) pulled, like a taut cable between a steamer and a tug, from beginning to end. It lapses and lapses along a trifle too liquidly—and is too *much* conceived (I think) in dialogue—I mean considering that it isn't con-

131

ceived like a play. Another reflection the Western idiot makes is that he is a little tormented by the modern mixture (maddening medley of our cosmopolite age) of your India (vast, pre-conceived and absently-present) and your subject not of Indian essence. The two things—elements—don't somehow illustrate each other, and are juxtaposed only by the terrible globe-shrinkage. But that's not *your* fault—it's mine that I suffer from it. Go on and go on—you are full of talent; of the sense of life and the instinct of presentation; of wit and perception and resource. Voilà.

It would be much more to the point to *talk* of these things with you, and some day, again, this must indeed be. But just now I am talking with few—wintering, for many good reasons, in the excessive tranquillity of this tiny, inarticulate country town, in which I have a house really adapted to but the balmier half of the year. And there is nothing cheerful to talk of. South Africa darkens all our sky here, and I gloom and brood and have craven questions of "Finis Britanniae?" in solitude. Your Indian vision at least keeps *that* abjectness away from you. But goodnight. It's past midnight; my little heavy-headed and heavy-hearted city sleeps; the stillness ministers to fresh flights of the morbid fancy; and I am yours, dear Mrs. Cotes, most constantly,

Henry James

1. Mrs. Cotes, the former Sara Jeannette Duncan (1862–1922), a Canadian novelist, had sent HJ her latest novel, *His Honour and a Lady*.

To H. G. Wells
Ms Bodleian

Lamb House, Rye
January 29*th* 1900

My dear Wells.

It was very graceful of you to send me your book—I mean the particular masterpiece entitled *The Time Machine*,[1] after I had so *un*gracefully sought it at your hands. My proper punishment would have been promptly to have to pay for it—and this atonement I should certainly, for my indiscretion, already have made, had this muddy village facilitated the transaction by placing a bookseller's shop, or stand, in my path. (No Time Machine, as it happens, would suffice to measure the abysmal ages required by the local stationer to get a volume, as he calls it, down. Several, artlessly ordered by me, have been on their way down for months.) So I have had, as the next best thing, to bow my head to the extremity of simply reading you. You are very magnificent. I am beastly critical—but you are in a still higher degree wonderful. I re-write you, much, as I read—which is the highest tribute my damned impertinence can pay an author. I shall now not rest content till I have made up several other deficiencies—grossly accidental—in my perfect acquaintance with you. (Stay your hand—the aids to that extension are precisely the volumes on their way down. You *shall* cost me something—if it takes all my future—and all your own past.) So I am very particularly and knowingly grateful. I hope you and Mrs. Wells have kept warmer and drier and brighter and braver than I have done since my last parting with you. The weather, the news,[2] the solitary stress of January, Rye and the newspapers combined, have darkened my days and bedevilled my nights. I have felt like your Time Traveller at the bottom of his shaft. However, I suppose we all feel much alike—and shall have still more reason to yet. I hope poor Bob Stevenson[3] is resisting successfully his remedial agencies. If he does *that* there will indeed be hope for him. I think of him with pangs and pains and pities and send him my tender remembrance. Good night and all good wishes. With kind remembrances to your wife, yours most truly

Henry James

1. Published in 1895.
2. The British forces in the Boer War initially had suffered a succession of disasters.
3. R. A. M. Stevenson, cousin of Robert Louis Stevenson, who lived near Wells, was recuperating from a stroke.

To Katherine Prescott Wormeley
Ms Yale

Lamb House, Rye
February 8*th* 1900

Dear Miss Wormeley.[1]

I have wonderful missives to thank you for and I've only waited in order to do so with the deliberation becoming to my sense of their dignity and value. Please believe that I deeply appreciate the admirable and generous labour that prepared for me the ms. notes to Balzac's Letters and that accompanied the proof of the Preface to your translation. I am almost heart-broken at the thought of the immense trouble you took—(all your white, still Christmas day—I seem to see and feel it in your New Hampshire hills)—over such magnificent fatiguing copying and putting *à ma porté*. It gives me the measure of your heroic capacity for application and production. But let me tell you first that I immediately of course forwarded your letter to Heinemann—with a *glowing* note of my own. *He* will immediately, also, have written straight to you, I don't doubt—but I enclose his reply to me, to cover any accident. He *will*, of course, take up your *Life*, in time—but what he says is alas, fatally true, about the blight on everything by the war. This is not the least horrid of its (indirect) consequences—books are "nowhere," and one's little market, so small at the best, for anything not vulgar, is completely closed. But it will open again.—I have read with care every word of your preface and your notes—as I had already read the *Roman d'Amour*, and bought and read much of the *Lettres à l'Etrangère*.[2] I say "much" rather than most, for our great man is, to me, I must frankly say, one of the *least* engaging of letter writers, the heaviest, least easy or happy. You may say: how could [he] be anything *but* the least, with his overwhelmed and colossal life?—a question to which, I admit, there is no answer. And in this big, dull, magnificent volume we have, I quite feel with you, the best of him—I mean *all* of him, the whole tormented, incredible man. I am with you, wholly, in your strictures on *Un Roman d'Amour* and think you altogether make out your case. The mere *literary* evidence is enough: it is impossible to believe that (execrable taste as he sometimes had) he *wrote* the vulgar and evidently interpolated stuff in the long letter to his sister. Only nobody *cares*, alas, in all England or the U.S.—nobody heeds, or considers, or understands, one scrap. You speak of the stupidity of the *Athenaeum* notice, but anything but a stupid, an abysmally idiotic notice of him, or of anything relating to him, is *unthinkable* now in this country or the U.S.—but more here, even, I think, than there. I find your zeal, your devotion, your thoroughness, your mastery of your subject beyond praise—and agree with you thoroughly as to Louvenjoul's[3] asininity and frivolity; though I think he gains something by his local nearness to the Balzac personal *tradition*—tracks etc. legend, history etc. He knows many things transmitted, repeated, believed, etc. But I don't at all remember, I am sorry to say, reading any account of the dissemination of papers etc., after Mme de Balzac's death—at least I remember it—on dim reflection—very vaguely; and I am afraid it's a matter in which my help is feeble. I only (and *this* vaguely) remember *hearing* something of the sort from the Edward Lee Childes[4] in Paris—years ago. His sister (if you know who he is—nephew of General Lee—lived all his life in France and married, first Mme Delessert (née de Triqueti) and then Mlle de Sartiges—) married a Pole and was a great friend, at the end of her days, of Mme de Balzac. She became, the sister, *déconsidérée*, and he—Lee Childe—ceased to see her;—but in connection with some mention of her by his first wife, I seem to remember the latter's telling me that extraordinary *dispersals*, depredations, were taking place over B[alzac]'s (Mme de B.'s) papers. But that is all—and everyone is dead!—I don't know that I understand your critical feeling as to Balzac's *character* and life—I doubt if any man *ever* understands any woman's critical basis and method. Moreover I think you are in danger of tending or desiring too much to reconstruct a B. in conformity with Anglosaxon ideas, conceptions, "forms," which would have been so much Hebrew to him. He was a magnificent *special* creature (not in the least, I think, a *gentleman*— heaven forbid!)—with all sorts of abysmal things in him. But the Hanska history is, clearly, a very honest and noble matter—though beware of Anglicising, either, *any* abysmal She-Slav! *That*, and his dauntless courage, and his filial piety, are the best things in his life—except his genius! But I don't mind spots and stories and mixtures in him any more than in the kindred insoluble Shakespeare—I *want* them and love them; I feel them (I mean the whole ragged mantle of *life* draping and tripping him), a part of his tangible and merciful humanity. Beware of *seeming* to give our English-spoken attitude toward him anything of that parti-pris view of impeccability which people (*our* people only) set up on the subject of the divine William and from which they have had so remarkably and awkwardly to climb down. However, the purpose, dear Miss Wormeley, of these few crude acknowledgments is only and exclusively to express my gratitude for your lights and your labours. I shall in time profit by them all. I've promised to do four or five articles for the *North American Review* and a paper on B. apropos these last publications will *probably* be one of them. (They are grotesquely shy of any such good subjects—but I shall probably prevail.[5] Only it must come in its order, and not, probably, for a good many months.) Then I shall do you and your revendications all honour. And meantime I shall treasure and study the latter. Your biography will be *very* valuable.—Forgive my tired scrawl. It's late at night—my only letter time, and yet too often a slightly jaded one.—You've no idea how the sense of the War here brings me back the far-off sense of *ours*—with the same things happening, the same done, etc., the same deaths of young men and mourning of mothers. Only I don't behold *your* equivalent—that of the Sanitary Commission.[6] Yours always

Henry James

1. Miss Wormeley (1830–1908) translated Balzac's *Comedie Humaine* in forty volumes between 1855 and 1896. In 1892 she published *A Memoir of Honoré de Balzac.* She was a sister of Ariana Curtis, HJ's Venetian-American friend.
2. These were Balzac's letters to Eveline Hanska, the former Evelina Rzewuska (1801–1882), the Polish countess Balzac ultimately married.
3. Vicomte Charles de Spoelberch de Louvenjoul (1836–1907), a wealthy French bibliophile who collected Balzac and published the valuable bibliographical *Histoire des oeuvres de Balzac* (1879).
4. For HJ's friendship with the Childes, see *Letters* II, 61–62; III, 32.
5. HJ did not "prevail," but he wrote his 1902 essay on Balzac reprinted in *Notes on Novelists* (1914) and subsequently lectured on him in the United States.
6. Miss Wormeley had served with the U.S. Sanitary Commission during the American Civil War.

To W. Morton Fullerton
Ms Harvard

The Athenaeum
Pall Mall S.W.
March 22 1900

My dear, dear boy.

It is delightful to me to find myself again in genial communication with you; and, as always, by the action of some graceful and generous expression and motion of your own. I think nobody I know but you would have thought of making me the sign I have just received from you and which reaches me here—or rather I am very sure of it. Be therefore, as always, tenderly thanked and blessed. It makes little difference that I don't quite know—as yet—what my brother's Berlin honours are: he is still at Carquéiranne (Var.)[1] and hasn't communicated them to me: but I rejoice in them none the less, and particularly enjoy hearing of them from *you*. I think that, whatever they are, his genius has fairly earned them—for his genius struck me, when he was in England this autumn etc., as really *indiscutable*. I hope with all my heart that they may refresh and uplift his strength and his spirits.

This is a mere scrawled word—an affectionate, responsive hand-wave, hand-squeeze to you, in a hurried and hustled week. I am in town for ten days (which draws to an end), after a rustication prolonged and unattenuated, and I am delighted to find that even so limited a dose of London opens the fountains of homesickness— even in a flow that will float me homeward in two or three days more. I thought at first (on coming back to old haunts) that I had re-made myself, in exile, a virginity of curiosity, of amusability; but lo! that freshness is already *flétrie* and I am terrified at the stale taste of what life is supposed to have to offer one of most respectable and substantial. *Nature* is the only real freshness—the one that abides; and there is so little to be said for art, perhaps. They both combine, at any rate, in the kind, fond way I think of you and your friendship. I have a hundred things more to say—but they must wait for the easier conditions I shall presently recover. We sit here at a strange drama—but *you* see it from a still better place (on the whole) perhaps, and take it more intensely in. Your ideas—from your place—how I should like to hear them. I shall not be at home at Easter, by a chance: but I shall try and get you, drag you, to where I *may* hear them as soon thereafter as possible. My life is arranged— if arranged it can be called—on the lines of constantly missing you. Think thus what you *might* be (though so good is what you *are*) to yours always

Henry James

1. The French physiologist Charles Richet (1850–1935) had made his chateau near Hyères available to the William Jameses.

To Margaret Mary James
Ms Harvard

Lamb House, Rye
April 1*st* 1900

Dearest Peggot:

I have accidentally delayed to send on the enclosed to you, according to your mother's request, she having lately enclosed it to me. But here it is, with a pleasant—or at any rate interesting—breath of home in it. Don't "acknowledge" it—that is to me. Keep all your handwriting for Mamma and Dad. I think they will by this time have gone back to Costebelle where I hope everything will go on with them as well as it has the last few months. I hope, too, that your journey home a week ago was comfortable and easy and that some of the rather horrid figures and sounds that passed before us at the theater didn't haunt your dreams. There were too many *ugly* ones.[1] The next time I shall take you to something prettier. Tell your comrades, and give my love to the three—that I feel I owe you all this, and won't fail! Give my kindest regards also to Mrs. Clarke[2]—and a special remembrance to Rebecca. *Liebe wohl.* Ever your affectionate uncle

Henry James

1. HJ had taken his thirteen-year-old niece and some of her friends to a variety show and "cinematograph" and had been disturbed by the films of the Boer War (which were later confirmed as "fakes"). He reported to WJ that Peggy was "a highly developed pro-Boer (and seemed surprised that I was not)."

2. Peggy James was living with the Joseph Thatcher Clarkes. See letter to Mr. and Mrs. WJ, 9 August 1899.

To William James
Ms Harvard

Lamb House, Rye
May 12*th* 1900

Dearest William.

Your postcard with your account of arrival at N[auheim],[1] your fever and bleeding, worries and distresses me—but whatever the mysterious visitation I trust it's already ancient history. I mean, that you are quite free of it and have seen your new Doctor and have been directed and comforted. God send you a quiet and propitious period. I am very glad you are, during it, going to rest from writing. No news with *me* save that I have totally shaved off my beard, unable to bear longer the increased hoariness of its growth: it had suddenly begun these three months since, to come out quite white and made me *feel*, as well as look so old.[2] Now, I feel *forty* and clean and light. [Jonathan] Sturges is still here, but goes Tuesday! I send you the *Chronicle*. When Alice can write—and really about *you*—I shall affectionately bless her. This is all now. A p[ost] c[ard] from you will meanwhile greatly reassure. Ever your

Henry

1. WJ had gone to Bad Nauheim for the baths, which were said to be beneficial to heart patients.
2. HJ had worn a beard since the Civil War.

To Paul Bourget
Dictated Ts Private

Lamb House, Rye
May 15*th* 1900

Très cher ami.

Your charming signal from the Ponte Vecchio touches me in my tenderest places, and I acknowledge it in this form *senza complimenti* so as to leave you none of these pretexts for not reading me which my holograph more indulgently supplies. I was already deeply in your debt for *Drames de Famille*,[1] for which please receive thanks much too long deferred. The first of the tales contained in it was the only one I already knew. I have read the whole thing with the intensity *que je mets toujours à vous lire* and with no reserves at all, *in particular* to my relish of the way it is all, especially "Le Luxe des Autres," done. I say "in particular" because I am always conscious of a sort of a deviation from you on the ground of method, a different *sens* from your own as to certain parts of the presentative question. You tend often to make me take your *nouvelle* rather for an essay, a study (or *quelque chose d'approchant*) on the subject, than as a direct exhibition or exploitation of that subject, and this not at all from your famous excess of analysis, *qui ne fait rien à l'affaire*, but from a way you

139

have of going, somehow, in front of your story or action like an epiloguist who has arrived to meet it even from the first, and turns round to walk with it and bear it company on the road. You have anticipatory and discounting touches which move me occasionally to remonstrance. But all that is general, and I think the "Luxe des Autres" suffers from it, in fact, exceptionally little! And this story gains from all the *rest*, of your manner and mystery—gains admirably. This thing strikes me as one of the very best of your briefer works. The whole exposition is masterly—and the thing is all really *in* the exposition. That itself is the tragedy and comedy. It is more than Balzacian—it's Balzac and something more; real Balzac and real Bourget in short together. How you *have* profited by that gentleman. There is nothing I approve and admire more in your work than the fresh renewed recognition of him that so much of it constantly involves; so that when I read you I seem to myself to be performing an act of piety to *him* still over and above *tous ceux que je vous dois à vous.*

You are doing just now, you and Madame Paul, the thing in the world that one can do of the sweetest and the softest—I mean when one belongs, for misery and bliss, to our little trade: you are perching in an Italian city which perches *itself*, for you, on a finished task and a published and acclaimed book. Never mind the acclamation, or even, the publication, at any rate; it is the done thing, the launched boat, that has opened for you the old Etruscan gate and lubricates for you, with the sense of it, all commerce of Brufani's and Betti's. I can't form the letters of these sacred names, without sighing, without weeping for envy. My pale and hungry ghost sits with you and walks with you, leans with you on the great Umbrian parapet and bends with you to the small Umbrian predellas. To say I'm sick for not being with you can only make us all say, so painfully and unprofitably "Why the deuce then are you not?" that I give up, I have scarce spirit to try to explain. I'm not—wretchedly, odiously not; and that's all. It was on the cards from the first that there was to be no Italy for me this year. *Jouissez, vous autres;* drink deep, sink deep—stay under as long as you can.

I am sorry to say I have nothing at all to send you, and nothing interesting to tell you. I stick fast in my little corner, and am scarcely ever in London—though I do go up this afternoon for two or three days. I therefore see very few people, and I ought to have done a great deal of work. Well, so I have—but much of it un-profitable and unusable. Even of the rest, however, there is a blocked accumulation; I have done a goodish many things which come to light but piecemeal—yet I have the material for two or three books. Books don't, books can't, however, appear here now; if there were any literature in the country I should say the time was a curse on it. This interminable war keeps everything back. *Voilà.*

My brother, since he left Costebelle, has been at Geneva, and is now at Nauheim—but you are really more in possession of him than I. I have the hope that he saw as much of you as possible after moving nearer to you—a hope founded on three or four highly appreciative allusions to all your and Mme Paul's kindness, in his too few letters, or rather postcards. The history of this commerce I greatly long [for] from him. But that will not be for two or three months—if, as I hope, he comes back to England then. Commend me very kindly to Madame Paul and forgive the misery of this letter. The only thing it could now give me any pleasure to write to you would be that I am starting to join you. As that is out of the question, all else is despair and darkness. Yet it would be delightful to receive from you one echo of Perugia. Give my love, my tenderest, to the old green Pope in the old brown Piazza. But I send as much of it also to both of you. Yours always,

Henry James

1. A collection of tales published by Bourget earlier that year.

To Mrs. William James
Ms Harvard

Lamb House, Rye
May 22*d* 1900

Dearest Alice.

Very gross my late silence. Your letter of the 16th, with a p.s. from William, and enclosing one of Harry's, has lately rejoiced my heart, and I have also a postcard from William. I am overjoyed at what I gather to be your reassured and re-enlightened state on the new information—i.e. Riegel's.[1] It does me far-reaching good. Right glad does it make me. I hope you have settled down to due moderation of care and due elation of consciousness. It is still but stingily summerish here—may *your* conditions be more *genialisch*—though I believe that's vile German. I was away from here last week three days (a long and dull story to tell), and along of Helena Gilder,[2] in town, met Mark Twain, who told me he is in correspondence with William and gave me a muddled and confused glimpse of Lord Kelvin, Albumen, Sweden and half a dozen other things (on which I was prevented from afterwards bringing him to book); the whole (most embroiled) hint of which makes me wonder if some such mixture as that is the "card" which William speaks of having up his sleeve. But though M.T. looked rosy as a babe, and said it was all "Albumen" and he was putting W. on it, I didn't know Lord Kelvin was a "Doctor" and don't understand "why *Sweden!*"[3] However, these things will doubtless transpire. Yet I heartily hope you will prove to be needing nothing but Nauheim. When the packet comes that William speaks of (for me to open) I will inspect and advise. A box of books *has* (to-day) come. Forgive my late-at-night rather weary brevity. My correspondence has got fearfully in arrears through Jonathan Sturges's long visit: it is sad and strange that one of the most intelligent and *doué* mortals one knows should, inevitably, in fact, be the most (through his infirmity—which makes him *archi*-dependent) practically *draining.* I have a pile of letters chin-high before me—and am so working now, more and more, at fiction that, after my mornings, I feel quite depleted for even the most trivial forms of composition. And this grows as the fiction grows. So bear with my meagerness. All thanks for Harry's so interesting confidences. I greatly like to see them—though missing many of his allusions to people and not much knowing (and you will say caring!) who anyone is. But I greatly care who H. himself is. I hope Peggy keeps high and happy, and am always, dearest Alice, your affectionate

Henry

Thank you (P.S.) for telling me of Santayana's book (P. and R.)[4] which has come and which I find of an irresistible distraction. Charles Norton more or less due here—and the deadly Darwins expectant of a visit at Folkestone; I mean from me. And I must go!

1. Apparently one of WJ's doctors.
2. Helena De Kay Gilder, wife of Richard Watson Gilder.
3. Mark Twain had just returned from Sweden, where he had spent some time at the

health establishment of Henrik Kellgren—and HJ heard the name as Kelvin, the British physicist, which accounts for his confusion.

4. This was George Santayana's *Interpretations of Poetry and Religion,* just published, which WJ recommended to his brother.

To Ford Madox Hueffer
Ms Barrett

Lamb House, Rye
May 23*d* 1900

Dear F. M. Hueffer.

I take it very kindly that you have sent me your so curious and interesting book of verses,[1] with so friendly a letter, and I thank you on both heads. I think your doubt about the verses misplaced and unjustified—all those that I have yet read seeming to me to hold their own very firmly indeed. Those I have read—and re-read—are the little rustic lays—several of which I think admirable: terribly natural and true and "right," drawn from the real wretchedness of things. The poetry of the cold and the damp and the mud and the nearness to earth—this is a chord you touch in a way that makes me wonder if there isn't still more for you to get from it. But doubtless it is only feasible and, so to speak, bearable when it *comes,* and it mustn't, for one's philosophy, come too often! May your genuine note find handsome recognition. Shall you not again pass, soon, this way? I shall be very glad to see you, and I am yours very truly

Henry James

1. The 27-year-old Ford Madox Hueffer (1873–1939), later Ford Madox Ford, had sent HJ his just published *Poems for Pictures.*

To Cora Crane
Ms Columbia

Lamb House, Rye
June 5*th* 1900

Dear Mrs. Crane.

I have just seen the Moreton Frewens,[1] who, being at Brede, came in and found me, to my relief, at home, and who, I grieve to say, give me a bad account of their news from you of Crane. They speak of a telegram received today (Whitmonday) as unfavourable, and the effect of this is to make me regret I have not, as I fully intended any one of the last three or four days, got off sooner my response to the letter received from you while you were at Dover. Skinner[2] was to give me your new address, and twice have I been to ask for it without finding him. I have it now only from the Frewens. It is a shock to me that Crane is less well[3]—I was full of hope, and had been, in that hope, assuming that a good effect had come to him from his move: cheerful theories much disconcerted! I think of him with more sympathy and sorrow than I can say. I wish I could express this to him more closely and personally. On the Monday you were at Dover I was on the very point of going over to see you and had arranged for an absence of a day, domestically, the night before, but the A.M. brought with it a mass of proofs to be instantly attended to—I was under much pressure, and I lost the occasion, believing then that you were leaving—and leaving with all good omens—on the Tuesday. I learned afterwards that you had waited a day or two longer, but Skinner expressed doubts of Crane's having been able to see me even if I had gone—and that partly consoled me. I bicycled over to Brede with a couple of friends, a day or two after you had gone—to show them the face of the old house; but the melancholy of it was quite heartbreaking. So will it, I fear, always be to me. I won't pretend to utter hopes about Crane which may be vain—or seem to you to now, and thereby only irritating or, at least, distressing: but I constantly think of him and as it were pray for him. I feel that I am not taking too much for granted in believing that you may be in the midst of worries on the money-score which will perhaps make the cheque for Fifty Pounds, that I enclose, a convenience to you. Please view it as such and dedicate it to whatever service it may best render my stricken young friend. It meagerly represents my tender benediction to him. I write in haste—to catch the post. I needn't tell you how glad I shall be of any news that you are able to send me. I wish you all courage and as much hope as possible, and I am yours and his, in deep participation

Henry James

P.S. There must [be] a Banker at Badenweiler with whom you have dealings that will make the conversion of this cheque easy. So I trust.—H.J.

144

1. Moreton Frewen (1853–1924), an Englishman who traveled widely in the American West, had let Brede House to the Cranes. See Anita Leslie, *Mr. Frewen of England* (1966).

2. Dr. Ernest Skinner, the Rye general practitioner who was HJ's doctor.

3. Stephen Crane was dying at 29 of tuberculosis, and Cora had taken him to Germany in a special train in hope of a cure.

To Cora Crane
Ms Columbia

Lamb House, Rye
June 7*th* 1900

Dear Mrs. Crane.

Your miserable news has been with me—by the newspapers—two days, and yet I have not found till now a possible hour to put pen to paper to tell you of the sympathy with which I think of you. I wrote you on Sunday last—and at the moment I wrote the end of the poor boy's swift tragedy must have been near. It will have come before my letter reached you. Yet I hope it *has* safely reached you. I have been under constant sharp pressure these forty-eight hours, or this post-script to it would have followed sooner. Yet I feel I can say nothing to you that you haven't been saying again and again to yourself. What a brutal, needless extinction—what an unmitigated un-redeemed catastrophe! I think of him with such a sense of possibilities and powers! Not that one would have drawn out longer these last cruel weeks—! But you have need of all your courage. I doubt not it will be all at your service. Shall you come back—for any time at all—to Brede Place? You will of course hate to—but it occurs to me you may have things to do there, or possessions to collect. What a strange, pathetic, memorable chapter *his* short—so troubled, yet also so peaceful—passage there! If there is any chance of seeing you, I shall greatly value it. I don't know whom you may have with you at present—I hope such aid and service as may be needful. It occurs to me that your brother-in-law will perhaps have arrived. I think with much sympathy of your niece and the immersion of her happy youth in so much trouble and sorrow. Please assure her of this for me. I catch the post and beg you to believe in much that this hasty sign too imperfectly says. Believe me, dear Mrs. Crane, yours most truly

Henry James

To Viscountess Wolseley
Ms Hove

Lamb House, Rye
June 10*th* 1900

Dearest Lady Wolseley.

How much more kind than I can say your benevolent letter and your—that is also Lord Wolseley's—exquisite and delightful token! I thank him with really deep sentiment for his little keepsake of the collarstuds, or rather (flower of human ingenuity!) necktie-props! They are admirable, delightful; a new joy, altogether, I foresee, and I shall cherish them and flaunt them for life! I am greatly touched with all the *trouble* you've taken in this generous connection, and the production, from its nestling situation, of the illustrative shirt really brought tears from my eyes. But I like your calling it an "old" one! *Comme vous y allez, Madame!* I give a shiver at the thought that if you had glimpses of *my* wardrobe: its antiquities would in that case be scattered over the land! The shirt is really in the fair flower and heyday—the smoothest, stiffest, serenity, of its starched youth; and with deep gratitude for the admirable way it has performed its office, I restore it tenderly to the shelf from which it has so gracefully fluttered to me. It will travel back thither by post. It has seen—after these adventures—much of the world; but it has a long life before it.—Your passage across this narrow scene has left behind it a glory that doesn't—that will never—die out. Rye rather lacked History—now she *has* it.[1] You didn't leave me where you found me. I am inches and inches higher. I believe I could really do anything with the place. However, I shall only just go on meekly liking and even (though not at all meekly *that*) hoping for your appearance again in it. I have a young "priest" billeted on me (by urgent request—not mine!), the Bishop and his attendant train being here for five days for Ordination; and though the young priest "fasts" (on fish, eggs, vegetables, tarts, claret, cigarettes, coffee and liqueurs), I seem to be always face to face with him at meals—after waiting them for him while he roams elsewhere. It is now 11.30 P.M., and he hasn't come in! On the whole I prefer, for billets, the Military. I shall venture to hold you to your kind promise of letting me see Hampton Court[2] on Private View. I wish I had thoughts to ask you to be so good as to look, for me, at a vast and massive old

146

"desk" that Jarvis[3] is keeping for me—an escritoire that I am afraid to have him send down. I wished you to arm me with courage; and I fear I must wait for your next visit. I'm a little sorry he didn't go round with you: there is an out-of-the-wayness as to some of his things. Let me recommend a return. All thanks for the gardening paper, which will arrive, and on which I shall model yours, Lord Wolseley's and your daughter's very devotedly

Henry James

1. The Wolseleys had been visiting HJ a few days earlier when the news of the occupation of Pretoria by the British arrived and the town gave Viscount Wolseley (1833–1913), the former commander in chief of the British armies, an ovation.
2. The Wolseleys had an apartment in Hampton Court.
3. An antique dealer. HJ had six secretary-desks in Lamb House.

To Urbain Mengin
Ms Harvard

Lamb House, Rye
June 11th 1900

My dear Urbain Mengin.

Forgive my always writing you in my but semi-civilised native idiom. I would in your own—in Italian[1]—if it were not so expensive a process; costing, that is, so many more hours than I can give. Je vous écris comme ceci, en d'autres termes, parce que ma correspondence devient de plus en plus le triste fardeau de ma sombre vieillesse, que j'y économise autant que possible les derniers grains de sable de mon maigre sablier, et que si je vous écrivais en Français de France j'y dépenserais le triple de temps. Je vous écris donc, comme vous voyez, en pur patois de Rye. Je suis bien aise de vous savoir encore et si longtemps dans la douce et (comme dirait notre ami) meurtrière Italie. A défaut d'y être moi-même cela m'est toujours un plaisir personnel d'y savoir quelqu'un *al quale voglio proprio bene.* J'y suis trop peu—et j'en rêve toujours. Heureux enfant—d'être jeune et de l'être chez Giovannina Scarpa! Je suis vieux, et bien loin d'elle. Elle ne voudrait pas de moi! Enfin, contentez-la! Vous m'écrivez, comme toujours, de votre si charmante plume à vous, et ce que vous me dites de Bourget (et de l'espèce de politique que je le suppose, d'après votre allusion—pas absolument claire —en train de faire), m'intéresse et même m'attriste très-

147

particulièrement. Je n'y peux, cependent, mon cher Mengin, absolument rien. Je ne suis pas au courant; je vois peu, ici, les journaux
français—ou même aucun journal (fléaux du siècle qu'ils soit tous!)
et j'ai conscience de sentir presque toutes les choses actuelles (et
même d'autres encore), d'une façon trop différente de la sienne. Ce
n'est pas seulement son culte de Barrès, qui m'a fait m'en rendue
compte. Si je me mettais donc à le gourmander, ou du moins à le
sermonner sur toutes les questions de *feeling* et de jugement où
nous en somme pas d'accord, j'en aurais pour longtemps. Il me
semble, du reste, qu'en somme, *tout*, chez lui, se tient—parti-pris
social, ton et sujets, opinions politiques et réligieuses, ou que du
moins celles-ci vont très bien avec d'autres dispositions, d'autres
preventions et façons de sentir, dont toute son oeuvre fait foi. Il
est—pour moi—de plus en plus marqué chez lui qu'il ne s'intéresse
réellement qu'à la vie de grand luxe, qu'aux spectacles de la grande
richesse, de l'éternelle "élégance," dont, selon moi, il abuse—et
qu'il ne *peut* souhaiter pour son pays que les régimes qui, censé-
ment, font fleurir ce genre de beauté.—*There*, too simply stated, is
my general feeling about his tendencies and their inevitable drift.
The manner in which his imagination, his admirable intelligence
and his generous and sensitive soul have been led captive by a
certain abnormal vision of "high life" remains for me one of the
oddest and most indescribable facts with which literary, with
which moral criticism, just now, has to deal. He's a moralist so
strangely conditioned! At any rate he is under influences drawing
him as he is going (is not his wife, even, one?) much more strongly
than any arresting influence that I have quality, or authority or
competence to faire jouer. Trust him, moreover. He has so much
talent, so many resources, and quantities of good sense.—I hope you
are able to put in all this month with Giovannina. Venice in June
is the logical Venice, of which I can't talk to you without a nostalgic heartbreak. The Bourgets wrote to me lately from Perugia—
and I hope you may meet them somewhere.—I am fast anchored
here. Adieu, paniers—vendanges sont faites. J'ai 80 ans—je vis du
raison sec du souvenir. Il s'attache, mon souvenir, à vous—il s'y
arrête—il s'y délasse. Revenez me voir ici, comme l'année passée.
Le jeune Boyd est vautre, jusqu'au cou dans les tristes affaires du
Sud-Afrique. Je les sens, ces affaires, en somme, autrement que
lui—ce qui fait que de longs mois de silence se sont entassés

entre nous. Mais nous recauserons—quand ce ne sera que de *vous!*
Felicissima notte!—Tout à vous.

Henry James

1. Mengin, whose mother tongue was French and who spoke English fluently, had also mastered Italian.

To William Dean Howells
Dictated Ts Harvard

Lamb House, Rye
29th June 1900

My dear Howells,

I can't emulate your wonderful little cursive type on your delicate little sheets—the combination of which seems to suggest that you dictate, at so much an hour, to an Annisquam fairy; but I will do what I can and make out to be intelligible to you even, over the joy it is, ever and always, to hear from you. You say that had you not been writing me the particular thing you were, you fear you wouldn't have been writing at all; but it is a compliment I can better. I really believe that if I weren't writing you this, on my side, I *should* be writing you something else. For I've been, of late, reading you again as continuously as possible—the worst I mean by which is as continuously as the book sellers consent: and the result of *Ragged Lady*, the *Silver Journey*,[1] the "Pursuit of the Piano" and two or three other things (none wrested from your inexorable hand, but paid for from scant earnings) has been, ever so many times over, an impulse of reaction, of an intensely cordial sort, directly *at* you—all, alas, spending itself, for sad and sore want of you, in the heavy air of this alien clime and the solitude, here, of my unlettered life. I wrote to you to Kittery Point—I think it was—something like a year ago, and my chief occupation since then has been listening for the postman's knock. But let me quickly add that I understand overwhelmingly well what you say of the impossibility for you, at this time of day, of letters. God knows they *are* impossible—the great fatal, incurable, unpumpable leak of one's poor sinking bark. *Non ragioniam di lor*—I understand all about it; and it only adds to the pleasure with which, even on its personal side, I greet your present communication.

This communication, let me, without a shred of coyness, instantly declare, much interests and engages me—to the degree even that I think I find myself prepared to post you on the spot a round, or a square, Rather! I won't go through any simpering as to the goodness of your "having thought of me"—nor even through any frank gaping (though there might be, for my admiration and awe, plenty of that!) over the wonder of your multiform activity and dauntlessly universal life. *Basta* that I will write anything in life that anyone asks me in decency—and a fortiori that you so gracefully ask. I can only feel it to be enough for me that you have a hand in the affair, that you are giving a book yourself and engaging yourself otherwise, and that I am in short in your company. What I understand is that my little novel[2] shall be of fifty thousand (50,000) words, neither more, I take it, nor less; that I shall receive the sum mentioned in the prospectus "down," in advance of royalties, on such delivery. (I shall probably in point of fact, in my financial humility, prefer, when the time comes, to avail myself of the alternative right mentioned in the prospectus—that of taking, instead of a royalty, for the two years "lease," the larger sum formed by the so-much-a-word aggregation. But that I shall be clear about when the work is done; I only glance at this now as probable.) It so happens that I can get at the book, I think, almost immediately and do it within the next three or four months. You will therefore, unless you hear from me a short time hence to the contrary, probably receive it well before December. As for the absoluteness of the "order," I am willing to take it as, practically, sufficiently absolute. If you shouldn't like it, there is something else, definite enough, that I can do with it. What, however, concerns me more than anything else is to take care that you *shall* like it. I tell myself that I am not afraid!

I brood with mingled elation and depression on your ingenious, your really inspired, suggestion that I shall give you a ghost, and that my ghost shall be "international." I say inspired because, singularly enough, I set to work some months ago at an international ghost, and on just this scale, 50,000 words; entertaining for a little the highest hopes of him. He was to have been wonderful and beautiful; he was to have been called (perhaps too metaphysically) "The Sense of the Past";[3] and he was to have been supplied to a certain Mr. Doubleday who was then approaching me—had then approached me as the most outstretched arm of the reconstructed Harpers. The outstretched arm, however, alas, was drawn in again, or lopped off, or otherwise paralysed and negatived, and I was left with my little project—intrinsically, I hasten to add, and most damnably difficult—on my hands. Doubleday simply vanished into space, without explanation or apology; the proposal having been wholly his own and made, as pleaded, in consequence of a charmed perusal of the "Turn of the Screw." It is very possible, however, it is indeed most probable, that I should have broken down in the attempt to do him this particular thing, and this particular thing (divine, sublime, if I *could* do it) is not, I think, what I shall now attempt to nurse myself into a fallacious faith that I shall be able to pull off for Howells and Clarke. The damnable *difficulty* is the reason; I have rarely been beaten by a subject, but I felt myself, after upwards of a month's work, destined to be beaten by that one. This will sufficiently hint to you how awfully good it is. But it would take too long for me to tell you here, more vividly, just how and why; it would, as well, to tell you, still more subtly and irresistibly, why it's difficult. There it lies, and probably will always lie.

I'm not even sure that the international ghost is what will most bear being worried out—though, again, in another particular, the circumstances, combining with your coincident thought, seemed pointed by the finger of providence. What Doubleday wanted was two Tales—[both] tales of "terror" and making another duplex book like the *Two Magics*. Accordingly I had had (dreadful deed!) to puzzle out more or less a second, a different, piece of impudence of the same general type. But I had only, when the project collapsed, caught hold of the tip of the tail of this other monster—whom I now mention because his tail seemed to show him as necessarily still more international than No. 1. If I can at all recapture *him*, or anything like him, I will do my best to sit down to him and "mount" him with due neatness. In short, I will do what I can. If I can't be terrible, I shall nevertheless still try to be international. The difficulties are that it's difficult to be terrible save in the short piece and international save in the long. But trust me. I add little more. This by itself will begin by alarming you as a precipitate instalment of my responsive fury. I rejoice to think of you as basking on your Indian shore. *This* shore is as little Indian as possible, and we have hitherto—for the season—had to combat every form of inclemency. To-day, however, is so charming that, frankly, I wish you were all planted in a row in the little old garden into which I look as I write to you. Old as it is (a couple of hundred years) it wouldn't be too old even for Mildred. But these thoughts undermine. The "country scenes" in your books make me homesick for New England smells and even sounds. Annisquam, for instance, is a smell as well as a sound. May it continue sweet to you! Charles Norton and Sally were with me lately for a day or two, and you were one of the first persons mentioned between us. You were *the* person mentioned most tenderly. It was strange and pleasant and sad, and all sorts of other things, to see Charles again after so many years. I found him utterly unchanged and remarkably young. But I found myself, *with* him, Methusalesque and alien! I shall write you again when my subject condenses. I embrace you all and am yours, my dear Howells, always,

Henry James

I return Mr. Clarke's letter to you.

1. *Ragged Lady* and *Their Silver Wedding Journey,* both published in 1899; "Pursuit of the Piano" was a short story.
2. There is no indication which story HJ had in mind; he seems never to have written it.
3. HJ laid "The Sense of the Past" aside, resumed it in 1914, but never completed it.

To Jonathan Sturges
Ts Lubbock

Lamb House, Rye
Monday [10 July 1900]

My dear Jonathan.

The enclosed from poor Harland will interest you and perhaps move you to write him a word—as I have done at some length. (Don't preserve it for the purpose of returning it to me.) But he *will* get better and write other Snuffboxes, and they will, I trust, also sell (I see the '*Cardinal's*' is in its third edition).[1] Strange indeed, as he says, is the course of events. I am having my share of that course down here in about such measure as I can bear—by which I mean that the weeks go on and that my sense of general exposure and of the visited and looked-in-on state rather increases than shrinks: thanks to the most unencouraged accidents and even most deprecated developments, overtures, symptoms, tendencies. However, I survive, with a bleak smile, and even my work shines through too—with a cold northern light. But my hermitage seems on the path of many feet, and the deeply embowered privacy which I hoped it most to yield figures rather, to my troubled sense, as a sort of flag-flying top-of-the-hill condition. But let me not complain. I *have* just finished a book in 70,000 words (*The Sacred Fount*— planned originally for *7000!*)[2] and am on the point of sitting down to the 50,000 of another (an international tale of terror, bespoken from a respectable source).[3] And I won't trouble you with the detail of my processional entertainment—as it's ungracious to enumerate in the querulous key. *These* days are peaceful—only my young cousin, "Bay" Emmet, who has come over from Paris to paint my portrait,[4] breaks the solitude (save G. T. Lapsley[5] and his sister, who come down today to lunch!—and "Dodo" Benson[6] and Arthur Collins, who have proposed themselves together for the end of the week!) and she is soothing and easy and absolutely uninterfering, and will make me a pleasant picture. Charles Norton and his daughter were here more than a week ago, and I went over to Lewes with them on their way to Rottingdean and Lady Burne-Jones, and then called with them on the American Resident (a good friend of C.N.'s and whom it turned out that *I* knew—I had forgotten and misplaced him). I mean Edward Warren—*not* of Cowley Street— who proved a most interesting person, with a most interesting interior—replete with exquisite fragments, finds, treasures of currently-discovered Greek sculpture, of which he is the accredited purchaser for the Boston art-museum. The contrast—horsey Lewes, the Sussex downs, and a kind of Mount Athos monastery of marbles and gems!—But you, my dear Jon? This is but a chat at the foot of the stair before I go to bed. *That* it is well time for—being exactly midnight and fifty minutes. I try to focus you, and the lap of lionesses, as your habitat, alternates with the chintzier nest of the Haslemere cottage and the smoking-rooms of the great military families. May you have extracted right and left an agreeable sensation and a coherent moral. Yet it's truly an incoherent moment. That China—! But right they *are*! What a Mandarin I should be! Well, I nod to you sleepily for goodnight, as a fellow-such, along the length of the chimney-piece, and am yours always the Maecenas of Rye and the Master of Peter![7]

P.S. Peter has become truly the light of my eyes and the grace of my home. He is alike affectionate, intelligent, inodorous and chaste, a real little phantom of delight. And as for his smallness, he is to my spiritual eye colossal. And I've also bought a wire-haired fox-terrier pup—of beautiful marking and promise. There! You're welcome to your tigresses.

1. Henry Harland (1861–1905), editor of *The Yellow Book*, whose novel *The Cardinal's Snuff Box*, dealing with the love of an English novelist and an Italian duchess, had recently been published. Harland was slowly dying of tuberculosis.

2. *The Sacred Fount* was published on 6 February 1901 in the United States and nine days later in England.

3. See letter to Howells, 29 June 1900.

4. Bay Emmet completed the portrait that summer, and HJ placed it in his dining room in Lamb House where it remained until his death. It was later kept in the studio of his nephew William James, at 95 Irving Street, Cambridge, and is now owned by Leon Edel. (See page 164.)

5. Gaillard Thomas Lapsley. See letter to Lapsley, 15 September 1902.

6. E. F. Benson (1867–1940), son of the Archbishop of Canterbury (and brother of A. C. Benson), whose novel *Dodo* (1893) achieved considerable celebrity. He lived in Lamb House after HJ's death and wrote a series of novels about life in Rye—the "Lucia" novels.

7. The Lubbock typescript of this letter records no signature.

To James B. Pinker
Ms Yale

Lamb House, Rye
July 25*th* 1900

Dear Mr. Pinker.

I send you at last, today, the complete Ms of *The Sacred Fount*— as to the interminable delay of which I won't further expatiate. The reasons for this have been all of the best, and in the interest of the work itself—intrinsically speaking. It makes exactly 77,794 words—say, more roughly, about *seventy-eight* thousand. It won't do for serialisation—that is impossible, and it has the marks, I daresay, of a thing planned as a very short story, and growing on my hands, to a so much longer thing, by a force of its own—but a force controlled and directed, I believe, or hope, happily enough. It is fanciful, fantastic—but very close and sustained, and calculated to minister to curiosity. However, I can never descant on my own things. What I should like, as regards this, is almost any sum "down," that is *respectable,* for the English and American use of the book for any period short of surrender of copyright: three, five, seven years—in short whatever you can best do. The "down" is important.—What goes to you today is *one* complete type-copy (327 pages), and another—the duplicate—goes to you tomorrow. I have then still another at your service should you desire it.

I hope you bear up—though I'm afraid "trade" doesn't—under this temperature,[1] and everything else.

Yours very truly,
Henry James

1. The Boer War.

To Violet Paget (Vernon Lee)
Ms Colby

Lamb House, Rye
July 28*th* 1900

Dear Violet Paget.

You ask me not to "answer" your letter, and it would be difficult indeed to do so—so I write these few lines with as little view as possible of their coming under that head. Let them stand simply, then, for recognition, greeting, thanks, and even such imperfect response as may be.[1] I may well have regretted to have failed, of late years, of sight and profit of one [of] the few most intelligent persons it had ever been my fortune to know—and as to whom you are right in supposing that my interest hadn't dropped. I hold that we *shall* meet again—let us by all means positively do so; at some time of full convenience. That occasion will turn up—in Italy if not here— and will give great pleasure to yours, dear Violet Paget, always

Henry James

P.S. I immensely envy you your days at the genial (or exquisite) house from which you write me.

1. This terse letter suggests HJ's determination to have as little as possible to do with his former friend Violet Paget, who wrote under the name of Vernon Lee. She had satirized him six years earlier in a short story. See *Letters* III, 402–404.

To Urbain Mengin
Ms Harvard

Lamb House, Rye
August 7*th* 1900

Dear Urbain Mengin.

All my Shelleys, alas, including the Dowden,[1] are in London, in my apartment there, which I have sordidly *let,* furnished, according to the custom of this commercial country, for many months to come. Of all my books *not* "under glass" and thereby locked up, I've by contract given my *locataire* (who pays me an excellent *loyer*) the use, and it so happens that Shelley, Dowden, Forman & Co. are among the volumes on the open shelves and a part of my tenant's *jouissance.* I can't ask him for the six or seven large volumes without making rather a *gros trou* in the serried ranks of my—that is of *his—bibliothèque*—besides giving him the trouble of packing and sending them to me here. *But, tout de même,* I am having the two volumes of Dowden's *Life* sent you directly from another quarter of London and I beg you to accept them with my affectionate regards as a free and friendly contribution to your studies, the evolution of your thesis and the establishment of your glory. At no very distant date I *hope* to be able to send you Buxton Forman's volumes from my own library. There will be a possibility of my entering the place and changing a few books in the month of December. Can you *wait* till then? *Tâchez.* I will take up a few volumes from here, plant them in De Vere Gardens in place of Buxton F. and, coming away *muni de ces derniers,* cause them as promptly thereafter as possible to be expedited to you. *Cela vous va-t-il?* It's the best I can do.—I write you briefly—I should have gone to bed an hour ago. I send your little niece my hearty good wishes and much envy her uncle. I too have a niece with me—*mais une très-grande alors,* as we mainly make nieces *dans nos contrées. Àpropos de quoi (de nos contrées)* I went over to Dover (what a language we have—"over to Dover!"—it would have made Flaubert an even greater maniac than his own did!) the other day and saw our friends of Le Plantier.[2] He was working and they were well, but it struck me that they had come very far for very little. *Aussi*—not to add to their confusion—*ne le sermonnai-je pas.*—Dowden's book is of immense interest by the facts. *De ton, c'est de second ordre.* Good night and *bonne chance!* Yours always

Henry James

1. Urbain Mengin, after some years as a French tutor in England and then as a teacher in France, was working on his doctorate. His dissertation was *L'Italie des Romantiques* (1902), in which he traced minutely the voyaging and life in Italy of Byron, Shelley, and Keats.

2. The Bourgets.

To William Dean Howells
Dictated Ts Harvard

Read P.S. (August 14th) first!

Lamb House, Rye
August 9*th* 1900

My dear Howells.

I duly received and much pondered your second letter, charming and vivid, from Annisquam; the one, I mean, in reply to mine dispatched immediately on the receipt of your first. If I haven't since its arrival written to you, this is because, precisely, I needed to work out my question somewhat further first. My impulse was immediately to say that I wanted to do my little stuff at any rate, and was willing therefore to take any attendant risk, however, measured as the little stuff would be, at the worst, a thing I should see my way to dispose of in another manner. But the problem of the little stuff itself intrinsically worried me—to the extent, I mean, of my not feeling thoroughly sure I might make of it what I wanted and above all what your conditions of space required. The thing was therefore to try and satisfy myself practically—by threshing out my subject to as near an approach to certainty as possible. This I have been doing with much intensity—but with the result, I am sorry to say, of being still in the air. Let the present accordingly pass for a provisional communication—not to leave your last encompassed with too much silence. Lending myself as much as possible to your suggestion of a little "tale of terror" that should be also international, I took straight up again the idea I spoke to you of having already, some months ago, tackled and, for various reasons, laid aside. I have been attacking it again with intensity and on the basis of a simplification that would make it easier, and have done for it, thus, 110 pages of type. The upshot of this, alas, however, is that though this second start is, if I—or if *you*—like, magnificent, it seriously confronts me with the element of *length*; showing me, I fear, but too vividly, that, do what I will for compression, I shall not be able to squeeze my subject into 50,000 words. It will make, even if it doesn't, for difficulty, still beat me, 70,000 or 80,000—dreadful to say; and that faces me as an excessive addition to the ingredient of "risk" we speak of. On the other hand I am not sure that I can hope to substitute for this particular affair *another* affair of "terror" which will be expressible in the 50,000; and that for an especial reason. This reason is that, above all when one has done the thing, already, as I have rather repeatedly, it is not easy to concoct a "ghost" of any freshness. The want of ease is extremely marked, moreover, if the thing is to be done on a certain scale of length. One might still toss off a spook or two more if it were a question only of the "short-story" dimension; but prolongation and extension constitute a strain which the merely apparitional—discounted, also, as by my past dealings with it—doesn't do enough to mitigate. The beauty of this notion of "The Sense of the Past," of which I have again, as I tell you, been astride, is precisely that it involves without the stale effect of the mere bloated bugaboo, the presentation, for folk both in and out of the book, of such a sense of gruesome malaise as can only—success being assumed—make the fortune, in the "literary world," of every one concerned. I haven't, in it, really (that is save in one very partial preliminary and expository connection), to make anything, or anybody, "appear" to anyone: what the case involves is, awfully interestingly and thrillingly, that the "central figure," the subject of the experience, has the terror of a particular ground for feeling and fearing that *he himself* is, or may at any moment become, a producer, an object, of this (for you and me) state of panic on the part of others. He lives in an air of *malaise* as to the malaise he may, woefully, more or less fatally, find himself creating—and that, roughly speaking, is the essence of what I have seen. It is less gross, much less *banal* and exploded, than the dear old familiar bugaboo; produces, I think, for the reader, an almost equal funk—or at any rate an equal suspense and unrest; and carries with it, as I have "fixed" it, a more truly curious and interesting drama—especially a more human one. *But*, as I say, there are the necessities of space, as to which I have a dread of deluding myself only to find that by trying to blink them I shall be grossly "sold," or by giving way to them shall positively spoil my form for your purpose. The hitch is that the thing involves a devil of a sort of prologue or preliminary action—interesting itself and indispensable for lucidity—which impinges too considerably (for brevity) on the core of the subject. My one chance is yet, I admit, to try to attack the same (the subject) from still another quarter, at still another angle, that I make out as a possible one and which may keep it squeezable and short. If this experiment fails, I fear I shall have to "chuck" the supernatural and the high fantastic. I have just finished, as it happens, a fine flight (of eighty thousand words) *into* the high fantastic, which has rather depleted me, or at any rate affected me as discharging my obligations in that quarter. But I believe I mentioned to you in my last *The Sacred Fount*—this has been "sold" to Methuen here, and by this time, probably, to somebody else in the U.S.—but, alas, not to be serialized (as to which indeed it is inapt)—as to the title of which kindly preserve silence. The *vraie vérité*, the fundamental truth lurking behind all the rest, is furthermore, no doubt, that preoccupied with half a dozen things of the altogether human order now fermenting in my brain, I don't care for "terror" (terror, that is, without "pity") so much as I otherwise might. This would seem to make it simple for me to say to you: "Hang it, if I can't pull off my Monster on *any* terms, I'll just do for you a neat little *human*—and not the less international—fifty-thousander consummately addressed to your more cheerful department; do for you, in other words, an admirable short novel of manners, thrilling too in its degree, but definitely ignoring the bugaboo." Well, this I *don't* positively despair of still sufficiently overtaking myself to be able to think of. *That* card one has always, thank God, up one's sleeve, and the production of it is only a question of a little shake of the arm. At the same time, here, to be frank—and above all, you will say, in this communication, to be interminable—that alternative is just a trifle compromised by the fact that I've two or three things begun ever so beautifully in such a key (and only awaiting the rush of the avid bidder!)—each affecting me with its particular obsession, and one, the most started, affecting me with the greatest obsession, for the time (till I can do it, work it off, get it out of the way and fall with still-accumulated intensity upon the *others*), of all. But alas, if I don't say, bang off, that *this* is then the thing I will risk for you, it is because "this," like its companions, isn't, any way I can fix it, workable as a fifty-thousander. The scheme to which I am *now* alluding is lovely—human, dramatic, international, exquisitely "pure," exquisitely everything;[1] only absolutely condemned, from the germ up, to be workable in not less than 100,000 words. If 100,000 were what you had asked me for, I would fall back upon it ("terror" failing) like a flash; and even send you, without delay, a detailed Scenario of it that I drew up a year ago; beginning then—a year ago—to *do* the thing—immediately afterwards; and then again pausing for reasons extraneous and economic. (Because—now that I haven't to consider my typist—there was nobody to "take" it! The *Atlantic* declined—saying it really only wanted "Miss Johnson!")[2] It really constitutes, at any rate, the work I intimately want actually to be getting on with; and—if you are not overdone with the profusion of my confidence—I dare say I best put my case by declaring that, if you don't in another month or two hear from me either as a Terrorist or as a Cheerful Internationalist, it will be that intrinsic difficulties will in each case have mastered me; the difficulty in the one having been to keep my Terror down by *any* ingenuity to the 50,000; and the difficulty in the *other* form of Cheer than the above-mentioned obsessive hundred-thousander. I only wish you wanted *him*. But I have now in all probability a decent outlet for him.

Forgive my pouring into your lap this torrent of mingled uncertainties and superfluities. The latter indeed they are properly not, if only as showing you how our question does occupy me. I shall write you again—however vividly I see you wince at the prospect of it. I have it at heart not to fail to let you know how my alternatives settle themselves. Please believe meanwhile in my very hearty thanks for your intimation of what you might perhaps, your own quandary straightening out, see your way to do for me. It is a kind of intimation that I find, I confess, even at the worst, dazzling. All this, however, trips up my response to your charming picture of your whereabouts and present conditions—still discernible, in spite of the chill of years and absence, to my eye, and eke to my ear, of memory. We have had here a torrid, but not a wholly horrid, July; but are making it up with a brave August, so far as we have got, of fires and floods and storms and overcoats. Through everything, none the less, my purpose holds—my genius, I may even say, absolutely thrives—and I am unbrokenly yours,

Henry James

14*th* August

P.S. The hand of Providence guided me, after finishing the preceding, to which the present is postscriptal, to keep it over a few days instead of posting it directly: so possible I thought it that I might have something more definite to add—and I was a little nervous about the way I had left our question. Behold then I *have* then to add that I have just received your letter of August 4—which so simplifies our situation that this accompanying stuff becomes almost superfluous. But I have let it go for the sake of the interest, the almost top-heavy mass of response that it embodies. Let us put it then that all is for the moment for the best in this worst of possible worlds; all the more that had I not just now been writing you exactly as I am, I should probably—and thanks, precisely, to the lapse of days—be stammering to you the ungraceful truth that, after I wrote you, my tale of terror did, as I was so more than half fearing, give way beneath me. It *has*, in short, broken down for the present. I am laying it away on the shelf for the sake of something that *is* in it, but that I am now too embarrassed and preoccupied to devote more time to pulling out.[3] I really shouldn't wonder if it be not still, in time and place, to make the world sit up; but the curtain is dropped for the present. All thanks for your full and prompt statement of how the scene has shifted for you. There is no harm done, and I don't regard the three weeks spent on my renewed wrestle as wasted—I have, within three or four days, rebounded from them with such relief, vaulting into another saddle and counting, D.V., on a straighter run. I have *two* begun novels: which will give me plenty to do for the present—they being of the type of the "serious" which I am too delighted to see you speak of as lifting again, "Miss Johnson" permettendolo, its downtrodden head. I mean, at any rate, I assure you, to lift *mine!* Your extremely, touchingly kind offer to find moments of your precious time for "handling" something I might send you is altogether too momentous for me to let me fail of feeling almost ashamed that I haven't something—the ghost or t'other stuff—in form, already, to enable me to respond to your generosity "as meant." But heaven only knows what may happen yet! For the moment, I must peg away at what I have in hand—biggish stuff, I fear, in bulk and possible unserialisability, to saddle you withal. But thanks, thanks thanks. Delighted to hear of one of your cold waves—the newspapers here invidiously mentioning none but your hot. We have them all, moreover, *réchauffées*, as soon as you have done with them; and we are just sitting down to one now. I dictate you this in my shirt-sleeves and in a draught which fails of strength—chilling none of the pulses of yours gratefully and affectionately,

Henry James

1. HJ had begun writing *The Ambassadors*.
2. This parenthetic remark was inserted in HJ's hand. He is probably referring to Mary Johnston (1870–1936), the Virginia-born writer of romances whose *To Have and to Hold*, just published, was a sensational best-seller.
3. The uncompleted "The Sense of the Past" was published posthumously in 1917, edited by Percy Lubbock.

To James B. Pinker
Ms Yale

Lamb House, Rye
August 16th 1900

Dear Mr. Pinker.

I am much obliged to you for your cheque, today received, for £225, representing the amount received from Methuen & Co. on the agreement for *The Sacred Fount*, less your commission.

And it gives me great pleasure to know you are in relation with the Scribner's in respect to the American volume. Believe me

Yours very truly
Henry James

To James B. Pinker
Ms Yale

Lamb House, Rye
August 29th 1900

Dear Mr. Pinker.

I am greatly obliged for your warning about the importunate lady,[1] but have myself so vivid, or rather so dark, a view of her, that

I think I can assure you I am not in further danger. She is indeed, clearly, an unprofitable person, and I judge her whole course and career, so far as it appeared in this neighborhood, very sternly and unforgivingly. I sent her a contribution which reached her at the moment of Crane's death and which was really, out of pity for *him*, more substantial than I could afford, and yet I learn that the young local doctor here, who gave almost all his time to them, quite devotedly, during all Crane's illness, and took them to the Black Forest, has never yet, in spite of the money gathered in by her at that time, received a penny, and doesn't in the least expect to. It's really a swindle. So you see I understand.—I have received today my copies of *The Soft Side.*[2] Believe me yours very truly

Henry James

1. Cora Crane. HJ had written earlier to Pinker, "my heart, I fear, is generally, hard to her."

2. *The Soft Side,* containing twelve tales, appeared in England on 30 August 1900 and in New York in September.

To Margaret Mary James
Ms Harvard

Lamb House, Rye
September 25*th* [1900]

Dearest Peggy.

I have only been waiting to be able to give you news of your mother's safe departure and arrival to write and thank you as you deserve to be thanked for the delightful photos you sent me by her and which I prize as the best and bravest yet taken. I will return to them in a moment—only telling you first of how comfortably and serenely I saw the dear Being started, from Dover, on Saturday evening, by the Ostend boat, and how promptly and happily I today hear from her of her having been, on Sunday noon, reunited to your Dad. Of this she may by this time have written to yourself. At any rate she clearly finds him very, very much better; and very much more encouraged and more encouraging about himself. She is also, clearly, not less glad not to be far away on the billow; and so all's well that ends well. She brought me a very satisfactory account of you and your re-launched state and mood, as she last saw you, and *them:* and I give you on these things an uncle's most affectionate

163

Portrait of Henry James by Ellen (Bay) Emmet, 1900: "the smooth and anxious clerical gentleman in the spotted necktie" (James to Bay Emmet, 20 October 1901).

blessing. May studies, spirits, sports, leap and march and stride together in right military step and as if to martial music! I greatly miss you, dearest Peggot and my small dashes down into High Street are solitary and sad. But we will make it up later, for opportunities of further familiarity with Lamb House will not, I fondly hope, be wanting to you. Yes, I delight in the photos, and shall be most thankful if you can give me two or three more of (1) myself with my hands in my pockets and my head and eyes twisted a bit up and to one side, standing in a corner of the garden; (2) the back court, with the little shrubs in pots; (3) the house from the garden, with your mother and Theo[dora] Sedgwick retreating through the window. Also of the largeish head, in profile, of your Uncle, if you can get it a bit less dark. (On the other hand the two or three *lighter* ones of this that you sent, don't seem particularly successful.) The one of the court is charming; a very great success. Leslie[1] has taken a goodish many more on some new films I gave her, but some of them, for some reason, developed by the photographer, don't seem very brilliant. If some of the later ones come out better, I will send such as are interesting. I bicycle now out to the Farm, and have got a machine for Leslie; but the afternoons are woefully shortening and there isn't much time (out of the way as she is for the returns) to take good rides. We had the best of their time there—your mother and you and I—in those exquisite Walks to and fro. But it's past midnight and your uncle must tumble in. He has heard, alas, of the sudden *death* of little Peter at St. Leonard's—precious, beautiful little Peter, whom you never saw. I went over yesterday afternoon and brought him home, and this A.M. with George and Smith,[2] I buried him in the garden. But good night again, dear Peggot, and with lively hopes of a reunion not too long delayed. Do the photos at your leisure—I mean convenience; and without detriment to your learning or your "fun"—if you have any. I mean, only, any fun. The portrait of *me* in the garden-nook is, to my sense, the best I ever had taken. And the garden-nook is so pretty. Give my love, my blessing to my three young music-hall friends; and recall me very kindly to their father and mother. I embrace you, dearest Peg, on both cheeks, and am your always-affectionate uncle

Henry James

1. Leslie Emmet.
2. George Gammon, the gardener, and Smith, HJ's servant.

To Cora Crane
Ms Columbia

Lamb House, Rye
October 1st 1900

Dear Mrs. Crane.

I enclose you a letter—that is a brief note—addressed to the Secretary of the Royal Literary Fund supporting your application in as few words as possible. It occurs to me that your being, and Crane's having been, American, that is alien, not British subjects, and not long domiciled in England may be a bar to their entertaining it—and I think you right to get all the letters you can. One from Judge Crane would not be perhaps exactly practical—a letter from America to an English Fund. But I leave the matter to you, and my note represents the whole connection with it that I shall be able to find possible. I congratulate you on having got quarters of your own, and I am yours very truly

Henry James

To Mrs. William James
Ms Harvard

Lamb House, Rye
October 1st 1900

Dearest Alice.

I have your good letter of Friday last and two postcards, one from each of you since—yours to tell me you were not going to Geneva and William's to ask for boots etc. Two pair of boots went today by parcel-post, both *new*, as the new ones seemed to pack into closer compass. They are in *one* parcel. May they safely and swiftly arrive. Your letter tells me much of what Sir J. Scott tells you about going to Egypt—the preferable post-boats etc., and makes me feel with hope and cheer that you're really thinking of it. I heartily conjure you to do so—quite apart from the question of whether *I* can go. Believing as I do that it's the very best thing William can attempt, and yet being, alas, *very* sceptical about myself, I am *angoissé* to think of this benefit for him standing or falling at all by my frail possibility. My case is partly economical—but also partly, even

166

largely, embarrassed in another way. I this day at 3 o'clock in Walter Dawes's office, at last solemnly and triumphantly "completed the purchase" of this house, which is now therefore, beneficently mine (subject to a mortgage which I can certainly pay off easily in two or three years): that is, I paid to Mrs. Bellingham upwards of half the value of the house. The rest resides in two annual payments of interest on a mortgage, of £25 apiece—which the holder is but too glad to keep going. This disbursement has given me a sense of temporary depletion—not at all to the point of inconvenience so long as I stay quiet, and making me considerably shrink from plans of Eastern travel. In expectation and view of it, moreover, I a short time since covenanted for the delivery of a novel (to Constable and Co. here and Ch. Scribner's Sons in the U.S.) for publication in the autumn of 1901;[1] and this novel will *have* to be written during six or seven of the prior months of next year. I can't write it *now*, for I am writing now a novel to begin serialisation in Harper[2] also next autumn (the other one is to come *straight* out as a book); and this I am devoutly (as to regularity of "daily stint") now proceeding with and hoping to finish soon after the New Year. I can put *off* the Constable and Scribner book to 1902; but I quite awfully don't *want* to—there are reasons, as to order, interval, dates of subsequent works, so cogent as to keeping it just where it *is*. I feel as if the ghost of the unwritten book would interpose between me and all the pyramids and temples, and as if I should rather "eat my heart out" over the delay. Now that after such previous years of dropping out and languishment—by my own dire detachment from *ways*—the excellently effective Pinker is bringing me up, and round, so promisingly that it really contains the germs of a New Career, I don't want (at 57!) to sacrifice any present and immediate period of production—however brief—that I can stiffly (*and* joyously!) keep in its place. Such is the manner in which I am at present moved, for safety's and lucidity's sake, to put the case; but there will be time for us still to talk of it further: though the finishing of my *serial* book, now on the stocks (150,000 words), is truly also by itself a prospect requiring margin. (What I *yearn* to hear of is some *quand même* attitude toward Cairo and the Nile on William's and your part. Cultivate it, embrace it, cherish it.)—It's extremely sweet to me, now that it's done, this sense of real possession of L.H.—it brings a deep peace. (The house was, by the way, bought (after some years of hiring) by Francis Bellingham from Davis Lamb only in *1893*—so that it has been almost as recently Lamb as possible.) Many thanks for Billy's second letter—almost as delightful as the first. I'm sending it to Peg.—Baldwin[3] *doesn't* come down for a night—can't: rather to my relief. Gosse has been and gone and I walked him out to tea with Elly and Leslie[4] (he being delighted with the whole impression) yesterday P.M. The two W̧arrens[5] come down for a Sunday and Monday before the end of the month—then, for awhile, I ween, *plus personne.* I shall get your second lecture-copy (William), from MacA.,[6] in case you want it, and myself register and post it to you. He will, in response to your postcard, give you details, today, I suppose as to how he sent it. He tells me he put [it] into an envelope left with him, directed by you, for the purpose; but didn't register it. I should think you had better have the second copy without delay. But it's more than midnight. Goodnight. Much love.

Henry

1. This became *The Wings of the Dove.*
2. *The Ambassadors* was serialized in the *North American Review,* January–December 1903.
3. Dr. W. W. Baldwin. See *Letters* III, 177.
4. The Emmets were living near Rye at this time. See letter to Ellen Temple Hunter, 3 July 1897.
5. Edward Warren and his wife. See letter to Warren, 15 September 1897.
6. William MacAlpine, HJ's typist.

To W. Morton Fullerton
Ms Barrett

Lamb House, Rye
October 2*d* 1900

My dear boy Fullerton.

How can I thank you kindly, tenderly enough for your so interesting, so touching letter? Let this question itself represent for you such elements of "reply" as, in our so frustrate conditions of intercourse, may temporarily serve. Read into my meagre and hurried words—well, read into them *everything.* I as perfectly understand and embrace your practical impossibilities of migration as I completely retain the consciousness of my original impressible vision

168

of the spare, bare chance. Its very spareness and bareness endeared it to me, and I rocked its frail vitality in my arms as an anxious mother rocks the small creature of her entrails whose life is precarious. And now I have laid its shrivelled shape away to rest—as its little breathing-hour is over. Forgive this slightly gruesome image—which marks simply the moral that my absolute comprehension (ah, my hideous intelligence!) of your complex *asservissement* owes nothing to any attenuation of the sense that your not being able to be here leaves me face to face with it. I *am* face to face with it, as one is face to face, at my age, with every successive lost opportunity (wait till you've reached it!) and with the steady, swift movement of the ebb of the great tide—the great tide of which one will never see the turn. The grey years gather; the arid spaces lengthen, damn them—or at any rate don't shorten; what doesn't come doesn't, and what goes *does*.[1] I needn't ask you to believe that I don't say this to torment you, completely on your *side* as I am; I only say it to *feel*, myself, my loss; as I should have said it to feel my gain if you *had* been free. The next best thing to having you, in short, is thus to be *with* you *quand même. Don't* think, please, by the way, that I supposed you in any "oasis of calm" whatever. I saw the Paris of these months as a positive hell of worry and oppression for you—and that was why, was why . . . ! I only meant that, compared with some—so many other—past periods, your special *Times* tension[2] was presumably less great. I figure your actual predicament luridly enough—and every jangle of your bell-rope vibrates in my own nerves. Sit as tight as you *can:* it's all we can ever do. I rejoice heartily that you got the three weeks in May you tell me of. I wish I might have got them *with* you—but this too apparently, was not, heaven help us, to have been thinkable. Let me the more beg you to put in order your record, your impressions—to give them a form in which I may have cognition of them. In this cognition I should delight. Don't be more difficult for me, in detail, than you *must.* (N.B. This *is* not a technical, but a general prayer!) Your letter exhales a complexity, an obscurity of trouble, which has for me but one light—the inevitableness, in relation to it, of my wondering if I mayn't hold out the conception of *help* to you; or rather of my absolutely *holding* out the assurance of it.[3] Hold me then *you* with any squeeze; grip me with any grip; press me with any pressure; trust me with any trust. I wish I could help you, for instance, by satisfying your desire to know from "what port," as you say, I set out. And yet, though the enquiry is, somehow, of so large a synthesis, I think I *can* in a manner answer. The port from which I set out was, I think, that of the *essential loneliness of my life*—and it seems to be the port also, in sooth to which my course again finally directs itself! This loneliness, (since I mention it!)—what is it still but the deepest thing about one? Deeper about *me*, at any rate, than anything else: deeper than my "genius," deeper than my "discipline," deeper than my pride, deeper, above all, than the deep countermining of art. May that amount of information about it give you a lift! Take all this, at all events, my dear Fullerton, for the very soul of sympathy, and believe me always yours

Henry James

1. HJ echoes what he has just been writing in *The Ambassadors*—Strether's speech in the fifth part to Little Bilham about lost opportunities: "What one loses, one loses, make no mistake about that."

2. Fullerton was still an editor in the Paris bureau of the London *Times*.

3. While it is difficult to know what Fullerton wrote HJ, he seems as usual to have spoken vaguely of his own troubles. It was not until some years later that he was able to write to HJ with greater candor. His way of handling his own problems—problems that arose from his numerous amorous involvements and his conflict between trying to live the life of a leisured gentleman in Paris and having to cope with much newspaper drudgery—was to write sentimentally of large subjects such as loneliness, the question raised here. HJ, who was fond of him, always responded generously, and especially at this moment when he was writing of Lambert Strether's troubled aging.

To Edith Wharton
Ms Yale

Lamb House, Rye
Oct. 26th 1900

Dear Mrs. Wharton.

I brave your interdiction and thank you both for your letter and for the brilliant little tale in the Philadelphia repository.[1] The latter has an admirable sharpness and neatness: and infinite wit and point—it only suffers a little, I think, from one's not having a *direct* glimpse of the husband's provoking causes—literally provoking ones. However, you may very well say that there are two sides to that; that one can't do everything in 6000 words, one must narrowly choose (à *qui* le dites-vous?) and that the complete non-vision of Millicent—and her gentleman—was a less evil [thing] than the frustrated squint to which you would have been at best reduced. Either *do* them or don't (directly) touch them—such was doubtless your instinct. The subject is really a big one for the canvas—that was really your difficulty. But the thing is *done.* And I applaud, I mean I value, I egg you on, in your study of the American life that surrounds you. Let yourself go in it and *at* it—it's an untouched field, really: the folk who try, over there, don't come within miles of any civilized, however superficially, any "evolved" life. And use to the full your remarkable ironic and valeric gift; they form a most valuable, (I hold,) and beneficent engine. *Only,* the *Lippincott* tale is a little *hard,* a little purely derisive. But that's because you're so young, and with it, so clever. Youth *is* hard—and your needle-point, later on, will muffle itself in a little blur of silk. It *is* a needle-point! Do send me what you write* when you can kindly find time, and do, some day, better still, come to see yours, dear Mrs. Wharton, most truly

Henry James

* Oh, I'll do the same by you!

1. The "Philadelphia repository" was *Lippincott's Magazine,* which published Mrs. Wharton's short story "The Line of Least Resistance" in the October 1900 issue. The story deals with a wealthy man from Newport who discovers that his wife is unfaithful, but who maintains the social forms of his marriage.

To W. E. Norris
Ms Yale

Lamb House, Rye
December 23rd 1900

My dear Norris.[1]

I greatly desire that this shall not fail to convey you my sentiments on this solemn Christmas morn; so I sit here planning and plotting, and making well-meant *pattes de mouche,* to that genial end. A white sea-fog closes us in (in which I've walked healthily, with my young niece, out to the links—with the sense of being less of a golfist than ever); the clock ticks and the fire crackles during the period between tea and dinner; the young niece aforesaid (my only companion this season of mirth, with her parents abroad and a scant snatch of school holidays to spend with me) sits near me immersed in *Redgauntlet;* so the moment seems to lend itself to my letting off this signal in such a manner as *may,* even in these troublous times (when my nerves are all gone and I feel as if *anything* shall easily happen), catch your indulgent eye. I feel as if I hadn't caught your eye, for all its indulgence, for a long and weary time, and I daresay you won't gainsay my confession. May the red glow of the Yuletide log diffuse itself at Underbank, (with plenty of fenders and fireguards and raking out at night), in a good old jovial manner. I think of you all on the Lincombes etc., in these months, as a very high-feeding, champagne-quaffing, orchid-arranging society; and my gaze wanders a little wistfully toward you—away from my plain broth and barley-water. I in fact some three weeks ago, fled from that Spartan diet up to town, hoping to be in the mood to remain there till Easter, and the experience is still going on, with this week here inserted as a picturesque parenthesis. I asked my young niece in the glow of last August not to fail to spend her Christmas with me, as I then expected to be, Promethean-like, on my rock; and I've returned to my rock not to leave her in the lurch. And I find a niece does temper solitude—even though I've gathered from you that you occasionally find a daughter *doesn't.*[2] If her parents were willing (which, luckily for me, they're not!) I should be much tempted to convert her, by some form of adoption, into a daughter. But perhaps that, exactly, would spoil it!

London, at all events, seems to me, after long expatriation, rather thrilling—all the more that I have the thrill—the quite anxious throb—of a new little habitation—which makes, alas, the third that I am actually master of! I've taken (with 34 De Vere Gardens still on my hands, but blessedly let for another year to come, and *then* to be wriggled out of with heaven's help) a permanent room at a club (Reform), which seems to solve the problem of town on easy terms. They are let by the year only, and one waits one's turn long—(for years); but when mine the other day came round I went it blind instead of letting it pass. One has to furnish and do all one's self—but the results, and conditions, generally, repay. My cell is spacious, southern, looking over Carlton Gardens; and tranquil, utterly, and singularly well-serviced; and I find I can work there—there being ample margin for a typewriter and its priest, or even priestess. It all hung by *that*—but I think I am not deceived; so I bear up. And the next time you come to perch at a neighbouring establishment, I shall swoop down on you from my eyrie. It's astonishing how remote, cumbrous and expensive it makes 34 De Vere Gardens seem. Worse luck that that millstone still dangles gracefully from my neck!—

I saw of course Gosse, a few evenings ago; as light-hearted as a young duke just attaining his majority. He is flushed still with the pleasant social episode of his aged relative's demise. If he could only lose four or five a year I think he would be kept in spirits. The spoils of "Sandhurst" moreover, if not quite those of Poynton, appear to have proved richer than he feared; so his Christmas is probably as merry a one as we know.

I also met Rhoda B[roughton] twice, but Rhoda is rather thrown upon the world. She has let her Richmond house for six months, and perches on friendly boughs—which she causes perhaps to bend a little more than the soft south wind. It's really the end, I believe, of her Richmond life—her nephew having seceded.—I've now dined, and re-established my niece with the second volume of *Redgauntlet*—besides plying her, at dessert, with delicacies brought down, *à son intention*, from Fortnum & Mason; and thus with a good conscience I prepare to close this and to sally forth into the seafog to post it with my own hand—if it's to reach you at any congruous moment. I yesterday dismissed a servant at an hour's notice—the house of the Lamb scarce knew itself and felt like that of the Wolf—so that, with reduced resources, I make myself generally useful. Besides, at little huddled, neighbourly Rye, even a white December seafog is a cosy and convenient thing.

So good night and all blessings on your tropic home. May your table groan with the memorials of friendship, and may Miss Effie's midnight masses not make her late for breakfast and *her* share of them—which is a little even in these poor words from yours, my dear Norris, always

Henry James

1. From this time on HJ wrote an annual Christmas letter to Norris, who had befriended him after *Guy Domville* during his long stay at Torquay, South Devon, where Norris lived.

2. Norris's daughter lived with him.

To Jessie Allen
Ms Harvard

Lamb House, Rye
Christmas night 1900

Dear and unspeakable Miss Allen![1]

How can I bear with it at all—between emotion at the remembrance and anguish at the unbridled extravagance? It confirms every conviction as to the way you ruin your friends and make them a full-fed and ravening mob! *Of course* we're devouring monsters, when you've reduced it to a science to kindly see that we become so. Well, I thank you most humbly, blushingly and awkwardly—but I feel myself in the very act going straight downhill (odiously brandishing and boasting over my dear little old brass trophy—I more brazen, myself, than any part of it), not somehow to have made you keep it for yourself. As if you ever conceivably *would*, however; as if locking you up with it for a year even (and you *must* have been locked for many months!—since last June), would do anything toward making it take root on you! No—you'd bound out of confinement the last day and *rush* with it to somebody's door. Only that the somebody should be again wretched unremunerative *me*—that *does* show the very perversity of self-spoliation! Well, I bow my head—very low indeed—and I clutch (observe) the admirable creation. All Venice seems enclosed in its little brass parapet—and the cluster of charming objects figure to me the Salute, San Giorgio, the Dogana etc., rising out of the level lagoon. They are dear, dear things—these special relics—and I love them, tenderly, and I haven't another and never *had* had, and I thank you more than I can say; but all that is no reason and doesn't make the positive frenzy of your altruism less a case to be *watched!* Meantime *I* watch my treasure! My little niece, who is here alone with me, helps me to mount guard, and we turn on at moments a dear little wire-haired fox-terrier whom I've lately acquired and of whom we are now making a great companion. He already understands—positively understands *you* and your headlong course; knows all about it, in short, but proposes to swagger about the treasures of Lamb House, all the same, on all afternoon visits. He is twice the dog he was yesterday—and so, in truth, am I! I have just come up to a small upstairs study that I rejoice in here—after a tête-à-tête

174

with my niece over a colossal turkey on which we made no perceptible impression whatever; and I have left her alone, by the fire and the lamp in the little oak-parlour—if a young thing may be said to be alone who is deep down in Sir Walter [Scott]. The sea-wind howls in my old chimneys and round my old angles; but the clock ticks loud and the fire crackles fast within, and I wonder if I am not perhaps as humbly snug in my antiquated corner as your wonderful dollared friends (I am too utterly *dis*-dollared), with their Providential hot pipes. However *you* do the picturesque for them even as you do it for *me*—so it's as broad as it's long! Your returning warrior sounds quite like Drury Lane—and I hope he will be a big success and have a long run.—I find myself quite yearning again, even after but four or five days here, for the electric metropolis and the fringe of "South Belgravia." The country is dire in the short days—and my niece makes me jealous of Sir Walter. She doesn't read her uncle; and perhaps it's as well! The more I think the more I *do* suspect Sir Gerald. The only hitch is the "daughter"; but perhaps she is only humbug and a part of the game: do make me a sign when you get back—I shall be expectant; and shall instantly arrive to pour forth. Yours, meanwhile, most constantly and thankingly

Henry James

1. Elizabeth Jessie Jane Allen (1845–1918) was descended from the Allens of Cresselly (listed in Burke's Landed Gentry), and her great-great grandfather had been the Earl of Jersey. HJ had met Miss Allen in Venice during his 1899 visit at the Curtis's Palazzo Barbaro; he was delighted with her style, her conversation, and her accounts of visits to castles and country houses. His protest against her lavish Christmas gift mingled with his constant refrain that she played to excess the role of Lady Bountiful. She lived in a small corner house at 74 Eaton Terrace, where HJ faithfully took tea with her when he was in town. They gossiped endlessly about the Curtises in the 211 letters HJ wrote her during the remaining years of his life. John Singer Sargent called this "mischievous tattle about James's friends, whom she always tried to alienate from him."

2
The Edwardian Novels

1901–1904

2
The Edwardian Novels

With the advent of the new century, Henry James entered into the most fertile period of his life, a creative surge during which he had a great sense of health and happiness. He spent the next four years in Rye, even during long winters of storms that swept the coast and gave him a sense of isolation and distance from his old metropolitan world. In his own rural neighborhood he found himself with local friends and acquaintances, and certain fellow craftsmen. During 1900 Stephen Crane lived eight miles away, in Brede House, with Cora; Joseph Conrad was for a while at Winchelsea collaborating with Ford Madox Hueffer; H. G. Wells, becoming swiftly famous, settled at Sandgate. James became a familiar figure in the coastal town, as he took his daily walks, sometimes with neighbors, his typist, or his novelist friends. Kipling occasionally came to see him from the farther reach of Sussex in his new expensive motor car. James worked long hours in his Garden Room, the detached pavilion beside Lamb House, which looked down the descent to the High Street. The regularity of his life, his hours of dictation, and his leisurely local distractions and evenings of quiet reading enabled James to write his three large novels, *The Ambassadors*, *The Wings of the Dove*, and *The Golden Bowl*, in three years. Although completed first, *The Ambassadors* was published in book form after the *Wings*, for it had to wait on its serialization in the *North American Review*.

During these years James also assembled two collections of tales, *The Soft Side* and *The Better Sort*, in the second of which his masterpiece "The Beast in the Jungle" appeared. He was much distressed by the Boer War, and the death of Queen Victoria deeply moved him. He watched with a critical eye the accession of Edward VII. James had retained a perch in London, a room at the Reform Club, and he made occasional forays into the metropolis, but he was happiest with his house and garden, and his staff of servants. He had

had a husband and wife caring for him in De Vere Gardens. In Lamb House he had a maid and a houseboy, and later a housekeeper and a second maid.

After MacAlpine, James employed Mary Weld, who typed the three large novels and the two-volume life of William Wetmore Story which James published in 1903. Although he had a new generation of friends, he still corresponded with Mrs. W. K. Clifford, the busy playwright and novelist, of whom he was particularly fond, and with his old friend Rhoda Broughton. His family correspondence continued as before, as well as his letters to Grace Norton and Howells. In 1902 he began to correspond with Edith Wharton. His loneliness was partially offset by visits from his niece Peggy, William James's only daughter, now an adolescent. During this period we find him corresponding with Jocelyn Persse and writing more frequently to Howard Sturgis.

As he neared the end of his long writing of *The Golden Bowl* James experienced an acute desire to revisit the United States. He had not seen his native land since 1883, when his father died. In August 1904, with the *Bowl* in press, he sailed for New York, and started on the great travel adventure of his later years.

To Clara and Clare Benedict
Ms Basel

Reform Club
January 22*d* 1901

Dearest Benedicts.

I am much touched by your anxious telegram (which I am just answering)—as I was also delighted and spell-bound, my dear Eagle,[1] a few days ago, by your so brilliant and interesting letter. To proceed immediately to the point, the poor dear old stricken Queen is *rapidly* dying and by the time this reaches you will probably be no more—the fluctuations (very small really) caused by her obstinate vitality and the wonderful doctor-arts, being but flickers of the lamp of which the oil is spent. Blind, used up, utterly sickened and humiliated by the war, which she hated and deplored from the first (it's what has finished her) and by the way everything is going, she is a very pathetic old monarchical figure. She had been failing fast for days before it became public, and was far gone when the first news of her being ill came. It is a simple running down of the old used-up watch—and no winding-up can keep for more than from hour to hour. As I write (5.30 P.M.), she is reported as "rallying" a little, but it can only mean a postponement of a few hours.—I feel as if her death will have consequences in and for this country that no man can foresee. The Prince of Wales is an arch-vulgarian (don't *repeat* this from me); the wretched little "Yorks" are less than nothing; the Queen's magnificent duration had held things magnificently—beneficently—together and prevented all sorts of accidents. Her death, in short, will let loose incalculable forces for possible ill. I am very pessimistic. The Prince of Wales, in sight of the throne, and nearly 60, and after all he has done besides of the same sort, is "carrying on" with Mrs. George Keppel (sister-in-law of Lord Albemarle), in a manner of the worst omen for the dignity of things. His accession in short is ugly and makes all for vulgarity and frivolity. There will be tremendous obsequies, of course, even if they take place at Windsor, and not at the Abbey, as the nation will wish. (She has probably arranged to be placed at Frogmore with her husband—"Frogmore" for the Empress of India!!) and probably for a year's mourning. Wear it *you*, too (as good Americans ought, for she was always nice to us), for a month. Forgive this unsightly scrawl to catch the post. Your last letter full of fine things and filling me with rejoicing and recognition in respect to Nervi. Yes, I know it a little, and very pleasantly; but more . . .[2]

1. Clara Woolson Benedict, a sister of Constance Fenimore Woolson (see *Letters* III, Appendix), and her daughter Clare continued to correspond with HJ and to visit Europe every summer. HJ figured in these letters as the Dove, Mrs. Benedict as the Eagle.
2. The rest of this letter is missing.

To Margaret Mary James
Ms Harvard

The Reform Club
Tuesday [5 February 1901]

Dearest Peggot.

I rejoice to get your good report of your Saturday's adventures[1] and to know that you really saw and enjoyed—also that you got smoothly and safely home, and felt the affair generally a success. I myself did well enough, but the lady whose house I went to had invited too many people—especially ladies in high plumes and bows, so that as a lone and modest man I had the back seat, as it were, of all. However, I saw a good deal, and our windows were close to the show. I thought it very interesting. I thank you, too, greatly, for dear Billy's[2] delightful letter, which I will carefully keep for restoration to your mother. Billy's letters always make me long more and more to see him. I am hearing rather frequently from Rome and a short letter just received from your Dad is very cheerful about himself. He says he has "come up wonderfully" since Mrs. Myers' departure;[3] also that Mr. Clarke has been two days in Rome; which, of course, however, you know. I am glad *Dombey and Son* has woven such a spell, but remember that spells should always be sacrificed to spelling; by which I mean Education in general.—I am going to propose that we postpone our theatre for a week longer—a week, that is from next Saturday, so as to interspace our pleasures a little more; that is, not have two spectacular Saturdays running; besides which the shadow of the Funeral seems still, this week, a little too much over things. But I will write to you about this soon again, and arrange it comfortably. I send my kind regards to Mrs. Clarke, and am ever your affectionate Uncle

H.J.

P.S.—Don't think of "answering" this.

1. HJ had arranged with friends for his niece to have a good window seat for the funeral procession of Queen Victoria. He was invited to the George Vanderbilts' to view the same spectacle.
2. WJ's second son, named after his father.
3. F. W. H. Myers, WJ's friend and fellow psychical researcher, had just died in Rome, where the WJs were spending the winter.

To Edith Bronson, Contessa Rucellai
Ms Private

The Reform Club
February 15 1901

My dear Edith.

It is an extreme shock to me to receive from you today the announcement of your mother's death,[1] and I hasten to assure you of my complete participation in your great trouble—only full of sorrow at being so far away and having been so during these many sad and anxious months, as I am sure they must have been. I thought of her constantly, and I thought of you: but everything has made it impossible to me to go to Italy again, and a great gulf of time and space and silence—all insurmountable and inevitable—had come to open itself between us. She sent me a message of invitation for last summer, but it was not at all a manageable thing to me to go to Italy at that season; and, in short, I've been without news of her—save the vague and indirect—all these last months; and all the while thinking of her with helpless compassion and sadness. The strain for *you* must have been, for a long time past, immense: and for her I hope there was no marked suffering, was nothing but serenity. I can't put questions to you—you must be overwhelmed with more letters than you can ever answer; and I shall wait till some news of the things I would like much to know gradually makes its way to me. Meanwhile her death makes me feel strangely older and sadder. It is the end of so many things—so many delightful memories, histories, associations—some of the happiest elements of one's own past. It breaks into my tenderness, even for the dear old Italy and seems to alter and overshadow *that* cherished relation. From years ever so far back she was delightfully kind to me and I had for her the most sincere affection. Those long Venetian years will be for all her friends—had indeed already become so—a sort of legend and boast. I'm thankful for the four or five days I had with her at Asolo two summers ago. But heart-breaking are ends and one's sense of the Lash. Peace to her generous memory—and peace also to you and your home. I hope the latter has no other agitation than this. I am coming to Florence again, all the same, as soon as ever I can. With kind remembrances to your husband, I am yours, my dear Edith, always affectionately

Henry James

1. Katherine De Kay Bronson. See *Letters* II, 358–359.

To Oliver Wendell Holmes, Jr.
Ms Harvard

Reform Club
February 20 1901

My dear Wendell.[1]

I have too long owed you a letter—I mean an acknowledgment of your friendly reception of Montagu Barlow[2] and of your expression of that benevolence under date of January 6th. He came and dined with me as soon as he returned hither and spoke of you with enthusiasm and of the evening he spent with you as the pleasantest thing that had happened to him. I am sorry indeed that it was but one evening, but such is the inquiring Briton, to whom the casual compatriot, over here, is but (for swift passage) a joke. And they have up their sleeve *always* tiresome and irrelevant Newtons and Elmiras—and they tell one about them on their return and life becomes grey and mixed. *All* reports of the land of my birth, however, are, to me, bewildering now, and I know not what to think of anything—but *you.* You remain a part of the palpable past, I mean one of the few portions of it I can fit, at all, into the present as depicted and projected for me. Therefore do, for heaven's sake, come out again this summer. England is domestically interesting and picturesque now—rather!—to make up for her being so deplorable beyond her seas. I've been spending this winter (after two absent ones) in town, and have fallen upon pomps and pageants. We are going to have a pompous king, who will give us *Circenses* if not *Panem.* It remains to be seen to what they will lead but meanwhile they are the joy (even in the midst of deepest insignia of mourning) of a people long starved for opportunities of Asiatic prostration. We grovel before fat Edward—E. the Caresser, as he is privately named; and the thing has a good deal of ancient colour. But I mourn the safe and motherly old middle-class queen, who held the nation warm under the fold of her big, hideous Scotch-plaid shawl and whose duration had been so extraordinarily convenient and beneficent. I felt her death much more than I should have expected; she was a sustaining symbol—and the wild waters are upon us now. I stay here till Easter—then return to Rye for many months. Come and see me there. William is spending the winter in Rome and is, I trust, substantially more sound. He hopes to be able to deliver a course of lectures in Edinburgh in May. But he has resigned from Harvard. Yes, I am smooth-cheeked and strange now and shall remain so for it is tidier in one's declining years. If I can rummage out some lame photog. on going down to Lamb House next week, you shall have it with pride (I mean with *my* pride at your having it). My faithful love to your wife. Always yours,

Henry

1. Wendell Holmes was at this time Chief Justice of the Massachusetts Supreme Court.

2. A British parliamentarian to whom HJ had given a letter of introduction to Holmes.

To Mrs. Humphry Ward
Ms Barrett

Reform Club
March 15 1901

Dear Mrs. Ward.

Most kind your letter, most kind your invitation. In the face of all this benevolence I feel I need all my courage—or rather all my caution—not to be fully and immediately responsive. But the stern and sordid truth is that it is, alas, impossible to me to go abroad this spring. I am not free but bound, very intensely and inexorably. I've a terrible unfinished and belated book on my hands, which I can't get away from for a day, and which alone is a roaring lion in my path.[1] But in addition to this my brother and his wife arrive precisely *from* Italy to find me in England at Easter and to come down and spend a month with me, and to have left them there unvisited all winter in order to go just as they depart, crossing them on the way, would really disgrace me forever. However, I sufficiently rattle for you my chains. I talked only yesterday with a lady who knows your villa well (Mrs. L. A. Harrison, who used to be Alma Stretell),[2] and she made my mouth water for the thought of it. But I must, woe is me, wipe my mouth hard and sit down again to my task. Let me not however do so without expressing my liveliest appreciation of your remarks on the *Sacred Fount*[3]—as to which I almost blush to have made you suppose that, for the thing that it is, any at all were necessary. I say it really in all sincerity—the book isn't worth discussing. It was a remarkably accidental one, and the merest of *jeux d'esprit*. You will say that one mustn't write accidental books, or must take the consequences when one does. Well, I do take them—I resign myself to the figure the thing makes as a mere tormenting trifle. The subject was a small fantasticality which (as I *have* to write "short stories" when I can) I had intended to treat in the compass of a single magazine instalment—a matter of eight or ten thousand words. But it *gave* more, before I knew it; before I knew it had grown to 25,000 and was still but a third developed. And then, in the hand-to-mouth conditions to which I am condemned with my things (which I can scarcely place anywhere), I couldn't afford to sacrifice it; my hand-to-mouth economy condemned me to put it through in order not to have wasted the time already spent. So, only, it was that I hatingly finished it; trying only to make it—the one thing it *could* be—a *consistent* joke. Alas, for a joke it appears to have been, round about me here, taken rather seriously. It's doubtless very disgraceful, but it's the last I shall ever make! Let me say for it, however, that it has, I assure you, and applied quite rigorously and constructively, I believe, its own little law of composition. Mrs. Server is *not* "made happy" at the end—what in the world has put it into your head? As I give but the phantasmagoric I have, for clearness, to make it *evidential*, and the Ford Obert evidence all bears (indirectly) upon Brissenden, supplies the motive for Mrs. B.'s terror and her re-nailing down of the coffin. I had to testify to Mrs. S.'s sense of a common fate with B. and the only way I could do so was by making O. see her as temporarily pacified. I had to give a meaning to the vision of Gilbert L. out on the terrace in the darkness, and the *appearance* of a sensible detachment on her part was my imposed way of giving it. Mrs. S. is back in the coffin at the end, by the same stroke by which Briss is—Mrs. B.'s last interview with the narrator being all an ironic *exposure* of her own false plausibility, of course. But it isn't worth explaining, and I mortally loathe it! Forgive my weariness over my deadly backward present book, which *isn't* a joke—unless I don't know the difference. But I am miswriting for dizziness. May your villa be an Eden without the least little serpent! Yours, dear Mrs. Ward, very constantly

Henry James

1. *The Ambassadors.*
2. Mrs. L. A. Harrison, a musical and bohemian socialite, friend of Sargent's.

3. *The Sacred Fount*, a fantasy-novel in which HJ has the first-person narrator speculate about the "interpersonal" relations of the guests at a week-end party. The novel has provoked much critical speculation; and this passage suggests some of HJ's intentions.

To Violet Hunt
Ms Barrett

The Athenaeum
March 26*th* 1901

Dear Violet Hunt.[1]

The man about town will with great pleasure emerge from his Club at 5 o'clock on Wednesday next, to join the woman about town at *hers*. And the former is infinitely obliged to the latter for this delightful opportunity. Yours most truly

Henry James

1. HJ had known Violet Hunt (1866–1942) from her childhood. Daughter of the painter Alfred William Hunt and his novelist wife, Margaret Raine, Miss Hunt was herself a writer of fiction.

To Hendrik C. Andersen
Ms Barrett

Lamb House, Rye
4 May 1901

My dearest Boy Hendrik.

What an arch-Brute you must, for a long time past, have thought me! But I am not really half the monster I appear. Let me at least attenuate my ugly failure to thank you for certain valued and most interesting photographs. I spent the whole blessed winter— December to April—in London (save a week at Christmas), and returned here to take up my abode again but three or four weeks ago. It was only *then* that I found, amid a pile of postal matter unforwarded (as my servants, when I am away, have instructions only to forward *letters*), your tight little roll of views of your Lincoln. It had lain on my hall-table ever since it arrived (though I don't quite know when that had been); and my first impulse was [to] sit down and "acknowledge" it without a day's delay. Unfortunately—

with arrears here, of many sorts, to be attended to after a long absence, the day's delay perversely imposed itself—and on the morrow my brother and his wife, whom you saw in Rome, arrived for a long stay, with their daughter in addition. They are with me still, and their presence accounts for many neglects—as each day, after work and immediate letters etc.—I have to give them much of my time. But here, my dear boy, I am at last, and I hold out to you, in remorse, remedy, regret, a pair of tightly-grasping, closely-drawing hands. I've lost your studio address—can't find it high or low; but I send this to Sebasti's bank—on the advice of my brother—as *they* (he and his wife) can't remember the thing either. I also enclose a letter which has just come to you here. May it all not fall short! My companions speak of you with the extremest tenderness, found you delightful and had the greatest pleasure in seeing you. My brother is also very interesting to me on the subject of your Lincoln—as, having seen it, he can control somewhat my impression based only on photographs. The latter show me how big a stride with it you have made in this short time and how stoutly you must have sweated over it; but I won't conceal from you that there are things about it that worry me a little. That comes, inevitably, partly from the fact of my being, alas, of a generation nearer to Lincoln than you (the younger generation of his lifetime, though I never saw him in the flesh); and having been drenched in youth with feeling about him, the sense of him, photographs, images, aspects of him. A *seated* Lincoln in itself shocks me a little—he was for us all, then, standing up very tall: though I perfectly recognise that that was a condition you may have *had*, absolutely, to accept. However, I like the head—think it on the whole very fine and right (though rather too smooth, ironed-out, simplified as to ruggedness, ugliness, *mouth* etc.); and it is the figure, especially as seen from the side, that somewhat troubles me. I don't feel the length of limb, leg, shanks, loose-jointedness etc.—nor the thickness of the large body in the clothes—especially the presence of shoulders, big arms and big hands. It's in general a *softer*, smaller giant than we used to see—to see represented and to hear described. I do think he wants facially more light-and-shade, and more breaking-up, under his accursed clothing, more bone, more mass. He is, in general, more *placid* than one's own image of him, and than history and memory. Benevolent, but deeply troubled, and altogether tragic: that's how one thinks of him.—But forgive this groping criticism; far from your thing itself, I worry and fidget for the love of your glory and your gain; and I send you my blessing on your stiff problem and your, I am sure, whatever mistake one may make about it, far from superficial solution.—I hope you have had a winter void of any such botherations as to poison (in any degree) your work or trouble your brave serenity or disturb your youthful personal bloom; a winter of health, in short, and confidence and comfort. It has been a joy to me to be with any one who had lately seen you—and I wish that, without more delay, I could do the sweet same! There is much I want to say to you—but it's half past midnight, and I wax long-winded. So I bid you good night with my affectionate blessing. I count on seeing you here this summer. Give me some fresh assurance of the prospect. I have had a charming letter from Mrs. Elliott,[1] very happy over her Jack's finally-placed Boston show. *Meno male!* Yours, my dear Hans, always and ever

Henry James

1. The former Maude Howe. See letter to Andersen, 27 July 1899.

To Edmund Gosse
Ms Congress

Lamb House, Rye
May 14th 1901

My dear Gosse.

Your proposal in respect to Tolstoi, with the great honour it does me, greatly (I won't attempt to conceal from you) embarrasses and complicates my soul. I should like *much* to oblige and serve your case—how much I needn't say; but there are reasons why I am not in a position to produce at present, or within any *near* time, the needed 3000 words about our friend. Rather there is *a* grave reason—nay, there are two! The first is I don't materially *know* any of Tolstoi's work but his two or three great novels (and one or two Kreutzer Sonatas etc.); and that I see, of his later incarnation a list of ten or twelve volumes reproduced on the flyleaf of the issue of a single publisher. (Beside which there is other fiction.) *Or*, it so happens that I haven't at present *time* to read all or any of this stuff; it's impossible to me—other matters press on me too hard. And yet no estimate of him can have any value which doesn't take full account of them. I don't really, in other words, possess, at all, my whole Tolstoi; and I am afraid I must ask you accordingly to let me off. It must—the job—be done by some one who *does* possess him. This is a poor and scrambling scrawl—and I shall write you better—less scramblingly and more explicatively and personally (which I want greatly to do—and to arrange to see you), in a day or two. Forgive my impracticability and incompetence. I feel a great jadedness in your note and give it a still greater sympathy. Your life is a miracle to me; and it has the proportionate wonder and admiration of yours always

Henry James

To Muir Mackenzie
Ts Lubbock

Lamb House, Rye
June 15th 1901

Dear Grand Governess,[1]

You are grand indeed, and no mistake, and we are bathed in gratitude for what you have done for us, and, in general, for all your comfort, support and illumination. We cling to you; we will walk but by your wisdom and live in your light; we cherish and inscribe on our precious records every word that drops from you, and we have begun by taking up your delightful tobacco-leaves with pious and reverent hands and consigning them to the lap of earth (in the big vague blank unimaginative border with the lupines, etc.) exactly in the manner you prescribe; where they have already done wonders toward peopling its desolation. It is really most kind and beneficent of you to have taken this charming trouble for us. We acted, further, instantaneously on your hint in respect to the poor formal fuchsias—sitting up in their hot stuffy drawing-room with never so much as a curtain to draw over their windows. We haled them forth on the spot, every one, and we clapped them (in thoughtful clusters) straight into the same capacious refuge or omnium gatherum. Then, while the fury and the frenzy were upon us, we did the same by the senseless stores of geranium (my poor little 22/-a-week-gardener's idée fixe!)—we enriched the boundless recep-

With gardener, George Gammon, in the garden at Lamb House.

tacle with *them* as well—in consequence of which it looks now quite sociable and civilised. Your touch is magical, in short, and your influence infinite. The little basket went immediately to its address, and George Gammon (!!) my 22-shillinger, permitted himself much appreciation of your humour on the little tin soldiers. That regiment, I see, will be more sparingly recruited in future. The total effect of all this, and of your discreet and benevolent glance at my ineffective economy, is to make me feel it fifty times a pity, a shame, a crime, that, as John Gilpin said to his wife "you should dine at Edmonton, and I should dine at Ware!"—that you should bloom at Effingham and I should fade at Rye! Your real place is *here*—where I would instantly ask your leave to farm myself out to you. I want to *be* farmed; I am utterly unfit to farm myself; and I do it, all round, for (seeing, alas, what it is) not nearly little enough money. Therefore you ought to be over the wall and "march" with me, as you say in Scotland. However, even as it is, your mere "look round" makes for salvation. I am, I rejoice to say, clothed and in my right mind—compared with what I was when you left me; and so shall go on, I trust, for a year and a day. I have been alone—but next week bristles with possibilities—two men at the beginning, two women (postponed—the Americans) in the middle—and madness, possibly, at the end. I shall have to move over to Winchelsea! But while my reason abides I shall not cease to thank you for your truly generous and ministering visit and for everything that is yours. Which *I* am, very faithfully and gratefully,

Henry James

1. Miss Mackenzie, an expert gardener, had been appointed by HJ "Hereditary Grand Governess" of the Lamb House garden. HJ consulted her regularly as his garden took shape.

To James B. Pinker
Ms Yale

Lamb House, Rye
June 31*st* [1 July] 1901

Dear Mr. Pinker.

Yes, it *is* the case, to my great regret, in respect to my Constable-Scribner book. I have already had a word of inquiry from William Meredith,[1] in answer to which I was obliged to write him that I must ask for a delay to the end of the year—say *December 31st.* He has taken this very kindly—I've just heard from him; and should have immediately written to you even if I had not got your note. It is simply because from one of these last days to the other (absolutely), I was expecting to send you the last three Instalments of my Harper novel, that I hadn't communicated with you on the Constable question before. I hated to write without accompanying my letter with my packet of finally-finished fiction—as I am after all doing even now. Yesterday, today, tomorrow (literally) has it seemed certain this business would have had *Finis*—and it *will,* veraciously, in all probability have it tomorrow.[2] Then the stuff will instantly go to you—Parts Ten and Eleven being all ready. It has been a long, long job—and not from interruptions (of late), or disasters, for I've kept steadily and intensely at it. It's simply that the thing itself has *taken* the time—taken it with a strong and insistent hand.—This Constable one will, for intrinsic reasons, take less; besides being already well started. (I did *that* more than a year ago.) It is of high importance to me to delay it as little as possible—I hate the delay actually inflicted; and within the time I shall now positively work it. Constable & Co., as I say, are humane to me—and for those who are humane to me I will do anything. But will you very kindly write to Scribner on the subject of the inevitable delay and my regrets at it—and giving them the fresh date of the end of the year?—I shall be writing you again within the week.

Yours very truly
Henry James

1. Meredith, son of the novelist George Meredith, was associated with the publishing house of Constable. He was pressing for *The Wings of the Dove,* which HJ was to write as soon as he completed *The Ambassadors.*

2. *The Ambassadors,* now scheduled for serialization in the *North American Review.*

To James B. Pinker
Ms Yale

Lamb House, Rye
July 10 1901

Dear Mr. Pinker.

I enclose to you at last, by this post, the too-long retarded Finis of *The Ambassadors.* You will doubtless know what course to take with it.

I may mention that I've kept back (out of this to-be-serialized form) three or four chapters (three and one half strictly speaking), which I shall desire to include in the volume.[1] I have withheld them only for the shortness of the Parts, and they will be indispensable in the book.

Believe me yours ever
Henry James

1. These chapters were later inserted into the book, by a Harper editor, in the wrong order. See letter to Pinker, 11 August 1903.

To William M. Meredith
Ms Unknown

Lamb House, Rye
July 18*th* 1901

Dear Will Meredith.

Please consider that the ensuing is the title of my novel: *The Wings of the Dove.* It fits happily enough— is "pretty"—and I think will do generally. I trust, devoutly, it hasn't been used. *The Flight of the Dove* would, in that case, be second best; but would be less good. Kindly, therefore, use the *W. of the D.* for purposes of advertisement.—I am happy to say that I've got well launched into the book: and am only regretting that I've presently to go off to the New Forest to see a very old friend who is sick, there, unto death.[1] I shall be back, however, the end of next week and after that fixed here, till Christmas, without a break. I have relations with me for the first part of each month but shall be at most times free and delighted to put you up if you carry out your promise.—Believe me, yours ever
Henry James

1. HJ's old editor at the *Nation,* E. L. Godkin.

To Frances Carruth Prindle
Ms Private

Lamb House, Rye
August 1 1901

Dear Madam.

I am afraid I'm not able to help you much in the matter of the addresses of persons in the couple of fictions of mine concerning which you so kindly enquire—and I may add that in general my productions themselves contain and exhaust (as I hold that *any* decent work of art does, and should) the information to be desired or imparted about it. I haven't either *The Bostonians* or "The New England Winter" under my hand,[1] haven't seen them for years, nor re-read them since they were published—which must have been some fifteen years since; and I so detest, as it were, my books after they are done, and I've got rid of them, that I cherish no remembrances and can pass no examinations. I can only recall in respect to your questions that Miss Chancellor must have lived in Charles St. on the left side from Beacon; and that her house had one of the white doors, partly glass, that open on a short flight of steps before the house door proper is reached. But heaven forbid that I should risk a number! I only remember in the N.E.W. Mrs. Daintry as in Marlborough St.—and the other names you cite have passed from my recognition. Didn't the Tarrants, surely, live in a suburb, and isn't Cambridge specified? I seem dimly to recall Miss Birdseye lived in—oh, I forget! I must have meant one of the streets in the neighborhood of the old Worcester station—or the Boston and Albany. I think vaguely of *Essex*—or of something off it, and I *smell* the house, inside, even yet; but I can neither name or number it. Pardon my extreme helplessness—I haven't been to Boston for nearly twenty years, and that in itself is enfeebling. I am much obliged to you for the tribute of your interest and am yours

Very truly
Henry James

1. *The Bostonians* was published in 1885. The tale "A New England Winter" appeared in *Century Magazine,* August–September 1901, and was reprinted in *Tales of Three Cities* (1884).

To W. Morton Fullerton
Ms Princeton

Lamb House, Rye
August 9th 1901

My dear Fullerton.

This isn't to disengage you with violence from the coils of your boa-constrictor of a special wire,[1] nor to hustle nor harry you in any way, nor to admit for a moment that you may notice, by a sign, my demonstration; still less is it to explain to you the *Sacred Fount* or to report to you on your French exercitation (which I've not yet had half an hour of the proper detachment to read—but shall take to my room with me, for the night, a short time hence). It is simply to write into our baffled and blighted intercourse—the poor, pale idea of an intercourse only, *s'il en faut*, fit for a label, a catalogue, a glass case in a museum of dry specimens—well, anything that the occasion may yield ere it flies. It yields for instance the chance to thank you ever so kindly for your generous immediate letter of this morning; it yields in fine the fact that I thus sit with you a little again in the little sleeping town and under the midnight lamp. *You* sit like young Laocoon, even now, I fear, the centre of the convolutions of your monster (Laocoon *père* being of course the heavenward-gazing Blowitz);[2] and when I think of it the wonder and mystery and variety of life, the wide range of human histories, come over me—with *me* (born under *our* stars, not to say stripes), perched here in my little Cinque Port, over against the coast of France, reaching out to the capital of capitals, the Paris of Parises, where you, in strange, high, lighted chambers, with boulevards at your feet, and the glory thereof, and chancelleries in your ears and Europe, in short, in your hand, prompt the performance of the journal of journals and hold up to the morning the mirror of mirrors. It is all "kind of" Balzackish—and I can almost from my garden, at this hour, under the wondrous summer stars (do you know their terrible dry lustre this year? as if silver nails in the coffin of our knowledge!) see the long-armed ray of Cap Gris Nez. (From an eminence a little way off I can wholly see it.)—You speak of your *Cornhill* article as one always speaks and feels about one's potboilers; but that doesn't prevent me from having felt as I read it as if I were seated with you before that little *café-glacier* that has the summer shade, where we have been together, and you were telling me, happily passive, things out of your abundance, and I could put my hand on your shoulder and wish the occasion would last. Therefore I wish—as for a spectral substitute, makeshift for fond fancy—I wish, I say, for more articles. *Donnez-les moi tous.*—You say I didn't tell you of my brother, and, in effect, there *is*, thank goodness, more to tell of him than I mentioned. He is really, to all appearance, substantially better in health—his doctors, Schott, of Nauheim, i.e., speak of it as a Recovery. He was able, last winter in Rome, to finish writing ten lectures, and was able still more blessedly to deliver them in person, in May and June (before Edinburgh University—the first half of the so-called Gifford lot. He has confirmed his contract to come out next May and deliver the second half.) He has resigned his Harvard chair—but that is good, as well as necessary, for he wants absolutely, in what remains to him, to write two supremely expressive and characteristic books, and he can only do with freedom and with a rigid economy of his forces. The University moreover treats him very decently. When he was last here he read (this I *should* have told you) your *Patriotism and Science*,[3] at my suggestion, and was very greatly struck with the same. He spoke of it to me with unreserved appreciation. If he were going to be any appreciable or foreknowable time in Paris I would ask you to see him; but he sails for home on the 31st, and has to do an aftercure in the Vosges and put in ever so much time here before that; whereby I seem to doubt if he will even pass by your habitat at all. My niece Peggy (aet. 15), their only daughter, is now with me, and, as she is a most soothing and satisfactory maid, attached and attaching to her (poor old) Uncle, we are spending the summer days (amazing for unbroken beauty, but too rainless) here together in idyllic intimacy and tranquillity. (She has been at school in England for two years, and it's over.) There would be room for you between us, and I wish you had been with us this P.M. We take longish, late, afternoon walks— and this afternoon off—two miles—(by the Golfists-little-steam-train) to the beautiful sands of the shore, vast and firm and shining, with the dear old Romney marsh on one side, and the blue, blue sea of August on the other—where we wandered far and far and missed you awfully and awfully. Ah, you *must* come! *Voilà.*—You are perfectly right about such stuffs as the *Sacred Fount*—I can't, the least little bit, afford to write them; they lead to bankruptcy straight—and serve me right thereby. *That jeu d'esprit* was an accident, pure and simple, and not even an intellectual one; you do it too much honour. It was a mere *trade*-accident, *tout au plus*—an incident of technics, pure and simple—brought about by—well, if you were here I could tell you. But it isn't worth writing about, and I shall never do the like again. Don't think me ungracious to your poetic invocation: how can I *feel* so to an address in the character of Jehovah? Only these things are abysses, and I am, without them, always sufficiently yours beyond all sounding

Henry James

1. An allusion to Fullerton's dispatches to the *Times*.
2. Fullerton's superior in the Paris bureau of the *Times*.
3. *Patriotism and Science: Some Studies in Historic Psychology* (1893).

To William Dean Howells
Ms Harvard

Lamb House, Rye
August 10th 1901

My dear Howells.

Ever since receiving and reading your elegant volume of short tales[1]—the arrival of which from you was affecting and delightful to me—I've meant to write to you, but the wish has struggled in vain with the daily distractions of a tolerably busy summer. I should blush, however, if the season were to melt away without my greeting and thanking you. I read your book with joy and found in it recalls from far far away—stray echoes and scents as from another, the American, the prehistoric existence. The thing that most took me was that entitled "A Difficult Case," which I found beautiful and admirable, ever so true and ever so *done*. But I fear I more, almost, than anything else, lost myself in mere envy of your freedom to do, and, speaking vulgarly, to place, things of that particular and so agreeable dimension—I mean the dimension of most of the stories in the volume. It is sternly enjoined upon one here (where an agent-man does what he can for me) that everything—every hundred—above six or seven thousand words is fatal to "placing"; so that I do them of that length, with great care, art and time (much reboiling), and then, even then, can scarcely get them worked off—published even when they've been accepted. *Harper* has had a thing for nearly two years which it has not thought worth publishing—and *Scribner* another for some fifteen months or so; and my agent-man has others that he can't place anywhere. So that (though I don't know why I inflict on you these sordid groans— except that I haven't any one else to inflict them on—and the mere affront—of being unused so inordinately long—is almost intolerable) I don't feel incited in that direction. Fortunately, however, I am otherwise immersed. I lately finished a tolerably long novel, and I've written a third of another—with still another begun and two or three more subjects awaiting me thereafter like carriages drawn up at the door and horses champing their bits.[2] And àpropos of the first named of these, which is in the hands of the Harpers, I have it on my conscience to let you know that the idea of the fiction in question had its earliest origin in a circumstance mentioned to me—years ago—in respect to no less a person than yourself. At Torquay, once, our young friend Jon. Sturges[3] came down to spend some days near me, and, lately from Paris, repeated to me five words you had said to him one day on his meeting you during a call at Whistler's. I thought the words charming—you have probably quite forgotten them; and the whole incident suggestive—so far as it was an incident; and, more than this, they presently caused me to see in them the faint vague germ, the mere point of the *start*, of a subject. I noted them, to that end, as I note everything; and years afterwards (that is three or four) the subject sprang at me, one day, out of my notebook. I don't know if it be good; at any rate it has been treated, now, for whatever it is; and my point is that it had long before—it had in the very act of striking me as a germ—got away from *you* or from anything like you! had become impersonal and independent. Nevertheless your initials figure in my little note; and if you hadn't said the five words to Jonathan he wouldn't have had them (most sympathetically and interestingly) to relate, and I shouldn't have had them to work in my imagination. The moral is that you are responsible for the whole business. But I've had it, since the book was finished, much at heart to tell you so. May you carry the burden bravely!—I hope you are on some thymy promontory and that the winds of heaven blow upon you all— perhaps in that simplified scene that you wrote to me from, with so gleaming a New England evocation, last year. The summer has been

199

wondrous again in these islands—four or five months, from April 1st, of almost merciless fine weather—a rainlessness absolute and without precedent. It has made my hermitage, as a retreat, a blessing, and I have been able, thank goodness, to work without breaks—other than those of prospective readers' hearts.—It almost broke mine, the other day, by the way, to go down into the New Forest (where he has taken a house) to see Godkin, dear old stricken friend. He gave me, in a manner, news of you—told me he had seen you lately. He was perhaps a little less in pieces than I feared, but the hand of fate is heavy upon him. He has mitigations—supremely in the admirable devotion of his wife. And he is quartered for the time in the Forest of Arden. I am lone here just now with my sweet niece Peggy, but my brother and his wife are presently to be with me again for fifteen days before sailing (31st) for the U.S. He is immensely better in health, but he must take in sail hand over hand at home to remain so. *Stia bene, caro amico, anche Lei* (my *Lei* is my joke!) Tell Mrs. Howells and Mildred that I yearn toward them tenderly.

Yours always and ever,
Henry James

1. *A Pair of Patient Lovers* (1901).

2. *The Ambassadors* just completed, HJ had immediately set to work on *The Wings of the Dove*, which, because of the serialization of the former, came out ahead of it in book form.

3. See HJ's *Notebooks*, entry for 31 October 1895, 225–228, and the scenario for *The Ambassadors* in the same volume, 372–374.

To James B. Pinker
Ms Yale

Lamb House, Rye
September 13*th* 1901

Dear Mr. Pinker.

I send you today a complete duplicate of *The Ambassadors*, carefully revised, if you will be so good as to forward it to Harper & Bros. either through Albemarle Street or directly, or however your discretion may enjoin. It makes, as you will see—it goes separate from this—a bulky but not an unmanageable (I hope) packet. And I enclose herewith a letter which kindly send either with it or apart, as you think best—or return it to me, if you prefer, to post directly. I only wish to put it on witnessed record that I formally ask for duplicate *Proofs* of the serial, and that I as formally give warning that the volume is to contain a small quantity of additional matter. Believe me yours very truly

Henry James

To Hendrik C. Andersen
Ms Barrett

Lamb House, Rye
September 13th 1901

Dear, dear Hendrik!

Yes, your letter has been a joy, as I wired you this noon; I had rather dolefully begun to give you up, and I am now only sorry so many days must elapse before I see you. Don't, dearest boy, for heaven's sake, make them any more numerous than you need. Subject to that caution, I bow to your necessities, and can easily see that, for a week in London, you must have much to do. But make it, oh, make it, your advent, not a day later than Saturday 21st, will you not? I count on you intensely and immensely for *that* afternoon, when the 4.28 from Charing Cross, thoroughly handy for you, will (changing at Ashford) bring you here by 6.40, and I shall, at the station take very personal possession of you. You speak of being "free for a week" then—which is much less than I have been hoping of you; but I already put in an entreaty that the "week" shall terminate only (if it absolutely must even then) on Monday 30th. But I shall make you try to stretch it out further. However, we will talk of these things and of a million more—above [all] of all the blessed "good news" which, as you tell me, you've brought from Rome. I am eager for that. I am alone now—have been so this fortnight, and hope pretty confidently to be so while you are with me. You shall therefore have the best berth—such as that is—in the house: trust me for it. Put through your London jobs and mind your London ways: write me once more before you come, and come the first moment you can; and above all think of me as impatiently and tenderly yours

Henry James

To Jessie Allen
Ms Harvard

Lamb House, Rye
September 19*th* 1901

Dear bountiful and beautiful lady!

It is equally impossible to respond to you adequately and not to respond to you somehow. You flash your many-coloured lantern, over my small grey surface, from every corner of these islands and I sit blinking, gaping, clapping my hands, at the purple and orange tints to such a tune that I've scarce presence of mind left for an articulate "Thank you." How you keep it up, and how exactly you lead the life that, long years ago, when I was young, I used to believe a very, very few fantastically happy mortals on earth *could* lead, and could survive the bliss of leading—the waltz-like, rhythmic rotation from great country-house to great country-house, to the sound of perpetual music and the acclamation of the "house-parties" that gather to await you. You are the dream come true—you really do it, and I get the side-wind of the fairy-tale—which is more than I can really quite believe of myself—such a living—almost—*near* the rose! You make me feel near, at any rate, when you write me so kindly about the hideous American episode[1]—almost the worst feature of which is that I don't either like or trust the new President, a dangerous and ominous Jingo—of whom the most hopeful thing to say is that he may be rationalized by this sudden real responsibility. *Speriamo,* as we used to say in the golden age, in the heavenly mansion, along with the ministering angel, long, long ago. And all thanks meanwhile for your sympathetic thought. It must indeed—the base *success* of the act—cause a sinking of the heart among the potentates in circulation. One wonders, for instance, just now, who is most nervous, the poor little Tsar for himself or M. Loubet[2] for him. Let us thank our stars that we are not travelling stars, I not even a Loubet, nor you a Loubette, and that though we have many annoyances we are probably not marked for the dagger of the assassin.

20*th*, P.M.

I had to break off last night, and I resume—perhaps a trifle precariously at this midnight hour of what is just no longer Friday, but

202

about to be Saturday. I have seen, as it were, my two guests, and my tardy servants, to bed, and I put in again this illegible little talk with (poor) you! It has been a more convivial twenty-four hours than my general scheme of life often permits. A young American person (whom I've known from childhood) arrived yesterday afternoon. Two other American persons came down from town today to luncheon. At 4.45 I saw them off again (the childhood's friend helping—or rather, for that isn't it, the friend *while* herself, years ago, a child!) and by the same stroke met another guest—a British male. The British male and the childhood's friend I have now at last tucked into their respective apartments for the night—prior to the departure of the latter tomorrow A.M. But the British male remains, I seem to foresee till Monday. And tomorrow Saturday P.M. arrives another male, not British, but of mixed foreign and American origin[3]—while, pending these episodes, a below-stairs crisis that has been maturing fast for some time reaches, visibly, its acute stage. Such are the modest annals of Lamb House—or rather its daily and nightly chronicle. But don't let it depress you—for everything passes, and I bow my head to the whirlwind. But I hate the care of even a tiny and two penny house and wish I could farm out the same. If some one would only undertake it—and the backgarden—at so much a year I would close with the offer and ask no questions. I may still have to try Whiteley. But I shall try a winter in town first. I blush for my meagreness of response to all your social lights and shadows, your rich record of adventures.—I never saw our good Barbarites[4] again—I mean after my one glimpse just after their arrival. I spent a few hours in town early this month for a try, but they had then fled the Cork St. country with small reluctance I feel sure. They do cut out for themselves dreary summers in these parts! But one Barbaresque, one Angelic hour must make it all up! And if they have had—or are now (still) having Killarney in between—the parental sacrifice will have been still further sugared. Only I marvel at their fortitude—as exhibited at their age, the heroism that sustains them in a pilgrimage to the far, far island and through the grim tension of sojourning in the house of the mere, mere friend. *You* are capable of these exploits, but you haven't come to their years. Meanwhile it's manifest that what you gather of happy impressionism is inferior only to what you bestow. I am afraid I don't go to town till January 1st or so—but then to bide till May. I shall plant my feet in that interval very firmly indeed on your fender. *Con*found your "sick child"! What business has a sick child with ministers' caravansaries and railway stations—which is essentially the York mixture. If she is well enough for such exploits she is surely well enough to let you alone. But it's now—as usual over my letters—tomorrow A.M. (I mean 1 A.M.) and I am dear Miss Allen, very undecipherably but constantly yours,

Henry James

1. President McKinley died of his assassin's wounds on 14 September and was succeeded by Theodore Roosevelt.
2. Émile-François Loubet (1838–1929), President of the French Republic, had just received Tsar Nicholas II at Dunkirk.
3. The visitors were Lily Norton, Ida Higginson (who came only for lunch), the British journalist Bailey Saunders, and Hendrik Andersen.
4. The Daniel Curtises, in whose Palazzo Barbaro in Venice HJ had first met Jessie Allen.

To Mrs. William James
Ms Harvard

Lamb House, Rye
September 26th 1901

Dearest Alice.

It has been a joy to hear from you at last, for I've been as one who thirsted for your letter. William's, the day after you landed, stopped a little the gap, but your's of the 15th today received, and the enclosure of his to you from Chocorua, have set me again on my feet. I was, alas, afraid that the first bump up against the collective realities of home would be a shock that you would feel to your foundations, but that is an accident that is probably already more or less remedied by the lapse of the month, the improvement of the temperature and the rally of your friends—to say nothing of the return to order of your house. May these things all have happened, and the effect of them have been blessed. Your letter tells me much, and makes me deeply feel with you. I've missed you sore on my own side, and William has not more than I the sense of the beautiful vanished days. They have continued here, the beautiful days, of an exquisite quality, and all September has been worthy of the wonderful previous summer. That is for air and light and *general* sweetness; but I grieve to say Lamb House itself has been a scene of woe. The tidal wave I had long been expecting and dreading broke just a week ago—and has now, I am happy to say, spent its force. That is, the tragedy of the Doom of the Smiths has in the course of six or seven days been completely *acted* and is over.[1] The romance of sixteen years is closed, and I sit tonight amid the ruins it has left behind. The wretched S.'s departed on Monday last 23d, in charge, most blessedly, of her sister, who was within reach, at Ashford being wife to the gardener of the great little Alfred Austin,[2] the Laureate, who lives near thereby. I can't write you the details at all fully, though they would much interest you: they are so numerous and so miserable, and they have, all these last days, cost me so much precious time. Suffice it that the bottom fell out of the whole situation very suddenly at the last, though (after a delusive dream of going on a little longer, after my return from seeing you off) each successive day had been making me feel it looser. On the 18th Lily Norton came down to me for two nights, and the next day Ida Higginson joined her here, from town, for luncheon etc. That afternoon (19th) Bailey Saunders, my friend whom you'll remember, was to come, for three days, over from Eastbourne, and on the morrow I was expecting—also for three or four days—our young Norwegian Andersen, from Rome. The moment therefore was favourable and Smith, who had been more or less drunk and helpless each day and *all* day for many previous, was *most* so on this complicated occasion. I got, however, both Mrs. Higginson and Lily off without their suspecting the dire *dessous* of the situation, and Saunders and dear young A. remained with me through it and were really a comfort in my dismals. For when once one really *touched* it the whole fabric crumbled and the wretched creatures utterly collapsed. It was exactly as if they had been hanging but by a thread, and a breath had caused them to drop. Smith was *accumulatedly* so drunk that I got him out of the house—i.e. all Friday Saturday and Sunday—that though I had Skinner to him to medicate him I could really not communicate with him to the extent of a word, any more than with his wife, whom I made over wholly to her own sister. The latter, a most excellent superior little woman, came over on Saturday afternoon with her husband, stayed till Monday and took them off on that day, having packed, hard, all their accumulations of years etc. in the interval. She was in complete sympathy with me, as she couldn't but be, and was quite overwhelmed in presence of the revelations. When once the waters are opened the floods come up, and the revelations are sad—quite dreadful. The S.'s have had, all the years they've lived with me, excellent wages and *no* expenses—not even for clothes, for she has, it appears, bought none, for years (it was one reason she never left the house), and he has had all his from *me*. But it appears that they've not saved a single penny, and as they've done nothing else whatever with the money, they've simply, while in my service, spent hundreds and hundreds of pounds in drink—and left me still in debt for it. Mrs. Ticknor (the sister), producing at the last—under pressure from me—a bill of more than three pounds to a dealer here for liquor just lately supplied, which they were unable to pay; and this though they had had £5.00 from me within the month! They were, at the end, simply two saturated and demoralized victims, with not a word to say for themselves and going in silence to their doom; but great is the miracle of their having been, all the while, the admirable servants they were and whom I shall ever unutterably mourn and miss. Day before yesterday I went up to town and out to Walthamstow to get hold of his brother and make *him* take Smith himself off the hands of the Ticknors. By an equal blessing, he is as good a person as they (the T.'s) and is also a gardener—the keeper of the cemetery of the place, and he agreed to do his part; that is to come down to Ashford yesterday and remove the wretched S. This will have been done yesterday, so that they are each now in the hands of their respective relatives. It's an extraordinary "Providence" that they *had* any—otherwise my case would have indeed been queer. There would have [been] nowhere to put them—nohow to displace them. As it is of course I pay!—having (most profusely, as I now feel, *on* their rottenness) promised them a liberal allowance—an almost foolishly liberal one—weekly, for two months, to be paid to the sister and the brother, and two months' wages as well—"till they can turn round." They will never turn round; they are lost, utterly; but I would have promised *anything,* in my desire to get them out of the house before some still more hideous helplessness made it impossible. A new place is impossible to either; they wouldn't keep it three days; and their deplorable incriminating aspect alone damns them beyond appeal. What they looked like going to the Station! Mrs. Smith hadn't a "rag to her back"; I mean nothing to put on to be seen in—and it was, in short (I mean the whole episode has been) a perfect nightmare of distress, disgust and inconvenience. As a climax of the latter I sit here tonight without a servant, to call a servant, in the house. Little housemaid and the gnome Burgess,[3] with Mrs. Bourn, who sleeps here, to keep Fanny company, do what they can for me, and I get dinner at the Mermaid; but it's a return to first principles, and I miss Mrs. Smith's cuisine and Smith's hourly ministrations, with a sinking of the heart. I want to rub along here, somehow to January 1st, but I can't find—anyway get—here a cook or a parlourmaid that will carry me on, and yet to dive into the deep and dangerous sea of London rather appalls me. These last days, render[ing] all work (till this A.M. again) impossible, have made a shocking hole in my time—so that the thought of going up to town and putting in *more* precious sequences of hours almost makes me want to close the house and bolt altogether. But I shall do as I can, and I am ashamed of this preposterous long story as well as of my puerile wail. I treat you to so much detail (in spite of my saying I couldn't), on account of your interest in all the conditions. Alas, I've learned from Mrs. Bourn and Fanny since the event how much worse than I knew some of them had long been. Pray for me, but don't despair of me; and I will do as much, on my side, and as little, for you. Give my tender love to William and tell him to lift up his heart!—I mean till the blander course of events, with the lapse of the days and the subsidence of mere change, has taken him in hand. Change *as* change can be, alas, as baleful as it can be blissful. I am ravaged by your anecdote of Pegg's *beaux jours*. But tell her, with all her old uncle's fond love, that they are *not* passed—that we shall have them again and very much better; or at least, if that's too much to hope, quite as good. I hope that by this time Billy is with you and long for your news of him. Likewise of Francis,[4] whom you don't mention, though you do Jack Randall. Also do give me news of your mother. I ask these things shamelessly, knowing that you too are perhaps even still servantless and upheaved, but so greatly clinging to the silver cord of—well, of our last two years. But it's—yet again—1.15 A.M., and I am, dearest Alice, your ever affectionate

Henry

1. The Smiths, husband and wife, had been HJ's faithful servants for the past sixteen years. Their collapse into alcoholism had been accelerated by the move from De Vere Gardens to Lamb House. See letter to Navarro, 15 June 1898.

2. Alfred Austin (1835–1913), Poet Laureate since 1896, lived in Kent, near Ashford, the junction point for Rye.

3. HJ's bantamweight houseboy, Burgess Noakes.

4. Over HJ's protestations WJ had named his youngest son, born in 1890, Francis Tweedy James, in honor of family friends, the Edmund Tweedys (see *Letters* I, 21). In later years Francis renamed himself Alexander Robertson, choosing (as HJ had proposed) old James family names.

To Sarah Orne Jewett
Ms Harvard

Lamb House, Rye
October 5*th* 1901

Dear Miss Jewett.[1]

Let me not criminally, or at all events gracelessly, delay to thank you for your charming and generous present of *The Tory Lover*. He has been but three or four days in the house, yet I have given him an earnest, a pensive, a liberal—yes, a benevolent attention, and the upshot is that I should like to write you a longer letter than I just now—(especially as it's past midnight) see my way to doing. For it would take me some time to disembroil the tangle of saying to you at once how I appreciate the charming touch, tact and taste of this ingenious exercise, and how little I am in sympathy with the experiments of its general (to my sense) misguided stamp. There I am!—yet I don't do you the outrage, as a fellow craftsman and a woman of genius and courage, to suppose you not as conscious as I am myself of all that, in these questions of art and truth and sincerity, is beyond the mere twaddle of graciousness. The "historic" novel is, for me, condemned, even in cases of labour as delicate as yours, to a fatal *cheapness*, for the simple reason that the difficulty of the job is inordinate and that a mere *escamotage,* in the interest of ease, and of the abysmal public *naiveté* becomes inevitable. You may multiply the little facts that can be got from pictures and documents, relics and prints, as much as you like—*the* real thing is almost impossible to do, and in its essence the whole effect is as nought: I mean the invention, the representation of the old CONSCIOUSNESS, the soul, the sense, the horizon, the vision of individuals in whose minds half the things that make ours, that make the modern world were non-existent. You have to *think* with your modern apparatus a man, a woman—or rather fifty—whose own thinking was intensely otherwise conditioned, you have to simplify back by an amazing *tour de force*—and even then it's all humbug.

208

But there is a shade of the (even then) humbug that *may* amuse. The childish tricks that take the place of any such conception of the real job in the flood of Tales of the Past that seems of late to have been rolling over our devoted country—these ineptitudes have, on a few recent glances, struck me as creditable to no one concerned. You, I hasten to add, seem to me to have steered very clear of them—to have seen your work very bravely and handled it firmly; but even you court disaster by composing the whole thing so much by sequences of speeches. It's when the extinct soul talks, and the earlier consciousness airs itself, that the pitfalls multiply and the "cheap" way has to serve. I speak in general, I needn't keep insisting, and I speak grossly, summarily, by rude and provisional signs, in order to suggest my sentiment at all. I don't mean to say so much without saying more, and now I have douched you with cold water when I only meant just lightly and kindly to sprinkle you as for a new baptism—that is a *re*-dedication to altars but briefly, I trust, forsaken. Go back to the dear country of the *Pointed Firs, come* back to the palpable present-*intimate* that throbs responsive, and that wants, misses, needs you, God knows, and that suffers woefully in your absence. Then I shall feel perhaps—and do it if only *for* that—that you have magnanimously allowed for the want of gilt on the gingerbread of the but-on-this-occasion-*only* limited sympathy of yours very constantly,

Henry James

P.S. My tender benediction, please, to Mrs. Fields.[2]

1. Miss Jewett had sent HJ her historical novel. This letter shows HJ explaining that he sometimes writes "the mere twaddle of graciousness," but refusing to do so for the author of *The Country of the Pointed Firs* (1896).
2. See letter to Mrs. Fields, 5 September 1898.

To Rudyard Kipling
Ts Harvard

Lamb House, Rye
October 30*th* 1901

My dear Rudyard.

I can't lay down *Kim*[1] without wanting much to write to you: absolutely and most gratefully, coercive in that direction is, in fact, your magnificent book. And yet to write is to try to bridge such a dreadful interval of separation and silence that I almost feel as if I mightn't reach you—I mean as if the lapse in our commerce at the best so hindered (by the perversity that Rye isn't Rottingdean, nor Rottingdean Rye) were a thing of positive impenetrable thicknesses. I've a horrid sense that I've stupidly let these thicknesses grow (through a couple of crowded, complicated anxious summers etc., among other recent matters): though I shall in a moment assure you, properly, how little heart I've had to do that. I must in the first place simply *penetrate*, at any cost, so that here goes—and I beseech you to feel the silence in question crumble and send up a golden dust.

I overflow, I beg you to believe, with *Kim*, and I rejoice in such a saturation, such a splendid dose of you. That has been the great thing, I find; that one could sink deep and deep, could sit in you up to one's neck. Inevitably, at my age, and with the habits and arrears of my craft, I read with comment and challenge, in face of the material; in other words I have some small reserves and anxieties— as to your frequent *how* of performance. But these things haven't mattered. They floated away like upset boats and drowned sages in the current; and I've surrendered luxuriously to your genius. Don't scoff at me, nor let Mrs. Carrie scoff, nor your children (who must be pretty well up to scoffing age now), when I tell you that I take you as you are. It might be that I wished you were quite different— though I don't. I should still, after this, just fatalistically take you. You are too sublime—you are too big and there is too much of you. I don't think you've cut out your subject, in *Kim* with a sharp enough scissors, but with that one little nut cracked—so!—the beauty, the quantity, the prodigality, the Ganges-flood, leave me simply gaping as your procession passes. What a luxury to *possess* a big subject as you possess India; or, to pat you still more on the head, what a cause of just pride! I find the boy himself a dazzling conception, but I find the Lama more yet—a thing damnably and splendidly *done*. Bravo, bravo, Lama, from beginning to end, and bravo, bravo, the whole idea, the great many-coloured poem of their relation and their wild Odyssey—void of a false note and swarming with felicities that you can count much better than I. The way you make the general picture live and sound and shine, all by a myriad touches that are like the thing itself pricking through with a little snap—that makes me want to say to you: "Come, all else is folly—sell all you have and give to the poor!" By which I mean chuck public affairs,[2] which are an ignoble scene, and stick to your canvas and your paint-box. There are as good colours in the tubes as ever were laid on, and *there* is the only truth. The rest is base humbug. Ask the Lama.

Ask the Lama too, while you are about it, why you shouldn't come over to see me some merciful day when it would give me joy and support. Direct signals to this effect have long failed me: I've known of you, for half the year, nothing but that—these three winters, hideously, isn't it?—you've been overseas and beyond my imagination; and the other half, that is, for these three summers, I've known nothing of *anything* outside my anxiously-applied domestic consciousness, or in other words the walls of my house or garden, by reason of the constant pressure of my brother William and his fortunes, his ill condition, his wife and his, always, youngster or two (mainly a youngstress, Peggy). He has been long and wearily ill, and still isn't much other, and my existence has had that for pivot and centre. But he has lately returned to America, and I seem of late to have looked more over the wall. As I say, I wish I could pull *you* over it hitherward—you being, immediately, the largest animated object my searchlight rests upon. I only have a sinking sense that you accept no invitation for anything further than South Africa for the moment; also, I sit among the ruins of a smashed household—having had lately the pleasure of losing two servants, a man and wife; who had lived with me for sixteen years (and whom I finally dispensed with in sixteen hours); otherwise I would make my appeal straight to Mrs. Carrie. I go up to town after Christmas; to remain till May, and if so be it that you don't migrate again, this year, too headlong, I shall ask your leave to come down, one of the very first days, from the comparatively thinkable Victoria. Cross country journeys *hence*—save for return the following year—are superlatively unthinkable. Till Christmas I shall be occupied grinding my teeth and breaking my heart over the finish of a book[3] promised for January 1st, and on which my already oft-perjured life depends. Please take this ugly scrawl, meanwhile and plead with your wife to take it, as my issue from the longest tunnel in the world. I haven't, for months, looked at the serried row of the presentation copies, so richly bedight, that I owe you both, right and left—for I travel with the whole shelf, and in the tunnels they serve to read by—without feeling that, thus constantly and admirably addressed by you, I ought to be eternally, since I can't be anything like as eloquently—replying. I needn't tell you how much I hope you are both personally sound and scatheless, and that I involve you all in the affectionate interest of yours, my dear Rudyard, very constantly,

Henry James

1. *Kim* had just been published.
2. Kipling's patriotic verses about the Boer war.
3. *The Wings of the Dove.*

To Graham Balfour
Ms Scotland

Lamb House, Rye
November 15th 1901

Dear Graham Balfour.

Into my rural backwater books float a bit slowly and circuitously, so that it is only this evening that I have, after delayed acquisition, finished with emotion, your two admirable volumes.[1] But having done so, I can't delay to write to you, many though I feel the letters to be that they will have already piled up in your path. I reflect with pleasure, however, that not one of these can contain a grain of intelligent animadversion. I wondered how—in all the exciting conditions—you would find it possible to give the book the element of freshness, or in fact to do it with coherency at all; but so far as I did foresee you safely in port, you are there very much in the form—very solidly and successfully in it—that I supposed you to have in your mind. And the achieved and rounded thing is a thing, I think, to congratulate you on very heartily. You strike me as having shown infinite taste, discretion, happiness of touch and sense of proportion, and in particular, as having admirably *composed* or distributed it—with, moreover, a constantly fine and charming art of expression. The subject of course is nothing if not interesting, but your treatment has also an interest of its own, and I hope you feel that you have put up a very fair and shapely monument. Fanny Stevenson and Lloyd O.[2] must feel it, and I enter deeply into all it must be for you to know that you have gratified *her*. I shall immediately write to her—reading you makes *that* irresistible. It's in the second volume of course that your chance opens out, and I rejoice that as to the islands and Vailima³ you could take it so lucidly. (I had never understood his whole previous—to V.—mixed itinerary, and you in a manner make me.) Beautiful verily, furthermore, your final chapter—I mean your high and eloquent, but controlled summing up, your characterization from knowledge. The whole thing, the whole renewal of contact and revival of sight of him has greatly affected me, bringing back so the various wonder of him—so that one feels, as anew, *stricken;* and that is really the last thing your book makes one want to say. There are other things, other and different consequences (of all the cumulative publicity and commemoration) that make the critical spirit in me put a question; but the general emotion floats them away and brushes the question by—so at least *I* find. The question really is, however, for the critical spirit, whether Louis' work itself doesn't *pay* somewhat for the so complete exhibition of the man and the life. You may say that the work was, or *is*, the man and the life—as well; still, the books are jealous and a certain supremacy and mystery (above all) has, as it were, gone from them. The achieved legend and history that has *him* for subject, has made so to speak, light of *their* subjects, of their claim to represent him. In other words you have made him—everything has made him—too *personally* celebrated for his literary legacy. He had of course only to be then himself less picturesque, and none of us who knew him would have had him so by an inch. But the fact remains that the *exhibition* that has overtaken him has helped, and that he is thus as artist and creator in some degree the victim of himself. I speak as from the literary vision, the vision for which the rarest works pop out of the dusk of the inscrutable, the untracked. However, as I say, we must take R.L.S. as we now inevitably have him, all *together,* and all drenched with light—for the collective bunch, so, is splendid. And—I didn't mean to make so much of my point—it being past midnight and too late for me to make more! I've rejoiced to see how the book has sold. I am ashamed to say I shall have to send this c/o Methuen—having lost your Oxford address and mistrusting always mere post office wit. I don't deserve to know what news you have of Fanny S.—too silent have I been, too little attention shown. But

I really write now. Believe me, my dear Balfour, yours very grate-fully

Henry James

1. *Life of Robert Louis Stevenson* by Graham Balfour (1858–1929), published in October 1901.
2. Fanny Van de Grift Stevenson, the author's widow, and Lloyd Osbourne, Fanny's son by her first marriage.
3. Vailima, meaning "five waters," was the Stevensons' house in Samoa.

To W. Morton Fullerton
Ms Harvard

Lamb House, Rye
November 17*th* 1901

My dear Fullerton.

I retort, you see, without mercy;—I let myself go, and for the simple pleasure of reaching out to you in my solitude. This is tolerably unqualified in these days, and I can't *not* grasp at the golden apple of conversation with you—even though I get but a single bite—when the bough thus bends before me. It cheats a little the unamiable *fact*—the fact, I mean, that we are practically never together. So *let* it, for the moment—all too brief—cheat and cheat and cheat. I like your speaking to me, out of your wisdom, of my *Cornhill*-dosified Rostand;[1] and I need scarcely make the point that my "like" is not the like of slang, but that's, simply, of the old tender passion. *Vous parlez d'or*—but of course *I* couldn't in my British backwater; and there would have been no possibility there of a really ironic article. One can but dosify ever so tinily. I like (*now* it's ironic) your thinking, out of the *raffinement* of your re-finement, that one can say ten intelligible words, in this country, of the sort that are in solution (in their thousands) in the common-est air of criticism *autour de vous*. My little paper, I am sure, though no sort of echo of it has reached me, passes for fantastic up to the very limit. As for doing more, I will gladly do anything any one asks me—but almost no one ever does ask. Sidney Lee,[2] who deals much with the *Cornhill*, demanded of me the Rostand—which I wasn't eager to write, and I would, so emboldened, [have] proposed to him a Hervieu[3] on some early occasion, were it not that the discussion of H. inevitably exposes itself to difficulty in the

Smith and Elder circle,[4] through being almost impossible, save in the terms of the rankest adultery. *Vous en parlez à votre aise,* young heir not only of all the ages but of all the subjects. But if, as I seem to understand, *L'Énigme* is to be in the next *R[evue] de Paris* and you can put your hand on a copy of the same for my benefit, you would by so doing, warm up a lonely evening for me here not a little. And why not, by a still prompter post, send me the "psychologic" documents you speak of? You speak darkly, but you speak handsomely, and I will try piously to read into them everything you don't tell me about yourself. Furthermore I will immediately send you by anticipation and compensation a photograph for which even in that bristling little *salottino* of yours you may still find a hook— or at least an eye. It's admirable of my brother—but inferior of me, whom it causes to resemble her late Britannic majesty. *Je suis mieux que ça.* Still even of me it has merit. I am working here (to be plain with you) with extreme continuity—though my things *percer* so slowly. I've lately finished a long novel—delayed by the vulgarest Harper-"serialization," and am almost finishing another, which Will Meredith is to publish by the winter's end.[5] I have just done a Flaubert for an amazing Heinemann-translation series, and am as soon as possible to do a Balzac for the same.[6] I did ages ago a G. Sand on the basis of those so queer and interesting two vols. of *Russian Life* you helped me to buy that last hot summer day in Paris, but the *N.A. Review* has never yet published it. Such, in these *parages* is the glory of literature—and of *votre serviteur.* But I tear myself from you. Goodnight. Yours always

Henry James

1. In the *Cornhill Magazine* and the *Critic,* November 1901.

2. Sidney Lee (1859–1926), editor of the *Dictionary of National Biography* since 1891.

3. Paul Ernest Hervieu (1857–1915) wrote plays on domestic conflicts. *La Course du flambeau* (1901) was well received. *L'Énigme,* dealing with infidelity, was performed at the Théâtre Français on 5 November.

4. In addition to publishing the *Dictionary of National Biography,* Smith and Elder controlled the *Pall Mall Gazette* and the *Cornhill.* Sidney Lee, as editor of the latter, would not accept articles dealing with sexual promiscuity and adultery—the subjects of Hervieu's plays.

5. *The Ambassadors* and *The Wings of the Dove.*

6. HJ's prefaces to Flaubert and Balzac were included in *Notes on Novelists* (1914). Also included was the essay on George Sand, published in the *North American Review* (April 1902).

To Mrs. W. K. Clifford
Ts Lubbock

Lamb House, Rye
Friday P.M. December 13 1901

Dearest Lucy C.

I found your letter here after a somewhat belated return—that is on Wednesday night—Tuesday having been occupied with a pilgrimage—oh, so cold and sad, but so glad to *be*, at all!—down to dear old George Meredith at Boxhill; and in the evening with a call on Elizabeth Robins[1] (of which anon). I ought to have seen you after the play[2] but it was too scantly manageable—and what there is to say will keep well; I shan't forget it. (I really quite yearn, now, for town, and will come up at the first possible hour after January 5th.) I am greatly touched and interested by your expression of your feeling as agonized author-mother—which is very vivid and eloquent, though making me fear my note found you on a day of temporary disillusionment, or whatever. Oh, the days of temporary disillusionment—when by a mercy it *is* temporary! With me it's in permanence, and the stuff of all days; though I too am an author-mother, or at least, as harder-hearted over my young 'uns, an author-stepmother.

The "house" was very decent indeed on Monday, the stalls only *slightly* spotted with absences, and the back parts of the theatre, I thought, extremely well occupied. For an un-papered house it was perfectly honourable. Mrs. Leopold Rothschild and the Austrian Ambassador near me. I can't go now into the question of where I think the play halts—for I think the *subject* halts, to begin with, through our over-familiarity with the sentimental, the tragic side of the "double life" (as Chrissie[3] used to call it—of her own!). Also there are other things, but we will talk them over by a January fire. They are not of the essence—the essence (I mean of logic, interest, straightness, *effect*) is all of the best. One of them, e.g., is that the scheme of the wife's suicide, scheme of the steamer etc., has its unfortunate side, and the passage between the Kendals[4] in the saloon (though much *her* best bit of acting) inexorably loses intimacy and concentration from the locality, their queer unnatural privacy there etc. And that doesn't come from the K.'s having made the supernumeraries meagre, *more* supers would have been a still

216

greater detraction. But a truce to piecemeal remarks—all the more that my arrears of letters, on my return, are maddening. I only wanted to cheer you up if you are down, and if you are up, why then to cheer you upper. The other night showed me that you have, distinctly and preciously—by which I mean valuably—a *hearing:* you're *inside,* for a fresh go. And don't say the farcical comedy alone will do: the thing is the Drama of Life!—objective and ironic. And *without* Mrs. K., the most preposterous lamb of sacrifice that ever was seen on earth! She's the *butcher,* not the mutton. Elizabeth R., stout (almost *fat*) handsome, brilliant, charming, and returning I think every way to the charge. Ethel's Broceliande[5] verses the other night full, really, of poetry and mystery. I prefer them—ever—to anything, *any* news, correspondence, or editorial talent in any paper whatever. Goodnight, and brandish your spear! Ever yours,

Henry James

1. Elizabeth Robins (1863–1952), the American actress. See *Letters* III, 341.

2. Mrs. Clifford's play, *The Likeness of the Night,* ran at the St. James's from 20 October to 21 December.

3. Mrs. Rogerson. See letter to Mrs. Clifford, 24 January 1900.

4. William Hunter Kendal (1843–1917) and his wife, Madge (1849–1935), had the leading roles in Mrs. Clifford's play.

5. Ethel, Mrs. Clifford's daughter, later Lady Dilke. Broceliande refers to the mysterious and magical forest in Brittany, in the Arthurian legend, where Merlin was enchanted by Vivian.

To Henrietta Reubell
Ms Harvard

Lamb House, Rye
December 15th 1901

Dearest Etta Reubell.

It's a very sorry showing that I should be only today—or tonight (for my correspondence, in my declining years, becomes more and more nocturnal), thanking you for your beautiful kind letter of weeks and weeks ago. But somehow my gracelessness isn't *all* gracelessness, and *this* is very much what has happened. I waited, first, for the pleasure of looking forward to my letter and for that of leaving you to feel for awhile that you had written last, that I was in your debt, not you in mine, and that in short I hadn't with tactless promptitude turned up again on your hands. Only I *then,* accidentally, overdid my tact—was swept away by the current of life, swift even in this small backwater, past the date at which I judged I might gracefully appear before you. That *would* have been at least a month ago. It has taken me this month to fish myself out of the rapids. But a truce to explanations. They never explain. The only explanation between old friends is old affection. Well, mine for you is absolutely antique. It was *that* that didn't answer you. And the devil is that, as, perhaps, if I had written to you weeks ago I shouldn't be writing now, why, I bless my present pleasure, however *made* present. But I ought, the more, therefore, to have better things to tell you than this. The difficulty is that *au village* we have so little to tell—and I am positively *au village*. It more and more meets my bill, and I find myself reducing my time in London to three or four months in the year. I stay now till January 10th, and then depart—for town—but till the first days of May. I wish I could depart for *your parages*—but Paris is more and more to me of a cold, bright dream. *Speriamo purè*—for a better day. It's deadly dull *au village* at this season—but that is just one of my reasons for liking it. The autumn and winter charm of the country is the evenings—selfish and anti-social, with the firelight, the lamplight and the book—and always the same. It's rapture—a still unexhausted one (after long years of London), never to dine out. The weak point here, on the other hand, is the almost total absence of society—in the sense of three or four pleasant people to talk with, especially an agreeable woman or so, like yourself, *à quoi demander une tasse de thé*. On the other hand where *should* I find an agreeable woman or so, like yourself? It isn't as if I were really missing—through mistaken arrangements—what 42 Avenue Gabriel[1] only can offer. The only company one does get is what one has under one's roof—the inmate and the "stayer." Now the stayer, let me tell you, if you don't intimately know it, is at best more or less of a vampire. One's life, before him, and not less before *her*—especially when one is lone and singlehanded to meet the assault—goes quite to pieces. But I think you do intimately know it. Do you remember young Jonathan Sturges? *He* comes down on the 20th to remain till the *Nouvel An—pour le moins*. But he is full of talk and intelligence, and of the absence of prejudice, and is saturated with London, and with all sorts of contrasted elements of it; to which he has given himself up. Handicapped, crippled, invalidical, he has yet made his way there in a wondrous fashion, and knows nine thousand people, of most of whom *I've* never heard. So he's amusing, and to him (as I'm very fond of him), I make sacrifices. But they *are* sacrifices. I've just made another—that of going for a week's visit (a thing of the rarest with me now, so that I've just refused the Duchess of Sutherland—repeat it not!—to come to Trentham for the New Year) to a very ill American friend[2] at Torquay, where there was in the house a most *bavarde* and yet pleasant Mrs. Rives née Bininger (a sister of Mrs. Fred Post), now settled as a thrifty but horsey widow somewhere near Windsor.[3] I mention her because you may remember her from old Paris days, and because she was very amusing and lurid on the subject of the *new*, the second American duchess of Manchester, *née* Zimmerman, who had just been to see her, at home, with the little rotten twopenny Duke;[4] but it's too long a story to tell with justice to all its grotesquenesses. There was also in the house (at Torquay) old Mrs. Sands[5] (my hostess's, Mrs. Godkin's, and Harry S.'s mother), and she told me that the said Harry's apartment or rather *house*, in the Queen's Gardens where she had just been for a month with him, is to be so renovated and modernised and be-lifted etc., that the rise in the rent must send him—though so old a *locataire*—forth into the world. That makes me wonder about you. Are *you* to be revolutionized and be-lifted? Heaven forbid! I would *rather* palpitate on your stair than mount rocket like. Every pant is consecrated by tender associations. I believe, moreover, neither that they'll "rise on" you, nor rise *to* you— nor that you will dream of going forth. You'll "stay," like *my* friends, on your own terms, and they'll keep you (and be proud of it), as their private vampire. Forgive, meanwhile, the gross egotisms of the greater part of the foregoing. I feel you care more for my news—or would if I had any—than for vague ejaculations from me on your own. You wrote me from your usual Caux, after your usual Mrs. Shaw, who must be more usual by this time than ever. You are as faithful to her as she is to life—both of you in spite of everything. I read over your letter—meet your mention of Boit[6] at Vallombrosa etc., where he kindly asked me for last July–September. I spent a summer there eight or nine years ago, and the ingenuity and audacity of their making it a torrid *villeggiatura* from Paris leaves me confounded. But we live in a confounding age. I'm trying to think if I've seen any of your friends within any calculable time. Hamilton Aïdé[7] spent a couple of days with me early in the summer—75, still singing, and now starting for Egypt. He is fabulous. Practically about 55. Alma Harrison[8] last spring—having come (through Peter) into money and a pleasant old house in the country—which I knew (in Suffolk, close to the sea) before they had it. Her general cleverness comes out there strongly, I judge, in her brilliant gardening—the most diffused talent, one finds if one lives in the country, of the women, even the stupidest, of this land. They are natural gardeners—whereas I remain, as neither a woman nor a Britain, a most hopeless unnatural one. But goodnight, dear old friend; *felicissima notte*. I needn't tell you I pray for your health, your happiness, your New Year, and all that is yours. *I* am so, and that is the best guarantee for (affectionately)

Henry James

P.S. If you haven't done so you must absolutely read the two moderate sized volumes of Funck-Brentano:[9] 1/ *Affaire du Collier.* 2/ *La Mort de la Reine.* They *font comprendre* the French Revolution.

1. Miss Reubell's home in Paris.
2. E. L. Godkin.
3. Amélie Rives (1863–1945), Virginia-born novelist, who married the Russian Prince Troubetzkoy.
4. Helena Zimmerman, American heiress. See Hesketh Pearson, *The Marrying Americans* (1961).
5. Godkin had married his second wife, Katherine Sands, in 1884.
6. Edward Darley Boit, American painter. See *Letters* I, 356.
7. Charles Hamilton Aïdé (1826–1906), a Londoner of versatile accomplishments and familiar figure in society. See *Letters* III, 19.
8. Alma Harrison, the former Alma Stretell. See letter to Mrs. Ward, 15 March 1901.
9. Frantz Funck-Brentano (1862–1947), French historian.

To Violet Hunt
Ms Barrett

Lamb House, Rye
January 16*th* 1902

My dear Violet.

No, I am not yet in the field; but I come up to town on February 1st when I will immediately make you overtures for one of those so pleasant little talks in Sackville Street—which I like to "place," periodically. All thanks meanwhile for your so graceful remark about the poor dear old *Ambassadors*, by which I am touched, but which I was not writing when you were here. The *A's* were finished three, or more, years ago (before the *W. of the D.* were written), and had a long serialization in an American Review (hence the XII so marked "parts"). You are right about Mme de Vionnet's visit to Mrs. P[ocock], it gave her away and was intended to have for the reader that indirectly reaching virtue. Maria G. is, dissimulatedly, but a *ficelle*,[1]—with a purely functional value, to help me to expose Strether's situation, constantly, in the dramatic and scenic way, without elementary explanations and the horrid novelist's "Now you must know that—." She is not of the subject. Mme de V. *is*, of course, "of" the subject. But Strether *is* the subject, the subject itself. But we will talk of these interesting things. As for the already great bouncing *teething* New Year, *je vous la souhaite bonne et douce.* Yours always

Henry James

1. HJ explains the term *ficelle*—stage-trick—in his preface to *The Ambassadors* (New York Edition, XXI). His *ficelle* was Maria Gostrey, a character specifically created as a way of conveying information to the reader that would not otherwise be available unless the author himself intervened to explain. The *ficelle* was the "reader's friend" and "an enrolled, a direct, aid to lucidity," a puppet-creation for functional use that at the same time became a fully animated personage.

To William Dean Howells
Ms Harvard

Lamb House, Rye
January 25*th* 1902

My dear Howells.

It's a wonderful state of things that I am in your debt for two letters and that for the first in particular—the charming one at the summer's end, long months ago—my failure to make sign of payment—has been aggravated and odious. It's useless to attempt to excuse or palliate such baseness; there *are*, I daresay, attenuating circumstances—but my exquisite literary art, even, I fear, would fail to make them worthy of your consideration. There is only one of them that I'll mention. That I'm *going* to write to you is always a delicious thought to me, which I hug and cherish even as the prospect of some joy, some social joy, to come: only I know not *what* social joy, in my battered age, casts so graceful a shadow before. At all events there has been that amount of preliminary gloating to stay my hand. After all, however, I do gloat over *having* written you, as well, and this I am proposing to do an hour or two hence. Your most kind communication, meanwhile, in respect to the miraculously coloured "uptown" apartment-house has at once deeply agitated and wildly uplifted me. The agitation, as I call it, is airily but the tremor, intensity of hope, of the delirious dream that such a stroke may "bring my books before the public," or do something toward it—coupled with the reassertion of my constant, too constant, conviction that no power on earth can ever do that. They are *behind*, irremovably behind, the public, and fixed there for my lifetime at least; and as the public hasn't eyes in the back of its head, and scarcely even in the front, no consequences can ensue. The Henry James,[1] I opine, will be a terrifically "private" hotel, and will languish, like the Lord of Burleigh's wife, under the burden of an honour "unto which it was not born." Refined, liveried, "two-toileted," it will have been a short-lived, hectic paradox, and will presently have to close in order to reopen as the Mary Johnston or the K[ate] Wiggin or the James Lane Allen.[2] Best of all as the Edith Wharton! Still, your advertisement gave me an hour of whirling rapture, against which I almost began to draw cheques. Then, in a vision I saw the thing catching the eye of my multitudinous publishers and *in* the eye I distinguished benevolent pity. They never have any for *me*, but I feel they are now having it, amusedly, for their floundering fellow-speculator.—Very interesting as well, and scarce less tormenting—I mean in the way of making my mouth vainly water—the rest of your present letter, with its record of "big-sellers" to come, for you, or, what is almost as good, a prevision of "big-sellers" among the seats of the mighty. May the prevision be resoundingly made good. I am delighted at any rate that you are not, as your letter of the autumn rather sadly portended, letting fiction slip away from you. All success to your *risorgimento!* I await with barely decent patience the advent both of the serialized and the *lump* production.[3] You remain the sole and single novelist of English speech, now producing, whom I read— read the more, therefore, with concentrated passion. Where then should I be without you? The *little* American tale-tellers (I mean the two or three women) become impossible to me the moment

222

they lengthen. Mary Wilkins I have found no better than any other Mary, in the fat volume; and dear Sarah Jewett sent me not long since a Revolutionary Romance, with officers over their wine etc., and Paul Jones terrorizing the sea, that was a thing to make the angels weep.[4] You wrote me of some inky maiden in the West, I think, who was superseding these ladies, but I watch for her in vain, and beg you to direct her to me.—Àpropos of which articles (of diminutive fiction) you responded in your autumn letter to some remarks of mine—some, I fear, unmanly groans, on the subject of my difficulty in bringing my own diminutives to light; citing certain things of yours that had waited, in periodicals, ever so long. Your instances *were* very edifying—and the thing has no importance, save that I feel I appeared, seemingly, to have groaned out of tune. I didn't in the least mean that I was surprised at the small hospitality offered to things of 14,000, 15,000 words etc.; for of that I long since sounded the depths. My surprise (over my own case) was wholly in respect to things of six, seven, eight thousand words (I do no others now). Artfully—and oh, so difficultly—constructed of those dimensions, to conciliate the fastidious editor, they none the less languish in the dark backward for periods of two years at a time. I just observed advertized in the February *Scribner* a tiny thing that was "accepted" at a date remote by nearly that amount of time;[5] and my moral is all that even its tininess didn't smooth the way—more than this—for it. You'll say that they might perfectly have refused it altogether, and when I reflect that that is gruesomely true, I doubly wonder why I fall—*have* fallen—into this strain of vain interrogation (say) of the silent stars—as if you pretended to speak for them! It is only that in reading over your older letter just now, I found first your passage relating your own experience. And little must any individual experience abide with you, or weigh for you, amid such a wealth of production. I marvel at the quantity of your work, and at what I venture to suppose the facility by which it *has* in some degree to be explained. You are magnificent, at any rate, and make me feel stranded and afar— I mean, in especial, by your journalistic abundance. When *I* try journalism—but I never *do!* (There I was at it again—so I'll *pretend* I never do.) The rest of your summer's end letter, about your Maine ways and Maine woods, was very grateful to me, and I felt, almost resentfully, that it was *I* who ought to have been with you when you went astray with your young parson, over the haunted house, and *not* the young parson—if young he was—whose familiarity (with you) I tend to resent. There are no woods to get lost in here—though there *are* young parsons; with whom, however, I don't associate—so that I try to find it your one symptom of a compromised fortune that you are reduced to them in Maine. I should view a long drive with one—of the hereabouts pattern—as a confession of despair. However, that takes explanations—which wouldn't be interesting.—I scribble to you thus interminably, late, very late, at night—my only letter-writing time. A wild southwest gale howls round my old house, and I hear the lash of the rain in the intervals of the wind. My lamp burns still, my servants are long since at roost, and my faithful hound (a wire-haired fox terrier of celestial breed) looks up from his dozing in an armchair hard-by to present to me afresh his extraordinary facial resemblance to the late James T. Fields.[7] It's one of the funniest likenesses I ever saw (and most startling); and yet I can't write to Mrs. Fields of my daily joy in it. So I thus relieve myself to you, even though you too be, in a manner, a residuary relict. I've had a workful autumn and early winter, finishing a novel which *should* have by this time been published—that has been ready to be—but on which, as it is long, I fear too long, I've still several weeks work. It's to be lumped (by Constable here and Scribner in America), and has, I think, a prettyish title *The Wings of the Dove.* It's moreover, probably, of a prettyish inspiration—a "love-story" of a romantic tinge, and touching and conciliatory tone. I pray night and day for its comparative prosperity, but no publisher, alas (and they've had a mass of it for some time in their hands), have told me that it has "taken their fancy." So I'm preparing for the worst and yet at the same time panting (as *always* before the material has caught up with the mental finish of a book) to get immediately next two or three besetting subjects. Meanwhile, unfortunately, my way is temporarily, I hope but very briefly, stopped by my having suffered to be gouged out of me long ago by the Waldo Storys[8]—a history in itself—a promise first to "look at" the late W.W. S[tory]'s papers and then to write a memorial volume of some sort about him. I've delayed quite desperately, and at last, quite *must*, as I've also promised Wm Blackwood here. But there is no *subject*—there is nothing in the man himself to write about. There is nothing for me but to do a *tour de force*, or try to—leave poor dear W.W.S. *out*, practically, and make a little volume on the old Roman, Americo-Roman, Hawthornesque and other bygone days, that the intending, and extending, tourist will, in his millions, buy. But pray for me *you*, over this—to do all that and Please the Family too! Fortunately the Family is almost cynically indulgent—and I hope not to be kept Pleasing it more than three or four months. But my lamp burns low. You must be single and stricken (each of you—with all respect to the other) without Mildred. But I congratulate her on her winter tropics and send her the assurance of my affectionate interest—if she can accept a gift so stale as it that will be when it reaches her. You offered me her calendar—and I gave no sign, brute that I was—and now I suppose it's gone forever. It would still be a joy to me, little as I deserve it. I surround Mrs. Howells with the solicitude of an antediluvian friend, and I bless the Boy as much as ever one can bless up, for I seem to see him perched on vertiginous platforms, far out of the line of vision of the likes of yours, my dear Howells always

Henry James

1. An apartment house in Manhattan had been so named.

2. Mary Johnston's most popular romance had been *To Have and to Hold*. Kate Douglas Wiggin (1856–1923) wrote *Rebecca of Sunnybrook Farm;* James Lane Allen (1849–1925) wrote a series of Kentucky tales, *Flute and Violin*.

3. Probably Howells's *The Son of Royal Langbrith*, serialized in the *North American Review*, January–August 1904.

4. Mary Eleanor Wilkins (1852–1930), wrote short stories for *Harper's Bazar*. See letter to Sarah Orne Jewett, 5 October 1901.

5. "Flickerbridge," in *Scribner's Magazine*, February 1902, reprinted in *The Better Sort*.

6. James Thomas Fields (1817–1881) published James's first stories in the *Atlantic*, of which he was editor. Howells was at the time assistant editor.

7. See letter to Blackwood, 28 October 1897.

To Hendrik C. Andersen
Ms Barrett

105 Pall Mall S.W.
February 9*th* 1902

My dear, dear dearest Hendrik.

Your news[1] fills me with horror and pity, and how can I express the tenderness with which it makes me think of you and the aching wish to be near you and put my arms round you? My heart fairly bleeds and breaks at the vision of you *alone,* in your wicked and indifferent old far-off Rome, with the haunting, blighting, unbearable sorrow. The sense that I can't *help* you, see you, talk to you, touch you, hold you close and long, or do anything to make you rest on me, and feel my participation—this torments me, dearest boy, makes me ache for you, and for myself; makes me gnash my teeth and groan at the bitterness of things. I can only take refuge in hoping you are *not* utterly alone, that some human tenderness of *some* sort, some kindly voice and hand *are* near you that may make a little the difference. What a dismal winter you must have had, with this staggering blow at the climax! I don't of course know *what* fragment of friendship there may be to draw near to you, and in my uncertainty my image of you is of the darkest, and my pity, as I say, feels so helpless. I wish I could go to Rome and put my hands on you (oh, how lovingly I should lay them!) but that, alas, is odiously impossible. (Not, moreover, that apart from *you,* I should so much as like to be there now.) I find myself thrown back on anxiously and doubtless vainly, wondering if there may not, after a while, [be] some possibility of your coming to England, of the current of your trouble inevitably carrying you here—so that I might take consoling, soothing, infinitely close and tender and affectionately-healing *possession* of you. This is the one thought that relieves me about you a little—and I wish you might fix your eyes on it for the idea, just of the possibility. I am in town for a few weeks but I return to Rye April 1st, and sooner or later to *have* you there and do for you, to put my arm round you and *make* you lean on me as on a brother and a lover, and keep you on and on, slowly comforted or at least relieved of the first bitterness of pain—this I try to imagine as thinkable, attainable, not wholly out of the question. There I am, at any rate, and there is my house and my garden and my table and my studio—such as it is!—and your room, and your welcome, and your place everywhere—and I press them upon you, oh so earnestly, dearest boy, if isolation and grief and the worries you are overdone with become intolerable to you. There they are, I say—to fall upon, to rest upon, to find whatever possible shade of oblivion in. I will *nurse* you through your dark passage. I wish I could do something *more*—something straighter and nearer and more immediate but such as it is please let it sink into you. Let all my tenderness, dearest boy, do *that.* This is all now. I wired you three words an hour ago. I can't *think* of your sister-in-law—I brush her vision away and your history with your father, as I've feared it, has haunted me all winter. I embrace you with almost a passion of pity.

Henry James

1. The death of Andersen's brother Andreas, a painter.

To Hendrik C. Andersen
Ms Barrett

Lamb House, Rye
February 28*th* 1902

Dearest, dearest Boy, more tenderly embraced than I can say!—How woefully you must have wondered at my apparently horrid and heartless silence since your last so beautiful, noble, exquisite letter! *But*, dearest Boy, I've been dismally *ill*—as I was even when I wrote to you from town; and it's only within a day or two that free utterance has—to this poor extent—become possible to me. *Don't waste any pity*, any words, on me now, for it's, at last, blissfully over, I'm convalescent, on firm grounds, safe, gaining daily—only weak and "down" and spent, and above all like a helpless pigmy before my accumulation of the mountain of a month's letters etc. To make a long story of the shortest, I was taken in London, on January 29th—two days after getting there, with a malignant sudden attack, through a chill, of inflammation of the bowels: which threw me into bed, for a week, howling. Then I had a few days of false and apparent recuperation—*one* of which was the Sunday I wrote you from the Athenaeum on receipt of *your* direful letter. But I felt myself collapsing, *re*lapsing again, and hurried down here on February 11th just in time to save, as it were, my life from another wretched siege out of my own house. I tumbled into bed here and had a dozen wretched days of complicated, aggravated relapse: but at least nursed, tended, cared for, with all zeal and needfulness. So I've pulled through—and am out—and surprisingly soon—of a very deep dark hole. *In* my deep hole, how I thought yearningly, helplessly, dearest Boy, of *you* as your last letter gives you to me and as I take you, to my heart. I determined, deliberately, *not* to *wire* you, for I felt it would but cruelly worry and alarm you; and each day I reached out to the hope of some scrawl—I mean toward some possibility of a word to you. But that has come duly now. Now, at least, my weak arms still can feel you close. Infinitely, deeply, as deeply as you will have felt, for yourself, was I touched by your second letter. I respond to every throb of it, I participate in every pang. I've gone through Death, and Death, enough in my long life, to know how all that we *are*, all that we *have*, all that is best of us within, our genius, our imagination, our passion, our whole personal being, become then but aides and channels and open gates to suffering, to being flooded. But, it is better so. Let yourself go and *live*, even as a lacerated, mutilated lover, with your grief, your loss, your sore, unforgettable consciousness. *Possess* them and let them possess you, and life, so, will still hold you in her arms, and press you to her breast, and keep you, like the great merciless but still *most* enfolding and never disowning mighty Mother, on and on for things to come. Beautiful and unspeakable your account of relation to Andreas. Sacred and beyond tears. How I wish I had known him, admirable, loveable boy—but you make me: I *do*. Well, he is *all* yours now: he lives in you and out of all pain. Wait, and you will see; hold fast, sit tight, *stick hard*, and more things than I can tell you now will come back to you. But you know, in your courage, your genius and your patience, more of these things than I need try thus to stammer to you. And now I am tired and spent. I only, for goodnight, for five minutes, take you to my heart. And I'm better, better, better, dearest Boy; don't think of my having been ill. Think only of my love and that I am yours always and ever

Henry James

To Clare Benedict
Ms Basel

Lamb House, Rye
May 2*d* 1902

My dear Clare.

I send you both, your mother not less than myself,[1] my tenderest condolences on the death of poor little gallant, romantic Tello. It must be the loss of the most intimate of friends, almost the nearest of relations, a brave little black, barking son and brother! This end of his career takes me back in memory to the other end—the melancholy days in Venice when he came to you for refuge and you covered him with your charity. You can at any rate both reflect that you filled to the brim for years the cup of his capacity for happiness, and that while he lived he was probably the most important and glorious dog in the two hemispheres. I say these things with a certain ruefulness and awe, for, even while I write, the companion of my so much tamer adventures (than yours and Tello's), *my* little blacknosed brother and son, my small (yet not *too* small) fox-terrier, Nicholas by name, of the rough-haired (yet not *too* rough), slumbers gently at my elbow, and making me doubly feel for you, reminds me of the frailty of these attachments. He has climbed into my best drawingroom armchair, pillowed his charming black-and-tan little impudent head on my most Pompadour cushion; and so, though he is old enough to know better, he asserts his youth and his impunity. But—on the other hand—while you were making Tello the cosmopolite of his race, I committed to earth the three valued friends whose names are inscribed on the small tomb-stones in my garden—so I know the particular pang of loss. For you moreover Tello was born (at least your interest in him was), of a particular terrible passage in your lives—out of nothing resembling which, thank God, can any successor to him come to you. And I think of him with gratitude always—that he was there to take part of your feeling.—I am utterly abashed, I may add, all the same to be writing to you before I've answered your mother's grand letter—which *did* duly come to me. Give my love to her, and tell her that I've only waited—*been* waiting—to be grand enough to have a right to. I've had a perversely blighted winter (a rather dismal and protracted illness, and then a recurrence), which has thrown everything into pie. But I am at last quite well, and worthy to be in relation with her again, into which I shall speedily put myself. I well measure the amount of *missing*—in your bereavement—that she will now accomplish it. I'm glad you're at Berry Pomeroy—very,—liking to feel as I do that somebody beside myself is freezing (for I hope you're freezing), in grim rural consistency! Please take, my dear dear Clare, much love from yours ever constantly

Henry James

1. HJ makes a curious slip in this letter: writing of Miss Woolson's dog Tello (Othello), which had just died, he writes "myself" instead of "yourself"—suggesting, perhaps, a continued unconscious involvement with Miss Woolson after her suicide in Venice eight years earlier.

To Edmund Gosse
Ms Duke

Lamb House, Rye
Thursday P.M. [15 May 1902]

My dear Gosse.

I *have* indeed been much disconcerted at finding that though I gave you my Flaubert[1] in September last, eight months ago, it is now printed without a proof having been sent me. I find it good enough as I read it over, to think it might have been treated with that ordinary consideration. I find it a refinement of *torture*, always, to read a thing of which I have seen no proof—the things one *could* have amended and bettered are so pilloried there in an eternal publicity. There are in this thing no monstrosities of error, though there is a distressing misprint on page 35, toward the bottom, *vivify* for verify (please correct it in any copy under your hand); but to get off simply without *them* isn't what one bargains for, and there are many things I should have felt happier to have slightly altered. What does Heinemann mean? I think he will have difficulty in saying. Please, I beseech you—for I am nervous and anxious now—*insist* on my seeing a proof of the Balzac.[2] Now that this volume is out of its order in time, do make any needful further postponement to render this certain. I sent you a very rough copy, you will remember, on your assurance that proof was what I shall have; and the thing needs it *more* than the Flaubert. Delayed as it has been, its frankly best place, now, would be to wind up the series. There it is out of all pretence to order, and yet *is* an important finale. —Please think of this, and heal the gaping wound of yours ever

Henry James

1. The Flaubert essay was written for *Madame Bovary*, published by Heinemann in May 1902 as volume 9 in a series edited by Gosse, "A Century of French Romance." James was unaware that the volume was a bowdlerized version of the novel.

2. The Balzac essay, in the same series as the Flaubert, was appended to volume 7 in the series, a translation of *The Two Young Brides*, published in September 1902. HJ had sent this essay to Gosse on 4 April.

To Edmund Gosse
Ms Leeds

Lamb House, Rye
Friday P.M. [16 May 1902]

My dear Gosse.

I roll at your feet in the dust—crawl and grovel—an apologetic worm. My memory has remained all day a blank, utter and complete, as to my having *had* Flaubert proofs in October, and dealt with them; it's an extraordinary case of a perfect lapse and extinction (forgive this filthy paper!) of the impression made. But from the moment Heinemann has the dated and recorded *facts* about it he *must* be right, and I deeply regret having challenged his fidelity. Please express this to him. (There are some small stupidities in the published pages that I can't understand my not having amended.) But we live in darkness—and I've not been *willingly* black. For the bad quarter of an hour I've given you I will do any penance you impose—even to that—if you are ruthless—of forgoing the Balzac proof. Only, as you are now strong, be merciful and not impose that extremity if you are not yourself cruelly forced to it. Yours ruefully and wretchedly

Henry James

To Edmund Gosse
Ms British Library

Lamb House, Rye
June 26*th* 1902

My dear Gosse.

I have the highest opinion of the title Joseph Conrad would have, on literary grounds, to become one of your beneficiaries:[1] all the more that in spite of his admirable work he is not so known to a wide and promiscuous public that his claims may speak wholly for themselves. He has been to me, the last few years, one of the most interesting and striking of the novelists of the new generation. His production (you know what it consists of) has all been fine, rare and solid, of the sort greeted more by the expert and the critic than (as people say) by the man in the street. His successive books have been real literature, of a distinguished sort, the record of his experience, in navigating years, of eastern seas, strange climes and far countries, all presented in a form more artistic than has been given to *any* "Tales of the Sea" among English writers and that approximates more than anything we have to the truth and beauty of the French Pierre Loti. *The Nigger of the Narcissus* is in my opinion the very finest and strongest picture of the sea and sea-life that our language possesses—the masterpiece in a whole great class; and *Lord Jim* runs it very close. When I think moreover that such completeness, such intensity of expression has been arrived at by a man not born to our speech, but who took it up, with singular courage, from necessity and sympathy, and has laboured at it heroically and devotedly, I am equally impressed with the fine persistence and the intrinsic success. Born a Pole and cast upon the waters, he has worked out an English style that is more than correct, that has *quality* and ingenuity. The case seems to me unique and peculiarly worthy of recognition. Unhappily, to be very serious and subtle isn't one of the paths to fortune. Therefore I greatly hope the Royal Literary Fund may be able to do something for him. *Do* let me recommend him to you in the name of his charming, conscientious, uncommon work. It has truly a kind of disinterested independent nobleness.

Believe me yours always
Henry James

1. HJ was writing in support of a grant for Conrad from the Royal Literary Fund; it was awarded during the ensuing month.

To Owen Wister
Ms Congress

Lamb House, Rye
August 7*th* 1902

My Dear Owen.[1]

I have been reading *The Virginian* and I am moved to write to you. You didn't send him to me—you never send me anything; as to which, heaven knows, you're not obliged, and, conscious of your probably multitudinous preoccupations, I mention the matter only from the sense of my having felt, as I read, how the sentiment of the thing would have deepened for me if I *had* had it from your hands. The point is that the sentiment of the thing so appealed to me, interested me, convinced me, that I thus unscrupulously yield to the pleasure of making an however ineffectual sign of the same to you across the waste of distance and darkness. Signs are, in this void, poor things, and to talk with you would be the real delirium; still, I want it to pass as dimly discernible to you that what I best like in your book deeply penetrated even my weather-beaten, my almost petrified old mind. What I best like in it is exactly the fact of the *subject* itself, so clearly and finely felt by you, I think, and so firmly carried out was the exhibition, to the last intimacy, of the man's character, the personal and moral complexion and evolution, in short, of your hero. On this I very heartily congratulate you; you have made him *live,* with a high, but lucid complexity, from head to foot and from beginning to end; you have not only intensely seen and conceived him, but you have reached with him an admirable objectivity, and I find the whole thing a rare and remarkable feat. If we *could* only palaver (ah, miserable fate!) and you were to give me leave, there are various other awfully interesting things I should like both to say and to sound you on; these same, and connected, questions, elements of the art we practice and adorn, being, to my judgment, the most thrilling that can occupy the human mind. I won't deny that I have my reserves—perverse perhaps and merely personal in respect to some sides of your performance; but in the first place they don't touch the Essence; in the second they would take space (tremble at what you escape!) and in the third you haven't asked me for them—an indispensable condition, I hold, of offering such observations. The Essence, as I call it, remains—the way the young man's inward and outward presence builds itself up, fills out the picture, holds the interest and charms the sympathy. Bravo, bravo. *I* find myself desiring all sorts of poetic justice to hang about him, and I am willing to throw out, even though you don't ask me, that nothing would have induced me to unite him to the little Vermont person, or to dedicate him in fact to achieved parentage, prosperity, maturity, at all—which is mere *prosaic* justice, and rather grim at that. I thirst for his blood. I wouldn't have let him live and be happy; I should have made him perish in his flower and in some splendid noble way—as e.g. Loti makes Yann (with whom your friend has points in common) do so invaluably in *Pêcheur d'Islande.*[2] But I am letting myself loose among my reserves and I pull myself up. I only wanted to pat you officiously, and both violently and tenderly, on the admirably assiduous back. Bend this last possession again to—ah, not to the Virginian. *Don't* revive him again at your peril, or rather at his! I have an impertinent apprehension that you're promising yourself some such treat for his later developments. Damn his later developments—and yet I can't say Write me another Wild West novel all the same—for I believe the type you've studied and dismissed to be, essentially (isn't it?) *ce qu'il y a de mieux* in the W.W. But write me something equally American on this scale or with this seriousness—for it's a great pleasure to see you bringing off so the large and the sustained. How I envy you the personal knowledge of the W.W., the possession of the memories; that *The V.* must be built on, and the right to a competent romantic feeling about them. But it's one o'clock in the morning, and I am too long-winded. And I have made myself too late for inquiries or messages. Yet I involve you all, your wife, your mother, your children, your every circumstance (including your next book), in a common benediction, and am yours, my dear Owen, very delightedly

Henry James

1. Son of HJ's friend Sarah Butler Wister and grandson of Fanny Kemble, Wister, whom HJ had known since he was a boy, had just published his archetypal "western," *The Virginian.*

2. Pierre Loti, pseudonym of Louis Marie Julien Viaud (1850–1923), French naval officer and novelist, author of *Pêcheur d'Islande* (1886). See HJ's *Essays in London and Elsewhere* (1893).

To Edith Wharton
Ms Yale

Lamb House, Rye
August 17th 1902

Dear Mrs. Wharton.

I have just asked the Scribners to send you a rather long-winded (but I hope not hopelessly heavy) novel of mine that they are to issue by the end of this month (a thing called *The Wings of the Dove*), and I find myself wishing much not to address myself to you to that without doing so still more.[1] This has been made especially the case, I assure you, by my lately having read *The Valley of Decision*,[2] read it with such high appreciation and received so deep an impression from it that I can scarce tell you why, all these weeks, I have waited for any other pretext to write. I think in truth I have waited simply because, really, your book gives one too much to say, and the number of reflections it made me make as I read, the number of remarks that, in the tone of the highest sympathy, highest criticism, highest consideration and generally most intimate participation, I articulated, from page to page, for your absent ear, have so accumulated on my consciousness as to render me positively helpless. I can't discharge the load by this clumsy mechanism. The only possible relief would be the pleasure of a talk with you, and that luxury, thanks to the general perversity of things, seems distant and dim. I greatly regret it.—I seem to have the vision of our threshing out together, if chance only favoured, much golden grain. But I gather indeed from your admirable sister-in-law and niece,[2] who have been so good as to come and pay me a little visit, that chance *may* favour your coming hitherward—within these next few months. I shall pray for some confirmation of this—i.e. for your being able to be for a little in England. Even, however, were I prepared to chatter to you about *The Valley*, I think I should sacrifice that exuberance, to the timely thought that the first duty to pay to a serious, an achieved work of art, is the duty of recognition, *telle quelle*, and that the rest can always wait. In the presence of a book so accomplished, pondered, saturated, so exquisitely studied and so brilliant and interesting from a literary point of view, I feel that just now heartily to congratulate you covers plenty of ground. There is a thing or two I should like to say—some other time. You see what reasons I have for wishing a Godspeed to that talk. *The* particular thing is somehow mistimed while the air still flushes with the pink fire of the Valley; all the more that I can't do it any sort of justice save by expatiation. So, as, after all, to mention it in two words does it no sort of justice, let it suffer the wrong of being crudely hinted as my desire earnestly, tenderly, intelligently to admonish you, while you are young, free, expert, exposed (to illumination)—by which I mean while you're in full command of the situation— admonish you, I say, in favour of the *American Subject*. There it is round you. Don't pass it by—the immediate, the real, the ours, the yours, the novelist's that it waits for. Take hold of it and keep hold, and let it pull you where it will. It will pull harder than things of more *tarabiscotage*, which is a merit in itself. What I would say in a word is: Profit, be warned, by my awful example of exile and ignorance. You will say that *j'en parle à mon aise*—but I shall have paid for my ease, and I don't want you to pay (as much) for yours. But these are impertinent importunities—from the moment they are not developed. All the same *Do New York!* The first-hand account is precious. I could give you one, by the way, of Mrs. Cadwalader and Miss Beatrix, very fresh and accented, if it were not past midnight. We renewed and augmented our friendship and I rejoiced to see your sister-in-law always so brave and beneficent. She made me fairly feel that I *need* her here. There you have the penalty of the dispatriate. And the Bourgets are paying again one of their inexplicable little visits to England—spending three or four weeks at Bournemouth. *Non comprenny!*—I who know Bournemouth. But it gives me the chance to hope for them for a day or two much as I should be so glad some day to hope for you. Believe me, with kind regards to your husband, yours, dear Mrs. Wharton, most cordially

Henry James

1. HJ seems to be saying in this ambiguously worded sentence that he does not want to discuss his novel at this moment but rather wants to talk about the novel Mrs. Wharton has sent him.

2. Mrs. Wharton's two-volume historical novel, recently published, dealt with an eighteenth-century Italian aristocrat of liberal sympathies.

3. Mary Cadwalader Rawle married Edith Wharton's brother Frederic Rhinelander Jones when Edith was seven. The marriage was later dissolved. They had one daughter, Beatrix, later Mrs. Max Farrand.

To Mary Cadwalader Jones
Dictated Ts Harvard

Lamb House, Rye
August 20*th* 1902

Dear and bountiful Lady.

My failure, during these few days, to thank you for everything has not come from a want of appreciation of *anything*—or from a want of gratitude, or lively remembrance, or fond hope; or, in short, from anything but a quite calculating and canny view that I shall perhaps come in, during your present episode, with a slightly greater effect of direct support and encouragement than if I had come during the fever of your late short interval in London. It seems to be "borne in" to me that you may be feeling—*là où vous êtes*—a little lone and lorn, a little alien and exotic; so that the voice of the compatriot, counsellor and moderator, may fall upon your ears with an approach to sweetness. I am sure, all the same, that you are in a situation of great and refreshing novelty and of general pictur- esque interest. At your leisure you will give me news of it, and I wish you meanwhile, as the best advice, to drain it to the dregs and leave no element of it untasted.

My situation has, *en attendant,* been made picturesque by the successive arrivals of your different mementoes, each one of which has done its little part to assuage my solitude and relieve my gloom. Putting them in their order, Mrs. Wharton comes in an easy first; the unspeakable Postum follows handsomely, and Protoplasm—by which I mean Plasmon—pants far behind. How shall I thank you properly for these prompt and valued missives. Postum *does* taste like a ferociously mild coffee—a coffee reduced to second child- hood, the prattle of senility. I hasten to add, however, that it accords thereby but the better with my enfeebled powers of assimilation, and that I am taking it regular and blessing your name for it. It interposes a little ease after the long and unattenuated grimness of cocoa. Since Jackson *was* able to provide it with so little delay, I feel I may count on him for blessed renewals. But I shall never count on any one again for Plasmon, which is gruesome and medicinal, or at all events an "acquired taste," which the rest of my life will not be long enough *to* acquire.

Mrs. Wharton is another affair, and I take to her very kindly as regards her diabolical little cleverness, the quantity of intention and intelligence in her style, and her sharp eye for an interesting *kind* of subject. I had read neither of these two volumes,[1] and though the "Valley" is, for significance of ability, several pegs above either, I have extracted food for criticism from both. As criticism, in the nobler sense of the word, is with me enjoyment, I've in other words much liked them. Only they've made me, again, as I hinted to you other things had, want to get hold of the little lady and pump the pure essence of my wisdom and experience into her. She *must* be tethered in native pastures, even if it reduce her to a back-yard in New York. If a work of imagination, of fiction, interests me at all (and very few, alas, do!) I always want to write it over in my own

237

way, handle the subject from my own sense of it. *That* I always find a pleasure in, and I found it extremely in the "Vanished Hand"[2]—over which I should have liked, at several points, to contend with her. But I can't speak more highly for any book, or at least for my interest in any. I take liberties with the greatest.

But you will say that in ticking out this amount of Remingtonese at you I am taking a great liberty with *you,* or rather, of course, I perfectly know you won't, since you gave me kind leave—for which I shamelessly bless you. I relapsed into solitude and bad weather with your departure—the latter of which I fear you met, nastily, on your passage to Dublin. But we go on with the theory that there is some stored summer somewhere waiting to pop its cork like the champagne at a dull dinner, and when it comes, if it does come, I hope there will be enough to reach up, in far Scotland, to your end of the table. I have not been very exquisitely well, but I think I know why, in fact am sure I do, so that I see my way out with a little patience. In this stress Bobby has been my mainstay—a source of healing balm. His beautiful little nature endears itself more and more; though I am sorry to say his beautiful little back perplexes me with symptoms of itchability that make me—or that *will,* before you depart, make me—want to remind you of your promise of that healing lotion. It will be one more good thing I shall owe you. Meanwhile I apply, also under advice, paraffin, and it seems very decently to answer. But I stay my hand, or rather my voice, as the animal himself crouches near me like patience on a monument. He is waiting for his walk, dying for it, and the afternoon wanes. Good-bye, with innumerable good wishes. Please tell Miss Beatrix that these are addressed equally to her, as in fact my whole letter is, and that my liveliest interest attends her on her path. I hope, heartily, she is more and more acheless and painless. Yours and hers always affectionately

Henry James

P.S. I enclose sixteen stamps! Postum 7d. Plasmon 9d. So there you are.

1. Mrs. Jones had sent *Crucial Instances* (1901), a collection of Mrs. Wharton's tales, and a short novel, *The Touchstone* (1900).

2. James's memory of the title is inaccurate. *Crucial Instances* contains no story titled "Vanished Hand," but it does carry one called "The Moving Finger." HJ is recalling Mrs. Wharton's description of a painter who keeps touching up the portrait of a dead woman to represent her age—as though she were still aging.

To Ford Madox Hueffer
Ms Harvard

Lamb House, Rye
September 9th 1902

My dear Hueffer.

I thank you ever so kindly for your letter, which gives me extreme pleasure and almost for the moment makes me see the *Wings* myself, not as a mass of mistakes, with everything I had intended absent and everything present botched! Such is the contagion of your charming optimism. There is something, I suppose, by way of leaven in the lump; but I feel—have been feeling—mainly as if I had deposited in the market-place an object chiefly cognisable and evitable as a lump. Nothing, all the same, is ever more interesting to me than the consideration, with those who care and see, or want to, of these bottomless questions of How and Why and Whence and *What*—in connection with the mystery of one's craft. But they take one far, and, after all, it is the *doing* it that best meets and answers them.

The book had of course, to my sense, to be composed in a certain way,[1] in order to come into being at all, and the lines of composition, so to speak, determined and controlled its parts and account for what is and what isn't there; what isn't, e.g. like the "last interview" (Hall Caine[2] would have made it large as life and magnificent, wouldn't he?) of *Densher*[3] *and Milly.* I had to make up my mind as to what was my subject and what wasn't, and then to illustrate and embody the same logically. The subject was Densher's history with Kate Croy—hers with him, and Milly's history was but a thing involved and embroiled in that. But I fear I even then let my system betray me, and at any rate I feel I have welded my structure of rather too large and too heavy historic bricks. But we will talk of these things, and I think I have a plan of getting over to Winchelsea some day next week, when I shall no longer have three American cousins staying with me, and two others at the Mermaid![4] But I will consult you telegraphically first. I am hoping you *have* been able to pass the book on to Conrad. Yours most truly,

Henry James

1. HJ composed *The Wings of the Dove* in such a way as to omit all the big senti-

mental scenes—since he had chosen what today we would call a "soap opera" subject, a character dying of a nameless disease. Hueffer had apparently written asking why the big scenes were left out.

2. Sir Hall Caine (1853–1931), author of a series of best-selling sentimental novels such as *The Woman Thou Gavest Me* (1913).

3. Hueffer created the legend that he was the original of the passive-aggressive journalist character, Merton Densher. This does not fit the evidence, and a more credible "original" would be Morton Fullerton.

4. Various Emmet relations. The Mermaid Inn at Rye is a short distance from Lamb House.

To Gaillard T. Lapsley
Ms Harvard

Lamb House, Rye
September 15*th* 1902

My dear Gaillard.[1]

Don't you feel that you could, on the whole, if pressed, address me less grimly than as your dear *Mister*—? I like to be your dear, but I don't like to be your Mister. Say "my dear Henry J." and *n'en parlons plus*. It touches me much, at any rate, to hear from you in any form, and I can veraciously say that I missed you this summer. I miss you, in truth, at all times, and when you tell me that you too are solitary, am disposed to urge it upon you to chuck up your strange and perverted career and come over here and share *my* isolation. I live in this little corner practically without society and yours would be charming to me. I would let you "lecture" me all day long. Think of it earnestly. Your freshly-interesting letter (of August 31) puts before me again luridly enough your uncanny situation. I can't write of it to you—I can only take it in and feel it as a sort of nightmare. Yet it's beyond me, too—I can't deal with it anyhow, and it makes me cling to the ancient order in which I am sunk and sit tighter than ever amid the effects. How can I tell you, even, to bear up? Were I in your place I feel that I should be able to do nothing more heroic than flee. The moment you do, and in my direction at all, the more thoroughly I shall understand it and the more tenderly I shall welcome you. It's the great truth that you *énoncez*—the education of the men, in your *parages*, in mixed schools by women: it is *that* that is lurid and staggering! What unprecedented types, what race, what manners, what sort of a fu-

240

ture, is it going to make? We have invented in the U.S. many kinds of cheapness; but what kind of cheapness shall we have produced *so?* But that way madness lies, and I dash the dreadful subject away! No I don't, exactly, either—for I am much struck with what you say about the effect of the climate on the reading-habit—the extinction of the latter by the former; an extremely curious and gruesome phenomenon in its turn. Altogether it must be a sweet country! *Don't* fail to come and see me next summer, prepared to give me every detail. I'm afraid I've nothing to give you from *here*—if I had it would be like sending you the *Vicar of Wakefield* in return for *Gulliver's Travels.* Berkeley sounds *Gulliverian*—that's what it is! I've been here all summer, in arch-tranquility, as usual—that is with the recent pressure of three Emmet cousins at once. That indeed will sound to you Berkeleian! They will—two of them—come back, and then I will give them your message. Good-night; my letter-writing hour wanes—to A.M.; my heart goes out to you, and I am affectionately yours

Henry James

P.S. I am afraid you will find Fanny Stevenson a relation of questionable joy—old, changed, barbaric, weary, queer. You come too late.

1. Gaillard Thomas Lapsley (1871–1949) called on HJ in 1897 with a letter of introduction from Mrs. Gardner. A graduate of Harvard, which failed to find him a position, Lapsley taught in California until 1904, when he was elected Fellow and Lecturer of Trinity College, Cambridge. He became internationally known for his works in medieval constitutional history.

To James B. Pinker
Ms Yale

Lamb House, Rye
September 18*th* 1902

Dear Mr. Pinker.

Let me thank you for your cheque and fully acknowledge it—£269.18.0., representing A. Constable & Co.'s payment "down," on account of royalties, of £300 on publication of *The Wings of the Dove,* less your commission.

I am glad to hear you are expecting something from Scribners—yet am puzzled or muddled as to what it can be. I had a longish time ago £100 from them, through you, on account of something: wasn't it on account of this book? They agreed to pay it *then* in consideration of its not being more. Or am I confounding—as to *The Sacred Fount?* If I am, so much the better!—Believe me yours very truly

Henry James

P.S. Many thanks about the "Notice." I have seen but one—the one in the *Times*, but I shan't trouble you for any—as it is my eccentric practice to see as few as possible. No "press-cuttings" agency ever had access to me. This is the fruit of a long life.

To Mrs. Humphry Ward
Ms Barrett

Lamb House, Rye
September 23rd 1902

Dear Mrs. Ward.

All thanks for your kind and generous letter. I think I see the faults of my too voluminous fiction exhaustively myself: indeed when once my thing is done I see nothing *but* the faults. There are three or four major ones (or rather two maximum ones in particular) in the book that I think of very ruefully. Neither of them, I may say however, is the objection you raise—as to Kate's understanding with Densher, for that understanding was *in its explicitness* simply the subject of the book, the idea without which the thing wouldn't have been written. The subject is a *poor* one, I unaffectedly profess—the result of a base wish to do an amiable, a generally-pleasing love-story. But such as it is, it's *treated*, and it wouldn't have been treated if my pair hadn't *met* on the subject of Milly's money. The thing is essentially a Drama, like everything I do, and the drama, with the logic, the progression, the objectivized presentation of a drama, is all *in* their so meeting. The main field of it is, as the book is composed, in Densher's consciousness; that composition involves, for us, largely, the closing of Kate's, and there is no torment worth speaking of for Densher; there's *no* consciousness—none, I mean, that's at all dramatic—if their agreement hasn't been *expressed* and this expression, above all, been *the thing* he has subscribed to. Everything in Kate, meanwhile, has from the first led up to it by innumerable marks—or been meant to:

her offer to her father, in particular, being of course, but the appeal to be protected against herself (*in general*) by rupture with the danger of what she foresees in the *other* life. But it's long past midnight and my lamp burns low. I didn't mean to expatiate. What's done is done, and what isn't, alas, isn't. Kate is a very limited success, Mrs. Stringham is a charming idea not carried out, and Mrs. Lowder (and these are not the maximum faults, either!) has slipped away altogether. Milly and Densher are decent—at most.—And I, dear Mrs. Ward, am not even *that*; for I can't, I am very sorry to say, come to you next month. It won't be possible for me to leave home at present—I mean next month, at all—too many things keep me here. But I come up to town on January 10*th* to stay till May, and then I hope with all my heart to make up a little. But it *is* 1.15 A.M. Good night, good morning. Yours very constantly,

Henry James

To W. Morton Fullerton
Ms Princeton

Lamb House, Rye
October 18*th* 1902

My dear Fullerton.

I have liked keeping your letter by me, as it were, and eke your Sister's[1] interesting perpetration: I seem to put them, comparatively speaking, a little *from* me in making them a subject of utterance and acknowledgment. And yet, God knows, it's not that I don't like to utter to you! It's only that these things have, as it were, been squeezed in my silence and double-locked in my tenderness. And now I help the young lady, ever so gently, out and down: not, with every assistance, through the narrow door of the vehicle in which she has been perched—even though the process be a little ruffling to her charming feathers and frills, worn as if positively to be presented at court. The pages you send me are beautiful in their good faith, though a little painful in their admirable tension; and if they are like the distinguished model you have (and he is utterly unable to judge, himself), that is perhaps why he feels unable to get far enough from them to focus and estimate them. I really think this must be the ground of my difficulty. They *have*, probably, so close a relation to me that I seem not only to have written them, but to have written them many times over—from which springs a sense of delicacy, as well as a baffled *vision*, in respect to praising, or at least to measuring, them. Am I so much that *as* that? is what they make me ask myself—and the author, verily, seems to hold up the torch to me. *Tout y est*, my conscience tells me; or rather hers does: whereupon I can only marvel and hold my breath at the exquisite instrument that hers has made itself. It *is*, but too sensitively, too insanely *me*, and I feel, over the case, quite painfully responsible. It is all beautifully done, *as* me; but I am not good enough, not right enough to do so well, and even not good and right enough to do at all with that intensity. Kindly tell her, with my anxious benediction, that at these rates I won't answer for her. She may see a little where she's going, but I see where she's *coming*—and oh, the dangers scare me. I would have written, if I could, like Anthony Hope and Marion Crawford,[2] and I think she ought accordingly, to ask herself if her real tribute shouldn't be to do what the accident of my *self* only has prevented me from doing. Let her apply my inclination, my yearning, as I can't apply it. I want immense qualifying, and she presents me pure. Oh, so pathetically pure! She doesn't know what she is about. Hold her back. The great white light awaits—to engulf her. And she mustn't be engulfed. She must float and splash and scramble and remount the current, become distinct and distinguishable, with the jolly reminiscence of having been fished from the whirlpool.—It is by way of Jonathan Sturges that the news comes to me of your being about to proceed, as your organs say, to Madrid. It's a kind of a special shock to me, as well as an enthralling interest—I mean a shock because, after all, though I never see you, yet with you in Paris, I feel in a manner, in line with you, and as if, with a pull of the tense cord, I might work myself along to you. But Madrid is another planet, and it's a whole balloonery to learn. However I only want *not* to know this till I know it by *you*. If it makes something for you to give me let me save it up for you. Whatever befalls you the loss of my importunate attention shall *not*. Yours, my dear Fullerton, always and ever,

Henry James

P.S. I have had on a table for a long time two books I have wanted to send you—for sentiment's cumbersome sake: senseless volumes of a translated (book of) Flaubert and a translated (book of) Balzac, the only redeeming features of whose meretricious, and illustrative futility is, in each case, a "critical introduction" from my pen. These, as little things of France, I have had a disposition that you should receive, and the Flaubert was as to the fly-leaf inscribed with your name as long ago as last June, and then never (by some accident) sent. Ergo, it now occurs to me that, if you are *leaving* Paris, the last thing you want to be burdened with is two silly fat books— remembering but too well as I do the picturesque overgrowth of your collection in your most literary of *entresols*. You shall accordingly not have them (and a small loss!) till you come and view them here (which I wish to God you *could* do for three days, by way of a last farewell before you migrate to Mars). I only mention them —and be hanged to them!—that we may be harmlessly amused together at my fond intention.

1. Katherine Fullerton Gerould (1879–1944) was Morton Fullerton's cousin, but she had been reared in his family as if she were his sister. She later married Professor Gordon Hall Gerould of Princeton and published fiction and articles in magazines. She seems (like her cousin) to have begun as an imitator of HJ's style.
2. Two best-selling romantic novelists of the time.

To Mrs. Cadwalader Jones
Dictated Ts Harvard

Lamb House, Rye
October 23*rd* 1902

Dear Mrs. Cadwalader.

Both your liberal letters have reached me, and have given me, as the missives of retreating friends never fail to do, an almost sinister sense of the rate at which the rest of the world goes, moves, rushes, voyages, railroads, passing from me through a hundred emotions and adventures, and pulling up in strange habitats, while I sit in this grassy corner artlessly thinking that the days are few and the opportunities small (quite big enough for the likes of *me* though the latter be even here). All of which means of course simply that you take away my breath. But that was on the cards and it's not worth mentioning. Your best news for me is of your being, for complete convalescence, in the superlative hands you describe—to which I hope you are already doing infinite credit. I kind of make you out, "down there"—I mean in the pretty, very pretty, as it *used* to be, New York autumn, and in the Washington Squareish region trodden by the steps of my childhood, and I wonder if you ever kick the October leaves as you walk in Fifth Avenue, as I can to this hour feel myself, hear myself, positively *smell* myself doing. But perhaps there are no leaves and no trees now in Fifth Avenue—nothing but patriotic arches, Astor hotels and Vanderbilt palaces (my secretary was on the point of writing the great name "aster"—which I think the most delightful irony of fate! they are so flowerlike a race!). The October leaves are at any rate gathering about me here—and that I have watched them fall, and lighted my fire and trimmed my lamp, is about the only thing that has happened to me—though I *should* count in a visit from a delightful nephew,[1] who has just been with me for a fortnight, and left me for Geneva, where he spends the winter.

I assisted dimly, through your discreet page, at your visit to Mrs. Wharton, whose Lenox house must be a love, and I wished I could have been less remotely concerned. In the way of those I know I hope you have by this time, on your own side, gathered in John La Farge, and are not allowing him to feel anything but that he is well and happy—except, also, that I very affectionately remember him. I am hoping, by the same token, that your good offices are not to be too urgently required by Marion Crawford,[2] an account of whom, in a letter I have just had the pleasure of receiving from the Villa, makes me a little anxiously wonder. Mrs. Crawford writes me of his terrific siege of nose-bleed. I hope with all my heart that the flood is permanently stayed, and if it was the result (as I make bold, on the general evidence, to figure to myself) of too extravagant a cerebration I take a comfort in thinking you may find an art (among your many!) subtly to control that abuse, by detaining him, at due hours, in harmless sociability. This sounds a little as if he didn't, in talking with you, *have* to cerebrate—which isn't what I mean, for I know that *I* did. But, in fine, make him waste his time—even if it wastes yours. And begin, thereunto, by making him hear that I take a devoted interest in all news of him, and in everything he does and is. Be, in a word, not only good to, but good *for* him.

You were both of these things in respect to *me* when you so handsomely and promptly put me into communication with the papermonger of London Wall. They instantly sent me three or four specimens, out of which I picked an approach to my idea; and save that, once the article ordered, they took an eternity to supply it (for the bundle has but just come home) they have met every hope I entertained. I am too sorry that *this* can't be Waterloo and Sons, to show you how they've stamped me, enveloped me, and generally turned me out. To make up for that, however, I find myself thinking of you, as a link in the chain, every time I write (with my own hand) a letter. You pervade thus my correspondence.

But I am not thanking you, all this time, for the interesting remarks about the book I had last placed in your hands,[3] which you so heroically flung upon paper even on the heaving deep—a feat to *me* very prodigious. I won't say your criticism was eminent for the time and place—I'll say, frankly, that it was eminent in itself, and all full of suggestion. The fact is, however, that one is so aware one's self, even to satiety, of the rights and wrongs of these matters—especially of the wrongs—that freshness of mind almost fails for the discriminations, however benevolent, of others. Such is the price of having written many books and lived many years. The thing in question is, by a complicated accident which it would take me too long to describe to you, too inordinately drawn out and too inordinately rubbed in. The centre, moreover, isn't in the middle, or the middle, rather, isn't in the centre, but ever so much too near the end, so that what was to come after it is truncated. The book, in fine, has too big a head for its body. I am trying, all the while, to write one with the opposite disproportion—the body too big for its head.[4] So I shall perhaps do if I live to 150. Don't therefore undermine me by general remarks. And dictating, please, has moreover nothing to do with it. The value of that process for me is in its help to do over and over, for which it is extremely adapted, and which is the only way I can do at all. It soon enough, accordingly, becomes *intellectually*, absolutely identical with the act of writing—or has become so, after five years now, with me; so that the difference is only material and illusory—only the difference, that is, that I walk up and down: which is so much to the good.—But I must stop walking now. I stand quite solemnly still to send my hearty benediction to Miss Beatrix and I am yours and hers very constantly

Henry James

1. WJ's second son, Billy.
2. See letter to Mrs. Waldo Story, 17 June 1899.
3. *The Wings of the Dove.* See HJ's preface to the New York Edition, XIX, for his discussion of the "misplaced center."
4. *The Golden Bowl.*

To W. Morton Fullerton
Ms Barrett

Lamb House, Rye
November 7th 1902

My very dear Fullerton.

You see how you fetch me when you *do* write!—Only please don't take it as a warning. For your beautiful letter deeply delights and moves me—being *the* most beautiful, I really think, I ever received from *any* man: pervaded as it is by an exquisite intelligence (ineffable luxury!) as well as by the penetrating cordial of affection. Admirable, inspiring, inflaming, the sympathy with which you read me. Well, I deserve it too, I can say to *you*; for I do write from out of the deep and dire complexity of that sentient "machine" on which you put your unerring finger and to be encased in which *is* to be, *à toute heure* and forever, mortally isolated. But I am less so from your very naming of it to me—naming of your sense of it; which gives me the chance to say to you "Think of me so, *know* me so, always, and you will think of me tenderly." In short, for your lucid reflection of, disengagement of a response to, the soul, as it were, of my *too*-embodied book, I seize you gratefully fast, I hold you supremely close. You absolutely add to my wish, and to my need, to lead the life of—whatever I may call it!—my genius. And I *shall*, I feel, somehow, while there's a rag left of me. Largely thanks to you.

And how deeply interesting you are on the subject of your change of place; expressing yourself to me with a frankness and fulness which you have never used, which I have always (ah, ever so considerately!) desired, and which *I* need scarcely assure you I regard as a sacrosanct deposit. What you give me this brave glimpse of comes to me all, in my quiet corner, as the breath of the outer battle—even to the extent of making me feel rather ignobly aloof from it and as if I ought, if not for health's sake, at least for the glory of the clash of arms, to draw nearer. But I feel in you the strength of your sword and buckler, as well as that your cause is not a losing one. You are kept for great things—these last ten years have been for you, the clearest assertion of it. They *come*, all the while, and what is now happening to you is but one of their aspects and approaches. You'll bring Spain back into the family—you'll repay the debt to Columbus. Save that it takes you horribly *away,* I think of you with a free mind—in the interest of your *own* free one—at Madrid. And I try to think it thinkable to come some day and see you there. It will be my only chance. I don't say to see Madrid etc. (which I've never done); that is nothing. But to see you—which is *much;* much more than fate has apparently hitherto thought me particularly worth of.—However, the night wanes, and these are but stammering words. Your two little periodicals have just come in and I know afresh (or *you* shall) how little your practical bounty in these matters (it's the *practical* side that costs) is ever lost upon me. I immediately read the Zola in it—unseductive, ungarnished *grand homme* of art (or *even?*) strangely common specimen of big distinction; because I promised the ingenuous *Atlantic* to write a paper on him.[1] Your *Cornhill* thing will infallibly reach me by the operation of natural forces, and I delight to expect it. Likewise I send you, in their cumbrous elegance and ill-starred association, my Flaubert and Balzac Introductions; only what the *Devil* will you do with them? You must be *storing* books in Paris—have them packed at the bottom of some box. They will have an ultimate bibliographical value. And oh, T. A. Cook[2] is *not* my poor distinguished Densher—*ah, que non!* I never dreamed of him, good lusty chap as he is—and of course you don't suppose it. You do apparently suppose, on the other hand, that when I go to see George Meredith on the 22d (as I *do*) by domiciliary aid of Marie S., I go with an "unspeakable friend." I yearn to arrive at the friend's identity. Perhaps I shall; I don't as yet as much as suspect it; but Mrs. Marie,[3] may have surprises for me. Meanwhile you are "amazed" at my courage. It's too soon. Wait. I *shall*, doubtless, be equal to the occasion. At present I but rack my brain and squint at your obscurity. But my last word, with my good night, is a benediction and I am yours constantly and entirely

Henry James

1. HJ's article on Zola appeared in the *Atlantic Monthly,* August 1903, and was reprinted in *Notes on Novelists* (1914).

2. The allusion here may be to the eminent journalist E. T. Cook, founder of various journals such as the *Westminster Gazette* and the *Daily News* and a biographer of Ruskin. It is possible that Fullerton was in this way inquiring whether *he* was Densher.

3. This was probably Marie Meredith Sturgis (Mrs. Henry Parkman Sturgis), Meredith's daughter, who often acted as her father's hostess. Fullerton had met George Meredith in his younger days and was a friend of his son, Will Meredith.

To William Dean Howells
Ms Harvard

Lamb House, Rye
December 11*th* 1902

My dear Howells.

Nothing more delightful, or that has touched me more closely, even to the spring of tears, has befallen me for years, literally, than to receive your beautiful letter of November 30th, so largely and liberally anent *The W. of the D.* Every word of it goes to my heart and to "thank" you for it seems a mere grimace. The same post brought me a letter from dear John Hay, so that my measure has been full. I haven't known anything about the American "notices," heaven save the mark! any more than about those here (which I am told, however, have been remarkably genial); so that I have *not* had the sense of confrontation with a public more than usually childish—I mean had it in any special way. I confess, however, that that is my chronic sense—the more than usual childishness of publics: and it is (has been), in my mind, long since discounted, and my work definitely insists upon being independent of such phantasms and on unfolding itself wholly from its own "innards." Of course, in our conditions, doing anything decent is pure disinterested, unsupported, unrewarded heroism; but that's in the day's work. The *faculty of attention* has utterly vanished from the general anglo-saxon mind, extinguished at its source by the big blatant *Bayadère* of Journalism, of the newspaper and the *picture* (above all) magazine; who keeps screaming "Look at *me, I* am the thing, and I only, the thing that will keep you in relation with me *all the time* without your having to attend *one minute* of the time." If you are moved to write anything anywhere about the *W. of the D.* do say something of that—it so awfully wants saying. But we live in a lovely age for literature or for any art but the mere visual. Illustrations, loud simplifications and *grossissements*, the big building (good for John), the "mounted" play, the prose that is careful to be in the tone of, and with the distinction of a newspaper or bill-poster advertisement—these, and these only, meseems, "stand a chance." But why do I talk of such chances? I am melted at your reading *en famille The Sacred Fount*, which you will, I fear, have found chaff

250

in the mouth and which is one of several things of mine, in these last years, that have paid the penalty of having been conceived only as the "short story" that (alone, apparently) I could hope to work off somewhere (which I mainly failed of), and then *grew* by a rank force of its own into something of which the idea had, modestly, never been to be a book. That is essentially the case with the *S.F.*, planned, like *The Spoils of Poynton, What Maisie Knew*, "The Turn of the Screw," and various others, as a story of the "eight to ten thousand words"!! and then having accepted its bookish necessity or destiny in consequence of becoming already, at the start, 20,000, accepted it ruefully and blushingly, moreover, since, *given the tenuity of the idea*, the larger quantity of treatment hadn't been aimed at. I remember how I would have "chucked" *The Sacred Fount* at the fifteenth thousand word, if in the first place I could have afforded to "waste" 15,000, and if in the second I were not always ridden by a superstitious terror of not finishing, for finishing's and for the precedent's sake, what I have begun. I am a fair coward about *dropping*, and the book in question, I fear, is, more than anything else, a monument to that superstition. When, if it meets my eye, I say to myself, "You know you might not have finished it," I make the remark not in natural reproach, but, I confess, in craven relief.

But why am I thus grossly expatiative on the airy carpet of the bridal altar? I spread it beneath Pilla's[1] feet with affectionate jubilation and gratification and stretch it out further, in the same spirit, beneath yours and her mother's. I wish her and you, and the florally-minded young man (he *must* be a good 'un) all joy in the connection. If he stops short of gathering samphire it's a beautiful trade, and I trust he will soon come back to claim the redemption of the maiden's vows. Please say to her from me that I bless her—*hard*.

Your visit to Cambridge makes me yearn a little, and your watching over it with C. N[orton] and your sitting in it with Grace. Did the ghost of other walks (I'm told Fresh Pond is no longer a Pond, or no longer Fresh, only stale, or something) ever brush you with the hem of its soft shroud? Haven't you lately published some volume of Literary Essays or Portraits[2] (*since* the *Heroines of Fiction*) and won't you, munificently, send me either that *or* the

Heroines—neither of which have sprung up in my here so rustic path? I will send you in partial payment another book of mine to be published on February 27th.

Good-night, with renewed benedictions on your house and your spirit. Yours always and ever,

Henry James

1. Howells's daughter, Mildred.
2. The volume was *Literature and Life* (1902).

To Jessie Allen
Ms Harvard

Lamb House, Rye
December 12th 1902

Dearest and worst Miss Allen.

I shall really have to bring it (them)[1] back to you when I come up to town, and I from this moment hold them subject to your order, for restitution, and utterly refuse and decline to regard them as mine or as otherwise known to me than as impossible, unspeakable, unforgivable. I really, dear lady, can *not* again receive *any* object of value from your hands, of value or even of *no* value, and I loudly won't hear of so much as even cursefully growling Thanks at you for those before me. See what ungraciousness (most disagreeable to me and foreign to my sweet nature) your perversity reduces me to, and learn from it, I beseech you, a lesson. You wouldn't do it if you knew how I at last really *mind* it, and how I can't go on with any kind of comfort unless I have your solemn and serious promise that you won't do it again. And even thus the bearskins will be deposited at no distant date either on the top of your house or at its foundations, or thrust into one of its windows or down one of its chimneys; for I thought I had made all this plain last year. There!—And do you see what a Pig you make of me? And a Pig that I shall *remain*, that I shall continue to be, elaborately, inexorably, always, *always!* See, too, what you compel me to sit up nights writing about, when I might be either reducing my oil-bill or at least writing about Shakespeare and the musical glasses,[2] or the Kenmares and the crimes of the aristocracy. There is nothing *here* to write about whatever. I don't exist here save as an intensely

252

private individual, sitting with his feet in impossible bearskins and holding no commerce whatever with his kind; thereby also incurring no suspicion or communication of news. Which means that I went no longer ago than this afternoon to the house of certain well-meaning golf-playing, gardening, blundering Fuller-Maitlands,[3] to see two previously-theatrical little *plays*, and that I came away flabbergasted and terrorized at what apparently normal bipeds, not to be hanged if they *don't*, may be still observed to cheerfully and wantonly perpetrate in the provinces. I am so glad we don't have private theatricals at the Barbaro. I would rather go to Norway at once, I would rather eat my dinner in bearskins or go to bed in snow-shoes, than return again to the Fuller-Maitlands. I envy you your little indep[end]ent heartless life in Eaton Terrace. Your news of your great world round about it falls about me like the white, noiseless, ghostly snowstorm we lately had here. Kenmares and Herberts and Douglases[4] and the rest of your Dieudonné dinners and Carleton suppers fade away from me like phantoms and babble their names through a non-conducting air. It's many a day since I've looked upon the ailing beauty of Lady K[enmare] and it seems "borne in" upon me that I shall never look upon it again. Not that she seems to me likely to succumb to her ailments, but we live apart, almost like her ladyship and her ladyship's own Lord. I could scarce see less of her if I *were* that personage.—I wish you joy of your Derbyshire ice-house; you really, summer and winter, do lay out grand treats for yourself. The bearskins shall reach you in time to form part of your *trousseau* for that desperate hazard. I don't know, I fear, at all, the R[alph] Curtis's[5] address (only that it is near Villefranche, but am without postal lights on it altogether). *It*, also, is ghostly and hollow to me, as dear Daniel and Ariana are when once away from the Barbaro, that is when *they* are once away. They wander, for me, like hungry spectres, whose wanderings I stupidly thank the lord I am not condemned to emulate. They see all the greatness of the earth and bestrew their path with anecdotes and witticisms and other triumphs; but I snuggle down into my blankets here and rejoice that my aged legs have not their ways to tread. I *guess* they loathe Ralph's villa and Ralph's *milieu*; and, poor dears, my heart bleeds for them. I send you her charming letter—don't return it. I needn't add that I sit tight, tight here for Christmas; with nothing loose about the business whatever but the probable presence of one little ribald friend.[6] I am already giving a daily stir to the plum-pudding with the Pearl of Price[7]—that is I shall settle down to that as to the only event in the dear deadly, desert days as soon as I have slept off the dramatic *orgie* of this afternoon. And I must sleep it off quickly or the cock will crow. It is *1.15 A.M.*—as usual (it's *always* 1.15 when I write letters), and I am yours most unforgivingly, resentfully, punitively

Henry James

1. Two bearskins which Miss Allen, with her customary Yuletide generosity, had bestowed on HJ.
2. See Oliver Goldsmith, *The Vicar of Wakefield,* chapter 9: "They would talk of nothing but high life, and high-lived company, with other fashionable topics, such as pictures, taste, Shakespeare, and the musical glasses."
3. Edward Fuller-Maitland. See letter to Grace Norton, 18 December 1902.
4. Probably distinguished houses Miss Allen frequented.
5. Ralph Curtis, son of the Daniel Curtises (of the Palazzo Barbaro in Venice), and a close friend of Sargent's.
6. Jonathan Sturges, often called by HJ "the little demon."
7. HJ invariably referred to Mrs. Paddington, his housekeeper, as a "pearl of price." See letter to Louise Horstmann Boit, 12 August 1904.

To Jessie Allen
Ms Harvard

Lamb House, Rye
December 15, 1902

Dear Goody Two Shoes.[1]

Very good—I accept, I retire; I forbear the needed discipline, and I promise to wear the bearskins ĩn Bed in the blizzard that I feel to be now again preparing: BUT all on a condition—that I address you as above always (and that you answer to that name) for the rest of my life. The first money I put by (I've never put by a penny in my life—so the vow is safe!) I shall have a collar made (in Bond Street) properly to fit you, and with the full G.T.S. marked upon it in diamonds, and expect you to wear the same whenever I "take you out." So I think the matter can be arranged. If any further detail of it remain to be settled we can attend to that when I *do* take you out as soon as possible after I come up next month. I shall take you out and *shake* you a little, but I shall also be able I trust (if you will amiably accept it) to give you a good and pleasant airing. And I wish you meanwhile a fine old romping and roaring Derbyshire Christmas. Yours, dear and admirable Goody, very constantly

Henry James

P.S. It may interest you to know that the friend in Washington invites, presses me to come out and see her there this spring (I confess, you see, to a pressing *Her*); and in so doing enumerates the attractive people around her—"the black eyes" of one lady and the "crisp smile of Mrs. Slater!" What a picture of a society in which that desolating female is held out for an attraction! Decidedly, dear Goody, I can do better in London!

1. Henceforth HJ addressed Miss Allen as "Goody Two Shoes" and so inscribed his books to her. "Goody" was a well-known nursery character who was overjoyed when she was given two shoes—having always walked about with only one. The tale is attributed to Oliver Goldsmith.

To Grace Norton
Ms Harvard

Lamb House, Rye
December 18*th* 1902

Dearest Grace.

This abomination—as my silence—has terribly lasted; but I have already given you often enough the measure of that infamy; just as you have given me that of your superiority to all explanations, your repudiation of all need of them. I think I really don't write to you at these times because I *want* to so much! The want seems to make the *act* vast—like a spreading landscape—in proportion to it, and acts of such vastness to assert, by the same logic, their incompatibility with my little life. At the same time the moment I break through all logic, the moment I grasp my pen blindly and as with the smash of a window-pane I feel myself doing the homeliest, nearest, sweetest, most natural and consistent thing in the world—barring the queer consciousness—which does abide a little—of having nothing to "tell" you. You must put up therefore with that essential fact—of my telling you nothing as hard as ever I can. You have no idea of what a small personal world I live in, in having come to live so much as I do in the country, for William and Alice won't have been able to tell you—knowing as they do nothing about it!

They only know my personal world while they are here—which then becomes as huge as they inevitably make it. It shrinks in their absence to such a point—that if you could see it you would, I know, anxiously ask: "But do you really think such a life can be *good* for you?" To which I should reply, "Yes, beautiful for three quarters of the year. For the remaining quarter a certain amplification"—which I more or less get by going up to London. The *im*personal life is so provided for among my Sussex yokels that I only blush not to have more of the fruits of thought and concentration to show for it. I thought long ago that I knew how to live alone, but I am learning better with each revolving month. It is a lesson that has every merit save that of qualifying me to revisit the shades that you adorn: which (or something like which) I find myself more and more amiably entreated (really the word for it) to do—Boston, New York, Washington, all making the most insidious signs to me. The sweet art I have just mentioned having mastered to its last refinements—what would become of *it* as a response to these weird arguments? However, that's a complicated question, and, after all, not pressingly *actual* (I wish it *were!*)—also, moreover, the case might be met by my crowding the answer into my purely demoralized quarter of the year (though indeed that quarter *isn't*, by my practise "purely," but only feebly, guardedly, comparatively demoralized). I am already, for that matter, here, under the agitating shadow of Christmas, which we take very hard at Rye—that is so far as fearing its agitations and providing, without ruin (or trying to) against its financial liabilities. One has the sense of being "looked to" from so many "humble" quarters that one feels, with one's brass knocker and one's garden-patch, quite like a country gentleman, with his "people" and his church-monuments. I haven't monuments—but (did William tell you?) an Immemorial Pew, which "goes with" my house and which I have never been in but once! And two Harrisons, from Winchelsea, are coming over to luncheon tomorrow. It is very complicated—they being the brother and the sister-in-law of Mrs. Frederic[1] who was already a Harrison, and Frederic's cousin as well as his bride. They are very ugly, very destitute of enchantments to sense, very supposedly delightful and very new to our neighbourhood, having but lately bought rather a pleasant old house there. Also I am deeply and incurably sated with them (as I know *you* are), in advance! All the same there come on Christmas to dinner the Edward Fuller-Maitlands (a childless sketching and golf-ing couple lately established here), and with *them* I am likewise gorged, already, to such repletion that I am heavy even as with *their* heaviness. On which you say "Why *have* them?" And I gloomily reply "What will you have? The Squire—! One's 'people'!" I was lately, during three or four days in town, at Gertie Lewis's wedding, and if you don't know who Gertie Lewis[2] is Sally or Lily will tell you; and if they can't it won't matter. The point is only that I saw there, wedged into a dense thousand or two of people, Miss Hogarth,[3] looking very old and shrunken and, oh, of Another Time (that look!—with her great Dickens connection, in a world know-ing and heeding it not, all wan and wasted in her!)—but very friendly and pleasantly, almost tremulously, eager, eager above all to talk about you, which we did for some time, exclusively and tenderly, wedged *together* in this deep fusion. And I didn't feel, on my side, as unqualified as I may appear to you, for you glimmer upon me, phantasmagoric, in my Cambridge letters, and William writes me, e.g., that he takes long drives (or *has* taken them) with you. I don't suppose he takes them in these months; but I hope that (for him at least) your fireside replaces them. I don't suppose he has such a magnifying effect upon it as he and Alice have had, in their visits, upon mine (because you are primarily on the grander scale); but I am safe to believe that he doesn't drag it down. I know it has had, your fireside, dear Grace, this year, the loss of your devoted old friend of so many years, Ferdinand Bocher—which means that your life, and your future, and all your conditions of being, have had it. But I am not, as you see, pretending to speak of that—in any way but by the single tone and touch of *recognition*. What I am hoping is that you will speak to *me* of it—which will be much more to the point: as I would to *you* if I had an intimate friend to lose as a *presence* which, thank heaven, I haven't! For you yourself, dear Grace, are a presence so terrifically arranged as an absence. How-ever, the small hours overtake my letter, as they habitually do most of my letters (I am unable to write these, for reasons I won't bore you with, almost ever, save at night) and it is now in fact one o'clock in the morning. I should like to sit up with you longer, but the wind has gone down (it has been blowing a long wintry gale over our little roofed and chimneyed hilltop), and with the hush that has come the scratching of my pen and ticking of my clock sound almost alarmingly loud. My little old house, moreover, gives out, more and more, strange nocturnal sounds, inexplicable thumps and groans, unaccountable wandering noises, as if it really wished to live up to a proper psychic hauntability. All this makes for my getting my head under the bedclothes—so that it's already from there that I am, my dear Grace, ever so constantly yours

Henry James

1. Frederic Harrison (1831–1923), a prolific writer on historical and literary subjects.
2. Gertrude Lewis, daughter of the eminent solicitor Sir George Lewis (1833–1911).
3. Georgina Hogarth, youngest sister of Charles Dickens's wife, Catherine.

To Sarah Butler Wister
Ms Congress

Lamb House, Rye
December 21 1902

My dear Sarah Wister.

I have two delightful letters from you—that is one letter and an interesting note; and I have decently and decorously *waited,* as I think it always honorable to do with friends with whom my correspondence has a certain nobleness of *rhythm*—if there be any such besides yourself. It is a way, perhaps, of fondly treating myself to the belief that you may enjoy with a certain fulness the sense of a letter from me to *come.* But this quiet night of my small Sussex, and above all small solitary, Christmastide I can wait no longer; the spirit of the season works in me, and my voice, with it, goes strongly forth to you. Do you know of what I remind myself in these years when, much the most of the time remote from London embroilments, I *sit alone* in the evenings, with the lamp and the fire and the ticking of the clock? Of nothing less than of your mother as I used, for so many years, regularly to find her, inveterate and philosophic, though not so detached, really (luckily for *me!*) as the *form* of her attitude (so to speak) seemed to give out. And the resemblance is increased for me by the fact that the clock I listen to is one that she most blessedly left me in her will[1] (a small portable brass one which never leaves me), and to the peculiarly

258

loud and active tick of which, as well as its very deep and mellow and charming strike, I used to listen as I sat with her. But there are differences—in especial that of the fact that whereas when she "sat alone" I could, once a week, come in, when *I* do the same *I* have no nine o'clock visitor. None, that is, save the tramping *ghosts* of other years, of whom indeed she is not the least. They are, as my principal company—a company much more numerous now than the present and the palpable. I echo without the least reserve your declaration (from Aiken, S.C.) that I ought to come home again before the "romance" of Charleston and the like completely departs. My *feeling* is with you absolutely on the subject; all my sensibility vibrates to the truth you utter. *Vous prêcher,* in fine, *un converti:* my native land, in my old age, has become, becomes more and more, romantic to me altogether: *this* one, on the other hand has, hugely and ingeniously ceased to be. But the case is, somehow, absurdly, indescribably difficult; one's behaviour, one's practical possibilities, being (for these cumbersome reasons) much less on the side of one's right feelings than on that of one's wrong. If I could go home for six months and see just what I want in just the way I want, I would make any sacrifice, or effort, to do it. But that is, inevitably, what I shouldn't do—and every six months that are added to my span of life make it more impossible. You see I *am* "too late"; not yet too late for Charleston, etc., but too late for myself. It would be grotesque to treat the molehill of a "run" like the mountain of a repatriation (for that I am utterly too late—on all sorts of material grounds as well as others); but I don't, constitutionally, *run;* I creep and crawl and falter and fumble—and in short the question lives in a cloud of complications. But let me firmly establish that I am romantically, as it were, with you up to my eyes. And as for the "Morgesons" and "Two Men," I read them long years ago (the first in queer green paper covers) when they originally appeared (as *you* did), John La Farge, of all persons, having put me on the first named. I seem to remember having even "noticed" the second[2] (probably in the *Nation* and very badly). I recall (of them) an ugly crudity like the unintentional exhibition of the contents of a pocket, or of an un-"made" bedroom—which one thought was "strong" or weird or vivid because it was like the things one didn't know, like a family row, with slaps and indecencies, over a bad breakfast, or something of that sort! But I suspect the books are somewhat documentary as regards New England rural *manners,* as such (unbefogged by Wilkins and Jewett sentimentality etc.). But what dim deep limbo must hold them;—I have been thinking of you (to better purpose than so) over a different sort of book-business—in tackling the queer job, that is, of putting together a nondescript memorial volume on William Story; which of course reeks (the *job* does—in a strange, baffled superficialised way) with Rome; which, in its turn, still always, reeks with you, and that far-away winter.[3] It would take me long to tell you how four or five years ago the Waldo Storys tackled me on the subject of making some use of W.W.S.'s papers, and how I at first utterly declined, how they returned to the charge (fearing awfully, I surmise, that Edith Peruzzi[4] would have a go at it), and how at last *de fil en aiguille* I have come to the point of really putting the thing through—or the greater part of it, during these current weeks; with the prospect even, perhaps, of making a sufficiently agreeable and *nourri* volume. Tell it not in Gath, keep it, please (as from *me*) utterly to yourself, but W.W.S. is, on a near view (as he was from afar!) thinner than thin—as a theme for "literature and art"; so that one has had to (very artfully and ingeniously) invent a way, a *biais* for doing anything with him. But some of the materials they have given me *are* interesting, and there hangs about the whole the thing, after all, that made me succumb (ungraciously!) to pressure: the fact that it's all about (in its own fashion) Rome—all about Italy. (It isn't even all—but I make it as much so as I can). I hope to finish in six weeks, or perhaps less, and when the book comes out, whatever misbegotten thing it proves, of course I shall send it to you. Only, oh! there are things I should put into it the better for a chance to talk of them with you!

December 23*rd*

I had to break off here two nights ago, and now I must really say goodnight, as the small hours again creep in (I have been writing other letters), and I am on the edge of the morning of Christmas eve. I have again just read over your admirable letter, and I feel that I have responded, in detail, to almost none of it. You thrill me, haunt me, with your South, and with the types I might have known and shall never know, and you speak to much the same purpose, of persons (Alice Warren, S. G. Ward, Florence L. F. etc.)[5] to the name of each of whom I particularly vibrate, and so much old association is behind them. Sam Ward must be a prodigious survival and Florence a strange (in many ways) *revival*. But about *her*, I confess to you, what has always stuck in my crop has been her marriage—though I don't suppose it was any more *baroque* than her mother's. (Grant [La Farge] was *here* a year or two before it, and I saw him and got my impression.) But much right have I to talk! Mrs. Lockwood[6] was at any rate, in a way, consistently baroque. I should tell you, I feel, how little I see your sister,[7] though it's a dreary thing to tell. It comes largely from our *both* living in the country and not in the same one—far from town and they without a London habitation. But I was half an hour with her last summer and am under a (perfectly honest) promise to go to Hereford for three days the very first time she asks me. Country visits have now immensely dropped out of my life—in consequence of which I really enjoy them much more in their rarity than I used to in their frequency. I resent (and don't understand) the single state of your niece Alice, who is handsome, charming, and with all her capacities and, as one would say, opportunities. *Qu'y-a-t-il là-dessous*, unless she is so much married to her parents, as it were, that the other step would be bigamous! I desire a message to Owen,[8] but I seem to infer you are not near him, and I know not indeed where you are; enviable as your account of your unshackled hermitage appears to me. My hermitage here, is somehow full of shackles: and small prosy *attaches* like tapes, buttons and safety-pins, that tie one down and forbid me to wander. I am not even enchained by a passion or by a nursery. I had from Owen a very charming and interesting letter [in answer to one] that I wrote him about the *Virginian*, which I ought in my turn to thank him for and will yet; and in which his reply to an objection that I had made to his treatment of his subject in one particular (kindly tell him from me as a Christmas *gracieuseté* or geniality) left me stubbornly unconvinced; more so even with his subsequent gained *perspective* of it, than before. But I must deal with him directly on these things, and wish indeed I had the real, the personal, chance. I am more "versatile" than he even suspects. But really, good night, good morning. Yours always and ever

Henry James

1. Mrs. Wister's mother, the actress Fanny Kemble, willed a clock to HJ and wrote some Shakespearian verses to accompany it. HJ kept the verses, titled "With My Travelling Clock," and some of her letters, although he burned most of his papers.

2. Elizabeth Drew Stoddard (1823–1902) wrote realistic novels set in her native Massachusetts, among them *The Morgesons* (1862) and *Two Men* (1865). HJ wrote a review of the latter, but it seems never to have been published. It was destined for the *North American Review*. The *Nation* review of 26 October 1865 was by Howells. The manuscript of HJ's review is preserved in the Barrett Collection at the University of Virginia, and the text has been printed in *Studies in Bibliography*.

3. They had seen a good deal of one another during 1872–1873 in Rome. See *Letters* I, 324–325, 328.

4. The Countess Peruzzi was the former Edith Story.

5. Mutual friends of their Roman days—Alice (Bartlett) Warren (who had given HJ the idea for "Daisy Miller"); Samuel G. Ward; Florence La Farge, the former Florence Bayard Lockwood, who married Grant La Farge, a son of the painter John La Farge.

6. Mrs. Benoni Lockwood, mother of Florence. See *Letters* I, 471.

7. Frances Butler Leigh, Mrs. Wister's sister, had married the Reverend James Wentworth Leigh, a younger son of Lord Leigh. Their daughter was Alice Leigh.

8. See letter to Owen Wister, 7 August 1902.

To Houghton, Mifflin and Company
Dictated Ts Harvard

Lamb House, Rye
December 29*th* 1902

Dear Sirs.

I have waited a few days to answer your letter of the 11th, because, being rather definitely conscious of an inability to utter an immediate Yes to your proposal, I thought my view might possibly be modified by a little more reflection. But I am sorry to say that this is not what has happened, and I keep you waiting not an hour longer. I do not see my way to engaging with you for a Life of Lowell for the American Men of Letters series, and I have had to recognise that my mind is not likely to change. From the moment I say as much as this it seems scarcely worth while to speak of the why and the wherefore—beyond saying, that is, that the subject affects me, somehow, as wanting in freshness; unless I should rather say that I myself am wanting in freshness in respect to it. I can not help feeling, in the presence of Mr. Scudder's Biography,[1] of the publication of so many of Lowell's letters (Mr. Norton's two volumes etc.)[2] and perhaps also as a consequence of the profuse journalistic attention that he received during his time in this country, and of all of which I was a near witness, that, in proportion to the quantity—the amount—of his literary bequest and in consideration of the tranquillity in which the years of his life were spent, there is not much *remainder* of subject, of career and material generally, to treat. This is particularly the case, to my sense, for a volume that has to fall back, inevitably, on criticism and "appreciation"—the story itself, simple, at the best, in its lines etc., having been liberally told. Save for the "Biglow Papers"[3] and the moderate collection of his lyric verse, his few volumes are themselves only critical work, literary and political, of which I am far from contesting the distinction, as I am far from questioning the high character of the man. But I don't see matter for another *volume*—as proceeding, that is, from myself. If there were a good many more letters to publish, especially letters of his residence in this country and his subsequent visit here, these would considerably ease the question off and contribute to the making of a book. But I am afraid there are not to any great extent and of a publishable kind. If there were, moreover, they would be highly agreeable, but not markedly *interesting*, and would moreover not lend themselves to the scale of one of your Series Biographies. Especially they would put nothing much more under its "critical" feet. So there is my melancholy case—with the detail of which I have troubled you more than I meant. I may even in spite of this add that I have taken to my heart a warning, in respect to biography without a real Biographic subject, from my actual difficult job of trying to treat W. W. Story as one. You may be interested to know that I am doing my best for *him* and that I shall have produced, I hope, an entertaining book, as well as a somewhat larger one than I expected. (I have but a few weeks' more—four or five—work on it.) But the subject, owing to its intrinsic slightness, has been all to *make*—to make by a system of importation of helpful material *into* it, by a system, as it were, of manufactured interest which has really required a diabolical art. That is why the volume has necessarily *grown;* the brevity of the subject making amplification of some sort or other positively vital. I don't mean for a moment to compare Lowell's intellectual history (*for* such meagreness) with Story's; I only mean that I am more than ever struck with the fact that the interest of biographic work must depend on intrinsic richness of matter. If a man has had a quiet life, but a great mind, one may do something with him; as one may also do something with him even if he has had a small mind and great adventures. But when he has had neither adventures *nor* intellectual, spiritual, or whatever inward, history, then one's case is hard. One becomes, at any rate, very careful. In spite of this lesson I am almost tempted to add that I should like to do an American Man of Letters if I could only think of one in your probable list (as yet *not* done) in whom the conditions would meet. But I am afraid I can't think of one, and that you will be scarce able to suggest him. Believe me yours very truly

Henry James

1. Horace E. Scudder's life of James Russell Lowell was published in 1901.
2. Charles Eliot Norton's edition of Lowell's letters (1894). See *Letters* III, 440–442.
3. *Biglow Papers* (1862) contained two series of satirical verses in Yankee dialect opposing the Mexican War and supporting the North in the Civil War.

To [Mrs. Francis Bellingham][1]
Ms Barrett

Lamb House, Rye
New Year's Eve 1902

Dear Madam.

Mr. Stanning, of Lloyds Bank, communicated to me today your kind invitation to look at your son's beautiful King George's Bowl,[2] in his keeping, and I lose no time in thanking you for this much appreciated privilege. I was delighted to rest my eyes on this admirable and venerable object (it has a beautiful color—the tone of old gold—as well as a grand style and capacity); for anything and everything associated with this dear old house has an interest for me so deeply have I in these five years attached myself here. I have a feeling for every ascertainable fact of its history, and am only sorry such facts are not more numerous: which would seem but to prove, however, that that history has been happy and tranquil, as the good old house deserves. I believe you and your children had never lived here, and condole with you on the loss—feeling as I do personally indebted to your peculiarly civilized ancestor who kindly conceived and put together for my benefit, so long ago, exactly the charming, graceful, sturdy little habitation (full of sense, discretion, taste) that suits alike my fancy and my necessity, and in which I hope, in time (D.V.) to end my days. Believe, dear Madam, in the renewed thanks of yours most truly

Henry James

1. The holograph is addressed simply to "Dear Madam" and there is no indication of the recipient of the letter, but she seems most likely to have been Mrs. Francis Bellingham, mother of the late owner of Lamb House.

2. King George I spent a night in Lamb House after his ship was driven into Rye harbor during a storm. He arrived at the moment of the christening of a daughter in the Lamb family. The golden bowl was his gift to the child. This bowl may have suggested the title for the novel HJ was beginning to write.

To Urbain Mengin
Ms Harvard

Lamb House, Rye
January 1*st* 1903

My dear Urbain Mengin.

Your letter, your beautiful book, your faithful remembrance, your shining magnanimity—all, all confound and overwhelm me, so that I approach you crawling *à quatre pattes* and with my forehead in the dust. I won't undertake to explain or attenuate my long and unmannerly silence—to which, moreover, I have again and again exposed your exemplary patience. You know me for the most execrable of correspondents, and there is nothing to add to that. Your great handsome wide-margined large-printed, yellow-covered *Italie des Romantiques*[1] came to me safely more months ago than I have the courage to confess to in round numbers. Call it *100* and *n'en parlons plus*. I mean let us not speak of my base delay. Let us, on the contrary, speak—a little—of the volume itself; though, as I understand, it was for you a super-imposed and inevitable task, you won't care to have it judged as you would an utterance of your heart—I have in any case attentively and appreciatively read it; finding in it much entertaining matter very succinctly and agreeably presented; especially liking your Lamartine, your Chateaubriand and your Mme de Staël. How little they all *saw* compared with *nous autres!* And to have had to become "romantique," and break a thousand window-panes, to see even that little! The only thing one can say is that they saw more—(more beauty) than the Pres[ident] de Brosses.[2] But we would kick their posteriors today for what they *didn't* see—especially that big yellow-satin *derrière* of Mme de Staël. What I regret is that you can have treated a poet of a vertiginous lyric *essor* like Shelley's without in any way indi-

265

cating his quality and splendour—which I don't think *fair*, as we say. He is one of the great poets of the world, of the rarest, highest effulgence, the very genius and incarnation of poetry, the poet-type, as it were. But you speak only of the detail of his more or less irrelevant itinerary, and put in scarce a word for what he signifies and represents. I regret it for the reason that French readers have very rarely occasion to hear of him, so that when by chance they do I can't but be sorry that the case isn't stated for him more liberally as *poet*. He was the strangest of human beings, but he was *la poésie même*, the sense of Italy never melted into *anything* (*étranger*) I think, as into his "Lines in the Euganaean Hills" and *d'autres encore*. "Come where the vault of blue Italian day. . . !" is, for *me*, to *be* there *jusqu'au cou!* And *de même* for Keats, the child of the Gods! Read over again to yourself, but *aloud*, the stanzas of the *Adonais* (or I wish I could read them *to* you!) descriptive of the corner of Rome where they both lie buried,[3] and then weep bitter tears of remorse at having sacrificed them to the terrestrial *caquetage* of A. de Musset! Forgive my emphasis. I feel as if my poor friends had lost an opportunity in the doux pays de France. Mais il ne s'agit pas de ça. Il s'agit de vous y souhaiter pour vous-même mille douceurs pendant l'année qui commence. I hope you are happily adjusted to Melun and that Paris is well within your extended grasp. It appears to have ceased, alas, almost completely to be within mine. I am very much where you left me last—save that I am a great deal older and *plus gros* and *plus pesé* and *plus solitaire*. I spend eight months of the year in this place (favourable to work and health and poverty and much *too* favourable to thought) and four in London, for which place I presently depart. Travelling is less and less in my line, and except that I greatly yearn to go back, before I descend into the deep tomb, to dear old Italy for a year. There we must still meet. I foresee that you will never come again to England, and France, for me, is but an engaging dream.—The Paul Bourgets were here (in England), as you probably know, for a few weeks last summer; but I saw them but for a few hours, in London, and have had no news of them since. I don't know in what *île d'or* they are wintering—but you must be better informed. Good-night— good-day; it is past midnight and I am, my dear Mengin, very faithfully yours

Henry James

1. Mengin's recently-completed dissertation for the French *doctorat-ès-lettres*.

2. Charles de Brosses (1709–1777) known as the Président de Brosses, of Dijon, famous for a lengthy dispute with Voltaire. A series of his letters on Italy was published in 1836.

3. The Protestant Cemetery in Rome which figures in "Daisy Miller," and where Miss Woolson was buried not far from the graves of Keats and Shelley.

To Mary Weld
Ms Private

Reform Club
February 16*th* 1903

Dear Miss Weld.[1]

I go on Friday down to Lamb House for two days in consequence of the outbreak there of a sudden complication springing from the purchase by Gasson the dreadful,[2] of the house and garden in Mermaid Street, that menaces and (potentially by any building on the ground) would fatally injure the west end of my garden. I have had to buy the ground from him at an extortionate price and now have got to spend money on enclosing it, all of which makes me sick. But I shall none the less welcome the Rye bookbindery,[3] which I think an excellent and probably fruitful idea—in spite of the so bookless character of so much of the population, or rather of all of it. If your friend does join you, which I hope, I promise you my own patronage. But you must get up the subject well meanwhile. It is very interesting, but it's slow and it takes no end of work. Poor binding is an abject thing, good a divine. Go in for the latter. I have been sorry to hear of your cold, but I can't but think your festivities worth it, after your long claustration at Rye. I wish you more parties now but no penalties. I am still without the sign of a dog and no time to occupy myself with the question. My purpose is firm to stay here till the first days of May. I am for Rye and Remington.

Henry James

1. Mary Weld (d. 1953) daughter of a classical scholar, served as HJ's secretary from 1901 to 1904; he dictated *The Ambassadors*, *The Wings of the Dove*, and *The Golden Bowl* to her.

2. J. H. Gasson, a tradesman in Rye, from whom James bought the garden plot adjacent to Lamb House for £200.

3. Miss Weld had asked HJ if she might use the studio in Watchbell Street (which he had purchased with Lamb House) to pursue her hobby of bookbinding during her many leisure hours in Rye.

To Frances Sitwell
Ms Yale

Reform Club
April 29*th* 1903

Dear Mrs. Sitwell,

How charming and interesting your note, and how deeply touched I feel at having your news from you in this delightful way. It gives me the greatest pleasure and I very affectionately congratulate you both.[1] Besides being good, your intention is beautiful, which good intentions *always* aren't. And it has a noble poetic justice, in which there is a dignity matching even with that of the Monument. You talk of the crown of your romance coming late, but what do you say to the total absence (at the same lateness) of all crowns whatever, whether of romance or of anything else?—which is the chill grey solitary portion of your faithful old friend,

Henry James

P.S. Please give my particular love to S. C[olvin], as you will see him before I have the chance to give him the very consecrating handshake—as to my sympathy—that I am keeping for him.

1. Mrs. Sitwell (1839–1924), who had been called the early Muse of Robert Louis Stevenson, had written to HJ announcing her engagement to Sidney Colvin (1845–1927), keeper of prints and drawings at the British Museum (referred to in the letter as the Monument). The bride was 64, Colvin six years younger; their romance had lasted forty years (Mrs. Sitwell's long-estranged husband had recently died). HJ attended the wedding in June.

To Hendrik C. Andersen
Ms Barrett

Reform Club
April 30*th* 1903

My dear, dear Hendrik.

What a cold-blooded Brute my interminable silence must have made you think me! Yet it has been no part of the plan of my tenderness to you to bombard you with letters that you would have on your mind, at the end of weary days, as answerable things; and moreover, the only decent letter I could have addressed you, all these weeks and months would have been one to tell you that I was miraculously able to come to Italy. I am, most damnably, *not*, and never, all winter, have been near it at all, and I think it is merely having had *that* mean and meagre news for you that has made me feel it better to give you no news at all. It is the old story—with all (the few) of my Italian friends. The only thing *worth* sending them is an announcement of one of my eternally delayed visits, and what I yet must send if I break silence is the mere shabby statement that I "can't come." So I *don't* break silence, and I have been as mournfully mum to you, my dear, dear boy, as to the rest. But please feel now, none the less, that I lay my hands on you and draw you close to me. I am reduced to mere blank unknowing *hope* that your winter may have been kind to you, your work crowned with encouragement and your personal existence free from worry or anxiety. The knowledge that your mother is with you has given me a certain ease of mind about you. I have been sure that you are weary and worn, but I also have cherished the belief that you have had a home, a hearthstone and a *present* affection. I hope you have both been in good health and heart, and I send my very friendly greeting to your mother.—For myself, I am very decently well and have had a very convenient and occupied winter—wholly spent, since January 15th in London—which I leave again, however, for Lamb House, a fortnight hence. I am to be there, as usual, without budging, all the summer, and next autumn. I wish I could think with any confidence, that there is a likelihood of my seeing you there—so delighted would be as you sufficiently know, your welcome. But I don't clearly work it out and am full of doubts and fears. I seem to see you—in my ignorance—sailing for home, with your mother, from some Italian or French port. Yet if you come up to Paris to see (or pick up) your brother, that gives me a gleam of hope. Don't "chuck" me this year, dearest boy, if you can possibly help it. Write me a word when you have *easy* time, and give me something to hold on by. Don't tell me anything sadder or badder than you can help. Give me a notion of what you have done—and oh, if you can, give me a photograph? All at some moment when you are not too dismally tired. You shall have, as a bribe, a photograph of poor old me (taken the other day), as soon as I get back to Rye. (They happen to have been sent there.) Good night, dearest boy, meanwhile. It's long past midnight, and I am ever so constantly yours

Henry James

P.S. I hope your young brother has had a prosperous winter and that you have been easy about him.

To William James
Dictated Ts Harvard

Lamb House, Rye
May 24*th* 1903

Dearest William.

How much I feel in arrears with you let this gross machinery testify—which I shamelessly use to help to haul myself into line. However, you have most beneficently, from of old, given me free licence for it. Other benefits, unacknowledged as yet, have I continued to receive from you: I think I've been silent even since *before* your so cheering (about yourself) letter from Ashville, followed, a few days before I left town (which I did five days ago), by your still more interesting and "important" one (of May 3d) in answer to mine dealing (so tentatively!) with the question of my making plans, so far as complicatedly and remotely possible for going over to you for six or eight months. There is—and there *was* when I wrote—no conceivability of my doing this for at least a year to come—before August 1904, at nearest; but it kind of eases my mind to thresh the idea out sufficiently to have a direction to *tend* to meanwhile, and an aim to work at. It is in fact a practical necessity for me, *dès maintenant,* to know whether or no I absolutely want to go if, and when, I *can:* such a difference, in many ways (more than I need undertake to explain) do the prospect of going and the prospect of *not* going make. Luckily, for myself, I do already (as I feel) quite adequately remain convinced that I *shall* want to whenever I can: that is unless I don't put it off for much *more* than a year—after which period I certainly shall *lose* the impulse to return to my birthplace under the mere blight of incipient senile decay. If I go at all I must go before I'm too old, and, above all, before I mind being older. You are very dissuasive—even more than I expected; but I think it comes from your understanding even less than I expected the motives, considerations, advisabilities etc., that have gradually, cumulatively, and under much study of the question, much carefully invoked *light* on it, been acting upon me. I won't undertake just now to tell you what all these reasons are, and how they show to me—for there is still plenty of time to do that. Only I *may* even at present say that I don't despair of bringing you round, in the interval (if what is beyond the interval *can* realise itself) to a better

270

perception of my situation. It is, roughly—and you will perhaps think too cryptically—speaking, a situation for which six or eight months in my native land shine before me as a very possible and profitable remedy: and I don't speak *not* by book. Simply and supinely to shrink—on mere grounds of general fear and encouraged shockability—has to me all the air of giving up, chucking away without a struggle, the one chance that remains to me in life of anything that can be called a *movement:* my one little ewe-lamb of possible exotic experience, such experience as may convert itself, through the senses, through observation, imagination and reflection now at their maturity, into vivid and solid *material,* into a general renovation of one's too monotonised grab-bag. You speak of the whole matter rather, it seems to me, *à votre aise;* you make, comparatively, and have always made, so many movements; you have travelled and gone to and fro—always comparatively!—so often and so much. I have practically never travelled at all—having never been economically able to; I've only gone, for short periods, a few times—so much fewer than I've wanted—to Italy: never anywhere else that I've seen everyone about me here (who is, or was, anyone) perpetually making for. These visions I've had, one by one, all to give up—Spain, Greece, Sicily, any glimpse of the East, or in fact of anything; even to the extent of rummaging about in France; even to the extent of trudging about, a little, in Switzerland. Counting out my few dips into Italy, there has been no time at which *any* "abroad" was financially convenient or possible. And now, more and more, all such adventures present themselves in the light of mere agreeable *luxuries,* expensive and supererogatory, inasmuch as not resolving themselves into new material or assimilating with my little acquired stock, my accumulated capital of (for convenience) "international" items and properties. There's nothing to be done, by me, any more, in the way of writing, *de chic,* little worthless, superficial, *poncif* articles about Spain, Greece, or Egypt. They are the sort of thing that doesn't work in at all to what now most interests me: which is human Anglo-Saxondom, with the American extension, or opportunity for it, so far as it may be given me still to work the same. If I *shouldn't,* in other words, bring off going to the U.S., it would simply mean giving up, for the remainder of my days, all chance of such experience as is represented by interesting "travel"—and which in this special case of my own would be much more than so represented (granting the travel to be American). I should settle down to a mere mean oscillation from here to London and from London here—with nothing (to speak of) left, more, to happen to me in life in the way of (the poetry of) motion. That spreads before me as for mind, imagination, special, "professional" labour, a thin, starved, lonely, defeated, *beaten*, prospect: in comparison with which your own circumgyrations have been as the adventures of Marco Polo or H. M. Stanley.[1] I *should* like to think of going once or twice more again, for a sufficient number of months, to Italy, where I know my ground sufficiently to be able to plan for such quiet work there as might be needfully involved. But the day is past when I can "write" stories about Italy with a mind otherwise pre-occupied. My native land, which time, absence and change have, in a funny sort of way, made almost as romantic to me as "Europe," in dreams or in my earlier time here, used to be—the actual bristling (as fearfully bristling as you like) U.S.A. have the merit and the precious property that they meet and fit into my ("creative") preoccupations; and that the period there which should represent the poetry of motion, the one big taste of travel not supremely missed, would carry with it also possibilities of the prose of *production* (that is of the production of prose) such as no other mere bought, paid for, sceptically and half-heartedly worried-through adventure, by land or sea, would be able to give me. My primary idea in the matter is absolutely economic—and on a basis that I can't make clear to you now, though I probably shall be able to later on if you demand it: that is if you also are accessible to the impression of my having *any* "professional standing" *là-bas* big enough to be improved on. I am not thinking (I'm sure) vaguely or blindly (but recognising direct intimations) when I take for granted some such Chance as my personal presence there *would* conduce to improve: I don't mean by its beauty or brilliancy, but simply by the benefit of my managing for once in my life not to fail to be on the spot. Your allusion to an American Pinker as all sufficient for any purpose I could entertain doesn't, for me, begin to cover the ground—which is antecedent to that altogether. It isn't in the least a question of my trying to make old copyrights pay better or look into arrangements actually existing; it's a question—well, of too much more than I can go into the detail of now (or, much rather, into the general and comprehensive truth of); or even that

I can ever do so long as I only have from you Doubt. What you say of the Eggs (!!!), of the Vocalisation,[2] of the Shocks in general, and of everything else, is utterly beside the mark—it being absolutely *for* all that class of phenomena, and every other class, that I nurse my infatuation. I want to see them, I want to see everything, I want to see the Country (scarcely a bit New York and Boston, but intensely the Middle and Far West and California and the South)—in *cadres* as complete, and immeasurably more mature than those of the celebrated Taine when he went, early in the sixties, to Italy, for six weeks, in order to write his big book.[3] Moreover, besides the general "professional" I have thus a conception of, have really in definite view, there hangs before me a very special other probability—which, however, I must ask you to take on trust, if you can, as it would be a mistake for me to bruit it at all abroad as yet. To make anything of this last-mentioned business I must be on the spot—I mean not only to carry the business out, of course, but to arrange in advance its indispensable basis. It would be the last of follies for me to attempt to do *that* from here—I should simply spoil my chance. So you see what it all comes to, roughly stated—that the six or eight months in question are all I have to look to unless I give up the prospect of ever stirring again. They are the only "stir" I shall ever be able to afford, because, though they will cost something, cost even a good bit, they will bring in a great deal more, in proportion, than they will cost. Anything else (other than a mere repeated and too aridly Anglo-American winter in Florence, perhaps, say) would almost only cost. But enough of all this—I am saying, *have* said, much more than I meant to say at the present date. Let it, at any rate, simmer in your mind, if your mind has any room for it, and take *time*, above all, if there is any danger of your still replying adversely. Let me add this word more, however, that I mention August 1904 very advisedly. If I want (and it's half the battle) to go to the West and the South, and even, dreamably, to Mexico, I can only do these things during the winter months; it wouldn't do for me to put in all that part of the summer during which (besides feeling, I fear, very ill from the heat) I should have simply to sit still. On the other hand I should like immensely not to fail of coming in for the *whole* American autumn, and like hugely, in especial, to arrive in time for the last three or four weeks of your stay in Chocorua—which I suppose I should do if I quitted this by *about* mid-August. Then I should have the music of *toute la lyre*, coming away after, say, three or four Spring weeks at Washington, the next April or May. But I *must* stop. These castles in Spain all hang by the thread of my finding myself in fact economically able, fourteen months hence, to *face* the music. If I am not, the whole thing must drop. All I can do meanwhile is to try and arrange that I *shall* be. I am scared, rather—well in advance—by the vision of American expenses. But the "special" possibility that shines before me has the virtue of covering (potentially) all that. One thing is very certain—I shall not be able to hoard by "staying" with people. This will be impossible to me (though I *will*, assuredly, by a rich and rare exception, dedicate to you and Alice as many days as you will take me in for, whether in country or town.) Basta!—I talk of your having room in mind, but you must be having at the present moment little enough for anything save your Emerson speech,[4] which you are perhaps now, for all I know, in the very act of delivering. This morning's *Times* has, in its American despatch, an account of the beginning, either imminent or actual, of the Commemoration—and I suppose your speech is to be uttered at Concord. Would to God I could sit there entranced by your accents—side by side, I suppose, with the genial Bob![5] May you be floated grandly over your cataract—by which I don't mean have any manner of *fall*, but only be a Niagara of eloquence, all continuously, whether above or below the rapids. You will send me, I devoutly hope, some report of the whole thing. It affects me much even at this distance and in this so grossly alien air—this overt dedication of dear old E[merson] to his immortality. I hope all the attendant circumstances will be graceful and beautiful (and *not* either Ellen or Edward[6] for the centre of the firewheel). I came back hither, as I believe I have mentioned, some six days ago, after some eighteen weeks in London, which went, this time, very well, and were very easy, on my present extremely convenient basis, to manage. The Spring here, till within a week, has been backward and blighted; but Summer has arrived at last with a beautiful jump, and Rye is quite adorable in its outbreak of greenery and blossom. I never saw it more lovely than yesterday, a supreme summer (early-summer) Sunday. The dear little charm of the place at such times consoles me for the sordid vandalisms that are rapidly disfiguring, and that I fear will soon quite destroy it. Another scare for me just now is the threatened destruction of the two little charmingly-antique silver-grey cottages on the right of the little vista that stretches from my door to the church—the two that you may remember just beyond my garden wall, and in one of which my gardener has lately been living. They will be replaced, if destroyed, by a pair of hideous cheap modern workingman's cottages—a horrid inhuman stab at the very heart of old Rye. There is a chance it may be still averted—but only just a bare chance. One would buy them, in a moment, to save them and to save one's little prospect; but one is, naturally, quite helpless for that, and the price asked is impudently outrageous, quite of the blackmailing order. On the other hand, let me add, I'm gradually consoling myself now for having been blackmailed in respect to purchase of the neighbouring garden I wrote you of. Now that I have got it and feel the value of the protection, my greater peace seems almost worth the imposition. This, however, is all my news—except that I have just acquired by purchase a very beautiful and valuable little Dachshund pup of the "red" species, who has been promising to be the joy of my life up to a few hours since—when he began to develop a mysterious and increasing tumification of one side of his face, about which I must immediately have advice. The things my dogs have, and the worries I have in consequence! I already see this one settled beneath monumental alabaster in the little cemetery in the angle of my garden, where he will make the fifth. I have heard, most happily, from Billy at Marburg;[7] he seems to fall everywhere blessedly on his feet. But you will know as much, and more, about him than I. I am already notching off the days till I hope to have him here in August. I count on his then staying through September. But good-bye, with every fond *vœu*. I delight in the news of Aleck's free wild life—and also of Peggy's (which the accounts of her festivities, feathers and frills, in a manner reproduce for me). Tender love to Alice. I embrace you all and am always yours,

Henry James

1. Sir Henry Morton Stanley (1841–1904) who made a famous expedition to Central Africa in 1871 in search of the explorer David Livingstone.

2. In his letter to HJ of 3 May 1903, WJ mentioned that his brother might find it strange to see Americans putting butter on boiled eggs and wrote of their "ignobly awful vocalization."

3. In addition to his celebrated history of English literature, Hippolyte Adolphe Taine (1828–1893) published *Voyage en Italie* (1866).

4. WJ spoke in Concord at the centenary of Emerson's birth, 25 May 1903.
5. Robertson James.
6. Emerson's children.
7. WJ's second son was studying in Germany.

To Edward Warren
Dictated Ts Huntington

Lamb House, Rye
May 24*th* 1903

My dear Edward.

Forgive me, first of all, this cold and mechanical form. I am obliged to dictate letters this morning, in order to make a sweep (or to help toward it) of arrears of correspondence that the fatal London (up to the time I left it a few days since) had caused, by its devilish arts, dreadfully to accumulate. So I make you profit by the legibility that is in the air, so to speak; all the more that it's important I shouldn't delay another hour to write you. This had been my full intention at each hour that preceded my quitting London; but even you too, in your noble impeccability, know what sometimes becomes, in Pall Mall and Piccadilly, of intentions in themselves irreproachable. So much spilled milk at every corner and crossing. It was imperative, not less than it was deeply desirable, that I should remind you of what you had said about my putting your name down for the Reform—remind you, that is, that, for this purpose, I should be accompanied, on the Candidates' Book, either by a proposer or by a seconder: preferably, it seems to me, in your interest, by the former. All the while I should have sent you a Members' List that you should look it over for some convenient name. I blush to say that I came away without possessing myself of a copy of the same, and that I am thus stupidly and helplessly writing to you without being able to send one. I am forced to go up to town, however, for Friday night, and I will then clutch the same.

Meanwhile, in truth, I am yearning to see you scarcely less about another matter—a dreadful little "preservation of picturesque character of Rye" question, which, suddenly sprung upon us here out of the blue, has, these last days, deeply disconcerted me: though not beyond feeling that (as with most of my disconcertments) half-an-hour's talk with you would help either to entertain a gleam of hope or to swallow, to gulp down, the black draught of despair. I am wondering, in short, whether there is any possibility of your coming down for a night, the sooner the better, one of these very next days. Rye is lovely at this hour (barring the little hideous black cloud I speak of), and almost as much worth your seeing in herself as if you had never seen her before. The little black cloud is that the pitiless, the almost infamous Whiteman, my opposite neighbour and proprietor of the two little old-world whitey-grey cottages at the end of my garden wall, threatens them with imminent and remorseless destruction unless the horror can be very quickly averted. I am trying, with feeblest resources, and another person or two is trying, to avert it if possible; but, so far as I myself am concerned, I should derive no end of moral support, by such brief communion with you on the spot (and face to face with the threatened treasure) as would morally (I speak only of moral aid) back me up. You remember well of course the small quaint structures I mean—to the right of the little eternally-sketched vista stretching from my doorstep toward the church: of which the one nearest me has the pretty little small-paned, square-cornered bay-window resting its short pedestal on the cobble-stones. Both have their little old gables, colour, character, almost silvery surface, and have always been the making—the very *making*—of the hundred or so water-colour sketches of the Vista annually perpetrated from in front of my door. It would *go*, without them—vista, character, colour, subjects, composition, everything: above all the very tradition of the little old bit of street itself, and the long-descended pleasant legend of its sketchability. What Whiteman proposes is to put up two raw, cheap, sordid workingmen's cottages and let them at eight shillings a week apiece. My gardener has for the last year occupied the hither one (the position is of course perfect for him, and for me). I have tried to intervene and supplicate, and with the effect of the *possibility* either of purchase (not by *me*—his terms are of course colossal) or of a lease, on conditions scarcely less exorbitant, in which I *should* have, ragingly, to play my part. The latter would be a "repairing" lease—and it is on *that* matter that I pine for some kindly light from you: as to what it would cost me, currently, to meet the repairing obligation.[1] The only thing is that time rather sickeningly presses. Whiteman is shakey, and his devilish little builder, Ellis, who has completed the horrible new plans for him, is, I fear, unremittingly and intensely poisoning his mind. I am trying to get him to give me (and the other person) to the end of the week to turn round. If you can't come for a night could you, possibly, for a few hours of the day?—though I fear that my importunity makes, at the best, ducks and drakes, for you, of golden minutes, each with its beauty and its sanctity. Still, the moment *is* (apart from the Horror) quite adorable here. My blessing on you all. Yours, my dear Edward, always (plaintively),

Henry James

1. HJ probably took care of the repairing lease; the old cottages were not destroyed, and HJ's gardener continued to live in his house long after HJ's death.

To Frederick Macmillan
Ms British Library

Reform Club
June 22<i>d</i> 1903</div>

My dear Macmillan.

Your letter and form of agreement meet me here today, on my return hither from three days absence from Rye, to which I return on Wednesday. With thanks, after signing, I enclose herein the agreement for "London Town"—or whatever it seems (shall seem) best to call it in default of mere "London" rendered practically unavailable by W. Besant[1] and by reason of one's wishing to mark that it isn't a question, exactly, of London *City*—alone. But this is as yet a detail and I am yours always truly

Henry James

1. Walter Besant (1836–1901) published in 1892 a volume on London as part of his series of volumes, *Survey of London*. HJ assembled this and other volumes, including Loftie's *History of London* (1883), Stow's *Survey of London* (1908), Sheppard's *Memories of St. James's Palace* (1894) and Milman's *Annals of St. Paul's Cathedral* (1868), in preparation for the book on London he planned to write for Macmillan. The book was never written. A pocket notebook in the Houghton Library contains penciled scribbles of his walks and observations during 1907–1908. See *Notebooks*, 325–330. He described the proposed book to Gosse as destined to be "a romantic-psychological, pictorial-social volume."

To Jocelyn Persse
Ms Harvard

The Athenaeum
July 16 1903

My dear, dear Jocelyn.[1]

Your letter reached me yesterday just as I was taking the train for this bewildering Babylon, and I have not, in the hurly burly, had a minute till now to thank you for it. I snatch my minute, at present, between other, but no more interesting, preoccupations. You were as happily inspired to write me so humanely as when you had that other inspiration—days ago—of coming to see me at the Reform. Cultivate always, in the future, inspirations as happy and as generous. I am lunching, tea-ing, dining out—till tomorrow, but finding it all less good, by a long shot, for soul and sense, than the least moment of that golden westward walk and talk of ours on Monday afternoon. A blessing rested on that, still rests, will ever rest. It will rest better still if you will remember that you promised to send a photograph to yours always and ever

Henry James

P.S. Let me find the photograph at Lamb House when I go back.

1. HJ met Dudley Jocelyn Persse (1873–1943), a Persse of Galway and a nephew of Lady Gregory's, at the Colvin wedding. This letter marks the beginning of a deeply affectionate correspondence. Hugh Walpole described Persse as "a young man-about-town, hunting, social, extremely good-natured." Shane Leslie said Persse "supplied something which HJ could not find elsewhere in his life." Persse wrote to Leon Edel on 31 August 1937, "HJ was the dearest human being I have ever known. Why he liked me so much I can't say." Walpole on one occasion said to Rupert Hart-Davis, "Believe it or not, HJ was madly in love with him." See the chapter "An Exquisite Relation" in Edel, *The Master* (1972).

To Jocelyn Persse
Ms Harvard

Lamb House, Rye
July 21*st* 1903

My dear Jocelyn.

Coming back late last night from an absence of several days I found your photograph and note awaiting me: in which I so rejoiced that I presently asked myself what the "blow" would (or wouldn't) have been had the gift failed me, or had I been fool enough not to invite it—and for exactly that hour. It welcomed me (with Maximilian's aid)[1] home to my empty halls and made them seem for the moment less lonely. Your portrait is good enough to be a satisfaction, in spite of belonging to the vicious order of the "licked" and stippled—the elaborately retouched: with its value of resemblance, however, not quite *all* pumice-stoned away. So, to cherish you the better, I have you already under glass and in a frame of modest richness—from which, to make room for you, I have evicted an old photograph of an old friend (of whom I have a later and much better one). I only regret that your brave young name, in your remarkable young fist, doesn't complete the presentment. For you are one of those of whom the beholder asks Who you are. However, you are not for the staring crowd.—My absence, of which you gently inquire, dragged and seemed long to me, from day to day; but I did the things that were necessary, both in town and country, and the rising tide of a more private existence now begins to cover the sandy space. From Friday P.M. to Monday morn, down close to Leith Hill in Surrey I had indeed rather a sense of peace in a lovely land and with some old American friends who have taken a house there. On Saturday I had quite a wondrous drive—in that miraculously rural, almost romantic Surrey country which is so absurdly near the dire South London. But these will seem pale adventures to *you*, luxurious youth, whom I seem to see launched on the huge (and agitating) wave of the King's visit, and into endless Irish junketting. May these things not float you too direfully far—far, I mean, from the virtuous *grind* of life and the sober realities that a homely friend can hope to share with you! The waters, here, verily, threaten to close a good deal over my own patient head . . .[2] more shallow inkpot. It is meant to do nothing of the kind—it isn't a bombardment (though it looks so like one) to reduce you. Don't be reduced; keep your course and bide your time. Only have it present to you— and never doubt of it—that no small sign of your remembrance will ever fail even of its most meagre message to yours, my dear Jocelyn, always

Henry James

1. HJ's dachshund, usually abbreviated to Max.
2. The letter is torn here.

To Violet Hunt
Ms Barrett

Lamb House, Rye
August 11th 1903

My dear Violet.

I am obliged for your Ferocious letter—you *have* a "rum" collection of places of resort. Lamb House, on your departure, relapsed into ascetic gloom, which has deepened hourly till the present 11.30 P.M. on this Tuesday, which is a climax of howling and desolating tempest. I trust you are not still on the roads. The whole constitution of things here has mourned you—inasmuch as the annual Flowershow taking place today, and the darling of Rye's heart, proved (through the weather) a blighted abortion, unredeemed by the fact that my despised little gardener took four "first prizes" and that no one else took more than one. Such is our homely news. With Shakespeare and the musical glasses you have obviously fared otherwise. Your comparison of genius to the passenger on the "liner" with his cabin and his "hold" luggage is very brilliant and I should quite agree with you—and *do*. Only I make this difference. Genius gets at its *own* luggage, in the hold, perfectly (while common mortality is reduced to a box under the berth); but it doesn't get at the Captain's and the First Mate's, in *their* mysterious retreats. Now William of Stratford (it seems to me) *had* no luggage, could have had none, in any part of the ship, corresponding to much of the wardrobe sported in the plays.[1] But I am writing a letter when I meant but to wave a hand. Goodnight—it's already Wednesday A.M.—for since beginning this I've had to go through the poignant drama of getting Max to bed. I envy you, quite, the great humane city, cool and convenient and wet—while the country is thus reduced to nought. Nevertheless you must risk the same indeed for us again. Yours, believe me, always
Henry James

1. One of a series of allusions to Shakespeare which led to HJ's being called a "Baconian," although he also said later to Miss Hunt, "I find it *almost* as impossible to conceive that Bacon wrote the plays as to conceive that the man from Stratford, as we know the man from Stratford, did."

To James B. Pinker
Ms Yale

Lamb House, Rye
August 13*th* 1903

Dear Mr. Pinker.

I just get your note about Methuen's request for expedition. I have indeed done everything in my power, but the Harpers have been of a mortal slowness in sending me proof of the last third of the Book—which I received but three or four days ago, and returned to Albemarle Street immediately, after due correction, to be sent as fast as possible back to New York. It is this remaining third that has not yet been supplied to Methuen, and, as the proof in question will have left for New York only yesterday, I am afraid there will be at least twenty days delay in its returning hither again with the numerous corrections embodied. The thing therefore is for the New York people immediately to be cabled to that they send a full set of proof of this portion (*exactly the same chapters and pages they last sent to me through Albemarle Street*) again, without delay, straight to you, to be handed over to Methuen—I mean without waiting for the corrections; though I shall thus quite tiresomely have to make them all again in Methuen's proof. This botheration would have been obviated if the New York people had shown the least heed for my re-iterated request for duplicates of proof, of the serial form, from the first. This request was made them from the first, both by letter and by personal supplication in Albemarle Street, but entirely without result. I went to see McIlvaine[1] about it myself, and he interviewed me on the subject in the attesting presence of Mr. Sidney Brooks, declaring that my request should have effect—but all to no purpose. I am writing to Albemarle Street today to ask them, urgently, to cable, but shall be greatly obliged to you if, without prejudice to this, you will kindly prod them in the same sense as hard as ever you can. They require all that can be administered of that. And will you also render me a small service which will help?—send, namely, over to Bedford Street and procure for me the *North American Review* which is due to be issued by Heinemann on the 15th, and have it immediately despatched to me here? It requires a small interpolation that I shall be able to make, but when I then post it off to Methuen the latter will have received, for setting up the Book, eight out of the twelve numbers of the Serial. Up to now he has sent me proof of a quantity represented but by three—so there is still a margin for his going forward. Let me add, moreover, that I shall be able to help him materially by sending him a duplicate Type-Copy of my MS., which I fortunately have clung to, and have not sent him hitherto because the printed text of the Serial contains inevitable little amendments and alterations. (Besides this I am afraid I lack duplicate of some passages omitted in the serial form and subsequently supplied to Harpers for insertion in the Book.)[2] However, these things will help to sustain Methuen in patience till the still wanting proof arrives from New York. I am myself writing to him today in this full sense. Pardon my long-windedness. Yours very truly

Henry James

1. Clarence W. McIlvaine, who joined Harper in 1891 and established the London office at 45 Albemarle Street.

2. Harper's failure to provide all the proofs resulted in a publishing error that exists in all American editions of *The Ambassadors* published during HJ's lifetime. An editor inserted into the book in the wrong order sections that HJ had omitted from the serialization in the *North American Review* (see letter to Pinker, 10 July 1901). The English edition, which HJ himself saw through the press, was accurate. Later, in revising the book for the New York Edition, he used a paste-up of the American version, thus perpetuating the error in that otherwise carefully edited and elaborately prepared edition.

To Jocelyn Persse
Ms Harvard

Lamb House, Rye
September 15*th* 1903

My dear Jocelyn.

Had I obeyed the impulse of the moment, on receipt of your letter from Norfolk I would have acknowledged it on the spot and with the liveliest signs of appreciation. "This, my dear Jocelyn, is charming—this is liberal and lovely—this does equal credit to your head and heart!"—Some such bundle of compliments would I have sent flying at you by return post. You wrote to me in a manner that gave me great pleasure and all my *disposition* was that you should straightway know it. But I have it always on my conscience to play fair in these matters, and I stayed my hand in order that you shouldn't too soon be crushed to earth by the sense of again *owing* a letter (not indeed that I believe this is a consciousness that so very

utterly flattens you out!). I preferred that you should have the pleasure (such as it is for you) of *my* owing you one, and I have left that
to you, these days, to make the most of. May it have counted a little
among the familiar joys of your actual romantic (as it strikes me)
career! I seem to see you roll, triumphant, from one scene of amiable hospitality and promiscuous social exercise to another; and,
sitting here, on my side, as tight as I can, with a complete avoidance
of personal rolling, I quite rejoice in the bright brave vision of you,
who are willing to do these things (that I *can't* do) for my mind, and
to take me with you, so to speak, in thought—so that, even while
I crouch in my corner, I get through you, more or less, the vibration
of adventure and the side-wind of the unfolding panorama. May
you, to the end of the feast, retain a stout young stomach! Which
is a manner of saying—may you suffer yourself to be pelted with as
many of the flowers of experience as you can (we won't talk just
now of the thorns); so that when we next meet you shall have at
least some of the withered leaves to show me and let me sniff. I
meanwhile am also a good deal pelted (pelted, not petted!) but I feel
as if my experience were more thorn and bramble. I sit (as I say) as
tight as I can, but it hasn't prevented these last weeks here from
being a time of really rather sharp discipline for me—in the way of
making some sort of terms with invasions, interruptions, complications, that I seem powerless to prevent.

I have been pressed with retarded work (which greatly interests
me), and have had at the same time to keep putting up and "doing
for" visitor after visitor, and running a crowded and quite un-
lucrative little hotel. People *chez moi* and howling storms (*chez
moi*, quite enough, too); these have been the chief of my diet ever
since you left me; and the end is not yet. The rest of this month
threatens to be much compromised and complicated, and I have
been anxiously studying your remark about the probability of your
being accessive to me in town (for the question of our evening
together), "about September 25th or October 1st." It looks at
present (to my great regret) as if I should be tied here by entangle-
ments straight *over* the 25th; and it also looks as if a friend abroad,
who comes to me for a week within the next three or four, would
precisely choose for his visit the time *from* October 1st. That will
force me to wait for my little rush to London, for his departure.
However, I take it, that you mean that you come back then for more
or less *permanence* on that latter date—and not that you are merely

there between a couple of prolonged absences. This simplifies and only makes necessary a short delay. I will write you of the earliest date in October that I shall be able to propose—I mean I will write as soon as I see my way a little clearer. I pat you affectionately on the back meanwhile and am yours, my dear Jocelyn, always and ever

Henry James

To James B. Pinker
Ms Yale

Lamb House, Rye
October 25*th* 1903

Dear Mr. Pinker.

I have not been unmindful that I promised Copy for *The Golden Bowl* to Methuen for the end of November—if humanly possible; and I have been gouging away at it with great constancy ever since the date of that vow, having this in view. As the case stands—and as I fear is always inevitably the case with me—I am not now as far toward completion as I should like—and being overpressed maddens me and destroys my work. Still, I am not, I think, too backward, and I shall be considerably less so five weeks hence. I have in good order, "highly finished" and copied, some 110,000 of the (about) 170,000 words of which it is my plan that the Book shall consist. What I can at present say is therefore that I shall in all probability by the end of November be able to deliver about three-quarters of the whole, following them up at a quick rate with the final quarter: this in case it be convenient to Messrs. Methuen to have that quantity in advance. It will enable them, I should say, practically to judge of the *whole* quantity, and even to begin to set up. I have been for the last ten days direfully interrupted by having absolutely to produce a promised article for the *Quarterly*,[1] as to which all procrastinations and pleadings had exhausted themselves. This has taken me off, but I shall presently get back and go straight again. You might enclose the present to Messrs. Methuen. Yours ever

Henry James

1. "Gabrielle D'Annunzio," *Quarterly Review*, April 1904, reprinted in *Notes on Novelists* (1914).

To Jocelyn Persse
Ms Harvard

Lamb House, Rye
[26 October 1903]

My dear Jocelyn.

This is but a poor word, omitted three days ago, very stupidly, to say that I have written to have a copy of *The Ambassadors* sent you—every copy I have succeeded in being possessed of here having successively melted away. Don't write to "thank" me for it—but if you are able successfully to struggle with it try to like the poor old hero, in whom you will perhaps find a vague resemblance (though not facial!) to yours always

Henry James

Monday P.M.

To Howard Sturgis
Ms Harvard

Lamb House, Rye
November 8*th* 1903

My dear Howard.

I send you back the blooming proofs[1] with many thanks and with no marks or comments at all. In the first place there are none, of the marginal kind, to make, and in the second place it is too late to make them if there were. The thing goes on very solidly and smoothly, interesting and amusing as it moves, very well written, well felt, well composed, well written perhaps in particular. I am a bad person, really, to expose "fictitious work" to—I, as a battered producer and "technician" myself, have long since inevitably ceased to read with *naïveté*; I can only read critically, constructively, *re*constructively, writing the thing over (if I can swallow it at all) *my* way, and looking at it, so to speak, from within. But even thus I "pass" your book very—tenderly! There is only one thing that, as a matter of detail, I am moved to say—which is that I feel you have a great deal increased your difficulty by screwing up the "social position" of all your people so very high. When a man is an English Marquis, even a lame one, there are whole masses of

The Green Room in Lamb House, James's winter workroom.

Marquisate things and items, a multitude of inherent detail in his existence, which it isn't open to the painter *de gaieté de cœur* not to make some picture of. And yet if I mention this because it is *the* place where people will challenge you, and to suggest to you therefore to expect it—if I do so I am probably after all quite wrong. No one notices or understands *any*thing, and no one will make a single intelligent or intelligible observation about your work. They will make plenty of others. What I applaud is your sticking to the real line and centre of your theme—the consciousness and view of Sainty himself, and your dealing with things, with the whole fantasmagoria, as presented to him only, not otherwise going behind them.—And also I applaud, dearest Howard, your expression of attachment to him who holds this pen (and passes it at this moment over very dirty paper): for he is extremely accessible to such demonstrations and touched by them—more than ever in his lonely (more than) maturity. Keep it up as hard as possible; continue to pass your hand into my arm and believe that I always like greatly to feel it. We are two who can communicate freely.—I send you back also *Temple Bar*,[2] in which I have found your paper a moving and charming thing, waking up the pathetic ghost only too effectually. The ancient years and images that I too more or less remember swarm up and vaguely moan round about one like Banshees or other mystic and melancholy presences. It's *all* a little mystic and melancholy to me here when I am quite alone, as I more particularly am after "grand" company has come and gone. You are essentially grand company, and felt as such—and the subsidence is proportionally flat. But I took a long walk with Max this grey still Sabbath afternoon—have indeed taken one each day, and am possessed of means, thank goodness, to make the desert (of being quite to myself) blossom like the rose.

Good-night—it's 12.30, the clock ticks loud and Max snoozes audibly in the armchair I lately vacated. I needn't assure you I will bury ten fathoms deep the little sentimental secret (of another) that you gave me a glimpse of. Yours, my dear Howard, always and ever,

Henry James

1. The proofs Sturgis sent HJ were of a novel called *Belchamber*, to be published in 1904. Its subject was an English nobleman, familiarly called "Sainty," who is lured into an unconsummated marriage, and whose faithless wife presents him with an heir. Sainty tolerates his wife's behavior and shows great affection for the child.

2. Sturgis's reminiscences, "A Sketch from Memory," appeared in *Temple Bar* 118–233.

To Henry Adams
Ms Mass. Historical

Lamb House, Rye
November 19*th* 1903

My dear Adams.

I am so happy at hearing from you *at all* that the sense of the particular occasion of my doing so is almost submerged and smothered.[1] You did bravely well to write—make a note of the act, for your future career, as belonging to a class of impulses to be precipitately obeyed and, if possible, even tenderly nursed. Yet it has been interesting, exceedingly, in the narrower sense, as well as delightful in the larger, to have your letter, with its so ingenious expression of the effect on you of poor *W.W.S* [*tory*]—with whom, and the whole business of whom, there is (yes, I can see!) a kind of *inevitableness* in my having made you squirm—or whatever is the proper name for the sensation engendered in you! Very curious, and even rather terrible, this so far-reaching action of a little biographical vividness—which did indeed, in a manner, begin with me, myself, even as I put the stuff together—though pushing me to conclusions less grim, as I may call them, than in your case. The truth is that any retraced story of bourgeois lives (lives other than great lives of "action"—*et encore!*) throws a chill upon the scene, the time, the subject, the small mapped-out facts, and if you find "great men thin" it isn't really so much their fault (and least of all yours) as that the art of the biographer—devilish art!—is somehow practically *thinning*. It simplifies even while seeking to enrich—and even the Immortal are so helpless and passive in death. The proof is that I wanted to invest dear old Boston with a mellow, a golden glow—and that for those who know, like yourself, I only make it bleak—and weak! Luckily those who know are indeed but three or four—and they won't, I hope, too promiscuously tell. For the book, meanwhile, I seem to learn, is much acclaimed in the U.S.—a better fate than I hoped for the mere dissimulated-perfunctory. The Waldo Storys absolutely *thrust* the job upon me five, six, *seven* years ago—and I had been but dodging and delaying in despair at the meagreness of the material (*every*—documentary—scrap of which I have had thriftily to make use of). At last I seemed to see a *biais* of subjective amplification—by which something in the nature of a *book* might be made, and then I could with some promptness work my little oracle. Someone has just written to ask me if the family "like it," and I have replied that I think they don't know whether they like it or not! They are waiting to find out—and I am glad on the whole they haven't access to *you*. I wish I myself had—beyond *this*. But even this, as I tell you, has been a great pleasure to yours, my dear Adams, always and ever

Henry James

1. Adams's long letter to HJ had been written on the preceding day in Paris. He told HJ, "You have written not Story's life, but your own and mine . . . I feel your knife in my ribs." His central argument was that HJ had demonstrated the provincialism of Boston in the half-century from 1820 to 1870. The text of Adams's letter appears in *Letters of Henry Adams 1892–1918*, ed. Ford (1938), pp. 413–415.

To Anne Thackeray Ritchie
Ms Harvard

Lamb House, Rye
November 19*th* 1903

Dearest Anne Ritchie.[1]

All sorts of things have happened since I got a beautiful letter from you several days ago—one of which is that I have been up to town for three or four nights; that I there, on Sunday last in particular, strove hard, and hoped exceedingly, to get to St. George's Square, but was beaten by combinations—and had to come home again baffled and rueful. I *did* on the Sunday P.M. make my pilgrimage to Hyde Park Gate[2]—and the time consumed therein—and in being afterwards carried off elsewhere by Sidney Lee,[3] whom I found there, was one of the reasons. The great reason, however, was all adequate, for I paid the dear man Leslie a *long* visit, almost—by his insistence—and found him (and left him I think) brighter and firmer than I had ventured to hope. He is as infinitely touching and backward-reaching as you say, and particularly beautiful in his humourous, kindly patience with his long ordeal. He is so gentle and friendly to me that he almost makes me cry—*does* make me indeed, so that I have to wink very hard to carry it off and not get forbidden the house—as a source of demoralization. And when all's said and done, it's a very handsome, noble, gentle end, full of all the achievement behind it and surrounded with such beauty in present and past—beautiful ghosts, beautiful living images (how beautiful Vanessa!)[4] beautiful inspired and communicated benevolence and consideration on the part of everyone. He lay there always *reading*—and I blessed, for him and *to* him, his invulnerable eyesight, and was able to tell him of two or three French books of some newness. He spoke with visible emotion of your assiduous tenderness to him—felt it, clearly, so that to speak of it—and of your and his long *link,* and your long fidelity, almost made him break down.—How can I thank you enough for taking our poor *W. W. S [tory]*—so kindly and *seeingly?* You know the difficult job it was with my so meagre material—and how I *had* to invent an attitude (of general evocation and discursiveness) to fill out the form of a book at all. And now I feel that in *this* you might have helped me more than I even *let* you—when I did ask you what you remembered etc. The lady Mrs. Procter quarrelled with Kinglake about was Mme Blaze de Bury[5] (no great figure of romance). And how I want to talk to you! But *pazienza*. I come up to town in January for three or four months and then we'll make it up. Yours meanwhile always and ever

Henry James

1. Lady Ritchie, HJ's friend of his dining-out days in London, was the eldest daughter of Thackeray and the sister of Leslie Stephen's first wife, Harriet Marian Thackeray, who had died in 1875. See *Letters* II, 157, 160, 209.
2. Residence of Leslie Stephen, who was dying of cancer.
3. See letter to Fullerton, 17 November 1901.
4. Vanessa Stephen, later Mrs. Clive Bell, Stephen's oldest daughter and the sister of Virginia Woolf.
5. Adelaide Anne Procter, whom HJ admired during his early London days. See *Letters* II, 199–201; III, 104–106. A. W. Kinglake (1809–1891), whom HJ had met at London dinner tables, famed as author of *Eothen*, a book of travels in the Middle East. See *Letters* II, 94. Mme Blaze de Bury moved in Paris and London artistic circles in the 1870s and 1880s. See *Letters* II, 53.

To Clara and Clare Benedict
Ms Basel

Lamb House, Rye
November 21st 1903

My dear old friends,—(for this applies also to the antiquity of Clare):

I am dazzled and delighted by your energy, patience and humour, over which I have been poring, pensively, all day. I say pensively because I am almost awestruck by such an exhibition of *universal* resources—beginning with the antiquity—or rather more even quality—of paste and scissors and culminating in what would seem the free play of the gift of prophecy. I sit here quaking and shaking at the far-off prospects—and suddenly you make me *believe* in it, put it before me in a manner not to be denied. I see as I linger, again and again, over the pleasing panorama,[1] that this is the way it *will* happen, the way it *must:* all the while that I have been doubting that it could happen at all. You and Clare *make* it happen, and your picture-packet seems to become my Travelling Bible and Guide, to be kept about from now on, and in the light of which I am to read my fate and arrange my conduct. I will be gentle with you even through my worst necessities, and endeavour to make Clare suffer as little as possible. I *feel* it, having to make her do so at all,—yet you render me the great service of helping me to get accustomed to the idea. May I not hope a little that she—knowing thus *her* fate—will be able to make some successful effort to do the same? Moreover I can't believe that we shan't at least *meet*, through some happy hazard—on some possibly crowded crossing or in some lightning-elevator, and I can assure her that if this does happen (your sybilline leaves omit the precarious page), I shall betray as marked a shade of recognition as—well, as the situation seems at the time to permit.—A week ago, being two or three days in town, I went out to the dreary Tilbury Docks to "see off" (by an "Atlantic Transport") an old friend and her daughter[2] who were embarking rather helpless and alone, and going aboard with them and with the herd of other compatriots (and almost into their very bunks) in the electric-lighted dark of the day, I said to myself "Now or never is my chance; stay and sail—borrow clothes, borrow a toothbrush, borrow a bunk, borrow $100: you will never be so near to it again. The worst is over—the arranging: it's all arranged *for* you, with two kind ladies thrown in." So strong was this feeling that if I had only had a thicker overcoat, and they, my kind ladies, had only had one extra bunk, I would have turned in *with* them and taken my chance. As it was I shoved my way out of the encumbered tubular passages—I stopped my ears against the national squeak—I turned and fled, bounding along Tilbury docks in the grimy fog and never stopping till I clutched at something that was going back to London. And *now* I see why this was so—why I funked the frugal "Minnehaha." I was reserved for your and Clare's extra bunk, on another line and at another date. It's *you* that will lend me a toothbrush and perhaps even $100—so it is evidently written. Alas, otherwise, it is the 100 $ that are the lion in my path. I want to "go" as much as ever, and it seems to be known over there that I do; but, intensely as I sit here and brood with desire, no opening through which that indispensable sum can come to me so much as glimmers on my anxious eyes. Everything else seems favourable—my banker's account alone is not. So unless the sum is paid in to it before August next (and for me to draw upon with an unrestrictedly free hand), the American people will see the cup dashed from their lips—I being *in* it, will come down hard. But I just drop that remark, without insisting. It would not be delicate of me to insist. Yet I read over and over again a passage in a letter I have just had from an English friend (W. E. Norris, the novelist), who has been returning through the U.S. from a tour more or less round the world.—I find, alas, I've destroyed it—but it was practically this: "All my American friends said 'You want to go, in N.Y., to the Waldorf-Astoria'—though heaven knows there was nothing I 'wanted' less. But I went—I *had* to—and I fought with the management, over everything (I *had* to) as with beasts at Ephesus. It's an awful place, and my bill was the awfullest part of it." So *I* sit and brood. But you and Clare mustn't let my broodings tinge your Vienna winter with even the mildest violet grey. I hope you are taking music, clothes, coffee and Butterbrödchen in all the usual appropriate doses. I am taking coffee again—for the first time for two years, and oh it's a real "first aid to the wounded." But I am taking neither bread nor butter nor clothes nor even music—for I am growing painfully fat, and that is affected by all these things: the Butterbrödchen making it worse, the clothes making it (or rather it making them) impossible—they won't "meet," and the music exercising the soul at the expense of the body (whereas it's just the reverse I want). Happy you, Clare, thin daughter of thinner mother! I have had here a very motionless (save for daily walks), and miserably moist autumn and suppose myself to stay till toward February 1st, when my only motion will be to London. You make me wonder where *you* are, with easy respiration, to roam—but I don't much care (as it were), if you are only punctual at the wharf. I shall *live* meanwhile in the precious Panorama—I am yours, both, very constantly and gratefully

Henry James

1. Mrs. Benedict, in a note to this letter, describes the "panorama" as a kind of scrapbook devised as a joke to show HJ traveling through the United States "surrounded by the leaders of fashion" and journeying in luxurious style. The Benedicts invited HJ to travel with them on their return journey to America, on the "Kaiser Wilhelm II," the following summer. He accepted and booked his passage for 24 August 1904.

2. This was Mrs. John La Farge, the former Margaret Perry, and her daughter.

To Howard Sturgis
Ms Harvard

Lamb House, Rye
November 23 *d* 1903

My dear Howard.

I return, not in silence, the inedited text[1]—for I must at least break my silence with thanks. Beyond this, however, it is difficult to write—comment and criticism would take me too far, and it is clumsy work (I mean c. and c. are); so that we must wait and *jaw*, and then I shall try and be—all proportions kept—as interesting to you as you are to me. Suffice it for the present that I am perhaps just a wee bit disappointed in the breadth of the celebrated nuptial night scene—though I don't think I confess that Miss Cholmondeley[2] will find it "adorable." Then I see, on reflection, that what keeps the scene, after all, decent, is that with the key in which you keep Sainty it can't not be. Resistance, pressure, the turn of the trodden worm—these things would have brought the crude fact to the surface, and only these *could*. It's kept under by his not pulling, not stirring it up. I re-wish immensely that I might have talked with you while the book was a-writing; in the interest of a Sainty with a constituted and intense imaginative life of his own, which would have been to be given (given more than anything else), out of which all relations with people would have come as baffled and tragic *excursions*—mangled and bewildering days (or nights) "out." But see already how clumsy it is to try to talk! We will make it up later. Start next year *another* book and let me anonymously collaborate. I *will* come down with joy for a night or two as soon as I am in town on a basis. And you will be—you *are* daily avenged, meanwhile, for my coarse invocations of what *might* have been by the humiliating difficulty I am having here over my own stuff—in which I've come nearer to sticking fast than ever in anything. Continue at any rate to remit—and to *per*mit—and believe yours always

Henry James

1. Of *Belchamber.*
2. Mary Cholmondeley (d. 1925), English novelist, best known for *Red Pottage* (1899), which deals with scandalous goings-on in English society.

To Howard Sturgis
Ms Harvard

Lamb House, Rye
December 2*d* 1903

My dear Howard.

I came back last night from a small, complicated absence—the "week's end" the other side of London and a night in London thrown in—to find your too lamentable letter, in which you speak of "withdrawing" your novel—too miserably, horribly, impossibly, for me to listen to you for a moment. If you *think* of anything so insane you will break my heart and bring my grey hairs, the few left me, in sorrow and shame to the grave. Why should you have an inspiration so perverse and so criminal? If it springs from anything I have said to you I must have expressed myself with strange and deplorable clumsiness. Your book will be the joy of thousands of people, who will very justly, find it interesting and vivid, and pronounce it, "disagreeable" etc., vivid and lively, curious and witty and *real.* My esoteric reflections over the subject will occur to nobody else at all, and the whole thing will excite marked attention. So if you love me let your adventure take care of itself to the end. Forgive, otherwise, this scrawl—I find a pile of letters awaiting me here. Send on *la suite prochainement* and believe me yours my dear Howard always and ever

Henry James

To Howard Sturgis
Ms Harvard

Lamb House, Rye
December 7*th* 1903

My dear Howard.

I am as usual backward in returning you your valued sheaf of prose—so much prose (even of my own especially) has, *ces-jours-ci,* been resting on me. I've had to pass and approve my own—a very different matter from so easily and yet tenderly chalking off yours. I'm afraid you haven't, all the same, waited for my chalk—but I nevertheless don't fail even now of meeting your three little queries. (*Do* forgive my beastly slowness.)

295

(1) There is assuredly no such English vocable as "onto"—and your proof-reader is there right. I dislike even "on to" (save in two or three particular applications—such as catching-on to etc.). *I* would say "taking the matter *to* very unsafe ground"—without any on.—But I would perfectly (2) say "reason you shouldn't"—and there your idiot is wrong. It is absolutely *good* English colloquial usage. As for (3) "if this thing was true," *were*, in the connection, *is* what it should be. But it *wouldn't* always be! Here "if" is as "whether." As for the rest, all the pages devoted to Sainty's relation to the Child are beautifully done and, on the whole, I think, the best in the book. Don't be depressed about it—it all holds the attention from beginning to end, and has never a dull nor an ineffectual page nor moment. So the public voice will declare. There are many things more I shall like to say about it when we next meet; but I can't help taking up now something you said in one of your last notes—to the extent of controverting it. You spoke of the part of the book after Sainty's marriage as the part in which "nothing happens to him." Why, my dear Howard, it is the part in which *most* happens! His marriage itself, his wife *her*self, happen to him at every hour of the twenty-four—and he is the only person to whom anything does. *Claude* above all, happens to him, and I regret that the *relation*, in which this would appear, so drops out. What happens to Cissy[1] is at all events comparatively naught—beside what is happening to S. all the while. And further, it seems to me, it wasn't at all a question (which you say you *should* have done) of making Sainty "resist." That isn't at all necessary for interest in the situation—what the subject only asks is that he shall *feel*. If he had only felt everything else as he feels his wife's baby (from the moment he hears him say, onward) the subject would have been fully expressed. But it is the baby, as a baby, that he actually feels—for a pleasure!—most. Goodnight, all the same! *Auf Wiedersehn!* Yours always

Henry James

1. In *Belchamber*, Cissy is the woman Sainty marries and Claude is his worldly cousin. See letter to Sturgis, 8 November 1903.

To Viscount Wolseley
Ms Harvard

Lamb House, Rye
December 7th 1903

Dear Lord Wolseley.

I feel I must absolutely not have passed these several last evenings in your so interesting and vivid society without thanking you almost as much as if you had personally given me the delightful hours or held me there with your voice. I have read your two volumes[1] from covers to covers and parted from you with a positive pang. They form a "human document" of a fascinating order, and I greatly rejoice that you were moved to produce them. Last winter, in London, when you once mentioned to me that you were doing this work, you said something a little sceptical, I remember, about the value of, or the warrant for, autobiography in general; to which I hadn't then the full and ready reply. This warrant is, for yours, that it renders your friends (even such old ones as me—to say nothing of your enemies, if you need ever, save in a campaign, have thought of *them*) the service of making them know you ever so much better still than they presumed to think they did. And you do this in such a naturally and inevitably gallant, familiar, unconscious way, that one's affection, if I may say so, is as much quickened as one's knowledge and admiration are enlarged. It's a beautiful, rich, *natural* book—and happy the man whose life and genius have been such that he has only to *talk*, veraciously, and let memory and his blessed temperament float him on, in order to make one live so with great things and breathe so the air of the high places (of character and fortitude). To a poor worm of peace and quiet like me—yet with some intelligence—the interest of communicating so with the military temper and type is irresistible—and of getting so close (comparatively!) to the qualities that make the brilliant man of action. Those are the qualities, unlike one's own, that are romantic and wonderful to one, and when I think that you have lived all your days by them and with them and for them, I feel as if I had never questioned you nor sounded you enough, nor (in spite of the charm of intercourse!) got half that one might "out of" you. However, men of genius never can explain their genius, and you have clearly been a soldier and a paladin, and understood that

297

mystery, very much in the same manner as Paderewski plays[2] or as Mr. Treves[3] removes appendices; so that we have to make the best of you at that. But what, as a dabbler in the spectacle of life, I think I most envy you, is your infinite acquaintance, from the first, with superlative *men*, and your having been able so to gather them in, and make them pass before you, for you to handle and use them. They move through your book, all these forms of resolution and sacrifice, in a long, vivid, mostly tragical procession—and many of them must have half haunted you, while you wrote, in the quiet days of Glynde. You have led, at any rate, so many lives, and the book tells but half of them. It even now almost takes my breath away to see that when I first knew you, years ago, in exquisite Portman Square, you were almost fresh from the shambles of "Cadmassie," [Kumasi][4] and yet you had so much other freshness too that you have had to wait till today to find them worth mentioning. What the book, meanwhile, does tell it tells admirably—with such good nature, spontaneity and juvenility. To have done and seen it all, and still be young and *write* young, and *read* young—well, that is to lead many lives, as I say. It has all been to me a piece of intimate (and rather humiliating) experience. I would give all I have (including Lamb House!) for an hour of your retrospective consciousness, one of your more crowded memories—that for instance of your watch, before your quarters, during the big fight in Ashantee, when the fellow was eyeing you to see if you wouldn't get out of it. All the Ashantee pages carry one immensely along. *But I feel like that fellow*—such is the effect of your style.—Well, the effect of mine will be to make you wish I would stop. Please don't dream, overloaded with letters as you must be, that this is susceptible of the slightest "acknowledgement." I scarcely dare, for common shame, let me add, to send Lady Wolseley any message save that I am conscious of the depths of my guilt to her and that I am preparing even now a full confession, for her private and particular eye. I haven't communicated with her for so long, in spite of urgent reasons why I should, that I should violate every law of proportion by tacking on mere "regards" to her, however affectionate, here. And yet I am with equal attachment and constancy hers and yours always and ever

Henry James

1. *The Story of a Soldier's Life* (1903), by Viscount Garnet Wolseley.

298

2. Ignacy Jan Paderewski (1860–1941), the Polish pianist, then at the height of his career.

3. Sir Frederick Treves (1853–1923) had removed Edward VII's appendix the previous year.

4. Wolseley commanded the expedition sent against King Koffee of Ashanti in 1873 and occupied Kumasi in 1874. Ashanti is the core of the old kingdom of Ghana annexed by Britain in 1902.

To Grace Norton
Ms Harvard

Lamb House, Rye
December 13*th* 1903

My dear Grace.

No indeed, it shall not be a "year" though it is already more months or at least weeks, than I meant it should be. My letter will still, however, in gratitude for your last, come into you pretty securely on the long lambent wash of the murmurous Christmas wave (at least so I pray), and will in that manner somewhat save the situation. You see I figure you, in the light of (supposed) British analogy, a good deal "washed" on Christmas—in the sense at least of the postal high tide breaking upon you in the white foam of letters. Your own beautiful last, then, to be plain—it now lies before me—is of August, a further backward try than I supposed (I mean remembered); a preserved flower of the dead summer which was born dead with us here (to the degree that we had none at all, and have been naturally further than ever from having one since). I write you, as usual, as with the feeling of the Eddystone Lighthouse a good deal around me—perched up on a rock over the sea, with the night winds of winter roaring and wailing about: they happen to be at it with rather particular fury and melancholy tonight. You will be moreover the only person I have spoken to (other than in some mere household connection) today or for many days—which I mention but as conducing to the local colour of our recent so rigorous history. You'll say this social void gives me, or ought to, such time to write to you that this should have been (since I heard from you) my fifth letter at least. But I feel, fortunately, no "void" at all—that is no practical one to throw me back on desperation (pardon the turn of my phrase). The days depart and pass, laden somehow like processional camels—across the desert of one's solitude. So you see I have in my way, all the multi-coloured "life" of my caravan. And every now and then I go up to London for two or three days (I do so, e.g., tomorrow P.M. for twenty-four hours): and every now and then somebody comes down here for the week's end; and after the New Year, February 1st or before, I resort to town for three whole months or more; so that my desolation has limits. And in the late spring and summer I am exposed, really, to the full force of the human throng—so that you mustn't think of me as merely and chronically sea-bound. It is only that in my situation—local situation—in itself—there isn't a cat (but only my dear little yellow dog) to speak to: which counts at times as a positive element of bliss.—I read over your letter and I come upon the Berensons,[1] whom I don't know, and as to *him*, confess to him by others, (and by his association with that "writing upon art") pedagogically, which I have long since come to feel as the most boring and *insupportable* identity a man can have. I am so weary, weary of pictures and of questions of pictures, that it is the most I can do to drag myself for three minutes every three years into the National Gallery. If *you* are not so it is only because you live at Cambridge Mass. You *would* be if you lived—at Rye, Sussex. And then you speak of Howells, the dear man, and of his having been to see you and telling you a sad and interesting thing about his melancholy and his living under the dominion of "fear" etc. which I *place* in him perfectly, from impressions received in long past years (I've scarce seen him for more than twenty); though not received from his verse, which I never have (so far as knowing it) felt *as* verse, very much, or found engaging, even from the melancholy (which I like and like *only*, in verse) to read. I think, however, that, real as this condition in him is, in a degree, it is yet a thing disconnected, in a manner, from his *operative* self, and that never has been the least paralysing, or interfering, or practically depressing, but on the contrary, very stimulating to endeavour. If his verse expresses it, his prose, so copious, expresses it not at all—and he has in short been so inordinately and cheeringly and cheerfully "successful." Still, I've always known that he has a strange, sad kind of subterraneous crepuscular *alter ego*, a sort of "down cellar" (where they keep the apples of discord) of gloom and apprehension. I can quite believe of his benevolence that he tried to point out my merits to your unperceiving mind—and should enjoy his zeal and deplore your darkness even more had I not reached a state of final beatitude in which one cares not a fraction of a straw what any one in the world *thinks* of one. How they *feel* for one, yes—or even against one; that as much (almost!) as ever. But how they *judge*—never again, never! And it is a peace worth having lived long and wearily to have attained.—Lowes Dickinson,[2] whom you also mention, I don't know (though he is a friend of several of my friends); as I know almost no Cambridge folk—going there almost never. But I've read a charming little Greek history-book from his hand, and have another volume I mean to read. You mention other persons and seem to have still others up your sleeve—but I have none, by way of anecdote and illustration, to match them with—my friends somehow make no show on paper. Besides, they are not *here*—thank goodness (though Phil Burne-Jones, by the way,—who has never been here—was to have come down, precisely, for this Sunday and couldn't). On the other hand London bristles with folk, as you know, and to touch it even for three days is to get again the sense of social quantity, if nothing else. Yet it is also more filled for me (almost) with ghosts than with the living.—I won't say more in respect to your so vehement gesticulations of deterrence—won't say it tonight at least—and that I *want* to "visit" the U.S. more than ever. I increasingly desire to—precisely to do that "visit the country at large"; but as I am also increasingly frightened, myself, at my desire, you may take comfort—my fear will perhaps paralyse me. If *yours* (of seeing me) also increases, why not come out and live in Lamb House during my absence and lend me Kirkland Street? A fair exchange. Think of this—or at any rate think somehow or other (better) of yours my dear Grace, always and ever

Henry James

1. Bernard Berenson (1865–1959), the American art critic, and his wife, Mary Logan Smith. Sponsored by C. E. Norton and Isabella Stewart Gardner, the future creator of I Tatti had established himself as an eminent authority on Renaissance art.

2. Goldsworthy Lowes Dickinson (1862–1932), of Trinity College, Cambridge, author of *The Greek View of Life* (1896).

To Millicent, Duchess of Sutherland
Ms Private

Lamb House, Rye
December 23*rd* 1903

My dear Duchess.[1]

I fear there is little chance this will reach you on Christmas Day in your remote stronghold, but let it take you none the less my warmest Christmas greeting and my lively appreciation of the kindness of your charming letter about poor dear W. W. S[tory], and my effort to perform in that record, in a manner, the operation of making bricks without straw and chronicling (sometimes) rather small beer with the effect of opening champagne. Story was the dearest of men, but he wasn't massive, his artistic and literary baggage were of the slightest and the materials for a biography *nil*. Hence (once I had succumbed to the amiable pressure of his children), I had really to *invent* a book, patching the thing together and eking it out with barefaced irrelevancies—starting above all *any* hare, however small, that might lurk by the way. It is very pleasant to get from a discriminating reader the token that I have carried the trick through. But the magic is but scantly mine—it is really that of the beloved old Italy, who always *will* consent to fling a glamour for you, whenever you speak her fair.

It's ill news, however, that you have been ill, though if I brightened an hour of that I shall not have laboured, as they say, in vain. I don't know that you make in Scotland as much of Christmas as we make—say, at Rye—perhaps because if you *did* make much your machinery of mirth (by which I mean your war-dances and frolic pipings generally) might bring down the vault of heaven. But I trust you are able to face, by this time, bravely, whatever demonstrations the discretion of the national character permits.

Take, meanwhile pray, the *Ambassadors* very easily and gently: read five pages a day—be even as deliberate as that—but *don't break the thread*. The thread is really stretched quite scientifically tight. Keep along with it step by step—and then the full charm will come out. I *want* the charm, you see, to come out for you—so convinced am I that it's there! Besides, I find that the very most difficult thing in the art of the novelist is to give the impression and illusion of the real *lapse of time, the quantity* of time, represented

302

by our poor few phrases and pages; and all the drawing-out the reader can contribute helps a little perhaps the production of that spell. I am delighted meanwhile to hear that you are to be in town a little later on. I go up next month—some time—to stay a goodish many weeks, and nothing will make me feel more justified of my adventure than the great pleasure of seeing you. Perhaps you will then even tell me more about the composition you have been busy with—there are literary confidences that I am capable of rejoicing in. But I shall rejoice more to know that health and strength possess you and that they dedicate you to a secure and prosperous New Year. I invoke a friendly benediction on all your house, and am, my dear Duchess,

Yours very cordially and constantly
Henry James

1. Lady Millicent Fanny St. Clair Erskine, eldest daughter of the fourth Earl of Roslyn, was married to the fourth Duke of Sutherland. Her interests were literary, and she published several novels.

To H. G. Wells
Ms Bodleian

Lamb House, Rye
January 24th 1904

My dear Wells.

You have done me the honour more than once to compliment me very handsomely on my faculty, such as it is, of Expression, but I think I must have won from you by this time at least an equal tribute to my power of silence. I won't pretend to enumerate the attenuating circumstances that cluster round my fault—I find it a simpler course to admit frankly that I have been graceless and abominable. The absurd part of the matter is, too, that I've *wanted,* day after day, to write—wanted to quite intensely from the day I read your two so munificently-conferred books. The more distinctively prophetic of the two has been the same "intellectual treat" to me as its predecessors; I mean that it has affected me, in the same way, as a record of romantic adventure of which You are the Hero. As such M[ankind] in the M[aking] thrills and transports me—so little does the interest ever flag that hangs about your brilliant gallantry in the sorest stress—about your dire exposure, your miraculous resource and your final hairbreadth escape. For you do escape, thank heaven, for other palpitations to come—the sense of which is one of the consolations of my life. Seriously, I found myself singularly subjugated by your volume and in abject agreement with its main thesis—which nothing, it seems to me, can stand up against. And the humanity and lucidity and ingenuity, the pluck and perception and patience and humour of the whole thing place you before me as, simply, one of the benefactors of our race. But my sense, too, is really all summed up in my vision, as I say, of the essential gallantry of your mind. It becomes, as one reads, inordinately objective, heroic, sympathetic, D'Artagnanesque.

Of the little Tales in t'other book[1] I read one every night regularly, after going to bed—they had only the defect of hurrying me prematurely to my couch. They were each to me as a substantial coloured sweet or bonbon—one pink, the other crimson, the other a golden amber or a tender green, which I just allowed to *melt* lollipop-wise, upon my imaginative tongue. Some of the colours seemed to me perhaps prettier than the others, as some oranges are the larger and some the smaller, in any dozen. But I (excuse me!) sucked *all* the oranges.

And with all this experience of you I had, in its season, that of knowing, in an imperfect roundabout way, that you made that admirable effort for poor Gissing *in extremis*[2]—my failure to thank you for which at the time must have affected you as an ugly note. When I say to "thank" you I mean—well, I mean *just* that, after all—though you may very well not have noticed whether I was audible or not. I was in truth, at the time you must have returned, audible only as a groaner and even curser under the discipline of the gout-fiend—having had, shortly after the New Year, to tumble into bed with a violent attack, and then to spend tiresome days in my chair, which I have only lately quitted. These conditions made writing, for a long spell, a highly avoidable effort. And *now* I can't write of Gissing with any pertinence, for I am concerned only with the prospect, some day not too long hence, of asking you, face to face, for the story of your surely most dismal, as it was a most generous, pilgrimage. I wish I could name the day for this by telling you that I am myself ready (under a luckily brighter star) to peregrinate to Folkstone—but I should have to strain the point of veracity to do so. My damnable gout attack has knocked my time into Smithereens; I am obliged to go to London next week, for some stay, and I fear that this is the only winter journey that, in my actual conditions, I can aspire to. What has become meanwhile of your own London pied-à-terre—and is there no chance of my seeing you *there?* I shall really be in town (105 Pall Mall, S.W.) till Easter— whereby can't you cultivate some simultaneity? I go to America to "look after my interests" on August 24th, and from Easter till then shall not budge (further than Folkestone), I devoutly hope, from *this* spot. All of which means that I should like immensely, and much rather sooner than later, to see you. I send meanwhile more and more comprehensive salutations to your house and am yours, my dear Wells, very cordially and constantly

Henry James

1. *Twelve Stories and a Dream* (1903).
2. Wells went to Gissing in St. Jean-de-Luz, when he learned that Gissing was dying, and remained with him to the end. See Wells, *Experiment in Autobiography* (1934).

To William James
Ms Harvard

Lamb House, Rye
May 6*th* 1904

Dearest William.

Your "Grigsby"[1] letter, which has just come in, would be worthy of the world-laughter of the Homeric Gods, if it didn't rather much depress me with the sense of the mere inane silliness of this so vulgarly chattering and so cheaply-fabricating age—the bricks of whose mendacity are made without even as many wisps of straw as would go into the mad Ophelia's hair. My engagement to *any one* is—as a "rumour"—exactly as fantastic and gratuitous a folly as would be the "ringing" report that Peggy, say, is engaged to Booker Washington, *ouf!* or that Aleck is engaged to Grace Norton. There *is* a Miss Grigsby whom I barely know to speak of, who has been in London two or three June or Julys (a friend of the H. Harlands and of Marie Meredith (Sturgis), George Meredith's daughter (whom I have seen, in *all*, five or six times, in the company of a dozen people—and *once* alone, for ten minutes, when in consequence of three or four DECLINED invitations from her I called on her at the Savoy Hotel. She is, I believe, a Catholic, a millionaire and a Kentuckyian, and gives out that she is the original of the "Milly" of my fiction *The Wings of the Dove,* published before I had ever heard of her apparently extremely silly existence. I have never written her so much as three words save two or three times, at most, to tell her I wouldn't come up from Rye to lunch or dine with her (I've never done it!) and I hadn't till your letter (entailing these so burdensome denegations—for a busy pen and a minding-one's-own-business-spirit) so much as been conscious of the breath of her name for practically a year—since about last June, that is, when I met her once at dinner in London (being there for a few days), and *never* afterwards beheld her or communicated with her in any fashion whatever. *She* must have put about the "rumour" which, though I thought her silly, I didn't suppose her silly *enough* for. But who—of her sex and species—isn't silly enough for *anything,* in this nightmare-world of insane *bavardage?* It's appalling that such winds may be started to blow, about one, by not so much as the ghost of an exhalation of one's own, and it terrifies and sickens me for the prospect of my visit to your strange great continent of puerile *cancans.* Who and what, then, is safe? When you "deny," deny not "simply by my authority," please, but with my explicit derision and disgust. The friends I cross (I suppose—still!) to N.Y., from Southampton with, are poor Mrs. Benedict and her daughter, C. Fenimore Woolson's sister and niece,[2] whom I have known these twenty-five years or so (having a house at Cooperstown and originally introduced to me by Henrietta Pell-Clarke). They come regularly, and have always come, to all the Bayreuth festivals, and *always* by the North German Lloyd boats, of which they know every officer, servant, nook and cranny. They go back from Bayreuth, as usual, this year (have been in Germany all winter), and wrote some time ago, begging me to let them make all arrangements for me on their ship—*exactly* my projected date; so that I should have nothing to do but to come aboard at Southampton, and find them, *dès* Bremen, having prepared place at table and everything else for me. As a lone and inexpert man I simply and naturally *assented* to that very kind proposal—as saving me all research and giving me peace of mind—so that if all goes well I shall probably be extremely glad to have done so. But that is the only witchcraft I am using. And I deplore having, in such haste, to write you about such rubbish, when there are "real" things to write about, such as they are, for which I have just now too little time. One of them is, precisely, that I must hurry down to the Station in a few moments, to meet Howells, who comes over from Folkestone to spend two or three days with me—leaving his daughter there because, apparently, eternally and interferingly "tired." They are out here without Mrs. H., who comes out with John later—for the summer and autumn, and were in London for three weeks before I came back here (Howells very pleasant indeed again to commune with, and the girl charming in her way)—which I did a few days ago. I brought my three months in London to a close with the liveliest sense of the good part they had played in attenuating—always—my big annual dose of Rye; but now it's a blessing to be here again, sticking as fast as possible till I "sail." There are some links still missing in the prospective sailing process—but they will in one way or another supply themselves, and it is my conviction that nothing but the jealousy of the gods in the form of some grave accident will keep me—*can* keep me—from embarking. So I am treating the matter as a prayed-for certainty. The great link missing is the question of any "let" of the house. *That* presumably is not to be, but even over that, even over its possibly costing me the services of Mrs. Paddington (she *hates* to be left here alone—I mean workless and masterless for long periods—which comes from her being so good a servant), I shall not worry. And I *may* be able to LEND the house to one or other of two or three possible subjects of beneficence—though I shall choose them very carefully. But this is all for today. I continue to found my life on Fletcher.[3] He is immense—thanks to which I am getting much less so. I hope (and gather) with all my heart that Billy is restored to comfort and beauty. I embrace you straight round and am always your hopelessly celibate even though sexagenarian

Henry

1. Emilie Busbey Grigsby, mistress of the Chicago traction magnate Charles T. Yerkes, had met HJ during the spring of 1903 in London and asked him whether she didn't look like his heroine, Milly Theale, in *The Wings of the Dove*. HJ was noncommittal but flattered, and had tea with the publicity-seeking Miss Grigsby at the Savoy. Thereafter she announced herself as his heroine, and soon the press began to rumor their engagement. See the chapter "The Reverberator" in Edel, *The Master* (1972).

2. See letter to the Benedicts, 21 November 1903.

3. HJ had recently begun to "Fletcherize"—that is, to chew his food into liquidity, as recommended by the popular food faddist Horace Fletcher.

To Henry James III
Ms Harvard

Lamb House, Rye
July 26th 1904

Dearest H.

Your letter from Chocorua, received a day or two ago, has a rare charm and value for me, and in fact brings to my eyes tears of gratitude and appreciation! I can't tell you how I thank you for offering me your manly breast to hurl myself upon in the event of my alighting on the New York dock, four or five weeks hence, in abject and craven terror—which I foresee as a certainty; so that I accept without shame or scruple the beautiful and blessed offer of aid and comfort that you make me. I have it at heart to notify you that you will in all probability bitterly repent of your generosity, and that I shall be sure to become for you a dead-weight of the first water, the most awful burden, nuisance, parasite, pestilence and plaster that you have ever known. But this said, I prepare even now to *me cramponner* to you like grim death, trusting to you for everything and invoking you from moment to moment as my providence and saviour. I go on assuming that I shall get off from Southampton in the Kaiser Wilhelm II, of the North German Lloyd line, on August 24th—the said ship being, I believe, a "five-day" boat, which usually gets in sometime on the Monday. Of course it will be a nuisance to you, my arriving in New York—if I do arrive; but that got itself perversely and fatefully settled some time ago, and has now to be accepted as of the essence. Since you ask me what my desire is likely to be, I haven't a minute's hesitation in speaking of it as a probable frantic yearning to get off to Chocorua, or at least to Boston and its neighbourhood, by the very first possible train, and if may be on the said Monday. I shall not have much heart for interposing other things, nor any patience for it to speak of, so long as I hang off from your mountain home; yet, at the same time, if the boat should get in late, and it were possible to catch the Connecticut train, I believe I could bend my spirit to go for a couple of days to the Emmets',[1] *on the condition that you can go with me*. So, and so only could I think of doing it. Very kindly, therefore, let them know this, by wire or otherwise, in advance, and determine for me yourself whichever you think the best move. Grace Norton writes

308

me from Kirkland Street that she expects me there, and Charles N[orton] writes me from Ashfield that he expects me *there*, and Mrs. Gardner writes me from Brookline that *she* absolutely counts on me; in consequence of all of which I beseech you to hold on to me tight and put me through as much as possible like an express parcel, paying fifty cents and taking a brass check for me. I shall write you again next month, and meanwhile I'm delighted at the prospect of your being able to spend September in the mountain home. I have all along been counting on that as a matter of course, but now I see it was fatuous to do so—and yet rejoice but the more that this is in your power. I received with your own a lovely letter from your Mother, for which I tenderly thank her—meaning certainly to write her within a few days. She gives me a happy report of everyone; which I earnestly pray these next months may confirm. There is little more to tell you before I again communicate— save that we are having a blazing hot and dry summer here; with a greater continuity of drought and heat than I remember for many a year. We have had it as quasi-tropical (for England) before, but have never had it for so many weeks on end. But Lamb House bears up under it, and the garden and garden-room are pure and unmitigated blessings. I write this in the latter, late in the evening, with a great deal of open window, through which not a stir of draught passes. So if you are to introduce me to a residuum of heat, I shall arrive quite acclimatised. But good-night, dearest H.—with many caresses all round, ever your affectionate

Henry James

1. Ellen (Bay) Emmet, HJ's painter-cousin, had married William Blanchard Rand and was living on a farm in Connecticut.

To Hendrik C. Andersen
Ms Barrett

Lamb House, Rye
August 10*th*1904

My dear dear Hendrik.

No letter from you was ever more charming and touching to me than your last from Montefiascone—wonderful romantic spot of which I envy you (even till I *ache* with) the so intimate and friendly knowledge. Every word of you is as soothing as a caress of your hand, and the sense of the whole as sweet to me as being able to lay my own upon *you*. It's so much money in my pocket—that of my otherwise so baffled spirit—to know you are at your ease in a good high place, with the rest and peace and idleness and cool air and brown cheeks and glorious wine all keeping you company; to say nothing of your still more human companions—whose being with you I more and more rejoice in and to whom I am particularly glad (both for him and for you) to know that your brother Arthur is added. Make him a sign of my ever so kindly remembrance. Stay as long and lie as loose as you by a stretched possibility can—you will be of ever so much more value to yourself and to the world in the end—to say nothing of your being of more, my dear, dear Hendrik, to your poor fond old H.J. I only groan over its being so beastly long, of necessity, before I can hope to get from your lips the charming echo and side-wind of your Italian summer—even as I had from you so beautifully, last year, the story of your primitive Norcia. I "sail," heaven help me, on August 24th—not to return, very probably, till late in the spring—all of which means, doesn't it?—dreary and deadly postponements. But may the time be full, for you, of triumphant completions and consummations—without a solitary blink of giddiness. It was after I last wrote you that your photos arrived and I haven't as yet so much as thanked you for them directly. But I find them, dear Hendrik, difficult to speak of to you—they terrify me so with their evidence as of *madness* (almost) in the scale on which you are working! It is magnificent—it is sublime, it is heroic; and the idea and composition of your group-circled fountain, evidently a very big thing. Only I feel as if it were let loose into space like a blazing comet—with you, personally, dangling after like the tail, and I ask myself where my poor dear confident reckless Hendrik is being whirled through the dark future, and where he is going to be dropped. I want to be there, wherever it is, to catch you in my arms—for my nerves, at all events, give way, with the too-long tensions of your effort, even if yours don't. And I yearn, too, for the *smaller* masterpiece; the condensed, consummate, caressed, intensely filled-out thing. But forgive this obscure, this wild and wandering talk. The photographs are admirably interesting and give the impression of an immense effect; but to know where I am, and where *you* are, I ought to *be* there, in front of each group, with my questions to ask and your brave answers to take, while my arm is over your shoulder; and for all that *ci vuol' tempo*, alas. Meanwhile, at any rate, my dear boy, I pat you on the back lovingly, tenderly, tenderly—and I am, with every kindest message to your blessed companions, yours my Hendrik, always and ever

Henry James

To Louise Horstmann
Ms Unknown

Lamb House, Rye
August 12th 1904

Dear Miss Horstmann.[1]

Don't think that I have forgotten that I promised a week ago to give you by letter, for the sake of distinctness, the principle heads of our little understanding about this house. I came back from Ascot and from London to rather a complication of calls upon my time, but have been meaning to make you a proper sign.

I give you up the house then on Saturday, September 3rd, as it will be all ready for you on that date, and you can send things on, which will be duly taken care of, even if you should not yourselves arrive immediately. And I understand that you take the house for six months from the said Saturday, September 3rd—that is, say, as the best estimate, to the first Saturday in March—with option to you certainly, of taking it on at the same rate for two or three months longer if you should feel so disposed.

You pay me Five Pounds a week for the same, and as I suggested the other day at Laleham, you make three payments of two months each: the first on taking possession; the second at the end of two months; the third at the end of two months more. This includes everything, I paying the Servants' wages, and you being liable, naturally, for no rates or taxes: except always the Gas-bill contracted during your stay, as is customary in such cases.

I make the house over to you, practically, just as I have been living in it and you will find it, I make bold to say, in very good and tidy condition. I leave all the Servants, who amount to five in number, including the Gardener and the Houseboy. The latter has

311

his meals in the house, but doesn't sleep, and the Gardener of course does neither, having his cottage close by the garden gate. You will find this functionary, George Gammon, an excellent, quiet, trustworthy fellow in all respects—a very good carpenter into the bargain and thoroughly handy at mending anything that gets broken in the house. I have endowed him with a small hand-cart, which is kept in the vault beneath the Garden-room, highly convenient to the House door, and which I find quite sufficient for the conveyance of my luggage, or that of visitors, to and from the Station for all comings and goings. The distance is so short that it means, save in some extraordinary rain, the complete suppression of flies—which is a great simplification.

The Cook-Housekeeper, Mrs. Paddington, is really, to my sense, a pearl of price; being an extremely good cook, an absolutely brilliant economist, a person of the greatest order, method and respectability, and a very nice woman generally. If you will, when you let her see you each morning, in the dining-room after breakfast, just also suffer her to take you into the confidence, a little, of her triumphs of thrift and her master-strokes of management, you will get on with her beautifully—all the more that she gets on beautifully with her fellow-servants, a thing that all "good" cooks don't do. She puts before me each week, with the Tradesmen's books, her own weekly book, by the existence of which the others are distinctly, I think, kept down. But these are matters that you will of course know all about.

The Parlour-maid, Alice Skinner, has lived with me for six years—that is with an interval of no great length, and is a thoroughly respectable, well-disposed, and duly competent young woman. And the Housemaid is very pretty and gentle—and not a very, *very* bad one. The House-boy, Burgess Noakes, isn't very pretty, but is on the other hand very gentle, punctual and desirous to please—and has been with me three years. He helps the Parlour-maid, cleans shoes, knives, doorsteps, windows etc. and makes himself generally useful. Also takes letters to the Post-Office and does any errands. Naturally he brushes clothes and "calls," in the morning, those of his own sex who may repose beneath the roof. Lastly, though of such diminutive stature, he is, I believe, nineteen years old.

The Servants will of course tell you just what tradesmen I

employ. I should be glad if you could go on with the same. They are in fact the inevitable ones of the place, and are all very decent, zealous, reasonable folk. I leave almost everything "out" save some books, of a certain rarity and value, which I lock up; and there is, I think, a full sufficiency of forks and spoons etc. as well as of all household linen.

Lastly, I take the liberty of confiding to your charity and humanity the precious little person of my Dachshund Max, who is the best and gentlest and most reasonable and well-mannered as well as most beautiful, small animal of his kind to be easily come across— so that I think you will speedily find yourselves loving him for his own sweet sake. The Servants, who are very fond of him and good to him, know what he "has" and when he has it; and I shall take it kindly if he be not too often gratified with tid-bits between meals. Of course what he most intensely dreams of is being taken out on walks, and the more you are able so to indulge him the more he will adore you and the more all the latent beauty of his nature will come out. He is, I am happy to say, has been from the first (he is about a year and a half old) in very good, plain, straightforward health, and if he is not overfed and is sufficiently exercised, and adequately brushed (his brush being always in one of the bowls on the hall-table—a convenient little currycomb) and Burgess is allowed occasionally to wash him, I have no doubt he will remain very fit. In the event, however, of his having anything at all troublesome the matter with him, kindly remember that there is an excellent "Vet" a dozen miles away, who already knows him, and would come by to see him for a moderate fee on any sign made. This person is "Mr. Percy Woodroffe Hill," Canine Specialist, St. Leonard's-on-Sea—a telegram would promptly reach him.

You may find it pleasant to belong to the little Golf Club out at Camber Links—to which a small and innocent steam tram jogs forth a number of times a day. I don't know that a six months' membership is worth a year's fee, moderate though the latter be; but it is sometimes a resource to have tea there of a Sunday afternoon, and if you will mention my name to the Secretary, Captain Dacre Vincent, he will gladly inscribe you on the easiest terms possible. There are lots of pretty late summer and early autumn walks—over field paths etc. I wish I might both carry out my American destiny and be at hand to put you up to my own rambles.

Perhaps, however, you are not like me, crimson ramblers—in which case you will walk about the garden!

Such is my simple showing—but I shan't scruple to add a post-script to this, later on, if any illuminating remark occurs to yours, your sister's, and John Boit's most truly

Henry James

1. Jessie Allen found tenants to occupy Lamb House during HJ's trip to America, and he got into touch with them. Louise Horstmann was about to marry John Boit, member of a family James had known in his early days in Rome.

3
The American Scene

1904–1905

3

The American Scene

Henry James returned to the United States after his long absence with anticipation and a confusion of feeling. He wanted to reassess his personal past, for he had reached his sixtieth year; and he wanted to write a kind of "Return of the Native," regretting that Thomas Hardy had used this title for one of his novels. The various papers he wrote mainly for *Harper's* and the *North American Review* became in the end *The American Scene,* one of the most searching and moving nonfictional works of his old age. He looked at the American land as one who had skipped twenty years of its life and he tried to connect the new tall buildings in Manhattan with his old and less sky-encumbered vision. In writing his earlier travel pieces in *English Hours*, those later included in *Italian Hours*, and his account of his travels in France, James had called himself "the sentimental traveller," or "the observant stranger." For his American journey he became "the restless analyst."

His visit was quite as startling as William James had predicted. He went first to stay with William and Alice at Chocorua, their summer home in the White Mountains, which he had never seen. Then he rewalked the streets of Boston and Cambridge, where he had acute memories of old strolls with Howells and the dreams of his ambitious youth. He revisited Concord and Salem; he re-examined New York, and went on to Philadelphia and to Washington, where he was invited to the White House and had a close view of President Theodore Roosevelt. His old friends were now in high places. Oliver Wendell Holmes, Jr., was on the Supreme Court, John Hay was secretary of state. Only Henry Adams remained immured in the pessimism and frustrations of his private life. As in the 1880s, Henry James felt Washington to be a rather empty, talkative city. He set out for the South, which he had never seen, in the hope of avoiding the coldest part of the winter. But the winter pursued him. He went to South Virginia, Richmond,

Charleston, Florida—to what had once been the Confederacy. Then, when it became clear that he could earn goodly sums of money by lecturing, he undertook to tell his fellow citizens about "The Lesson of Balzac." Audiences flocked to hear him, but more to see the man whose name had been known in America since his success with "Daisy Miller" and *The Portrait of a Lady* a quarter of a century earlier. He moved westward to Indianapolis, Chicago, St. Louis, and then on to California. This was new territory, and the shocks and impressions were surfeiting and exhausting. He fell back into New York State with relief and then into New England. After a spring and early summer in the East he sailed for home.

His letters tell us much less than does *The American Scene*. He was too busy to write many letters as he traveled. And he did not want to seem too critical of his homeland when he wrote to his English friends. But what we have of his journey, his hasty scribbles to Jessie Allen, Edmund Gosse, Edith Wharton, and his old friend Mrs. Wister, as well as certain others, hint at what his later New York tales revealed—his feeling that he could not accept the new America, its materialism and changed ways of life. As he later would tell Mrs. William James, who urged him to end his expatriation and live in Boston or New York, he could never make America his home. He found it rapacious, violent, ahistorical, and no place for his own subtle and analytic sensibility. The "crudity" of American wealth appalled him: everything existed to nourish commerce. "Business" was the national oracle, as distinct from Europe, where commerce, trade, and industry had their seats of affluence and power but had no cultural pretensions. He disliked the ways in which personal relations, the arts, the imaginative and intellectual life of America were subordinated to the tycoons he saw in the entourage of Teddy Roosevelt's "court" in Washington.

There is enough in the letters of these crowded months to disclose how James felt. His ripened views may be read in his prose-poem *The American Scene* and the tales of Manhattan in *The Finer Grain*, as well as in the masterly tale that was the outcome of his journey, "The Jolly Corner."

To Mr. and Mrs. William James
Ms Harvard

Deal Beach N.J.
Wednesday noon [31 August 1904]

Dearest W. and A.

Don't think me false and frail to have deflected into this adventure,[1] which Harry will have wired to you about and which I *knew* in my boots would more or less await me as a trap (very kindly) set on the wharf. I can't narrate it all now—everything since my landing has been and remains such a confusion of movement and mystery, and of being (ever so benevolently and agreeably) carried and done for. This place has even a *charm* (four or five miles from "Long Branch"); the weather, air, the light etc., are delicious, and poor dear old Mark Twain, who is here, beguiles the session on the deep piazza. But I expect to get to Boston and to rejoin Harry tomorrow night, Thursday, and I suppose we shall be with you by Friday P.M.—you know best the hour. Harvey is waiting to take me [on] a drive—and I don't scribble more, and I can find (amid much luxury) neither ink, paper nor stamps. Harry was a rare benediction yesterday at dock—amid *3000* people, and I left him to wire you and struggle with my extra luggage on to Boston. Voyage five days thirteen hours—ship colossal—but crowd excessive. Love in quantities—I am still tired. I have kept off two interviewing women for this P.M.—wishing to come down from P.M. Yours oh so yearningly

Henry

1. HJ was met on his arrival in the United States by his nephew, as planned, but he was almost immediately taken to the Jersey shore by his publisher, Colonel George Harvey, president of Harper and Brothers.

To Robertson James
Ms Vaux

Chocorua, N.H.
September 4 1904

My dear Bob.[1]

William tells me that he has just written you expressing the hope that you will come up here for as many days as possible while I am

319

here, and I add my voice, without delay, to assure you what pleasure you will give me by doing so. I got here night before last (having arrived from England—at N.Y.—on the previous Tuesday), and hope to stay as long as William and Alice do. I expect to spend October mainly in Cambridge etc. and one of the first things I shall then do will be to come over to Concord—especially if by that time Mary and Mamie shall have come back there. But meanwhile it will minister greatly to the richness of the family life, and the sense of reunion offered to my long-starved spirit, to have you here. The Dead we cannot have, but I feel as if they would be, will be, a little less dead if we three living can only for a week or two close in together here. I have come home at last (after twenty-two years since my last visit), to stay seven or eight months if possible (I have *let* my little house in England for six), and there are many things, in respect to feasabilities of seeing and doing here, that I want to talk to you about and which you may, I think, in some degree forward. So heaven speed your approach and our intimate meeting! I find this place more charming than I had fully apprehended it—though over here, for such a sodden absentee as I have long been, the *point of view* requires a good deal of taking. I greet the two Marys affectionately: please let them know at your first opportunity that I am only waiting to see them. Yours, dearest Bob, always and ever

Henry James

1. HJ's youngest brother lived in Concord, Massachusetts. The "two Marys" were his wife and daughter, later Mary James Vaux.

To Le Roy Phillips
Ms Harvard

Chocorua, N.H.
September 8*th* 1904

Dear Sir.

I am afraid I am really not able to help you or enlighten you in respect to the matter on which I just received your letter—the question of a "bibliography" of my productions early and late.[1] You see authors in general do not find themselves interested in a mercilessly complete resuscitation of their writings—there being always, inevitably, too many that they desire to forget and keep buried. This leads them to watch with some detachment the process of digging up. They of course cannot prevent it and must accept all manner of consequences—but they must at least keep their hands from the pick-axe and the spade. My own impression is that I have hitherto got off well and have been very little bibliographized, for I have escaped positively knowing of anything of the sort, and I have certainly escaped contributing to it. If you so generously enjoy the search I can only congratulate you on the zest of your curiosity—but I am at a loss to give you any general assistance and am yours most truly,

Henry James

1. Le Roy Phillips, a cousin of Morton Fullerton, a Boston bookman and a devoted reader of HJ, was not discouraged. He went on to publish the first full-length bibliography of HJ's work, including more than three hundred anonymous items in various American journals written during HJ's younger years. Phillips identified these by consulting the account books of the journals.

To James B. Pinker
Ms Yale

Chocorua, New Hampshire
September 14*th* 1904

Dear Mr. Pinker.

I promised you I would write you by the middle of this month, and I am extremely anxious not to fail of my vow, in spite of the fact that I have spent this fortnight, since my arrival in the great country, in such a manner as to make my communication, inevitably, rather less, than more, illuminating. I have been deep in these New Hampshire mountains—the sequestered country that is the *only* place to be at this season (and beautiful exceedingly), and it has represented no sort of contact with New York or Boston, as yet, completely desert and empty—and given me thereby no new or direct lights on the question of the advisability, or the bearings, of your coming over.[1] This is altogether what I was, when I last saw you, expecting—for the present. On the arrival of my ship in N.Y. I found an amiable representative of the house of Harper awaiting me on the dock, with urgent instructions, to take possession of me, and carry me down to the New Jersey coast to pay such visit as I

Henry James and William James, Cambridge, Massachusetts, 1905.

would to Col. Harvey and his wife: which in view of the general
lavish kindness displayed, was the course for me appreciatively to
take. I spent a day and two nights with them (with poor dear old
Mark Twain for fellow guest) and departed under the nursing care
of Harvey's private secretary, who restored me to N.Y. and sent me
on the way to Boston and this place, with every sort of zeal and
ingenuity for my comfort. In my first bewildered hours these things
were a great blessing. I had an assault of interviewers and escaped
them all for the time—all that is save one[2] who passed on here from
New York three days ago, and whom I couldn't cast forth (it was a
young woman with an introduction from the Scribners!) after a
journey of 250 miles. The Scribners have written me, that they are
immediately sending me proof of the *Golden Bowl*—but it hasn't
begun to come yet. It probably will in a day or two. Proof of my
Christmas tale for Harper has on the other hand come—and it has

been intimated to me (rather funnily!) that "the whole house" are particularly pleased with it![3]——I feel as yet, however, that nothing has occurred or may very soon occur to contribute to the question of timeliness, importance etc., of your coming, as far as I and my affairs are concerned. Enough time, none the less, has elapsed, for me to have been able to give the matter some thought, and now that I am really here and begin to be face to face, a little, with what I have already undertaken to do (as much as possible *while* here) I am asking myself whether my own interest ought to weigh at all heavily in the scale of your making so big a journey. The effect even of this short time has been to suggest to me that my book of Impressions, opening out very wide before me, will *by itself* give me plenty to do—and that your presence in respect to anything of mine that it is important to arrange this autumn may well represent a large effort without proportionate urgency. There is the matter of the Collective Edition—but mightn't that well stay over till the Spring? I seem to descry that I shall stick it out here, till (about) June next, and am thinking of settling the matter, as soon as I get back to Boston, by taking my passage in a Cunarder from *there*, for the first week in that month. Therefore if it seems to you that your visit will time itself for other matters as *well* at some date in the spring, I feel bound to suggest to you that it will time itself probably better for *me.* Troubled I am, you see, lest you should, coming now, find me provided for, as it were, for months to come—and should wonder why I hadn't spoken to you this particular word of warning. Therefore I speak it, for myself, and for conscience sake; but conscious of course, at the same time, that you may have many *other* good reasons—which you will estimate wholly for yourself. (I may add parenthetically, that it strikes me that the Collective Edition may perhaps be discussed better after I have been here six months than sooner.) So there is the case—and I needn't tell you I shall be delighted to see you if you do make the journey. If you could—or can—look at it sufficiently in the light of a holiday perhaps you will. My own so very rapid voyage—five days thirteen hours—made the bridge seem strangely short and easy. I forget what address will always be best. Yours, dear Mr. Pinker, ever

Henry James

1. Pinker, who had other business to transact, had offered to advance his journey to America if it could help HJ's immediate publishing arrangements.

2. The interviewer was Florence Brooks; the interview appeared in the New York *Herald* on 2 October 1904.

3. HJ's tale was "Fordham Castle" published in *Harper's*, December 1904, and reprinted in the New York Edition, XVI.

To Thoby Stephen
Ms Tate

> Chocorua, New Hampshire. U.S.A.
> September 16 1904

My dear Thoby.[1]

Your letter finds me in a far country—I left England a month (or upwards) ago, to spend eight or nine months in America. I am much interested in what you say of Professor Maitland's projected Life of your Father,[2] and well understand the value and necessity of some reproduction of his letters. But, alas, I am far from home, from my house and its contents; my papers are locked away in many places (I *let* my house before departing), and there is no one I can entrust with the task of diving into the very private accumulations in question. Therefore I can't *at present* satisfy myself—or satisfy all of you, as I should be delighted to do, as to what I may possess, in this order, from your Father's hand. I will make a point of looking into the matter as soon as I return to England—though I am afraid that that will be late in the day for Professor Maitland's purpose. This, however, remains true, meanwhile—that I *can't* have, in the nature of the case, very many of his letters. Living in London, as I did, for years and years, and as *he* did, and living mainly near him, we hadn't occasion frequently to correspond—for I saw him with a certain blessed frequency, as I like now to remember—like exceedingly and fondly and tenderly. What I occasionally had was a *note*— but he must have had many and more regular recipients of his letters.

It is very interesting to me to hear from you, and if we hadn't been so separated by all your absences and my own (living as I do in the country and very shy of London in the "full" time), I should have made a point of looking up Vanessa and Virginia. I send them my love and my blessing; I shall repair this long blank as soon as I am restored to dear old England. I hope you are settling or settled,

324

somehow and somewhere, and you have my very frequent remembrance and sympathy, all of you. Yours most truly

Henry James

1. Oldest son of Leslie Stephen's second marriage (to Julia Duckworth), Thoby Stephen was the brother of Vanessa Bell and Virginia Woolf.

2. Frederic W. Maitland's *Life and Letters of Leslie Stephen* (1906) contains no letters to HJ.

To Howard Sturgis
Ms Harvard

The Mount
Lenox, Mass.
October 17 1904

My dear Howard.

J'y suis, j'y reste—until you come, and until Monday next, 24th, on which night I shall have to be at Cambridge, Mass. I write you this ill-conditioned[1] scrawl meanwhile to cheer you on your way, to sustain and fortify your steps and light if need be your path. Also because I've a horror of facing you, dearest Howard, *without* having, before that, broken the horrid silence that has enveloped me since I parted from you and your admirable companion on that so intensely Japanese morning at Cotuit. I recognised *your* so handsome hand, as it seemed to me, in the address of a razor-strap so tiresomely forgotten by me there and so more than generously sent after me—an act I blush to the eyes to think I have never till now acknowledged. I have been in constant movement and almost *never* my own master for an hour—with other complications and hindrances, of which I will tell you. The social life, not unnaturally, is the note of this elegant, this wonderful abode,[2] where I have been since Saturday, and where your advent on Thursday next, will be extremely welcomed. It is an exquisite and marvellous place, a delicate French chateau mirrored in a Massachusetts pond (repeat not this formula), and a monument to the almost too impeccable taste of its so accomplished mistress. Every comfort prevails, and you needn't bring supplementary apples or candies in your dressing-bag. The Whartons are kindness and hospitality incarnate, the weather is glorious-golden, the scenery of a high class, and we yearn

325

for you and try to *tromper* the interval with talking of you without cessation. Your train is the 10.45 from the South Station—making 10.49 from the quieter little Trinity Crossing one, where I took it with greater comfort. You book (and check) through to *Lee,* but you change at *Pittsfield,* which you reach at 3, waiting there till 3.20. Then you take a little local train which brings you on, *past* Lenox, to Lee Station, which you reach at 3.40—for a drive of a short two miles to this house. I shall try my very best to meet you at Lee—though as I am lunching out that day there may be a shade of uncertainty. There is a dining-car on the train from Boston—which is huge in length (the train); being the Boston-Chicago express, all Pullmans. But lunch either early or late—the crowd thereat is considerable. But *à bientôt.* Yours dearest H. always,

Henry James

1. HJ added a footnote: "Ill-conditioned save for this marmorean paper."
2. Sturgis was in the United States at the same time as HJ, and they had arranged to be at Mrs. Wharton's together. The Mount was her recently built country house near Lenox.

To George Harvey
Ms Congress

The Mount
Lenox, Mass.
October 21 1904

Dear Colonel Harvey.[1]

Your letter of the seventeenth reaches me by devious ways, to this place, this A.M. and I lose not an hour in replying to it.

Your proposal of a dinner in New York next month, with Morley, Bryce & Co., is a very generously, quite nobly, hospitable idea, but I shall tell you the plain unvarnished truth (superficially ungracious as I may seem) when I say that such an occasion would have for me such unmitigated terrors and torments, that I shouldn't be able to goad myself, with whatever heroic effort, into being present at it. I should flee to Arizona or Alaska—I should run till I dropped. Such has had to be *always* my obedience to that constitutional infirmity, a rooted panic dread of banquets, toasts, speeches—any sort of personal publicity; in consequence of which

I have consistently, for long years, kept clear of them—in a manner that makes further, makes *final* consistency imperative. A dinner has been offered me, within the last few days in Boston (by the Tavern Club), and another in N.Y., by the Lotus, and I've dashed them both from my lips.

The great thing, however, is that during all my life in London, where such occasions abound, I have inveterately declined to be present at them even when the banquet has been offered, as it often has, to a close personal friend or a person for whom I had nothing but honour and admiration. I always gave my reason—that I never *went* to Dinners (with a big D.), and that if I should miraculously live to see one offered to myself that would be the one from which I should most be absent. Kindly consider then how I am committed to not greedily jumping at the demonstration, when complimentary to myself, that I would have nothing to say to when complimentary to others. And I beseech you very mercifully to take this rude response to your invitation as final and authentic—and to believe that I will do instead anything else in the world—instead—for you that you shall name![2]

I am very glad moreover to have this occasion of writing to you on another matter—that of your having patience with me (also!) in respect to my Impressionistic papers. I am very glad to be able to say that the stuff of them, the impulse toward them, gathers force and volume in my mind every day and every hour; so that, verily, I am moved inwardly to believe that I shall be able not only to write the best book (of social and pictorial and, as it were, human observation) ever devoted to this country, but one of the best—or why "drag in" one *of*, why not say frankly *the* Best?—ever devoted to any country at all. Only, *this* is what threatens a little to happen—and it's what I feared, at the back of my head, from the first: that the business of seeing, observing, noting, visiting, moving etc., in the right abundance and with the right surrender of one's time and feeling to it, takes up so *much* time and is such an affair all in itself, that one's opportunity to write, to sink into quiet *use*—of all one's stuff, is likely to be not a little crowded out while the formidable process goes on. I hold that one must follow up the formidable process—*that* is of the essence—as far as one can—the rest will come later and as it must.

I can't "knock off" things—and I want to produce a work of art, and shall. However, that will work itself out, and is already indeed doing so. I shall be able at no distant date to give you a first Instalment—a "New England," for which I have gathered in quite immense material. And meanwhile I have been bethinking myself much of my necessary kind of form and tone and feeling, how it *must* be absolutely personal to myself and proper to my situation. If Thomas Hardy hadn't long ago made that impossible I should simply give the whole series of papers the title of *The Return of the Native.* But as that's out of the question I have found myself thinking of, and even liking better—*The Return of the Novelist*[3]—if that doesn't seem too light and airy or free and easy. It *describes* really my point of view—the current of observation, feeling etc., that can float me further than any other. I'm so very much more of a Novelist than of anything else and see all things *as* such. But this determination isn't final, and doesn't doubtless, press—and I merely throw out the remark to help to keep you in patience. Believe me yours most truly

Henry James

P.S. My brother's house—95 Irving Street Cambridge Mass.—is an address (by itself) that now always finds me.

1. George Harvey (1864–1928) was one of Joseph Pulitzer's lieutenants on the *World.* He later owned the *North American Review,* for which HJ was writing his American impressions, and headed the publishing firm of Harper and Brothers, which he financially reorganized.

2. HJ finally consented to an intimate dinner without fanfare or speeches at the Metropolitan Club in New York. He sat between Mrs. Harvey and Mrs. Cornelius Vanderbilt. Mark Twain, Booth Tarkington, and Hamlin Garland were among the authors present.

3. The title ultimately found for the book was *The American Scene.*

To Jessie Allen
Ms Harvard

The Mount
Lenox, Mass.
October 22d 1904

My dear generous Goody.

It is the great complexity of things, in my American career (if career it be), that has kept me silent even when I have been on the point again and again of bursting into some sort of jabbery greeting; and I must ask you to set down to the same cause *all* my damnable dumbnesses and other roughnesses. My pen grows aged and infirm in the business of repeating to you, for conscience' sake, how little I pretend to keep up correspondences. I have absolutely no time for them, and ever so much less here than at home. Yet your two brave letters have been none the less a sweet note of dear old steadily-seated England (I like so to think that she's there, bless her grand-motherly heart), and have helped to keep it before me that, *after* all these most interesting and refreshing adventures and impressions she will still be there for me to wreak my constant homesicknesses (of the back of the head or the bottom of the heart) upon. I am finding my native land indeed a most agreeable and absorbing ad-venture and this golden glorious American autumn (*such* weather, as of tinkling crystal, and *such* colours, as of molten topaz and ruby and amber!) a prolonged fairy-tale. I came with a neat little project of paying no visits (of "staying") whatever, and have carried it out, still more neatly, by having spent but two nights at an hotel, and done nothing but proceed from one irresistably hospitable house to another. I can't give you chapter and verse for it, but it has all been a succession of extraordinary fresh and pleasant episodes, involving mainly old friends, and relations, but amid places and scenes en-tirely new to me (the *country* almost all) and of which the beauty has been almost a revelation. It is my good fortune, today, that I had seen in ancient years so exceedingly little of this mighty land: hence everything today has a really romantic freshness. I have lately been a week with our famous Mrs. Gardner (at her country-house, near Boston, which is full of the most delicious Venetian and Barbaresque associations). Her palace of art is closed and muffled, the petticoats thick until December, but I had such a glimpse of its outer precincts as to convince me that she is even more than I thought, a great and extraordinary little woman.[1] *Here* I am in an exquisite French chateau perched among Massachusetts mountains—most charming ones—and filled exclusively with old French and Italian furniture and decorations. The region, as I say, is lovely, and—or rather *but*—everyone is oppressively rich and COSSU (look up that French word if you don't know it!) and "a million a year" (£200,000) seems to be the usual income. I have been won over to motoring, for which the region is, in spite of bad roads, delightful—the mountain-and-valley, lake-and-river beauty extends so far, and goes so on and on that even the longest spins do not take one out of it. But I too go on and on, and I mustn't, now and here, as I've some thirty more letters to write. I hope you are in Italy at this writing and that the Barbaro in especial will have been "blest" to you. À propos of whose *padroni*, I went a month ago, in the White Mountains of New Hampshire to see (for the *day*, only) Miss Wormeley,[2] Ariana's sister, on her wonderful mountain perch, and found her exquisitely housed and established there, in presence of one of the most splendid of views and in charming conditions every way. On my *inextasiant* to her about them she said with melancholy and ironic amusement—"Yes, and yet for Ariana and Dan I'm always 'poor Kitty!' " She evidently communicated their commiseration, and as she frankly expressed it their "bigotry." They will evidently never see her more for she is rather aged and broken, and will never again come to Venice (*feeling*, besides, so differently from them about most things), any more than they will thinkably, ever come to America. But read this, for God's sake, to yourself, in the sweet privacy of dear little water-coloured 74 [Eaton Terrace], and not, aloud, under the resounding vaults of the Barbaro. You have written me much many-coloured picturing of your recent weeks—but I can't go into them, in response, but only breathe a benediction on your work and ways—save for a general conviction that "They" (the band of your vampires)[3] are, *must* be, *at* you again and doing their damnedest to bring you low. I go up to Boston (five or six hours) two days hence, but return here, after twenty-four hours there, for another week. See how *I* am brought low! This country is too terrifically big—and yet all this New England is but the corner of a corner of a corner. Fortunately the journeys, the long ones, are wonderfully comfortable (for feeding, sitting and all luggage arrangements; luggage so gratis, so "booked through"—through and through and so *safe*). But *basta*. Yours, my dear Goody, always and ever

Henry James

1. Mrs. Gardner's long-planned Venetian palace in Boston, Fenway Court, was nearing completion.

2. See letter to Katherine Prescott Wormeley, 28 November 1899.

3. HJ's euphemism for the beneficiaries of "Goody" Allen's attentions and generosity.

To Edmund Gosse
Ms Congress

The Mount
Lenox, Mass.
October 27*th* 1904

My dear Gosse.

The weeks have been many and crowded since I received, not very many days after my arrival, your incisive letter from the depths of the so different world (from this here); but it's just because they have been so animated, peopled and pervaded, that they have rushed by like loud-puffing motor-cars, passing out of my sight before I could step back out of the dust and the noise long enough to dash you off such a response as I could fling after them to be carried to you. And during my first three or four here my postbag was enormously—appallingly—heavy: I almost turned tail and re-embarked at the sight of it. And then I wanted above all, before writing you, to make myself a notion of how, and where, and even *what*, I was. I have turned round now a good many times, though still, for two months, only in this corner of a corner of a corner, that is named New England; and the postbag has, happily, shrunken a good bit (though with liabilities, I fear, of re-expanding), and this exquisite Indian summer day sleeps upon these really admirable little Massachusetts mountains, lakes and woods in a way that lulls my perpetual sense of precipitation. I have moved from my own fireside for long years so little (have been abroad, till now, but once, for ten years previous) that the mere quantity of movement remains something of a terror and a paralysis to me—though I am getting to brave it etc., and to like it, as the sense of adventure, of holiday and romance, and above all of the great so visible and observable world that stretches before one more and more, comes through and makes the tone of one's days and the counterpoise of one's homesickness. I am, at the back of my head and at the bottom of my heart, tran-scendently homesick, and with a sustaining private reference, all the while (at every moment verily), to the fact that I have a tight anchorage, a definite little downward burrow, in the ancient world—a secret consciousness that I chink in my pocket as if it were a fortune in a handful of silver. But, with this, I am having a most charming and interesting time, and seeing, feeling, how agreeable it is, in the maturity of age to revisit the long-neglected and long unseen land of one's birth—especially when that land affects one as such a living and breathing and feeling and moving great monster as this one is. It is all very interesting and quite unexpectedly and almost uncannily delightful and sympathetic—partly, or largely, from my intense impression (all this glorious golden autumn, with weather like tinkling crystal and colours like molten jewels) of the sweetness of the country itself, this New England rural vastness, which is all that I've seen. I have been only in the country—shamelessly visiting, and almost only old friends and scattered relations—but have found it far more beautiful and amiable than I ever dreamed, or than I ventured to remember, I had seen too little, in fact, of old *to* have anything, to speak of, to remember—so that seeing so many charming things for the first time I quite thrill with the romance of elderly and belated discovery. Of Boston I haven't even had a full day—of N.Y. but three hours, and I have seen nothing whatever, thank heaven, of the "littery" world. I have spent a few days at Cambridge, Mass., with my brother, and have been greatly struck with the way that in the last twenty-five years Harvard has come to mass so much larger and to have gathered about her such a swarm of distinguished specialists and such a big organization of learning. This impression is increased this year by the crowd of foreign experts of sorts (mainly philosophic etc.) who have been at the St. Louis congress and who appear to be turning up overwhelmingly under my brother's roof—but who will have vanished, I hope, when I go to spend the month of November with him—when I shall see something of the goodly Boston. The blot on my vision and the shadow on my path is that I have contracted to write a book of Notes—without which contraction I simply couldn't have come; and that the conditions of life, time, space, movement etc. (really to *see,* to get one's material) are such as to threaten utterly to frustrate for me any prospect of simultaneous work—which is the rock on which I may split altogether—wherefore my alarm is great and my project much disconcerted; for I have as yet scarce dipped into the great Basin at all. Only a large measure of Time can help me—to do anything as decent as I want: wherefore pray for me constantly; and all the more that if I can only arrive at a means of application (for I see, already, from here, my *Tone*) I shall do, verily, a lovely book. I am interested, up to my eyes—at least I think I am! But you will fear, at this rate, that I am trying the book on you already. I *may* have to return to England only as a saturated sponge and wring myself out there. I hope meanwhile that your own saturations, and Mrs. Nelly's, prosper, and that the Pyrenean, in particular, continued rich and ample. If you are having the easy part of your year now, I hope you are finding in it the lordliest, or rather the *un*lordliest leisure. I saw of course in Cambridge dear old C. E. Norton, very ancient and mellow now, àpropos of whose daughters and whose Dantesque fame this undergraduate pleasantry may, though irrelevant, interest you. The eldest of the three girls is much the prettiest, and they go declining, whereby they are known in college as Paradiso, Purgatorio and Inferno. The third is *very* plain. I commend you to all felicity and am, my dear Gosse, yours always,

Henry James

To Edith Wharton
Ms Yale

95 Irving Street, Cambridge
November 18 1904

Dear Mrs. Wharton.

I have really had it on my conscience not to write to you till I should have a definite presentable *occasion*—but for this occasion, and the support and color it would afford, I have all the while fondly yearned. Your so generous and interesting letter at last makes me feel that I may emulate G.W.S.[1] at a distance, without compunction—and indeed with some relief. For I figure to myself that your morning's work will have been spreading its wings in a stiller air than while a poor brother-author was trying so inveterately to raise the wind in a neighbouring apartment. Otherwise I should even now look toward you with a mystic finger (which you would yet understand) on my lips,—I shall rejoice to make the acquaintance of Mr. Updyke,[2] and to any sign I shall receive from him my response will be prompt. Only I shall not be on this spot *very* greatly longer. I am trying to make it possible to be in New York by the 6th or 7th of next month (though *I may* have to return here for a single week, shortly afterwards). But I shall look out meanwhile for the good Updyke, of whom your account is alluring. I feel as if I had succeeded in making my days here put on a respectable imitation of interest; but *il n'y a pas à dire*, Boston doesn't speak to me, never has, in irresistible accents, or affect me with the sweet touch of an affinity. My want of affinity with it in fact is so almost indecent that I have to resort to concealment and dissimulation. I ought, normally, to have more. But I have made two or three absences, and it was on a return from four days at Newport, night before last, that I found your letter. I found Newport quite exquisite, like a large softly-lighted pearl (and with the light partly of far-away associations); also the good August Jay[3] offered me a spin round the whole island, which the remains of a bad sore throat forbade my taking in the more or less icy air—this a sad sorrow to me. But he and his wife lunched with the Masons (Ella and Ida, with whom I was staying), and Mrs. Jay was very *brave* and ornamental. We lived over again, a little together, he and I, our wondrous Lenox day, and that makes me wonder if you have ventured to *badiner* again with "Smalley" since that so memorable collapse of *his* gallantry. I figure you rather as *revenue* from those adventures—sated and appeased even as Misa[4] with what she "leaves." In case you have any gain of leisure at any rate, I am venturing to send you an advance-copy of *The Golden Bowl* which comes out tomorrow. The Scribners have made so pretty a pair of volumes of it that I am comparatively brazen about thrusting it on people—the type and paper are so pleasing! Sustained by this sense I would in fact send a copy to Berry[5] in Washington if I had his address. Would you very kindly inscribe the same on a simple card and post it to me? And let me know, not less kindly, at your leisure, about when you yourself expect to migrate. If you are still as hospitably minded as you were during my blessed stay with you I should be delighted to profit by it for a week or two. I have seen almost nothing of Howard S.—he is too impenetrable at Wellesley. I greet Wharton very faithfully and am yours most constantly,

Henry James

1. George W. Smalley. See letter to Norris, 4 February 1896.

2. Daniel B. Updike (1860–1941), Massachusetts printer, whose Merrymount Press printed such early Wharton works as *The Touchstone* and *Madame de Treymes*.

3. Augustus Jay (1850–1919), U.S. diplomat, secretary of legation in Paris from 1885 to 1893.

4. Mrs. Wharton's elderly Pekinese.

To Sarah Butler Wister
Dictated Ts Congress

21, East Eleventh Street
New York City
January 1 1905

Dear S.W.

Forgive me, all mercifully, the outrage of this legibility, forced upon me by the pressure of notes and letters to write, and of a thousand things to do: the alternative to which, really is to sink into disaster and disgrace. So, for expedition's sake, I thus shamelessly, yet ever so gratefully, dictate. Your gentle letter from Washington found me, on my honor, at the very point of writing to you; as I had had it at heart to do from the moment that funny question was settled of my reading a Paper in Philadelphia. You can't think it funnier than I do myself—but there is a lurking reason in all things, and a fine method in my madness. Be patient with me while I horribly explain to you that on this coming tomorrow week, Monday, 9th, I am spending but that sole night in Philadelphia—pledged as I am to go on to Washington the next day, dine on that evening with John Hay, to meet the President, and then spend eight or nine days with Henry Adams. I thereafter come back here to complete a visit to Mrs. Wharton, beginning (this visit) tomorrow, but mutilated and *écourtée,* to her amiable resentment, by this said interlude at Washington. After *that,* I have rather intensely promised to spend a few days with Dr. William White[1] at Philadelphia, returning there for the purpose, and if you will *then* let me put in three with you at Butler Place I shall immensely appreciate the opportunity. I am cramped, crowded, consternated, almost overdone with the endeavour to reconcile conflicting occasions and desires: with very little time too to do it all *in*—considering there is much I am, even *with* all my helplessness, aiming at; matter for communication to you when I shall have the joy of seeing you. Don't come to my horrid little mercenary lecture if you

335

can possibly help it; but if you can't help it—though from Butler Place I should think nothing would be easier—come and brace yourself: brace yourself but (figuratively at least and sustainingly) *em*brace me! I shall see Owen at any rate, whom I really yearn to see (tell him, the wretch) and in short I shall get nearer news of you, which is what I crave. I am bearing up, but am half killed (with kindness); my good hostess here, Mrs. Cadwalader Jones, whom you wot of, having found nothing better to fit the view of it than to call me Célimare (le *Bien-Aimé*—of Labiche's farce.)[2] Remember thus what I shall have been accustomed to, and be easy and trustful (till he can patch it up better) with yours, dear S.W. always and ever

Henry James

1. Dr. J. William White (1850–1916), eminent Philadelphia surgeon, enjoyed an international reputation.
2. Eugène Labiche (1815–1888), writer of French farces, including *Célimare le bien-aimé* (1863), which deals with a man of many infidelities and cuckoldries who yet remains the spoiled darling of his womenfolk.

To William James
Ms Harvard

Rittenhouse Club
Philadelphia
January 10 [1905]

Dearest W. and A.

I scrawl this word while I wait for my train-hour to Washington and while Owen Wister awaits my going on the sofa behind me (to go to station *with* me) just to say that my performance last night[1] was a complete success, a brilliant one, an easy one, with no flaw save the immense and *foreseen* (this fortnight, by *me*) OVERDONE-ness of the occasion: *five or six hundred* people in a hall stuffed to suffocation, tho' very large and with perfect audibility, and making for a "literary address" an inevitably rather false and "fashionable" *milieu*. But it went beautifully—and I revealed to myself a talent for lecturing. Miss Repplier[2] introduced me admirably and was really lyrical at close. But more from Washington.

Henry

P.S. The practical and ideal *kindness* of the people here passes belief!

1. HJ's Philadelphia lecture, "The Lesson of Balzac."

2. Agnes Repplier (1855–1950), well known at the time for her witty and graceful essays. See letter to Gosse, 16–18 February 1905.

To Mary Cadwalader Jones
Ms Harvard

1603 H. St.
Washington D.C.
January 13 1905

Dearest Benefactress!

A word of thanks, heaped up and flowing over, for everything you have lately surpassed yourself in doing for me—for the exquisite bounty which follows my steps and hangs about me like the soft music in some gilded and flowered Masque or fairytale. I am, briefly, doing as well here as I can do without your magic and your mercy, and I am, above all, abundantly justified of my yearning little Southward move. It's ever so much blander and softer an air, already, and everything human and social is in mild harmony with that. Henry Adams, dear man, is a philosophic father to us, and La Farge, Saint Gaudens and even your unassuming Célimare expand and gently extravagate in the large license of Liberty Hall. We went (without Henry) last night to a big and really quite pompous function at the White House—where, supper being (for the comparatively select few) served at small—or smallish—tables, the President did St.-G. and H.J. the honour to put us at his—with Célimare next the lady who was at his right. If this is "royal favour" I suppose poor Célimare ought to bloom. Theodore Rex is at any rate a really extraordinary creature for native intensity, veracity and *bonhomie*—he plays his part with the best will in the world and I recognise his amusing likeability. McKim's[1] dinner was a big success and beautifully done—but the Eagle screamed in the speeches as I didn't know that that Fowl was still (after all these years and improvements) *permitted* to do. It was werry werry quaint and queer,—but so is *everything*, sans exception, and the sensitive Célimare absorbs it at every pore. His affair at Philadelphia, a (to *him*) dazzling success; a huge concourse, five or six hundred folk, a vast hall and perfect brazen assurance and audibility on Célimare's part. *Il s'est révélé conférencier*, and on the strength of it is to sing his little song again (for a heavy fee) at Bryn Mawr, on the 19th. I come back then to Philadelphia (the *most*, the fantastically, kind) and stay three days with J. William White and three days at Butler Place;[2] after which I retrace again my steps southwards *straight*,—without stopping here. I go for two days to Richmond and then for four or five down to Charleston to meet there Owen Wister, invalidical (nervously), but ever so amiable etc. This will make a *short* Washington—but a quite sufficient one (especially if I come back much later on for a few days). But farewell— my letters devour me; I have 390 still to write. I think I rather *did* make the point at suite 884[3] (at the last) that I *couldn't* come back there. A thousand thanks for the photographic service. Continue to be *invraisemblable*, give my love to Beatrix, the Earth-shaker, and believe in the affection of your clinging

Célimare.

1. Charles Follen McKim (1847–1909), leader of the neoclassical revival in architecture and member of the influential firm of McKim, Mead and White.
2. Mrs. Wister's Philadelphia home.
3. Mrs. Wharton's New York home, 884 Park Avenue.

To Jessie Allen
Ms Harvard

Washington
January 16th 1905

My dear generous Goody.

I am writing you under the inspiration of your ever so kind and charming letter of the 3d last—writing you thirty words though I haven't really time for thirteen or for three. But I *must* greet you and bless you, even though giving you an account of my accumulated impressions and adventures (though *that's* a wild word for really very mild matters) is out of the question. Arrears (oh, this horrible American blotting paper!) pile up and one can't remount, all breathlessly, the stream of time. I've been spending a month in the horrific, the unspeakable, extraordinary, yet partly interesting, amusing, and above all fantastically *bristling* New York, and now I am here (on my way to the south) for a fortnight, and find the conditions ever so much balmier and pleasanter. I am staying with an old friend who has a charming house—Henry Adams, of ancient

Presidential race—and, as everywhere, seeing more people than I have use for. They are all amiable, but of imperfect identity—and *il y en a trop, juste ciel, il y en a trop!* I go an hour hence to the capitol, to the Senate, for Cabot Lodge kindly to show me that august Body in session, I then hurry away to lunch at the Secretary of State's (John Hay's); I rush then to a literary conference by a French *littérateur* (Funck-Brentano) patronized by Mrs. Hay, in one of the saloons of the White House; I *try* afterwards to call on funny little Mrs. Slater to whom I have promised it, and I dine, subsequently, at the French Embassy.[1] Funny little Mrs. S., in much-"crushed" strawberry-coloured satin and many, many diamonds, accosted me three or four nights since at the annual "Diplomatic Reception" at the White House and fixed me, remindingly, insistently, with her little Punch-and-Judy smile—but I have neglected her till now (she *is* more *négligeable* here than was given out), and only want to go in order to amuse you with her by the dear little tea table at 74^2—bless its little Babylonianly buttressed walls!—At the said Reception, by the way, the President and Mrs. Roosevelt had invited me to stay over (with the select couple of hundred of the inner "*entrée*") to supper, and the former did me the honour to put me at *his* table (of ten persons), next to the lady (wife of a member of the Cabinet) who was next him; so that I had a great deal of his extraordinary talk and indescribable overwhelming, but really very attaching personality. We were all, at supper, at smallish tables, and the whole occasion, throughout, was a curious and striking example of the stride Theodore has taken toward "state and ancientry"—and of the way the American people (personally liking *him*) like it and submit. The White House is charming—and the thing was very well "done"; but so many *aides-de-camp* in uniform had never before been seen, nor so many crimson silk ropes to divide off the sheep from the goats. So much for *that*; but don't run away, in general, with your exaggerated ideas of wealth, luxury and, above all, of a "fascination" here. There is NO "fascination" *whatever*, in anything or anyone: that is exactly what there *isn't*. It is a quality that belongs to another order altogether. And don't make so much of all the loose and tiresome talk about the "luxury"—preposterous chatter! It is not much more true than the stuff and nonsense about the beauty of the women—which is *nil*, distinctly. At the White House the other night I didn't see *one* beautiful woman. The *comfort*, in several ways, is very respectable; in several other ways it is also absolutely *nil*; and the "wealth" in extent and diffusion, is as nothing to the no-wealth—and no-comfort-at-all. There is still more of *both*, and of Personal Beauty, in dear little dense and dingy old England than in all the millions of square miles that spread vacantly about me here. The more pity that I am about to try to traverse some of these! I go hence to Florida, to New Orleans, etc.—and I confess indeed that the sense of moving southward, the sense of the blander air and richer sun, extremely solicits me. I have only to sit (and *lie*) in my train, *from* here, long enough, and I slide into full tropical splendour—in the southern-most winter-resorts of Florida, where the resorts are used [for] bathing daily in blue tepid seas. It *is* verily a wonderful land (Personal Beauty, of the no. 74 type, apart.) I can't "take up" all your own thrilling history and anecdote—your Venice picture in especial making me heave such long, reverberating groans of felt privation and backward envy. I only console myself with the thought of how almost impossibly and intolerably exasperating the dear old C[urtises] must have become. AND, all the while, nothing can surpass the *howling* homesickness of yours, dear Goody, always and ever

Henry James

1. The French ambassador was Jules Jusserand (1855–1932), formerly member of the French embassy in London. See *Letters* III, 218.
2. Miss Allen's London residence, 74 Eaton Terrace.

To Edith Wharton
Ms Yale

1603 H St. Washington
January 16th 1905

Dear Mrs. Wharton.

If I have delayed writing to you it is in order not to resemble too much certain friends of ours who *don't*, in similar situations, delay—who send back Parthian shots, after leaving you, from the very next *étape*. But there have again and again, under the pressure of events, been words on my lips for which your ear has seemed the only proper receptacle—and which for want of that receptacle, I fear, have mostly faltered and failed and lost themselves forever. Let me make it distinct, at any rate, that things have been very convenient and pleasant for me, "straight along"—the reading of *une petite cochonnerie*, as Jusserand[1] says of his successive *oeuvres*, having constituted at the too amiable Philadelphia an almost brilliant scene—600 people listening (and to *what, juste ciel!*) like one. I felt as if I had really *me révélé conférencier* (to myself at least); but too late, at last, and after having lived too long in the deep dark hole of silence. I repeat the thing, at any rate, on the 19*th*, at the earnest Bryn Mawr—quite like a mountebank "on tour." The only drawback is that the really touching friendliness and *bonhomie* of all those people, their positively fantastic *obligeance* (it is really very special and beautiful and boring) bury one under such a mountain of decent response that the *place*, the funny Philadelphia itself, taken as a subject to play with a little, melts away from one forever. And the same, a little, with this so oddly-ambiguous little Washington, which sits here saying, forever, to your private ear, from every door and window, as you pass, "I am nothing, I am nothing, nothing!" and whose charm, interest, amiability, *irresistibility*, you are yet perpetually making calls to commemorate and insist upon. One must hold at one's end of the plank, for heaven only knows where the other rests! But, withal, it's a very pleasant, soft, mild, spacious vacuum—peopled, immediately about me here, by Henry Adams, La Farge and St.-Gaudens,[2]—and then, as to the middle distance, by Miss Tuckerman, Mrs. Lodge and Mrs. Kuhn, with the dome of the Capitol, the Corcoran Art Gallery and the presence of Theodore—Theodore I—as indispensable *fond!* I went to Court the other night, for the Diplomatic Reception, and he did me the honour to put me at his table and almost beside him— whereby I got a rich impression of him and of his being, verily, a wonderful little machine: destined to be overstrained perhaps, but not as yet, truly, betraying the least creak. It functions astoundingly, and is quite exciting to see. But it's really *like* something behind a great plate-glass window "on" Broadway. I lunch with the Lodges[3] today, I dine with the Jusserands tomorrow—he really delightful and she much better, a little "marked," but perfectly adequate, and after Bryn Mawr I go to spend three or four Philadelphian days with my old friend Sarah Wister at Butler Place. To remount *vers le Nord* chills me in thought—this relative mansuetude of the Washington air and prettiness of the Washington light, have affected me as such a balm. But I then come back to overtake or join (probably) the G[eorge] Vanderbilts,[4] and be personally conducted by them for three or four days at the formidable Biltmore. After that I possibly join Owen Wister (queerly, though I think but imaginatively and superficially blighted in health—only physical—and with a young medical attendant) at Charleston—or at any rate work down to Florida and New Orleans. Such is the only witchcraft I am being used with—for the present, though I *may* have roamed, delirious and flower-crowned, as far as the farthest West before I see you again. I seem to see patria nostra *simplify* as I go—see that the *main* impressions only count, and that these can be numbered on the fingers; which is truly a blessed vision. I hope meanwhile that the snow isn't too high by your doorstep, nor the doubt (of the immediate human scene) too heavy on your heart. How can you doubt of a scene capable of flowering at any moment into a Mrs. Toy.[5] By that sign you shall conquer. If you have seen Mrs. Chanler again she will have told you perhaps of the pilgrimage I made with her in the rain to the Washington Cemetery—for a chance *de nous soulager*, critically, unheard *que par les morts*. She was for those first days a resource—emotionally—that I greatly miss.[6] And, I miss, intensely, Walter Berry—and fear I shall continue to do so, as I seem destined to retire, sated (with everything but *him*) about the moment he comes back. But I have had from him a charming note. I hope you have the same—that is, I mean news of cheer and comfort from Wharton. And I am wondering further what you may perhaps be learning *de plus funeste encore* from Minnie-Paul. But never dream of writing to tell me, I shall hear, in time—for all the use I can be in the matter. Don't, I mean, begin to *croire* devils, "answer" this sprawling scribble which has really no dimensions at all—no more length than breadth or thickness. Only fight your own battle (like Prometheus—) with the elements (of civilization). We shall see them in due course somehow softened by springtime, and shall meet again under that benediction. Believe me yours very constantly

Henry James

1. See letter to Jessie Allen, 16 January 1905.
2. Augustus Saint-Gaudens (1848–1907), the American sculptor.
3. Senator Henry Cabot Lodge and his wife, the former Anna Davis.

4. See letter to Frances Morse, 7 June 1897.

5. Mrs. William (Nancy) Toy.

6. HJ had known Margaret Terry Chanler (1862–1952), daughter of the painter Luther Terry, since his Roman days. See *Letters* I, 335. He and Mrs. Chanler visited the grave of Mrs. Henry Adams (Clover Hooper; see *Letters* II, 361, 407) in particular to see the La Farge statue of a veiled figure Henry Adams had placed there.

To Henry Adams
Ms Mass. Historical

Jefferson Hotel
Richmond
February 1 1905

My dear Henry.

I have written first to thank R. U. Johnson[1] for crowning me with glory—and now I must thank *you* for guiding, straight to my unworthy and even slightly bewildered brow, his perhaps otherwise faltering or reluctant hand. Well, I am crowned—and I don't know that that makes much difference; but, still more, I am *amused*, and that very certainly does. An amusement the more, in the somewhat stale dream of existence, and suddenly clapped down before one, and for which there is nothing to pay—and which may go on and on and develop a richness all its own: this surely is more than one had seemed to one's self to be hoping for—and the charming list, already, seems to flush with the promise. I rejoice in the thought that it will be longer—for the amusement must now be in exact proportion to its length. There are candidatures I am waiting for— and altogether this dreary place, where I arrived last night on my diabolical journey (with a *harvest* of sweet impressions from Philadelphia), is quite warmed and lighted up by your contribution. Still, I am homesick, on my way to Florida—for the evenings when I used to listen to Moreton Frewcn[2] and to wish he were Mrs. Lodge. But good-night *cher confrère*. I hope you are thinking of our uniforms.[3] But keep it cheap—think what Theodore will want. Yours academically

Henry James

1. Johnson, HJ's former editor at the *Century*, was secretary of the National Institute of Arts and Letters, to which HJ had been elected when it was founded in 1898. The Institute was now creating an inner body to be known as the American Academy

of Arts and Letters, which would consist of fifty members of the Institute, and HJ had just been elected on the second ballot along with Henry Adams, Charles Eliot Norton, and Theodore Roosevelt. This explains his allusion to "Theodore." See Appendix I.

2. See letter to Cora Crane, 5 June 1900.

3. An allusion to the uniforms of the French academicians. The American academy created special insignia for its members, but no uniforms.

To Henry James III
Ms Harvard

Biltmore, North Carolina
February 4*th* 1905

Dearest Harry.

I arrived at this place, last P.M. in a driving snow storm (the land all buried, and the dreariness and bleakness indescribable), and the first thing that has happened to me, alas, has been to have a sharp explosion of gout in my left foot. But I hope to make this a *short* business (with bran footbaths—I've just *had* one, under domestic difficulties—and aspirin, to aid); only the conditions, of vast sequestered remoteness and "form," pompous machinery that doesn't *work*, are unfavourable to it; huge freezing spaces and fantastic immensities of *scale* (from point to point) that have been based on a fundamental ignorance of comfort and wondrous deludedness (though now, I think on poor George Vanderbilt's part, waked up from) as to what *can* be the application of a colossal French château[1] to life in this irretrievable niggery wilderness. (The country I passed through yesterday from Richmond!) But these are not the things I must write you of—only all tender sympathy for your miserable mumpishness and thanks, exceeding and abounding, for the Cunard service, so nobly and promptly performed. I wired you an hour ago that I would take 38, or its equivalent, in [the] *Saxonia* for July 4th, assuming that if this was to be had on the previous sailing it will be to be had on the later. I should *like* to say I would stay over to August 1st,—but this is a complicated question, *very,* for many reasons, and I must wait till I can talk of it with you face to face—only making sure of the *Saxonia* cabin, for July 4th (no. 38) for the present and meanwhile. The Cambridge summer *heat* scares me (with Chocorua let)—and there are other urgent reasons too. I hope to goodness your mumps have turned out mild and that you are already out of the woods. I wish there were some bran bath I could recommend you for *them*. I sit here rather lonely and disconsolate with mine—in a room *nothing* can make warm, with a hideous plate glass window like the door of an ice-house, no curtains to speak of (a *north* room, without shutters or blinds, and a view of vastnesses of snow): also with bells I can get no servant to answer—so that I have to hobble and hop along corridors for hot water from a remote bathroom. Pity the poor Biltmorean! But don't *breathe* these plaints outside the house—any more than, I hope, you have breathed any too indiscreet wail from Butler Place. I shall weather through even the tortures of Biltmore (which *aesthetically*—as to the *house*—moreover, are so real). But all this time I am not asking you to thank your mother and bless her for my finding the little *trunk* here awaiting me so safely. I embrace her tenderly in my gratitude—nothing could be more *right*, and rejoicing; but the levity of the things contained are strange irony in this Nova Solyma.[2] Heaven send I *do* need them yet, further on! These conditions, on this mountain top, *appal* me, and I shall get *on* as soon as I can travel; cutting down Charleston, too, as ruthlessly as possible. My state is such that getting as soon as possible under the wing of your Uncle Bob's Mary and Mamie at Daytona Florida glitter before me like an ideal of safety. My *other* front tooth (*not* handled at Philadelphia) came out last night, in bed, with the chattering of my jaws,—but I am utterly indifferent now. I think that "*c/o Mrs. Robertson J., The Bennett, Daytona, Fla.*" will really be the next best address for my letters after you receive this. I shall *strain* for it. I shall be at some hotel (I imagine the place a boardinghouse—but don't know). At any rate they will take care of them. All thanks for the pile I found here. Yours, dearest Harry, in all sympathy and with all love to all

Henry James

1. Biltmore, country residence of George Washington Vanderbilt (see 16 January 1905), built in 1890, was set amid 130,000 acres in North Carolina at a cost of $3,000,000. Several more millions were spent on decorations and furnishings.

2. *Nova Solyma, the ideal city; or, Jerusalem Regained,* an anonymous Latin romance written in the times of Charles I, attributed to Milton, but probably by Samuel Gott.

To Edith Wharton
Ms Yale

Biltmore, North Carolina
February 8*th* 1905

Dear Mrs. Wharton.

Literally, absolutely, your good letter has found me on the very point of writing to you; I should have done so today even if this consolation (to the rigour of my fate here) hadn't come in. For I have read the February morsel of the *House of Mirth*,[1] with such a sense of its compact fulness, vivid picture and "sustained interest" as make me really wish to celebrate the emotion. And the emotion of being here, moreover—that is another, and a very different matter— but one that put the pen, or the idea of the pen, ever so suggestively into my hand. And yet I feel that the mere pen, too, can do but scant justice to the various elements of my situation, the recent, the constant, and above all the acutely—*so* acutely!—actual, and that really to talk, about them, we must take some future N.Y. good fireside hour and then thresh them out and to the last straw. I arrived here (from two *drearissime* days at Richmond—dire delusion!) five days ago, and was instantly taken with a most deplorable and untimely little attack of gout (in my left foot—the much *éprouvé* on past occasions): the result of which has been that I have not once left the house, and but scantly my room. But I am sufficiently better to intend to depart, at any cost, tomorrow afternoon for Charleston. The whole land here is bound in snow and ice; we are 2,500 feet in the air; the cold, the climate, is well nigh all the "company" in the strange, colossal heartbreaking house; and the desolation and discomfort of the whole thing—whole scene—are, in spite of the mitigating millions everywhere expressed, indescribable. There has been no one here but little pleasant squinting Mrs. Hunt,[2] of Washington (the architect's daughter) and a pleasant (also) little old British soldier-man General Sir Thomas Fraser, who departed yesterday. I am now alone with the good George Vanderbilts and Huntina; and it has all been verily a strange experience. But I can't go into it—it's too much of a "subject": I mean one's sense of the extraordinary impenitent madness (of millions) which led to the erection in this vast niggery wilderness, of so gigantic and elaborate a monument to all that *isn't* socially possible

346

there. It's *in effect,* like a gorgeous practical joke—but at one's own expense, after all, if one has to live in solitude in these league-long marble halls and sit in alternate Gothic and Palladian cathedrals, as it were—where now only the temperature stalks about—with the "regrets" sighing along the wind of those who have declined. You who have accepted, for March, be careful (if I may presume, from this experience to advise); come late in the month rather than early,—then, if there has been a real change, you will get the benefit of the place itself—which I have wholly lacked, mounted all as it is in deep snow and with every distance one vast blur of sleet. In the early spring I can conceive it as admirable. And I feel that in speaking of it as I have, I don't do justice to the house as a phenomenon (of brute *achievement*). But that truly would take me too far! It's only as a place to live in, and in the conditions fatally imposed, that I, before it, threw up my hands—! But we will talk of it.—All this time, since we parted, I have seen nothing but Philadelphia and Washington—but very considerably well each of them, though I am more or less committed to going back to W. (if I *can*), late in spring—very late—for ten days—which I shall like. They really, the two places, are very much alike; I saw no very marked differences—except as I rather preferred Philadelphia as having rather more furnished, and peopled vistas, more consoling marble stoops, and yet imposing less frequent obligation to say one rejoiced in it. Quantities of people in both, but I could see no difference in most of them, and I think I found your Mitchell and Agnes Repplier as interesting as—well, I won't be too personal! I had rather a lurid four or five hyperborean days (lurid with a polar light) at Butler Place (Sara Wister's), but those again must wait. Verily, I am living through much. And I am cut down to the barest ten days in Florida, having *utterly* to be with my damnable Dentist in Boston again, for three days, on the 27th. This will give me, when I get away from here, but bare time to run down to Palm Beach and then *straight* back, from there (with appalling continuity) to Boston—I go then from Boston to Chicago, St. Louis and California—expecting to be back "East" again by about April 20th (though my brother assures me I shan't). I have taken my passage for England on July 4th—x x x x x x x

Since writing the above, I have been down to luncheon, and been able to see more of the house—and feel a bit shabby at failing to rise to my host's own conception of the results he has achieved. They *are*, in a way, magnificent and such a complicated costly mass has of course all sorts of splendid sides (I admire it as mere masonry), and contains innumerable ingenious features and treasures. Still, I repeat—for a tasteful Southern *home*, it merely makes me weep!—All this time I haven't expressed the smallest sympathy with your influenza—as to which you have my tender compassion. May he have left no blight behind. But I pity you still more, I think, for having had to affront the horrors of this winter in the New York streets—my own dire dismay at which had much to do with driving me away. When I get back to them for a while, as I must, it will be late, and I fear—with all thanks for your renewed invitation to Park Avenue but I shall have to be there with a certain wild freedom incompatible with genteel visiting—sounding the *bas-fonds*, shirking the "smart" set, giving decent time to a long list of good old cousins and ancient ties (I've had after all, one American tie!) wholly forever—to their wounded sensibility—in my last visit; and above all *working*, from a clear 10 A.M. to a clear 1.30, with a dictatee and a Remington and quantities of sprawling papers, notebooks and other impedimenta that wouldn't fit in to 884 [Park Avenue]. But there is time to talk of this—there is so much before me in the interval. I falter, I groan at the sight—I am already tired of my adventure—or *should* be, I had better say, if I weren't sure the West *must* be more characteristic and interesting. What I have seen since New York has *not* been that—interesting: nay, not a bit! But goodnight—I must hasten to dress for dinner and an evening with my hosts and Huntina *tout purs*. Don't dream this requires the least *réplique*, but remember that (forgive this blank page that I just discovered) my postal anchor is always 95 Irving Street, Cambridge. Yours, dear Mrs. Wharton, always and ever,

Henry James

P.S. Poor Smalley[3]—how reduced—how banished!

1. *The House of Mirth* was serialized in *Scribner's Monthly* from January to November 1905.
2. A daughter of Richard Morris Hunt, architect of Biltmore.
3. See letter to WJ, 20 April 1898.

With Mrs. Robertson James and her daughter Mary, St. Augustine, Florida, 1905.

To Edmund Gosse
Ms Congress

The Breakers Hotel,
Palm Beach, Florida
February 16*th* 1905

My dear Gosse.

I seem to myself to be (under the disadvantage of this extraordinary process of "seeing" my native country) perpetually writing letters; and I blush with the consciousness of not yet having got round to *you* again—since the arrival of your so genial New Year's greeting. I have been lately in constant, or at least in very frequent, motion, on this large comprehensive scale, and the right hours of *recueillement* and meditation, of private communication, in short, are very hard to seize. And when one does seize them, as you know, one is almost crushed by the sense of accumulated and congested matter. So I won't attempt to remount the stream of time save the most sketchily in the world. It was from Lenox, Mass., I think, in the far-away prehistoric autumn, that I last wrote you. I reverted thence to Boston, or rather, mainly, to my brother's kindly roof at Cambridge, hard by—where, alas, my five or six weeks were harrowed and ravaged by an appalling experience of American transcendent *Dentistry*—a deep dark abyss, a trap of anguish and expense, into which I sank unwarily (though, I now begin to see, to my great profit in the short human hereafter), of which I have not yet touched the *fin fond*. (I mention it as accounting for treasures of wrecked *time*—I could do nothing else whatever in the state into which I was put, while the long ordeal went on: and this has left me belated as to everything—"work," correspondence, impressions, progress through the land.) But I was (temporarily) liberated at last, and fled to New York, where I passed three or four appalled midwinter weeks (December and early January); appalled, mainly, I mean, by the ferocious discomfort this season of unprecedented snow and ice puts on in that altogether unspeakable city—from which I fled in turn to Philadelphia and Washington. (I am going back to N.Y. for three or four weeks of developed spring—I haven't yet (in a manner) seen it or cowardly "done" it.) Things and places southward have been more manageable—save that I lately spent a week of all but polar rigour at the high-perched Biltmore, in North

Carolina, the extraordinary colossal French château of George Vanderbilt in the said N.C. mountains—the house 2500 feet in air, and a thing of the high Rothschild manner, but of a size to contain two or three Mentmores and Waddesdons, the *gageure* of an imperfectly aesthetic young billionaire. Philadelphia and Washington would yield me a mild range of anecdote for you were we face to face—will yield it me then; but I can only glance and pass—glance at the extraordinary and rather personally-fascinating President— who was kind to me, as was dear J. Hay even more, and wondrous, blooming, aspiring little Jusserand, all pleasant welcome and hospitality. But I liked poor dear queer flat comfortable Philadelphia almost ridiculously (for what it is—extraordinarily *cossu* and materially civilized), and saw there a good deal of your friend—as I think she is—Agnes Repplier, whom I liked for her bravery and (almost) brilliancy. (You'll be glad to hear that she is extraordinarily better, up to now, these two years, of the malady by which her future appeared so compromised.) However, I am tracing my progress on a scale, and the hours melt away—and my letter mustn't grow out of my control. I have worked down here, yearningly, and for all too short a stay—but ten days in all; but Florida, at this southernmost tip, or almost, does beguile and gratify me—giving me my first and last (evidently) sense of the tropics, or *à peu près*, the subtropics, and revealing to me a blandness in nature of which I had no idea. This is an amazing winter-resort— the well-to-do in their tens, their hundreds, of thousands, from all over the land; the property of a single enlightened despot, the creator of two monster hotels, the extraordinary *agrément* of which (I mean of course the high pitch of mere monster-hotel amenity) marks for me [how] the rate at which, the way *in* which, things are done over here changes and changes. When I remember the hotels of twenty-five years ago even! It will give me brilliant chapters on hotel-civilization. Alas, however, with perpetual movement and perpetual people and very few concrete objects of nature or art to make use of for assimilation, my brilliant chapters don't yet get themselves written—so little can they be notes of the current picturesque—like one's European notes. They can only be notes on a social order, of vast extent, and I see with a kind of despair that I shall be able to do here little more than get my saturation, soak my intellectual sponge—reserving the squeezing-out for the subsequent deep, ah, the so yearned-for peace of Lamb House. It's all interesting, but it isn't thrilling—though I gather everything is more really curious and vivid in the West—to which and to California, and to Mexico if I can, I presently proceed. Cuba lies off here at but eighteen hours of steamer—and I am heartbroken at not having time for a snuff of that flamboyant flower.

Saint Augustine, February 18*th*

I had to break off day before yesterday, and I have completed meanwhile, by having come thus far north, my sad sacrifice of an intenser exoticism. I am stopping for two or three days at the "oldest city in America"—two or three being none too much to sit in wonderment at the success with which it has outlived its age. The paucity of the signs of the same has perhaps almost the pathos the signs themselves would have if there *were* any. There is rather a big and melancholy and "toned" (with a patina) old Spanish fort (of the 16th century), but horrible little modernisms surround it. On the other hand this huge modern hotel (Ponce de Leon) is in the style of the Alhambra, and the principal church ("Presbyterian") in that of the mosque of Cordova. So there are compensations—and a tiny old Spanish cathedral front ("earliest church built in America"—late 16th century), which appeals with a yellow ancienty. But I must pull off—simply sticking in a memento[1] (of a public development, on my desperate part) which I have no time to explain. This refers to a past exploit, but the leap is taken, is being renewed; I repeat the horrid act at Chicago, Indianapolis, St. Louis, San Francisco and later on in New York—*have* already done so at Philadelphia (always to "private" "literary" or Ladies' Clubs—at Philadelphia to a vast multitude, with Miss Repplier as brilliant introducer. At Bryn Mawr to 700 persons—by way of a *little* circle). In fine I have waked up *conférencier*, and find, to my stupefaction, that I can do it. The fee is large, of course—otherwise! Indianapolis offers £100 for 50 minutes![2] It pays in short travelling expenses, and the incidental circumstances and phenomena are full of illustration. I can't do it *often*—but for £30 a time I should easily be able to. Only that would be death. If I could come back here to abide I think I should really be able to abide in (relative) affluence: one can, on the spot, make so much more money—or at least I might. But I would rather live a beggar at Lamb House—and it's to that I shall

352

return. Let my biographer, however, recall the solid sacrifices I shall have made. I have just read over your New Year's eve letter, and it makes me so homesick that the bribe itself will largely seem to have been on the side of the reversion—the bribe to one's finest sensibility. I have published a novel—*The Golden Bowl*—here (in two volumes) in advance (fifteen weeks ago) of the English issue— and the latter will be (I don't even know if it's yet out in London) in so comparatively mean and fine-printed a London form that I have no heart to direct a few gift copies to be addressed. I shall convey to you somehow the handsome New York page—don't read it till then. The thing has "done" much less ill here than anything I have ever produced.

But good-night, verily—with all love to all, and to Mrs. Nelly in particular. Yours always,

Henry James

1. A card of admission to HJ's lecture, "The Lesson of Balzac," at Bryn Mawr College, 19 January 1905.
2. This would have been about $500.

To William James
Ms Harvard

The Washington
Saint Louis
March 8*th* 1905

Dearest William.

I have waited to write till my little mauvais quart d'heure (before 300 plain gapers of the Contemporary Club, in a room heated to suffocation and after a vast stifling dinner of the said 300) should be over and done with; but I pray God and the postman that this shall comfortably catch you before too late an hour of the 11th. I spouted my stuff last night "successfully" (the cheque slipped into my hand *coram publico* and almost before I had said my last word)—in the large room of this hotel, crowded to suffocation and with the exhaustion of a long preliminary dinner, preceded in *its* turn by 150 "presentations," well nigh undoing me. I got through, however, honourably, but more and more feeling that my lecture is too special and too literary—too critical—for these primitive promiscuities—but that it would do very well in *London*, and perhaps will in New York. At best, however, the "meeting" so many anonymous hundreds along with it, especially when that takes place, depletingly, before, is a heavy tax to pay, and I felt last night that I am truly earning my bread. I thank the powers (and *you* — your backing) that I named no smaller fee; I couldn't in that case go through with it. But I *shall* now. This vast grey, smoky, extraordinary *bourgeois* place seems to offer, in a ceaseless mild soft rain, no interest and no feature whatever; but I am to lunch with the Noonday Club (only men, business-men, thank heaven) today and to be "received" (with absolutely no speech) by the University Club tonight. Tomorrow I go to Chicago, and for the first two days (of my two Chicago lectures) to the *Hotel* (auditorium annex) decidedly, giving only Sunday and Monday to the Higginsons[1] and to the getting in and out from their suburb. The mixture of the social effort and exposure with the lecturing is, for *my* powers, really too upsetting. I expect to leave Chicago, *after* Indianapolis and Milwaukee, about Sunday week, and then to get to Los Angeles, Southern California, by the straightest most comfortable road I can (giving up probably New Orleans—the journey thence, to Los Angeles through the illimitable Texas etc. seeming so stopless and so appalling). It was appalling coming *here*—all the way from Detroit on Sunday, a single boundless empty platitude (from 8 A.M. to 10 P.M.); and we were four hours late—with no reason to give. Kindly continue letters (please tell Alice) to the Higginsons, Winnetka Ill., until I wire, or write from there. (I shall be puzzled, for forwarding, *after* that.) But I send you my blessing on your own wild way, and the same to Harry, with all love, on *his* so much tamer one. I hope to goodness he is really making good strides. Will you name to Alice to cover all contingencies (though I am feeling a bit rich) the exact amount of money of *mine*, that you leave in the bank? That is, will you give her a note of it? I wish you a serene and auspicious departure and endless happy reaction and refreshment, and "people, people, all the way" for your comfort (and ours), and a return in plenty of time before *my* sailing-time comes. With which I am more than ever your

Henry

1. George Higginson, a remote cousin of HJ's—the grandson of Jeannette James Barker, step-sister of HJ's father.

To Edward Warren
Ms Huntington

University Club
Chicago
March 19*th* 1905

Dearest Edward.

This is but a mere breathless blessing hurled at you, as it were, between trains and in ever so grateful joy in your brave double letter (of the lame hand, hero that you are!) which has just overtaken me here. I'm not pretending to write—I can't; it's impossible amid the movement and obsession and complication of all this overwhelming *Muchness* of space and distance and time (consumed), and above all of people (consuming). I start in a few hours straight for Southern California—enter my train this, Monday, night 7.30 and reach Los Angeles and Pasadena at 2.30 Thursday afternoon. The train has, I believe, barber's shops, bathrooms, stenographers and typists; so that if I can add a postscript, without too much joggle I will. But you will say "*Here* is joggle enough," for alack, I am already (after seventeen days of the "great Middle West") rather spent and weary, weary of motion and chatter, and oh, of such an unimagined dreariness of *ugliness* (on many, on *most* sides!) and of the perpetual effort of trying to "do justice" to what one doesn't like. If one could only damn it and have done with it! So much of it is rank with good intentions. And then the "kindness"—the princely (as it were) hospitality of these clubs; besides the sense of *power*, huge and augmenting, power, power (vast mechanical, industrial, social, financial) everywhere! This Chicago is huge, *infinite* (of potential size and form, and even of actual); black, smoky, *old*-looking, very like some preternaturally *boomed* Manchester or Glasgow lying beside a colossal lake (Michigan) of hard pale green jade, and putting forth railway antennae of maddening complexity and gigantic length. Yet this club (which looks old and sober too!) is an abode of peace, a benediction to me in the looming largeness; I *live* here, and they put one up (always, everywhere), with one's so excellent room with perfect bathroom and w.c., of its own, appurtenant (the *universal* joy of this country, in private houses or wherever; a feature that is really almost a consolation for many things). I have been to the South, the far end of Florida etc.—but prefer the far end of Sussex! In the heart of golden orange-groves I yearned for the shade of the old Lamb House mulberry tree. So you see I am loyal, and I sail for Liverpool on July 4th. I go up the whole Pacific coast to Vancouver, and return to New York (am due there April 26th) by the Canadian-Pacific railway (said to be, in its first half, sublime). But I scribble beyond my time. Your letters are really a blessed breath of brave old Britain. But oh for a talk in a Westminster panelled parlour, or a walk on far-shining Camber sands! All love to Margaret and the younglings. I have again written to Jonathan [Sturges]—he will have more news of me for you. Yours, dearest Edward, almost in nostalgic *rage*, and at any rate in constant affection,

Henry James

To Mrs. William James
Ms Harvard

Hotel del Coronado
Coronado Beach, California
Wednesday night,
April 5*th* 1905

Dearest Alice,

I must write you again before I leave this place (which I do tomorrow noon); if only to still a little the unrest of my having condemned myself, all too awkwardly, to be so long without hearing from you. I haven't, all this while—that is these several days, had the letters which I am believing you will have forwarded to Monterey sent down to me here. This I have abstained from mainly because, having stopped over here these eight or nine days to write, in extreme urgency, an article, and wishing to finish it at any price, I have felt that I should go to pieces as an author if a mass of arrears of postal matter should come tumbling in upon me—and particularly if any of it should be troublous. However, I devoutly hope none of it has been troublous—and I have done you best to let you know (in any need of wiring etc.) where I have been. Also the letterless state has added itself to the deliciously simplified social state to make me taste the charming sweetness and comfort of this spot. California, on these terms, when all is said (Southern C. at least—which, however, the real C., I believe, much repudiates), has completely bowled me over—such a delicious difference from the rest of the U.S. do I find in it. (I speak of course all of nature and climate, fruits and flowers; for there is absolutely nothing else, and the sense of the shining social and human inane is utter.) The days have been mostly here of heavenly beauty, and the flowers, the wild flowers just now in particular, which fairly *rage*, with radiance, over the land, are worthy of some purer planet than this. I live on oranges and olives, fresh from the tree, and I lie awake nights to listen, on purpose, to the languid lisp of the Pacific, which my windows overhang. I wish poor heroic Harry could be here—the thought of whose privations, while I wallow unworthy, makes me (tell him with all my love) miserably sick and poisons much of my profit. I go back to Los Angeles tomorrow, to (as I wrote you last) re-utter my (now loathly) lecture to a female culture club of 900 members (whom I make pay me through the nose), and on Saturday P.M. 8th, I shall be at Monterey (Hotel del Monte). But my stay there is now condemned to bitterest brevity and my margin of time for *all* the rest of this job is so rapidly shrinking that I see myself *brûlant mes étapes*, alas, without exception, and cutting down my famous visit to Seattle to a couple of days. It breaks my heart to have so stinted myself here—but it was inevitable, and no one had given me the least inkling that I should find California so sympathetic. It is strange and inconvenient, how little impression of anything any one ever takes the trouble to give one beforehand. I should like to stay here all April and May. But I am writing more than my time permits—my article is still to finish. I ask you no questions—you will have told me everything. I live in the hope that the news from William will have been good. At least at Monterey, may there be some! I asked you in my last to please forward any letters *next* to c/o Edward and Louisa[1] at Seattle, Washington. I don't know their address, after all, but have written him simply to Seattle. Bob will know (I suppose) if you can get to "phoning" with him. But goodnight—with great and distributed tenderness. Yours, dearest Alice, always and ever

Henry James

P.S. I shall let you know when to stop forwarding to Seattle—or say rather that you post for there only up to today week—that is the 13th.

1. Edward Holton James, HJ's nephew (son of Robertson James), and his wife, the former Mary Louisa Cushing. See letter to Edward Holton James, 15 February 1896.

To Walter V. R. Berry
Ms Unknown

Hotel Belvedere, Baltimore
June 11*th* 1905

My Dear Berry.

Forgive this unconventional (but eagerly expeditious) form of letting you know that I sail on the Cunard *Saxonia* from Boston on July 4th. I hear from Mrs. Wharton this very moment, that you are still shipless, and I have hopes that you may be moved or inspired, or providentially aided and supported. Try, at all events, try hard, and tell me, when we meet at Lenox—I go there for four or five days about the 24th—that you have succeeded. I have been spouting here and at Bryn Mawr College, Pa., and feel for the moment almost your neighbour.—The Boston embarkation will chill your fancy, but the ship is commodious, deliberate, sturdy and favoured by the first Boston Families. So take fire. I return tomorrow to 36 West 10th Street New York. Yours pressingly,

Henry James

To Edith Wharton
Ms Yale

36 West 10*th* St. (or, better,
95 Irving St., Cambridge, Mass.)
June 13*th* 1905

Dear Mrs. Wharton.

I approach the subject again, after your last good letter, with infinite *malaise*; but the stern reality of things presses upon me, and in fine, *Ich kann nicht anders.* So, I greatly fear, as the days come on and the future bristles with formidable detail of all I have to squeeze into my time between this and my departure (bristles even like the more fretful porcupine) I shall not be able to come to you on Saturday 24th, but only on Monday 26th. Next week is a particularly difficult one for me and it is absolutely necessary that I shall put in, make *sure* of, a clear day or two of it for Cambridge. The only way I can manage this is by clutching at Saturday 24th, aforesaid, as the *least* impossible day. Be indulgent over all this and

don't shoot—"I am doing my best!" On the 26th I will eagerly come
and try and squeeze in all experience between that day and the
following Saturday A.M. when I shall have, by the same immitigable
law, to depart. This sad little story has required to be told—but
"don't answer"! though I know you would with the best gentleness.
Anything else would embitter the few remaining drops of the cup—
the "America cup"—of yours not inconstantly

Henry James

P.S. I instantly wrote to W. Berry.

To Frederick Allen King
Dictated Ts Private

95 Irving Street
Cambridge, Mass.
July 2, 1905

My dear Sir.

I have been perpetually occupied and moving about since receiving your letter of June 23rd on the matter of the bibliography of
my writings, which you tell me you are at the trouble of preparing;[1]
and I am now reduced to answering your questions very briefly and
with this needful aid to expedition.

I feel that I almost answer them, with completeness, in frankly
telling you that I quite abhor bibliographies, so far as I myself, at
least, may be the subject of them, and that my principle (already
more than once put into practise) is to find it impossible to give
them any furtherance. I always think it over-much to ask of an
author, for instance, that he shall help to divest his early aberrations, his so far as possible outlived and repudiated preliminary, of
any blessed shelter of obscurity or anonymity that may luckily
have continued to cover them. With this sentiment on my part, you
may judge how little use your altogether flattering (I admit) but too
misguided undertaking can make of my befogged memory.

Since you mercifully ask me if your unearthing early unsigned
reviews (or at least the attribution of them) in *The Atlantic
[Monthly]*, *The North American* [*Review*], "meets my approval," I
brace myself to answer frankly that it fills me only with the bitterness of woe. I would much rather myself, with my own hand, heap

359

mountains of earth upon them and so bury them deeper still and beyond *any* sympathetic finding-out.

Of articles contributed to the "Balloon Post," Boston, 1871,[2] I have, quite candidly, no recollection whatever, and think you must be here on some false scent.

Almost the only thing I *can* tell you without anguish is that "Cousin et Cousine" in the *Revue des Deux Mondes*, October 1, 1876, must have been simply a translation of a little tale called "Four Meetings" contributed to I forget what American periodical,[3] and afterwards gathered into some volume of "short stories," but which particular volume I can't recall. With the differences of distribution, title, etc., between the American and the English issues of these various collections, I am nowadays quite at sea.

Let me add that your great good-will in the matter almost brings to my eyes tears of compassionate remonstrance for misapplied effort. You inquire for instance where the English subjects in "Transatlantic Sketches" originally appeared in serial form? —whereat any ability I might possess to brood over that point for revival of remembrance quite loses itself in wonder as to why and how any such wretched little question can matter, at this hour, to any human being endowed with the responsibility of intelligence. *Help* no intelligence to feed itself on such twaddle (millions of miles removed from any real *critical* play of mind) and believe me

Yours very truly,

Henry James

1. King's bibliography was published as an addendum to Elisabeth Luther Cary's *The Novels of Henry James* (1905).

2. HJ contributed a closet-drama, "Still Waters," to the 12 April 1871 issue of a publication called the *Balloon Post*, which was sold at a Boston fair in aid of French relief. The playlet is reprinted in *The Complete Plays of Henry James* (1949).

3. *Scribner's Monthly*, November 1877.

4
Revisions

1905–1910

4
Revisions

The creative power Henry James manifested just before his journey to America was matched by his re-creative power on his return. Between 1905 and 1910 he carried through the process of re-arranging and shoring up his works of forty years. For the New York Edition he revised his principal early novels, revised them often minutely, as if he were revising his own life, and selected only those works he deemed admissible to his final canon. The edition contains none of his "American" works save "The Jolly Corner." *Washington Square* and *The Bostonians* were set aside for possible revision later. James included rather his "international" works and his novels and tales of English life. At the same time he revised his various early and late travel writings, which became *English Hours* and *Italian Hours*. He also retouched *A Little Tour in France.*

During these years James also engaged in considerable critical activity. He wrote eighteen prefaces for the New York Edition which are essentially autobiographical: a writer's record of how ideas came to him and the methods by which he imagined and told his novels. He defined his exploration of the novel form, discussed his belief that novelists must create organic structures, and explained his many artistic innovations. The prefaces reflect James's joy in his skill and his craft, and his pride of invention. During these years he renewed his playwriting, turning the one-act *Summersoft* of the 1890s into a three-act comedy, *The High Bid*, for the Forbes-Robertsons and making a one-act play out of his short story "Owen Wingrave," a tale about a young military cadet's pacificism. He gathered his late tales into *The Finer Grain.*

These five productive years were busy social years as well: there were two visits with Edith Wharton in Paris, during the first of which (in 1907) he repeated part of his old tour of France and touched at some new places and then went on to Italy, knowing that it would be his last visit there. At the end of the decade he formed a friendship with the young Hugh Walpole, whose work he criticized but for whom he showed a marked affection.

When he found that the New York Edition was not selling, Henry James suffered the same kind of frustration and defeat he had experienced after his playwriting in the 1890s. A new depression put him to bed for many weeks. His doctors, including Osler and Mackenzie, could find nothing seriously wrong; his emotions swung between fear of aging and a kind of free-floating anxiety. His letters and cables caused William James to send his eldest son to Henry's bedside; and although William himself was seriously ill with his chronic heart ailment, he came abroad with his wife to see what solace he could offer his brother. A brief note in Mrs. James's diary that summer suggests her predicament while attending the two famous invalids: "William cannot walk and Henry cannot smile." The three went to the Continent, William to have another round of treatments in Bad Nauheim and Henry to see whether a change of scene might help. In midsummer Henry decided to accompany his ailing brother and his sister-in-law back to the United States. They had just settled back into their summer home in the White Mountains when William died.

Henry James mourned his brother profoundly, writing to many friends that William had been his "Ideal elder brother." Somerset Maugham, visiting America that winter, dined one evening at 95 Irving Street, and noted Henry's acutely anxious state. "I can remember nothing of the conversation at table, but it seemed to me that Henry James was troubled in spirit; after dinner the widow left us alone in the dining room, and he told me that he had promised his brother to stay at Cambridge for, I think, six months after his death, so that if he found himself able to make a communication from beyond the grave there would be two sympathetic witnesses on the spot ready to receive it. I could not but reflect that Henry James was in such a state of nervousness that it would be difficult to place implicit confidence in any report he might make. His sensibility was so exasperated that he was capable of imagining anything. But hitherto no message had come, and the six months were drawing to their end."[1]

1. Preface to *The Greatest Stories of All Time*, selected by W. Somerset Maugham (1939).

Mrs. William James did hold some seances, but we do not know whether Henry participated. William's death clearly had been a shock, and it gave him uneasy thoughts about his own mortality. By the spring of 1911, however, his depression had somewhat abated, and in due course he said goodbye to some of his old Cambridge friends—to Grace Norton, with whom he had corresponded during all the years of his expatriation, to Howells, and to the Irving street circle—knowing that these were last farewells. He returned to Lamb House feeling that he could no longer tolerate the loneliness of his Rye winters; and he was eager to write a book about William, which ultimately turned into an autobiographical record of the James family and the youth of the two celebrated brothers.

To Mrs. William James
Ms Harvard

Off Queenstown
Wednesday
R.M.S. Ivernia.
[12 July 1905]

Dearest Alice.

This is but a line ashore to tell you that I am in still decent fettle after a voyage made in remarkably good conditions—fair, though mixed, as to weather and admirable as to luxury of cabin space, air, and steadiness (unique) of ship. But she is too *slow*—we shall not be at Liverpool till Thursday A.M: the *Wilhelm II* would have been there yesterday. But it has done very well—though I am too utterly unfit for the sea, and the time is at best a purgatory for me. I have had two extremely agreeable companions—Elizabeth Robins[1] and Walter Berry and we have stuck together—(the others being all, verily, as nought, with the exception of young Roland Gray, attractive, and his mate the long, long young Walcott (Dr. W's) whom I much like). I fear you have stewed most of these days, and my sense of your sovereign virtue and heroism grows with each turn of the screw. But I hold you all to my heart and I beg you to not fail to have let William know of my letter to him at Chicago that may have gone astray, through lack of "Quadrangle" before University Club.[2] And I failed at the last to do what I most intensely meant—viz: to leave a particular affectionate farewell to your mother. I shall write from Lamb House as soon as I can turn round. Ever your

Henry

Wednesday (Queenstown) Only another word to renew my blessing and enclose—!

H.J.

1. See Elizabeth Robins, *Theatre and Friendship* (1932), 250–251.
2. The faculty club at the University of Chicago is called the Quadrangle.

To Charles Scribner's Sons
Ms Princeton

Memorandum   [30 July 1905]

My idea has been to arrange for a handsome "definitive edition" of the greater number of my novels and tales—I say of the greater number because I prefer to omit several things, especially among the shorter stories. I should wish probably to retain all my principal novels—that is with the exception possibly of one.

My impression is that my shorter things will gain in significance and importance, very considerably, by a fresh grouping or classification, a placing together, from series to series, of those that will help each other, those that will conduce to something of a common effect. My notion is, at any rate, very rigidly to sift and select the things to be included, thereby reducing the number of volumes to an array that will not seem, for a collective edition, very formidable. My idea is, further, to revise everything carefully, and *to re-touch*, as to expression, turn of sentence, and the question of surface generally, wherever this may strike me as really required. Such a process, however, will find its application much more in the earlier, the earliest things than in those of my later or even of my middle period. It is called for in *Roderick Hudson* and *The American* for instance, to my sense, much more than anywhere else. The edition will thus divide itself into about ten volumes of regular novel length, into a few volumes of distinctively *short* novels, not more than two of which, or three at the most, would completely fill a moderate volume; and into a considerable number of short stories, six or eight of which are longer than the common magazine short-story, and the whole list of which is susceptible of an effect

366

of revival by the re-classification that I have mentioned. A good many of these, which have all been collected in volumes, I shall wish, as I say, to drop; but the interest and value of the edition will, I think, rest not a little on the proper association and collocation of the others.

Lastly, I desire to furnish each book, whether consisting of a single fiction, or of several minor ones, with a freely colloquial and even, perhaps, as I may say, confidential preface or introduction, representing, in a manner, the history of the work or the group, representing more particularly, perhaps, a frank critical talk about its subject, its origin, its place in the whole artistic chain, and embodying, in short, whatever of interest there may be to be said about it. I have never committed myself in print in any way, even so much as by three lines to a newspaper, on the subject of anything I have written, and I feel as if I should come to this part of the business with a certain freshness of appetite and effect. My hope would be, at any rate, that it might count as a feature of a certain importance in any such new and more honorable presentation of my writings. I use that term honorable here because I am moved in the whole matter by something of the conviction that they will gain rather than lose by enjoying for the first time—though a few of the later ones have in some degree already partaken of that advantage—a form and appearance, a dignity and beauty of outward aspect, that may seem to bespeak consideration for them as a matter of course. Their being thus presented, in fine, as fair and shapely will contribute, to my mind, to their coming legitimately into a "chance" that has been hitherto rather withheld from them, and for which they have long and patiently waited.

My preference would be to publish first, one after the other, four of the earlier novels, not absolutely in the order of their original appearance but with no detrimental departure from it; putting *The American*, that is, first, *Roderick Hudson* second, *The Portrait of a Lady* third, and *Princess Casamassima* fourth. After this would come three or four volumes of the longer of my short stories—to be followed by *The Tragic Muse* in two volumes, a book which closes, to my mind, what I should call as regards my novels, my earlier period. I think, though as to this I am not positive, that I should then give three or four more volumes to completing the group of such minor productions; and should wind up with my five later novels, *The Awkward Age, The Wings of the Dove, The Ambassa-*

dors and *The Golden Bowl* in the order of their appearance. And I repeat that I am proposing nothing but my fiction.

If a *name* be wanted for the edition, for convenience and distinction, I should particularly like to call it the New York Edition if that may pass for a general title of sufficient dignity and distinctness. My feeling about the matter is that it refers the whole enterprise explicitly to my native city—to which I have had no great opportunity of rendering that sort of homage. And—last of all—I should particularly appreciate a single very good plate in each volume, only one, but of thoroughly fine quality. I seem to make out (though I have not been able yet to go into the whole of the question) that there would not be an insuperable difficulty in finding for each book, or rather for each volume, some sufficiently interesting illustrative subject.

There are two or three points more.

Messrs. Scribner's complete edition of Rudyard Kipling offers to my mind the right type of form and appearance, the right type of print and size of page, for our undertaking. I could desire nothing better than this, and should be quite content to have it taken for model. (But I think, also, by the way, that I should like a cover of another colour—to differentiate—than the Kipling.)

As for time of delivery of first copy I should find it convenient to be able to take from the present date to the 25th September to send the two first books, completely revised (with the very *close* revision and re-touching that for these cases I have spoken of) and with their respective Prefaces, of from 3000 to 5000 words. The revision, the re-manipulation, as I may call it, of *The American* and *Roderick Hudson* is demanding of me, I find, extreme (and very interesting) deliberation; which will tend, however, absolutely to improvement (and not to say, perhaps, even to making of the works in question, in their amended state, unique—and admirable, exemplary— curiosities of literature).

I should not omit, finally, to note that in the foregoing I have, inevitably left the question open of the inclusion or the non-inclusion of my longer novel *The Bostonians.* I cannot take time, have not freedom of mind to decide this minor matter just now; but I shall do so later on, and if in the affirmative a convenient place in the whole order will be found for the book.

Henry James

July 30 1905

To Hendrik C. Andersen
Ms Barrett

Lamb House, Rye
August 6th 1905

My dear, dear Hendrik!

Your letter from Gibraltar is a sad enough story—which I bear a little less badly, however, for having felt myself, as the days have gone on, prepared for it. That I *should* have you here at this lovely moment (for it is of the loveliest here) was somehow too good to be true, and as your silence lengthened out I felt, more and more, that I was losing you. It is very horrible—but I understand well how difficult, how not to be managed, with your so much more direct and economic road to Italy, it must have been for you to come this way. It was only that, in those last hours at Newport,[1] you seemed to believe the thing possible. So *I* believed for a while—and I looked forward, and the pang of the loss is sharp; but, clearly, you have done the right thing. Short and scant—pitifully—with this annihilation, do those few American moments seem to me—and lighted with the strange light of our common uneasiness and outsideness there. But I remember ever so tenderly our first hour together in Boston, and our drive to the railroad with my trap and then our other and better and longer drive at Newport (which was quite lovely),—coloured with the beauty of our seeming then destined soon to meet again. When the Devil *shall* we meet, at this rate?—and when, ah when, shall I be able to go back again, at the right moment and in the right way, to the loved Italy? The grim years pass, and don't bring me that boon! Still, we *must* meet, and I must somehow arrange. What consoles me a little is to hear that your weeks in America did tend, did eventuate, in some way, to your profit and your gain—though I wish to heaven I were near enough for you to tell me more without the impossible trouble of your writing it. *That,* about nothing, must you have. Yet it's all pretty wretched, this non-communication—for there are long and weighty things—about your work, your plan, your perversity, your fountain, your building on and on, and up and up, *in the air,* as it were, *and out of relation to possibilities and actualities,* that I wanted to say to you. We would have *talked* them beautifully and intimately here, these things—but now it's as if they had to wait and wait. Yet they mustn't wait too long. *Make the pot boil, at any*

369

price, as the only real basis of freedom and sanity. Stop building in the air for a while and build on the ground. *Earn* the money that will give you the right to conceptions (and still more to executions) like your fountain—though I am still wondering what American community is going to want to pay for thirty or forty stark naked men and women, of whatever beauty and lifted into the raw light of one of their public places. Keep in relation to the *possible* possibilities, dearest boy, and hold on tight, at any rate, till I can get you somehow and somewhere and have you *back* me. But good night, dearest boy; it's ever so late, and it's hideous that you're not here and that you won't be. How long and close, in imagination and affection, I hold you! Feel, Hendrik, the force and the benediction of it and all the applied tenderness of your constant old friend

Henry James

P.S. It's a delight to me that you can speak of yourself as so cleared off, physically, and so confident, and oh, how I yearn after you to Montefiascone!

1. HJ and Andersen had visited Newport together during HJ's final days in the United States.

To Robert Herrick
Ms Chicago

Lamb House, Rye
August 7*th* 1905

Dear Robert Herrick.[1]

It has been charming to hear from you—but I am always miles and miles behind all proper forms of correspondence. When I have done a day's stint of work—that is of "literary composition"—with any intensity, any power to write further—in *any* manner—dreadfully abandons me; I am depleted and exanimate, and letters come off as they can—the larger proportion of them never coming off at all. But I must thank you for the gentle gift of *The Common Lot* too, which I want to read and shall read: it rests on my table only till I shall have got into the traces again, for dragging my cart in its customary ruts. I have been since my return from the U.S. much derailed—but things are running more smoothly. I rejoice heartily that your Breton conditions prove so charming to you, and may you [enjoy?] the romantic experiences. Why do you speak of "sparing" me the expression of your "unregenerate enthusiasm" for them? I shouldn't have supposed that at this time of day *j'en étais encore* at having to prove *my* haunting preoccupation with the things of France. You didn't even come—you told me—to my fanatical Balzac lecture!—All thanks at any rate, for your so serious and urgent remarks on the matter of my revisions in respect to some of the old stuff I spoke of to you in connection with the plan of an *edition définitive*. I am greatly touched by your having felt and thought strongly enough on the matter to take the trouble to remonstrate at the idea of my retouching. The retouching with any insistence will in fact bear but on one book (*The American*—on *R. Hudson* and the *P. of a Lady* very much less); but in essence I shouldn't have planned the edition at all unless I had felt close revision—wherever seeming called for—to be an indispensable part of it. I do every justice to your contention, but don't think me perverse or purblind if I say that I hold myself really right and you really wrong. Its *raison d'être* (the edition's) is in its being selective as well as collective, and by the mere fact of leaving out certain things (I have tried to read over *Washington Square* and I *can't*, and I fear it must go!) I exercise a control, a discrimination, I treat certain portions of my work as unhappy accidents—(many portions of many—of all—men's work are). From that it is but a step further—but it is 1 o'clock A.M. and I've written seven letters, and I won't attempt to finish that sentence or expand my meaning. Forgive my blatant confidence in my own lucid literary sense! If I had planned not to retouch—that is to revise closely—I would have reprinted all my stuff and that idea is horrific. You, also, will be ravished! Trust me—I shall be justified. But good night and pardon my untidy scrawl and my belated incoherence. Recall me kindly to your wife and believe me, yours always

Henry James

1. HJ had met the novelist Robert Herrick (1868–1938) in Chicago during his recent visit. *The Common Lot* was published in 1904.

To Antonio de Navarro
Ms Private

Lamb House, Rye
November 1st 1905

My dear Tony.

Your letter touches and interests me, and I thank you, very tenderly, for all the sympathy it expresses and to which I unreservedly respond. But, alas, I shall not be able to be in town for at least three weeks to come——I have to keep my immersions in that complicated element within very definite limits. I had been up a good many days when we met, that evening [*Oliver Twist*] under Tree's fantastic influence,[1] and I was obliged to march back here (where strenuous occupation holds me fast) immediately afterwards. But I am very sorry to hear of your depressions and lassitudes. I scarce know what to say to you about them. The want of a commanding, that is of an imperative occupation is a fertile source of woe—to an *âme bien née*—and you are in some degree paying the penalty of your "material advantages" themselves, your freedom of expatriation, your fortune, your living in a terrific "modernity" of cosmopolite ease (which has the drawback of not working you actively into the scheme of things here). My own conditions resemble yours—that is as to ease of expatriation, and putting aside fortune and other *agréments!*—but I am luckily possessed of a certain amount of corrective to our unnatural state, a certain amount of remedy, refuge, retreat and anodyne! From the bottom of my heart I pity you for being without some practicable door for getting out of yourself. We all need one, and if I didn't have mine I shouldn't—well, I shouldn't be writing you this now. It takes at the best, I think, a great deal of courage and patience to live—but one must do everything to invent, to force open, that door of exit from mere immersion in one's own states. You are young and gallant and intelligent—so, *allons donc*, there are still horizons! We must indeed talk of these things together—and some time in January I come up to town for three months: *songez donc*, three great months! Then I will reach out my hand to you—will put my arm round you like a brother. Sit tight till then—we can always sit tight, and it always pays to have held on fast through everything. On this I embrace you and bid you goodnight. I hope your poor little boy came bravely through the oculist's hands the other day, and I greet very heartily his radiant mother. And I am, my dear Tony, your always affectionate old friend

Henry James

1. Herbert Beerbohm Tree (1853–1917) produced a dramatized version of the Dickens novel.

To Edith Wharton
Ms Yale

Lamb House, Rye
November 8*th* 1905

Dear Mrs. Wharton.

You cannot say that I have bombarded you with letters, and I should be very sorry if I had put any such statement into your power. I have had, had perhaps to excess, a conscience about writing to you, having become aware, for myself, more and more as I grow older, of the several things—interest—that life would, would be more fully, more needfully applicable to, if it were not for its letters. So many of them are not *fair!* And I have wanted immensely, where you are concerned, to *be* fair. So I have measured what I was doing—as well as what I wasn't—and have said again and again "No, no—not yet!" The limit I fixed myself was when the final numbers of the *House of Mirth* should have come out: "When I've read that," I said to myself, "I'll write." Half an hour ago, or less, I laid down the November *Scribner*, and now I have no scruple. Let me tell you at once that I very much admire that fiction, and especially the last three numbers of it: finding it carried off with a high, strong hand and an admirable touch, finding it altogether a superior thing. There are things to be said, but they are—some of them—of the essence of your New York *donnée*—and moreover you will have said them, to a certainty, yourself. The book remains one that does you great honour—though it is better written than composed; it is indeed throughout *extremely* well written, and in places quite "consummately." I wish we could talk of it in a motorcar: I have been in motor-cars again, a little since our wonderful return from Ashfield; but with no such talk as that. There are fifty things I should like to say—but, after so long an interval there are

373

so many I want to, in general; and I think that my best way to touch on some of the former would be by coming back to the U.S. to deliver a lecture on "The question of the *roman de moeurs* in America—it's deadly difficult." But when I do that I shall work in a tribute to the great success and the large portrayal, of your Lily B[art]. She is very big and true—and very difficult to have *kept* true—and big; and all your climax is very finely handled.[1] Selden is too *absent*—but you know that better than I can make you. I hope you are having a boom. Have you read *Les Deux Soeurs?*[2]—and have you read the amazing little Mme Tinayre's *Avant l'amour?*[3] You are sure to have done both; so oh, for an hour of the motor again. The French, in the Tinayre light, are *impayables;* and so is our poor Paul Bourget, frankly, I think in the *poncif*[4] light—and even in the "Amour" light too—this *Amour* light of his latest manner. But as a surrender to the *poncif,* in all the force of the term, the thing—his latest book—is, I think, for a man of his original value, one of the strangest literary documents conceivable. Not that the *poncif* was not always in some degree—in a great degree—present in his fiction (though never in his criticism etc.); but the way it has now invaded his "morality," as well as his form, deprives me of any power to acknowledge his so inveterate and so generous, gifts of his volumes! It affects me as a painful *End.* So I have no news whatever of that couple—they haven't come (as usual) to England this summer, and the tidings you brought home were my last.—I despatched Mrs. Jones and Beatrix back with as much Impression as their two brief little stations in London (during which I went up to attend them) permitted me to stuff into them. Beatrix, I thought, less well than she ought to be—but every ill would fade from her if she would give up Doctors and Waters and really and sacrificially commit herself to the divine Fletcher (who, now that I have got back to my own good conditions, here, for worshipping him, has renewed the sources of my life.) I have made a few short absences, but the *pax britannica* of this (to me) so amiable and convenient retreat, awaited me, on my return from my American adventure, with such softly-encircling arms that I have, for the most part, sunk into it deep, and shall be here for two or three months to come. I go to spend a couple of days, in a week or two, with Mrs. Humphry Ward—and I haven't even yet read *William Ashe,*[5] which she has handsomely sent me, as a preparation. But I have had practically to *tell* her that all power to read her has abandoned me—though I have put it as the power to read any fiction. But she will extract from me when I see her that I *have* read Mrs. Wharton, and what I think of that—being very gentle about it, though, for she also greatly admires Mrs. Wharton. Of this, however, you will have personal evidence, as she appears to be really intending to go over and see you in the course of the winter. What a prodigious drama it will be—her tumbling herself bodily into the circus of her millions, and how little either the millions or she will make the other party out. *Pourvu qu'elle en réchappe!* You must give me news of the commotion, into which I foresee you inevitably dragged and engulfed. But news of Walter Berry I greatly want too, who, after having greatly endeared himself to me, in the summer, *par son naturel, ses dons et ses malheurs,* vanished from my sight on his mad Italian errand—and has left me since a prey to wonder and fear. I have—I had—heard of, and wept over, his "ill luck," the *guignon* pursuing him—but I see it now to be in the consummate art with which he invokes that goddess. I tried to save him—hard; but he rushed (full of fractures) on his fate and I don't know at all what has become of him (in what *gargote* he sank by the wayside); and I still lie awake at night thinking of it—that being the force of the impression he made on me.—I am very busy "in my poor way," trying to make my ten months in America, the subject of as many *Sensations d'Italie*[6] as possible and finding, strangely, that I have more impressions than I know what to do with or can account for—and this in spite of finding that, also, they tend exceedingly to melt and fade and pass away, flicker off like the shadows from firelight on the wall. But I shall draw a long breath when I have worked them off—which it looks as if it would take me perhaps *two* (separate) volumes (of Impressions, pure and simple) to do: whence I fear that it may be very fantastic and irrelevant stuff I am producing—for I don't see, I repeat, where it all comes from. And the queerest part of the matter is that, though I *shall* rejoice when it is over, I meanwhile quite like doing it. *Entre temps* my thoughts wing their way back to Pagello[7] and his precious freight (have you read the luridly interesting little volume, *George Sand et sa Fille,* by the way?) and hover about him as he so greatly adventures and so powerfully climbs *m'attachant à se pas,* to his flights and his swoops,—and even more to his majestic roll in the deep valleys, with a wistfulness in which every one of those past hours lives again. Most of all lives, I think, perversely, and even a little hauntingly, that leave-taking of ours at the Ashfield[8] door last June—and poor dear Charles's unforgettable fixed smile of farewell (here below) to *me*, and poor Margaret's pathetic glare. But I wouldn't for anything not have had that experience, so beautiful, of our whole going and coming, or not have rendered them that visitation and I thank you again, even at this distance of time, for having made it so exquisitely possible to me.—I know about your shock and your pang in connection with poor Miss Crane's strange and terrible annihilation, but I can't speak of it, any more than I can of those unhappy overdarkened Dixeyd (with my impression of the boy in the pride of his youth, a great ornament and *panache* to them), and of their existence there, as I saw it, all of such innocent, *un*ironic comedy. Heaven help us all!—The Pagello-sense has been with me a little, here,—again this autumn—notably during four or five splendid October days spent with Ned Abbey[9] (and his wife—R.A.!) in Gloucestershire, who have a wondrous French machine and who, in the insolence of their art-gains want to buy some fine old Jacobean (or other) house and estate. I roamed with them far over the land to look at three or four, and found it a most interesting and charming pursuit; in fact in a capacious luncheon-stacked car, the very summit of human diversion. This absurd old England is still, after *long* years, so marvellous to me, and the visitation of beautiful old buried houses (as to "buy"—seeing them as one then sees them) such a refinement of bliss. Won't you come out with Pagello, and a luncheon basket, and feign at least an intention of purchase—taking me with you to do the lying? I will show you all those the Abbeys haven't yet bought. Submit this programme to Mr. Edward, please, with my very cordial regards. I hope his health and "form" are, in all his splendid applications of them, of the best.

But it's long past midnight, while I write—past 1 A.M., and I bid you at once good night and good morning. Don't be morbid *you*, in the matter of our postal relation, please, and believe me yours, dear Mrs. Wharton, very constantly,

Henry James

1. HJ is recalling the final hours of Mrs. Wharton's heroine Lily Bart, when she plans her suicide.
2. Paul Bourget's short novels *Les Deux Soeurs* and *Le Cour et le métier* (1905).

3. Marguerite Suzanne Marcelle Tinayre (1872–1948), French novelist, who married the engraver Jules Tinayre. The theme of women's emancipation runs through her novels, such as *Avant l'amour* (1897) and *Hellè* (1899). She also wrote a biography of Madame de Pompadour (1925).

4. HJ is using the noun in its figurative sense: "poor, conventional or commonplace work."

5. Mrs. Ward's *The Marriage of William Ashe* appeared in 1905.

6. Bourget's travel sketches, *Sensations d'Italie* (1905), which HJ greatly admired.

7. Dr. Pietro Pagello, the handsome Italian surgeon who attended George Sand's lover Alfred de Musset in Venice in 1834 and became Sand's lover in his place. See HJ's discussion of this affair in *Notes on Novelists* (1914). One may speculate that Pagello veils a mutual friend in this discussion, probably W. Morton Fullerton, whom Mrs. Wharton had met and who would later become her lover. The name, as can be seen, is also applied to her motorcar.

8. Their visit together to Charles Eliot Norton at his summer home.

9. Edwin Austin Abbey (1852–1911), the American muralist, and his wife, Mary Gertrude Mead, lived at Morgan Hall in Gloucestershire.

To H. G. Wells
Ms Bodleian

Lamb House, Rye
November 19*th* 1905

My dear Wells.

If I take up time and space with telling you why I have not *sooner* written to thank you for your magnificent bounty, I shall have, properly, to steal it from my letter, my letter itself; a much more important matter. And yet I *must* say, in three words, that my course has been inevitable and natural. I found your first munificence here on returning from upwards of eleven months in America, toward the end of July—returning to the mountain of Arrears produced by almost a year's absence and (superficially, thereby) a year's idleness. I recognized, even from afar (I had already done so) that the Utopia[1] was a book I should desire to read only in the right conditions of *coming* to it, coming with luxurious freedom of mind, rapt surrender of attention, adequate honours, for it of every sort. So, not bolting it like the morning paper and sundry, many, other vulgarly importunate things, and knowing, moreover, I had already shown you that though I was slow I was safe, and even certain, I "came to it" only a short time since, and surrendered myself to it absolutely. And it was while I was at the bottom of the crystal well that Kipps suddenly appeared, thrusting his honest and inimitable head over the edge and calling down to me, with his note

377

of wondrous truth, that he had business with me above. I took my time, however, there below (though "below" be a most improper figure for your sublime and vertiginous heights), and achieved a complete saturation; after which, reascending and making out things again, little by little, in the dingy air of the actual, I found Kipps, in his place, awaiting me—and from his so different but still so utterly coercive embrace I have just emerged. It was really very well he was there, for I found (and it's even a little strange) that I could read *you* only—AFTER YOU—and don't at all see whom else I could have read. But now that this is so I don't see either, my dear Wells, how I can "write" you about these things—they make me want so infernally to talk with you, to see you at length. Let me tell you, however, simply, that they have left me prostrate with admiration, and that you are, for me, more than ever, the most interesting "literary man" of your generation—in fact, the only interesting one. These things do you, to my sense, the highest honour, and I am lost in amazement at the diversity of your genius. As in everything you do (and especially in these three last Social Imaginations),[2] it is the quality of your intellect that primarily (in the Utopia) obsesses me and reduces me—to that degree that even the colossal dimensions of your Cheek (pardon the term that I don't in the least invidiously apply) fails to break the spell. Indeed your Cheek is positively the very sign and stamp of your genius, valuable to-day, as you possess it, beyond any other instrument or vehicle, so that when I say it doesn't break the charm, I probably mean that it largely constitutes it, or constitutes the force: which is the force of an irony that no one else among us begins to have—so that we are starving, in our enormities and fatuities, for a sacred satirist (the satirist *with* irony—as poor dear old Thackeray was the satirist without it), and you come, admirably, to save us. There are too many things to say—which is so exactly why I can't write. Cheeky, cheeky, cheeky is *any* young man at Sandgate's offered Plan for the life of Man—but so far from thinking that a disqualification of your book, I think it is positively what makes the performance heroic. I hold, with you, that it is only by our each contributing Utopias (the cheekier the better) that anything will come, and I think there is nothing in the book truer and happier than your speaking of this struggle of the rare yearning individual toward that suggestion as one of the certain assistances of the future. Meantime you set a magnificent

378

example—of *caring*, of feeling, of seeing, above all, and of suffering from, and with, the shockingly sick actuality of things. Your epilogue tag in italics, strikes me as of the highest, of an irresistible and touching beauty. Bravo, bravo, my dear Wells!

And now, coming to Kipps, what am I to say about Kipps but that I am ready, that I am compelled, utterly to *drivel* about him? He is not so much a masterpiece as a mere born gem—you having, I know not how, taken a header straight down into mysterious depths of observation and knowledge, I know not which and where, and come up again with this rounded pearl of the diver. But of course you know yourself how immitigably the thing is done—it is of such a brilliancy of *true* truth. I really think that you have done, at this time of day, two particular things for the first time of their doing among us. (1) You have written the first closely and intimately, the first intelligently and consistently ironic or satiric novel. In everything else there has always been the sentimental or conventional interference, the interference of which Thackeray is full. (2) You have for the very first time treated the English "lower middle" class, etc., without the picturesque, the grotesque, the fantastic and romantic interference, of which Dickens, e.g., is so misleadingly, of which even George Eliot is so deviatingly, full. You have handled its vulgarity in so scientific and historic a spirit, and seen the whole thing all in its *own* strong light. And then the book has, throughout, such extraordinary life; everyone in it, without exception, and every piece and part of it, is so vivid and sharp and *raw*. Kipps himself is a diamond of the first water, from start to finish, exquisite and radiant; Coote is consummate, Chitterlow magnificent (the whole first evening with Chitterlow perhaps the most brilliant thing in the book—unless that glory be reserved for the way the entire matter of the *shop* is done, including the admirable image of the boss). It all in fine, from cover to cover, does you the greatest honour, and if we had any other than skin-deep criticism (very stupid, too, at [th]at), it would have immense recognition. I repeat that these things have made me want greatly to see you. Is it thinkable to you that you might come over at this ungenial season, for a night,—some time before Christmas? Could you, would you? I should immensely rejoice in it. I am here till January 31st—when I go up to London for three months. I go away, probably, for four or five days at Christmas—and I go away for next

Saturday–Tuesday. But apart from those dates I would await you with rapture.

And let me say just one word of attenuation of my (only apparent) meanness over the *Golden Bowl.* I was in America when that work appeared, and it was published there in two volumes, and in very charming and readable form, each volume but moderately thick and with a legible, handsome, large-typed page. But there came over to me a copy of the London issue, fat, vile, small-typed, horrific, prohibitive, that so broke my heart that I vowed I wouldn't, for very shame, disseminate it, and I haven't, with that feeling, had a copy in the house or sent one to a single friend. I wish I had an American one at your disposition—but I have been again and again depleted of all ownership in respect to it. You are very welcome to the British brick if you, at this late day, will have it. I greet Mrs. Wells and the Third Party very cordially and am yours, my dear Wells, more than ever,

Henry James

1. *A Modern Utopia,* published, like *Kipps*, in 1905.
2. *Anticipations* (1902), *Mankind in the Making* (1903), and *A Modern Utopia.*

To William James
Ms Harvard

Lamb House, Rye
November 23d 1905

Dearest William.

I wrote not many days since to Aleck, and not very, very many before to Peggy—but I can't tonight hideously further postpone acknowledging your so liberal letter of October 22d (the one in which you enclosed me Aleck's sweet one), albeit I have been in the house all day without an outing, and very continuously writing, and it is now 11. P.M. and I am rather fagged: my claustration being the result first, of a day of incessant bad weather, and second of the fact that Grenville Emmet[1] and his Indian bride spent yesterday and last night here, much breaking into my time, and third that I go tomorrow up to town, to proceed thence, under extreme and cogent pressure, to pay a thirty-six hours' visit, in the country, to the Humphry Wards. She and Humphry go to America after the New

Year, and I think she wants me greatly to indoctrinate and *avertir* her. She will in sooth be lionized limb from limb. But don't you and Alice think it necessary to lift a finger. *I* am not in any degree "beholden" to them—I regard it quite as the other way round; and she, amiable and culture-crammed woman as she is, is strangely stupid. (*Burn* and repeat not this—such reverberations—of imbecility—come back to me from the U.S.!) Grenville's Squaw is much better than I thought she'd be—facially ugly, but vocally and intelligently good and civilized, and with a certain "air"; and he (in addition to being in his way a "dear") is, for a lawyer, almost fabulously ingenuous. One gets such strange *bouffés* from those young people, of the general blankness of the home over which the Kitty T[emple] of our youth later presided. I am having a very good and peaceful autumn—(the best one I have ever had here, with *enormous* profit from Fletcher), and shall prolong my present phase till February 1st, going then up to town till (probably) May. I am working off my American book very steadily (*absit omen!*)—or rather the stuff which is taking, irresistibly and inevitably, the form of two moderately-long books (separate, of course, not two vols; which wouldn't at all do, but a sort of First and Second Series, with an interval between, the first winding up with Philadelphia and Washington and the second beginning with two papers on the South and going on with all the rest of my so unaccountably-garnered matter). I have practically *done* the first, and serial publication of it begins in December. I shall be mightily glad to have tapped it all off, for the effort of *holding rather factitiously on* to its (after all virtual) insubstantiality just only to convert it into some sort of paying literature is a very great tension and effort.[2] It would all so melt away, of itself, were it not for this artificial clutch! (But I am hoping to have made the whole thing, really, a short job for the way it will have been done.) You tell me what is good of yourself and your more or less disposed-of college lectures, and of your probably not going to France next year (*'faudra voir!*) but you say nothing about California, and I am much puzzled by a mystery and ambiguity in all your Sequences—Peg's admission to Bryn Mawr, mixed up with her simultaneous social debut and your California absence etc. When do you go there, anyhow, and when does she go to B.M., and does she go to California with you, and if she doesn't who takes her out, at home and with whom does she abide?

However, I shall write to Alice for information—all the more that I deeply owe that dear eternal Heroine a letter. I am not "satisfied about her," please tell her with my tender love, and should have testified to this otherwise than by my long cold silence if only I hadn't been, for stress of composition, putting myself on very limited contribution to the post. The worst of these bad manners are now over, and please tell Alice that my very next letter shall be to her. Only *she* mustn't put pen to paper for me, not so much as dream of it, before she hears from me. I take a deep and rich and brooding comfort in the thought of how splendidly you are all "turning out" all the while—especially Harry and Bill, and especially Peg, and above all, Aleck—in addition to Alice and you. I turn you over (in my spiritual pocket), collectively and individually, and make you chink and rattle and ring; getting from you the sense of a great, though too-much (for my use) tied-up fortune. I have great joy (tell him with my love) of the news of Bill's so superior work, and yearn to have some sort of a squint at it. Tell him, at any rate, how I await him, for his holidays, out here—on this spot. And I wish I realized more richly Harry's present conditions. But I am probably *incapable* of doing it—and he must judge me so. I await him here not less.—

I mean (in response to what you write me of your having read the *Golden B.*) to try to produce some uncanny form of thing, in fiction, that will gratify you, as Brother—but let me say, dear William, that I shall greatly be humiliated if you *do* like it, and thereby lump it, in your affection, with things, of the current age, that I have heard you express admiration for and that I would sooner descend to a dishonoured grave than have written.[3] Still I *will* write you your book, on that two-and-two-make-four system on which all the awful truck that surrounds us is produced, and *then* descend to my dishonoured grave—taking up the art of the slate pencil instead of, longer, the art of the brush (vide my lecture on Balzac). But it is, seriously, too late at night, and I am too tired, for me to express myself on this question—beyond saying that I'm always sorry when I hear of your reading anything of mine, and always hope you won't—you seem to me so constitutionally unable to "enjoy" it, and so condemned to look at it from a point of view remotely alien to mine in writing it, and to the conditions out of which, *as* mine, it has inevitably sprung—so that all the intentions that have been its main reason for being (with *me*) appear never to have reached you at all—and you appear even to assume that the life, the elements forming its subject-matter, deviate from felicity in not having an impossible analogy with the life of Cambridge. I see nowhere about me done or dreamed of the things that alone for me constitute the *interest* of the doing of the novel—and yet it is in a sacrifice of them on their very own ground that the thing you suggest to me evidently consists. It shows how far apart and to what different ends we have had to work out (very naturally and properly!) our respective intellectual lives. And yet I can read *you* with rapture—having three weeks ago spent three or four days with Manton Marble[4] at Brighton and found in his hands ever so many of your recent papers and discourses, which having margins of mornings in my room, through both breakfasting and lunching there (by the habit of the house), I found time to read several of—with the effect of asking you, earnestly, to address me some of those that I so often, in Irving Street, saw you address to others who were not your brother. I had no time to read them therein. Philosophically, in short, I am "with" you, almost completely, and you ought to take account of this and get me over altogether.—There are two books by the way (one fictive) that I permit you to *raffoler* about as much as you like, for I have been doing so myself—H. G. Wells's *Utopia* and his *Kipps*. The *Utopia* seems to me even more remarkable for other things than for his characteristic cheek, and *Kipps* is quite magnificent. Read them both if you haven't—certainly read Kipps.—There's also another subject I'm too full of not to mention the good thing I've done for myself—that is for Lamb House and my garden—by moving the greenhouse away from the high old wall near the house (into the back garden, setting it up better—against the *street* wall) and thereby throwing the liberated space into the front garden to its immense apparent extension and beautification. The high recaptured wall is alone worth the job—though the latter has been proving far more abysmal and long-drawn than I intended. But hot-water pipes and a radiator fed from the new greenhouse stove, or boiler, pass straight into the garden room now and warm and dry it beautifully and restore it to winter use. But oh, fondly, goodnight! Ever your

Henry

1. Grenville Temple Emmet was a son of Katherine (Kitty) Temple Emmet, sister of Minny Temple. He had just married Pauline Anne Ferguson in Minnesota, and they were on their honeymoon.

2. In the end HJ published only one volume, *The American Scene* (1907).

3. HJ is responding in this letter to WJ's critique of *The Golden Bowl*. WJ had written: "Why don't you, just to please Brother, sit down and write a new book,˙with no twilight or mustiness in the plot, with great vigor and decisiveness in action, no fencing in the dialogue, or psychological commentaries, and absolute straightness in style" (Ms Harvard, 22 October 1905).

4. Manton Marble (1834–1917) had been proprietor and editor of the New York *World* from 1862 to 1876. He now lived in Brighton, where HJ occasionally visited him.

To Edith Wharton
Ms Yale

Lamb House, Rye
December 18 1905

Dear Mrs. Wharton.

Your letter gives me warrant, and I throw discretion to the wind and answer it by return of post. Besides, I must thank you very kindly, with no delay, for the so handsome photograph in which you *baissez les yeux* so modestly before the acclamations of the world. They are all transcribed for you, however, by the *soins* of Romeike,[1] I surely make out, in that compendium you are reading; so that you look thoroughly in possession of your genius, fame and fortune. It is a very charming picture, as charming, that is, as a picture can be, which doesn't none the less, "do you justice." But I take it gratefully for my *étrennes* and place it, ever so conspicuously among quaint tributes already beginning to cluster on my mantel shelf. You make me a still handsomer present, however, in your dazzling news of your (intended) February voyage. This is a delight to hear, and immediately so *furnishes* for me the rather vacant prospect of the spring that I feel as if, with an empty new house on my hands and no money left to garnish it, I had suddenly inherited a "centre-table" or a chandelier; and I am already, on the strength of it, excitedly moving in. This is verily a brave showing, and I can't tell you how well-inspired I think you both. I go up to town February 1st, to stay a good two weeks, and hope to learn there, promptly, of your arrival in the almost neighbouring capital. After that, I shall pull on the London string as hard as I know how—to bring you over without too much delay. Would that Pagello *were* in your train, or, failing that, even Cook,[2] prince of Pagellists—it would make me believe so in the dream of a spin with you. I *have* had a few here, this

384

Edith Wharton in 1905.

autumn, and the sense of the way England *s'y prête* made my mouth water.—I can't tell you meanwhile how mighty I think it of you to be spending the Christmastide at Biltmore—I myself only going to Brighton and thinking even that formidable. May those marble halls not expand, but *contract,* to receive you, and may you have, as you of course will, one of the *apartements* of state, and not a bachelor bedroom, as I did, in the wing looking over an ice-bound stable-yard, and that even the blaze of felled tree didn't warm. But there must be always this about Biltmore, that it thoroughly fills the mind, while one is there—little as the mind can do to fill *it.*

Your letter opens up deeps that call unto deeps, of various sorts—and we must really do everything to make the Poncivite of Paul and Minnie (for *she's* in it, much) "keep" till we meet; in company with the unattenuated Tinayre[3] and many other things besides. I must tell you a small anecdote of the unattenuated Tinayre—culled during a Sunday spent not long since, with Mrs. H[umphry] W[ard], at Stocks. The two ladies had somewhat foregathered "morally," during Mme T.'s brief visit to England two years ago, and after *François Barbazanges,*[4] sent by the author to that of Robert Elsmere, the latter had written remonstrantly, pleading to know whether the "facts of life," as Tolstoy and Turgénieff handled them, didn't constitute "freedom" enough for the novel, and whether Mme T. hadn't really better think it over. Mme T. replied that she would think it over indeed—and promised very deferentially and sympathetically—and then in due course (of a year or two) sent Mrs. W. *Avant l'amour* with another sweet letter saying that she *had* thought it over and that this was the result. (It appears that the volume in question is an early-published thing, out of print,—which accounts for a certain ambiguity in it—now revived, reconsidered, retouched and above all *châtiés;* therefore offered to Mrs. W. as the fruit of her example.) This Mrs. W. retailed to me with bewildered gravity, as so strange a miscalculation of the French mind! But I see it as a *calculation* (of the French mind!) altogether—with the irrepressible *malice* of the demonic little Tinayre having made all the *frais* from the first, and with the ineffable *Avant l'amour* ("*avant*"!!!) re-vamped perhaps even really just *for* the trick on her correspondent. I understood it after the tone in which our Mrs. W. mentioned to me her suggesting to her Tolstoy and Turgénieff—but Mrs. W. (she is really an absolute dear) has never understood it to this hour.—These things, however, take me too far, and make me desire to burn my letter. You will miss Mrs. Ward in New York—she is definitely, I think, and quite sublimely, to go in the spring. But let not that make you change your plan. I am afraid my little mill has ground no personal news of interest since I last wrote you. I continue to sit very tight here (and I like the quiet conditions in this misty-browny-purply and essentially *toney* South of England autumn, which is far from having your Lenox etc. sublimities—but which *is*, truly, *tonier*):[5] having the cogent motive of the mind to put through *à tout prix*, the squeezing-out of my American stuff, in order both to keep ahead of it before it *goes* (really an heroic feat), and, more particularly, to clear the ground of it to be free for more inspiring work. It's very good [of] you to speak of your regret at the relegation of *that*. I do myself feel it waiting at the door and scratching there, like my little hound, to be let in. But the threshing out [of] my American matter in this form will really enable me to use some of it (I mean some of the *sense* of it) in the fictive form better. I shall read the *House of Mirth* again, over, in the "final" state. I go back with you in spirit to the little Park Avenue House, of which I have, really, a thrillingly romantic recollection. I vibrated much there and got a great deal out of it. Don't "answer" this—only make me a sign when your sailing is fixed. I enclose a special benediction to Mr. Teddy and I think tenderly of dear demented Walter B. Yours, dear Mrs. Wharton, always and ever

Henry James

1. The clipping agency.
2. Mrs. Wharton's chauffeur, Charles Cook.
3. See letter to Mrs. Wharton, 8 November 1905.
4. Tinayre's novel *La Vie Amoureuse de François Barbazanges* (1904).
5. Apparently a coinage by HJ and a pun on Tinayre.

To Paul Bourget
Dictated Ts Private

Lamb House, Rye
21 December 1905

Mon cher ami.

I have sent you today a small volume containing a couple of mercenary Conférences[1] that I delivered in a few places, last spring, in America: which please let serve as a belated, dreadfully belated, acknowledgement of your kind care in possessing me promptly of "Les Deux Soeurs."[2] This volume I read with immediate attention and with the highest appreciation; but I had returned only a few days before from the great country, returned to formidable arrears of work, and of occupation of every kind; which pressure has been my portion from that moment, and has, on the whole, permitted me to make, right and left, these four or five months, terribly sincere excuses for everything.

I went to America saddled with the engagement, the inevitable, to produce a book of Impressions; but if the Impressions didn't fail to assault me, nor I (as I think), to catch them on the wing, it proved a very different matter to pluck them of their feathers and truss them up properly and serve them at table. I came back, in short, victim in all ways to the immense incoherence of American things. I found matter for plenty of Copy, but the copy has had only *now* to get itself done, and I am gouging it out as I can. You are in a perfect position for giving me all sympathy: in return for which I promise you my probable two volumes as soon as they are published. (They are meanwhile, of course, appearing, journalistically, in morsels).[3]

My time of nearly eleven months *là-bas* was full of interest to me, but I found the country formidable and fatiguing (I went to Florida and California); and I also failed to arrive at a single conclusion, or to find myself entertaining a single *opinion*. I was conscious of plenty of sensations, agreeable and *horripilantes*; but that is as far as I got, and all that my report of my experience may pretend to. One of the last and pleasantest things that happened to me (at the end of June) was to spend a few days, at Lenox, with Mrs. Wharton, in the happiest conditions of season, temperature and general *agrément*. I had been with them for a longer time in the autumn, but the splendour of the early summer in that region, the beauty of the land, the charm of their admirable house—without counting the merit of the hostess—made the moment I speak of a delightful last impression. The good Teddy was far away in Canada, fishing, but long and admirable motor-hours (they had just acquired a valiant new machine) consoled me at least for his absence. À propos of both of whom, you are already aware, no doubt, that they expect to sail for Europe toward the end of February. She has just kindly announced me this good news. *Je vous en fais part*, if you don't already know it. Their idea is apparently to be first for some little time in Paris and then to come to England. Won't you both come here *with* them? I don't see, unless you do, how I am to tell you half of my traveller's tale—any more than to extract from you those arrears of your own history that I greatly desire. You must hear from me of Mrs. Gardner, who is *de plus en plus* remarquable and whose *palais-musée* is a really great creation. Her acquisitions during the last ten years have been magnificent; her arrangement and administration of them are admirable, and her spirit soars higher still. Her spirit is immense, and proof against time and fate. It has greatly "improved" her in every way to have done a thing of so much interest and importance—and to have had to do it with such almost unaided courage, intelligence and energy. She has become really a great little personage.

But I must not go on as if I were pretending to write to you. I can only greet you, very affectionately, both, and give you as we say, all the compliments of the season. I have no notion of where this will find you; I hope in Paris, and I hope at peace with yourselves and the world. Commend me earnestly to Madame Paul, and believe me, *mon cher ami*, very faithfully yours,

Henry James

1. HJ had sent Bourget *The Question of Our Speech* (1905), containing his Bryn Mawr commencement address and his lecture on Balzac, which had just been published in the United States.
2. See letter to Mrs. Wharton, 8 November 1905.
3. *The American Scene.*

To W. Morton Fullerton
Ms Barrett

Lamb House, Rye
January 4 1906

My dear, dear Morton.

Only a word, before I go to bed, to tell you how intensely I am moved, and how deeply penetrated, by your beautiful, your exquisite letter.[1] There, my dear boy, are high and noble affinities and sympathies, exchanges of intelligence as rich as lovers' vows, and I ask myself under the blessing of them, why a strange fate keeps us so hideously separate. Your admirable perceptions and vibrations represent for me *all* the response that the genius of poor H.J. seems likely to be permitted to have become sensible of, and I consider of them with a kind of timorous joy, as if with my breathing on them so much as mere gratitude and recognition, they might mock me with sudden evanishment. Meanwhile I sink into your so full and lucid expression of what you so all-acutely feel as into a bath of some rare and fragrant essence, more grateful than I can say to my rather aching sense. I am safe with you, and I am *whole* to you, and the thought of my being any good—of any fine use—to you—well, that crowns the edifice. There is more to say—even though you yourself have spoken with so generous an eloquence; but this is all now—save that I somehow hoped and believed you were no longer ridden by the powers of darkness.[2] It deeply disconcerts me to hear (to 'gather) that this is not so; and I am horribly tempted almost to wish you some turn of the screw that *will* throw you with a felt weight on yours always

Henry James

1. HJ seems to be responding in this veiled language to Fullerton's praise of his newly published American lectures.
2. Fullerton's complicated love affairs in Paris.

To Jocelyn Persse
Ms Harvard

Lamb House, Rye, Sussex
January 9th 1906

Very dear Jocelyn.

It breaks my heart to have had to wait a little to make you a sign of response to your note. But I have been furiously pressed finishing some work and tidying up my situation a little before making an absence here of some duration (pressed catching the American post of today really), and as every half hour has made a difference I have been distressfully sacrificing you. My packet went off before dinner today, and though I am face to face now with fifteen letters, and an imminent renewal of my job, I clutch my pen of friendship and with it in my hand, give you, very affectionately, the *accolade* for the New Year. (If you don't know what accolade—which I oughtn't to have underlined—means, look it up in the Dictionary!) I come up to town on Tuesday, February 5th—mark that Date; and hereby invoke your company for *Major Barbara*[1] (with me) on the 7th P.M. (no, I mean *Wednesday* 6th, P.M.) if you haven't already, or shan't have by that time, seen it too damned often. Will you let me know if you have—and keep away from it as much as possible meanwhile? It will be an old story in London by that time—must be in fact already—but I, you see, have had no opportunity of beholding it. I was in town for forty-eight crowded and fleeting hours on my way back from a rather outstretched and very tranquil and convenient Christmastide at Brighton. I came quickly back here to put in this very necessary interval before returning there for a longish stay. Forgive my hurling so many hardhitting little china pots at your unfortunate head, or rather at your beautiful chin; it is too absurd. But the little history was that I wanted, extremely, being in town, to put my hand on some object that I could send you as a New Year's offering (I having been, during the time precedent to Christmas, remote from the arts and the places); but during a rapid and too hurried look round I beheld but the mere residuum, as it seemed to me, of superfluous rot; whereupon I said to myself: "Go to, I won't pick up on the run some base object that he doesn't want, but will wait till I see him, and then artfully discover if there be not some convenient accessory that he *does* desire and lack—which I will then most officiously thrust upon him." Such is my belated purpose still; so think it obligingly over. Meanwhile the little shaving pots are but a prosaic stopgap. So good night my dear boy. I spell it cunningly out that things are decently well with you. I hope this odious looking little 1906 announces itself, the vile brat, good-naturedly enough to the individual Jocelyn. It is very vacant and very moist and very mild here; but I think it must be very good for me, for the weeks dash by like motor cars breaking the law (and their inmates' necks). We will also visit the French Comedy. Go you meanwhile to see *Jonathan Sturges* at Long's. He asked about you the other day with interest and desire; and he is wretchedly unwell there and laid up with a nurse. But he sees people at times, and the best hours are the afternoon. Try him, at any rate, and if he isn't well enough, or whatever, try again. (He *can't* go out.) I renew the accolade. Yours, my dear Jocelyn, always and ever

Henry James

1. Shaw's *Major Barbara*, which had been produced for a number of matinees during December 1905, was now to have a six-week run at the Court Theatre under the Vedrenne-Barker management.

To the Earl of Lovelace.
Ts Lubbock

Lamb House, Rye
January 14*th* 1906

Dear Lord Lovelace.

I left home at Christmas for a few days' stay, which became a fortnight's absence, and, on my return a week ago, found the very handsome, remarkable and interesting volume which you had been so good as to send me. I wished to take real possession of it before having the pleasure of thanking you, and I have now done so by a very attentive, and in fact fascinated perusal.

Let me tell you at once that I am greatly touched by your friendly remembrance of my possible feeling for the whole matter, and of your own good act, perhaps, of a few years ago—the to me ever memorable evening when, at Wentworth House, you allowed me to look at some of the documents you have made use of in "Astarte." Ineffaceably has remained with me the poignant, the in fact very romantic interest of that occasion.[1] And now you have done the thing which I then felt a dim foreshadowing that you would do— but the determination of which must have cost you, as you show indeed, infinite consideration, and you have done it all after a man-ner of your own, and in a form, and with a weight and an authority, a general overwhelming massiveness, before which, at first, one catches a little one's breath. I caught mine, when I recognised your purpose and the extent of it, but as I went on I saw your act, I can honestly say, as a high and grave inevitability absolutely complete in itself, and justified by the very terms in which you perform it. It is an incantation out of which strange tragic ghosts arise, and other grimacing shapes, and thick troubling fumes of a past that seems to serve for them as a dark underworld; but such an effect was the essence of your case, and could only come, of itself, from the mo-ment you began to speak, as you have done, from the only real knowledge of what you are talking about (in connection with the matter) that our chattering time has seen. This knowledge, in its kind, strikes me as your warrant, and still more as your necessity (for the act) and great is the pleasure of seeing a thing so immit-igably *done*. For if you evoke the Ghosts you send them also, with as firm a hand, back to their shades, and I think there is not one of them (least of all the dreadful one of Hayward, whom I distressfully remember) who will ever rise again for an hour. Great is the virtue of History—when it has waited so long and so consciously to be written, and to be enabled to proceed to its clearing of the air. Between the covers of the book shapes itself the *last word* about Byron—absolutely the last word, strange, portentous and poly-syllabic, but admitting now of none other whatever after it. It seems to me equally true that your justice to Lady Byron has the same final and conclusive character, allowing of no rectification in any sense, and I can't sufficiently congratulate you on not having yielded to any insidious but considerable temptation to dress her in any graces, in any shade of colour whatever, not absolutely her own. To have spoken for her so sincerely and with such effect, and yet with such an absence of special pleading—I mean with so perfectly leaving her as she was—can't have been an easy thing, and remains, I think, a distinguished one. Clear she was, and you have kept her clear; and amid the all too heavy fumes one puts out one's hand to her in absolute confidence. I think her spirit, somewhere in the universe, must be putting out its hand to *you!*

As for some other questions—by which I mean the form and scheme of the book on the side of illustration and reference and citation—there would be much to say, to my sense, if it were not one o'clock A.M. and I hadn't already written you as long a letter as you will care to read. On the one hand the miscellany is extraor-dinarily rich and entertaining—and I can but admire and envy you the magnificence of your *Fund*, on which you so royally draw—I mean your fund of reading and historic saturation. Likewise it's interesting to encounter so many vivid and dauntless personal opinions, and so competent a defence of them. I nevertheless think I should have ventured to contend with you on the literary con-nection, into which, in some places, you expand, and am not sure, in short, that I wouldn't rather have argued for your bundle of precious relics wrapped in a plain white napkin—instead of in your cloth of gold. But these are things to talk of—of which I think with the greatest pleasure. May I ask to be very kindly commended to Lady Lovelace? I come up to town early in February for a longish stay and shall then give myself an early occasion for finding her, if possible, at home. Believe me yours most gratefully and truly,

Henry James

1. Ralph Gordon Noel King, second Earl of Lovelace (1839–1906) and Lord Byron's grandson. His *Astarte* (1905), privately printed, was a vindication of his grandmother, Lady Byron, and dealt also with Byron's love affair with his half-sister, Augusta Leigh. The "occasion" HJ refers to was his visit to Lord Lovelace on 4 February 1895, when he wrote in his notebooks that he was "shown some of their extremely interesting Byron papers; especially some of those bearing on the absolutely indubitable history of his relation to Mrs. Leigh, the sole *real* love, as he emphatically declares, of his life" (*Notebooks*, 181–182).

To Hendrik C. Andersen
Ms Barrett

Lamb House, Rye
January 31*st* 1906

Bravo, bravo, dearest Hendrik, for the vivid little note and the still vivider little photos of the vividest big group: a more than adequate and altogether beautiful response to my poor New Year's letter, which was only meant to bless and cheer you and never to hurry and worry you at all. Noble and admirable your two lovers united in their long embrace, and quite, to my sense, the finest of all your fine contributions to this wonderful (and interminable) series! It won't, by its nature, help the great nude army to encamp in the heart of the American city, but when I have said *that,* I shall have exhausted the sum of my strictures upon it—with the exception perhaps of saying that I don't think I find the *hands,* on the backs, *living* enough and participant enough in the kiss. They would be, in life, very participant—to their fingertips, and would show it in many ways. But this you know, and the thing is very strong and (otherwise) complete. There is more flesh and *pulp* in it, more life of *surface* and of blood-flow *under* the surface, than you have hitherto, in your powerful simplifications, gone in for.[1] So keep at *that*—at the flesh and the devil and the rest of it; make the creatures palpitate, and their flesh tingle and flush, and their internal economy proceed, and their bellies ache and their bladders fill—all in the mystery of your art. How I wish (to God) I could stand there with you in your crowded workshop and talk of these things. But patience, patience, that *still* will happen.

You say no word of your head and your health—so I try to take the Kissers for favourable evidence, and I scan the so handsome fatigued face of the rabbit-picture for signs reassuring and veracious. I don't know to what extent I make them out: you're so beautiful in it that I only hope you're exempt from physical woe. I take hold of you ever so tenderly and am yours ever so faithfully

Henry James

1. Referring again to Andersen's statue of the embracing couple, HJ scribbled on the flap of the envelope: "His hand is the better and his knees ever so interesting and magnificent."

To Witter Bynner
Dictated Ts Harvard

Lamb House, Rye
1st February 1906

Dear Witter Bynner.

I have your graceful letter about *The Troll Garden*[1] which duly reached me some time ago (as many appealing works of fiction duly reach me); and if I brazenly confess that I not only haven't yet read it, but haven't even been meaning to (till your words about it thus arrive), I do no more than register the sacred truth. That sacred truth is that, being now almost in my 100th year,[2] with a long and weary experience of such matters behind me, promiscuous fiction has become abhorrent to me, and I find it the hardest thing in the world to read almost *any* new novel. Any is hard enough, but the hardest from the innocent hands of young females, young American females perhaps above all. This is a subject—my battered, cynical, all-too-expert outliving of such possibilities—on which I could be eloquent; but I haven't time, and I will be more vivid and complete some other day. I've only time now to say that I *will* then (in spite of these professions) do my best for Miss Cather—so as not to be shamed by your so doing yours. Believe me, yours ever,

Henry James

1. HJ had met the poet Harold Witter Bynner (1881–1968) in New York during his American trip. Bynner now sent him Willa Cather's first collection of short stories, published in 1905. So far as we know HJ never commented on the book.
2. HJ was in his sixty-third year.

To Paul Harvey
Dictated Ts Lubbock

Lamb House, Rye
March 11, 1906

My dear Paul.

It would take some little explanation to tell you why, rejoicing greatly in your admirable letter, I didn't thank you for it without the delay of more than a day or two (instead of after this rather more graceless interval). In three words, however, it came to me amid the hurly-burly of a visit to town after a long interval and amid (by the same token) many consequent complications—whereby seeing, from one day to another my return hither and my recovery of time for a correspondence frustrated all round, I possessed my soul in patience till this hour. I came back to this east-windy place (comparative) a couple of days ago, and give you almost immediately and very gratefully the benefit of it. It is delightful to me, please believe, not wholly to lose touch of you—ghostly and ineffective indeed as that touch seems destined to feel itself. I find myself almost wishing that the whirligig of time had brought round the day of your inscription with many honours on some comfortable "retired list" which might keep you a little less on the dim confines of the Empire, and make you thereby more accessible and conversible. Only I reflect that by the time the grey purgatory of South Kensington or, wherever, crowns and pensions your bright career, I, alas, shall have been whirled away to a sphere compared to which Salonica and even furthest Ind are easy and familiar resorts, with no crown at all, most probably—not even "heavenly" and no communication with you save by table-raps and telepathists (like a really startling communication I have just had from—or through—a "Medium" in America (near Boston), a message purporting to come from my Mother, who died twenty-five years ago and from whom it ostensibly proceeded during a séance at which my sister-in-law, with two or three other persons, was present. The point is that the message is an allusion to a matter known (so personal is it to myself) to no other individual in the world but *me*—not *possibly* either to the medium or to my sister-in-law; and an allusion so pertinent and *initiated* and tender and helpful, and yet so unhelped by any actual earthly knowledge on any one's part, that it quite

396

astounds as well as deeply touches me. If the subject of the message had been conceivably in my sister-in-law's mind it would have been an interesting but not infrequent case of telepathy; but, as I say, it couldn't thinkably have been, and she only transmits it to me, after the fact, not even fully understanding it. So, I repeat, I am astounded!—and almost equally astounded at my having drifted into this importunate mention of it to you! (But the letter retailing it arrived only this A.M. and I have been rather full of it.)—I had heard of your present whereabouts from Edward Childe, who wrote me at the New Year his usual very faithful but *grincheuse* and pessimistic little letter (he doesn't "see life steadily and see it whole!") and I give you my word of honour that my great thought was, already before your own good words had come, to attest to you, on my own side, and pen in hand, my inextinguishable interest in you.[1] I came back from the U.S. after an absence of nearly a year (eleven months) by last midsummer whereupon my joy at returning to this so little American nook took the form of my having stuck here fast (with great arrears of sedentary occupation etc.) till almost the other day. I had engaged to "do a book" of Impressions—and had hoped to do it on the spot; but had found that so utterly impossible that it has been all to do since in these more detached conditions. (When the thing appears *as* a book you shall have, I promise you, a copy; but the successive portions of it are all being, for base profit, periodically "serialized" first—to the delay of the actual volume.) I found my native land, after so many years, interesting, formidable, fearsome and fatiguing, and much more difficult to see and deal with in any extended and various way than I had supposed. I was able to do with it far less than I had hoped, in the way of visitation—I found many of the conditions too deterrent; but I did what I could, went to the far South, the Middle West, California, the whole Pacific coast etc., and spent some time in the Eastern cities. It is an extraordinary world, an altogether huge "proposition," as they say there, giving one, I think, an immense impression of material and political power; but almost cruelly charmless, in effect, and calculated to make one crouch, ever afterwards, as cravenly as possible, at Lamb House Rye—if one happens to have a poor little L.H., R., to crouch in. This I am accordingly doing very hard—with intervals of London inserted a good deal at this Season—I go up again, in a few days, to stay till about May. So I am not making history, my dear Paul, as you are; I am at least only making my very limited and intimate own. *Vous avez beau dire,* you, and Mrs. Paul, and Miss Paul, are making that of Europe—though you don't appear to realize it any more than M. Jourdain[2] did that he was talking prose. Have patience, meanwhile—you will have plenty of South Kensington later on (among other retired pro-consuls and where Miss Paul will "come out") and meanwhile you are, from the L.H. point of view, a family of thrilling Romance. And it *must* be interesting to *améliorer le sort des populations*—and to see real live Turbaned Turks going about you, and above all to have, even in the sea, a house from which you look at divine Olympus. You live with the gods, if not like them—and out of all this un-utterable Anglo-Saxon banality—so extra-banalized by the ex-tinction of dear Arthur Balfour. I take great joy in the prospect of really getting hold of you, all three, next summer. I count, fondly, on your presence here and I send the very kindest greeting and blessing to your two companions. The elder is of course still very young, but how old the younger must now be!

I am sorry to say I see Lady Gregory[3] much less than of old. She is so immersed in her Erse—I had almost said in her Hearse! Yours, my dear Paul, always ever

Henry James

1. HJ had known Paul Harvey (1862–1948) since his visit to the Edward Lee Childes at their estate in the French Gâtinais in 1876. See *Letters* II, 62–63. Harvey, the child of a French painter and an English governess, was orphaned young. After attending Oxford he served as a secretary to the Marquess of Lansdowne during the Rosebery government. Later he was in the diplomatic service, and in his old age he compiled the Oxford Companions to English and French literature respectively.
2. Molière's principal character in *Le Bourgeois Gentilhomme*.
3. Augusta Lady Gregory (1852–1932), *née* Persse, whom HJ had known for many years. See *Letters* III, 291; also *Notebooks*, 145–147.

To Witter Bynner
Ms Harvard

Lamb House, Rye
26*th* March 1906

Dear Witter Bynner.

I feel pretty sure you know much about my friend H. G. Wells, who sails for New York tomorrow and to whom I am giving such help as is possible to his making some profit of his short stay [t]here. (I mean H. G. Wells of the *War of the Worlds, Kipps,* the admirable Kipps, which I hope you have read and appreciated, and all the other notable things.) I write this word to make you my confession that, interesting and sympathetic as he is, I have given him a note of introduction to you—but not at all to appeal to you for any general trouble about him; only, rather, to ask you to do one definite and, as I suppose, easy thing. Could you put him down at the Player's Club for the brief time he is there?—and thereby greatly oblige the author of these lines. Wells is, to my sense, a really brilliant little genius, and personally an interesting, charming man: very much the most remarkable of the younger literary generation here. He will send you my little note, and I am sure won't otherwise prove a burden to you. He goes to America to inquire and inform himself, and I am sure will be intensely immersed, all over the place, in that process. If you haven't read *Kipps,* read it—and find it remarkable enough to give you a pretext of gratitude for my having made the author known to you. I shall not for a long time, if ever, hurl anyone else at you, and I thank you again now, in advance, and am yours most truly,

Henry James

To Edith Wharton
Ms Yale

The Reform Club
April 2nd [1906]

Dear Edith Wharton!

I rejoice in your so interesting and auspicious letter,[1] make a single greedy leap to the finest point in it. *Bien sûr que I'll* meet you at Dover on the 25th, or anywhere in the world—*this* world—you suggest, and motor with you as long as the machine consents to resist my weight. I respond in other words to that charming idea, or to any modification of it, very heartily, and shall await, later on, your further commands. I regard it as an enchanting prospect. And *how* I want to hear about everything! our dear Névrosis, the translations, the dramatizations, the asphyxiating milieu of H[oward] S[turgis] (about whose strange drop into dullness you are sadly right!), the latest "returns" from the H[ouse] of M[irth] and whatever else you may confide to me as we spin. I really am exquisitely grateful to both of you for the motor-chance. I have set my foot *almost* into none since I tore myself last from Pagello.[2] (I will explain the almost.) Tout à vous, Madame,

Henry James

1. Mrs. Wharton had just arrived in Paris.
2. See letter to Mrs. Wharton, 8 November 1905.

To Edith Wharton
Ms Yale

The Reform Club
April 4*th* 1906

Dear Mrs. Wharton.

Your letter this A.M. received makes me still further rejoice. I will do my very best to be prepared with a pleasing itinerary—of the kind you have in your eye—by the date of your advent, and in fact to meet you with it at Dover on the 25th. With it or without it I will meet you. If we start from D. on the 26th A.M., I vote that we come southward through Kent and Sussex—we must keep south of London—and begin by lunching that day at Lamb House. In that case we might sleep at (I should think) Chichester, and make our way so, by Winchester and Salisbury, into the interesting Somersetshire of old houses (Montacute the beautiful!!) by *Wells*, on the way. Thence along the North Devon coast first, then across Devonshire southward to a wind up at Sidmouth on the south coast. (Ilfracombe is rather awful.) But this is a very rough hint. Don't resent the few monuments if thrown in and *met*—not sought and gone out of the way for; in this small country they come in (the occasional cathedrals etc.) of themselves. But *nous causerons de cela*. How much you are laying up on your side to tell me! Save every crumb—make in due course your further signals and believe me always yours

Henry James

Reform Club, Pall Mall, S.W.
May 4*th* [1906]

Beloved Ones!

I wrote you, feverishly, last Saturday—but now comes in a blest cable from Harry telling of your being as far on your way home as at Denver and communicating thence in inspired accents and form, and this, for which I have been yearning (the news of your having to that extent shaken off the dust of your ruin)[1] fills me with such joy that I scrawl you these still agitated words of jubilation— though I can't seem to you less than incoherent and beside the mark I fear, till I have got your letter from Stanford which Harry has already announced his expedition of on the 28th. (This must come in a day or two more.) Meanwhile there was three days ago an excellent letter in the *Times* from Stanford itself (or P.A.)[2] enabling me, for the first time, to conceive a little, and a trifle less luridly to imagine, the facts of your case. I had at first believed those facts to be that you were thrown bedless and roofless upon the world, semi-clad and semi-starving, and with all that class of phenomena about you. But how do I know, after all, even yet—? and I await your light with an anxiety that still endures. I have just parted with Bill, who dined with me, and who is to lunch with me tomorrow—(I going in the evening to the "Academy Dinner.") I have—since the arrival of Harry's telegram, or cable of "reassurance"—the second to that effect, not this of today, which makes the third and best—I have been, as I say, trying, under pressure, a three days' motor trip with the Whartons, much frustrated by bad weather and from which I impatiently and prematurely and gleefully returned today: so that I have been separated from B. for forty-eight hours. But I tell you of him rather than talk to you, in the air, of your own weird experiences. He is to cross to Paris on the 6th having waited over here to go to the Private View of the Academy, to see me again, and to make use of Sunday 6th (a *dies non* in Paris as here) for his journey. It has been delightful to me to have him near me, and he has spent and re-spent long hours at the National Gallery, from which he derives (as also from the Wallace Collection) great stimulus and profit. I am extremely struck with his *seriousness* of spirit and intention—he

401

seems to me *all* in the thing he wants to do (and awfully intelligent about it); so that in fine he seems to me to bring to his design quite an exceptional quality and kind of intensity. He is in every way a comfort and an interest to behold and to deal with, and comes within a measurable distance of being as fine, in his way, as Harry—which is verily saying all. What a family—with the gallantries of the pair of *you* thrown in! Well, you, beloved Alice, have needed so exceedingly a "change," and I was preaching to you that you should arrive somehow at one or perish—whereby you have had it with a vengeance, and I hope the effects will be appreciable (that is not altogether accurst) to you. What I really now *most* feel the pang and the woe of is my not being there to hang upon the lips of your conjoined eloquence. I really think I must go over to you again for a month—just to listen to you. But I wait, and am ever more and more fondly your

Henry

1. The WJs had been at Stanford during the San Francisco earthquake, and for some days HJ had been deeply anxious, not knowing their exact whereabouts.
2. Palo Alto, California.

To Charles Scribner's Sons
Ms Princeton

Reform Club
May 9th 1906

Dear Sirs.

I am in receipt of your interesting letter of the 27th April and respond to its different points in order.

Only let me say, as a preliminary, that I rather regret your decision not to send me back the revised mass of *Roderick Hudson* to be typed. I would gladly have had this done under my eye here (and pretty quickly), and would have sent you immaculate Copy. However, I shall be very gratified meanwhile for the patience of your compositors and shall not put it again to any such strain. I shall send you *The American* completely re-typed, as I am here also obliged to riddle the margins practically as much as in the case of R.H. And I shall send you *The Portrait of a Lady* with all the worst pages (I mean the most amended ones) re-copied—though my retouchings of this book are fewer and *no* passages so intricately altered as in the two others.[1] These *three* early books thus dealt with, the worst will be over; nothing else in the series will demand (or receive) so much re-manipulation. And let me add that I shall be obliged to send you the *P. of a L.* BEFORE the *American*, as it will be the easiest revision for me to finish (not having to be so close). I don't think there is any objection whatever to the appearance of the *P. of a L.* SECOND, and of *The American* third. I am on the point of escaping from three months of this Babylon and returning for the rest of the year to the quiet of the country—whence I shall very quickly send you the Preface of *R.H.*—sending that of *The Portrait* with the Copy.

For the rest I think I can but, to begin with, give a general and very satisfied assent to all the rest of your questions.

I very much like the specimen page you set up and am quite content with it—especially with the improvement of one more line of length and the *m* of width. It seems to me handsome and charming, and abates nothing of the *dignity* of aspect which was, for this presentment of my books, my dream and desire. If this page enables you to make then, by art of paper, etc., one not too "chunky" volume of *R.H.* and of *The American*, each, so much the better. The same for *The Awkward Age*.

I quite adhere to my original idea as to the total number of volumes and as to the number of those for my shorter productions. I regard twenty-three volumes as sufficient for the series and have no wish to transcend it.[2] I shall *make* what I wish to "preserve" fit into the number and only desire to sift and re-sift, in selection,—so as to leave nothing but fine gold! So far as I can at present absolutely say, therefore, Four Volumes for the Shorter Novels and Four for the Tales may be regarded as quite definite—the only shade of doubt being as to whether I may not, in close quarters with my selection, decide to make the Tales Five and the Shorter Novels Three. (In length indeed these two classes shade into each other.) But take it that I am perfectly satisfied with Eight Volumes for the two classes.

As for the approximate number of words of these various Eight Volumes I am not as yet very definitely prepared to say; but I should like to take a *safe number as a maximum and abide by that*. Should you consider 150,000 for these volumes excessive? This number would cover all contingencies in each case. But I rather infer that you would prefer a smaller one. Please tell me in this case your ideal maximum—as for instance 120,000? I would undertake to manage with 100,000, even, for each volume, but I don't think I should be able to do myself justice below that figure.

Lastly, I am quite content, in fact much relieved, to postpone the question of *The Bostonians* for the present.[3] And I of course rejoice in the two volumes for each of the main novels but the three excepted.

I shall be able to send you *The Portrait* very rapidly.

I was photographed the other day, by an American operator here, for a frontispiece (very well, artistically and suitably, as I believe), and am expecting proofs from day to day. Believe me, dear Sirs, yours very truly

Henry James

P.S. It gives me great pleasure to hear of Mr. Brownell's[4] interest and attention, and I shall be grateful for any help he can give the enterprise.

1. Ever since his return from the United States HJ had been minutely revising his early works for the New York Edition of his novels and tales which were to be published by Charles Scribner's Sons. He had sent them a much-revised copy of *Roderick Hudson* with its margins so illegibly scrawled as to present considerable difficulties to the typesetters. *The American* and *The Portrait of a Lady* were more extensively and profoundly revised than HJ here suggests, as were many of the early tales.

2. From the beginning HJ decided that he would keep his edition within the limits of twenty-three volumes. I have suggested that he chose this odd number in emulation of the first definitive edition of Balzac's *Comédie Humaine*: see Edel, "The Architecture of Henry James's New York Edition," *New England Quarterly* 24, no. 2 (June 1951): 169–178.

3. *The Bostonians* was finally excluded from the edition.

4. William Crary Brownell (1851–1928), critic and editor, was placed in charge of the production of the New York Edition.

To Hendrik C. Andersen
Ms Barrett

Lamb House, Rye
May 31st 1906

Carissimo Enrico Mio.

Of course, I've had punctually all your beautiful and blessed missives, and of course I've tenderly loved you, and yearningly embraced you, and passionately thanked you for them—but equally of course I've had to wait till tonight to do these things otherwise than all silently and hinderedly and, oh, so distantly. I won't take up precious time and space in telling you why I've *waited*—for you will feel always a felicity in this, as in the sense of the beautiful consciousness of something to happen, in good and fortunate time between us; your looking for my letter on the one hand, and my having the sense of its going forth to you on the wings of my affection, and your at last taking it in and being glad of it, there by your yellow Tiber, on the other. In short here we are together again—after a meagre and dismal and frustrated fashion I admit; but more at least than when neither of us is thus, with a poor vain pen, invoking the other. Your brave and charming letter of last month gave me much greater joy than my delay can, after all, have suggested to you, and that, and the numerous little photographs of your work, and the wondrous architectures and elevations and now, within a few days, the beautiful little new note with the three kodak-views of your self, your mother and the friend, have immensely comforted and cheered me. For they tell, and you speak so handsomely yourself, of your health and energy and *might*—so that I wonder at you and am proud of you, and send up hosannas and hymns of praise to the skies. I take your word for it that when you say you are well—with your old ailments conjured away—and say it so emphatically, you really mean it, dearest boy, and are not talking in the air. So I feel that you *must* be well, for if you weren't, with your prodigious and heroic production, which implies such a possession of life and sanity (don't read that word as *vanity*), you would by this time be sleeping in the cold tomb. Your production *is* prodigious and heroic and very beautiful and interesting to me— so much so that, dearest Hendrik, I affectionately and heartily declare, even while seeing less than ever where this colossal multiplication of divinely naked and intimately associated gentlemen and ladies, flaunting their bellies and bottoms and their other private affairs, in the face of day, is going, on any *American* possibility, to land you. I won't attempt to go into this last question now—you know already how it perplexes and even not a little distresses me. So I content myself with paying my tribute to your noble imagination and your splendid sense of the body and the members, your wealth of composition, combination, creation! The small photographs, as I say, immensely interest me, just as the rate at which you go takes away my breath. I look your kodaks (as I suppose them) over again, while I write, and they make me groan, in spirit, that I'm not standing there before the whole company with you—when I think I should find, if you would let me try, so much to say about them! There would be things, as I see the different figures thus, that I should, ever so affectionately, contend with you about, but that I can't touch on now and here. (I should go down on my knees to you, for instance, to individualize and detail the *faces*, the types ever so much more—to study, ardently, the question of doing that—the whole face-question. I should cheekily warn you against a tendency to neglect *elegance*—to emphasize too much the thickness and stoutness of limb, at the risk of making certain legs, especially from the knee down, seem too short etc.—and arms also too "stocky" and stony. The faces too blank and stony—the hair, for me, always too merely *symbolic*—and not living and *felt*. These offensive things I should say to you—in such a fashion that you would but love me better and our friendship would be but the tenderer and closer. But it's wretched work trying to talk at this damnable distance and I prefer to dwell on the things of great beauty that you constantly do. Of all the small photos accompanying your letter the two I enclose again (return by way of identifying them) strike me as the finest. But your whole overflowing vision and your whole *revel* of creation are unutterable. Delightful to me the small snapshots of your so loveable looking mother, and beautiful your own charming image with the gun on your shoulder. There, dear boy, you do look straight and strong and gallant and *valid*; for which the Powers—whoever they are—be praised. But how it only the more makes it a poor thing for me that the months are added to the months and we only don't meet. I want to ask you about your possibilities for this summer—but I have a feeling that they look bad for us. Is it your expectation that your mother will pass the summer in Italy? Will Mrs. Olivia[1] come back? Is there any chance of your being able to cross the Alps?—by which I mean, of course, to come here for a week? Tell me of these things won't you? in some brief easy way, at your earliest opportunity. We *must* meet somehow; we must talk of it and manage it. There is no place so peaceful as here—but of course unless you do for other reasons come northward I can't dream of asking you to make the big journey. Don't, however, oh don't, pass me—so near—on the wide waters. That does cast me down. But goodnight, dearest Hendrik. I draw you close and hold you long and am ever so tenderly yours

Henry James

1. Mrs. Olivia Cushing Andersen, widow of Hendrik Andersen's brother.

To Charles Scribner's Sons
Dictated Ts Princeton

Lamb House, Rye
12th June 1906

Dear Sirs.

All thanks for your letter of June 1st in answer to mine of May 9 and 12; which leaves me little to do but assent then to what you say about the restriction of the Eight Volumes of the Shorter Fictions generally to as nearly as possible 120,000 words apiece. I feel with you the importance of these volumes not being in any degree lumpish—and in short I will so manage at whatever cost. The "cost" will be a little, I am afraid, that of some critical animadversion on certain things missed by the reader, things that might rather confidently have been looked for: or perhaps I had better say that I *should* apprehend something of that sort were there more serious or attentive criticism nowadays to reckon with. I am not without the sense that the question of a supplementary volume or two—putting quite new books aside—may have to come up in the fulness of time; and for this possibility any omitted things that are really characteristic enough to mar completeness by their absence may meanwhile wait.

What does loom a little formidable to me, I confess, is the question of the "illustrations"; which makes me feel distinctly helpless at the view of getting into close quarters with it. I spent yesterday afternoon in being again "artistically" photographed here on my own premises by a young American expert, A. L. Coburn,[1] who had already done me in London, but without satisfactory success, and who came down from town for an earnest second attack. He is quite the best person going, here, I think, and this time I hope for good results; which he promises me within ten days, when I will promptly send you the best. I will also see if the reproduction of the little picture of the Florentine villa for volume II for R.H.[2] has not been by this time properly achieved, and in this case you shall have the two together. But please use the Villa-subject only if you absolutely approve of it: if it does really pass muster I don't suppose there is any harm in having it as one illustration, even if the difficulty of the others does prove past dealing with. It consists, this difficulty, in our really not wanting at all the common black-and-white drawing, of the magazine sort (and of however much character or cleverness); and wanting instead some scene, object or locality, and associated with some one or other of the tales in the volume, both consummately photographed and consummately reproduced. To *find* more than twenty such felicitous and characteristic bits, rather scattered about Europe as they really are, and then get them beautifully captured, represents more time (counting in only that element) than I can now command for the purpose, so I merely stare at the prospect, as you see, in humiliated impotence. Let me add on the other hand that if you should have in mind any really charming artist for twenty *drawings* of passages in the tales, I should be willing to take their charm for granted from you and leave you all the trouble. I should be quite at a loss to put my hand on such a treasure myself. I like Albert Sterner,[3] for instance; but are twenty Albert Sterners desirable or even thinkable—???

I am sending you immediately, that is in a very few days, revised copy for 300 or more of the 500 pages of *The Portrait*, to accelerate your being able to set up the other 200 now following as fast as possible, and Copy for *The American* as fast as possible after that. This has proved, in the close quarters of revision, slower (as well as really more beneficent) work than I fondly dreamed; as I have had to have a great many of the *Portrait* pages lucidly typed, to simplify the labour of your compositors; and it will be *all* in type that you will receive the revised *American*. Have a little more patience with me over these first three productions, which have been on a different footing, as regards the quantity of re-touching involved, from any of those to follow: so that future steps will be much more rapid and easy. Also let me add, for more explicitness than I have yet used, that I have absolutely no doubt whatever of the benefit I shall have conferred on each of them—and I mean of course benefit not only for myself, but for the public at large.[4] It is beyond any question with me, for instance, that what I have just been very attentively doing for the "Portrait" must give it a new lease of such life as it may still generally aspire to. I am very glad to have your announcement of proofs of R.H., which shall receive my immediate attention. Believe me, yours very truly

Henry James

1. Alvin Langdon Coburn (1882–1966), a young American photographer whose work had attracted considerable attention in London and been highly praised by Bernard Shaw.

2. This may have been a painting by Lizzie Boott of the Villa Castellani on Bellosguardo, where HJ had set certain scenes of *Roderick Hudson* and *The Portrait of a Lady*.

3. Albert Sterner (1863–1946), an American artist who did much work in black and white.

4. Charles Scribner had expressed to HJ's agent the misgiving that "Mr. James should so transform his early books that those who had known and delighted in them should feel disappointed with the new edition, owing to loss of freshness."

To James B. Pinker
Ms Yale

Lamb House, Rye
14th June 1906

Dear Mr. Pinker.

Your letter this morning received, on the questions of illustrations, re-animates and inspires me. It isn't that I don't see what an ornament a thoroughly good one to each volume will be to the series, but only that I have been rather frightened and flustered at the thought of having to give time to the invention and preparation of them—in addition to providing (which, however, I *shall* enjoy!) some sixteen or seventeen perfect Introductions. The prospect clears beautifully if you will kindly write to our friends in New York that I will gladly aid and abet them with suggestion and sympathy on this ground, if they see their way to taking over, themselves, the *procuring* and, as it were, working out of the pictures. When I spoke of the little villa-panel subject, by the way, in writing both to you and to New York a couple of days ago I had a stupid confusion of mind about its being wanted for *Roderick*. Of course it isn't, for that one volume, but if it's a practicable production, artistically speaking, it will serve excellently for one of the volumes of *The Portrait*, where a Florentine villa is again closely involved. Therefore, if I have my photograph for Volume I of the series, and the little villa-panel does successfully lend itself, there are two subjects secured to start with. Also, I think I can, beyond doubt, get a pleasing and artistic thing of this house, from the garden, and also procure a good reproduceable, slightly nebulous view of the English country house (Hardwicke, near Pangbourne, on the Thames) which I had vaguely and approximately in mind, years ago, for the opening of the *Portrait* (the place belongs to Charles D. Rose, M.P., with whom I had then been staying there, and I can easily write to them about it). These things I will set my young American photographer upon, as soon as I have received from him the result of our second and probably much more successful portrait attempt.[1] All thanks, I repeat, for your offer to communicate to the Scribners my full assent to their occupying themselves with the illustrations as far as ever they can. Please say to them, with this, that I will willingly, as far as possible, and as ingeniously contribute. I only recoil in terror from undertaking *too much.*

You shall receive for forwarding upwards of 350 pages of the *Portrait* as soon as I myself receive from town the last of the considerable number of fully-retyped pages of which said copy partly consists. Yours very truly

Henry James

1. From the time of this letter there began HJ's closer relationship with Alvin Langdon Coburn, the 28-year-old American photographer, who had already acquired a name in his art. HJ had always objected to black and white illustration of his works: he held pictures to be an affront to the written word. But the photographic representation, in which symbolic scenes could be used, seemed to him ideal, and, as further letters will show, HJ entered into the choice of the scenes with much enthusiasm. The result was the famous series of illustrations, much reprinted since their appearance in the New York Edition.

To Elizabeth Jordan
Ms NYPL

Lamb House, Rye
June 27*th* 1906

Dear Miss Jordan.[1]

Your letter is very pleasant to get, but I don't think I should (after a bit, now) have really been *needing* it as a reminder—inasmuch as the idea we exchanged notes about last summer has at last been coming up for me again, and I was positively coming to the point of myself advising you of the same. I am very glad that on your side the matter is still present to you. I will do with pleasure, for the Bazaar two or three papers of the kind you speak of, and of the length, or rather brevity—in fact I shall see my way best if I commit myself to doing *three,* of 3000 words each, and to letting you have them almost immediately. I think they should make a little *explicit trio* on the subject of our Women's Speech—entitled "The Speech of our Women," "A Talk on Tone" (I, II, III) or something of that sort. However, this is a detail, and I will send you a single one first and soon—very soon. But there are other cognate questions— on manners, address, the Public Behavior of our Girls etc. which ferment in my mind and at which I should like to have a go—only we will talk of these later. The thing is to make a beginning!

I rejoice greatly in your good account of Howells, dear man—of whom I am too much and too miserably deprived. I am down here in crouching seclusion (away from the madding London for work's sake, and quiet's), so I haven't yet seen the Harveys. But I am much hoping they will motor down soon to luncheon with me. Believe me yours very truly

Henry James

1. After HJ's commencement address at Bryn Mawr in 1905, "The Question of Our Speech," Elizabeth Jordan, editor of *Harper's Bazar,* invited him to write a series on the subject of American women. "The Speech of American Women" appeared in the November and December 1906 issues and "The Manners of American Women" in the April to July 1907 issues.

To Jessie Allen
Ms Harvard

Lamb House, Rye
July 6th [1906]

Dear, lavish, ruinous Goody!

Three baggy Buns, please, are (as I mentioned originally) all I can manage! You very kindly press upon me the conception of a Menu (or *Ménu,* as English lips love it!) but I beseech you to remember the delicacy of my appetite, the temperance of my life and the corpulence of my person. I am *no luncher at all,* and least of all in torrid weather, and I touch at that hour neither flesh of beast, of bird, nor even of any finny, bony fried or boiled thing. I eat, here, *one* small thing at 1.45—some cooked fruit, or a baked egg or a cool salad, or a hermit's portion of bread and cheese. PLEASE, dear pampering Goody, keep it, for *me*, down to that. I think I can make it, Monday, *1.45*, if you can kindly give me till then. And while I champ my crust we will discuss everything else. I leave every thrilling theme to that occasion. Only, with all your red-headed and stony-hearted friends, how have you a crust left? I'll keep a cold muffin over from the Osterley[1] breakfast. It affects me in advance as a cold Osterley altogether. Yours none the less ardently

Henry James

1. Osterley Park, at Osterley in Middlesex, residence of Lord and Lady Jersey, which HJ had visited often in the past, having been introduced there by James Russell Lowell during his time as U.S. minister to England.

To Hendrik C. Andersen
Ms Barrett

Lamb House, Rye
July 20 1906

My dearest old boy.

Charming to me your little note; very interesting your two little pictures; very touching your telling me that you affectionately think of me and reach out toward me. Yet formidable too, I confess, the vision of your pegging away there through the Roman summer at the rate of a pair of twins, or even triplets, a month, and with no other reward, for the time, than the sight of your so expensive family. My brain reels dearest Hendrik, for the thought of you, and the mad dance of your lusty images makes me fear they may whirl you back into *your* old "blind staggers." But you say nothing of that, and God forbid it. Only you say nothing either of any chance of your getting away into country coolness for a bit, and I would willingly sacrifice half a twin or the third of a triplet to think you might. It eased me off, when you were at Montefiascone etc., to feel that there you *couldn't* add to your family—splendid family as it is. But you must live as you can, and as you will, and I can only pray for you. Your fertility and power seem to me marvellous, and the two kodak figures of your note testify to that as wondrously as ever. They are very beautiful to me, as to everything but their faces—I am quite impertinently unhappy (as I told you, offensively, the last time) about your system of face. Also I sometimes find your sexes (putting *the* indispensable sign apart!) not quite intensely enough differentiated—I mean through the ladies resembling a shade too much the gentlemen (perhaps, as in the case of this last *ballerina*, through your not allowing her a quite sufficient luxury—to my taste—of hip, or to speak plainly, Bottom. She hasn't *much* more of that than her husband and I should like her to have a good deal more.) But no matter—they are both full of life and beauty and power—though I fear they will presently, in the mazes of the dance, tear their baby limb from limb. How many babies they do have—how they do keep at it, making you, to a tremendous tune, a grandfather! Admirable this back view of them in especial. But who, all this while, is *seeing* them, Enrico mio? and to what degree is the world the wiser? But you can't write me any answer to that—remember well how little pressure I *ever* put on you to write, spent as you eternally are with all this fierce creation. Therefore you *must* come and tell me about all such matters, about everything, here, and we must absolutely arrange it for the autumn! The only thing is that I *may* be very little alone in September, and I like to have you to myself. But there will probably be times, too! Write to me at the first real gleam of your seeing your way, and I'll be hanged if I shan't be able to help—! I rejoice your mother is well, and I send her my blessing. I trust that Arthur really prospers. I take you, my dear old Boy, to my heart, and beg you to feel my arms round you. Your devotissimo

H.J.

To Mrs. Humphry Ward
Ms Barrett

Lamb House, Rye
September 25*th* 1906

Dear Mrs. Ward.

I think it superlatively virtuous, yea even heroic, of you to have written me so liberal and beautiful a letter at a time when I so

With Mrs. Humphry Ward.

414

intensely understand how strain and stress and fatigue not only explain, but necessitate, every silence and *consecrate* the impossibility of every other effort. The letters of life, in general, become more and more its *poison*, moreover, surely—and are a matter against which, for myself, my heart is rapidly casing itself in impenetrable steel. One must at last go in, absolutely, for life-saving (the "life" being our own); and they are verily life-wrecking. Let me say at once that I will come to you with the greatest pleasure for Sunday November 19th—come, that is, without fail, on the afternoon of the 18th. In this I shall greatly rejoice.—Likewise I think it heroic of you to plough through the *Golden Bowl* which nothing could have induced *me* to do if I hadn't been its author. The work has merit, but it's too long and the subject is pumped *too* dry, even; that is, the pump is too big for it (it isn't itself so big), and tends thereby to *usurp* space in it. I shall never again do anything so long-winded. I find, myself, as I go on, that I can't read new fiction, and am lost in wonder at the strange law that condemns me to write it—and to assume, to that extent, a reading of the same *by* others—unlike myself! This, however, I very *scantly* assume—luckily for what really happens. But the disposition to read it—that is the *inability* of reading—has become in me almost a malady and a mania—though I find the reading of other things (including some old fiction) a greater boon than ever. However, we will talk of these things and of much else—above all of the wondrous idea of your going to America—heaven speed it!—as to which you must let me indoctrinate you up to the eyes! Fletcherise hard, first, at any rate; they will allow you no time for it there—so "put in" all (all the Fletcher) you can beforehand. Am I a convert? you ask. A *fanatic,* I reply. I began it upwards of two years ago (with instant and ardent conviction, from which I haven't for a moment departed); but I found the perpetual gregarious and loquacious feeding of the U.S. very detrimental to it, and though I clung to the theory there the practice went a good deal to pieces (as much as it ever *can* after the divine Light has once descended). I have got back to it completely, however, since my return—and again am clear that it's the greatest thing that ever was. Grapple it to your soul with hoops of steel. I rejoice to know that you've begun. It's none the less supremely difficult—*really* to do it (and I really do it): all life and conversation are so arrayed against it. I will confess to you that I am jealous of it before everything else—so jealous (e.g.) that I sigh in advance to think that even Stocks may have to be enjoyed at the cost of a minute's deflection. Here I spend fifty minutes (I spent 'em tonight) over a cold partridge, a potato (three potatoes) and a baked apple—all with much bread (indispensable with soft things); which means that I munch unsociably and in passionate silence, and that it is making me both unsociable and inhospitable (without at the same time making me in the least ashamed of so being. I brazenly glory in it.) The dear George Protheros[1] have been here (at *Rye*), for ten days and I haven't bidden them to a single meal. I am capable of sitting next to Mrs. Asquith[2] *mum* and with mere headshakes and finger-pointings; but you will see! I wish, and envy, you, indeed, a quiet inspired finish at the inspiring Versailles, and I am with all regards to Humphry, and much responsive interest in what you tell me of Dorothy and the others, yours, dear Mrs. Ward, very constantly,

Henry James

1. Fanny Prothero and her husband, George Walter Prothero (1848–1922), the Cambridge historian and editor of the *Quarterly Review*, lived in London at 24 Bedford Square. They also occupied Dial Cottage in Rye, where Fanny in particular became an intimate of Lamb House, kept an eye on HJ's servants, and increasingly provided him with the gossip of the town.
2. See letter to Margot Asquith, 9 April 1915.

To Alvin Langdon Coburn
Dictated Ts Barrett

[2 October 1906]

Memoranda to A. L. Coburn
For the Paris Subjects[1]
This is to make definite to you that the principal streets to look in for the portal of the old "aristocratic" *hôtel*[2] are the R. de l'Université, the R. de Lille, and the R. Bellechasse, the R. du Faubourg St. Germain, and even the short Rue Monsieur and (possibly) Rue Madame. There are even possibly three or four such *portes-cochère* on the quays of the Left Bank: the Quai Malaquais, for instance, the Quai Voltaire, the Quai d'Orsay, and etc., which are over there very much together. But look, for a grand specimen of the *type*, as I told you, at the British Embassy, in the R. du Faubourg St. Honoré. You will know it by its being on your left, in that street,

not long after you have passed the Rue Royale, and by its having the big escutcheon of lion and unicorn above it. Ask for *l'ambassade d'Angleterre:* anyone thereabouts, most of all your cabman, will show you. And there are two or three others, very nearly as majestic, in the same street: only these are too modern, and also too majestic. But I repeat for you that, once you get the Type into your head, you will easily recognise specimens by walking about in the *old* residential and "noble" parts of the city: by which I mean particularly Faubourg St. Germain. (Not but what there are there plenty of featureless houses too). Tell a cabman that you want to drive through every street in it, and then, having got that notion, go back and walk and stare at your ease. Add to the streets I named above, the *R. St. Dominique* and the *R. de Varenne,* which both cross the R. de Bellechasse, as does also the possible *R. de Grenelle.* So there you are for *that.*

Place de la Concorde, etc.

Look out *there* for some combination of objects that won't be hackneyed and commonplace and panoramic; some fountain or statue or balustrade or vista or suggestion (of some damnable sort or other) that will serve in connection with *The Ambassadors,* perhaps; just as some view, rightly arrived at, of *Notre Dame* would also serve—if sufficiently bedimmed and refined and glorified; especially as to its Side on the River and Back ditto. Above all don't forget I yearn for some outside aspect of the Théâtre-Français, for possible use in *The Tragic Muse;* but something of course of the same transfigured nature; some ingeniously-hit-upon angle of presentment of its rather majestic big square mass and classic colonnade. If by the same token, you could do something of the *Odéon Theatre* and *its* classic colonnade (the bookstalls are haunted by students of the Latin Quarter), there is a passage in *The Ambassadors,* where the hero lingers under the arcade, which might enable me to work it in.

Note that the Odéon is close to the *Luxembourg Gardens,* and there is another passage in the same book about his sitting *there* against the pedestal of some pleasant old garden-statue, to read over certain letters with which the story is concerned. Go into the sad Luxembourg Garden, straight across from the arcade of the Odéon, to look for my right garden-statue (composing with other interesting objects)—against which my chair was tilted back. Do bring me something right, in short, from the Luxembourg. These are the principal things I think of; though if you could rake in one or two big generalising glimpses or fragments (even of the Arc de Triomphe say) there are one or two other places—as second volume of *Princess Casamassima*, where suchlike might come in. My blessing on your inspiration and your weather!

Henry James

1. In *Alvin Langdon Coburn, Photographer: An Autobiography* (1966) Coburn wrote, "my first adventure in connection with the James frontispieces was a visit to Paris," for which he received "a detailed document." The memorandum here given is the document to which he refers. In all, he provided six pictures of Paris for the New York Edition.
2. HJ wanted an appropriate Parisian carriage-entrance to an old house for *The American*.

To Joseph Conrad
Ms Berg

Lamb House, Rye
November 1st, 1906

My dear Conrad.

I have taught you that I am lumbering and long, but I haven't, I think, yet taught you that I am base, and it is not on the occasion of your beautiful sea green volume[1] of the other day that I shall consent to begin. I read you as I listen to rare music—with deepest depths of surrender, and out of those depths I emerge slowly and reluctantly again, to acknowledge that I return to life. To taste you as I do taste you is *really* thus to wander far away and to decently thank you is a postal transaction (quite another affair), for which I have to come *back,* and accept with a long sad sigh the community of our afflicted existence. My silence is thus—after your beautiful *direct* speech to me too—but that I['ve] been away *with* you, intimately and delightfully—and my only objection to writing to you in gratitude is that I'm not reading you, but quite the contrary, when I do it. But I *have* you now, and the charm of this process of appropriation has been to me, with your adorable book for its subject, of the very greatest. And I am touched in the same degree by the grace of your inscription,[2] all so beautifully said and so generously felt. *J'en suis tout confus,* my dear Conrad, and can only

418

thank you and thank you again. But the book itself is a wonder to me really—for it's so bringing home the prodigy of your past experience: bringing it home to me more personally and directly, I mean, the immense treasure and the inexhaustible adventure. No one has *known*—for intellectual use—the things you know, and you have, as the artist of the whole matter, an authority that no one has approached. I find you in it all, *writing* wonderfully, whatever you may say of your difficult medium and your *plume rebelle*. You knock about in the wide waters of expression like the raciest and boldest of privateers,—you have made the whole place your own *en même temps que les droits les plus acquis et vous y avez les plus rares bonheurs*. Nothing you have done has more in it. The root of the matter of *saying*. You stir me in fine to amazement and you touch me to tears, and I thank the powers who so mysteriously let you loose with such sensibilities, into such an undiscovered country—*for* sensibility. That is all for tonight. I want to see you again. Is Winchelsea a closed book? Are the Ford Madoxes still away? (What a world *they* must then have been let loose into!) I am looking for some sign of them, and with it perhaps some more contemporary news of you. I hope the smaller boy is catching up, and your wife reasserting herself, and your "conditions" favourable? Ah, one's conditions! But we must *make* them, and you have on every showing, *de quoi!* I pat you, my dear Conrad, very affectionately and complacently on the back and am yours very constantly

Henry James

P.S. *Milles amitiés* to the fireside and the crib!

1. *The Mirror of the Sea* (1906).
2. Conrad had inscribed the book in French, writing the equivalent of a letter on the endpapers. See Joseph Conrad, *Lettres Françaises*, ed. G. Jean-Aubry (1929), 77.

To Jocelyn Persse
Ms Harvard

The Athenaeum
November 4*th* 1906

My dear Jocelyn.

I greet you, I miss you, I love you—but on the whole I don't envy you! Dank and dark and dreary must bonnie Scotland be in this rigour of the season, and calculated to make *me* (were I in your place) homesick for the very stink of the motor-busses in Piccadilly. However, I daresay your beautiful genius for life rises superior even to the discipline you are getting—and if I had your genius perhaps I could bear your weather. London is mild and rather golden—wondrously so for November, and I am enjoying it in the manner of a shy country cousin who gapes at the commonest objects. I have been to two plays with female friends—and supped after one of them at the Ladies'Athenaeum (Gerald du Maurier very pleasing in *Raffles*, but the play too infantile). I have been breakfasting here and am writing this in the Library, in the holy Sunday calm, and the yellow sunshine from Carlton Terrace pours peacefully in. I stay till Wednesday—then I tumble home. I count it a black loss that we haven't had an evening together. We must quite intensely make it up on the first next occasion. I rejoice heartily that you did what I longed you should over the C. Club matter. Bravo, Bravo! Of course give my love to Mrs. Gaskell, from me—you will find her most easy to live with! Take notes for me on the whole thing. Bear up generally and believe me always, my dear Jocelyn your

H.J.

To H. G. Wells
Ms Bodleian

Lamb House, Rye
November 8 1906

My dear Wells.

I came back last night from five days in London to find your so generously-given "America,"[1] and I have done nothing today but thrill and squirm with it and vibrate to it almost feverishly and weep over it almost profusely (this last, I mean, for intensity of mere emotion and interest). But the difficulty is that I am too dazzled by your extraordinary, your (to me) fascinating, intellectual energy for all the *judgment* of you that I should like to be able to command. The mere sight and sense and sound of your prodigious *reactions* before the spectacle of all actualities, combined with your power of making all those actualities—by a turn of the hand—consist of

420

amazing, fermenting, immeasurable passionate "questions" and social issues, comes near affecting me as the performance of a "strong
man" or a conjurer (juggler); seems to show you playing with your
subject and its parts as with the articles those *virtuosi* cause to
rebound and fly about. This amounts to saying that what primarily
flies in my face in *these* things of yours is *you* and your so
amazingly active and agile intellectual personality—I may even say
your sublime and heroic cheek—which I can't resist for the time,
can't *sufficiently* resist, to allow me to feel (as much as I want to)
that you tend always to simplify overmuch (that is as to large
particulars—though in effect I don't think you do here as to the
whole). But what am I talking about, when just this ability and
impulse to simplify—so vividly—is just what I all yearningly envy
you?—I who was accursedly born to touch nothing save to compli-
cate it. Take these fevered lines tonight then simply for a sign of my
admiring, panting, more or less gasping impression and absorption
of your book. When I think of the brevity of the process, of the
direct and immediate experience, from which it springs, the intensity and superiority of the projection of the realization, leave
me, I confess, quite wonderstricken, and I ask myself if such a
quantity of *important* observation—so *many* of such—have ever
before sprung into life under so concentrated a squeeze. I think not,
and your vividness and your force and your truth, and your caught
and seized images, aspects, characteristics and conditions are infinitely remarkable, for all your precipitation. I seemed to see, for
myself, while I was there, absolutely *no* profit in scanning or attempting to sound the future—the present being so hugely fluid
and the direction (beyond mere space and quantity and motion so
incalculable—as to the *whole*); and yet here you come and throw
yourself *all* on the future, and leave out almost altogether the
America of my old knowledge; leave out all sorts of things, and I am
gripped and captured and overwhelmingly beguiled. It comes of
your admirable communicative passion for the idea, and from your
wealth of ideas, and from your way of making intensely interesting
each one that you touch. I think you, frankly,—or think the whole
thing—too *loud,* as if the country shouted at you, hurrying past,
every hint it had to give and you yelled back your comment on it;
but also, frankly, I think the right and the only way to utter many
of the things you are delivered of *is* to yell them—it's a yelling

country, and the voice must pierce or dominate; and *my* semitones, in your splendid clashing of the cymbals (and *theirs*), will never be heard.[2] But there are still more things to say than I can so much as glance at, and I've only wanted to put to you, before I go to bed, that your book is, to my vision, extraordinarily full and rich and powerful and worthy, for all its fine fury of procedure—or perhaps just by reason of the same—of the vast uncomfortable subject. How glad you must be to have cast it from you! I don't know where this will find you—amid what blooming of citrons—but may it find you safely and assure you both that I am, as by communication, breathlessly yours

Henry James

1. *The Future in America,* published by Chapman and Hall in 1906.
2. HJ's *The American Scene* was to be published by the same publisher during the coming year.

To Alice Dew-Smith
Ms Unknown

Lamb House, Rye
November 12 th, 1906

Dear Mrs. Dew-Smith,

Very kind your note about the apples and about poor R.H.![1] Burgess Noakes[2] is to climb the hill in a day or two, basket on arm, and bring me back the rosy crop, which I am finding quite the staff of life.

As for the tidied-up book, I am greatly touched by your generous interest in the question of the tidying-up, and yet really think your view of that process erratic and—quite of course—my own view well inspired! But we are really both right, for to attempt to retouch the *substance* of the thing would be as foolish as it would be (in a *done* and impenetrable structure) impracticable. What I have tried for is a mere revision of surface and expression, as the thing is positively in many places quite *vilely* written! The essence of the matter is wholly unaltered—save for seeming in places, I think, a little better brought out. At any rate the deed is already perpetrated—and I do continue to wish perversely and sorely that you had waited—to re-peruse—for this prettier and cleaner form.

However, I ought only to be devoutly grateful—as in fact I am—for your power to re-peruse at all, and will come and thank you afresh as soon as you return to the fold; as to which I beg you to make an early signal to yours most truly,

Henry James

1. An allusion to *Roderick Hudson*, which had been extensively revised for the New York Edition and which HJ had described to his Rye neighbor Mrs. Dew-Smith. HJ's argument that his was "a revision of surface" did not alter the fact, as textual studies of his revisions have demonstrated, that substance was changed in the process.
2. HJ's servant.

To William James
Ms Harvard

The Reform Club
November 17*th* 1906

Dearest William.

I had a few days ago a very interesting and valuable letter from you—written even though you pleaded in fatigue and fag—and I scrawl this acknowledgement at the end of a rather darksome and drenching twenty-four hours spent in town, under a particular necessity whence I go back to Rye a couple of hours hence accompanied by T. S. Perry (for three or four days); he having come over a week ago from France and having put him up here at the Athenaeum and introduced him at the British Museum Lib[rary]. All, I think to his great delectation. We dined together last P.M. at the Athenaeum, and my principal impressions of him (for I saw him practically but once in America) bear on the extraordinarily small change in his mind, nature and above all expression, since our juvenile days—and on the premature antiquity of appearance which so belies his inward youth—as also, so happily for him, his still remarkable physical hardness and vigour.[1] But he is very genial and amusing—and told me last night that honorary members of the Athenaeum being made but for "distinction," the hall-porter on his coming-in, was always asking him for what he was distinguished: to which he had had to only reply—"For my appetite." He has seen a good deal of Bill at Giverny[2] etc. and speaks of him with great kindness and affection. Your letter breathed as to yourself a certain

423

exhaustion—which on the part of so great and heroic a lecture-maker I well understand; but it gave me the news of your having retreated from the Paris undertaking; which has quenched in me rather a haunting anxiety. I didn't, I couldn't believe in that essentially bristling and bustling—that in every way formidable and arduous, business for you—and I really hoped that time would bring a revision of your judgment. It wouldn't have led to *my*—as far as Paris is concerned—seeing much of you, for Paris has become to me, with time, a place of terror, almost—in fact almost every other place than L[amb] H[ouse] has! But since you've cast the terror of Paris *from* you, you must take up instead with the peace of L.H. and come over with Alice and put in a part of the time that was to have been there.—

November 18*th*

I broke off this, for interruption, yesterday, and an hour or two later came back here (to Lamb House) accompanied by T.S.P., who sits down by the drawingroom fire amply content with books while, as it's drearily and dismally wet, I drive this retarded and (so far as this paper is concerned) embarrassed, pen. T.S.P. is very genial and pleasant and talkative (immensely "improved")—a very easy inmate to entertain. But we have been living here for three weeks in a deluge—paying for our long beautiful rainless summer that lasted from the end of May to the end of October. Yesterday after your letter comes one from Bill enclosing me one from his mother to him and thereby giving me later news of you (November 5th), of your sleeping better and of your Lowell Lectures about to begin. May a huge *retentissement* attend these and promote the same for the sale of the Book afterwards. But invent a vulgar (comparatively) and mercenary name for it, and don't, oh don't, spell it heartbreakingly.[3] You speak of Harry as "stern" and of Aleck as tall and taciturn and of Alice as also comparatively bereft of speech, and the picture somehow as making for righteousness; that is for repose and for the social minor key—that is for the benefit of your nerves, the tranquillity and unity of your house and the possession of your powers and hours. Peggy has written me an interesting, touching perhaps just slightly agitated and overwrought letter; not, however, breathing depression—only suggesting that she may become sated with that medium before she has done all her time there. But even then she will, clearly, have got a good deal out of it—she gets a good deal—so much—out of everything she comes in contact with. I can give her (I immediately wrote to her) very little interesting history from this dull (thank God!) house just now—where I hope to prolong the dullness till the end of January. Some time in February I shall go over to Paris, without fail to see Bill. In the note from him accompanying your letter, dearest Alice, last night he says he finds in his work at Julian's "more interest and more fun than ever." Also that he is staying on at his little hotel for the present, and that Loulie Hooper has left for Switzerland (she was also staying there). So he won't marry *her*,—at any rate just yet.[4] But you will know of these things more than I. I yearn meanwhile over Aleck, please tell him, with my love, and over the noble sacrifice Ryley (though understanding the sacrifice) and even over the cool young Sidney Lovett his friend, so vividly remembered for his high urbanity. I seem to gather (in another connection) that Mrs. Piper[5] comes out—has perhaps actually come out to England and wish I could learn, dear Alice,—what people or circle—who she comes *to* and where she is to be, for ever since that message you sent me in the spring I've had such a desire for the possibility of something further—even to the degree of an obsession? Will the Cambridge people have hold of her? Mrs. Verrall, Mrs. Myers etc.? Can you in any way help me to her—wholly—out of all the psychical connection as I am here—save perhaps by those two women. But I judge Mrs. Myers *néfaste*. This is all for now. Have you read H. G. Wells's American ("Future") book? I find it full of interest, though shouted as through a gramophone by a man who was there—with that large order (the Future) but five weeks about; full of ideas and refreshing freedoms, ironies, and of a colossal but delectable "cheek"—of the extraordinary rude force and passion that make him the only one of the younger "literary" generation here except Lowes Dickenson and to some extent the too trickly and journalistic Chesterton (who has reduced to a science the putting of everything *à rebours*) presenting any interest whatever. But I must go down and look after my guest—and another who comes to dinner. My hot water pipes (excellently installed, now that all the dire upheaval is over) prove the most blessed success. They will really make me here a most blessed little winter climate and minister thereby to my whole prosperity, save me in fires, add to the value of the property. Your all-loving

Henry

P.S. You can stay here now, William, perfectly at any season.

1. HJ had been out of touch with T. S. Perry, friend of his youth, since the 1880s. See *Letters* III, 203–205.

2. The young Billy James was studying art at the Académie Julian in Paris. Perry had met Claude Monet at Giverny some years earlier.

3. WJ's Lowell Institute lectures were published with the title *Pragmatism, A New Name for Some Old Ways of Thinking* (1907).

4. HJ's joke about his nephew's marrying refers to Henry Adams's niece, Louise (Loulie) Chapin Hooper, later Mrs. Ward Thoron, who was a bit older than Billy.

5. Mrs. William J. Piper, the well-known medium, used by WJ in his explorations of spiritualism. See letter to Harvey, 11 March 1906.

To Alvin Langdon Coburn
Dictated Ts Barrett

Lamb House, Rye
6*th* December, 1906

Dear Alvin Langdon!

I have just written to Miss Constance Fletcher,[1] in Venice where she lives, at periods (with her infirm old mother and her mother's second husband, Eugene Benson, also I fear invalidical and a little played-out, but a painter of refined and interesting little landscapes of the Venetian country), in the *Palazzo Capello, Rio Marin'*; which is the old house I had more or less in mind for that of the Aspern Papers. I have told her exactly what I want you to do, outside and in, and as she is a very kind and very artistic person, you can trust yourself to her completely for guidance. She will expect you, and will, I am sure, respond to my request on your behalf in a cordial and sympathetic spirit. Your best way to get to the Rio Marin' will be to obtain guidance, for a few coppers, from some alert Venetian street-boy (or of course you can go, romantically, in a gondola). But the extremely tortuous and complicated walk—taking Piazza San Marco as a starting point—will show you so much, so many bits and odds and ends, such a revel of Venetian picturesqueness, that I advise your doing it on foot as much as possible. You go almost as if you were going to the Station to come out at the end of the bridge opposite to the same. Now that I think of it indeed your very best way, for shortness, will be to go by the Vaporetto, or little steamboat, which plies every few minutes on the Grand Canal, straight to the Stazione, and there, crossing the big contiguous iron bridge, walk to Rio Marin' in three or four minutes. It is the old faded pink-faced, battered-looking and quite homely and plain (as things

426

go in Venice) old Palazzino on the right of the small Canal, a little way along, as you enter it by the end of the Canal towards the Station. It has a garden behind it, and I think, though I am not sure, some bit of a garden-wall beside it; it doesn't moreover bathe its steps, if I remember right, directly in the Canal, but has a small paved Riva or footway in front of it, and *then* water-steps down from this little quay. As to that, however, the time since I have seen it may muddle me; but I am almost sure. At any rate anyone about will identify for you Ca' Capello, which is familiar for Casa C; *casa,* for your ingenuous young mind, meaning House and being used, save for the greatest palaces, as much as palazzo. You must judge for yourself, face to face with the object, how much, on the spot, it seems to lend itself to a picture. I think it *must,* more or less, or sufficiently; with or without such adjuncts of the rest of the scene (from the bank opposite, from the bank near, or from where-ever you can damnably manage it) as may seem to contribute or complete—to be needed, in short, for the interesting effect. I advise you to present your note first—unless you are so much in the humor the moment you arrive in front of the place as to want then and there to strike off something at a heat. My friends will help you by any suggestion or indication whatever, and will be very intelligent about it; and will let you see if something be not feasible from the Garden behind; which also figures a bit in the story. What figures most is the big old Sala, the large central hall of the principal floor of the house, to which they will introduce you, and from which from the large, rather bare Venetian perspective of which, and pref-erably looking toward the garden-end, I very much hope some re-sult. In one way or another, in fine, it seems to me it ought to give something. If it doesn't, even with the help of more of the little canal-view etc., yield satisfaction, wander about until you find something that looks sufficiently like it, some old second-rate pal-ace on a by-canal, with a Riva in front, and if any such takes you at all, do it at a venture, as a possible alternative. But get the Sala at Ca' Capello, without fail, if *it* proves at all manageable or effective.

For the other picture, that of *The Wings,* I had vaguely in mind the Palazzo Barbaro, which you can see very well from the first, the upper, of the iron bridges, the one nearest the mouth of the Grand Canal, and which crosses from Campo San Stefano to the great Museum of the Academy. The palace is the very old Gothic one, on your right, just before you come to the iron bridge, after leaving (on the vaporetto) the steamboat-station of the Piazza. Only one palace, the Franchetti, a great big sort of yellow-faced restored one, with vast Gothic windows and balcony, intervenes between it and the said iron bridge. The Barbaro has its water-steps beside it, as it were; that is a little gallery running beside a small stretch of side-canal. But in addition it also has fine water-steps (I remember!) to the front door of its lower apartment. (The side-steps I speak of belong to the apartment with the beautiful range of old *upper* Gothic windows, those attached to the part of the palace concerned in my story.) But I don't propose you should attempt here anything but the outside; and you must judge best if you can rake the object most effectively from the bridge itself, from the little campo in front of the Academy, from some other like spot further—that is further toward the Salute, or from a gondola (if your gondolier can keep it steady enough) out on the bosom of the Canal. If none of these positions yield you something you feel to be effective, try some other palace, or simply try some other right range of palaces, in some other reach or stretch of the Canal; ask Miss Fletcher to please show you, to this end, what I have written to her about that. And do any other odd and interesting bit you can, that may serve for a sort of symbolised and generalised Venice in case everything else fails; preferring the noble and fine aspect, however, to the merely shabby and familiar (as in the case of those views you already have)—yet especially *not* choosing the pompous and obvious things that one everywhere sees photos of. I hope this will be, with my very full letter to Miss Fletcher, enough to provide for all your questions. I will write the note to Miss F. to-night and send it on to you tomorrow. Let me know when, having seen Pinker again, you start. Indeed if you will give me two or three days notice I will send you the note to Miss F. *then*, in preference; as my letter, posted to her today, may bring a reply *before* you start—in which case I might have to write a fourth communication!

Yours,
Henry James

P.S. It will much help if you will take two or three subjects to *show* to Miss Fletcher and Benson: the *Porte-Cochère* ("American")—the St. John's Wood Villa—the antique-shop, Portland Place etc.—or my Hall (for an interior). H.J.

1. HJ had known Constance Fletcher (1858–1938), who wrote under the name of George Fleming, for many years. See *Letters* III, 461. Eugene Benson, the American painter, had been among HJ's acquaintances in the American artist colony in Rome during his stay there in 1873. See *Letters* I, 347.

To Alvin Langdon Coburn
Dictated Ts Barrett

Lamb House, Rye
7 December 1906

Dear A.L!

I wrote you yesterday, but here is another go, in answer to your note this morning received. I peruse your List, but we are not right yet about all the Subjects, and it takes a good deal of worrying out, as I find face to face with all the things I have to combine and reconcile and fit in; and I must beg you to be patient. We are *almost* right, but this having to settle so much ahead, by reason of your departure, forces my hand a good deal, and I must take a little more time. I have made a mistake or two, I find, by being too precipitate; and among other things, by tumbling into the detail of the matter too breathlessly in town, on Wednesday etc., having in particular omitted a couple of important things. I strangely and stupidly forgot, for instance, one whole Book, *The Awkward Age*, which is, by good luck, to be also (like the two others) in One Volume; and for which some English subject that I don't at all yet see must somehow be managed. A London morsel is not impossible for it, but it will take more thinking of, and I will let you hear, on this score, further, and try to do something about it with you on one of the last days of the year. There will be then another thing that I haven't mentioned, for "In the Cage": a London corner, if possible, with a grocer's shop containing a postal-telegraph office. This will be very good, and rather amusing to hunt for, if the right one be findable. It will all depend upon that, but a good deal of hunting may do it—all the more that I'm not sure the thing need absolutely be a corner. Look for grocer's shops with post-offices inside. Fortunately the few mistakes and confusions I have made don't bear on any of the things already done, except the Roman bit and the Place de la Concorde bit that we have spoken of. But I don't think I shall want any Studio, and probably shall not want Washington Square. (This

429

I spoke of to you as merely possible.) On the other hand I *shall* want, for a little tale called "Europe" an American view that we didn't speak of, that ought to be at Cambridge, Mass., if at all remotely findable—but which, alas, will be very hard to find. I must leave it open and contingent.

There *are* meanwhile to be Twenty-Three Volumes.

Six Novels in Two.

Three Novels in One.

Four Volumes of "Shorter Novels."

Four Volumes of Short Stories.

Twelve and Three, you see, make Fifteen, and Four make Nineteen and Four make Twenty-Three.

We have either made or definitely fixed on Plates for all the novels except *The Awkward Age* just mentioned; and this last we will do before you leave. But I will explain about the others when I next see you: suffice it for the present that nothing already *done* need be sacrificed. I shall *probably* want only one New York view, and one other American view in addition to the "Four Meetings." The great thing is that it all makes only twenty-two subjects required in addition to the *Portrait*, and these we can certainly make up. It really comes over me this morning, in fact, that it *may* not be necessary—in spite of my letter of yesterday—for you to go to Venice. It will depend on Claude Phillips's[1] giving leave for Room 21 of Wallace Collection. If he does so I can put "Aspern Papers" in the same volume with *Spoils of Poynton*, and make *Spoils* plate serve.[2] In this case I wouldn't ask you to go all that midwinter way simply for *one other* picture. Take no step, therefore, till I hear about Room 21; on which subject I have already written. Even this, however, leaves me with four subjects yet to find: one for *The Awkward Age*, one for the second volume of Short Stories (for the Tomb of "Beast in the Jungle" won't at all do—I *think!*) Another is wanting for Volume Third of Short Stories—this one very difficult. The "Four Meetings" picture provides for Fourth Volume of this series; and the Shorter Novels will be practically, now, settled. But I absolutely can't straighten this out completely till I see you again. I will leave nothing open, when it's time for you to go, but the things you may do in America.

Yours ever,
Henry James

1. Claude Phillips (1846–1924), keeper of the Wallace Collection.
2. This plan was changed, and each had its own frontispiece.

To Alvin Langdon Coburn
Dictated Ts Barrett

Lamb House, Rye
Sunday 9 December 1906

Dear Alvin Langdon.

Here is the Permit for the Wallace Collection—perhaps you could go *tomorrow*. Please note the day and *hours: Mondays* 9–12. And Mr. Phillips, the Keeper, has asked me to tell you to ask the Attendant if he will *see* you, as he would like to do, if he is on the premises. (He probably doesn't get there till after 10.) And take the beautiful Subject *obliquely*, won't you?—and with as much of the damask on wall as possible. And, further, please give the attendant, as a tip, 2/6 for me: (I will send you a postal order for same in the morning—I can't buy one today Sunday). I also enclose my own card.

And now, in spite of this, I think, on further and intenser reflection, that you HAD better go to Venice and proceed as we have arranged. I *want* the Casa Capello, and will arrange (in order, purposely to *get* it) to change my order of combinations somehow—putting "In the Cage" with "The Spoils" and the "Aspern Papers" with something else where its picture will still be so valuable. The more *foreign* plates we have the better. Still I MAY want the London grocery shop too, and will speak of it to you later, as well as of *The Awkward Age:* for which an easy idea comes to me.[1] Therefore start for Venice on Thursday if you are still minded—and do both subjects. I will send you letter *tomorrow*. (Such an explicit and full letter has gone to my friends that three words will serve for *your* note). If you can't do Room 21 tomorrow, wait till you come back—though the Christmas holidays are a bad time generally. May every luck and success attend you!

Yours ever
Henry James

P.S. The "January 31st 1906" [on the permit] must be a slip of the pen for 1907—as the date itself, of the Permit, proves.

1. The "easy idea" was to have Coburn photograph Lamb House.

To Paul Bourget
Ms Private

Lamb House, Rye
ce 19 décembre 1906

Mon cher ami.

Si je suis affreusement en retard avec vous, c'est la honte même et l'abaissement du remords qui me tient depuis si longtemps privé de paroles. Votre beau livre de critique,[1] au gentil épigraphe à la feuille volante, m'a fortement remué, il y a tant de semaines, sans m'aider pourtant à deserrer les dents; et peut-être souffrirais-je encore mon triste penchant au mutisme en raison directe, et sans le poids accablant du nombre de choses que j'ai à dire, sans le fait de vous avoir lu au *Temps*, il y a peu de jours, sur ce pauvre et sombre Brunetière,[2] et d'en avoir été irrésistiblement touché. Cela m'était arrivé aussi cet été à propos de votre admirable discours à l'occasion de la statue de Dumas *fils*, qui m'a enthousiasmé—et dont je n'ai pas profité pour vous le dire sur le champ, comme tout m'y poussait sauf la triste rouillure de ma syntaxe française qui est responsable de tous mes manquements. Il faut tant de syntaxe pour causer avec un Gallo-Latin doublé d'un Académicien! Je ne vous lis jamais cependant, sans désirer infiniment que nous puissions recauser—quand même ce ne serait que de l'étrange Brunetière, qui trouvait moyen d'être—pour moi—en même temps rébarbatif et sympathique. Vous en avez parlé avec un sentiment bien juste et une parfaite netteté. Mais que de choses, que de gens, que d'idées et d'objets il haïssait—quelle place dans l'appréciation intellectuelle, il faisait à la haine et au parti-pris! Il était à mon sens, pourri de parti-pris, et avec cela intelligent et sincère! Drôle d'esprit, en somme, mais sans pauvreté et qui a dû souffrir de lui, n'est-ce pas? plus que de toute autre chose. Je vous félicite encore beaucoup de la belle qualité des articles du volume bleu—mais ce n'est pour entrer dans aucun détail que je vous écris maintenant—c'est surtout pour ne pas avoir la rougeur au front quand je vous verrai comme je l'espère à Paris au mois de Février. Je compte sérieusement y passer quatre ou cinq semaines: j'y ai mon neveu (second fils de mon frère W.) qui y est établi pour l'étude de la peinture (chez Julian seulement encore), et auquel j'ai promis de lui rendre la visite, très bienfaisante, qu'il me fit ici cet été. Mrs. Wharton aussi (obéissant

432

aux lois de la pendule et du cheque-book—car je ne mets pas cela au nom de Teddy) s'installe, le mois prochain, 18 Rue de Varenne, comme vous devez du reste bien le savoir et comme elle vient de m'en faire la douce confidence. J'ai été à Londres me mettre aux pieds (si extraordinairement actifs) de la grande Isabelle [Gardner]—et je me rends demain pour assister aux tristes obsèques de mon très vieil ami, ce cher et excellent H. Aïdé,[3] qui vient de mourir (très subitement!) à l'âge de 80 ans! Si je vous trouve à Paris j'aurai beaucoup de chose à vous dire et à vous demander—que cet avertissement ne vous décide donc pas à l'exil! Je vous envoi à tous deux all the good wishes of the season, et me recommande de tout dévouement à Madame Paul. Croyez-bien, mon cher ami, à mon affectueux souvenir,

Henry James

1. *Études et portraits,* which contained various papers written between 1889 and 1906.
2. Ferdinand Brunetière (1849–1906), literary historian and critic, editor of the *Revue des Deux Mondes* from 1893.
3. See letter to Anne Thackeray Ritchie, 21 December 1906.

To Anne Thackeray Ritchie
Ms Harvard

The Reform Club
December 21*st* 1906

Dearest Anne Ritchie!

I am here—in town—till tomorrow—because I came up for dear old Hamilton's Memorial Service (which I thought quite beautiful and touching), and here your so characteristically charming and tender note reaches me. I looked for you helplessly, yesterday, in that concourse of many and highly heterogeneous faces, but the confusion was great, at the issue, and I missed many more old friends than I found, or at least could speak to. I think I was struck, though, with their being (considering the immensity of H. Aïdé's social circle) rather less of an affluence than I had expected; till, at least, I remembered how he had outlived, dear man, so much and so many, and that many who weren't there weren't there because, simply, they were dead. And it was of these, many, I was more thinking, as I sat there—and it made Aïdé's charming kindly friendship go back very, very far even for myself—as well as made me feel how he had been the soul of amiability and pleasantness and gentleness, and even the soul of (what shall one call it?) *mondanité*, in a way to make mundanity the most benignant and blessed of attributes. I am so glad we were together there (at Ascot) last summer, in that genial and graceful way; when under the slightly hard strain of a certain lady (not You!) he had such a mellowness of patience and good manners. But I shall miss him, oddly (*we* shall miss him) beyond even the use, as it were, that we had for him; he was such a pleasant part of one's past going on into one's present and vouching still for the reality of vanished things. *Requiescat!*—And he *will* rest, if ever a man may have needed to, from "Society"!—I like scarcely less the reminder you make me of that delightful verandah-day at Howard S[turgis]'s—to whom I came up three weeks ago and spent another Sunday (in view of his starting to take poor sweet tattered Mildred Seymour abroad). They have gone, poor Howard himself rather tattered, and tending to fall to pieces (rather more than one wants to see) as a simple affect of having never consented, all his life, to feel that he needn't be the sentimental factotum and consolatory convenience and man-of-all-work of quite such a numerous circle. His reward may be in some better and kinder world, but I am afraid he will go on here knowing nothing but his penalties, till they at last overwhelm him.

And how of the melancholy matters it seems I can only write you this dusky Christmastide! I haven't really borne to *think* of the bereavement of those brave and handsome young Stephen things (and Thoby's unnatural destruction itself)[1]—and have taken refuge in throwing myself hard on the comparative cheer of Vanessa's engagement[2]—quite as if it were an escape, a happy thought, I myself had invented. So I cling to it and make grossly much of it, and your sympathetic words contribute. Maitland's book[3] is really, I think, a thing of Beauty—ever so handsomely and feelingly done, and giving Leslie all the light he needed to be seen in to be loved as one *ended* by loving him. One loves M. himself and I shall as soon as possible [write] to tell him so. With so much affection in the air let me however divert the expression of some of it to you and yours, my dear old friend. May you be steeped, these days, in all the peace and good will—or even some of it will serve—that you so endlessly merit! Yours ever so constantly

Henry James

1. Thoby Stephen had recently died of typhoid fever after a trip to Greece.
2. To the future art critic Clive Bell.
3. F. W. Maitland's *Life and Letters of Leslie Stephen*, recently published.

To Mrs. W. K. Clifford
Ts Lubbock

Lamb House, Rye
February 17*th* 1907

Dearest Lucy C!

How glad I am to be talking with you this quiet Sunday morning in this (comparatively) quiet place—for no place now but tends every day to lose that virtue, and the curse (of invasion and alteration and complication) is steadily creeping on even here. And I say "talking" though I don't know quite how or where my voice will reach you, as you give me no *standing* address—and apparently are just leaving the curst Viareggio—and I can't send my letter to Ethel[1] to be forwarded, as I quite forget her number! The only thing I can do will be to throw myself upon the conscience of Chilworth Street with a petition outside. Your brave and bountiful letter from the dreary winter Viareggio—which *I* would earnestly have warned you against—came to me last night, making my heart rather blue for all your winds and your wounds and your wanderings in search of the southern balm that has apparently so consistently eluded you everywhere. But keep up your great hearts—you have at least not been in frozen England (perfectly *ravaged* now with Influenza-pestilence which stalketh by noon-day); and the relenting season *must* be bringing you now from day to day something of the real blest breath of Italy. Even here indeed (yesterday—for today it blusters and rattles rather more again) there begin to be delicious far-off hints and promises of better things, with the lengthening lingering light and the kinder colour of the air. I have just come back from a fortnight in town (which I took to escape, sixteen days ago, from really dread East wind here). I am not "settling" in London this year in my usual winter-end way, because I nurse the dream of going for a while to Paris on March 1st (I have in fact promised, absolutely, to spend ten or twelve days of the time with Mrs. Wharton, who has a temporary house there). Meanwhile I am putting in what diligence I can in this still life-saving retreat—diligence against the banded havoc of one's death-dealing *leisurely* friends. I saw some of *yours* in London—but meagrely, for I *can't* now, any more, rattle my old bones (more and more easily wearied and dislocated) from house to house and dinner to dinner and tea to tea etc. However, I lunched very pleasantly with the Fred Pollocks in their very pretty but noisy new house—the papa and mamma and Jack and Alice (without S.W.)[2] and they were all charming (even Fred quite graceful and sinuous and serpentine and overflowing); and we talked with tremendous tenderness of you and Turkey—quite held each other's hands and kissed and wept and "went on" round about you. There popped in Elizabeth Robins—but on such a footing of universal engagement and entanglement and with not a minute to be able to arrange for, not a single solitary *one*, for a whole fortnight, that after subsequent vain reachings out and telephonings and strugglings and yearnings, I had to come away with no other glimpse of her but that poor frustrated instant (she arriving after I had risen to go). The fury of social submersion in which she elects to live and "work" staggers my intelligence—the whole thing rendered extraordinarily acute now, moreover, by first, her up-to-the-eyes immersion in the sea of the Suffragettes, and second, her immense complications over her impending play—I suppose you know she *has* a "Gertrude Kingston" play (*but keep it deadlily to yourself!*)—all a crisis of ructions and convulsions and complications of many sorts; Mrs. Pat. C[ampbell] being, I believe, piled somehow on top of Gertrude K., and the two pulling different ways and distractedly tugging and kicking.[3] And in the midst of it all the subject and idea of the thing (Play) fine and strong and of a high "actuality"—the suffragette movement hot from the oven. However, I *know* nothing definite—only quite feel the thing *will* be produced and will probably profit much by its subject and connection. Only I ask myself how any really careful or finished piece can come out of such conditions—such a squash of perpetual people and scramble and fever of perpetual appointments. Only repeat me, quote me, betray me not—and burn my letter with fire or candle (if you have *either!* Otherwise wade out into the sea with it and soak the ink out of it). I think, I fear, that I saw no one else in particular to tell you of—I circulated as little as I could, and it was only fifteen—or rather thirteen—days. Jack Pollock[4] walked away across the Park with me—most charming and sympathetic youth I find him (and not black-hearted as the H[olman] H[unt]s do), but he is having for his rudimentary intellectual credit to pass, apparently, certain Law examinations (in order not to have been, publicly, too much of a featherhead even if he doesn't—as he never, never *will*—practise); and that now woefully obliges him to grind—to the detriment of everything else. Alice Waterlow I thought particularly pretty and charming. She is really, with adversity (I'm told Sydney is really much reduced as to resources—through folly of his father—but burn, burn!) proving a very nice courageous creature. And *apropos* of courage, above all, oh yes, I went to see Vanessa Stephen on the eve of her marriage (at the Registrar's) to the quite dreadful-looking little stoop-shouldered, long-haired, third-rate Clive Bell[5]—described as an "intimate friend" of poor, dear, clear, tall, shy, superior Thoby—even as a little sore-eyed poodle might be an intimate friend of a big mild mastiff. However, I suppose she knows what she is about, and seemed very happy and eager and almost boisterously in love (in that house of all the Deaths, ah me!)[6] and I took her an old silver box ("for hairpins"), and she spoke of having got a "beautiful Florentine teaset" from you. She was evidently happy in the latter, but I winced and ground my teeth when I heard of it. She and Clive are to keep the Bloomsbury house, and Virginia and Adrian to forage for some flat somewhere—Virginia having, by the way, grown quite elegantly and charmingly and almost "smartly" handsome. I liked being with them, but it was all strange and terrible (with the hungry *futurity* of youth); and all I could mainly see was the *ghosts*, even Thoby and Stella, let alone dear old Leslie and beautiful, pale, tragic Julia—on all of whom these young backs were, and quite naturally, so gaily turned. I heard afterwards that the Vanessas, so to speak—for she is the whole housefront—almost missed their marriage altogether (for the time) by scrambling into the Registrar's after their hour and just as he was about to close (I *think* it was a Saturday afternoon). What a nuptial "solemnity!" But how I am scribbling on! I've got alas an accumulation of a hundred unwritten letters to write! I'm putting in these days in as mouselike a fashion as possible here—trying to wind up jobs and tuck in loose ends before crossing the channel for the first time in more absurdly numerous years than I venture to count. Even now I'd give anything to stop here quietly and mind my business—I have so much to mind—rather than gad wastefully about. However, I am absolutely committed and, once the spiritless spell broken, I shall be glad and pick up some pleasure. I am only *certain* of four or five weeks in Paris, but shall try to get down to Italy for May (even if I have to come back here for an interval and start afresh). Therefore we may meet—but where, oh where? We shall have time to discuss that, only how long, and till when, do you remain away? I yearningly, burningly hope that in spite of winds and weathers and throats and drains and boring Butcheresses (*I've* just got to go and welcome the Protheros—of whom I'm fond—who are, since yesterday, arrived for convalescence from *ten* attacks of "Flu" at Mrs. Dew-Smith's—a specimen of the rush of Rye!) you've really found the game worth the candle—and don't repent, either of you, of your wasted treasure and beauty. How sweetly you speak of the fat red American book![7] I thank you all effusively for your generous sympathy! Yes, though I never see any "notices" (of any book of mine) that I can invidiously escape I believe this one *has* had, or is having, what the Publishers call a "remarkable" reception—receiving a very honourable sort of attention. But it *can't* have a sale other than the most modest—it's not the kind of thing that can. If it could the Public would be a very different sort of big Booby than it *is*—and that miracle will never happen. If you will only give me a certain and safe address I will *send* you the corpulent volume—which I yearn to do on the chance of its giving you the illusion of a few hours of the fond author's company. But my luncheon has been long waiting—it consists, I believe, of two baked eggs which will have got coagulated and hard. But for your sweet sakes who cares? I hope you will now come in for really rewarding ethereal mildness; I yearn over you constantly both—in fact I embrace you, both, violently and am ever your affectionate old grand (and great-grand) father

Henry James

1. See letter to Mrs. Clifford, 13 December 1901.
2. Sydney Waterlow. See letter to Waterlow, 9 January 1911.
3. Elizabeth Robins, who had played in HJ's *The American* in 1891, had since become a suffragette and a novelist and was involved in production of a play (much of which she wrote) called *Votes for Women*. Apparently she had some assistance in its staging from the actress-manager Gertrude Kingston and the popular actress Mrs. Patrick Campbell (Beatrice Stella Campbell, 1867–1940).
4. John (Jack) Pollock, son of HJ's old friend Sir Frederick Pollock, prepared for the bar, but his primary interest was the stage. He wrote plays and married an actress.
5. HJ had from the first reacted negatively to Clive Bell, and he formed an intense dislike of him.
6. HJ here sketches the history of the pre-Bloomsbury Stephens: the recent deaths

of Thoby and Leslie, the earlier deaths of Julia Duckworth Stephen and her daughter Stella. See letters to Leslie Stephen, 6 May 1895, and to Anne Thackeray Ritchie, 21 December 1906.

7. *The American Scene.*

To Mrs. W. D. Howells
Ms Harvard

Lamb House, Rye
February 24*th*, 1907

Dear Mrs. Howells,

It is delightful to hear from you in such humane form—even though you write to me out of the void of space, as I seem to feel—desperately baffled of attaching to you (little though you may be of an Airy Nothing) a local habitation; and even though too you speak to me of dear W.D.H. so inveterately as "Mr. Howells" to *me* who "go back" to exactly forty years ago (before your children were born), and who breakfasted with you in Sacramento Street, in pre-historic days, in company with the ichthyosaurus Bayard Taylor.[1] When you talk of Mr. Howells I feel moved to call *you*, in passionate protest, Sacramentina. And then my mid-Victorian teas in Berkeley Street—of which I most fondly remember stewed prunes and Venetian beads and *Atlantic* proofs as the central elements; I never thought of *them* as stepping-stones to so very much higher things than our sweet familiarities then prevailing. However, you breathe upon me, all benignantly, the rich concert of New York, where my imagination pursues you from elevator to elevator and indeed seems to make out that you are being now more or less permanently elevated. You tell me of your having "ordered" an apartment that looks out on the Park (the way you people *create* your conditions, out of the primal void, as with deific attributes!) and my imagination, as aforesaid, is moving you into it, for sweet settlement's own very sake, and taking out all those books, and pressing you down in easy chairs with them, faster than the mightiest moving-firm can bang you in, or than Mildred[2] can meantime whirl in Caribbean dances. Tell me, when you *are* in, and send me the key in your letter, that I may keep it in my pocket. It's humiliating to me here to feel my continuity so spiritless and perpetual. I have even been as yet, this winter, very little in London. I have had

439

hot-water pipes and radiators put into my house, and I stick fast here where I may pat them and hang about them as if they were fruits of the tropics. However, I go early next month to Paris for a few weeks and farther southward, a little, if possible. I am afraid I scarce see, often, any of the country neighbours you—so floridly—impute to me; only H. G. Wells once in a long time, and mainly in London to which he much resorts. He is a great, but a rude talent, and I fear the rudeness isn't as convertible into the something or other that one prefers as one originally hoped. However, he has force and wit—precious possibilities. "Fluffy" Hodgson Burnett[3] I never see—did you ever see in our yearning youth "Mrs. E. D. E. N. Southworth"?[4] Fluffy is the Southworth of our age. And people hereabouts who live at 10×15 miles distance from each other *across country*, and not on the railway, never meet unless they have motors. On the other hand when they have motors (that is the sentiment here) nobody wants to meet them. I'm all but cut for my radiators—and it takes all my amiability to counteract them. I send my best love to dear Mr. Howells—I do so yearn for a fierce N.Y. talk with him. I seem to guess he has been worried over the Long-fellow occasion[5]—which I am glad I couldn't be reached by. I am writing to John [Howells], with my blessing—it will explain itself—rejoicingly. Write me, I beseech you, on paper stamped with the name and address of the new-fangled Flat—*then* I shall enter in. If you can order the flat you *must* order the paper. Yours, dear Mrs. Howells, all and always.

Henry James

1. Bayard Taylor (1825–1878), American poet and novelist, best known for his translation of Goethe's *Faust*.

2. Howells' daughter.

3. Frances Eliza Hodgson Burnett (1849–1924), who wrote *Little Lord Fauntleroy* and other sentimental romances.

4. Emma Dorothy Eliza Nevitte Southworth (1819–1899), writer of popular American novels, some sixty in number, bearing titles such as *The Curse of Clifton* (1852) and *The Hidden Hand* (1859).

5. The Longfellow centenary.

To Jessie Allen
Ms Harvard

Hotel Guichard
Pau, B[asses] P[yrénées]
March 28 1907

Dear gallant Goody.

It's horrible the way I haven't written you since I had that heart-rending letter from you after you had emerged with bare life from that darkest nest of vampires lurking in the crypt of Lichfield. How I would like to smoke them out! But I couldn't wait to light my brand and proceed to the good work: I was so pressed with occupation before leaving home. Then in Paris, for a fortnight, I was pressed still tighter, though with urgencies of a slightly different order; and now immersed in a wondrous motor-tour through the centre and the wide and entire south of this wonderful and most interesting country, I have only the smallest gaps of breathingtime—with handfuls of forwarded letters awaiting me from stage to stage, and only bad ink and ricketty tables, as big as pocket-handkerchiefs, to write on. I greet you affectionately and cheeringly, at any rate, from the heart of my hurly-burly, and promise you floods of interesting discourse on my return. France seen in this intimate and penetrating way (for that's how we *are* seeing it) is of a captivating charm (to the intelligent mind), and my companions—Edward Whartons—are full of kindness, sympathy, curiosity and all the right elements of amenity and convenience— to say nothing of travelling arrangements (with servants sent on ahead by train everywhere to have our rooms ready and our "things out"), which makes the whole thing an expensive fairy-tale. (As I pay my own hotel bills, of course, the mere being attached to such a party makes my charges particularly handsome—a proof again of the old story that it's one's rich friends who cost one!)[1] But I blush for such sordid details in the face of my high entertainment—of which a wondrous social fortnight in Paris, in the heart, and more or less in the lap, of the Faubourg St. Germain will not have been the palest item. I will give you every detail about Mesdames de Fitz-James, de Béarn, d'Humières, d'Arenberg etc.[2]—but meantime please close your lips tight over them—and also believe that the star of Eaton Terrace has not in the least intermitted a twinkle for

441

me. I only pray, and yearn to hear, that the twinkling has, on the spot, not been *wholly* snuffed out by the beating up against it of bat-like vampire wings! We are staying three days here—and return to Paris by ingenious and unusual stops and stages—so I am a fond captive awhile yet, and shall also be, I apprehend for a week or two *after* my return to *58 rue de Varenne*, which remains my present address. But I now go into waiting again—I had (*we* had) a wondrous afternoon yesterday for a run up into deep Pyrenean gorges, and the day before for a most curious one at Lourdes. The way our admirable motor and sane, discreet, deliberate American chauffeur, *master* a country and make such a variety of experience of it easy and intelligible reconciles me really to the monstrous process and machine. But keep praying all the same, for your far-flying yet ever-faithful old friend

Henry James

1. The central portion of this letter, about the cost of traveling with the rich, is pasted over in the manuscript, presumably by the discreet (if herself gossipy) Miss Allen, who dutifully obeyed HJ's injunction to secrecy. It can be read, however, if held up to the light.

2. HJ enumerates some of Mrs. Wharton's Faubourg St. Germain friends and acquaintances—the Countess René de Béarn; the Princess and Duchess d'Arenberg, whose husband, Auguste Louis Almeric, had a German princedom and a French dukedom; and above all the Countess Robert de Fitz-James (*née* Rosalie de Gutmann), of Austrian Jewish extraction, a friend of the Bourgets. See Wharton, *A Backward Glance* (1934), 264–282.

To Howard Sturgis
Ms Harvard

58 Rue de Varenne, Paris
April 13*th* 1907

Dearest Howard,

I find your beautiful tragic wail on my return from a wondrous, miraculous motor-tour of three weeks and a day with these admirable friends of ours, who so serve one up all the luxuries of the season and all the ripe fruits of time that one's overloaded plate will hold. We got back from—from everywhere, literally—last night; and in presence of a table groaning under arrears and calendars and other stationery I can but, as it were, fold you in my arms. You talk of sad and fearful things—Benido P's[1] suicide was a horror I had yet

442

to learn—and I don't know what to say to you (at least in this poor inky, scratchy way.) What I should like to be able to say is that I will come down to Rome and see you even now; but this alas is not in my power without my altering all sorts of other pressing arrangements and combinations already made. I do hope to go to Rome for a little—a very little—stay later; but not before the middle or 20th of May; a time—a generally emptier, quieter time—I greatly prefer there to any other. It is of extreme importance to me to be (to remain) in Paris till May 1st—I haven't been here for years and shall probably never once again be here (or "come abroad" once again, like you) for the rest of my natural life. *Ergo* I am taking what there is of it for me—I can't afford, as it were, not to. And I have made my plans (if they hold) for approaching Italy by South Germany, Vienna, Trieste, Venice etc.—all of which will bring me to Rome by the 20th of May about, when, I fear, you will well nigh—or certainly—have cleared out altogether. From Rome and Florence (a few days of F.—where the thought—the image—of Edith P[eruzzi] appals me—what a climax!) I shall return straight home—where at least, then, I must infallibly see you. Or shall you pass through this place—homeward—before May 1st? The gentlest of lionesses bids me tell you what a tenderest welcome you would have from them. Hold up your heart meanwhile and remember, for God's sake, that there is a point beyond which the follies and infirmities of our friends and our *proches* have no right to ravage and wreck our own independence of soul. That quantity is too precious a contribution to the saving human sum of good, of lucidity, and we are responsible for the *entretien* of it. So keep yours, shake yours, up—well up—my dearest friend, and to this end believe in your admirable human use. To be "crushed" is to be of no use; and I for one insist that you shall be of some, and the most delightful, to *me.* Feel everything, *tant que vous voudrez*—but *then* soar superior and don't leave tatters of your precious person on every bush that happens to bristle with all the avidities and egotisms. We shall judge it all sanely and taste it all wisely and talk of it all (even) thrillingly—and profitably—yet; and I depend on your keeping that appointment with me. This is all, dearest Howard, now. I almost blush to break through your obsessions to the point of saying that my three weeks of really *seeing* this large incomparable France in our friend's chariot of fire has been almost the time of my life. It's the old travelling-carriage way glorified and raised to the 100th power. Will you very kindly say to Maud Story[2] for me, with my love, that I am coming to Rome very nearly *all* to see her. I bless your companions and am your *tout dévoué*

Henry James

1. Benido Peruzzi, son of Edith Story (Countess Peruzzi) and grandson of William Wetmore Story.
2. Mrs. Waldo Story. See letter to Blackwood, 28 October 1897.

To George and Fanny Prothero
Ms Harvard

58 Rue de Varenne, Paris
April 13th 1907

My dear George and Fanny Prothero.

I have touching and interesting communications from each of you, and you will condone the fond economy if I lump you together in one yearning response. It's a retarded one, for I returned but last night from a wondrous and absolutely incessant motor-tour of three weeks and a day (over all the south of this splendid and astonishing country) and find here many inevitable arrears. Let me say immediately, dear Mr. George, that I have been rather *at* than *in* the Pyrenees, for it was too early and snowy to penetrate (in a motor) up to the higher roads and the deeper gorges etc. We didn't go to Luchon or Bagnières de Bigarre or Eaux-Bonnes etc. but we did nonetheless see some places (notably the *very* charming Argèles and the sweet Eaux-chauds etc.—to say nothing of (twice!) the ineffable Lourdes (which however is *outside* the mountains). Also the very pleasing and salutary Salies de Béarn. We spent five or six days at Pau, and did those things as excursions of a day or part of a day; but deeper researches are only possible from May on. But *from* the first days of May I should think everything would be, from hour to hour, more and more possible and delightful. I had, before, never been nearer to that general part of France than by a month spent years ago at Biarritz (detestable) and Bayonne (suburban to it); and, with my good compatriot host and hostess (with whom I'm again putting in a week or two here), I was immensely charmed with the whole Pyrenean impression—aspects, beauty, "sym-

444

pathies" (of nature and people); general amenity and sweetness. It is *the* most sympathetic part of France, really never more so than the Riviera (Gascony Provence etc. by which we returned). We thought *Argèles* (less than two hours of motor—from Pau) adorable and desirable—with high cool air and a most immaculate and obliging inn. (Ah the good food and good manners and good looks everywhere! Ah, poor frowsy tea-and-toasty Lamb House!) *Try* the impurpled hills under a warmer sun—and I am sure you will have good news of them. They and their so pleasant people only ask to please. I rejoice that you are on your way hither. Aren't you to stop in Paris and won't you make me a prompt sign here if so? Don't fail of this at your joint peril. I deplore your continued visitations and promise you high benefit from a change of sky and of tone. I tenderly thank gentle Mrs. George for her report of Rye upheavals (I brace myself for all) and her other engaging expressions. But I must merely dash this off—sending it to Bedford Square. I should otherwise have so much to tell you. I am prostrate under my so big impression (so big yet so detailed as the magical monster the touring Panhard, makes it—the *only* way to travel at ease and with power now) of the grand style and inordinate interest of this incomparable France. Ah Grignon and Vézelay!—Ah the lovely rivers and the inveterately glorious grub! But these memories will keep and we'll have them all out together (yours too) in our pleasant walks and over our summer tea and toast.

Always your *tout dévoué*

Henry James

To Elizabeth Jordan
Ms NYPL

58 rue de Varenne, Paris
May 3rd 1907

Dear Miss Jordan.

I have, to my shame, two or three unanswered communications from you, and I can only let the fact of my being in Paris still (these nine weeks, with a couple more to come) plead for me; since that represents an agitated and abnormal life, with a terrible, even though profitable and inevitable leakage of precious hours—that of the writing table in particular. One of your letters replied to my proposal about a few short American "impressionist" papers—to the effect that the *Bazar* would find use for three if they should take the form of being specifically addressed to women. This I well understand to be your necessity—though I am not sure I had it as distinctly present to me when I made you my proposal. I am not sure either, that I shall be quite *able* to give them that complexion in an adequate degree—though again, with a swing of the pendulum I remember that I mostly feel myself able to do anything I sufficiently try. (I had to sufficiently try to do the Married Son, for instance.)[1] At any rate I *will* try, and if the things don't seem to me to come in a shape exactly to correspond with your need I won't send them to you. In fine I will do this only if they come out specifically right—I shall ask you to kindly leave the question open till I break with the agitated life and get back to the peace of home; which will be by the middle of June (I go down very briefly to Rome and Venice meanwhile). And then you sent me Mrs. Phelps Ward's[2] contribution to the *Whole Family*—which I began to read the other day, but which immediately affected me as subjected to so pitiless an ordeal in the searching artistic light and amid the intellectual and literary associations of Paris that I tenderly forebore, and laid it away to await resuscitation in a medium in which I shall be able to surround my perusal of it with more precautions. Lastly there comes your note asking me to consult, on the question of my favourite fairy-tale the dreadfully dim and confused and obscure memories of my antediluvian childhood.[3] I'm not very sure I *had* a favourite fairy-tale—so beguiling and absorbing to me were *all* such flowers of nursery legend (I mean when I was very infantine indeed) for I seem to make out that I got through them, through Perrault and Mme D'Aulnoy,[4] through the Brothers Grimm and H. C. Andersen, very early indeed and began to prefer "stories of Real Life" (amid which I ranked promiscuously Robinson Crusoe, Nicholas Nickleby, The Parents' Assistant, *The Initials*[5]—a novel "of manners" new and much esteemed at that time—and several of the productions of Captain Marryat).[6] However I *had* thrilled by the nursery fire, over a fat little Boys'—or perhaps Children's Own Book which contained all the "regular" fairy-tales, dear to that generation—an enormous number, amid which I recall "Hop o'my Thumb," *Le Petit Poucet*, as my small romance of yearning predi-

446

lection. I seem to remember that story in some other particularly thrilling and haunting form, with a picture of the old woodcutter and his wife sitting at night in the glow of the fire and the depths of the wood and plotting for the mislaying of their brood; a very dreadful and romantic image of a strange far-off world in which the enchanting heroism of the small boy, smaller than one's self, who had in that crisis gained immortality, gave one's fond fancy the most attaching of possible companions. There was no boy one had ever heard of one would have given so much to know—and one focussed him as a tiny brown mite much more vividly and saliently, in the picture, at the great moment, than any of the terrible big people by whom he was surrounded. It is the vague memory of this sense of him as some small precious object, like a lost gem, or a rare and beautiful insect on which one might inadvertently tread, or might find under the sofa or behind the window-curtain, that leads me to think of Hop-o'-my-Thumb as my earliest and sweetest and most repeated cupful at the fount of fiction.

Yes, the photograph Evelyn Smalley, poor dear invincible heroine must have given you, will have reached my house *after* I left home and be lying actually on my table, in all safety, with other matter of the packet or extensive kind that is never forwarded to me. But I shall find it as soon as I return, and will carefully and zealously write upon it to you with every precaution.

Yours most truly
Henry James

1. HJ's participation in a composite novel called *The Whole Family*, initiated by Miss Jordan at *Harper's Bazar* and published in 1908, in which each author contributed one chapter. HJ wrote "The Married Son."

2. Elizabeth Stuart Phelps Ward (1844–1911), Massachusetts author of emotional religious novels.

3. HJ's account of his favorite fairy tale was reproduced from this letter in a volume titled *Favorite Fairy Tales: The Childhood Choice of Representative Men and Women* (1907).

4. Marie-Catherine d'Aulnoy (1650[?]–1705), who wrote a volume of fairy tales containing "The Yellow Dwarf" and "The White Cat."

5. A novel by Baroness Jemima Montgomery Tautphoeus (1807–1893).

6. Frederick Marryat (1792–1848), a naval captain, who wrote novels about sea life such as *Peter Simple* (1834).

To James B. Pinker
Ms Yale

58 Rue de Varenne
Paris May 5*th* 1907

Dear Mr. Pinker.

All thanks for your note of yesterday—in relation to the subject of which it occurs to me to make this further point (though I had already, in writing to you, alluded to the matter). In your further reference to their whole rudeness about my American articles etc., with the Harpers kindly (or, rather, as sternly as you please!) bring home to them, as an illustration of their general extraordinary *sans façons* treatment of the same, that fact I have mentioned to you of their real *mutilation* of my volume[1] by the perfectly wanton suppression of the page headlines. I had supplied these with all ingenuity and care, to the Chapman and Hall sheets sent out to them for copy for the Volume—and these indications of the contents and subject of successive pages, made as vivid as possible etc., were—and are—an essential element in the readability of the book. The Harpers simply pay no attention to them at all, leave the poor book to make shift without them and accompany the act neither with any question, notification, apology or sound or syllable of any sort. I think the proceeding fairly monstrous—but I wrote them no word on receipt of the book, though moved by high disgust to do so, because while my interests were under discussion with them at your hands I thought it not right to put in my oar. But it's a point on which I do hate they should go "Scot free!" Yours ever

Henry James

1. *The American Scene* was published in London by Chapman and Hall on 30 January 1907. Harper published it in the United States on 7 February. The book included four sections that had not been serialized; those on the Bowery, Concord and Salem, Charleston, and Florida. Section VII of the essay on Florida, as well as the "running" headings, were omitted in the Harper edition.

To William James, Jr.
Ms James

Hotel de Russie, Rome
May 30*th* 1907

Dearest Bill.

Fully hideously have I delayed to acknowledge your bounties and services—the precious proofs,[1] all safe and exactly *right*; your good letter and your Dad's wonderful one—the latter supplementing an admirable one I had just had from him myself—but which, as it's almost *all* a series of very interesting restrictions, reserves and happy *damnations*, or almost, in respect to my American book, I don't send on to you; keeping your own meanwhile for reperusal here and to hand back to you in Paris. Their news, generally, seems very good, and the fruits of his liberation in particular first-class. I know well what he means by the rich sense of that new freedom— and I rejoice over them altogether. Meanwhile if I have rejoiced so *silently* here, it is that Rome has proved much more of a *trap*—of people and sessions and engagements than I thought it was so late in the season likely to be and the hours have melted in my hands (while I have endeavoured to concentrate my mornings into some urgency of work—till *déjeuner*, and laboured heroically to keep the *déjeuner* itself to myself). Apart from this the floodgates have been opened and a great hole made in the middle of each afternoon by my *having*, in common kindness, to sit to Hendrik Andersen for my Bust. !!—to an end as yet not positively or richly rejoiceful. But there will be something. The Season is warm (and not too warm— the nights delicious for coolness after the good Roman sort—till late in the summer); and the great sense of the old place is still more or less with one; but the abatements and changes and modernisms and vulgarities, the crowd and the struggle and the frustration (of real communion with what one wanted) are quite dreadful—and I really quite revel in the thought that I shall never come to Italy *at all* again—in all probability. However I am as glad to have come as I am impatient to turn my face homeward now—and am only at present waiting (to get on to a very brief dealing with Florence and Venice) because I've promised to put in two or three more sittings for the Bust, with which H.A. is taking ardent pains. I shall get off to Florence on Monday or Tuesday—and shall thence get on

449

On the terrace at Cernitoio, near Vallombrosa, 1907. James standing; Howard Sturgis at left with Mr. and Mrs. Edward Boit.

[to] Venice after the very fewest days possible. In Venice I shall probably spend six or seven—at *Palazzo Barbaro, San Stefano, Venezia* (with my good friends the D. S. Curtises.) I hope you thrive and triumph, dear Bill. Forgive my hurried meagreness and believe still in

Your fond old Uncle,
Henry James

1. Some galleys of the New York Edition.

To Jessie Allen
Ms Harvard

Palazzo Barbaro
Canal Grande, Venezia
Monday June 24 1907

Dear brave and ever-prized Goody.

You will wonder what has been "becoming" of me—but not more, with my prolonged absence, than I have wondered what has been becoming of myself. I am at last on the near "home stretch," and I yearn for that goal—but though I shall thus see you the sooner I feel that I shan't be able to meet you with any clearness of conscience unless I shall have made you a sign from these ever adorable (*never* more so!) marble halls and sent you some echo of our inimitable Barbarites—who are quite as inimitable as ever. I came here five days ago—from a week in Florence and previous month, almost, in Rome and Naples—all of which time Ariana was pulling awfully hard at one end of my scant tether. I am now the only guest—the full-blown summer is divine (even if pretty torrid), D. and A. are kindness and hospitality unlimited (or limited only by my condemnation to *sneaking* relations with everyone else—it would *never* be possible, on this ground, for me to stay here again); and in short Venice is really (thanks to the glow and large ease of the season) more characteristically exquisite and loveable than I've *ever* known it. I have this vast cool upper floor—all scirocco draughts and easy undressedness quite to myself; I go out with Ariana at 5, in the cool (comparative), and then again by moonlight; so that if I'm not madly in love with her what influence is wanting? Dan'l visits the matutinal Lido in the torrid A.M. hours—just as of yore—but if he yearns, yearns in vain for my society. Angelo[1] the everlasting has his white-gloved forefinger (as of yore) on almost every morsel that goes down my throat, and Angelino, worthy offshoot of such a scion, gets my hat off my head and my stick out of my fond clutch almost before I'm half up the grand staircase. So you see the dear old Barbarism is an element undefiled and uncorrupted—and that every note strikes true from the cool dim dawn, when the canal is a great curly floor of dark grim marble, to the still cooler blue night when I go forth with my Lady to be cradled by the plash outside the Guidecca. But of all this I must tell

451

With the "heroic young sculptor" Hendrik Andersen in his studio in Rome, 1907.

you—and of the new heartbreak it is just only to feel this enchantress (I allude now to the terrible old Venice herself!) weave her spell just again supremely to lose her. One dreams again so of some clutched perch of one's own here. But it's the most drivelling of dreams. Our friends leave for England on the 29th and I the day before—next Friday. I go to Milan and Lausanne (by the Simplon orifice) and then to Paris—Dover—Rye. I come up to town for three or four days about July 12th. Then for a jaw! Such a fine old feast as it will be to see you—and I allude neither to lunch nor to dinner. You will probably even see D. and A. first. That is *best!* Forgive this mere scrap of a hand-wag from your faithful old

Henry James

1. The gondolier of Daniel and Ariana Curtis at the Palazzo Barbaro.

To W. Morton Fullerton
Ms Princeton

Lamb House, Rye
August 8th 1907

My dearest Morton!

My difficulty is that I love you too fantastically much to be able, in intercourse and relation with you, in such a matter as answering your celestial letter, to do anything *but* love you, whereby the essence of the whole thing is simply that you divinely write to me and that I divinely feel it: all of which indeed, in respect to all your special and beautiful import itself doesn't, I am perfectly aware, see you much "forrarder." You touch and penetrate me to the quick, and I can only stretch out my hand to draw you closer. Infinitely sweet is it to my artistic soul to feel myself *felt* so exquisitely as you convey to me that you feel—and convey it so admirably and generously and luminously—so that I think the better of my *pensées moyennes* for your thinking well of them and only wish to *me tenir* in order to give you again anything I have to give. *Voila tout-ce-que j'ai à vous dire*—which is but a form of saying that it's miserable not more to see you and be with you. *Arrivez donc, arrivez donc,* and then we'll talk. You speak of the alternatives of the two ships, but don't mention the date of either—leaving me, however, all yearningly to clap you into the Lusitania—if I am right

453

in supposing that to be the one as to which you *don't* pay the beastly 800 francs down. This small possible complication looms that I am practically booked to go to Scotland for several days on some date between August 25th and about September 10th—but the particular day of going is more or less shiftable and I haven't to fix it yet. Let me hear if you conveniently can of your settled arrangement when it *is* settled, and so long as I can possess you for three days I shall be able easily to straighten out the rest. We are having a devil of a summer for cold and wind and damp, but there are lucid intervals, and this place retains a sweetness. Robert d' Humières and his wife lunched here yesterday from Paris, or rather on their way back to it by Folkestone.[1] When you come, at all events, I will explain to you as how there won't and can't be, *à l'heure qu'il est,* any second or "Californian" volume of the American stuff—it has inevitably fallen to the ground: thanks to lapse of time, re-intervention (fatal) of "Europe," original meagre documentation (my "Western tour" having been too cramped and contracted and brief) and, above all, through the so dire *thinness* of the picture *là-bas,* which makes it woefully fade and evanish unless held very tight for early and prompt reproduction. My Western impressions *went*—while I was writing the volume you've read— for I wasn't there long enough and immersedly enough (to do a second book *now* I should have to go again); and my four recent months on the continent here brushed them wholly away. One can't revert to such things (unless one has a bigger and more accumulated mass) over the head of France and Italy. And then this published volume appears to have had no "success" whatever over there—your letter and my brother's (which I read you) being the only echoes of any sort that have come back to me—save (in a sense) the sullen silence of the publishers. I *have* a great many other and *inédites* impressions—but shall have to use them in some other and "indirect" way. Trust me, dear Morton, for the indirection! As for your Notes—recorded and unrecorded—on poor dear H.J., I think of them with ineffable tenderness and pride. His communion with your exquisite intelligence is poor dear H.J.'s supreme luxury and source of thankfulness—and to feel you play that fine burning-glass over him from any point of vantage or seat of authority whatever is an idea to make him sit as still and as tight as possible, lest he cry out, when scorched, with the beautiful intensity of the sensation!

454

From that Bryn Mawr rostrum, and mothered (the possibility, as it were) by your subtle sister,[2] what a poetic justice! But I kind of want you to kind of *wait*. There are *four* intimately revised and seen through the Press first Novels all ready—but there is still some practical delay about beginning the issue. Still, I hope for *Roderick Hudson* in the autumn. Je vous embrasse bien!

Henry James

1. Robert Marie Aymeric Eugène Vicomte d'Humières (1868–1915), French poet, translator of Kipling and Barrie, who helped Marcel Proust with his translations of Ruskin. He was killed in action in France in 1915.
2. See letter to Fullerton, 18 October 1902.

To Mr. and Mrs. Edward Wharton
Ms Yale

Lamb House, Rye
August 11th 1907

My dear Edith and my dear Edward.

The d'Humières[1] have just been lunching with me, and that has so reknotted the silver cord that stretched so tense from the first days of last March to the first of those of May[2]—wasn't it?—that I feel it a folly in addition to a shame not yet to have written to you (as I have been daily and hourly yearning to do) ever since my return from Italy about a month ago. You flung me the handkerchief, Edith, just at that time—literally cast it at my feet: it met me, exactly, bounding—rebounding—from my hall table as I recrossed my threshold after my long absence; which fact makes this tardy response, I am well aware, all the more graceless. And then came the charming little picture-card of the poor Lamb House hack grinding out his patient prose under your light lash and dear Walter B[erry]'s—which *should* have accelerated my production to the point of its breaking in waves at your feet: and yet it's only tonight that my overburdened spirit—pushing its way ever since my return, through the accumulations and arrears, in every sort, of absence, puts pen to paper for your especial benefit—if benefit it be. The charming d'Humières both, as I say, touring—*training*—in England, through horrid wind and weather, with a *bonne grâce* and a wit and a Parisianism worthy of a better cause, amiably lunched with me a couple of days since on their way from town to Folkestone and so back to Plassac (don't you *like* "Plassac," down in our dear old Gascony?) the seat of M. de Dampierre—to whom, *à ce qu'il paraît*, that day at luncheon we were all exquisitely sympathetic! Well, it threw back the bridge across the gulfs and the months, even to the very spot where the great nobly-clanging glass door used to open to the arrested, the engulfing and disgorging Car—for we sat in my little garden here and talked about you galore and kind of made plans (wild vain dreams, though I didn't let *them* see it!) for our all somehow being together again. They appeared, that highly-civilized young couple, to the greatest advantage: a little more pedestrian and mackintoshed of aspect than under your (*pardon*—our!) gilded *lambris*, but delightfully conversible—in the key of that milieu; and she with her pretty salient eyes and her pretty salient gesture,[3] so vague, and yet so rounded and *invoking*, all as pretty as ever. But oh, I should like to remount the stream of time much further back than their passage here—if it weren't (as it somehow always is when I get at urgent letters) ever so much past midnight. It was only with my final return hither that my deep draught of riotous living came to an end, and as the cup had originally been held to my lips all by your hands I somehow felt in presence of your interest and sympathy up to the very last, and as if you absolutely should have been *avertis* from day to day—I did the matter that justice at least. Too much of the story has by this time dropped out; but there are bits I wish I could save for you. I spent four or five days in Paris, only, on my way home (exclusive of three in grim Lausanne with an afflicted relative)—after leaving Milan at 3.20 in the afternoon and reaching the Hotel Gibbon door, by the wondrous Simplon Tunnel, at 10.30 that night: an *approximation* of the compatriot-poisoned Italy (of early summer, drenched by the "Southern route")—which thrilled me even through the rage of that poison. And in Paris I called rue Barbet[4] and found Minnie at first alone and very charmingly *acceuillante*; full of the fact that they were (the first week in July!) "more *mondains* than ever," and that Paul had dined out every night for *nine* on end; also that he wanted to spend the whole summer so and never stir from rue Barbet, never *never* again. At last Paul came in, quite "decent" and pleasant, but with all his usual detachment and irrelevancy of attitude, tone and direction, and with no more question of what had happened to one or where one had been and how occupied in the two months than if we had broken off the day before. But I must break off—it's 1.15 A.M.!

August 12th

I wrote you last from Rome, I think—didn't I? but it was after that that I heard of your having had at the last awful delays and complications, awful *strike*-botherations, over your sailing. I knew nothing of them at the time, and in fact I'm not sure I *did* hear of them till Minnie B. spoke of them to me on my re-passage through Paris—she told me you had been infinitely incommoded. I can only hope that the horrid memory of it has been brushed and blown away for you by the wind of your American kilometres. I remained in Rome—for myself—a goodish while after last writing you and there were charming moments, faint reverberations of the old-time refrains—with a happy tendency of the superfluous, the incongruous crew to take its departure as the summer came on; yet I feel that I shouldn't care if I never saw the perverted place again, were it not for the memory of four or five adorable occasions—charming chances—enjoyed by the bounty of the Filippis.[5] For that really quite prodigious pair arrived from Paris in due course, *par monts et vaux*, by strange passes and détours, by Venice and Macerata and heaven knows what else beside, and I saw again a good deal of them—with interest, and as regards the handsome blowsy Caroline, with a good deal of a certain dim compassion. She is happy, but has after all married a little demonic *positif* Piedmontese bourgeois— she who is of a large and free and easy transalpine and even transatlantic tradition. It tells in all sorts of ways, as one sees them more—and they are in short decidedly interesting, and he all that you saw him in Paris, and she considerably more; but my point is that they carried me in their wondrous car (he drove it himself all the way from Paris via Macerata, and with four or five more picked-up inmates!) first to two or three adorable Roman excursions—to Fiumincino, e.g., where we crossed the Tiber on a mediaeval raft and then had tea—out of a Piccadilly tea-basket—on the cool sea-sand, and for a divine day to Subiaco,[6] the unutterable where I had never been; and then, second, down to Naples (where we spent two days) and back; going by the mountains (the valleys really) and Monte Cassino, and returning by the sea—i.e. by Gaeta, Terracina, the Pontine Marshes and the Castelli—quite an ineffable experience. This brought home to me with an intimacy and a penetration unprecedented how incomparably the old *coquine* of an Italy is the most beautiful country in the world—of a beauty (and an interest and complexity of beauty) so far beyond any other that none other is worth talking about. The day we came down from Posilippo in the early June morning (getting out of Naples and roundabout by that end—the road from Capua on, coming, is archi-damnable) is a memory of splendour and style and heroic elegance I never shall lose—and never shall renew! No—you will come in for it and Cook will picture it up, bless him, repeatedly—but I have drunk and turned the glass upside down—or rather I have placed it under my heel and smashed it—and the Gipsy Life *with* it!—for ever. (Apropos of smashes, two or three days after we had passed the level-crossing of Caianello, near Caserta, *seven* Neapolitan "smarts" were *all* killed dead—and this by no coming of the train, but simply by furious reckless driving and a deviation, a *slip*, that dashed them against a rock and made an instant end. The Italian driving is *crapulous,* and the roads mostly not good enough.) But I mustn't expatiate. I wish I were younger. But for that matter the "State Line" would do me well enough this evening—for it's again the stroke of midnight. If it weren't I would tell you more. Yes, I wish I were to be seated with you tomorrow—catching the breeze-borne "burr" from under Cook's fine nose! How is Gross, dear woman, and how are Mitou and Nicette[7]—whom I missed so at Monte-Cassino? I spent four days—out from Florence—at Ned Boit's wondrous—really quite divine—"eyrie" of Cernitoio,[8] over against Vallombrosa, a dream of Tuscan loveliness and a really adorable *séjour*, along with poor dear Howard S[turgis] and Mildred Seymour and the Babe, and five or six other waifs and strays—without counting the quite charming daughters. Howard has found a harbour of refuge there for the summer, and a much needed—for he is literally in pieces, as far as "character" goes, and I don't see his future at all. It's the strangest disintegration of a total of which so many of the pieces are so good—and produced by no cause, by no shocks, reverses, convulsions, vices, accidents; produced only by charming virtues, remarkable health and the exercise of a *cossue* hospitality. It's all irritatingly gratuitous and trivially tragic. The Babe rallies really excellently—all his friends rally. *Sans ça*—! But *même avec ça,* as I say, it seems to me an end! I spent at the last two divine weeks in Venice—at the Barbaro. I don't care, frankly, if I never see the vulgarized Rome or Florence again, but Venice never seemed to me more loveable—though the vaporetto rages. They keep their cars at Mestre! And I am devotedly yours both

Henry James

1. See letter to Fullerton, 8 August 1907.

2. HJ stayed with the Whartons in Paris from 7 to 21 March; then motored with them in central and southern France, returning to Paris on 2 April; stayed with them in Paris again until 10 May; went to Italy, where he remained until late June; and returned to Lamb House on 7 July.

3. HJ describes her as he described Mrs. Brook in *The Awkward Age.*

4. 20 rue Barbet de Jouy, where the Bourgets lived.

5. Filippo de Filippi (1869–1938), Italian Alpinist, traveler, and early enthusiast of motoring, and his American wife, Caroline. Filippi had the English manner of hospitality, presiding over elaborate dinners with his dark southern features and powerful voice.

6. HJ incorporated his account of this trip into *Italian Hours* (1909), as "A Few Other Roman Neighbourhoods."

7. Mrs. Wharton's dogs.

8. See letter to Henrietta Reubell, 15 December 1901.

To Clare Benedict
Ms Basel

Lamb House, Rye
September 13*th* 1907

My dear Clare.

What a very great silent oblivious brute you must think me! Returning to this place early in July after a long absence abroad (more than two months in Paris and then two in Italy) I found the March *Atlantic*[1] in a great heap of waiting postal matter on my table, but, amid arrears and immediate duties and labours lying in wait for me, didn't at once realize the gem that lurked in its unpenetrated recesses. Then at last I did so—your mother's charming card fell out (or was it, more gracefully still even, yours?) and I addressed myself to your delicate discreet little story—which, so far from itself "romping over the ruins of the language," walks a minuet, rather (with the figures it makes) in a swept and garnished, a charmingly preserved and ordered corner, of that desolation. I have been slow, again, to make you this sign of fond appreciation, because in the first place my power of correspondence partakes now of the senile decay of all my faculties and organs, and because in the second I am at this season of the year exposed to assaults, agitated by alarms and visitations, that make much havoc with my time. But I have had you constantly in mind, taken infinite comfort in knowing you safely tucked in at Pomeroy Place (the card with that address shone—still shines—with a light that never was on Dampfschiff or Schnellzug or Vienerhof or even Bayreuth Ring, any more than on Tammany!) and cursed to feel this present utterance accidentally arrested even when it was about to gush from my pen. To me the peace of Home (after the Summer flurry passes) is every month of my life more precious, and I should scarce be able to bear the ache of knowing that you twain don't sometimes take, if not quite deep draughts, at least sweet ladylike sips of it.

If you begin to Write you'll find it—the fostering habitation—still more endeared to you—and let me tell you that I am right glad you do begin to write. You do it, my dear Clare, with excellent taste, grace and humour—and with an excellent clear and conservative form. You write distinctly *well*, and the idea of your anecdote is a very happy and touching little find—without a word too much or a stumble by the way. This is good and of good omen, but what is particularly good is your liking, your yearning even (as I seem to make out) to do it: in spite of all the Dampfschiffs and Schnellzugs. May it bring you all sorts of quiet pleasure—or rather the one sort it best brings,—as you go farther and cut deeper and find the whole thing open out—as you *will* find it. Nothing would have stirred in your aunt Connie (than to see you thus feeling your way) a tenderer wonder and more amused participation. In relation to whom let me say that the most beautiful thing in Italy, almost, seemed to me in May and June last, the exquisite summer luxuriance and perfect tendance of that spot—I mean of course that very particular spot—below the great grey wall, the cypresses and the time-silvered Pyramid.[2] It is tremendously, inexhaustibly touching—its effect never fails to overwhelm. I spent May and part of June in Rome, a few days in Florence (sad and overdarkened for me by dismal and sinister *Story* tragedies and miseries and follies which I heed in a manner—suicide of Benido Peruzzi,[3] babble of his distracted mother etc.—to be confronted with and immersed in); and was in Venice, after that to the first days of July. I did, from Rome (with friends) a little wondrous *motoring*—down to Naples and back, by different ways etc., and that

460

shows you the lovely land with an easy power that nothing does; but Venice was nevertheless the only place I feel—ever *shall* feel again—the *ache* of desire to go back to. Everything else is now too profaned and vulgarized—swimming in a sauce that might have been cooked (it often seems to one) at Oshkosh. Now I sit *here* tight for months to come. But let me, all the same, before too long, see you and your mother pass; when Pomeroy Place is well below zero. And when I say "see" I mean *hear*—with that unsurpassed rustle of Viennese millinery. You'll be wanting *more*—it's then I look for you: so make the Schnellzug stop within touch of this. I send my best love to your mother and am yours and hers ever faithfully

Henry James

P.S. The beastliest, wettest, windiest cruellest summer known here for six centuries, only a *gleam* now.

1. Containing Clare Benedict's short story "Roderick Eaton's Children." Miss Benedict's mother, sister of Constance Fenimore Woolson, had enclosed a card quoting a sentence from HJ's article on Richmond, Virginia, published in the *Fortnightly Review*, November 1906, in which he referred to little tales "mostly by ladies, and about and for children, romping over the ruins of the English language in the monthly magazines."
2. HJ had once again visited Miss Woolson's grave in the Protestant Cemetery in Rome.
3. See letter to Howard Sturgis, 13 April 1907.

To Edith Wharton
Ms Yale

Lamb House, Rye
October 4*th* 1907

My dear Edith.

All thanks for your luminous reply to my question about the "personality" paper—that reply being quite what I expected. As the matter stands, however, the seed having been dropped, by however crooked a *geste*,[1] into my mind, I am conscious of a lively and spontaneous disposition to really dedicate a few lucid remarks to the mystery of your genius,[2] and I am writing today to the inquirer whose letter I sent you that if he can explain his so highly imaginative statement about your expressed wish (really, evidently, a barefaced, and as I judge, common trick of the trade), I will send him 3,000 words; waiting however for the appearance of *The Fruit*

461

of the Tree to do so. I trust their appearing in his organ—which I have had an opportunity of asking about (to learn that it's recognised)—won't displease you. The organs all seem to me much of a muchness. So I shall sharpen my pen. (I lost the sequences of the F. of the T. while abroad those four or five months—it was inevitable—and then decided to *wait*. And I am intensely waiting. It has been cruel.)

I am immensely thrilled by your news of your prospective repatriation *là-bas*. It affects me as a most majestic manœuvre—displaying in fact an almost insolent *maîtrise* of life. But your silver-sounding toot that invites me to the Car—the wondrous cushioned *general* Car of your so wondrously india-rubber-tyred and deep-cushioned fortune—echoes for me but too mockingly in the dim, if snug, cave of my permanent *retraîte*. I have before me an absolute year of inspired immobility—I am in short on the shelf. But, ah, how from the shelf I shall watch you on the Aubusson carpet! Dear old Aubusson carpet—what a more and more complex minuet it will see danced, with the rich Oriental note of Rosa[3] flashing through (doubtless more closely still) and binding and linking the figures! What sequels you will see to what beginnings. And into what deeper depths of what abysses you will find yourselves interested to gaze! It's all really a mighty thought and I yearn, unspeakably, over you both, but perhaps *most* unspeakably (tell him with my love) over Teddy. But goodnight. I have lately been motoring a goodish deal (in a small way—only over the so rich and charming Kentish country), with some friends—old London ones who have a wondrous Renaud that has the belly of an elephant and yet takes the steep hills like a swallow—and who have had for the summer Laureate Lodge, the Garden that you (are supposed to) Love. *Parlez-moi de ça—tant que vous voudrez:* these mild domestic pleasures. Also I spent five adorable days at John Cadwalader's grousemoor with Mary C.J. and Beatrix and in exquisite weather—an unforgettable experience. (As M. Arnold said of the Theatre: "Organize *Scotland*—Scotland is irresistible." It has so—in its own so different way—the intense classicism of Italy.) A charming melancholy word from Walter B[erry] has just come to me out of the Mount and I am writing to thank him. (Ah do indeed work *him* into the minuet—if only for the sake of my need of his news of it!) I am trying to get at Gaillard T. [Lapsley] even now—for the love of *his* actual news. I wish you Fullerton rather more than I believe in his playing up: he's so incalculable. Not so your plain unvarnished and devoted

Henry James

P.S. Ah do some time tell me what you mean by Cook's having become as one of the foolish! It's a shock unspeakable—that my idol has feet of clay??

1. A New York editor named Markeley had written to HJ claiming Mrs. Wharton had suggested HJ write an article for him on her new novel, *The Fruit of the Tree*. Mrs. Wharton promptly denied she would under any circumstances have done this. HJ, as this letter shows, briefly entertained the idea, but after reading the novel he told his agent he was "so little eager to write the article that unless he [Markeley] gives you real guaranties of proper and punctual payment I had much rather be rid of him altogether" (*Ms Yale*, 31 October 1907). The article was never written. HJ wrote a short story instead, called "The Velvet Glove" (1909), in which a literary Princess (with a motor car like Mrs. Wharton's) flirts with a famous dramatist in order to get him to praise her new novel. See letter to Mrs. Wharton, 24 November 1907.

2. Mrs. Wharton's comment on this remark to Scribner's was that it sounded as if HJ "meant to make mincemeat of me."

3. The Countess Robert de Fitz-James; see letter to Jessie Allen, 28 March 1907. In his letters to Mrs. Wharton, HJ frequently made playful allusions to her entourage as dancing symbolic minuets and sarabandes on her Aubusson carpet.

To James B. Pinker
Ms Yale

Lamb House, Rye
October 14th 1907

Dear Mr. Pinker.

Here's a go, and you must help me please! Read, to that end, the enclosed I and II from Forbes-Robertson,[1] who I judge, will write to you after receipt of the answer to II that I have written to him tonight. I have said to him practically *Yes*, I am willing to assume that we shall arrive at an agreement on the question of a possible brief and momentary curtain-drop! And I have done so because I confess that I am charmed by an actor-manager's wanting to play *all* my text, every syllable of it, instead of demanding the most brutal and bloody cuts. So, as I say, he will approach you, to "treat," and I fear I am unable to give you any particular *mode* for so doing. He ought to have the use of it—the piece—for a *term* only—(five years?)—*that* strikes me; and it further strikes me that the thing

463

ought to be viewed and discussed as a thing of value and distinction. The true inwardness of the question of the "breaks" (for *me*) furthermore would seem this: that if the little play thus becomes a "bill" in itself (but for the perfunctory forepiece) it should be *treated* of as a thing of that importance. I don't know to what extent you feel that your general experience will serve and inspire you here: therefore you will know what I mean when I say that you will doubtless be interested in very special and *expert* theatric light that may come to you as to what are the best terms and conditions in so particular (as it were) a case. My impression of F. R. is that he is very decent and reasonable. One of my other impressions is that there ought to be a question—a limit of delay—as to the *when* of production. Also sound your conscience or that of the treaty-making interest—as to a *sum down*—etc! Believe me ever yours

Henry James

P.S. On top of which it comes over me that I am perhaps leaving you a little in the vague as to the thing we are talking about. It is the one act play I told you of but the other day, which Ellen Terry never produced and which I put into the volume (Heinemann) called the *Two Magics*, to eke out "The Turn of the Screw": put it in absolutely in its scenic form, with amplifications of business etc. *written in* so as to give it the outward form and vain semblance of a Tale. Forbes-Robertson wrote to me *then* (ten years ago) to ask it of me for himself and Mrs. Patrick Campbell—and I then refused. It's after all this time that he returns to the charge!

H.J.

Should you care to *see* me and would you come down for the night?—after hearing from F.R.?

1. The eminent actor Johnston Forbes-Robertson read HJ's story "Covering End" in *The Two Magics* (1898) and proposed that the novelist turn it into a play for him. HJ replied that the story had originally been a play, the one-act *Summersoft* he had written in 1895 for Ellen Terry. This letter deals with the question of turning it into a three-acter.

To William James
Ms Harvard

Dearest William.

Your liberality, the way you have lately (and for so long past) written to me *sans compter,* you and Alice and Harry and all of you, your munificence, I say, is celestial; for this evening comes in your blessing of eight pages from under the Bryce Intervale roof[1]—at the very time of my being most bowed down under the long shame of all my accumulated (though somehow these many months practically insurmountable) silence. It's late at night, but I seize my pen to at least begin a letter to you and tell you how all summer—and from my time in Paris, even, last March–April etc. and in Italy through May–June, your so meanly acknowledged, and scarce acknowledged at all, outpourings have enriched and delighted me. And I had a *divine* letter from Alice, the other day only, still unanswered, and one just now, a joy to me, from Aleck; and though I owe also, now, responses to *him* and Peg and Harry and Bill, all urgently, I let everything slide till I've been a bit decent to *you.* I seem to have followed your summer rather well and intimately and rejoicingly, thanks to Bill's impartings up to the time he left me, and to the beautiful direct and copious news aforesaid from yourself and from Alice, and I make out that I may deem things well with you when I see you so mobile and mobilizable (so emancipated and unchained for being so), as well as so fecund and so still overflowing. Your annual go at Keene Valley (which I'm never to have so much as beheld) and the nature of your references to it—as this one tonight—fill me with pangs and yearnings—I mean the bitterness, almost, of envy: there is so little of the Keene Valley side of things in my life. But I went up to Scotland a month ago, for five days at John Cadwalader's (of N.Y.) vast "shooting" in Forfarshire (let to him out of Lord Dalhousie's real principality), and there, in absolutely exquisite weather, had a brief but deep draught of the glory of moor and mountain, as that air, and ten-mile trudges through the heather and by the brae-side (to lunch with the shooters) delightfully give it. It was an exquisite experience. But those things are over, and I am "settled in" here, D.V., for a good quiet time of urgent work (during the season here that on the whole I love best, for it makes for concentration—and *il n'y a que ça*—for *me!*) which will float me, I trust, till the end of February; when I shall simply go up to London till the mid-May. No more "abroad" for me within any calculable time, heaven grant! Why the devil I didn't write to you after reading your *Pragmatism*[2]—how I kept from it—I can't now explain save by the very fact of the spell itself (of interest and enthralment) that the book cast upon me; I simply sank down, under it, into such depths of submission and assimilation that *any* reaction, very nearly, even that of acknowledgment, would have had almost the taint of dissent or escape. Then I was lost in the wonder of the extent to which all my life I have (like M. Jourdain)[3] unconsciously pragmatised. You are immensely and universally *right,* and I have been absorbing a number more of your followings-up of the matter in the American (Journal of Psychology?) which your devouring devotee Manton Marble[4] of Brighton (whom I was capable of re-spending two days with lately—difficult to face as is the drench of talk which his opulent chosen isolation makes him discharge on one from pent-up sources) plied, and always on invitation does ply, me with. I feel the reading of the book, at all events, to have been really the event of my summer. In which connection (that of "books"), I am infinitely touched by your speaking of having read parts of my *American Scene* (of which I hope Bill has safely delivered you the copy of the English edition)[5] to Mrs. Bryce—paying them the tribute of that test of their value. Indeed the tribute of your calling the whole thing "*Köstlich* stuff" and saying it will remain to *be* read so and really gauged, gives me more pleasure than I can say, and quickens my regret and pain at the way the fates have been all against (all finally and definitely now) my having been able to carry out my plan and do a second instalment, embodying more and complementary impressions. Of course I *had* a plan—and the second volume would have attacked the subject (and my general mass of impression) at various *other* angles, thrown off various other pictures, in short *contributed* much more. But the thing was not to be. My Western journey was (through the complication of my having to get back to N.Y. remuneratedly to "lecture" and that of the mere scrap of time left for it by the then so devilish and now so life-giving Roberts) too brief and breathless for an extended impression or an abiding saturation, a sufficient *accumulation* of notes; and though even this wouldn't have prevented my doing something could I have got at that part of my scheme *quickly,* the earlier mass of the same delayed me till so much time had elapsed that here, and at a distance, and utterly out of actual touch, the whole thing had faded, melted for me too much to trust it as I should have needed to. I should have to go back for six months; and embark on impossible *renewals,* to do that second volume. And yet without it the first affects me as a mere rather melancholy lopsided fragment, infinitely awkward without its mate. But I must go to bed and finish tomorrow!

October 18*th*

A melancholy, dreary, diluvian day, and succession of days altogether, so that much confinement to the house—beyond the limit of what makes for righteousness and continuity of application—prepares for you a correspondent congested and oppressed (a bad autumn and winter here—or anywhere in the country—are rather fatal. But it remains to be seen if these shall be *too* bad.) I am having a good deal of decent quiet and independence, without invasion from London and a new excellent amanuensis from thence, a young boyish Miss Bosanquet,[6] who is worth all the other (females) that I have had put together and who confirms me in the perception, afresh—after eight months without such an agent—that for certain, for most, kinds of diligence and production, the intervention of the agent is, to *my* perverse constitution, an intense aid and a true economy! There is no comparison! I am very busy, though it doesn't outwardly show much—but I won't reveal the secrets of the prison-house more than to say that it will be an immense relief to me when the famous Edition is off my hands. You must wonder what has become, or is becoming, of it; but it is very much to the fore of my consciousness, with the very great application that the very copious amount of minute revision and beautification I have gone in for has taken and is taking even yet, and the very great deal of time devoured by the proof-reading of twenty-three (amended) volumes, and the writing for seventeen volumes of seventeen Prefaces of the most brilliant character and of 7000 words each. (Some of the books of course—six of them—appear in two volumes.) The prefaces are very difficult to make *right,* absolutely and utterly, as they supremely have to be. But they are so right, so far, that the Scribners, pleased with them to the extent quite—for publishers—of giving themselves away—pronounce them "absolutely unique!" Their (the Scribner's) deliberation is in their very just desire to have almost all the volumes in hand and ready—to avoid any possible *after* hitch or delay—before they begin to publish at all. *Then* they will issue them rapidly, as I understand, and *coup sur coup;* at the rate of two books a month—really handsome ones, I make out. What I am doing in the way of revision is equally "unique"—but overwhelmingly enlightened, inevitable and interesting; any judgment *a priori* (or even subsequently) to the contrary being simply fifteenth-rate!) Reading over your last night's letter again, in its beautiful charity, makes me participate to intensity in the divine difference your reprieve from immemorial college-labour[7] must mean for your days and nights and all your goings and comings, and throw myself into all the questions of your life as so modified and embellished. *Otium cum dignitate*[8]—putting independent labour, so comparatively otiose, for dependent. And your *dignitas* now so immense and so consummately earned, every particle of it so paid for over the counter!—it thus ought to be a very good period of life for you, your palpable essential youth and mobility backing all the rest up. I haven't *dignitas* and I haven't *otium,* but on the other hand I have Fletcher who is fully worth, I feel, *both,* and who helps me to a luxurious *im*mobility (*à peu près*) which is almost as good as Youth! How Alice must profit too by your emancipation—profit, I mean "sympathetically," and in spite of having you more thereby on her hands (unless by an increase of your mobility she has you *less;* in which case she won't have gained so much, for she'll have you more on her mind, and her mind, like all fine minds, is a more restless seat of occupation, and even of anxiety, than her hands). You are very interesting and "pathetic" about the receding and unpeopled Chocorua, with its irremediable *desertion* of hands, but I can't help hoping that in spite of everything, all changes, I mean, you will still be able to hold on to it and *sufficiently* exploit it—so much did my all too brief vision of it seem to say to *me.* Brief, brief and all too frustrated and fragmentary (partly through being so Roberts-ridden though he *was* to be such a "blessing in disguise") does almost all my American time affect me now as having been; all consisting of baffled snatches and prevented chances and stinted indulgences and divided claims—in proportion to what I *wanted* to

468

get out of it. Perhaps I wanted too much—I certainly did in proportion to my powers of dealing with it: for it seems after all, in retrospect, *formidable* more than aught else (I mean contacts and efforts and relations—not relatives—seem), and the whole thing couldn't doubtless have been other than it was! Besides I am in possession of unused and yet usable material from it still.——But it's into the status of your children that I throw myself most, and into all that it must say to you and to Alice to have them so interesting and so valuable. It says indeed almost as much to *me* as it can to you both! What you speak of as to *Bill* as you find him on his return is most truly felt: he strikes me as essentially and intensely *entire*; and it's all right to be entire if it doesn't mean you're prematurely concluded. He has visibly great power of growth. Harry is a blessing to me "all the time"—of Harry I can't trust myself to speak. And will you tell Aleck that I am hovering on the very brink of answering a Delicious Letter I've just had from *him!* I owe one, as I have said, to Peg as well, but hers shall go straight to Bryn Mawr. *She* sounds most handsome and precious. Also I've been overjoyed at your reports and at Alice's of your happy impression of Bob. It brings tears to my eyes to think of him at last in quiet waters—if they *be* waters unadulterated. Heaven grant he be truly a spent volcano. Apropos of whom Bill will have told you of the presence of Ned[9] *here*, with him, two or three times—and will probably have left me nothing to add. I hope I don't do him—poor Ned—injustice, but he strikes me as irremedially without form and void—as he is strangely and unhappily without attraction and breeding. I don't know what impression he makes, about, as he goes—I can't think a very pleasing or helpful (to himself) one; though on the other hand I judge him really amiable and without harshness or tortuosity. But he is untutored and untutorable—and is now in Paris (as yet alone, in the Latin quarter) "studying sociology," for the winter. Louisa, I believe, is to go over, but they evidently don't "stay together" more than they can help—and she *dégagée*, to my sense, no feeblest, faintest ray of magnetism. But I am writing on too far into the dead unhappy night, while the rain is on the roof—and the wind in the chimneys. Oh your windless (gale-less) Cambridge! *Choyez-le!* Tell Alice that all this is "for her too" but she shall also soon hear "further" (!!) from yours and hers all and always

Henry

1. WJ had stayed with Lord and Lady Bryce in their rented house in New Hampshire, where they were spending the summer.

2. *Pragmatism: A New Name for Some Old Ways of Thinking* (1907).

3. The chief character in Molière's *Le Bourgeois Gentilhomme*, a vain and ignorant man who tries to figure as a man of quality.

4. See letter to WJ, 23 November 1905.

5. HJ inscribed this copy to his brother, who had so frequently criticized his later style: "To William James, his incoherent, admiring affectionate Brother, Lamb House, August 21st, 1907."

6. Theodora Bosanquet (d. 1961), a young and literary Englishwoman, learned to type in order to apply for the position of amanuensis to HJ, and worked for him until his death. She wrote a lively essay entitled "Henry James at Work," published by the Hogarth Press in 1924.

7. WJ had just retired from Harvard.

8. "Ease or indolence with dignity."

9. See letter to Edward Holton James, 15 February 1896.

To William James
Dictated Ts Harvard

Lamb House, Rye
November 13 1907

Dearest William!

This is a small scrap of a sign; partly because I wrote you at rather inordinate length no long time since, and partly because I have designs, immediate and intense, on each other of *les vôtres;* though, thanks to a mountain of "correspondential" arrears, which flings its dark shade over the otherwise smiling (*unberüfen!*) champaign field of my present state, I shall have to tick-out my love on this so public-looking system—which I am returning to, for general labour, after eight months' severance from it, with deep and particular appreciation. What I am really wanting to say to-day is what I might have said two or three weeks ago, viz: that a man I don't particularly know, though I have known him a little for some years, one C. Lewis Hind,[1] a London journalist, ex-editor of *The Academy* and one thing or another has written to tell me that you are the person in America he wants utterly most to see during a short stay he is just beginning there, and that he will take it gratefully if I say a good word to you for him in advance, in case he shall be able to approach you during his days in Boston. (He doesn't ask me for a letter, and I wouldn't give it to him if he did, for I used to think him rather a donkey and am under no obligation to him whatever—he

470

rather to me. But he is a perfectly decent, respectable, and I believe amiable man; "interested in Philosophy" and, I infer, supremely in Pragmatism; so that if he comes along and makes you a sign, please understand that I have written you this explanatory, but not urgent nor insistent word.

And there is another like matter—only much more interesting. Do you remember my old (though not aged) and remarkable friend Elizabeth Robins, formerly on the stage, and whom you must have met when with me at the initial time of *The American* play-business? She is more remarkable than ever, and in every way eminent and intelligent, really distinguished; whereby, having naturally, some years since, utterly cast off the theatre and all its works, she has gone in for literature, Female Suffrage, the Colour Question in the U.S. (she springs from Louisville Kentucky) and various other activities. She writes me confidentially that she has just taken an engagement to do a Book on said Colour Question, and that she leaves for America almost immediately to prepare it; with plenty of openings on the Southern view—having, among other things, a winter *pied-à-terre* in Florida—but with a lack of good chances of *renseignement* in the North. She asks me if I could put her in contact with any good source of Inspiration on the subject there; and I have simply ventured to suggest You as the best source of Inspiration I know upon anything. Therefore I shall give her a note to you, just that you may tell her a few things; which I wouldn't dream of doing did I fear to launch her at you the least as a Bore or a Bother. She won't be in the slightest degree one or the other; but is really so interesting, charming and accomplished a person that she will pay her way with you abundantly by the interest and pleasure of talking with her. She has lately hurled herself with ardent conviction into the Suffragette agitation,[2] but not in the obstreperous, police-prodding or umbrella-thumping way of many others, and is, I believe, their most valued platform oratress, swaying multitudes like a heroine of Ibsen. All of which is just to tell you that I'm giving her a little letter. She asked me if I could put her up to Jerome of N.Y.; but, besides that I never saw him but once, I don't know that he would be particularly helpful to her; and at any rate you can tell her about this.

But I overflow too far; especially as, between sentences, I this morning dash out to tree-planting in the garden which, tell him with all my love, I wish Harry were here to have a finger in: as my principal small exploit has been, within half an hour, to get in a small but very good-looking Walnut tree: in place of that fourth-rate tall balsam-poplar, in the studio-angle of the lawn, that has been for the last two years sickening, decaying, dying, and poisoning by fabulously big and ugly roots, an incredible complicated wilderness of them, all the surrounding surface. The rest of you will, I trust, see the slow and sturdy walnut develop (I have reacted against quick trees) but I shall only see it started. This is all just now—save that I go on the 23rd to Liverpool to meet poor Lawrence Godkin, who arrives there with dear little Katherine G's cold ashes for interment near E.L.G[odkin] at Hazelbeach, the so oddly, so perversely fixed little out-of-the-way Northamptonshire church-yard in which their father and husband was (as I feel) so erratically laid after his death near Torquay several years ago. You will doubt-less have heard of poor Katherine's long, wretched struggle for life, these last months, and of her death a week ago. L. was, had become, as time went on, exceedingly attached to her; and now comes out all alone on this melancholy and already wintry mission; and has cabled to me practically to ask if I won't meet him and see him through: to which I have unreservedly responded. Fortunately Alice and Betty Lyon, her devoted friends, are here, and will have been of great utility. But it is all dreary—and, as an "arrangement" so strangely "felt." I hope you are having a glorious late autumn; it has been on the whole very decent here, and everything about us never so handsome. But good-bye

Ever yours
Henry James

1. C. Lewis Hind (1862–1927), journalist and art critic.
2. See letter to Mrs. Clifford, 17 February 1907.

To W. Morton Fullerton
Ms Princeton

Lamb House, Rye
November 14th 1907

My dearest Morton.

I have had your letter since yesterday, and if I have waited a little since, for a free hour to articulate, its immensely interesting and touching, its really overwhelming *contenu*,[1] has only the more deeply sunk into my spirit, so that, verily, the waves of my emotion have closed over it as those of some clear tropic sea might over some imperilled swimmer striking out for the moment below the surface. When I say "overwhelming," of all the sense of your troubled words, I only mean—very simply—that you stir my tenderness even to anguish: a fig for any tenderness (for that matter) that isn't so stirrable. Regret what you must and what you may, but for God's sake waste no further mere vain semblance of sense ever again on any compunction for the fact of your having so late, so late, after long years, brought yourself to speak to me of what there was always a muffled unenlightened ache for my affection in my not knowing—simply and vaguely and ineffectually guessing as I did at complications in your life that I was utterly powerless to get any nearer to, even though I might have done so a little helpfully. I seem to feel now that if I had been nearer to you—by your admission of me (for I think *my* signs were always there) something might have been advantageously different, and I think of the whole long mistaken perversity of your averted *reality* so to speak, as a miserable *personal* waste, that of something—ah, so tender!—in *me* that was only quite yearningly ready for you, and something all possible, and all deeply and admirably appealing in yourself, of which I never got the benefit. The clearing of the air lifts, it seems to me, such a load, removes such a falsity (of defeated relation) between us, that I think *that* by itself is a portent and omen of better days and of a more workable situation. The difference, I agree, is largely that of my "aching," as I say, intelligently now, where I only ached darkly and testified awkwardly before; but I can't believe I can't somehow, bit by bit, help you and ease you by dividing with you, as it were, the heavy burden of your consciousness. *Can* one man be as mortally, as tenderly attached to another as I am to you, and be at the same time a force, as it were, of some value, without its counting effectively at some right and preappointed moment for the brother over whom he yearns? I launch that question at you, and I believe in your solid basis and your final *trempe*; in other words in your assured future. I wish to God I could say on the spot *the* thing, the mere practical plain thing that would clear the air of your nightmare more than anything—that thus and so the sense you mention can be imaginably compassed. But even as to that light will break and patience find its account. Don't worry over *worrying*—nothing

473

takes the *particular* inconvenient form we fear; it only, at the worst, takes some other—in which we don't know it and fear it for the same. The letter I return to you—exquisite and sacred—represents a value of devotion, a *dedication* to you, so absolute and precious that I should feel but one thing about it in your place (as for that matter I perceive you to feel)—that it will be more than anything else, than all together, the thing to see you through. So sit tight and sit firm and *do* nothing—save indeed look for that money;[2] for while [*sic*] I wish to goodness I could *help* you to look, better than my present impotence permits. But even this may miraculously happen. I am losing this evening's post after all—this won't go till tomorrow A.M. But it takes you, my dearest Morton, the ever so much less wasted and wandering wealth of affection of yours, all and always,

Henry James

P.S. *Destroy* these things—when you've made them yours.

1. Fullerton's former mistress, Henrietta Mirecourt, had rifled his desk and obtained letters concerning his lively and varied sexual life with such personalities as the Ranee of Sarawak (Margaret Brooke), the stage designer Percy Anderson, and Lord Ronald Gower—and perhaps even his more recent involvement with Edith Wharton. HJ expressed a certain discomfort of affection in the situation and seems to have felt Mirecourt could be bought off and the papers recovered. He rightly saw that the blackmail could have little effect in the cosmopolite and journalistic society to which Fullerton belonged. It is to be noted that although HJ urged Fullerton to destroy his own letters, they were ultimately confided to Fullerton's cousin, Katherine Fullerton Gerould. On her death they were given to Princeton by her husband.
2. See letters to Fullerton, 19 and 26 November 1907.

To W. Morton Fullerton
Ms Princeton

Lamb House, Rye
November 19*th* 1907

Dearest Morton.

Your letters would make me weep salt tears if I hadn't almost outlived them, and I unspeakably ache and yearn, at the same time that I howl and gnash my teeth over you—though absolutely without detriment to my conviction of being able somehow to help you, to watch over you and prevent grave harm. Believe this, believe *in* this, lean on me hard and with all your weight—ça vous raffermira and will steady your nerves—your case being largely—on your own side—I can't but feel, a matter of exacerbated and hypnotized nerves: *they* indeed being no small matter, I allow. For the rest, throw yourself outside of the damned circle with a *cultivated* and systematic intensity, throw yourself on your work, on your genius, on your art, on your knowledge, on the Universe in fine (though letting the latter centrally represent H.J.)—throw yourself on the blest *alternative* life—which embraces all these things and is what I mean by the life of art, and which religiously invoked and hand-somely understood, je vous le garanti, *never* fails the sincere invoker—sees him through everything, on the contrary and reveals to him the secrets of and for her doing so. She has seen *me* through everything, and that was a large order too. So keep very still and very busy and very much interested in things—il y en a (and *practically*, I mean) more interesting than your case, and you will find that you are simply, therewith, keeping cool and sitting firm. And feel *all* the while round you the mighty mantle of the steadfast adhesion and infinite tenderness of yours all and always

Henry James

To Edith Wharton
Ms Yale

Adelphi Hotel
Liverpool
November 24*th* 1907

My dear Edith.

Forgive this uncanny whereabouts and this paper so tainted with the same. A woeful office of friendship has dragged me hither to meet poor Lawrence Godkin,[1] arriving from New York, and proceed with him to the melancholy (and really arduous) interment of dear little lately-extinct (as you probably know) Katherine G. in the extremely out-of-the-way Northamptonshire churchyard where her husband lies—a black drive of two hours, tomorrow, from Market Harborough—to which we have first to get, across country, from here. They are all such old and valued friends of mine that I have found myself involved in their lives and in their deaths; but at least during this grey Sunday in this grim place I may ask the detach-

475

ment of writing you these few lines too long delayed. I haven't yet thanked you for the copy of *The Fruit of the Tree* (admirable work!) nor told you—since indeed this has but just become apparent—that I shall probably *not* find myself at all well-advised to do that paper on your Personality for the mendacious Markeley of the "International Press Service," or whatever he calls it, whose letter of application I confided to you.[2] He wrote me such a very lame and unattenuated explanation of his preposterous statement that you had "expressed a wish" etc. that I felt I must cause inquiries to be made about him and his mysterious periodical—as I was able to do; and these have eventuated in nothing reassuring. I don't feel that I can "enthuse" over you in a hole-and-corner publication—it doesn't seem to me the proper place for either of us. Yet—apart from this—I am embarrassed as I am in no intimate relation at present with either the *Atlantic* or the *North American Review* which latter has behaved very rudely and in fact offensively to me over the whole progress of my American papers. If Scribner had for *deux sous* of inspiration (left over from that it employs in getting you to write in it) *it* would invite me to wrestle with your Personality in the bright arena of its pages; but I am not, for particular reasons, by way of *offering* anything to *ces messieurs* at all. I *want* to enthuse over you, I yearn to, quite—but I must wait for the right and bright and honourable occasion for so doing. *Ne craignez rien*—so to speak (as if you cared!) I say to myself at least that the thing won't lose or spoil by keeping or waiting. I have read *The Fruit* meanwhile with acute appreciation—the liveliest admiration and sympathy. I find it a thing of the highest and finest ability and lucidity and of a great deal of (though not perhaps of a completely) superior art. Where my qualifications would come in would be as to the terrible question of the composition and conduct of the thing—as to which you will think I am always boring. About this side I think there are certain things to say—but as against it the whole has intensely held and charmed me, and *Dieu sait si je suis* (in my blighted age) a *difficult* reader (of "new fiction"). The element of good writing in it is enormous—I perpetually catch you at writing admirably (though I do think here somehow, of George Eliotizing a little more frankly than ever yet; I mean a little more *directly* and avowedly. However, I don't "mind" that—I like it; and you do things which are not in dear old Mary Ann's[3] chords at all). However, there are many more things to say than I can go into now—and I only attempt to note that you have to my mind produced a remarkably rich and accomplished and distinguished book—of more *kinds* of interest than anyone now going can pretend to achieve.

Fullerton was with me on his way home for just one night—from 6.30 one P.M. to 9.30 the next A.M. and the only visit he has paid me in all these years. But he brought me indeed brave messages from you, and the beautiful Terrace photograph (elegant entirely and stirring within me a perfect pang of memory!) together with the charming news of your final installation in the *Revue de Paris*[4]—in which I immensely rejoice for everyone concerned. *Allons*, I shall have a letter awaiting you about December 12th rue de Varenne, but it won't, alas, tell you that I shall be able to come to you again this year. That, painful to relate, is really *de toute impossibilité*—an all insurmountably impracticable thing! Forgive this horrid little crudity of statement. The truth is I shall never, never, never cross the Channel again—but live and die henceforth a more and more *encroûté* Briton and your and Teddy's none the less tenderly affectionate

Henry James

1. See letter to WJ, 13 November 1907.
2. See letter to Jessie Allen, 28 March 1907.
3. George Eliot (Mary Ann Evans).
4. Charles du Bos's translation of *The House of Mirth* was being serialized in the *Revue de Paris*.

To W. Morton Fullerton
Ms Princeton

The Reform Club
November 26*th* 1907

Dearest Morton.

I returned but last night (to find your letter here) from a four days' ordeal—lugubrious and funereal—of "going to meet" an old American Friend (Laurence Godkin) at Liverpool and seeing him through the dreary and complicated business of effecting the internment of a near relation (the mortal *dépouille* brought over)—who was a still older friend of mine—in a terribly out of the way and inaccessible part of the Midlands—a *pays perdu* of Northamptonshire twelve

W. Morton Fullerton, Paris, around 1907.

miles from a station—and such bleak and dreary and dreadful and
death-dealing miles. But it's over—only my letters have been piling
up here *en attendant*—and yours is the first, *bien entendu,* that I
(oh so tenderly and responsively, my dear Morton, my hideously
tormented friend) deal with. Sickened as I am by what *you* have to
deal with, and with no pang of your ordeal muffled or dim or faint,
to me, I yet find myself very robustly conscious of two things. (1)
That you are *hypnotized* by nearness and contact and converse—
hypnotized by the utterly wrong fact of being—of remaining—
under the same roof with the atrocious creature into a belief in her
possible *effect* on any one she may so indecently and insanely
approach that has no relation to any potential reality. She can
possibly appear to no one but as a mad, vindictive and obscene old
woman (with whom, credibly, you may well, in Paris, have lived
younger, but who is now only wreaking the fury [of] an *idée fixe* of
resentment on you for not having perpetrated the marriage with her
that it was—or would be—inconceivable you *should* perpetrate).
She can only denounce and describe and exhibit *herself,* in the

character of a dangerous blackmailer, and thereby render very dangerous and absolutely compromising *any* commerce held with her. If you were not breathing the poisoned air of her proximity and her access you would *see* this and feel it—and the whole truth and reality and proportion and measure of things. The woman can *do* nothing but get (in literal truth) "chucked out," with refusal to touch or look at her calumnious wares—her overtures to your people at home, e.g. simply burned on the spot, unlooked at, as soon as *smelt.* And so throughout, she can absolutely in the very nature of the case and on the very face of it—but inspire a *terror* not only of intercourse, credence or reciprocity—but of the act or appearance *of attention* itself—for she will reek with every sign of vindictive and demented calumny. No one will *touch,* or listen to, e.g., anything with the name of the Ranee¹ in it—it will serve only to scare them. As for R[onald] G[ower],² he is very ancient history and, I think, has all the appearance today of a regularized member of society, with his books and writings everywhere, his big movement (not so bad) to Shakespeare, one of the principal features of Stratford on Avon. However, I didn't mean to go into any detail—if you [have] known him you've known him (R.G.); and it is absolutely your own affair, for you to take your own robust and frank and perfectly manly stand on. Many persons, as I say, moreover, knowing him at this end of Time (it is my impression); the point is what I especially insist on as regards your falsified perspective and nervously aggravated fancy. I have a horror-stricken apprehension of your *weakening,* morbidly to her: the one and only thing that could lose you. You have but one course—to say: You most demented and perverted and unfortunate creature, *Do* your damnedest—you *m'en donnerez des nouvelles.* If after this you make any pact or compromise with her in the interest of an insane (for it would be *that* in you, compassion), *then,* dearest Morton, it would be difficult to advise or inspire you. It is detestable that you should still be under the same roof with her—but if you should remain so after she had lifted a finger to attempt to *colporter* her calumnies—you would simply commit the folly of your life. My own belief is that if you really *break* with her—utterly and absolutely—you will find yourself *free*—and leave her merely beating the air with grotesque *gestes* and absolutely "getting" nowhere. If any echo of her deportement should come back to you send anyone to *me*—they will find *à qui parler.* But for God's sake after any *act* (though her dealings with you are indeed now all acts) don't again in any degree however small or indirect, temporize an inch further, but take your stand on your honour, your manhood, your courage, your decency, your intelligence and on the robust affection of your old, old, and faithful, faithful friend

Henry James

1. Margaret Brooke, Ranee of Sarawak. See letters to Minnie Bourget, 8 April 1899, and to Fullerton, 14 November 1907.

2. Lord Ronald Sutherland Gower (1845–1916), younger son of the second Duke of Sutherland, sculptor, politician, author, and art critic. He was the sculptor of the Shakespeare memorial in Stratford-on-Avon.

To W. Morton Fullerton
Ms Princeton

The Reform Club
November 29*th* 1907

Dearest Morton!

Your letter beautifully reassures me—save that I did mean only by my allusion to the "same roof" the same house: I didn't impute to you the same apartment. However, I understand what you mean by your advantage in being where you can to a certain extent observe her proceedings, and I defer in every way to your discretion as I rejoice to depend on your fortitude. I am with you, in the intensity of my imagination and my affection, at each moment of the day— and I immensely cultivate the feeling that you know I am and that such knowing, such an absolute consciousness and confidence, does say something valuable to you. "*Voici de fait*" etc.—one does (or one easily might) really hope she *will* hurl herself into that perdition—a grotesque give-away of her affair after which there would in truth be nothing whatever left for her (I don't say to "lose"—that is needless, but what is more important) not to gain! *She* only, ridiculous, impossible and odious, would appear in it. *Je vous embrasse bien* and am always yours

Henry James

To Ada Leverson
Ms Barrett

Lamb House, Rye
December 19*th* 1907

Dear Mrs. Leverson.[1]

Jocelyn Persse brought me duly your very kind and munificent letter which has left me almost bowed beneath the weight and mass of its liberality. But I find you a very penetrating and intelligent, as well as a very gentle and generous reader and I am much touched in short, by your so comprehensive appreciation. A poor artist's gropings are at the best but tentative motions and signals in the dark—therefore when some responsive light glimmers afar off he feels rather like a precarious voyager in a shaky or leaky vessel who sees a boat with a friendly lantern at the prow put forth from a vaguely looming coast to show him that his predicament is noticed. My "people" are all dead to me (after the vivid, though tormented life of thrice getting born) so long as I myself only name them. But when other lips kindly do so I see them sit up in their graves and look quite expressive and grateful. Yes, any charming person is like Jocelyn, I think, just as *he* is like any happy creation whatever, almost as he is the type of happy creation and the charming person almost and all but inhuman in his adequate and consistent realization of it. He promises to be human enough, however, to bring me some day to tea with you and I am yours most truly,

Henry James

1. HJ had never met the witty and generous Ada Leverson, the former Ada Esther Beddington (1862–1933), closest woman friend of Oscar Wilde, whose salon now included Jocelyn Persse.

To W. E. Norris
Ms Yale

Lamb House, Rye
December 23*rd* 1907

My dear Norris.

I want you to find this, as by ancient and inviolate custom, or at least intention, on your table on Christmas A.M.; but am convinced that, whenever I post it, it will reach you either before or after, and not with true dramatic effect. It will take you in any case, however, the assurance of my affectionate fidelity—little as anything else for the past year, or I fear a longer time, may have contributed to your perception of that remembrance. The years and the months go, and somehow make our meetings ingeniously rarer and our intervals and silences more monstrous. It is the effect, alas, of our being as it were antipodal Provincials—for if even one of us were a Capitalist the problem (of occasional common days in London) would be by so much simplified. I am in London less, on the whole (than during my first years in this place); and as you appear now to be there never, I flap my wings and crane my neck in the void. Last spring, I confess, I committed an act of comprehensive disloyalty; I went abroad at the winter's end and remained till the first days of July (the first half of the time in Paris, roughly speaking)—and on a long and very interesting, *extraordinarily* interesting, motor-tour in France; the second in Rome and Venice, as to take leave of *them* forever. This took London almost utterly out of my year, and I think I heard from Gosse, who happily for him misses you so much less (I mean enjoys you so much more—but no, that isn't right either!) than I do, that you had in May or June shone in the eye of London. I am not this year, however, I thank my stars, to repeat the weird exploit of a "long continental absence"—such things have quite ceased to be in my real *mœurs*—and I shall therefore plan a campaign in town (for May and June) that will have for its leading feature to encounter you somewhere and somehow. Till then—that is to a later date than usual—I expect to bide quietly here where a continuity of occupation—strange to say—causes the days and the months to melt in my grasp, and where, in spite of rather an appalling invasion of outsiders and idlers (a spreading colony and a looming menace), the conditions of life declare themselves as emphatically my rustic "fit" as I ten years ago made them out to be. I have lived *into* my little old house and garden so thoroughly that they have become a kind of domiciliary skin, that can't be peeled off without pain—and in fact to go away at all is to have, rather, the sense of being flayed. Nevertheless I was glad, last spring, to have been tricked, rather, into a violent change of manners and practices—violent partly because my ten weeks in Paris were, for me, on a basis most unprecedented: I paid a *visit* of that monstrous length to friends (I had never done so in my life before), and in a beautiful old house in the heart of the Rive Gauche, amid old private *hôtels* and hidden gardens (Rue de Varenne) tasted socially and *associatively,* so to speak, of a new Paris altogether and got a bellyful of fresh and nutritive impressions. Yet I have just declined a repetition of it inexorably, and it's more and more vivid to me that I have as much as I can tackle to lead my own life—I can't *ever* again attempt, for more than the fleeting hour, to lead other people's. (I *have* indeed, I should add, suffered infiltration of the poison of the motor—contemplatively and touringly used: that, truly, *is* a huge extension of life, of experience and consciousness. But I thank my stars that I'm too poor to have one.) I'm afraid I've no other adventure whatever to regale you with. I am engaged none the less, in a perpetual adventure, the most thrilling and in every way the greatest of my life, and which consists of having [for] more than four years entered into a state of health so altogether better than any I had ever known that my whole consciousness is transformed by the intense *alleviation* of it, and I lose much time in pinching myself to see if this be not, really, "none of I." That fact, however, is much more interesting to myself than to other people—partly because no one but myself was ever aware of the unhappy nature of the physical consciousness from which I have been redeemed. It may give a glimmering sense of the degree of the redemption, however, that I should, in the first place be willing to fly in the face of the jealous gods by so blatant a proclamation of it, and in the second find the value of it still outweigh the formidable, the heaped-up and pressed together burden of my years.—But enough of my own otherwise meagre annals. E[dmund] G[osse] spent a couple of days with me a month ago, in very practicable pleasant form, and showing for quite the image of the middle-aged paunchy person who, having struggled up the hill of Difficulty and found it very long, is at last taking breath ever so comfortably and gracefully on the social summit and surveying all the kingdoms of the earth. There is a very interesting fact about him, or possibility, rather (of a very happy order) which I mayn't yet speak of (and which you may, by his confidence, know about). If it becomes a reality (as I surmise it soon will) we shall then sniff it in the very air and delightedly congratulate him—as on being so handsomely brushed by the wing of Romance.[1] (And the Romance *isn't* his being raised to the Peerage—though I see you inferring that, and though that too will doubtless come!) Meanwhile kindly not mention this allusion of mine—if you should happen to be exchanging with him the compliments of the Season. But I must catch my post. I haven't sounded you for the least news of your own—it being needless to tell you that I hold out my cap for it even as an organ-grinder who makes eyes for pence to a gentleman on a balcony: especially when the balcony overhangs your luxuriant happy valley and your turquoise sea. I go on taking immense comfort in the "Second Home," as I beg your pardon for calling it, that your sister and her husband must make for you, and am almost as presumptuously pleased with it as if I had invented it. I am myself literally eating a baked apple and a biscuit on Christmas evening all alone: I have no one in the house, I never dine out here under *any* colour (there are to be found people who do!) and I have been deaf to the syren voice of Paris, and to other gregarious pressure. But I wish you a brave feast and a blameless year and am yours, my dear Norris, all faithfully and fondly

Henry James

1. Gosse was about to receive a considerable legacy after certain legal difficulties.

To Charles Scribner's Sons
Dictated Ts Princeton

Lamb House, Rye
31 December 1907

Dear Sirs.

It has been the greater pleasure to me to receive the two beautiful first volumes of The New York Edition, accompanied by your letter of the 17th that I was still taking that modest view of any imminence of publication which all my own extreme deliberations have at least had the merit of teaching me. Therefore I greatly rejoice, as I say, and thank you for the most welcome possible New Year's present. I am delighted with the appearance, beauty and dignity of the Book—am in short almost ridiculously proud of it. No reserves whatever have I to express—I am serenely content. The whole is a perfect felicity, so let us go on rejoicing. The only point is *this*— that I see your Prospectus (as to which I, further, treat my critical sense as in complete and happy abeyance!) announces the later

Long Novels as publishable directly after *The Awkward Age*—makes this succession, in other words, uninterrupted by any volume of Shorter Things. This I hadn't quite understood to be your view; but, on consideration, I am entirely ready to make it my own—I in fact seem to see it as so much better an arrangement (to make a sequence of all the regular Novels together) that I wonder I had taken anything else for granted. I shall send you next at once the Preface and Text of *What Maisie Knew* and so forth, because I have them all but ready; but after that I shall send you straight the revised *Wings of the Dove* and its two successors. But will you very kindly, therefore, despatch to me by book-post a Copy of your two-volume *Wings*, and the same of the *Golden Bowl?* I blush to say I am possessed of neither (having repeatedly dispossessed myself for ingratiating friends); and the one-volume English edition is in each case much less convenient for revision. Those three last of the Regular Novels will go fast; and that gives me great convenience for dealing with the shorter Eight. So please let us consider this order fixed, and believe me, with renewed assurances of high satisfaction, and my best wishes, all round, for the New Year, yours very truly

Henry James

P.S. I will send you by the next mail a note of the disposition I shall like you to make of the Copies you are so good as to place at my disposal.

To Edith Wharton
Ms Yale

Lamb House, Rye
January 2*nd* 1908

My dear Edith.

G. T. Lapsley[1] has gone to bed—he has been seeing the New Year in with me (generously giving a couple of days to it), and I snatch this hour from out the blizzard of Christmas and Year's End and Year's Beginning missives, to tell you too belatedly how touched I have been with your charming little Christmas memento—an exquisite and interesting piece for which I have found a very effective position on the little old oak-wainscotted wall of my very own room. There it will hang as a fond reminder of *tout ce que je vous dois.* (I am trying to make use of an accursed "fountain" pen—but it's a vain struggle, it beats me and I recur to this familiar and well-worn old unimproved utensil.) I have passed here a very solitary and *casanier* Christmas-tide (of wondrous still and frosty days, and nights of huge silver stars), and yesterday finished a job of the last urgency for which this intense concentration had been all vitally indispensable. I got the conditions, here at home thus, in perfection—I put my job through,[2] and now—or in time—it *may* have, on my scant fortunes, a far-reaching effect. If it does have, you'll be the first all generously to congratulate me, and to understand why, under the stress of it, I couldn't indeed break my little started spell of application by a frolic absence from my field of action. If it, on the contrary, fails of that influence I offer my breast to the acutest of your silver arrows; though the beautiful charity with which you have drawn from your critical quiver nothing more fatally-feathered than that dear little framed and glazed, squared and gilded *étrenne* serves for me as a kind of omen of my going unscathed to the end. Gaillard has come down from Trinity, very handsomely, to spend, as I say, these three nights, looking a bit wasted and overworked, and saying—(confessing, alas) that he's not well; yet less *accablé* than when I last saw him, and visibly better, I fondly fancy, than when he got here Tuesday evening. I feel sure he would have something *gentil* for me to send you if he were at my elbow, but I'm alone with the lamp, the fire and the sleeping stillness of this huddled little hilltop, and he deep, I hope, in restorative slumbers. He has spoken to me ever so charmingly of the felicity of his stay with you at The Mount last summer; that nothing sweeter or more sympathetic could be imagined, and was wondrously vivid, droll and discriminating today at dinner about Lily Norton, Lily's *fagotage,* Lily's red nose, Lily's everything of that sort, but Lily's social serenity *quand même,* her "character" and fine ease about herself[3]—which I've always thought remarkable, and rather of the "great" tradition. I admit that it's horrible that we can't—*nous autres*—talk more face to face of the other phenomena; but life is terrible, tragic, perverse and abysmal—besides, *patientons.* I can't pretend to speak of the phenomena that are now renewing themselves round you; for *there* is the eternal penalty of my having shared your cup last year—that I must *taste* the liquor or go without—there can be no question of my otherwise handling the cup. Ah I'm conscious enough, I assure you, of going without, and of all the rich arrears that will never—for me—be made up—! But I hope for yourselves a thoroughly good and full experience—about the possibilities of which, as I see them, there is, alas, all too much to say. Let me therefore but wonder and wish!——And only tell me *this*. The Scribners send me two volumes of my Revised Works (the first published) and tell me of a few others—other copies—to be held, throughout, at my disposition. I want you to receive the *whole* awful series (twenty-three volumes) in their gradual order as they appear; but to this end will you kindly let me know by as brief a word as may be, if by any chance *they*, the said Scribners themselves, are sending you the volumes of their own munificent movement—since I don't want you to be burdened, in your travelling trim, with duplicates. I hope heartily not, for, this being so, I will then immediately instruct them as to how to dispose, throughout, of *one* copy of my allowance of each successive book. In fact, I will, on second thoughts, do that immediately—without your troubling to say anything about the matter. (The books must be— these two first issued: *Roderick H.* and *The American*—only within a day or two out *là-bas.*) But it's long past midnight, and I am yours and Teddy's ever so affectionate

Henry James

1. See letter to Lapsley, 15 September 1902.
2. Expanding the one-act play *Summersoft* into a three-acter, *The High Bid*, for Johnston Forbes-Robertson.
3. Elizabeth Gaskell Norton, daughter of C. E. Norton. HJ uses the French word *fagotage* in the sense of "to dress like a fright."

To Edith Wharton
Ms Yale

Roxburghe Hotel
Edinburgh
March 23rd 1908

My dear Edith!

This is just a tremulous little line to say to you that the daily services of intercession and propitiation (to the infernal gods, those of jealousy and *guignon*) that I feel sure you have instituted for me will continue to be deeply appreciated. They have already borne fruit in the shape of a desperate (comparative) calm—in my racked breast—after much agitation—and even today (Sunday) of a feverish gaiety during the journey from Manchester, to this place, achieved an hour ago by special train for my whole troupe and its impedimenta—I travelling with the animals like the lion-tamer or the serpent-charmer in person and quite enjoying the caravan-quality, the *bariolé* Bohemian or *picaresque* note of the affair. Here we are for the last desperate throes—but the omens are good, the little play pretty and pleasing and amusing and orthodox and mercenary and *safe* (absit omen!)—cravenly, ignobly *canny*; also clearly to be very decently acted indeed: little Gertrude Elliott, on whom it so infinitely hangs, showing above all a gallantry, capacity and *vaillance*, on which I had not ventured to build.[1] She is a scrap (personally, physically) where she should be a presence, and handicapped by a face too *small* in size to be a field for the play of expression; but allowing for this she illustrates the fact that intelligence and instinct are *capables de tout*—so that I still hope. And each time they worry through the little "piggery" it seems to me more *firm* and more intrinsically without holes and weak spots—in itself I mean; and not other, in short, than "consummately" artful. I even quite awfully wish you and Teddy were to be here—even so far as that do I go! But wire me a word—*here*—on Thursday A.M.—and I shall be almost as much heartened up. I will send you as plain and unvarnished a one after the event as the case will lend itself to. Even an Edinburgh public isn't (I mean as we go here all by the London) determinant, of course—however, *à la guerre comme à la guerre*, and don't intermit the burnt-offerings. More, more, very soon—and you too will have news for yours and Edward's right recklessly even though ruefully

Henry James

1. This letter is of a piece with HJ's exuberant and nervous correspondence about the theatre in the years 1890–1895; see *Letters* III. Gertrude Elliott, the American actress, wife of Johnston Forbes-Robertson, had the leading role of an American tourist who visits an old English country house and ends by marrying the owner, a secondary role assumed in this instance by Forbes-Robertson. The play's short-story version, "Covering End," appears in *Collected Tales*, X, and the play itself in *The Complete Plays of Henry James* (1949).

To Jocelyn Persse
Ms Harvard

Roxburghe Hotel
Edinburgh
March 24 (P.M.) 1908

Dearest Jocelyn.

I wired to you an hour or two ago at the Hotel Chatham, where I hope you won't miss my telegram. A very breathless journey from Rome you seem to be making, and frankly, my dear, dear boy, I am touched, infinitely, by your being ready to start off on the long run to this place the morning, as I understand it (that of Thursday) after arriving—and perhaps storm-tossed—from Paris. Very generous and gallant of you I feel this to be and hope to goodness you be not all knocked up with it, so as to arrive here a mere rag of sacrifice, so to speak. If you come from King's Cross, as I sort of assume— starting 10 A.M.—you are due here at 6.15 which, if you are punctual, allows you a decent margin—play being at 8.15. I think from King's Cross the *normal* way for you to come, and I shall take it for granted by *probably* being at the station at said 6.15 to meet you—bringing you thereafter straight to this hotel, where I shall have your room ready and where you will of course be my guest. You shall not have a penny of expense in the *whole* matter that I can spare you— whereby (for I warned you some time back I would) I enclose you a cheque for £6.0.0 to pay for your return ticket; said ticket costing, as I see by the ABC £5.9.6 and the 10.6 over being for cabs and food and tips—*voilà!* You see I want to make very sure of you. As for your proposal about your friends in the country, dearest Jocelyn, I *can't* now go to stay with . . .[1]

1. The rest of the letter is missing.

To Theodora Bosanquet
Ms Harvard

Reform Club
March 30*th* 1908

Dear Miss Bosanquet.

Just a bare word to say that I shall be at home on Wednesday P.M. I'm expecting to take the 4.28 that day and to begin operations again on Thursday.

In the confusion of telegrams and letters at Edinburgh (whence I returned Friday night) I can't for my life remember whether I wired you or not, there was so much to do. But the Play was an unmistakeably complete and charming and rewarding success. This it will give you pleasure, I am sure, to know—even if I have, distractedly, till now, omitted to record it for you. I hope you have passed your days conveniently to yourself.

Yours very truly,
Henry James

To Henry Adams
Ms Mass. Historical

3, Place des États-Unis
May 8*th* 1908

My dear Henry.

I am kept here in gilded chains, in gorgeous bondage, in breathless attendance and luxurious *asservissement*[1]—otherwise I should have acknowledged sooner your magnificent and magnanimous bounty.[2] I am deeply and proudly grateful—and I promise myself an experience of the rarest quality as soon as I sit down to you in calmer conditions than these or than those I shall *immediately* find on my return (tomorrow) to England. My brother William and his wife are there—"Hibbert" lecturing[3] at Oxford and I shall have to be there—at Oxford—and in town with them, in a good deal of a social and other hurly-burly, the whole of the rest of this month and doubtless a little of June—after which they will come down to stay with me in the country. All that will not make for the devout and concentrated communion with you of which I dream—but I shall defy the Fates, all the same, to keep me from getting at you

490

more or less—and I foresee that I shall be borne aloft on billows of ecstatic comment. But of these things you shall hear from yours all constantly and gratefully

Henry James

P.S. I take the liberty of suggesting that you remain not too unaware of the fact that my hostess here, who has been reading you with a great overflow of delight, entertains for you such sentiments as will make any attention or attendance you may be able to render a thing of joy to her!

1. Although HJ had said he would never cross the Channel again, he changed his mind after the production of his play and the completion of another section of the New York Edition. He visited Edith Wharton from 24 April to 10 May. "Let me come, please," he had written her, "utterly incognito and wholly masked in motor goggles." He saw something of two old friends who were in Paris, Howells and T. S. Perry, and met a limited few of the Wharton circle. He also sat for his portrait to Jacques-Emile Blanche. See letter to Ellen Emmet Rand, 2 November 1908.

2. Adams had just sent HJ his privately printed *The Education of Henry Adams* (1907).

3. WJ's Hibbert Lectures at Manchester College, Oxford, published as *A Pluralistic Universe* (1909).

To Thomas Sergeant Perry
Ms Colby

Reform Club
May 20*th* 1908

My dear Thomas.

Just a word to thank you for your *petit mot* and to wish you a bomb-proof holiday in poor dear old Muscovy. How thrilling to drive in a droshky and to drink vodkha and to dine with a barina and to be served by a moujik and to exercise on a steppe—and in short do all the intimate and knowing Turgeneffian things!—I am rather relieved that you don't like my awful aspect as reported on by Blanche.[1] I didn't (in all confidence) myself—but I felt I had no right to an opinion. With Lilla and you to back me I shall continue (secretly and bitterly) to blush for it, a melancholy monster enough! Don't dally too long by the Volga, but take copious notes and then come over and pour them into the lap of yours, both, very constantly,

Henry James

P.S. There *is* one thing you perhaps can do for me: i.e. ascertain at Petersburg whether an old and very amiable Russian friend of mine, an artist, and at one time a very *intime* court personage (friend of the late Emperor and the present Dowager Empress) by name *Paul Joukowsky*,[2] be alive or dead? ? ? ? ? ? It isn't that I really know who you could *ask*—but the right person *would know!!*

1. The portrait of HJ by Jacques-Émile Blanche (1861–1942), now in the National Portrait Gallery of the Smithsonian Institution.
2. Paul Joukowsky (Zhukovski), friend from HJ's first Parisian days in 1875. See *Letters* II, 46, 49–50.

To Mrs. George Cornwallis-West
Ms Private

Reform Club
October 9 1908

Dear Mrs. West.[1]

Your letter overtakes me in town. I am much thrilled by your idea of possible lectures in the U.S.A. and give you with pleasure the benefit of my very limited experience upwards of four years ago. I say very limited because that describes the real *accident* or the particularly circumscribed nature of my small performance. I went to America (the first time for twenty-four years)[2] with no such notion and nothing prepared, but was almost immediately *asked*— promptly written to by the secretaries of three essentially American Institutions known as Ladies' Clubs which swarm all over the country. They earnestly proposed my addressing them on some "literary or other subject" and under competent advice I responded on trial—first to Philadelphia—I had an old sketched lecture (a mere beginning) on Balzac (planned and laid aside two years before). This I sent to England for, and "worked up" and finished—and this I delivered to about twenty (only) of the said Ladies' Clubs—and only in the big places. It was a bad subject—nevertheless one had a degree of success and one saw thereby the place—the people (copiously!) and the manners as perhaps one would not have done otherwise. A "personal" subject would have had of course much more success—and if I had gone with a plan I should have done differently. But I had nothing to do with any agent or big or-

492

Portrait of Henry James by Jacques-Émile Blanche, 1908; now in the National Portrait Gallery, Smithsonian Institution, Washington.

ganisation. *That* I could never have stood—ruin, madness, illness or perhaps money would have overwhelmed me. I simply said Yes to the best and most important of the Ladies' Clubs and absolute *no* to the rest. (That selection works best by the clue of fees. When they inquired as to my fee I said fifty pounds and closed with those who would give that. Twenty gave me the said £50 on my tour from New York to Los Angeles. I delivered the one poor literary lecture warning them as to exactly what it would be. It was interesting, amusing and *very* fatiguing! Meeting the number of people involved is the drawback—all very pleasant and kind but of a terrific monotony and indistinguishability! The being "run" by a regular Agency must be awful and fatal—though if done on high tones likely to be proportionately lucrative—I mean as lucrative as dreadful! However, *you* can't possibly fail, I am sure, to have a huge success and vulgarly speaking a big harvest! The only thing is to be able to *stand it!* Speak to them of your personal experiences and observations. That is really all they want and *to look at you for all they are worth.* Yours most truly

Henry James

1. The former Lady Randolph Churchill (Jennie Jerome), mother of Winston Churchill and in her second marriage wife of George Cornwallis-West.
2. It had been twenty-one years.

To Edith Wharton
Ms Yale

Lamb House, Rye
October 13*th* 1908

My very dear Friend.

I cabled you an hour ago my earnest hope that you *may* see your way to sailing with Walter B. on the 20th—and if you *do* manage that this won't catch you before you start. Nevertheless I can't not write to you—however briefly (I mean on the chance of my letter being useless) after receiving your two last, of *rapprochées* dates, which have come within a very few days of each other—that of October 5th only today. I am deeply distressed at the situation you describe[1] and as to which my power to suggest or enlighten now quite miserably fails me. I move in darkness; I rack my brain; I gnash my teeth; I don't pretend to understand or to imagine. And yet incredibly to you doubtless—I am still moved to say "Don't *conclude!*" Some light will *still* absolutely come to you—I believe—though I can't pretend to say what it conceivably may be. Anything is more credible—conceivable—than a mere inhuman *plan.* A great trouble, an infinite worry or a situation of the last anxiety or uncertainty are conceivable—though I don't see that such things, I admit, can explain *all.* Only sit tight yourself *and go through the movements of life.* That keeps up our connection with life—I mean of the immediate and apparent life; behind which, all the while, the deeper and darker and the unapparent, in which things *really* happen to us, learns, under that hygiene, to stay in its place. Let it get out of its place and it swamps the scene; besides which its place, God knows, is enough for it! Live it all through, every inch of it—out of it something valuable will come—but live it ever so quietly; and—*je maintiens mon dire*—waitingly! I have had but that one letter, of weeks ago—and there are *kinds* of news I can't ask for. All this I say to you, though what I am really hoping is that you'll be on your voyage when this reaches the Mount. If you're not you'll be so very soon afterwards, won't you?—and you'll come down and see me here and we'll talk *à perte de vue,* and there will be something in that for both of us—especially if we are able then in a manner to "conclude."

Believe meanwhile and always in the aboundingly tender friendship—the understanding, the participation, the *princely* (though I say it who shouldn't) hospitality of spirit and soul of yours more than ever

Henry James

1. The situation was that of her difficult marriage to Teddy Wharton and her involvement with the volatile Morton Fullerton.

To Gertrude Elliott
Ms Private

Lamb House, Rye
October 22*d* 1908

Dear Mrs. Forbes-Robertson.

It has been very interesting to me to hear from you and of your intention and prospects even though these appear to include no very early production of *The High Bid.* I greatly regret to learn that its apparent effect on returns during its few country performances in the spring was a *downward* influence—this I take in for the first time, and the view is of course not exhilarating. I can only hope that an experience on a larger scale and in the longer piece, as it were, will point another way. I have no fixed, no hard and fast view whatever, as you seem to suppose, of the difference between the attitude of London and provincial audiences *on the whole* in respect to any work of mine, but quite incline to believe that these attitudes are—on the whole, as I say, pretty even as regards *all* productions. I only conceive that the London conditions are *generally* better and that the trial there gives a longer and fairer test. In the long run (of returns) no doubt the cases are equal—as to favor or disfavor.—When you come to the question of the Second Act and its effect and its possibilities and impossibilities I *don't*, I confess altogether follow—and perhaps I don't understand you. I only get the sense that you are asking of the little play, with its exceedingly simple and limited origin, that one-act essence of it, stamped on its every square-inch of surface, a range of appeal and effect, a *bearing* that it didn't and couldn't pretend to have, and that can no more be inserted into it after the fact than seeds, say, can be inserted into a (seedless) California orange (I have just eaten one for lunch!) after the tight-skinned golden ball has been exposed on the fruit-stall. I think you mix things and—pardon the expression!—earnestly and eloquently "muddle" them in your plea for "bed-rock!" My small comedy treats its subject—and its subject is Mrs. Gracedew's appeal and adventure—on Mrs. Gracedew's grounds and in Mrs. Gracedew's spirit, and any deflection from these and that logic and that consistency would send the whole action off into a whirlwind of incoherence. Remember that my little piece was conceived quite primarily for *American* production (it was largely on that delusive ground that it took birth in response to Miss Terry's appeal—and she immediately started for America waving it over her head). That character intensely abides in it, and *can* only intensely do so, and stared out of it from the outset, and had so to be reckoned with.

If however you ask me whether then I can't entertain the idea of taking the second act, and especially its central part, in hand again on the possibility of making it go better, my reply is, on the contrary, that it will interest me greatly to see what I *can* do, as soon as I can get a free mind. It is always interesting to measure and reconsider things in the light of their apparent effect (or non-effect) on audiences[1]—if they [are] not things of the *essence.* I claim for myself infinite ingenuity in the whole dramatic and theatric mystery and craft, and I am quite ready to say that I will give the thing the benefit of my most earnest attention in the light of those resources—and in the measure of the possible. I can imagine, I think, already a more amusing *breaking-up*—of the centre of Act II—amusing in the sense of more generally attaching and thrilling and dramatic. But the very *stuff* of the thing can only remain of course—and there it is. Leave me, however, to shut myself up with it. I will see what I can do. Only I must wait till I have some very urgent present work off my mind, and as I gather that you expect to run your present play *through* your season at Terry's this leaves a margin. But will you please meanwhile send me the text of the alteration of the beginning of the first act of the H[igh] B[id]—the Cora and Young Man bit—which are not *with* the three bound acts (of the whole) you sent me some time since? I am appalled at what has "come out" of the play as I see the scale of the streaked excisions in these three volumes.—I've had no copy of my own since long ago. It will at least give attraction to the idea of putting something in!—I am very glad to infer that you have a country refuge, and hope it is doing you both great good, but as it may be only for Sundays—or week-ends—I address this to the Theatre. Believe me yours very truly

Henry James

1. Gertrude Elliott complained that her plea in *The High Bid* for the preservation of old "show" houses in England was evoking no response from audiences, while they applauded the reply of her husband, the leading man, that many in England had no housing to "show" at all.

To James B. Pinker
Ms Yale

Lamb House, Rye
October 23rd 1908

My dear Pinker.

All thanks for your letter this A.M. received. I have picked myself up considerably since Tuesday A.M., the hour of the shock,[1] but I think it would ease off my nerves not a little to see you, and should be glad if you could come down on Monday next, 26th, say—by the 4.25, and dine and spend the night. If Monday *isn't* convenient to you, I must wait to indicate some other near subsequent day till I have heard from a person who is to come down on one of those dates and whom I wish to be free of. I am afraid my anti-climax *has* come from the fact that since the publication of the Series began no dimmest light or "lead" as to its actualities or possibilities of profit has reached me—whereby, in the absence of special warning, I found myself concluding in the sense of some probable fair return—beguiled thereto also by the measure, known only to myself, of the treasures of ingenuity and labour I have lavished on the ameliorations of every page of the thing, and as to which I felt that they couldn't *not* somehow "tell." I warned *myself* indeed, and kept down my hopes—said to myself that any present payments would be moderate and fragmentary—very; but this didn't prevent my rather building on something that at the end of a very frequented and invaded and hospitable summer might make such a difference as would outweigh—a little—my so disconcerting failure to get anything from the Forbes-Robertsons. The non-response of *both* sources has left me rather high and dry—though not so much so as when I first read Scribner's letter. I have recovered the perspective and proportion of things—I have committed, thank God, no anticipatory *follies* (the worst is having made out my income-tax return at a distinctly higher than at all warranted figure!—whereby I shall have early in 1909 to pay—as I even did last year—on parts of an income I have never received!)—and above all, am aching in every bone to get back to out-and-out "creative" work, the long interruption of which has fairly sickened and poisoned me. (*That* is the real hitch!) I am afraid that moreover in my stupidity before those unexplained—though so grim-looking!—figure-lists of Scribner's I even seemed to make out that a certain $211 (a phrase in his letter seeming also to point to that interpretation) *is*, all the same owing me. But as you say nothing about this I see that I am probably again deluded and that the mystic screed meant it is still owing *them!* Which is all that is wanted, verily, to my sad rectification! However, I am now, as it were, prepared for the worst, and as soon as I can get my desk *absolutely* clear (for, like the convolutions of a vast smothering boa-constrictor, such voluminosities of Proof—

of the Edition—to be carefully read—still keep rolling in), that mere fact will by itself considerably relieve me. And I have *such* visions and arrears of inspiration—! But of these we will speak—and, as I say, I shall be very glad if you can come Monday. Believe me, yours ever,

Henry James

1. The shock was the smallness of his royalties for the early volumes of the New York Edition. In his expectations HJ had not considered the cost of obtaining "permissions" from the original publishers of his early novels.

To Ellen Emmet Rand
Ms Harvard

Lamb House, Rye
November 2*d* 1908

Dearest and most beloved Bay!

Yes, I have been hideously and horribly silent—but it has all been part and parcel of a *general* state of utterly coerced dishumanised separation from letters and brutality to correspondents (on my part) that has gone on for more than a year and that has had its odious and absolute reasons—my having got launched in a job (the closely revised and rewritten! collective—and *se*lective—Edition of my "Works," in twenty-three volumes), the whole preparation and seeing through the press of which—with endless Prefaces to each and other insidious titivations and abysmal traps to labour, to ingenuity, and, above all, to *time*, was to prove so much more exhausting and overwhelming a business than I had conceived in advance that my only way through it, I had early to recognise, was to sit tight, neglect everything else, never answer a *note* that I hadn't to, be a pig and a horror, in fine to every one and about everything else, and just get through by the skin of my teeth—since after the printers and publishers in the two countries had got at my heels I felt their fierce pursuit and pressure behind me and could neither lose nor waste a minute. I am just *now* only out of the wood, rather spent and sore, but the Edition a reality and an honour (though I say it who shouldn't)—only rather expensive in its multitude, with its beauty, and at its cost, alas, to chuck about much, in complimentary fashion. I am sending the lot to three or four authors only who send me *their* editions—and remain piggish to the end. Yes I *have* taken moments, beloved Bay, to weep, yes to bedew my pillow with tears, over the foul wrong I was doing *you* and the generous and delightful letter I so long ago had from you—and in respect to whose noble bounty your present letter, received only this evening and already moving me to this feverish response, is a heaping, on my unworthy head, of coals of fire. It is delightful at any rate, dearest Bay, to be in relation with you again, and to hear your sweet voice, as it were, and to smell your glorious paint and turpentine—to inhale, in a word, both your goodness and your glory; and I shall never again consent to be deprived of the luxury of you (long enough to notice it) on any terms whatever. Let me say at once, however, how distressed I am at your echoes of suffered bereavement, poor dear little Minnie's loss of her husband[1] and Jane von Glehn's[2] of her mother. The former of these strokes must have come to you all as a shock—occurring so in the flower of the brother-in-law's youth and activity. I had never seen him—but supposed him good for everything and anything but *that*. I think ever so tenderly of the (to me) ever so gentle and sympathetic Minnie, and bless the Fates that have given her that precious little boy who will I hope be for her something thoroughly safe and sound to hold onto and by. Will you tell her from me, please, that I am thinking of her ever so faithfully?

November 3 *d*

I had to break off last night and go to bed—and as it is now much past midnight again I shall almost surely not finish, but only Scrawl you a few lines more and then take you up to London with me and go on with you there, as I am obliged to make that move, for a few days, by the 9.30 A.M. Among the things I have to do is to go to see my portrait by Jacques Blanche[3] at the Private View of the New Gallery autumn show—he having "done" me in Paris last May (he is now quite the Bay Emmet of the *London*—in particular—portrait world, and does all the billionaires and such like: that's where *I* come in—very big and fat and uncanny and "brainy" and awful when I last saw myself—so that I now quite tremble at the prospect, though he has done a rather wondrous thing of Thomas Hardy—who, however, lends himself. I will add a word to this after I have been to the New Gallery and if I *am* as unnatural as I fear you must settle, really, to come out and avenge me.) Blanche is rather a

500

queer "mondain" do-you-any-way-you-like sort of painter, with a large English connection and a great love, and a strange, for a Frenchman, of England, to which he pays, always, an intimate annual and professional visit; but I found him extraordinarily agreeable to sit to (the whole thing being, I needn't say, *his* proposition and insistence from first to last—to do me as a sort of *pendant* to Hardy, I think, though on a grander scale!)—agreeable and ravishing to sit to by reason of his extraordinary conversational powers; by which he systematically holds his sitters wreathed in smiles and with a look of infatuation on their faces—which makes them thus very brilliant to paint. I don't know what system *you* have developed, dearest Bay—you are ravishing to sit to on any terms; but Blanche's power to coruscate with the tongue and the brush at the same time, and perhaps still *more* with the tongue than with the brush, partakes of the prodigious and the magical. When you see William, to get on again with *his* portrait[4]—in which I am infinitely and yearningly interested—as I am in every invisible stroke of your brush, over which I *ache* for baffled curiosity or wonderment—when you *do* go on to Cambridge (sooner, I trust, than later) he and Alice and Peggy will have much to tell you about their quite long summer here, lately brought to a close, and about poor little old Lamb House and its corpulent, slowly-circulating and slowly-masticating master. It was an infinite interest to have them here for a good many weeks—they are such endlessly interesting people, and Alice such a heroine of devotion and of everything. We have had a wondrous Season—a real golden one, for weeks and weeks—and still it goes on, bland and breathless and changeless—the rarest autumn (and summer, from June on, known for years); a proof of what this much-abused climate is capable of for benignity and convenience. Dear little old Lamb House and garden have really become very pleasant and *developed* through being much (and virtuously) lived in, and I do wish you would come out and add another flourish to its happy legend. But I *must* go to bed, dearest Bay—I'm ashamed to tell you what sort of hour it is. But I've not done with you yet.

105 Pall Mall
November 6*th*

I've been in town a couple of days without having a moment to return to this—for the London tangle immediately begins. What it

501

will perhaps most interest you to know is that I "attended" yester-day the Private View of the Society of Portrait Painters' Exhibition and saw Blanche's "big" portrait of poor H.J. (His two exhibits are that one and one of himself—the latter very flattered, the former not.) The "funny thing about it" is that whereas I sat in almost full face, and left it on the canvas in that bloated aspect when I quitted Paris in [May] June, it is now a splendid Profile, and with the body (and *more* of the body) in a quite different attitude; a wonderful *tour de force* (the sort of thing *you* ought to do if you understand your real interest!)—consisting of course of his having begun the whole thing afresh on a new canvas after I had gone, and worked out the profile, in my absence, by the aid of fond memory ("secret notes" on my silhouette, he also says, surreptitiously taken by him) and several photographs (also secretly) taken *at* that angle while I sat there with my *whole* beauty, as I supposed, turned on. The result is wonderfully "fine" (for *me*)—*considering!* I think one sees a little that it's a *chic'd* thing, but ever so much less than you'd have supposed. He dines with me to-night and I will get him to give me two or three photographs (of the picture, not of *me!*) and send them to you, for curiosity's sake. But I really think that (for a certain *style*—of presentation of H.J.—that it has, a certain dignity of in-tention and of *indication*—of who and what, poor creature, he *is!*) it ought to be seen in the U.S. He (Blanche) wants to go there himself—so put in all your own triumphs first. However, it would *kill* him—so his triumphs would be brief; and yours would then begin again. Meanwhile he was almost as agreeable and charming and beguiling to sit to, as *you*, dear Bay, in your own attaching person—which I think somebody once remarked to me explained *half* the "run" on you!—I delight in all your brave news of everyone but the dear bereft Minny and bereft Jane—as to the latter of whom please tell her I miss her and Wilfrid (whom I had planned to attract this autumn) ever so tenderly and sorely. Dear Gilliard Lapsley[5] (I hope immensely you'll see *him* on his way to Colorado or wherever) has given me occasional news of Eleanor and Elizabeth[6]—in which I have rejoiced—seeming to hear their nurseries ring with the echo of their prosperity. As they must now have children enough for these to take care of EACH OTHER (haven't they?) I hope they are thinking of profiting by it to come out here again—where they are greatly desired. I see Mary Clark[7] but at longish worldly intervals—

and fear she isn't *well.* But she bears up nobly and beautifully, and I've been at her new little admirable centre-of-Hyde-Park home to feel what an immense benediction that retreat has been to them, and will be for the rest of their days. The last time I was there (one lovely day last June—to be in their exquisite garden), I saw Bertie and Mrs. Bertie (mature, plain and worthy) and judged that *those* appendages have now lost most of their worrying power—if only by thoroughly exhausting it. The whole situation is evidently more *peaceful* than ever before—and their (dear good Stanley's and grand fine—and so "human" Mary's) afternoon of life more "golden" and genial than some of its previous times. But, beloved Bay, I must get this off now. I send tenderest love to the Mother and the Sister; I *beseech* you not to let your waiting laurel, here, wither ungathered, and am ever your fondest,

Henry James

1. Bay Emmet's oldest sister, Mary Temple Emmet Peabody, had just lost her husband, Archibald Russell Peabody.

2. Jane Emmet, a cousin, married Wilfrid von Glehn, a painter.

3. See letter to T. S. Perry, 20 May 1908.

4. Bay Emmet's portrait of WJ is at Harvard.

5. HJ often spelled Gaillard Lapsley's name Gilliard, as it was pronounced.

6. Eleanor and Elizabeth were daughters of Eleanor Temple Emmet, who had married a relative of Lapsley's, John Willard Lapsley.

7. Widow of Sir John Clark. See *Letters* II, 366–368.

To Anne Thackeray Ritchie
Ms Harvard

Lamb House, Rye
December 3d 1908

Dearest old Friend!

A brave and delightful postscript to our too-brief meeting your little grey card superscribed with mystic and intricate characters! I take it as a token and symbol of your beautiful fidelity and undying grace and should like to wear it round my neck like some mystic figured amulet or consecrated charm. I make out on its kind, gentle, vivid words—and, rather than not, the fact that you were amused and beguiled (by the aid of your unquenchable fancy and humour) at Lady Pollock's afternoon sing-song. There also flushes through the crushed strawberry glow of Vanessa's beauty and credulity, and the promise of Virginia's printed wit and the felicity of Hester's return.[1] These things I note as items of your always enviable sense of the things about you—of which I wish it were often given me to partake. But the so sweet and savoury *to be,* perceptibly and spiritually, you—and when I am with you I get all the fragrance and all the distinction. Therefore I *must* be with you again soon—as soon as the dire complications of our massive maturity (that is of *mine*) show the first sign of intermitting a little. I am scribbling this in my little old celibatoirean oak-parlour before being called to dinner—and oh so wish I were going to hand you in—to cold beef and pickles! for which you will say Thank-you! Here comes the mild announcement, and I proceed to munch and mumble alone—such a contrast to that bloated last Monday. However, *you* saved that, and now there is *nobody* to save your fondly clinging old friend

Henry James

1. HJ alludes here to Vanessa Bell and the future Virginia Woolf and to Mrs. Ritchie's daughter Hester. Vanessa and Virginia had spent some weeks at Rye; in a letter to Sara Norton Darwin, 11 September 1907, HJ had written: "Leslie Stephen's children three of them—the three surviving poor dear mild able gigantic Thoby, gathered in his flower—have taken two houses near me (temporarily) and as I write the handsome (and most loveable) Vanessa Clive-Bell sits on my lawn (unheeded by me) along with her little incongruous and disconcerting but apparently very devoted newly acquired sposo. And Virginia, on a near hilltop, writes reviews for the *Times*—and the gentle Adrian interminably long and dumb and "admitted to the bar." marches beside her like a giraffe beside an ostrich—save that Virginia is facially most fair. And the hungry generations tread me down!"

To James B. Pinker
Ms Yale

Lamb House, Rye
4*th* December 1908

My dear Pinker.

I send you tonight, apart from this, registered, "The Top of the Tree"[1] as I call the sufficiently pretty production (I think) that you will exercise your discretion about. Other things being equal, or even a little unequal—not *too* much so!—I should rather like it, than not, to follow my fiction of this month in the blue, the *English Review*. I like the way one's stuff is presented on that rather handsome page. But you will decide as to advisabilities, I leave it in your hands, and am yours ever

Henry James

P.S. I have succumbed to pressure on the question of going up to town tomorrow to see St. John Hankin's new Play[2] given by the Stage Society at the Haymarket on *Sunday;* and on that of going with [J. M.] Barrie, after dining with him, to see his own production on Monday. I shall return here Tuesday, and shall then in a very few days (within a week, I hope) have the small abomination ready for Alden.[3] When that is the case I shall ask you to be so good as to communicate with him on the side of the matter touching which nothing has passed between us.

1. This was the story, renamed "The Velvet Glove," in which HJ used the incident of his being asked to "puff" Edith Wharton's novel *The Fruit of the Tree.* See letter to Mrs. Wharton, 4 October 1907.

2. Edward St. John Hankin (1869–1909), whose play *The Last of De Mullins* was produced on 6 December 1908.

3. Henry Mills Alden (1836–1919), editor of *Harper's Monthly.* The "abomination" was probably HJ's story "Crapy Cornelia" published in *Harper's* in October 1909.

To Walter Berry
Ms Unknown

Lamb House, Rye
December 12*th* 1908

My dear dear Walter!

I am infinitely affected and charmed by your beautiful letter— and this even though it gives another turn to the dire screw under which a man of my age perpetually winces and gasps; the fell instrument by which the fact of the flight of the vital hours, the lapse and leap and bound of the days and weeks and seasons, makes perpetually deeper and deeper incision on the scant remainder of his consciousness. The recentness with which you were here, with your adventure all before you, and before *us*, and the immemorial blandness with which now, instead of that, the great grandmotherly Sphinx evidently looks down on you[1]—these things make me try to stay my ebbing breath even while they put vividly to me the *haute allure* of your career. Evidently the whole thing is going to be thoroughly refreshing and charming and interesting and brilliant for you, and next summer you are coming back here to tell me all about it. Meantime I treasure your letter as one of the most penetrating tributes and precious tokens I have ever received. I should like to tell you *par le menu* the entire sequel to that poignant hour of our loss of you, mine and the gracious Lady of Lenox's[2]—as it would indeed be much a matter of the *menu*, with the part every sort of furious feasting has played in it. But the theme is too large, and the whole thing defies, by volume and quantity, my lame epistolary muse. She has been having indeed, after a wild, extravagant, desperate, detached fashion, the Time of her Life. London, and even the Suburbs, have opened their arms to her; she has seen everyone and done everything and is even now the occasion of some great houseparty away off in the Midlands (at Stanway—the Elchos')[3] whence she comes back to more triumphs and will I imagine, be kept on here, in one way or another, till the New Year and the arrival of Teddy. She has really been much amused and pleased, and, with her frame of steel, it has all been remarkably good for her. But *what* a frame of steel, and what a way of arranging one's life! I have participated by breathless dashes and feverish fits, but then had to rush back here to recuperate and meditate. Here I hope, between honest toil, *la promenade et la lecture,* to stick fast for the next few months. But I envy you great livers—for you too, in your own way, have taken up the great romantic bow of Ulysses. Do, if Paul Harvey[4] is still at Cairo—for I don't exactly *know*—address yourself to him as a trusty and well-beloved friend of mine, and tell him I particularly asked you to do so. He is a remarkably distinguished and delightful person, whom I have known from long back; and on the smallest certainty (of his still being there) I would write to him about you. Good night, my dear Walter. Please believe how much I'm yours

Henry James

1. Walter Berry had gone to Egypt as a member of the International Tribunal, a position he held for three years.

2. Mrs. Wharton's house, The Mount, was situated at Lenox, Massachusetts.

3. Hugo Lord Elcho, eldest son of the tenth Earl of Wemyss. Stanway was in Gloucestershire.

4. See letter to Harvey, 11 March 1906. Harvey was in the British Foreign Service.

To Hugh Walpole
Ms Texas

Lamb House, Rye
December 13*th* 1908

My dear young friend Hugh Walpole.[1]

I had from you some days ago a very kind and touching letter, which greatly charmed me, but which now that I wish to read it over again before belatedly thanking you for it I find I have stupidly and inexplicably mislaid—at any rate I can't tonight put my hand on it. But the extremely pleasant and interesting impression of it abides with me; I rejoice that you were moved to write it and that you didn't resist the generous movement—since I always find myself (when the rare and blest revelation—once in a blue moon—takes place) the happier for the thought that I enjoy the sympathy of the gallant and intelligent young. I shall send this to Arthur Benson with the request that he will kindly transmit it to you—since I fail thus, provokingly, of having your address before me. I gather that you are about to hurl yourself into the deep sea of journalism—the more treacherous currents of which (and they strike me as numerous) I hope you may safely breast. Give me more news of this at some convenient hour, and let me believe that at some propitious one I may have the pleasure of seeing you. I never see A. C. B[enson] in these days, to my loss and sorrow—and if this continues I shall have to depend on you considerably to give me tidings of him. However, my appeal to him (my only resource) to put you in possession of this will perhaps strike a welcome spark—so you see you are already something of a link. Believe me very truly yours,

Henry James

1. Walpole (1884–1941) was beginning his career as book reviewer and novelist. He had written to HJ asking to meet him and sending recommendations from A. C. Benson and Percy Lubbock.

To Max Beerbohm
Ms Harvard

Lamb House, Rye
December 19*th* 1908

My dear Max Beerbohm.

I won't say in acknowledgment of your beautiful letter[1] that it's exactly the sort of letter I like best to receive, because that would sound as if I had *data* for generalizing—which I haven't; and therefore I can only go so far as to say that if it belonged to a class, or weren't a mere remarkable individual, I *should* rank it with the type supremely gratifying. On its mere lonely independent merits it appeals to me intimately and exquisitely, and I can only gather myself in and up, arching and presenting my not inconsiderable back—a back, as who should say, offered for any further stray scratching and patting of that delightful kind. I can bear wounds and fell smitings (so far as I have been ever honoured with such—and indeed life smites us on the whole enough, taking one thing with another) better than expressive gentleness of touch; so you must imagine me for a little while quite prostrate and overcome with the force of your good words. But I shall recover, when they have really sunk in—and then be not only the "better," but the more nimble and artful and alert by what they will have done for me. You had, and you obeyed, a very generous and humane inspiration; it charms me to think—or rather so authentically to know, that my (I confess) ambitious Muse does work upon you; it really helps me to believe in her the more myself—by which I am very gratefully yours

Henry James

1. "I could not resist writing to Henry James about 'The Jolly Corner' and about his writings in general, and I have had such a *very* lovely letter from him." Max Beerbohm, *Letters to Reggie Turner*, ed. Rupert Hart-Davis (1964), 178. The tale had just appeared in the December issue of *English Review*.

To Edith Wharton
Ms Yale

Lamb House, Rye
January 11*th* 1909

Dearest Edith.

Your word of today (Monday) gives me a world of satisfaction. I feel a good deal like dear old "Sainte-Beuve" (in the 'thirties or whenever), between interesting Her and interesting Him[1]—yet with a highly appreciative sense of having still finer material to deal with. Immensely relieved and fortified am I at any rate that what I felt from far back—viz: that the darkest enigma would get light if you could only travel on to the possibility of a *talk* has justified that constant conviction. I couldn't put it to you more definitely, for I hadn't the right, and I was indeed myself not a little puzzled and at a loss; but *en somme* I was sure—and couldn't accept at all the possibility of a non-clearance—from the moment a *meeting* remained possible or could again become so. But this I had very much—like a tactful old Sainte-Beuve—to keep to myself. (I doubt if he would in fact at all have equalled me.)—Of course I hadn't expected you would now *tell* me anything beyond your simple allusion to Morton's hell of a summer; and my question for myself has only been as to what may have been going on since. I knew everything up to last May or June—but have practically not heard from him since then—any more than you had, for the greater part; and I most intensely wish he could make it possible to get over to me here for three days during these next weeks. The thought of the tune to which he must want a holiday is heart-breaking to me—and a poor enough snippet of one would that be; but it would be something, and I am presently writing to him in that sense, and on, I fear, the bare chance. Glad am I that we "care" for him, you and I; for verily I think I do as much as you, and that you do as much as I. We can help him—we even can't *not*. And it will immensely pay.—I thank you most kindly for Bourget's play.[2] I am intensely occupied and haven't had much of a go at *it*—but it strikes me as a bit heavy and not particularly original sin (by which I mean, inevitably, of course, his particular one—in which it had its origin). What interests me I confess more is dear Howard [Sturgis]'s having given you that chance for him in Paris—which must have turned out to him a big thrill and joy and treasure *so* laid up at Qu'acre. And how delightful for you to have had him—so genuine and special and charming a social value, and all "our own"—to produce in a society so deeply sentient of such values. I back dear little Rosie[3] not to have been *au dessous* the sense of him indeed. So bless you both—and all. Burgess awaits my letter—*ce détail* will speak to you, and I am your ever so distormented and reconsoled

Henry James

1. Morton Fullerton's indecisiveness in his multiple and dangling love affairs had resulted in his neglect of Mrs. Wharton between the time of HJ's visit to her in Paris the previous May and her recent social whirl in England. She apparently confided in HJ, and had been seeing Fullerton again. His reference to the critic Charles-Augustin Sainte-Beuve (1804–1869) is to his love affair with Victor Hugo's wife.
2. Bourget's play was *L'Émigré*, published in November 1908.
3. The Countess Fitz-James. See letter to Mrs. Wharton, 4 October 1907.

To Bernard Shaw
Dictated Ts Harvard

Lamb House, Rye
20*th* January 1909

My dear Bernard Shaw.

Your delightful letter is a great event for me,[1] but I must first of all ask your indulgence for my inevitable resort, today, to this means of acknowledging it. I have been rather sharply unwell and obliged to stay my hand, for some days, from the pen. I am, thank goodness, better, but still not penworthy—and in fact feel as if I should never be so again in presence of the beautiful and hopeless example your inscribed page sets me. Still another form of your infinite variety, this exquisite application of your ink to your paper! It is indeed humiliating. But I bear up, or try to—and the more that I *can* dictate, at least when I absolutely must.

I think it is very good of you to have taken such explanatory trouble, and written me in such a copious and charming way, about the ill-starred *Saloon*. It raises so many questions, and you strike out into such illimitable ether over the so distinctly and inevitably circumscribed phenomenon itself—of the little piece as it stands— that I fear I can meet you at very few points; but I will say what I can. You strike me as carrying all your eggs, of conviction, appre-

510

ciation, discussion etc., as who should say, in one basket, where you put your hand on them all with great ease and convenience; while I have mine scattered all over the place—many of them still under the hens!—and have therefore to rush about and pick one up here and another there. You take the little play "socialistically," it first strikes me, all too hard: I use that word because you do so yourself, and apparently in a sense that brings my production, such as it is, up against a lion in its path with which it had never dreamed of reckoning. Yes, there literally stands ferocious at the mouth of your beautiful cavern the very last formidable beast with any sop to whom I had prepared myself. And this though I thought I had so counted the lions and so provided the sops!

But let me, before I say more, just tell you a little how *The Saloon* comes to exist at all—since you say yourself "WHY have you done this thing?" I may not seem so to satisfy so big a Why, but it will say at least a little How (I came to do it); and that will be perhaps partly the same thing.

My simple tale is then that Forbes-Robertson and his wife a year ago approached me for the production of a little old one-act comedy written a dozen years or so previous, and that in the event was to see the light but under the more or less dissimulated form of a small published "story."[2] I took hold of this then, and it proved susceptible of being played in three acts (with the shortest intervals)—and was in fact so produced in the country, in a few places, to all appearances "successfully"; but has not otherwise yet affronted publicity. I mention it, however, for the fact, that when it was about to be put into rehearsal it seemed absolutely to require something a little better than a cheap curtain raiser to be played in front of it; with any resources for which preliminary the F.R.'s seemed, however, singularly unprovided. The matter seemed to be important, and though I was extremely pressed with other work I asked myself whether I, even I, mightn't by a lively prompt effort put together such a minor item for the bill as would serve to help people to wait for the major. But I had distractingly little time or freedom of mind, and a happy and unidiotic motive for a one-act piece isn't easy to come by (as you will know better than I) offhand. Therefore said I to myself there might easily turn up among all the short tales I had published (the list being long) something or other naturally and obligingly convertible to my purpose. That would economise immensely my small labour—and in fine I pounced on just such a treatable idea in a thing of many years before, an obscure pot-boiler, "Owen Wingrave" by name—and very much what you have seen by nature. It was treatable, I thought, and moreover I was in possession of it; also it would be very difficult and take great ingenuity and expertness—which gave the case a reason the more. To be brief then I with consummate art lifted the scattered and expensive Owen Wingrave into the compact and economic little Saloon—very adroitly (yes!) but, as the case had to be, breathlessly too; and all to the upshot of finding that, in the first place, my friends above-mentioned could make neither head nor tail of it; and in the second place that my three-act play, on further exploitation, was going to last too long to allow anything else of importance. So I put *The Saloon* back into a drawer; but so, likewise, I shortly afterwards fished it out again and showed it to Granville-Barker,[3] who was kind about it and apparently curious of it, and in consequence of whose attention a member of the S[tage] S[ociety] saw it. That is the only witchcraft I have used!—by which I mean that that was the head and front of my undertaking to "preach" anything to anyone—in the guise of the little Act—on any subject whatever. So much for the modest origin of the thing—which, since you have read the piece, I can't help wanting to put on record.

But, if you press me, I quite allow that this all shifts my guilt only a little further back and that your question applies just as much, in the first place, to the short story perpetrated years ago, and in the re-perpetration more recently, in another specious form and in the greater (the very great alas) "maturity of my powers." And it doesn't really matter at all, since I am ready serenely to answer you. I do such things because I happen to be a man of imagination and taste, extremely interested in life, and because the imagination, thus, from the moment direction and motive play upon it from all sides, absolutely enjoys and insists on and incurably leads a life of its own, for which just this vivacity itself is its warrant. You surely haven't done all your own so interesting work without learning what it is for the imagination to *play* with an idea—an idea about life—under a happy obsession, for all it is worth. Half the beautiful things that the benefactors of the human species have produced would surely be wiped out if you don't allow this adventurous and speculative imagination its rights. You simplify too much, by the same token, when you limit the field of interest to what you call the scientific—your employment of which term in such a connection even greatly, I confess, confounds and bewilders me. In the one sense in which *The Saloon could* be scientific—that is by being done with all the knowledge and intelligence relevant to its motive, I really think it quite supremely so. That is the only sense in which a work of art can be scientific—though in that sense, I admit, it may be so to the point of becoming an everlasting blessing to man. And if you waylay me here, as I infer you would be disposed to, on the ground that we "don't want works of art," ah then, my dear Bernard Shaw, I think I take such issue with you that—if we didn't both *like* to talk—there would be scarce use in our talking at all. I think, frankly, even, that we scarce want anything else at all. They are capable of saying more things to man about himself than any other "works" whatever are capable of doing—and it's only by thus saying as much to him as possible, by saying, as nearly as we can, all there is, and in as many ways and on as many sides, and with a vividness of presentation that "art," and art alone, is an adequate mistress of, that we enable him to pick and choose and compare and know, enable him to arrive at any sort of synthesis that isn't, through all its superficialities and vacancies, a base and illusive humbug. On which statement I must rest my sense that all *direct* "encouragement"—the thing you enjoin on me—encouragement of the short-cut and say "artless" order, is really more likely than not to be shallow and misleading, and to make him turn on you with a vengeance for offering him some scheme that takes account but of a tenth of his attributes. In fact I view with suspicion the "encouraging" *representational* work, altogether, and think even the question not [an] *a priori* one at all; that is save under this peril of too superficial a view of what it is we have to be encouraged or discouraged *about*. The artist helps us to know this,—if he have a due intelligence—better than anyone going, because he undertakes to represent the world to us; so that, certainly, if *a posteriori*, we can on the whole feel encouraged, so much the better for us all round. But I can imagine no scanter source of exhilaration than to find the brute undertake that presentation without the most consummate "art" he can muster!

But I am really too long-winded—especially for a man who for the last few days (though with a brightening prospect) has been breathing with difficulty. It comes from my enjoying so the chance to talk with you—so much too rare; but that I hope we may be able before too long again to renew. I am comparatively little in London, but I have my moments there. Therefore I look forward—! And I assure you I have been touched and charmed by the generous abundance of your letter. Believe me yours most truly,

Henry James

1. Shaw wrote to explain why the Incorporated Stage Society rejected HJ's one-act ghost-play *The Saloon*. In his letter Shaw said that as a socialist he could not accept HJ's having his young pacifist hero murdered by the ghost; he urged HJ to rewrite the play to have the hero kill the ghost instead.
2. HJ reverts here from *The Saloon* to "Covering End," which became *The High Bid.*
3. Harley Granville-Barker (1877–1946), stage director and dramatist.

To Bernard Shaw
Dictated Ts Harvard

Lamb House, Rye
23rd January 1909

My dear Bernard Shaw.

This is but a word to say No, I am not "evading,"[1] the least little scrap; though alas you will think I am when I say that I am still worried with work and correspondence put into sad arrears by my lately having been unwell and inapt. I am only conscious, I think, that I don't very well even *understand* your contention about the "story" of *The Saloon*—inasmuch as it seems to me a quarrel with my subject itself, and that I inveterately hold any quarrel with the subject of an achievable or achieved thing the most futile and profitless of demonstrations. Criticism begins, surely, with one's seeing and judging what the work has made of it—to which end there is nothing we *can* do but accept it. I grant of course that we may dislike it enough neither to criticise it nor to want to—only that is another matter! With which, too, I seem not to understand, further, what you mean by the greater representational interest of the "man's getting the better of the ghost," than of the "ghost's getting the better of the man"; for it wasn't in those "getting the better" terms on one side or the other that I saw my situation at all. There was only one question to me, that is, that of my hero's within my narrow compass, and on the lines of my very difficult scheme of compression and concentration, getting the *best of everything*, simply; which his death makes him do by, in the first place, purging the house of the beastly legend, and in the second place by his creating for us, spectators and admirers, such an intensity of impression and emotion about him as must promote his romantic glory and edifying example for ever. I don't know what you could have more. He wins the victory—that is he clears the air, and he pays with his life. The whole point of the little piece is that he, while protesting against the tradition of his "race," proceeds and pays exactly like the soldier that he declares he'll never be. If I didn't shrink from using the language of violence I would say that I defy you to make a man in a play (that shall not be either a comedy or an irony, that is a satire, or something like) proceed consistently, and go all lengths, as a soldier, and do his job, and *not* pay with his life,—not do so without exciting the execration of the spectator. My young man "slangs the ghost" in order to start him up and give him a piece of his mind; quite on the idea that there may be danger in it for him—which I would again defy you to *interest* any audience by any disallowance of. Danger there must be therefore, and I had but one way to prove dramatically, strikingly, touchingly, that in the case before us there *had* been; which was to exhibit the peril incurred. It's exhibited by the young man's lying there gracefully dead—there could be absolutely no other exhibition of it scenically; and I emphasise "gracefully"! Really, really we would have howled at a *surviving* Owen Wingrave, who would have embodied for us a failure—and an ineptitude. But enough—I think it is, really; and I don't and won't use the language of violence. You look at the little piece, I hold, with a luxurious perversity; but my worst vengeance shall be to impose on you as soon as possible the knowledge of a much longer and more insistent one, which I may even put you in peril of rather liking. But till then I am yours most truly

Henry James

1. In reply to HJ's letter of 20 January, Shaw wrote on 21 January that James was evading the issue and that victory in *The Saloon* could be given to either side.

To William James
Ms Harvard

The Athenaeum
Pall Mall. S.W.
February 26*th* 1909

Dearest William.

Two things have happened since I last wrote (to Alice): first the arrival of your excellent letter of February 13th (after your receipt of my first about my "heart"); second my visit yesterday to the good, the most satisfactory Dr. James Mackenzie[1] (17 Bentinck St. W.) who examined me minutely and exhaustively an hour (by strange machineries and processes), and who is extraordinarily encouraging and reassuring—not to say exhilarating. (If he had only been there for *you* to go to at your bad time instead of the infernal Thorne,[2] I reckon you might have been spared much woe.) He at any rate finds so little the matter with me that it's rather difficult to say what he does find. Absolutely nothing grave or ominous at any rate— irregular action of the heart, but "of the common or garden sort, such as *everyone* has after sixty and such as he himself has had for fifteen years." He finds that it *has* been brought on by prolonged abandonment of exercise and by too great increase of fat—by which I mean that my undue and uncomfortable *sensations* had. He holds strongly that Fletcherism had nothing to do with the matter—he *enjoins* upon me strongly to continue it, to practise it just as I *have* been doing (thank the powers!) He has the highest opinion of its virtue and has practised complete mastication and insalivation himself and disseminated it systematically (without knowing especially about Fletcher) for a long time past. The only thing he definitely enjoins on me is to exercise—i.e. to walk since that's my only form—*superabundantly and up to the limit of exhaustion,* and to reduce my "figure." He is the absolute reverse of an alarmist and thinks the tendency to flurry and worry over so-called bad heart-conditions greatly overdone. When I asked him if [he] thought I should go to Nauheim he replied with immediate emphasis: "Most certainly not!—unless for a holiday or for recreation." He is in no hurry whatever to send people to Nauheim and told me of two men who had lately (within the year past) come to him, one who had been "ordered" to N., but after having been two weeks in bed first, and to whom he had said: "Go neither to bed nor to Nauheim, but go to *Norway* instead, and knock about there," and who had accordingly done it with the greatest profit. The other was an American—rich—travelling with his physician and on his way to Nauheim stopped to see him and whom he—after examining him—persuaded to make a *tour* of three or four months—instead, and who came back to him at the end perfectly well! So if I do go there with you and Alice it will probably be *all* for the pleasure of your society. I am feeling constantly and extraordinarily better and much appreciating the opportunities that London gives one for large and frequent circulation—and the more up-cheering Mackenzie gave me has of itself greatly contributed further to fortify me and straighten me out. (He is a plain, elderly, homely Scot, but full of kindly sense, humour, attention and interest and he inspired me with absolute confidence in his knowledge and wisdom.) It was above all a benediction to have him confirm just what *I* had found out—that is apprehended—about the cause and the remedy of and for my condition; and to have him further assure me that Fletcherizing *hasn't* the connection my too short tests were appearing to indicate; for already the benefit, digestive, symptoms attendant for me on not doing it had begun to loom dark—and in fact it's so impossible *continuously* to give it up that I see I was really draining myself as to its being accountable—and that for my recovery resumed motion and altered *quantity* of feeding are alone accountable. But this is all for tonight—I am sleepy and nod over my paper. I will write better another day.—The week's performances— all afternoons—of the small comedy came to an end today, and the F.R.'s go forth on their spring tour with their insufferable "vulgar" play.[3] But he tells me they have had very good audiences—much the best of *any* of the set of plays given in the same "Afternoon" conditions at the same theatre; and I feel as if the thing had done definite good to my "reputation" and position. Also it's hung up, but not abandoned, and it will remain and revive. On the other hand, alas, I shall have made almost no money by it—since the sum "down" on account of royalties paid me before the Edinburgh production a year ago. The few performances will scarcely have done more than wipe that out, but I can't tell for a day or two. What I mainly yearn for is to go further and do more—as soon as I'm free of near waiting jobs that the Edition has left me muddled up with. Ever your

Henry

1. Sir James Mackenzie (1853–1925), eminent heart specialist, recorded this consul-

tation after HJ's death without naming the novelist. He published it as Case 97 in his book *Angina Pectoris* (1923) but gave away HJ's identity by alluding to a ghost story written by his patient in which two children are haunted and one dies in the arms of the narrator: an allusion to "The Turn of the Screw." Mackenzie asked his 66-year-old patient to describe how he created terror, and the author replied that he sought to make his reader's imagination "run riot and depict all sorts of horrors." Mackenzie replied, "It is the same with you, it is the mystery that is making you ill. You think you have got angina pectoris and you are very frightened lest you should die suddenly." He then proceeded to reassure HJ as described in this letter.

2. Beasley Thorne, another heart specialist, had treated William James.

3. Forbes-Robertson, having produced an enormous success, "The Passing of the Third Floor Back" by Jerome K. Jerome, had given only a limited series of matinees of HJ's *The High Bid*.

To Edith Wharton
Ms Yale

Lamb House, Rye
April 19*th* 1909

My dear Edith!

I thank you very kindly for your so humane and so interesting letter, even if I must thank you a little briefly—having but this afternoon got out of bed, to which the Doctor three days ago consigned me—for a menace of jaundice, which appears however to have been, thank heaven, averted! (I once had it, and *basta così*); so that I am a little shaky and infirm. You give me a sense of endless things that I yearn to know more of, and I clutch hard the hope that you will indeed come to England in June. I *have* had—to be frank—a bad and worried and depressed and inconvenient winter—with the serpent-trail of what seemed at the time—the time you kindly offered me a princely hospitality—a tolerably ominous cardiac crisis—as to which I have since, however, got considerable information and reassurance—from the man in London most completely master of the subject—that is of the whole mystery of heart-troubles. I am definitely better of that condition of December-January, and really believe I shall be better yet; only that particular brush of the dark wing leaves one never quite the same—and I have not, I confess (with amelioration, even), been lately very famous (which I shouldn't mention, none the less, were it not that I really believe myself, for definite reasons, and intelligent ones, on the way to a much more complete emergence—both from the above-mentioned and from other worries). So much mainly to explain to you my singularly unsympathetic silence during a period of anxiety and discomfort on your own part which I all the while feared to be not small—but which I now see, with all affectionate participation, to have been extreme. Poor dear Teddy, poor dear Teddy—so little made, by all the other indications, as one feels, for such assaults and such struggles! I hope with all my heart his respite will be long, however, and yours, with it, of such a nature as to ease you off.[1] Sit loose and live in the day—don't borrow trouble, and remember that nothing happens as we forecast it—but always with interesting and, as it were, refreshing differences. "Tired" you must be, even you, indeed, and Paris, as I look at it from here, figures to me a great blur of intense white light in which, attached to the hub of a revolving wheel, you are all whirled round by the finest silver strings. "Mazes of heat and sound" envelop you to my wincing vision—given over as I am to a craven worship (*only* henceforth) of peace at any price. This dusky village, all deadening grey and damp (muffling) green, meets more and more my supreme appreciation of stillness—and here, in June, you must come and find me—to let me emphasize that—appreciation!—still further. You'll rest with me here then, but don't wait for that to rest somehow—somewhere *en attendant.* I am afraid you won't rest much in a retreat on the Place de la Concorde. However, so does a poor old croaking barnyard fowl advise a golden eagle!—You are a thousand times right to allude on a note of interrogation to Morton's article[2]—and no note is sharp enough to pierce, I fully see, the apparent obscurity of my behaviour. All will be well, but there is a special explanation—reason *for*—my having, lash myself as I would, been inevitably paralysed (that is embarrassed—up to now—fairly to anguish) over it. But that explanation I shall immediately, I shall in a day or two, make to him, if you will meanwhile lay me, all grovelling and groaning, at his feet. Kindly assure him of my absolutely consistent affection and fidelity and ask him to have a very small further—a scrap of divine—patience with me. I plead—I plead; also I bleed (with—attenuated—shame). Everything shall still be right and I am, dearest Edith, all constantly and tenderly yours

Henry James

1. Mrs. Wharton's husband was in increasingly disturbed mental health.

2. Fullerton's fulsome article on the importance of the New York Edition, published in the April issue of the *Quarterly Review,* called HJ the Homer of the international novel.

To Hugh Walpole
Ms Texas

Lamb House, Rye
April 27th 1909

My dear, dear Hugh.

Not in many vain words, yet without dull (or vainer) delay do I assure you of my exceeding great pleasure in your delightful, your admirable and beautiful letter. Your confidence and trust and affection are infinitely touching and precious to me, and I all responsibly accept them and give you all my own in return. Yes, all "responsibly," my dear boy—large as the question of "living up" to our splendid terms can't but appear to loom to me. Living up to them—for *me*—takes the form of wanting to be more sovereignly and sublimely—and ah so tenderly withal!—good for you and helpful to you than words can well say. This is, in vulgar phrase, a large order, but I'm not afraid of it—and in short it's inspiring to think how magnificently we shall pull together, all round and in every way. See therefore how we're at one, and believe in the comfort I take in you. It goes very deep—deep, deep, deep; so infinitely do you touch and move me, dear Hugh. So for the moment enough said—even though so much less said than felt. It won't be long, no—before we shall meet again; I *don't* come up on Saturday, but I do as early as possible next week—and my days go, and I suppose yours do. Hold me in your heart, even as I hold you in my arms—though verily I think no gallant youth less of a Baby. Say "*Très*-cher Maître," or "my very dear Master" (for the present),[1] and believe how faithfully I am yours always and ever

Henry James

1. HJ's affectionate letter is in reply to one from Walpole thanking him for his first visit to Lamb House and expressing admiration and loyal friendship—and also asking how to address him. In his diary Walpole called HJ "by far the greatest man I have ever met."

To Edith Wharton
Ms Yale

Lamb House, Rye
May 9*th* 1909

Dearest Edith!

Your letter gives me extraordinary pleasure—for my poor efforts don't meet with universal favour. Two American "high-class (heaven save the mark!) periodicals" declined poor John Berridge and the Princess[1]—which was a good deal *comme qui dirait* declining *you;* since *bien assurement* the whole thing *reeks* with you—and with Cook, and with *our* Paris (Cook's and yours and mine): so no wonder it's "really good." It would never have been written without you—and without "her." At any rate, as I seem to be living on into evil days, your exquisite hand of reassurance and comfort scatters celestial balm—and makes me *de nouveau* believe a little in myself, which is what I infinitely need and yearn for. While I *do* the Velvet Gloves I quite succeed in believing—but at all subsequent stages, when they are done, everything seems to address itself to dispelling the fond illusions (one amiable friend—"lady-friend"—said to me of the V.G. just after its appearance: "I *can't* say I think it's up to your usual mark!"); so that, in short, dearest Edith, you are a direct agent of the Most High for keeping alive in me the vital spark. You've blown upon it so charmingly today that it's quite a brave little flame again. Add to that that I've just lately begun to believe again that I shall "recover my breath to some extent"—and that the day here is most exquisite—divine and windless for a change—and you may feel that you've done a good stroke of work. But oh how I want your news, the real, the *intime*—how I want it, how I want it! I have been intending a movement on London for some days—but many things have conspired to delay it: however I do, I believe, absolutely go up for a while on the 12th, though with such country-*douceur* breaking out all about us here I ask myself how I can think of Pall Mall. If I think too much ill I shall retreat again. At any rate I go down to Howard from Saturday to Monday next. *Comme vous nous manquerez*—but how we shall jaw about you! I shall then perhaps hear a little when you are "due"—if the influences contribute as I infinitely supplicate the gods to make them. I mean by this if they will only leave poor dear

521

Teddy a little in peace.—I wrote a few days ago to Morton and shall very soon be writing him again—will you kindly mention to him on the first occasion, with my love? *En voilà un* a little of whose news—real and intimate—I should also like! But the things, the things, the things—i.e. the details—I yearn for—! Never mind; I believe I *shall* see you a bit effectively. And meanwhile I am ever so gratefully and tenderly and revivingly yours

Henry James

1. HJ's tale about Edith Wharton's Paris, "The Velvet Glove," had appeared in the *English Review* in March 1909. In the story John Berridge, a successful playwright, meets a beautiful American-born "princess," Amy Evans, and soon realizes that she is simply seeking a preface from him for one of her melodramatic novels. The story contains the account of a long motor ride through Paris in the Princess's car; hence HJ's allusions to Cook, Mrs. Wharton's chauffeur.

To Arthur Christopher Benson
Ms Bodleian

Queen's Acre
Windsor
June 5th 1909

My dear Arthur.

Howard S[turgis] has given me so kind a message from you that it is like the famous coals of fire on my erring head—renewing my rueful sense of having suffered these last days to prolong the too graceless silence that I have, in your direction, been constantly intending and constantly failing to break. It isn't only that I owe you a letter, but that I have exceedingly wanted to write it—ever since I began (too many weeks ago) to feel the value of the gift that you lately made me in the form of the acquaintance of delightful and interesting young Hugh Walpole. He has been down to see me in the country, and I have had renewed opportunities of him in town—the result of which is that, touched as I am with his beautiful candour of appreciation of my "feeble efforts," etc., I feel for him the tenderest sympathy and an absolute affection. I am in general almost—or very [often]—sorry for the intensely young, intensely confident and intensely ingenuous and generous—but I somehow don't pity *him*, for I think he has some gift to conciliate the Fates. I feel him at any rate an admirable young friend, of the

522

openest mind and most attaching nature, and anything I can ever do to help or enlighten, to guard or guide or comfort him, I shall do with particular satisfaction, and with a lively sense of being indebted to you for the interesting occasion of it. Of these last circumstances please be very sure.

I go to Cambridge next Friday, for almost the first time in my life—to see a party of three friends[1] whom I am in the singular position of never having seen in my life (I shall be for two or three days with Charles Sayle, 8 Trumpington Street), and I confess to a hope of finding you there (if so be it you *can* by chance be); though if you flee before the turmoil of the days in question, when everything, I am told, is at concert pitch, I won't insist that I shan't have understood it. If you are at any rate at Magdalene I should like very much to knock at your door, and see you face to face for half-an-hour; if that may be possible. And I won't conceal from you that I should like to see your College and your abode and your *genre de vie*—even though your countenance most of all. If you are not, in a manner, well, as Howard hints to me, I shan't (perhaps I *can't!*) make you any worse—and I may make you a little better. Meditate on that, and do, in the connection, what you can for me. Boldly, at any rate, shall I knock; and if you are absent I shall yearn over the sight of your ancient walls.

I am spending a dark, cold, dripping Sunday here—with two or three other *amis de la maison*; but above all with the ghosts, somehow, of a promiscuous past brushing me as with troubled wings, and the echoes of the ancient years seeming to murmur to me: "Don't you wish you were still young—or young again—even as *they* so wonderfully are?" (my fellow-visitors and inexhaustibly soft-hearted host). I don't know that I particularly do wish it—but the melancholy voices (I mean the *inaudible* ones of the loquacious saloon) have thus driven me to a rather cold room (my own) of refuge, to invoke thus scratchily *your* fine friendly attention and to reassure you of the constant sympathy and fidelity of yours, my dear Arthur, all gratefully,

Henry James

---

1. These were Charles Sayle, a librarian; A. Theodore Bartholomew, an assistant librarian; and Geoffrey Keynes, then at Pembroke College. They had sent a card to HJ inviting him to visit them at Cambridge. An account of his weekend there is given in Geoffrey Keynes, *Henry James at Cambridge* (1967), which contains the entire correspondence relating to the visit.

To Charles Sayle
Ts Keynes

Reform Club
Pall Mall, S.W.
June 16*th* 1909

My dear Charles Sayle,

I want to send you back a grateful—and graceful—greeting—and to let you all know that the more I think over your charming hospitality and friendly labour and (so to speak) loyal service, the more I feel touched and convinced. My three days with you will become for me a very precious little treasure of memory—they are in fact already taking their place, in that character, in a beautiful little innermost niche, where they glow in a golden and rose-coloured light. I have come back to sterner things; you did nothing but beguile and waylay—making me loll, not only figuratively, but literally (so unforgettably—all that wondrous Monday morning), on perfect surfaces exactly adapted to my figure. For their share in these generous yet so subtle arts please convey again my thanks to all concerned—and in particular to the gentle Geoffrey and the admirable Theodore, with a definite stretch toward the insidious Rupert—[1] with whose name I take this liberty because I don't know whether one loves one's love with a (surname terminal) *e* or not. Please take it from me, all, that I shall live but to testify to you further, and in some more effective way than this—my desire for which is as a long rich vista that can only be compared to that adorable great perspective of St. John's Gallery as we saw it on Saturday afternoon. Peace then be with you—I hope it came promptly after the last strain and stress and all the rude porterage (*so* appreciated!) to which I subjected you. I'll fetch and carry, in some fashion or other, for *you* yet, and am ever so faithfully yours,

Henry James

P.S. Just a momentary drop to meaner things—to say that I appear to have left in my room a *sleeping-suit* (blue and white pyjamas—jacket and trousers), which, in the hurry of my departure and my eagerness to rejoin you a little in the garden before tearing myself away, I probably left folded away under my pillows. If your brave Housekeeper (who evaded my look about for her at the last) will very kindly make of them such a little packet as may safely

reach me here by parcels' post she will greatly oblige yours again
(and hers),

H.J.

1. HJ had been taken punting at Cambridge by Rupert Brooke (1887–1915) and been
smitten by Brooke's physical beauty—hence "insidious."

To Howard Sturgis
Ms Harvard

Lamb House, Rye
July 11th 1909

Dearest Howard.

It was almost as beautiful of you to write me on the occasion of
Percy's admirable and exquisite article[1]—which I have written to
thank him for and express my emotion (not half-copiously enough)
in presence of as it was for that gentlest of our friends himself to
build (and as with a wave of his so very fine young wand) the
shapely monument. It is a very superior and a charmingly distinguished thing, the lovely paper, and I intensely and gratefully
and almost tearfully appreciate it. If he is with you at this moment,
dear creature, please repeat to him that I have assured you thus of
the high and rare pleasure he has given me—from which I can't help
feeling that appreciable benefits and glories will flow to both of
us.—As for our aquiline Edith, *elle plâne,* for the hour, just over this
province—and the matutinal telegram from her, supplementary to
the nocturnal (of last evening) leads me to hope for her *séjour* with
me for at least tomorrow to Tuesday. I daresay it is written in the
book of fate that I shall even motor with her to Folkestone and wait
upon her departure there. But these things are in the lap of the
goddess herself. The iridescent track of her Devastation—the phos-
phorescent lights of her wake—suffer, I suppose, at Qu'acre, gradual
extinction, and I can only hope your rest-cure flourishes and that
the dose is proportionate to the disorder! So much only, dearest
Howard, for this crowded hour. I have a friend staying with me—a
simple scene enough after your Cave of the Winds of friendship, but
the burden, again, is to be measured by the beast! The sense of your
splendid gallantry for the past month or two abides with me, and
on that sense my affection for you feeds and "battens." I must

renew our contact before too long again; my spirit has acquired, as it were, the fatal habit of you. Also of the firm, free William[2]—to whom I beg you kindly to commend me. Yours dearest Howard, all constantly

Henry James

1. Percy Lubbock (1879–1965) had begun to win a reputation as a young man of letters and an authority on Pepys. He had just published a study of Mrs. Browning. His anonymous article, a survey of HJ's achievement in the light of the New York Edition, appeared in the *Times Literary Supplement*, 8 July 1909.

2. Sturgis's companion William Haynes Smith, affectionately called "the Babe."

To Howard Sturgis
Ms Harvard

Lamb House, Rye
July 16*th* 1909

My dearest Howard!

I find your excellent note here after many days—days spent at the tip of the tail of our *so* high-flying Kite,[1] and of which I have a couple of times flashed you a dim telegraphic hint. The crisis began on Monday evening last—with her ineluctable descent and her unappeasable summons (even as those of the grim jailers of the Conciergerie to the appointees of the scaffold), and the sequel terminated by that 5 o'clock yesterday, when I separated from her at Canterbury, she to go on to Folkestone and the Métropole (with the doubtless weather-frustrated plan of crossing to Boulogne today), and I to sneak back here more dead than alive. We did in the interval—four full days—the whole country of Sussex in detail and from stem to stern—and, *vu* the weather!—she *may* be back this evening! It was almost worth it all, however, to be beguiled and regaled by your beautiful and wonderful letter about the *oiseau de feu*[2] and the majestic Baddingtonia, which is really a comic masterpiece and which the Fire-Bird was convulsed by and infinitely charmed with, but not, I make bold to say, to her faintest amendment or amelioration. Her amusement at any cost and in any quantity that suits her she *will* have, let who will pay (vitally, conveniently and temporally speaking) the piper. So she set the piper piping hard—and I danced till my aged legs would no more—and

526

(the worst is) it was all beautiful and interesting and damnable. (The country and the weather—for an interlude—so exquisite and delightful, I mean.) But I come back to a mountain of arrears—of which a ton of letters has to be dealt with first. I renew my affection to you, dearest Howard, and am ever yours (and William's, and even, a little, Mary's) devotissimo

Henry James

P.S. Percy's article[3] is having a *succès-fou* among my friends—and deeply deserves it.

1. Mrs. Wharton.
2. HJ had seen the Diaghilev ballets, then the rage of London, and now began to call Mrs. Wharton the "Firebird," after Stravinsky's *Oiseau de Feu*.
3. See letter to Sturgis, 11 July 1909.

To Edith Wharton
Ms Yale

Lamb House, Rye
July 26th 1909

Dearest Edith.

I could really cry with joy for it!—for what your note received this noon tells me: so affectionate an interest I take in that gentleman. How admirable a counsellor you have been, and what a *détente*, what a blest and beneficent one, poor tortured and tethered W.M.F. must feel! It makes me, I think, as happy as it does you. And I hope the consequence will be an overflow of all sorts of practical good for him—it *must* be. Of course, I shall breathe, nor write, no shadow of a word of what I have been hearing from you to him—but if he should in time—and when he *has* time (he can't have now), the pleasure I shall take in expressing my sentiments to him will be extreme.[1]

Your telegram arrived in time to keep me from writing Macmillan otherwise than in the sense it expressed; but I have now written him in *this* sense: that I am aware of matters in Morton's situation that make me think a sum of money will be highly convenient to him, I named them a little, and that if M. write to propose an advance I shall like greatly to send them, the Macmillans, a cheque for £100 that they may remit him the amount of as from themselves, I remaining, and wishing to remain, wholly unmentioned in the affairs. But send me no cheque, please, not only till I have let you know what reply I have had from Macmillan, but till Morton tells you he *has* made the request.

I hope the sum he has to pay to the accursed woman isn't really a very considerable one, or on which the interest for him to pay will be anything like *as* burdensome as what he has been doing. And 53 rue de Varenne?—But you will tell me of that at your leisure. I'm delighted you're to have Miss Bahlmann[2] with you. Paul Harvey[3] comes to me here for the night and I think will be able to give me some news of Walter B[erry]. I am greatly touched by your so gentil little *envoi* of the étude of the Praslin story. I haven't immediate time to master it, but have sampled it a little, and have known it more or less before. I remember Mrs. Deluzy Field in the U.S., and her coming one day to see my mother when I was there—a very expressive and demonstrative white-puffed person, impressing *les miens* as a Frenchwoman of the most insinuating and dazzling manners. She was a méridionale Protestant (of origin), I think—and that worked badly for her relations with the Duchess etc. But how when we were *tout-jeunes* in Paris the closed and blighted and *dead* closed *hôtel* P[raslin] used to be pointed out to us as we walked in the Rue St. Honoré![4]

Ever and always yours
Henry James

1. Morton Fullerton was still threatened by the blackmail he had first mentioned to HJ in 1907 (see letter to Fullerton, 14 November 1907). The ensuing letters show how Mrs. Wharton and HJ solved his problem for him.

2. Anna Bahlmann, Mrs. Wharton's childhood governess, who served as Mrs. Wharton's secretary after 1904.

3. See letter to Berry, 12 December 1908.

4. Mrs. Wharton had sent HJ an account of the celebrated murder in which the Duc de Choiseul, Charles Laure Hugues Theobald Praslin (1805–1847), stabbed his Duchess, Altarice Rosalba Fanny Sebastiani, to death. Mrs. Deluzy Field was the former Henriette Deluzy-Desportes, a governess in the Duke's household, who created the friction between the ducal pair that ultimately resulted in the Duke's using three knives to dispose of the Duchess. The crime occurred in 1847, and the James family, in Paris in 1855, still heard echoes of it. HJ remembers the Hotel Praslin, winter home of the family, in the rue du Faubourg St. Honoré. The Duke committed suicide after the crime; Mlle Deluzy was arrested as an accessory but was released. She married an American, the Reverend Henry M. Field, and became renowned in New York as hostess and conversationalist. Mrs. Wharton toyed with the idea of using the story in a novel; a descendant of Mlle Deluzy, Rachel Lyman Field, wrote a successful novel based on this family history, *All This and Heaven Too* (1938).

To Frederick Macmillan
Ms British Library

Lamb House, Rye
July 26*th* 1909

My dear Macmillan.

I am greatly interested in the fact that my accomplished and greatly valued friend of many years Morton Fullerton, is to do a book on Paris for you—which fact has after reflection made me think of *this* and decide to write to you. I know something—a good deal, of his personal and family situation, and especially of the financially depleting effect on him, lately aggravated, of the condition of his father, ill and helpless these many years in the U.S., and to whom he has had constantly to render assistance. It strikes me as not unlikely that he may have to write and ask you for some advance on the money he is to receive from you, for getting more clear and free for work at his book—and I should like to send you a cheque for £100, say, that he may profit by to that end, *without his knowing it comes from me.* Would you be willing to send it to him, as a favour to me, *as* from yourselves (independently of anything you may yourselves send him?) and with no mention whatever, naturally, of my name in the matter? I ask you this frankly as the only way I can see to give him the advantage of the money, which I believe would be a great convenience to him—for I am far from sure of his not sending it (the £100) back to me were I to propose it to him straight. Pardon this slightly complicated proposition—I shall feel it a great service if you are able to act on it—and believe me yours always

Henry James

To Edith Wharton
Ms Yale

Lamb House, Rye
August 3*d* 1909

Dearest Edith.

Deeply interesting your letter this A.M. received, and in nothing more so than in its wonderful and beautiful account of the change wrought in Morton by recent events, and which it verily enchants me to hear from you. It brings home to me with a force under which one fairly winces as for pain, the degree of the pressure of the incubus under which he had so long been living—and which one knew and infinitely pitied him for, with the sense that the normal and possible expanding and living man was lost in it, lost to himself and lost to *us*. Now that we have got him—and it's *you* absolutely, who have so admirably and definitely pulled him out—we must keep him and surround him and help him to make up for all the dismal waste of power—waste of it in merely struggling against his (to put it mildly) inconvenience. You speak of his having "recovered the possessions etc." of his own that she had in detention; but will you (at your leisure—when you write) mention whether she has surrendered the papers, letters, scraps of writing containing references to people etc. which he mentioned to me, originally, that as they were private things all, she threatened to make God knows what injurious and public use of? Those, I imagine, were what is most essential to his tranquillity that he *should* get back. But I indeed infer from what you say that his recovered tranquillity means precisely that he *has* got them. They are—they *must* be—*le plus clair* of the real finishing of the affair.

As for your proposition of lending him the sum you mention, through me (if he can't manage to arrange it otherwise), I can only accede to the beautiful, the noble beneficence of this on your part, with an extreme appreciation of all that it represents—and even though it puts *me*, poor impecunious and helpless me, in the ridiculous nominal position of a lender of *de facto sommes!* That, however, is *la moindre des choses;* so please consider that I will play my mechanical part in your magnificent combination with absolute piety, fidelity and punctuality—if it should *come* to the combination. That he should *let* you do it will seem to me in that case almost as beautiful as that you should do it; and of the beneficence of it, in converting a stricken and comparatively sterilized life into a life worthy of his admirable intelligence and capacity, I can't speak in terms adequate—or without emotion. Therefore I regard it as *all* worthy of three children of light and of honour. You will let me in time, if necessary, hear more about it.—Kindly meanwhile say to Morton that I did receive his Boulogne letter and am still belatedly replying to it. I want to write him *now*—ever so discreetly and *generally*, but ever so attachedly. My delay was inevitable at the time—through my immediately hearing from you of the tension of the situation in Paris that at once set in, and that made everything (nominally) outside malapropos for the moment.—You rejoice me further by what you tell me of Walter B[erry] and of his of course coming on from you to England. I shall have a letter waiting for him by the 15th—and I have *de plus* my little vision. You will probably motor him to Boulogne—after which why shouldn't you let him ferry *you* over? With which you would both come *here* to me for two or three days—and I would (at your convenience) go back with you—to Folkestone (and all this evening Walter is straining the leash to rush to the arms of Lady G.) You will tell me about this—*j'y compte.* It's horribly cold and damp here now—Novemberish altogether, but the other scale must come up—or go down; and we shall have good times yet. Poor dear worried Teddy—I think of him ever so kindly. But it's a normal anxiety—and so far almost a good one. All and always yours

Henry James

To Frederick Macmillan
Ms British Library

Lamb House, Rye
August 3*d* 1909

My dear Macmillan.

Pardon my having had to delay a day or two thanking you for your letter about Morton Fullerton, the Paris book etc. Let me definitely say then that I will with pleasure become surety for such a sum in case of your advancing him, on the Book, and at his request, the Hundred Pounds I wrote you of—in addition to the one I understand you already to have offered him. Should the book, in that case, not in due time be forthcoming, in other words, you are to call on me for the Hundred Pounds additionally supplied (advanced) and I will immediately respond to your call. But I greatly *believe* in the book.

Please say to Mrs. Macmillan that I should like nothing better than coming to pay you a little visit at Cromer—but that this month is unfavourable to me, always, through the frequency of small visitations of others to me here; which always leaves me much pressed with occupations between times. Will you kindly leave the question open to September, when I think I shall have a cleared field, and when I shall greatly enjoy proposing myself for a couple of days if I can grasp the right ones—and that shall suit you as well. Such a happy chance will have all the charm for me of a voyage of discovery—and a first acquaintance with your so eminent part of the world. And I risk and face with confidence the limits of your establishment. With kindest regards yours, my dear Macmillan, ever

Henry James

To John Galsworthy
Ms Unknown

[Lamb House, August 1909]

I answer your appeal on the censor question[1] to the best of my small ability. I *do* consider that the situation made by the Englishman of letters ambitious of writing for the stage has less dignity—thanks to the Censor's arbitrary rights upon his work—than that of any other man of letters in Europe, and that this fact may well be, or rather *must* be, deterrent to men of any intellectual independence and self-respect. I think this circumstance represents accordingly an impoverishment of our theatre; that it tends to deprive it of intellectual life, of the *importance* to which a free choice of subjects and illustration directly ministers, and to confine it to the trivial and the puerile. It is difficult to express the depth of dismay and disgust with which an author of books in this country finds it impressed upon him, in passing into the province of the theatre with the view of labouring there, that he has to reckon anxiously with an obscure and irresponsible Mr. So-and-So who may by law peremptorily demand of him that he shall make his work square, at vital points, with Mr. So-and-So's personal and, intellectually and critically, speaking, wholly unauthoritative preferences prejudices and ignorances, and that the less original, the less important and the less interesting it is, and the more vulgar and superficial and futile, the more it is likely so to square. He thus encounters an arrogation of critical authority and the critical veto, with the power to enforce its decisions, that is without a parallel in any other civilised country and which has in this one the effect of relegating the theatre to the position of a mean minor art, and of condemning it to ignoble dependences, poverties and pusillanimities. We rub our eyes, we writers accustomed to freedom in all other walks, to think that this cause has still to be argued in England.

[Henry James]

1. A Joint Select Committee of Lords and Commons held an inquiry in 1909 into the question of licensing of plays in England. From the early eighteenth century control of the stage was exercised by the Lord Chamberlain. The committee recommended that he should continue to license plays, but that it should be optional to submit a play for license and legal to perform an unlicensed play. However, no legislative action followed the report of this committee. On 12 August 1909 John Galsworthy read, as part of the testimony given by authors and dramatists during the hearings, HJ's letter of protest. The letter is reproduced in the committee's report of 1909, published by His Majesty's Stationery Office. The Lord Chamberlain continued to be responsible for the licensing of plays until 1968.

To Violet Hunt
Ms Barrett

Lamb House, Rye
November 2*d* 1909

Dear Violet Hunt.

I should be writing to you tonight to say that it would give me great pleasure to see you on Saturday next had I not received by the same post which brought me your letter one from Ford Madox Hueffer which your mention of the fact that you have known of his writing enables me thus to allude to as depriving, by its contents, our projected occasion of indispensable elements of frankness and pleasantness. I deeply regret and deplore the lamentable position in which I gather you have put yourself in respect to divorce proceedings about to be taken by Mrs. Hueffer;[1] it affects me as painfully unedifying, and that compels me to regard all agreeable and unembarrassed communication between us as impossible. I can neither suffer you to come down to hear me utter those homely truths, nor pretend at such a time to free and natural discourse of other things, on a basis of avoidance of what must now be most to the front in your own consciousness and what in a very unwelcome fashion disconcerts mine. Otherwise, "Es wäre so schön gewesen!" But I think you will understand on a moment's further reflection that I can't write you otherwise than I do, and that I am very sorry indeed to have so to do it. Believe me then in very imperfect sympathy

Yours
Henry James

1. Violet Hunt's affair with Ford Madox Hueffer had been of long duration, but this had not troubled HJ, who had on previous occasions received her at Lamb House with both amusement and his customary fastidiousness. He called her his "Purple Patch." Her diaries record that she "drifted about" Lamb House in a "white Chinese dressing gown," and that HJ "wants my news but never more than half of it, always getting bored or delicate." His forbidding her his house at this juncture stemmed in part from the reasons he gave, but also from the fact that Hueffer's wife was about to sue for "restoration of conjugal rights," and that HJ wanted to avoid any possibility of being mentioned in the attendant publicity.

To Violet Hunt
Ms Barrett

Lamb House, Rye
5 November 1909

Dear Violet Hunt.

I am obliged to you for your letter of Wednesday last, but, with all due consideration for it, I do not see, I am bound to tell you, that it at all invalidates my previous basis of expression to you on my receipt of F. M. Hueffer's letter. It appeared from that that the person best qualified to measure the danger feared your name might be made to figure in divorce proceedings instituted by his wife—I really don't see how an old friend of yours could feel or pronounce your being in a position to permit of this anything but "lamentable," lamentable—oh lamentable! What sort of a friend is it that would say less? I wasn't for a moment pretending to characterize the nature of the relations that may conduce to that possibility—relations, on your part, I mean, with the man to be divorced, which in themselves are none of my business at all. But your *position*, as a result of those relations—if I had it to speak of again I am afraid I could only speak of it so. That is not the point, however; the ground of my writing to you as I did was another matter, as to which your letter again makes me feel how right I was. I could see you, after so hearing from Mr. Hueffer only on a basis of impossibly avoiding or of still more impossibly hearing of his or his wife's private affairs, of which I wish to hear nothing whatever; and you immediately illustrate this by saying "as you know" they have been separated for years. I neither knew, nor know, anything whatever of the matter; and it was exactly because I didn't wish to that I found conversing with you at all to be in prospect impossible. That was the light in which I didn't—your term in March!—forbid you my house; but deprecated the idea of what would otherwise have been so interesting and welcome a *tête à tête* with you. I am very sorry to have had to lose it, and am yours in this regret,

Henry James

To Ford Madox Hueffer
Dictated Ts Harvard

Lamb House, Rye
November 8 *th* 1909

Dear Ford Hueffer.

Very pressing occupation has prevented till this moment my writing you these few words in reply to your last letter—though there really is nothing for me of importance to write. The nearest approach to that is my thus saying that I haven't for a moment pretended to judge, qualify or deal with any act or conduct of V.H.'s in the connection, as a matter of fact to which you called my notice; that whole quantity being none of my business and destined to remain so. What I wrote to her that I deplored and lamented was the situation in which, whatever it had or hadn't been, her general relation with you had landed or were going to land her—the situation of her being exposed to figure in public proceedings. I don't see how any old friend of hers can be indifferent to that misfortune. But these things, surely are your own affair together, and I wish for you very heartily that your complications may work out for you into some eventual "peace with honour."

Yours ever,
Henry James

To Hugh Walpole
Ms Texas

Lamb House, Rye
December 9th [10th] 1909

Dearest Hugh.

I respond with no end of tenderness to your beautifully-inspired little letter—I hold out my hand on the spot to clutch all affectionately your own generously-presented paw. I came back only this evening from the ten—the twelve—days to which my stay in town inordinately, though not unprofitably stretched itself—very mainly, at the last, through an urgent appeal on the part of Lady Lovelace[1]—made far back at Ockham—that I should wait over long enough to give her yesterday P.M.—with John Buchan again—over the unspeakable Byron papers. I obliged her in this at much cost to my convenience, but that—interesting—chapter is now completely closed, thank goodness—for I can do no more. Helen Lascelles graced the board at Wentworth House, and the name of H.W. graced of course—at every turn—my affable conversation with her. I wish to the devil you had come round on Tuesday afternoon to the box, at the Afternoon Theatre, to which I had accompanied my old (and so agreeable) friend Elizabeth Robins; we could well have made a place for you, and you would have profited by our enlightened and ingenious discourse. (She was the creatrix of *Hedda G.* fifteen years ago in England, and that Russian performance[2] affected us as a pale and ineffectual, and above all a completely un-Ibsenite thing.) I was for an hour and a half, at the Haymarket, in Mme. Maeterlinck's box,[3] last evening (after Byron dinner and Helen L.)—and wondered if you weren't there—but didn't discern you in the great dim swarm. It's hideous and unnatural our being, anywhere, near and not close; therefore come *at* me, for God's sake, wherever and whenever your younger eyes make out the possibility of your fond old friend, dearest Hugh, always and ever

Henry James

1. HJ had seen the Byron papers during Lord Lovelace's lifetime; see letter to Lovelace, 14 January 1906. HJ recorded in his pocket diary on 9 December 1909: "went to tea, Lady Lovelace and John Buchan." Buchan recorded in *Memory Hold-the-Door* (1940), 151–152: "an aunt of my wife's, who was the widow of Byron's grandson, asked Henry James and myself to examine her archives in order to reach some conclusion on the merits of the quarrel between Byron and his wife. She thought that those particular

papers might be destroyed by some successor and she wanted a statement of their contents deposited in the British Museum. So, during a summer week-end, Henry James and I waded through masses of ancient indecency, and duly wrote an opinion. The things nearly made me sick, but my colleague never turned a hair. His only words for some special vileness were 'singular'—'most curious'—'nauseating, perhaps, but how quite inexpressibly significant.' " The text of the HJ-Buchan opinion was signed by Buchan on 4 April 1910 and by HJ on 7 April. It is reproduced in Janet Adam Smith's *John Buchan: A Biography* (1965). The statement seems mainly to have been intended to confirm Lord Lovelace's version of the relationship between Byron and his half-sister, Augusta Leigh, as against that of R. Edgcumbe, whose *Byron: The Last Phase* had just been published.

Lord Lovelace had been unable to use the evidence contained in Byron's intimate letters to Lady Melbourne, although he had taken copies of them. These letters, written during the three years preceding Byron's marriage, were the ones read by James and Buchan. The two novelists concurred in calling Edgcumbe's theory (that Byron had a liaison in the summer of 1813 with his early love Mrs. Chaworth-Musters) "a house of cards." They concluded that Byron wrote of Mrs. Chaworth-Musters "with perfect respect and indifference; at this very time he was answering Lady Melbourne's remonstrances and expressing contrition as to that connection of which he himself said that it had an element of the *terrible* which made all other loves seem insipid."

2. Lydia Yavorska, Princess Bariatinsky (d. 1921), a Russian actress who had recently come to London, played Hedda Gabler in the revival of Ibsen's play.

3. Maurice Maeterlinck (1862–1949), the symbolist and allegorical dramatist who wrote *Pelléas and Mélisande* (made memorable by the music of Debussy), *The Blue Bird,* and other successful plays. Years later he recalled this meeting and spoke of HJ's "pure French, purer than any spoken by a Frenchman." Maeterlinck received the Nobel Prize for literature in 1911, the year HJ was a candidate.

To Edith Wharton
Ms Yale

Lamb House, Rye
December 13*th* 1909

Dearest Edith,

I'm horribly in arrears with you and it hideously looks as if I hadn't deeply revelled and rioted in your beautiful German letter in particular—which thrilled me to the core. You are indeed my ideal of the dashing woman, and you never dashed more felicitously or fruitfully, for my imagination, than when you dashed, at that particular psychologic moment, off to dear old rococo Munich of the Initials[1] (of my tender youth), and again of my far-away 30th year. (I've never been there *depuis.*) Vivid and charming and sympathetic *au possible* your image and echo of it all; only making me gnash my

537

teeth that I wasn't with you, or that at least I can't ply you, face to face, with more questions even than your letter delightfully anticipates. It came to me during a fortnight spent in London—and all letters that reach me there, when I'm merely on the branch, succeed in getting themselves treasured up for better attention after I'm back here. But the real difficulty in meeting your gorgeous revelations as they deserve is that of breaking out in sympathy and curiosity at points enough—and leaping with you breathless from Schiller to Tiepolo—through all the Gothicry of Augsburg, Würzburg, *und so weiter.* I want the rest, none the less—*all* the rest, after Augsburg and the Weinhandlung, and above all how it looks to you from Paris (if not Paradise) regained again—in respect to which gaping contrast I am immensely interested in your superlative commendation of the ensemble and well-doneness of the second play at Munich (though it is at *Kabale und Liebe* that I ache and groan to the core for not having been with you).[2] It is curious how a strange deep-buried Teutonism in one (without detriment to the tropical forest of surface, and half-way-down, Latinism) stirs again at moments under stray Germanic *souffles* and makes one so far from sorry to be akin to the race of Goethe and Heine and Dürer and *their* kinship. At any rate I rejoice that you had your plunge—which (the whole pride and pomp of which) makes me sit here with the feeling of a mere aged British pauper in a workhouse. However, of course I shan't get real thrilling and throbbing items and illustrations till I have them from your lips: to which remote and precarious possibility I must resign myself.

Blanche has been here (in London—he lunched with me) yes—and was very genial and intelligent and gentil; though impressing me more than ever with his genius for pushing his fortune par toutes les voies (we surely aren't *in* it with the French there!) but I fear I didn't do anything else very amusing in town except have a turn of gout again, in bed and in my unhappier foot; and see the Russian actress, Princess Bariatinsky,[3] in private and in public (very expert and artful, but not very interesting or rare); and attend the première of *L'Oiseau Bleu* at the Haymarket in Madame Maeterlinck's box—and sup with her (and him and a few others!) afterwards. I vulgarly liked Georgette,[4] and found the accommodating Maurice shy and sympathetic—being accommodating myself; though I didn't probe either of them to disgraceful depths. And now I am back here for—I

With Prince and Princess Bariatinsky at Lamb House.

hope—many weeks to come; having a morbid taste for some, even most—though not all—of the midwinter conditions of this place. Turkeys and mince pies are being accumulated for Christmas, as well as calendars, penwipers and formidable lists of persons to whom tips will be owing; a fine old Yuletide observance in general, quoi! A lonely stranded friend who is *mal* with his wife (she having retired overseas), and who rather bores me, comes to spend the three or four days with me;[5] and my amanuensis Miss Theodora Bosanquet, with a pal or second-self of hers (a lady-pal) has been secured for dinner. I can't say fairer than that, foul as it will doubtless all appear to you in the lurid light of your meilleur monde. While I was in London I had a yearning cry from Howard, whom I haven't seen for months, and arranged to go out to him for tea and dinner; but on the eve came a telegram putting me off by reason of such bad news that he couldn't see me. The bad news proved to be that his nephew Dick Seymour had been operated for appendicitis at Berlin and that his state caused some anxiety; but he is now rapidly recovering, and I didn't therefore get to Howard, who wrote me afterwards that he "couldn't at that time have received even the Angel Gabriel"; but that also, fortunately, the Babe had been a "perfect tower of strength and support"! I felt that with the towering Babe my visit might have been possible, but *enfin il n'y a que lui*, poor dear victim of consanguinity, for being so prostrated by the inevitable accidents of a numerous, too numerous, circle. That Walter B. is with you again, after *quelle odyssée* I know by a couple of charming signals, from him—this A.M. received, and which I shall immediately acknowledge. I sit and wonder at such heroic oscillations. *Il parait qu'on y survit pourtant.* I hope Teddy feels firm on his feet and that the long *épreuve* of the Crillon draws to an end. I think twenty times a week of W.M.F[ullerton], and wish it could make some decent difference to him. But good night—*tanti saluti affetuosi.* Ever your

H.J.

1. A favorite novel of HJ's childhood, *The Initials*, by the Baroness Tautphoeus (Jemima Montgomery), describing life in Germany.
2. Schiller's classical play (1784) dealing with corruption in the petty courts of Germany.
3. The Princess Bariatinsky's acquaintance with HJ is mentioned in Ezra Pound's *Canto* LXXIX:

> . . . her holding dear H.J.
> (Mr. James, Henry) literally by the button-hole . . .
> in those so consecrated surroundings
> (a garden in the Temple, no less)
> and saying, *for once*, the right thing
> namely: "Cher maître"
> to his checqued waistcoat, the Princess Bariatinsky,
> as the fish-tails said to Odysseus, ἐνί Τροίῃ . . .

4. Maeterlinck was then married to the actress Georgette Leblanc.
5. The journalist Baily Saunders.

To Mrs. J. T. Fields
Ms Huntington

Lamb House, Rye
January 2*nd* 1910

Dear Mrs. Fields.

How long I have been in answering your good note on the subject of dear Sara Jewett's letters, and how much ashamed I am! But there have been reasons, and my delay rather inevitable! I was making a long stay in London when your inquiry came, and I wanted to make *sure* before replying that my fear of having kept nothing from her hand was a justified fear: which I could do only by waiting till I could get back here—where my papers and possessions abide. So I waited, and when I came home found that I have preserved nothing—(I never had *many* letters from her at all) even as I supposed was the case. And that depressed and abashed me, in respect of writing to tell you so—and then came the pressure of rather urgent and overwhelming Christmas postal matter (a very formidable business by the good old British tradition); so that from these sad deterrents or delays my hand has been considerably stayed. Well, such now is the rather sad and sorry little case—that I find our admirable friend's occasional communications have submitted to the law that I have made tolerably absolute these last years and as I myself grow older and think more of my latter end: the law of not leaving personal and private documents at the mercy of any accidents, or even of my executors! I kept almost all letters for years—till my receptacles would no longer hold them; then I made a gigantic bonfire and have been easier in mind since—save as to a certain residuum which *had* to survive. You see that of Sara Jewett's, even beloved as one felt her, there were very few—and those ante-dating her accident and her illness; when I never expected to survive her and wish to deal with her memory. *After* those troubles I scarcely heard from her at all—or only in two or three painful and pathetic fragments, as it were, which it was pure sadness to keep. I wish I could help you more. I will with the greatest joy in any *other* way—if any memorial of her is in course of taking shape to which I might contribute a few pages. So the case has shaped itself. I wish you strength and cheer to do anything and everything to which you may put your wise and tender hand, and am, dear Mrs. Fields, your all-faithful old friend

Henry James

P.S. I would for instance with pleasure address you a letter, as Editor—a "letter" of reminiscence and appreciation and making twenty-five pages of print or so, which would serve, if you cared, as Introduction to your Volume: a thing very frank, familiar, *as* a thorough Friend, etc.; and oh so tender and so *admiring*—as I *do* admire her work!

To James B. Pinker
Dictated Ts Yale

Lamb House, Rye
3*rd* January 1910

My dear Pinker.

I have been for some little time in correspondence with J. M. Barrie and Granville Barker—very auspicious correspondence, I am happy to say—over the preparations on their side for the three act Comedy I have been doing for Frohman[1] (for whom, as I told you, they are acting) and which, he being as yet absent in America, they have had for two or three weeks past in their hands. Barker writes me under date of January 1st that the "business arrangement" about it should be proceeded with, and that he will inform the "business people" to that effect; and I have replied to him that you will act for me if they will communicate with you—which is what I suppose they will presently do. I am a little sorry not to be able to see you before this question is taken up; though I don't imagine it will present any great difficulty when once we establish the principal fact. This principal fact is that the play was asked of me, and that I have done it, for Repertory use by Frohman, and for Repertory use only; the limitation involved in that (by which I mean the act-ability of the thing for two or three nights in the week, with perhaps a matinee, only) being made up for, so far *as* made up, by one's freedom to contract for it with other Repertories, and with as many as one will or can. This represents of course much less actu-ally than it does potentially; but even actually there *are* other Repertory Theatres: at Glasgow, at Manchester, at New York! At any rate such is the basis on which I was originally approached; as I dare say it's the basis on which my stuff will prove most practicable. May such enlightened institutions therefore multiply! I suppose, at any rate, that we may ask for a "sum down"—and I suppose, in short, if I may say so without indiscretion, that any such arrangement as you made for J. Galsworthy's *Strife* would serve rather as a precedent as to what you can do for *The Outcry*. Barrie and Barker have immediately begun to cast the latter for me, speculatively; further definiteness on this score only awaiting their receipt a couple of days hence of some ultimate compressions of my Act Third; though Barker writes me that he considers the manuscript already delivered. It will be at any rate by Wednesday—and, confidentially speaking, it appears that they regard John Hare and Gerald Du Maurier as "vital" to my two principal men; to whom Barrie has just added the proposal of Dennis Eadie for a third.[2] Barker has meanwhile asked me for the part of my younger woman, or technical "heroine," on behalf of his wife, Miss Lillah McCarthy; to which I with a base diplomatic prudence have cheerfully assented—though she isn't my dream. But I have no one definitely better to propose, and as he, G.B., is to "produce" the play, the presence of his wife in it will (at least I hope) add strength to his elbow. What considerably pleases me is that Hare, having apparently some general understanding with Frohman about his coming in (after rather a prolonged absence from the stage) on the contingency of some part that shall appeal to him, Barker, directly he had read my play (I mean directly Barker had read it) pronounced him absolutely indispensable to the most important character. Hare himself is yet to read the play—but Barker and Barrie seem to have no doubts, and this means—it all means—a question of pretty early rehearsals and early production. All of which abysmal things will interest you.

So will another matter—that of my having had an appeal from Duneka[3] just before Christmas on the question of a serial for Harper's. I have replied to him that I will with pleasure do them one, at my earliest possibility, on an American subject, if what I call a "short one," namely 100,000 words will suit them; and, giving him some limited particulars of the subject, I have proposed a thing in positively and definitely Eight Numbers of 12000 words each. I have no reason to doubt, from the manner of his letter, that they will not assent to this; and I want, and need, to produce such an article really soon, soon enough, and definitely see my way to do it. Therefore if I hear from him again in the sense I expect I will let you know, so that you may arrange.

January 4*th*[4]

I wrote (or dictated) the above yesterday, but meant to add a postscript before sending it off—and publish it in the one piece that Putnam[5] will so injuriously cut; so wouldn't it be possible to make an immediate receipt of the money from Putnam a condition *sine qua non*—they returning you the story if they won't now pay for it? I wish much this might be so. I remember no such recovery of payment difficulty since the time of Ortmanns and *Cosmopolis*.[6] Believe me yours ever

Henry James

P.S. And *please*, if they do pay, insist with Putnam on their sending me *proofs*.

P.P.S. But I will write you again about the Duneka time-question.

1. Charles Frohman (1860–1915), the American producer, was planning a repertory season at the Duke of York's Theatre which would feature plays by Galsworthy, Shaw, Barrie, Granville Barker, and Henry James. HJ had just completed *The Outcry*, a three-act comedy, for Frohman.

2. John Hare was a veteran London actor-manager; Gerald Du Maurier, the highly successful actor son of HJ's old friend George Du Maurier; and Dennis Eadie, a younger actor-manager who had recently played in Granville Barker's social drama *Waste*.

3. F. A. Duneka, an editor at Harper's. HJ seems to have intended to give him *The Ivory Tower*, which he had begun to sketch in his notes.

4. The rest of the letter is in HJ's hand.

5. HJ shifts here from the play to the serialization of his long tale "The Bench of Desolation," which was appearing in *Putnam's Magazine*, and of which the final section was due in the current month.

6. F. Ortmanns edited an international journal called *Cosmopolis*. During its brief life it published two stories by HJ, "The Figure in the Carpet" (January–February 1896) and "John Delavoy" (January–February 1898).

To Edith Wharton
Ms Yale

Lamb House, Rye
February 2, 1910

Dearest, dearest Edith!

My progress is but very gradual[1] and I am as yet but a poor incommoded thing; though sitting up awhile today for the third successive time (day). However *eppur' si muove!* This is a most baffled scrawl to tell you how *divine* I hold your two letters (the one of yesterday, and the previous message through Morton's heroic medium); but that really I am not absolutely and positively not—in need. I am on a very decent and easy financial basis, with a *margin* of no mean breadth, a most convenient balance at my bank, and a whole year quite provided for even if I should do no work at all. You see I have my modest "independent" income (my share of our—my father's patrimony)[2] *and* this house; which constitutes here a real *aisance!* Moreover it so happens that I have definite arrangements for this year (on the basis of production) which will represent—from the moment I get to work again—a bigger budget than I have *ever* been in for. And slowly, but sensibly, I *am* coming round. I am sitting up today for the third time; four to five hours yesterday—six today—and feel within, with slow but sure distinctness, that the worst is well over. *Absit omen!*—I shall be at work again by—as before—the 1st of next month; and *never* has the fire of genius burned more luridly or impatiently within me. So, I *supplicate* you, don't have these lurid fears and soothe your angelic spirit to rest and confidence. Your general conditions have been as a nightmare to me—a real impediment to recovery; but the beginnings of the latter have come with the appearance that your worst is over. Tragic munificent Paris—always the Heroine, always *en scène*— not to say *en Seine!* And now for God's sake do let me know what has been decided about Teddy and about your going over. This latter image is too deplorable, and I hope and pray it is to be the other way, without knowing, however, how, in so bad a business, you yourself see it. What dire complications—and you knocking off "sellers" in the midst of them. You are prodigious and magnificent and that I am more and more your devoted old

Henry James

1. "Went to bed very ill," HJ wrote in his pocket diary on 22 January 1910. The Rye doctor, Ernest Skinner, found nothing organically wrong, but HJ was unable to take food and generally seemed in a state of depression, with some palpitations and shortness of breath. Skinner installed a nurse in Lamb House, and Mrs. Wharton promptly wrote offering financial help if needed.

2. This was the inheritance of Syracuse real estate that HJ shared with his brother. It had yielded him in the 1890s about $100 a month. Recently Henry James III had reorganized the property, and with higher rents HJ's share had increased to $250 a month.

To William James
Ms Harvard

Lamb House
February 8th 1910

Dearest William and Alice and All!

I intend to cable to you cheeringly tomorrow, but meanwhile it is high time this should go off to you by the next American post (which is tomorrow), and I am preparing it as you see by this rude medium which is for the moment easier to me than still a bit shaky ink-slinging.[1] I have waited till I could write you *firmly* and emphatically that I am on my way to real valour, or at least validity, again—and that has had to come little by little. But I am very steadily and smoothly getting the last dismal six weeks well behind me—and such is the manner in which I was hoping to go on before speaking of them at all. I mean my wish was all to be able to delay speaking of them at all till I could refer to them absolutely in the past tense. Well, that is indeed what is now quite conveniently and cheeringly happening. Skinner, who has been excellent and devoted, told me a few days since that his having had your cable and answered it very reassuringly and also written you—which is why I have put off these signals of my own for a lapse of days numerous enough to be more cheering than reassuring still. I am getting well again without a break or a flaw and am already quite lustily and ably convalescent. The blest Skinner took me out for the third time, this A.M., in his motor-car for an hour and a half—his wide round of the country side, and I sat at farmhouse and cottage and other doors while he made his calls—to my immense refreshment and sustainment. The weather is still and always of the meanest—yet everything in the way of outer air works straight for my good, and my strength is excellently coming back. I *eat* steadily a little more and more—and with *that* the blest process of recovery works. For I have had, really, a pretty dismal and dreary time, or *had* had, till a few days since (of more confirmed improvement) from three or four days after Christmas. It has all been, frankly and briefly, the last rude remainder of the heritage of woe of too-prolonged and too-consistent Fletcherism[2]—a final and conclusive (I trust) debt of suffering to that fond excess to be paid off. I think it will *all* have been paid off this time—and I can't give you my reasons in this first rather faltering scrawl. But my diagnosis is, to myself, crystal clear—and would be in the last degree demonstrable if I could linger more. What happened was that I found myself at a given moment more and more beginning to fail of power to eat through the daily more marked increase of a strange and most persistent and depressing stomachic crisis: the condition of more and more sickishly *loathing* food. This weakened and undermined and "lowered" me, naturally, more and more—and finally scared me through rapid and extreme loss of flesh and increase of weakness and emptiness—failure of nourishment. I struggled in the wilderness, with occasional and delusive flickers of improvement (of a few hours) for many days—and with Skinner co-operating most kindly—and then eighteen days ago I collapsed and went to bed and he instantly sent in an excellent Nurse (who is still with me for a few days more); whereby the worst of the burden was lifted and the worry and anxiety soothed and the fairly dismal "lonesomeness" assuaged. I had some rather depressing discouragements for a fortnight—ten or twelve days—but no complications of any sort; nothing but a slow gradual and successful struggle to be able to want food enough to swallow it, and on that basis I have got better—and shall know how to remain so. But it has all been a queer and indescribable history— that is a "ruin" and strange consciousness in the light of my Fletcheristic and "through mouth-treatment" past. *I hadn't intermitted that jealously and intently and intensely enough after the mortal warnings of last (the later) summer and the autumn that I wrote you of—and a greater vigilance—of intermission and violation was all the while insidiously required.* Failing it, came the angry and at first most obscure crisis. But at the darkest hour in bed light broke—"more artfully and more scientifically and more grimly *dis*Fletcherise and you'll get well"; and that has been the basis on which I began visibly, sensibly, traceably, regularly to do so. I make this queer egotistic and possibly incoherent statement for the benefit of your certain curiosity and wonderment and tenderness; but I mustn't write any more now. I have been sitting up all day—that is from 10 A.M. to this 9 [P.]M.—and Nurse reminds me of bedtime. She will stay four or five days more—then I shall cease to need her at all. Skinner has been devoted, Mrs. Paddington[3] perfect, and this house equally perfect as a "nursing home." I only pray now for weather. But I will write you more and better in a very few days. Have no fear nor anxious thought for me now. I have yearned over you—but was silent from poor writing power without alarming you. I mean I feared to by my shaky scrawl or statement. And I cudgel my brain to know how you knew—enough to cable Skinner. You will tell me, oh for a letter! If my so admirable friends the Protheros are with or near you will you explain to *them*—for she has beautifully written me two or three times—I write her most *soon*. And I send you all such love! Ever your restored

Henry

1. HJ was writing in pencil, propped up in bed.
2. In the absence of other symptoms, HJ decided he had for too long "Fletcherized"—that is, followed the food fad of Horace Fletcher, who advocated chewing one's food until it was reduced to liquid. He now abandoned this practice.
3. HJ's housekeeper.

To Theodora Bosanquet
Ms Harvard

Lamb House
March 2*d* 1910

Dear Miss Bosanquet.

Alas, I have been making no "strides"—except backward, and things have been very bad with me; too bad for me to write or make any sign. In short I am still having a very difficult and uphill time, with the one mitigation that one of my Boston nephews, the eldest, has just come out from America to be with me, and is a blessed support.[1] But the end is not yet—nor do I see it in sight. I got up this A.M. from nine days again in bed. I thank you very kindly for your letter. Everything seems "hung up," blighted and indefinitely postponed. There can be no production of *The Outcry* without my personal participation at preparation and rehearsal—and till there is a possibility of that no calculating. There can even be no casting of the piece without my presence in London. So all that is dark. History is strangely written—I don't know where, or how, you heard of my stay at Wittersham![2] I have no more been able to stay at Wittersham than in Kamschatka! I hope your London and your establishment "work", through everything; and I greet Miss Bradley very kindly. But I am sorry to be able to give you no more brilliant news of your poor old blighted

Henry James

P.S. There is a plan for my somehow seeing a very high authority[3]—the highest, doubtless—next week.

1. Henry James III.
2. Where WJ's friend Joseph Thatcher Clarke and his wife lived and where HJ's niece Peggy had boarded at the turn of the century.
3. The eminent physician Sir William Osler.

To Mrs. William Darwin
Ms Harvard

Garlant's Hotel
Suffolk Street, Pall Mall
March 15 1910

Very dear Sally.[1]

Beautiful and delightful to me your letter—though I could tell you so much better than in this poor way if I had not for many weeks (since just after Christmas) been very drearily and dismally ill—so that this is really my first expenditure of *ink*, if not of effort, for this very long time. (I have been reduced to the pale and stumbling pencil—but am now trying to reform.) A fortnight ago my dear nephew Harry came out from Irving Street most mercifully, to my aid; and on Saturday last, three days ago, succeeded in bringing me up to town to see Dr. Osler[2] (who kindly came on from Oxford for the purpose yesterday), and who has already given me so cheering and reassuring and sustaining an account of myself that I already feel very much better. Harry is obliged to sail again on the 25th, but I shall probably try to stay on here—after very many solitudinous and afflicted months at Rye; that is if I am fit to go back to my quarters in Pall Mall. Meanwhile your news is full of interest and sympathy to me—and especially touched am I by your so sweet and generous tribute to the poor old *Italian Hours*.[3]—Tricked out in their abandoned ancientry, and their great out-of-printness, to make—or to seek—some sort of fresh little fortune. I delight to think that they bear at all the test of being read again in the so dangerous presence of the unutterable scenes they tried to give their rude reflection of!—You make me, you leave me a bit uneasy about Lily,[4] to whom I send my bestest old love. I'm glad, ever so glad you have been able to take a convenient draught of the bland Bordighera—of which I have only far away but tender, genial and slightly overheated memories. I earnestly pray I may see you both in London in May.—Your allusion to dear E[dith] W[harton] opens up a big subject—but one that has cleared up for me greatly this last winter. I now realise that she has adopted the only habitat (and with its consequences—many very interesting ones) that is really possible for her; that she must have a winter home, that New York is without form and void, and that the Mount will eventually go. Teddy is cerebrally and nervously bad, (I fear very bad) again; and a catastrophe is sooner or later due there. But it's a long story! Bless you both. Ever your faithful

Henry James

1. The former Sarah Sedgwick, sister of Charles Eliot Norton's first wife, long married and living in England.
2. Sir William Osler had found HJ "splendid for his age" and prescribed a period of rest and relaxation.
3. HJ's collected writings about Italy, a counterpart to his volume *English Hours,* published five years earlier.
4. See letter to Mrs. Wharton, 2 January 1908. Lily Norton had been staying at Bordighera in Italy.

To Jocelyn Persse
Ms Harvard

Lamb House, Rye
April 28*th* 1910

Dearest, dearest Jocelyn!

If I have been so long and so woefully silent it is alas that I have been continuously and drearily ill, and that the end is not yet. I had your two notes as you started for Ceylon—but absolutely couldn't then write or report of myself, and haven't been able to since, in any definite or encouraging way. My nephew came out from America and was with me, very helpfully, for three weeks or so, but had to go back. However, his parents, my brother and my sister-in-law replaced him three weeks ago, and are an unspeakable Godsend and blessing, without which I should, I think, quite have gone under. My *nervous* condition—trepidation, agitation, general dreadfulness—has been deplorable, and it is now the thing that is primarily the matter with me—producing inability to *feed* adequately—and being in turn aggravated by it. In short things have been dismally bad. Yet there *is* an amelioration—but the thing is to keep it, amid relapses and *rechutes*. Forgive my sorry tale. Don't propose to come down and see me—it wouldn't be *workable* now. Only have the patience with me that I myself am trying to have with the endless ordeal of yours all dismally and devotedly

Henry James

To Hugh Walpole
Ms Texas

Lamb House, Rye
May 13th 1910

Dearest, Dearest Hugh.

I have been utterly, but necessarily, silent—so much of the time lately quite too ill to write. Deeply your note touches me, as I needn't tell you—and I would give anything to be able to have the free use of your "visible and tangible" affection—no touch of its tangibility but would be dear and helpful to me. But, alas, I am utterly unfit for visits—with the black devils of Nervousness, direst, damnedest demons, that ride me so cruelly and that I have perpetually to reckon with. I am mustering a colossal courage to try—even tomorrow—in my blest sister-in-law's company (without whom and my brother, just now in Paris, I couldn't have struggled on at all) to get away for some days by going to see a kind friend in the country—in Epping Forest.[1] I feel it a most precarious and dangerous undertaking—but my desire and need for change of air, scene and circumstance, after so fearfully overmuch of these imprisoning objects, is so fiercely intense that I am making the push—as to save my life—at any cost. It *may* help me—even much, and the doctor intensely urges it—and if I am able, afterwards (that is if the experiment isn't disastrous), I shall try to go to 105 Pall Mall for a little instead of coming abjectly back here. Then I shall be able to see you—but all this is fearfully contingent. Meanwhile the sense of your personal tenderness to me, dearest Hugh, is far from not doing much for me. I adore it.

I "read," in a manner, "Maradick"[2]—but there's too much to say about it, and even my weakness doesn't alter me from the grim and battered old *critical* critic—no *other* such creature among all the "reviewers" do I meanwhile behold. Your book has a great sense and love of life—but seems to me very nearly as irreflectively juvenile as the Trojans, and to have the prime defect of your having gone into a subject—i.e. the marital, sexual, bedroom relations of M. and his wife—the literary man and his wife—since these *are* the key to the whole situation—which have to be tackled and faced to mean anything. You don't tackle and face them—you *can't*. Also the whole thing is a monument to the abuse of voluminous dialogue, the absence of a plan of composition, alternation, distribution, structure, and other phases of presentation than the dialogue—so that *line* (the only thing *I* value in a fiction etc.) is replaced by a vast formless featherbediness—billows in which one sinks and is lost. And yet it's all so loveable—though not so *written*. It isn't written *at all*, darling Hugh—by which I mean you have—or, truly, only in a few places, as in Maradick's dive—never got expression *tight* and in close quarters (of discrimination, of specification) with its subject. It remains loose and far. And you have never made out, recognized, nor stuck to, *the centre of your subject*. But can you forgive all this to your fondest old reaching-out-his-arms-to you

H.J.?

1. To Hill Hall, country house of Mrs. Charles Hunter, sister of the composer Ethel Smyth.
2. *Maradick at Forty*, just published, was Walpole's second novel, preceded the previous year by *The Trojan Horse*. Of HJ's criticisms Walpole's biographer, Sir Rupert Hart-Davis, wrote in *Hugh Walpole* (1952): "many young writers would have quailed before such devastating strictures, but for Hugh they were spurs to fresh endeavour." See also Leon Edel's essay on Walpole, dealing with the cumulative effect of such criticisms, in *Stuff of Sleep and Dreams* (1982).

To Hendrik C. Andersen
Ms Barrett

[Hill Hall]
May 21*st* 1910

Dearest Hendrik.

Yes, I have been miserably and interminably ill these five months—and the end is not yet. My *nervous* condition presents apparently almost insurmountable difficulties—and I know not what the end may be. Meanwhile I am down, down, down; so think of me pitifully and tenderly. My sister-in-law (my brother William's wife) is with me for the present; otherwise I should be down for good and all. But you see I can't write—in spite of your letter, and the fine, the splendid framed picture you lately sent me—(but with the legs of your hero persistently too short). I can only be yours ever so affectionately, and your mother's and Olivia's.

Henry James

To William Dean Howells
Ms Harvard

Lamb House, Rye
May 27*th* 1910

My very dear old Friend.

A letter from Tom Perry just brings me news of the straight and heavy blow[1] that has descended on you, and this is a poor sign of the intensely tender participation with which it makes me turn to you. A poor—the very poorest—sign, I say, because I have been interminably and wearily and dismally ill these five months (ever since Christmas) and although the light of amendment has at last begun to break I am limited as yet but to feeble demonstrations. I think of this laceration of your life with an infinite sense of all it will mean for you—a sense only equalled by that of which your long long years of exquisite, of heroic devotion, the most perfect thing of the kind one has ever known, will always have meant for *her*. To think of her, moreover, is, for me, to recall the far backward stretch—from our melted, our unbearable-to-remind youth—of her unbroken gentleness and graciousness, the particular sweetness of

553

touch, through all my close association with your domestic fortunes, in every phase of them, and your public fame. But one can't *speak* of these things—especially with a lame pen and a broken utterance; and you will know how little I feel you, or fail Mildred, to appeal to my insistence. May all this coming time now wind you two closer and more helpingly together. T. S. P[erry] says you come out—so I shall see you before too long: though I am *trying* to go abroad (with my sister-in-law, for a few weeks—to first join William at Bad Nauheim). I have had a black and heavy time (with your beautiful letter of the winter unanswered), but am at last gradually working through. As T.S.P. gives me the impression of your starting *soon* I think best to send this to Albemarle Street or no—rather—that doesn't seem explicit enough—so I infer *Kittery* for the moment and send it there. Yours and Mildred's, my dearest old Friend's, more and more than ever

Henry James

P.S. No—on the whole—Harpers.

1. The death of Howells's wife, Elinor Mead Howells.

To Edith Wharton
Ms Yale

Bittongs Hotel Hohenzollern
Bad Nauheim
June 10th 1910

Dearest Edith.

Your kindest note met me here on my arrival with my sister last evening. We are infinitely touched by the generous expression of it, but there had been, and could be, no question for us of Paris—formidable at best (that is in general) as a place of rapid transit. I had, to my sorrow, a baddish drop on coming back from high Epping Forest (that is "Theydon Mount") to poor little flat and stale and illness-haunted Rye—and I felt, my Dr. strongly urging, safety to be in a prompt escape by the straightest way (Calais, Brussels, Cologne, and Frankfort) to this place of thick woods, groves, springs and general *Kurort* soothingness, where my brother had been for a fortnight waiting us alone. Here I am then and having made the journey, in great heat, far better than I feared. Slowly but definitely

I *am* emerging—yet with nervous possibilities still too latent, too in ambush, for me to do anything but cling for as much longer as possible to my brother and sister. I am wholly unfit to be alone—in spite of amelioration. That (being alone) I can't even as yet think of—and yet feel that I must for many months to come have none of the complications of society. In fine, to break to you the monstrous truth, I have taken my passage with them to America by the Canadian Pacific Steamer line ("short sea") on August 12th—to spend the winter in America. I must break with everything—utterly—of the last couple of years in England—and am trying if possible to let Lamb House for the winter—also am giving up my London perch. When I come back I must have a better. There are the grim facts— but now that I have accepted them I see hope and reason in them. I feel that the completeness of the change *là-bas* will help me more than anything else can—and the amount of corners I have already turned (though my nervous spectre still again and again scares me) is a kind of earnest of the rest of the process. I cling to my companions even as a frightened cry-baby to his nurse and protector—but of all *that* it is depressing, almost degrading to speak. This place is insipid, yet soothing—very bosky and sedative and admirably arranged, *à l'allemande*—but with excessive and depressing heat just now, and a toneless air at the best. The admirable ombrages and walks and pacifying pitch of life make up, however, for much. We shall be here for two or three months [weeks] longer (I seem to *entrevoir*) and then try for something Swiss and tonic. We must be in England by August 1st.

And now I simply *fear* to challenge you on your own complications. I can *bear* tragedies so little. *Tout se rattache* so *à the* thing—the central depression. And yet I want so to know—and I think of you with infinite tenderness, participation—and such a bare and helpless devotion. Well, we must hold on tight and we shall come out again face to face—wiser than ever before (if that's any advantage!) This address, I foresee, will find me for the next fifteen days—and we might be worse *abrités*. Germany has become *comfortable.* Note that much as I yearn to you, I don't nag you with categorical (even though in Germany) questions. I affectionately greet Minnie and Beatrix—out of my numbness—and of Morton I ache always and habitually to think. Ever your unspeakablest, dearest Edith,

Henry James

To Edmund Gosse
Ms Congress

Hotel Hohenzollern
Bad Nauheim, Germany
June 13*th* 1910

My dear Gosse.

Forgive a very ill and afflicted man, amid all his difficulties, more silence than he would fain be guilty of—for speech is *supremely* difficult to him. My blest sister-in-law brought me here eight days ago to join my brother, himself very unwell and making a cure here. I can't be *alone*—it is of the last impossibility, and moreover I had been hoping much from absolute change of conditions. This benefit has not yet been realized—on the contrary—my damnable nervous state, chronic, but breaking out too in acute visitations—is a burden almost not to be borne. It has a definite physical basis—and that basis is nominally now of smaller extent—I have turned, in respect to strength, some part of the physical corner. I can *walk* a good deal, and that helps a little. But black depression—the blackness of darkness and the cruellest melancholia are my chronic enemy and curse—and it is because of that—the wanting not to *write* just blackly—that, my weakness aiding, I lapse into silence and gloom. If I report a gleam of improvement it's all on me again—and then congratulations come as in bitter mockery. My fight is hard, believe me—but, with an immense patience, I expect to come out; the very devil as the bristling dragon of such a condition of nerves is. My brother and sister are angels to me—and I have asked *him* to write you also a brief account of me; which I am sure he will do in a rosier sense than I myself feel ground for. But I leave you to his impression. Meanwhile the monstrous truth is that I go to America with them sometime in August—our date not yet fixed. I cling to them unspeakably: such is my terror of solitude, at once—and my unfitness for society. I shall try to let Lamb House for several months—the whole autumn and winter; and when I come back shall try and have some small flat or house (for the winter months, regularly, in town—no more of *them* at Rye), instead of my contracted perch in Pall Mall. Such at least are my present vague poor plans. I have thought of you much and yearningly in all the present and recent turmoil of your, and "our" history, and am, my dear

Gosse, always your and your wife's struggling and clinging though infinitely and equally afflicted and attached friend

Henry James

To Edith Wharton
Ms Yale

Lamb House, Rye
July 29th 1910

Dearest Edith.

It's intense joy to hear from you, and when I think that the last news I gave you of myself was at Nauheim (it seems to me), with the nightmare of Switzerland that followed—"Munich and the Tyrol etc.," which I believe I then hinted at to you, proved the vainest crazy dream of but a moment—I feel what the strain and stress of the sequel that awaited me really became. That dire ordeal (attempted Nach-Kurs for my poor brother at *low* Swiss altitudes, Constance, Zurich, Lucerne, Geneva, etc.) terminated however a fortnight ago—or more—and after a bad week in London we are here waiting to sail on August 12th. I am definitely much better, and on the road to be *well*; a great gain has come to me, in spite of everything, during the last ten days in particular. I say in spite of everything, for my dear brother's condition, already so bad on leaving the treacherous and disastrous Nauheim, has gone steadily on to worse—he is painfully ill, weak and down, and the anxiety of it, with our voyage in view, is a great tension to me in my still quite *struggling* upward state. But I stand and hold my ground none the less, and we have really brought him on since we left London. But the dismalness of it all—and of the sudden death, a fortnight ago, of our younger brother in the U.S. by heart-failure in his sleep[1]—a painless, peaceful, enviable end to a stormy and unhappy career—makes our common situation, all these months back and now—fairly tragic and miserable. However, I am convinced that his getting home, if it can be securely done, will do much for William—and I am myself now on a much "higher plane" than I expected a very few weeks since to be. I kind of *want*, uncannily, to go to America too—apart from several absolutely imperative reasons for it. I rejoice unspeakably in the vision of seeing you and Walter

557

[Berry] here—or even in London or at Windsor—one of these very next days. I think I should be able to get in the course of the (of next) week a couple of nights in town and could come out to a tea or lunch, or even dinner with Howard [Sturgis]—especially if *She*[2] should be with you and open her arms and wings to, and for, me. I might manage it for Tuesday or Wednesday—or for Wednesday and Thursday—especially (again) if you should motor over from Folkestone and pick me *up* here and take me. Don't fail of this. I might manage that last even if you come, as I hope and pray, Monday. But I hurry this off to the post. You tell me nothing of Teddy—but you *will*. I send my unstinted love to Walter—brazen that thus out in spite of being abjectly in his debt. But I shall address him in spite of being abjectly in his debt. But I shall address him the "Strike but hear me!" in a way to bring the house down. Come from Folkestone to tea or lunch at *any* rate. Monday, only remember, is Bank Holiday—but that doesn't matter for Her the least little bit. Ever your all-affectionate, dear Edith,

Henry James

1. Robertson James (1846–1910), HJ's youngest brother.
2. Mrs. Wharton's motorcar.

To Howard Sturgis
Ms Harvard

Lamb House, Rye
Tuesday August 2d 1910

Dearest Howard.

Our famous and invincible Firebird[1] announces herself to me as flashing down here on Friday A.M. and culling me, as she passes, to present me as a limp field-flower that evening at Qu'acre. I needn't tell you that I can only, for the occasion, be all predestined limpness, and where the devastating angel catches me up there I shall yield to my fate—and where she produces me again there (since it's to be at Qu'acre) you will yield to yours. But let me, while even in the coruscating claws, let me make you this small squirming sign—let me wish you to have it from myself too at least that I am thus to be hurled on your hospitality. I shall come with her prepared to spend the night if you will allow me—and I shall rejoice so

intensely to see you that I lose the sense of the beautiful violence
to which I—I can't say consent!—in the *douce perspective* of not
failing of you. All must be well, I seem to feel, that begins so well,
and I am with an impatience that emulates even the Firebird's own,
all yours and William's (and hers!)

Henry James

1. This letter, read alongside the preceding one to Edith Wharton, amusingly illustrates HJ's addiction to hyperbole in describing Mrs. Wharton, and suggests his lively
social duplicities. Having invited Mrs. Wharton to make a trip to Sturgis's, HJ now
pretends he is the victim of the "Angel of Devastation" who is also the "Firebird."

To Grace Norton
Ms Harvard

Chocorua, N.H.
August 26th 1910

Dearest Grace.

I am deeply touched by your tender note—and all the more that
we have need of tenderness, in a special degree, here now. We
arrived, William and Alice and I, in this strange sad rude spot, a
week ago to-night—after a most trying journey from Quebec
(though after a most beautiful, quick, in itself auspicious, voyage
too), but with William critically, mortally ill and with our anxiety
and tension now (he has rapidly got so much worse) a real anguish.
The main mark of his state is a difficulty of breathing that it's
painful and terrible to see—and he at present lies constantly, as the
only thing possible, under the influence of morphia. Alice is, and
has been for weeks (he had gone down and down so before we
sailed), of a miraculous devotion, but we have the defense well
organized, for all the remoteness and isolation that strikes me here
as almost sinister; the "local" Doctor, nine miles off, being really
very good and competent, and his son, an excellent young physician
as well, installed in the house as valuable and efficient nurse and
taker of responsibilities. The telephone and automobile make nothing *very* difficult, and last night we had up from Boston a very
intelligent and I think able heart specialist, or more or less such,
one Smith by name, for consultation and further light. He went
back this A.M. early, but with a good effect on the situation left

behind him (he holds that dear William has "a fighting chance"—though my own heart sinks down and down over it); and we are further to have today a trained woman-nurse in addition to young Doctor Shedd—so that, in this better air (though the heat has been suffocating), we are probably in more favoring (and as practicable) conditions than we should find in Irving Street. Alice is terribly exhausted and spent—but the rest she will be able to take must presently increase, and Harry, who, after meeting us at Quebec, started with a friend on a much-needed holiday in the New Brunswick woods (for shooting and fishing) was wired to yesterday to come back to us at once. So I give you, dear Grace, our dismal chronicle of suspense and pain. My own fears are of the blackest, I confess to you, and at the prospect of losing my wonderful beloved brother out of the world in which, from as far back as in dimmest childhood, I have so yearningly always counted on him, I feel nothing but the abject weakness of grief and even terror. But I forgive myself "weakness"—my emergence from the long and grim ordeal of my own peculiarly dismal and trying illness isn't yet absolutely complete enough to make me wholly firm on my feet. But *my* slowly recuperative process goes on despite all checks and shocks, while dear William's, in the full climax of his intrinsic powers and intellectual ambitions, meets this tragic, cruel arrest. However, dear Grace, I won't further wail to you in my nervous soreness and sorrow—still, in spite of so much revival, more or less under the shadow as I am of the miserable, damnable year that began for me last Christmas-tide and for which I had been spoiling for two years before. I will only wait to see you—with all the tenderness of our long, long unbroken friendship and all the host of our common initiations. I have come for a long stay—though when we shall be able to plan for a resumption of life in Irving Street is of course insoluble as yet. Then, at all events, with what eagerness your threshold will be crossed by your faithfullest old

Henry James

P.S. It's to-day blessedly cooler here—and I hope you also have the reprieve!

P.S. I open my letter of three hours since to add that William passed unconsciously away an hour ago—without apparent pain or struggle. Think of us, dear Grace—think of us!

To Thomas Sergeant Perry
Ms Colby

Chocorua, N.H.
September 2*nd* 1910

My dear old Thomas.

I sit heavily stricken and in darkness—for from far back in dim-mest childhood he had been my ideal Elder Brother, and I still, through all the years, saw in him, even as a small timorous boy yet, my protector, my backer, my authority and my pride. His ex-tinction changes the face of life for me—besides the mere missing of his inexhaustible company and personality, originality, the whole unspeakably vivid and beautiful presence of him. And his noble intellectual vitality was still but at its climax—he had two or three ardent purposes and plans. He had cast them away, however, at the end—I mean that, dreadfully suffering, he wanted only to die. Alice and I had a bitter pilgrimage with him from far off—he sank here, on his threshold; and then it went horribly fast. I cling for the present to *them*—and so try to stay here through this month. After that I shall be with them in Cambridge for several more—we shall cleave more together. I should like to come and see you for a couple of days much, but it would have to be after the 20th, or even October 1st, I think; and I fear you may not then be still in *vil-leggiatura. If* so I *will* come. You knew him—among those living now—from furthest back with me. Yours and Lilla's all faithfully,

Henry James

To H. G. Wells
Ms Bodleian

Chocorua, N.H.
September 11*th* 1910

My dear Wells.

We greatly value, my sister-in-law and I, your beautiful and tender letter[1] about my beloved Brother and our irreparable loss. Be very gratefully thanked for it, and know we are deeply moved by your admirably-expressed sense of what he *was*, so nobly and magnanimously. He did surely shed light to man, and *gave*, of his

561

own great spirit and beautiful genius, with splendid generosity. Of my personal loss—the extinction of so shining a presence in my own life, and from so far back (really from dimmest childhood) I won't pretend to speak. He had an inexhaustible authority for me, and I feel abandoned and afraid, even as a lost child. But he is a possession, of real magnitude, and I shall find myself still living upon him to the end. My life, thank God, is impregnated with him. My sister-in-law and his children are very interesting and absorbing to me, and I shall stay on here (in America I mean) for some months—so that we may hold and cling together. And I hope in the future never to be without some of them. When I return to England I shall see you promptly—and you have perhaps meanwhile an inadequate idea of the moral and aesthetic greed (enriched by criticism) with which I read you. Yours all faithfully

Henry James

1. Wells, who had known WJ, wrote: "I can imagine something of what his death must be to you. I'm filled with impotent concern for you. That all this great edifice of ripened understandings and charities and lucidities should be swept out of the world leaves me baffled and helplessly distressed." See Edel and Ray, *Henry James and H. G. Wells* (1958).

To Howard Sturgis
Ms Harvard

Hotel Belmont
New York
October 18 1910

Dearest Howard.

Yes, I have been hideously silent since the receipt of your last, your best letter of participation in what I have lately had to go through; but this is precisely because I have had to go through *much.* I brought to an end a week ago—or less—the ordeal of my staying at Chocorua, where on August 27th my beloved Brother succumbed, in dismal suffering, before our eyes, to the rapid progress of his ill[ness]—against our fond reckoning (and in some measure his own) that, getting back there, to his summer refuge of twenty-three years and that he greatly loved, he would rally, among his children, and find strength for another fight. Now I am, can only be, glad that he has ceased to *have* pitifully to fight—but these seven weeks have been, as it is, pretty well as dismal as any drawing-out of the agony would have been—for after at first surprising myself by my own capacity to bear all the pain and privation (I had always *counted* so intensely on my brother) I was overtaken by a grave relapse—from which I have, however, at the end of three or four weeks—again more or less emerged. I broke away from Chocorua and its dismal associations (mixed up with so much beauty of mountain, forest, lake and stream—the whole thing gorgeous American autumn and that golden weather which is given us here as through open floodgates), I broke away, I say, nine days ago, and have been a large part of the time since with you will easily guess whom when I tell you that the appeal to my co-operation of almost every hour was not to be resisted. I came on to New York, in other words, only a few days after the silver steam-whistle of the Devastating Angel reached my ear; and, strange to say, the being devastated (in another way, for a change, from the one in which I *had* been) has done me perceptible good. You perhaps don't know that she brought Teddy out here a month ago under stress of fresh desperation and alarm, to see their old intimate and eminent N.Y. physician, Kinnicott, who has disposed of the rather terrible issues for the time. Teddy departed two days ago for a tour round the world—nothing less, if you please; departed all tragically and in tears, as if the great Chicago express were the bloody tumbril of the scaffold. He went under the care of an admirable devoted and indeed to my sense heroic friend, Johnson Morton, whom you may have *entrevu* with them in Paris or in London. The latter has undertaken the job, for a consideration—but heaven pity him, and them both, given poor Teddy's extreme and utterly wearing disintegration of spirit, of sense, of temper, of appearance, of everything. Edith, in moral, that is nervous and intimately personal (by which I don't mean mere material) *rags*, but as sublime and unsurpassable and as *paillettée* as ever, embarked for Cherbourg this A.M. on the *Kronprinzessin Cecilia* (or whatever); which is why I have time at last (or one of the reasons why) to write to you. I have been spending a few days in this prodigious and unutterable hotel (almost as transcending all *formulae* as the great and genial Devastatrix herself), in order to be near them—and last night she and Walter Berry and Morton Fullerton dined with me here in quarters that were as those of the Gonzagas, as who should say, at Mantua. Berry sails this week for Paris (to *abide*), Morton F. has broken off his twenty years' Paris connection with the *Times* and is having a great journalistic and periodical *acceuil* here (he will gain, as to the employment of his great talent, immensely by the change); and I, after paying, from tomorrow, a short visit to a friend here, go back to Cambridge Mass. to remain till the New Year with my dear sister-in-law and my nephews and niece. We cleave intensely together, and though I have as yet no definite plan I shall remain on this side of the sea as long as may be in order not to be far from them. It's an ineffable blessing to me that they are one and all such delightful dears and that they positively treat me almost as if I too were almost something of the sort. After the New Year I shall probably come back to this fantastic place for a few weeks; for with all its monstrosity so mixed with platitude that you can hardly tell which is which, it kind of draws me, and literally seems to agree with me better than chaster or finer things. It has immensely developed and spread, skyward, earthward, hell-ward, since I was here six years ago, and the season being still even too balmy (as with almost Neopolitan heat), the beauty of the light and atmosphere that play among the purple perspectives and the more than Babylonian towers is something not to be said. But, beloved Howard, I must check my confused gabble; there looms awfully, crushingly before me such a list of unwritten letters. May the gods have lately been merciful to you. *Cambridge, Mass.* will always find your fondestly faithfullest

Henry James

P.S. I'm fond and faithful to William [Haynes Smith] and Percy [Lubbock] too.

To James B. Pinker
Ms Yale

95 Irving Street
Cambridge, Mass.
November 15*th* 1910

My dear Pinker.

I am posting you a copy of *The Saloon* with this, in response to your so interesting cable. If Miss Kingston[1] *is* moved to produce it, on perusal, I shall much rejoice, in spite of the great drawback of my sad absence from rehearsal and preparation. It's in itself a very dramatic, interesting, effective and skilfull thing (*I* hold!!)—but difficult to do full justice to. At the same time if she is really intelligent able and ambitious (*capable* and interested) it is, I think, immensely the thing for her. I leave the arrangement, if it comes to an arrangement, to your best judgment, of course—I am too much out of the way here to have gathered any impression or echo as to how her enterprise "pans out." I only, of course, don't want to part with the rights to her for a long—a really long—time. I am writing to an intelligent, and very theatrically-minded young friend of mine, Jack Pollock[2] (who is also a friend of G.K's—and I think must have told her about the play which he knows) and request that he will so far as possible represent me and act for me at rehearsals—if rehearsals there are to be!

I was rather *down* when I wrote you last, but have re-bounded and am going on well. Tiresome little relapses overtake me—but then I overtake them, and I am back at work. You shall soon have proof of it, and I am yours ever

Henry James

P.S. I must have a second copy of the play put away at L.H., but difficult to run to earth; and this is a very good one.

1. Gertrude Kingston, the actress-manager, produced *The Saloon* in due course for a brief run in London.
2. See letter to Mrs. Wharton, 13 December 1909.

To Margaret La Farge
Ms N.Y. Historical

95 Irving Street
Cambridge, Mass.
November 15 1910

My dear Margaret.[1]

I want you much to know, and I want your mother above all to know, with what intimate participation I think of you, and of her, today—the news coming in to me for which I have of late been prepared and which you all must have been sadly enough expecting. It affects me as the end of so much trouble and pain and suffering long drawn-out, that I give way with relief to the sense that peace and rest and a heavenly immunity from tormenting questions and endless labours and sharp personal ills have descended upon him. And with this, too, the memory of the old years, when I saw him so much oftener and when the interest and fascination of his wondrous intelligence and rare and distinguished personality were really a feature of my life—all that rises before me in vividness and brightness, and I think of him as one of the very small number of *truly* extraordinary men whom I've known. He was that rare thing, a *figure*—which innumerable eminent and endowed men (and particularly in this country) haven't been. And he was the intellectual or temperamental artist as no one else has ever been here. Great, on that score, in the vastly vulgar air, should be his glory, should remain his example. But I didn't mean, my dear Margaret, to write you all this.—I only wanted to show you both how little I am really absent from what momentously concerns and happens to you. I would show you better hadn't I lately been myself sadly stricken and for many months very dismally ill. I am better of *that*, but I still have relapses and have only just come to the end of a fortnight spent largely in bed. Hence these feeble lines. Don't dream of "acknowledging." I know myself, of course, what submersion through the post office can be, or still is a good deal, for us here. You will be submerged. This is a mere all but *dumb* sign to you—to give please, my tender love to your Mother, and to believe me, my dear Margaret your all-faithful, old friend

Henry James

1. Margaret La Farge's father, the painter John La Farge, had just died.

5
Terminations

1911–1916

5
Terminations

Henry James's illness of 1910 and the death of his beloved brother renewed the pattern of his depression of 1895–1900. At that time one of his remedial steps had been to withdraw from London and by this change of scene put his painful experiences behind him. Now he reversed this experience. Lamb House for his old age was too lonely. He found a flat in Carlyle Mansions, Cheyne Walk, Chelsea, a part of London filled with literary associations and his own remote memories, and here he settled into the final work of his long creative life. The writing of his autobiographies renewed his sense of the past. He dealt with his childhood in *A Small Boy and Others*, and in its sequel, *Notes of a Son and Brother*, documented his and his brother's young manhood against the background of the James family. He also began to write *The Middle Years*, which would have told much about his early London life, but only a fragment was completed. Following the pattern of his gathering-in of older work, he assembled *Notes on Novelists* (1914) and set to work on an American novel Scribner's had asked for, offering him large royalties at Edith Wharton's secret instigation (see Appendix II). This was *The Ivory Tower*, which with a fragment of an earlier novel, *The Sense of the Past*, was published incomplete after his death.

A heart condition declared itself, and James lived and worked on a reduced scale, aided by his loyal amanuensis Theodora Bosanquet. He had lived for so long in the Victorian and Edwardian worlds of a civilization that seemed to be progressing toward large human decencies that the advent of the 1914 war came as a terrible shock. A note in his pocket diary for 4 August 1914 records: "Everything blackened over and for the time blighted by the hideous Public situation. This is (Monday) the August Bank Holiday—but with horrible suspense and the worst possibilities in the air. Peggy and Aleck came down on Saturday to stay."

James still had a year and a half to live, and he summoned his old powers to describe his feelings about the collapse of the world as he had known it. His letters of this time are among the most eloquent of any he wrote. He pictured himself as dipping his pen in ink and finding it dripping blood; he described the war as a total descent into barbarism. He promptly threw himself into Belgian Relief and then began to visit wounded soldiers in London's hospitals, mainly at St. Bartholomew's. James's letters to his own servant, Burgess Noakes, who was wounded at the front, are touching reminders of his ability to state simple truths and factual detail in the humblest kind of prose. The war, said James, was "a nightmare from which there is no waking save by sleep." He became a British subject half a year before his death. King George V bestowed the Order of Merit on him in the New Year's Honors List of 1916. James was then on his deathbed, and had dictated his final notes (printed in Appendix V). He died on the last day of February 1916; Mrs. William James took his ashes back to Cambridge for burial in the James family plot in the Cambridge cemetery.

To Sydney Waterlow
Ms Private

21, East 11*th* Street, N.Y.
January 19*th* 1911

My dear Sydney.[1]

I am immensely touched and gratified by receiving from Jack P[ollock] and you, here, your most kind cable about the *Saloon*, which you must so generously have come up to town to help give a generous lift to; and all the more gratefully affected as I have a beautiful letter from you, of the other week, or month, which is still haplessly unacknowledged. I rejoice exceedingly in your good impression, and dear Jack's, of the "effect" of the black little play— as to which my sense of the possibly fatal consequences of my remoteness from all control of rehearsals, preparations, compressions etc., has made me (given the barbarous vulgarity of the theatric mind in general, when left to itself) dreadfully nervous and pessimistic in advance. The thing was a difficult and unusual sort of thing to interpret, as the fact of Miss Kingston's quite clutching at it in spite of that made me to a certain extent trust her intelligence and her courage. Time only can show whether I have been justified and meanwhile perhaps I shall hear from a friend or two as to how, in detail, the performance went, the actors (especially Owen Wingrave) acquitted themselves, and as to how in particular the climax theatrically worked. I am counting on Jack for a word of further charity on the whole matter.—I am, as you see, in New York—paying a rather elastic visit to a friend or two and finding myself, measured by the *long* price, more and more conscious of a continuous approach to a normal state of health. My progress has been slow, by reason of my continued habit of miserably dropping back for a series of days, or even of weeks; but it goes on, nevertheless, and New York seems positively favourable to it, as the *Strom der Welt*, or doing things, seeing people, moving about and circulating as much as I can, has to all appearance a definitely remedial side. There are urgent reasons none the less for my hanging on here as long as possible—so that though I have just taken my passage "home" (never have I felt so ecstatically the joy of applying that term to my beloved little corner—or even to the dense rich totality—of Britain!) I have done so for the 14th June only—in the swift Mauretania. Your brave letter, open here before me, is redolent of Rye and of every cherished association. I hope to put in a long and secure summer there (probably never again so much winter)—from the end of June! I thought of you with a fond intensity all through the Election; it brought back to me the sinister clouded week (to me personally) of the previous year, when I had "assisted" as through a glass darkly. But how I should like to talk with you about the present outlook! Out of the midst of *this* unalterable or incalculable Democracy I don't, I confess, at all ardently democratise! The U.S.A. are prodigious, interesting, appalling. Will you say very kind things for me to all who remember or miss me— beginning with Mrs. Alice? I greet Mrs. Dew[2] all affectionately. I am slowly more and more in the straight path of health. Yours, my dear Sydney, all faithfully and fondly

Henry James

P.S. Cambridge, Mass. always finds me.

1. Sydney Waterlow (1878–1944), Cambridge contemporary of Leonard Woolf and other Bloomsbury figures, had married Alice Pollock, daughter of HJ's old friends Sir Frederick and Lady Pollock. Waterlow's brother-in-law, Jack Pollock, involved in the theatre, was instrumental in having *The Saloon* produced. Waterlow, later ambassador to Greece, lived near Rye and often walked with HJ. See Leon Edel, "Henry James and Sir Sydney Waterlow: The Unpublished Diary of a British Diplomat," *Times Literary Supplement*, 8 August 1968.

2. Alice Dew-Smith, HJ's neighbor in Rye.

To Edith Wharton
Ms Yale

95 Irving Street
Cambridge, Mass.
February 9*th* 1911

Dearest Edith.

Hideous and infamous, yes, my interminable, my abjectly grace-less silence. But it always comes, in these abnormal months, from the same sorry little cause, which I have already named to you to such satiety that I really might omit any further reference to it. Somehow, none the less, I find a vague support in my consciousness of an unsurpassable abjection (as aforesaid) in naming it once more *to myself* and putting afresh on record that there's a method in what I feel might pass for my madness if *you* weren't so nobly sane. To write is perforce *to report of myself* and my condition—and nothing has happened to make that process any less an evil thing. It's hor-rible to me to report darkly and dismally—and yet I never venture three steps in the opposite direction without having the poor ef-frontery flung back in my face as an outrage on the truth. In other words, to report favourably is instantly—or at very short order—to be hurled back on the couch of anguish—so that the only thing has, for the most part, been to stay my pen rather than *not* report favourably. You'll say doubtless: "Damn you, why report *at all*—if you are so crassly superstitious? Answer civilly and prettily and punctually when a lady (and 'such a lady,' as Browning says!) gener-ously and *à deux reprises* writes to you—without 'dragging in Velasquez'[1] at all." Very well then, I'll try—though it was after all pretty well poor old Velasquez who came back three evenings since from twenty-three days in New York, and at 21 East 11th Street, of which the last six were practically spent in bed. He had had a very fairly flourishing fortnight in that kindest of houses and tenderest of cares and genialest of companies—and then repaid it all by mak-ing himself a burden and a bore. I got myself out of the way as soon as possible—by scrambling back here; and yet, all inconsequently, I think it likely I shall return there in March to perform the same evolution. In the intervals I quite take notice—but at a given mo-ment everything temporarily goes. I come up again and quite well up—as how can I not in order again to re-taste the bitter cup? But here I *am* "reporting of myself" with a vengeance—forgive me if it's too dreary. When all's said and done it will eventually—the whole case—become less so. Meanwhile, too, for my consolation, I have picked up here and there wind-borne *bribes*, of a more or less authentic savour, from your own groaning board; and my poor old imagination does me in these days no better service than by enabling me to hover, like a too-participant larbin, behind your Louis XIV chair (if it isn't, your chair, Louis Quatorze, at least your larbin takes it so). I gather you've been able to drive the spirited pen without cataclysms, and that Teddy's tremendous tour (let alone his companion's) does follow, heroically, the greater curves of the globe. I take unutterable comfort in the thought that two or three months hence you'll probably be seated on the high-piled and *done* book—in the magnificent authority of the position; even as Catherine II on the throne of the Czars. (Forgive the implications of the comparison!) Work seems far from *me* yet—though perhaps a few inches nearer. A report even reaches me to the effect that there's a possibility of your deciding on Teddy's return to come over and spend the summer at the Mount, and this is above all a word to say that in case you should do so at all betimes you will probably still see me here; as, though I have taken my passage for England, my date is only the 14th June. Therefore should you come May 1st—well, Porphyro grows faint! I yearn over this—since if you shouldn't come then (and yet should be coming at all), heaven knows when we shall meet again. There are enormous reasons for my staying here till then, and enormous ones against my staying longer.

Such, dearest Edith, is my meagre budget—forgive me if it isn't brighter and richer. I am but *just* pulling through—and I am doing *that*, but no more, and so, you see, have no wild graces or wavy tendrils left over for the image I project. I shall try to *grow* some again, little by little; but for the present am as ungarnished in every way as an aged plucked fowl before the cook has dealt with him. May the great Chef still see his way to serve me up to you some day in some better sauce! As I am, at any rate, share me generously with your I am sure not infrequent *commensaux* Walter B. and Morton F. and ask them to make the best of me (an' they love me—as I love *them*) even if you give them only the drumsticks and keep the comparatively tender, though much shrivelled, if once mighty, "pinion" for yourself! Morton is much—immensely—on my mind, but I escape from that into the golden chambers and corridors, the prospective ones at least, of his Paris book. I hope Walter, whom I embrace no less, is engaged in as noble an architecture. I saw no one of the least "real fascination" (*excusez du peu* of the conception!) in N.Y.—but the place relieved and beguiled me—so long as I was *debout*—and Mary Cadwal and Beatrix were as tenderest nursing mother and bonniest *sœur de lait* to me the whole day long. I really think I shall take—shall risk—another go of it before long again, and even snatch a "bite" of Washington (Washington pie, as we used to say), to which latter the dear H. Whites[2] have most kindly challenged me. Well, such, dearest Edith, are the short and simple annals of the poor! I hang about you, however inarticulately, *de toutes les forces de mon être* and am always your fondly faithful old

Henry James

1. HJ had been staying once again with Mrs. Wharton's sister-in-law, Mary Cadwalader Jones, who had various pet names for him, the previous and more enduring one having been Célimare.
2. See letter to Navarro, 15 June 1898.

To Hugh Walpole
Ms Texas

21, East 11*th* Street, N.Y.
April 15*th* 1911

Belovedest little Hugh!

Your dearest little convalescent letter—the Lord be praised—brings tears to my aged eyes. It is moreover no fond figure of speech, but the very stiffest stretch of veracity, that even if it hadn't come I should have absolutely been writing to you—as of late intensely and yearningly intended and again and again foully frustrated—either today or tomorrow. What a hell of a black, or rather fiery red, little time you must have been having, and what a dismal hour for my irrepressible Hugh when he found himself gloomily conveyed by cowled ministrants from Glebe Place, or wherever ("as I say"), to grey and sinister and suburbs. I take heart, however, from your evidence of the way it has clearly answered—I hug the sweet thought that if you have in the course of a fortnight got more or less

574

out of the wood the great jolly highway along which the sight of your leaps and bounds has hitherto endeared you to so many hearts (for who the devil is the dedication-wretch of "Mr. Perrin," who has—the brute!—"more understanding and sympathy than ANY ONE *you have ever* met?")[1] will already have opened to your view. I'll forgive you all—by which I mean all of that most insidious and invidious of digs—straight into my soft and aching substance—if you'll now only go softly and smoothly. Feel me, dearest boy, seated, discreetly, even on your hospital cot (my finger in Mr. Perrin—but stuck fast, so pointingly, at the so objectionable preliminary page); feel me hang over you, and hover about you, feel me lay my faithful hand on you with the tenderest, let us say frankly divinest, healing and soothing influence. By the time this reaches you your attendant dragons and gorgons, all the cowled ministrants, will doubtless have opened your door a little to profaner presences, and I feel that were I by date in London nothing would prevent my getting at you. Let me then get at you a little this way—I mean all *but* as intimately as if I were bringing you jelly or grapes or the *Strand Magazine* or even Arnold Bennett's last up to that hour. Make me another sign, I beseech you, as soon as they begin to let you loose. I hope your mother has been to see you—even if she has had to come up from Edinburgh for the fond purpose. But that may be none of my business, and I write you, you see, in almost thick darkness, relieved only by the blest shimmer of your own fair—or at least fairly quite normal—hand. I have of course your previous little letter—written from the House of Lords and telling me you were leaving Chelsea—making other inscrutable arrangements. That communication and the precious Mr. Perrin I have had it much at heart to acknowledge—while in a personal state—still, however, that represents a sad and constant leak in my powers of execution—as distinguished from my inward yearnings and dreams. I am immensely better from the condition in which I left England, but the ground I have gained only seems to tell me more and more from how very, very far away I have had, and shall still have, slowly to struggle back; witness the frequent breaks and arrests and interruptions, direfully sickening and depressing, into which I am still liable to sink up to my neck. I don't know where I find courage, but I do more or less continue to find it—and I bore you with these dark references only that you shall be easy with your poor shipwrecked and but just barely saved old friend, dearest Hugh; be easy always and ever. I rejoice with you heartily over your rich disposal of Mr. Perrin, as I understand, in these strange parts. Strange they are ineffably, and huge and incommensurable and indescribable the monstrous Public and its mighty maw. There is nothing in England like this latter—and the fodder of the gigantic beast is mixed and tossed and pitchforked on a scale that takes millions of miles square for the process. If you enter—as Mr. Perrin—into the mixture, may you indeed have brave news of it all! I congratulate you ever so gladly on Mr. Perrin—I think the book represents a very marked advance on its predecessors. I am an atrocious reader, as you know—with a mania for appreciation, or in other words for criticism, since the latter is the one sole gate to the former. To appreciate is to appropriate, and it is only by criticism that I can make a thing in which I find myself interested at all *my own.* But nobody that I have encountered for a long time seems to have any use for any such process—or, much rather, does almost every one (and exactly the more they "read") resent the application of it. All of which is more or less irrelevant, however, for my telling you that I really and very charmedly made your book very *much* my own. It has life and beauty and reality, and is more closely *done* than the others, with its immense advantage, clearly, of resting on the known and felt thing: in other words on depths, as it were, of experience. If I weren't afraid of seeming to you to avail myself foully of your supine state to batter and bruise you at my ease (as that appears to have been for you, alas, the main result of my previous perusal of your works) I should venture, just on tiptoe— holding my breath, to say that—well, I should *like* to make, seated by your pallet and with your wrist in my good grasp and my faithful finger—or thumb—on your pulse, one or two affectionately discriminative little remarks. One of these is to the effect that, still, I don't quite recognize the *centre of your subject,* that absolutely and indispensably fixed and constituted point from which one's ground must be surveyed and one's material wrought. If you say it's (that centre) in Mr. P.'s exasperated consciousness I can only reply that if it *might* be it yet isn't treated as such. And, further, that I don't quite understand why, positing the situation as also part of the experience of Mr. Traill, you yet take such pains to demonstrate that Mr. Traill was, as a vessel of experience, absolutely *nil*—

recognising, feeling, knowing, understanding, appreciating, that is absolutely nothing that happened to him. Experience—reported—if interesting, is *recorded* to us, according to some vessel (the capacity and quality of such) that contains it, and I don't make out Mr. Traill's capacity at all. And I note this—*shall* you feel, hideously?—because the subject, your subject, *with* an operative, a felt centre, would have still more harmoniously and effectively expressed itself. Admirable, clearly, the subject that you had before you; and which, when all is said, dearest, dearest Hugh, has moved you to write a book that will give a great push to your situation. So (as that recognition is so great a point), don't feel that your infatuated old friend discriminates only to destroy—destroy, that is, the attachment to him that it is his very fondest dream all perpetually and intensely to feel in you!

I have been spending some weeks in New York—which is a very extraordinary and terrific and yet amiable place, as to which my sentiment is a compound of an hourly impression of its violent impossibility and of a sneaking kindness for its pride and power (it's so clearly destined to be the great agglomeration of the world!) born of early associations and familiarities—of the ancient natal order. I return to Boston and its neighbourhood (very different affairs) presently, and my plan still holds for sailing for England on June 14th—whereby, I ought, if all goes well, to reach "town" by the 20th. I send you herewith a small photograph of a life-sized head of me lately done by my very able and promising painter-nephew. The thing is pronounced a miracle of resemblance, and is excellently painted, but has suffered much from the reduction to smallness. Try to fancy, at any rate that my grave but kind eyes are fixed on *you*, dearest Hugh, and believe me your faithfully fond old

Henry James

1. Walpole's new novel, *Mr. Perrin and Mr. Traill*, was dedicated "To Punch—because you have more understanding and sympathy than anyone I have ever met." "Punch" was Percy Anderson, the stage designer

To Josiah Royce
Ms Harvard

Nahant[1]
June 30*th* 1911

Dear Professor Royce.[2]

I snatch too hurried a moment to express to you my great appreciation of your so generous and luminous treatment of my dear Brother's work and influence in your Phi Beta address yesterday—read by me in last night's *Transcript*. It affects me as a beautiful performance of a very difficult task—that of simplifying comprehensively and richly, and being ample and interesting within such limits. Strange how with Death and recession a man of genius becomes a *figure*—a representative of two or three stateable things, or things that have to be *made* stateable—to the public at large; save for the few who knew him best and saw the whole complexity, always. But for them even with Death there hasn't been recession! You have said much, however, and said it very happily—and the More will take care of itself. I hope myself to be able to help *that*[3] a little, and am yours very truly and gratefully

Henry James

1. HJ had gone to stay with his old friend George Abbott James (no relative) on the North Shore to escape the Boston heat.
2. Josiah Royce (1855–1916) had been brought from the west coast by William James to be a professor of philosophy at Harvard.
3. HJ's plan to write a book about his brother.

To Mrs. William James
Ms Harvard

On board the Mauretania
August 6*th* (Sunday P.M.) [1911]

Dearest Alice.

We expect to reach Fishguard tomorrow, and this is not too soon, D.V., (Sunday afternoon) to tell you that all has been and continues very well. I've never made, of course, an easier or quicker passage—great runs of 565 to 585 miles a day—and my sensations and sentiments have been attuned to the wondrous process. The enormous ship has only half its complement of passengers (at this mid-season time), and that has meant a luxury of space, service and general ease and amplitude. I sat, very agreeably, for meals—by his invitation—with George Meyer,[1] Secretary of the Navy and three or four other "prominent" New York men, whose "tone" and general *allure* has been illuminating—yet not wholly uplifting to me. The breeding and culture—or cultivation and civilization—the general amenity and finish one may be a prominent New York man and yet lack! *C'est à ne pas y croire!* But I like Meyer—much as a man and almost a gentleman. (He goes out on naval inquiry matters.) *Do send this to Harry*, though I shall try to write him a word. The great bland simple deaf street-boy-faced Edison[2] is on board, and I have talked with him and he has asked very kindly and sympathetically about Peggy. I thought he had known William a little, and he said "No, but I know his charming daughter." (His wife etc. are in Europe—his young son alone with him.) Well, I think of you all with unutterable tenderness—and will show it you better when I get on a better footing. The sea is poison to me at best—well as I have done. I feel I shall be *well* ten days after we land. Burgess[3] was kept from winning the first prize in a foot-race on deck yesterday only by not having like his competitors India-rubber soles—he slipped a little on a turn. But as it was he won prize second. It has been muggily hot till today. But now the air more normal. I embrace you so fondly all. Ever your

Henry

1. George von Lengerke Meyer (1858–1918), Secretary of the Navy from 1909 to 1913 under President Taft.
2. Thomas A. Edison (1847–1931), the inventor.
3. Burgess Noakes, HJ's valet, had accompanied him to America.

To Miss Frith
Ms British Library

Lamb House, Rye
August 15*th* 1911

Dear Miss Frith.

A word but to say that I arrived in England but last week again, and that I have sent *The Soft Side* (with "The Real Right Thing" in it) to Miss Braddon[1]—at the address your good letter of the 8th gives me—inscribed with a friendly word. It is a great pleasure to me to

579

acknowledge in any way to her, my recollections of the spell cast on my younger time by the "fine old fiction" as I said, yes, of those her so highly productive years. The connection recalls to me so many of the fond impressions and associations of youth—irrecoverable, unspeakable time! I am very glad that she knew, that she learnt, something of the charm she could work on wary minds even, and I am yours and hers most truly

Henry James

1. Mary Elizabeth Braddon (1837–1915) had written thrillers since 1862, when she published her best-selling *Lady Audley's Secret*. HJ had reviewed her as early as 1865 in the *Nation* (9 November).

To Hendrik C. Andersen
Ms Barrett

Lamb House, Rye
August 16*th* 1911

Dearest Hendrik.

I haven't the least idea where this will find you in your mad career—if restored to the blest Italy and to the shady Vallombrosa so much the better; though I could have wished you all something more to the point than to have escaped from the American hell (pure and simple!) only to betake yourselves with all your absorbed and stored-up *calore* to the less refreshing and reviving side of the Alps. I have had these several—that is these four—weeks your Newport letter in my fond grasp—with the immense comfort of knowing by it that you *will*, I devoutly trust, have got off by the 26th July—and by the big smooth *Olympic*, thank God, as well; even as I escaped on August 2d by the big smooth and even swifter, I believe, *Mauretania*—from which I disembarked at Liverpool on the A.M. of the 8th (we had put ashore a hundred passengers at Fishguard on the 7th). I have therefore been at home here a week—and though even here too horrid drought and heat prevail (*what* an infernal summer!) everything is of a holy peace and calm after the American *furia*, and I am ravished just to crouch for the time in this snug little garden that you know. I *ought* to have got a word off to Newport to you before you sail—from Nahant, where I was awaiting my own date; but, dearest Hendrik, I was utterly played-out with the torments and complications of the temperature and most of the other circumstances; so that, pen, ink and paper dropping from my perspiring hand, I allowed the dreadful days to pass and promised myself to write you better from these more possible conditions. Now I can only send my letter to Rome—in the hope it may be safely passed on to you. What a distracted time you must have had in the Awful Country—and how your poor dear mother must have suffered and shrunk. It's an amazing feat you performed—and you may be all proud of yourselves and of each other for it. But do make me another sign, dearest Hendrik—just a small sign to the effect that this *has* reached you. It's a sad business, this passage of all the months and years without our meeting again save in this poor way—and I wish to heaven we could relieve it a little by finding ourselves again fondly face to face. I want so to see you—and I so hold out my arms to you. Somehow it may still come—but it seems far off. Well, may life still be workable for you, with the mighty aid of art. *Ci vuol anchea* little intimate affection too, *pure* (as they say)—che diavolo! Therefore let us manage it somehow! Good-bye at any rate for now—*per ora*. I embrace you, dearest Hendrik, ever so tenderly! I send my good love to your mother and Olivia, and I am yours all affectionately, my dear boy,

Henry James

To Walter V. R. Berry
Ms Unknown

Lamb House, Rye
September 27th 1911

My Dear Walter.

The Angel of Devastation writes me that if I will join you within a day or two in Paris you will very kindly lead me forth into Lombardy for magnificent operations—up and down the Italian Kingdom! This is a hurried word (I found her letter here but last night—coming home for the first stay since I returned from the Belmont!)[1] to say that, as no such "great time" can now be in question for me, you are not to have me on your mind for a moment as to restrict for that space your freedom of actions. I really am entirely unable to start for any such glorious frolic—I have only within these twenty-four hours got Home (and there is no place, as we know, like Home!)—and got there with the most passionate determinations to stick fast for the rest of my life. I have the most urgent necessities here. I have written our incomparable friend—as the worm may write to the eagle. That is the Eagle's only fault that she exposes one often to wormlike consciousnesses. (I like to do my worming in private and feel as if I am doing it now in the eyes of all Italy.) For you it's different; you're of aquiline race (your nose betrayeth you) your spirit is attuned to great gyrations. So go and *girare*—be bold and free and happy—and tell me later all about it. Now that both she and you have so put your affairs in ordre *là-bas* I feel that I can count on your brave beaks (for I maintain I am a toothsome worm) to come and peck at me once in a while. *Vada pure!* I do feel deprived—but not of the grand tours (I have absolutely no use for them more); only of the genial, the generous jaw. I stayed here but nine days on my return to England—I found the South Coast depressingly hot and *blafard* and rain-starved; and the postponement of settling that I then advisedly made has terminated but now. Now it must take intense effect. I've just come back from ten days in Scotland—Scotland is "good enough for me"! I charge you with no message—it would kind of have the air of an aggravation; but I bless you both and envy you well—and await your appearance here. Does that aggravate? Well, I do hold on to you *de toutes les forces* of

> Your faithful old,
> Henry James

1. See letter to Sturgis, 18 October 1910.

To Alice Runnells
Ms Harvard

Lamb House, Rye
October 4*th* 1911

My very dear Niece.[1]

I must tell you at once all the pleasure your beautiful and generous letter of the 23rd September has given me. It's a genuine joy to have from you so straight the delightful truth of the whole matter, and I can't thank you enough for talking to me with an exquisite young confidence and treating me as the fond and faithful and intensely participating old Uncle that I want to be. It makes me feel—all you say—how right I've been to be glad, and how righter still I shall be to be myself confident. How shall I tell you in return what an interest I am going to take in you—and how I want [you] to multiply for me the occasions of showing it? You see I take the greatest and tenderest interest in Bill—and you and I feel then exactly together about that. We shall do—always more or less together!—everything we can think of to help him and back him up, and we shall find nothing more interesting and more *paying*. I expect somehow or other to see a great deal of him—and of you; and count on you to bring him out to me on the very first pretext, and on him to bring you. He is splendidly serious and *entier;* it's a great thing to be as *entier* as that. And he has great ability, great possibilities, which will take, and so richly reward, all the bringing out and wooing forth and caring and looking out for that we can give them—as faith and affection can do these things; though of a certainty they would go their own way in spite of us—the fine powers would—if, unluckily for us, they *didn't* appeal to us. I like to think of you working out your ideas—planning all those possibilities together—in the wondrous Chocorua October—where I hope you are staying to the end—and even if intensity at the studio naturally rather suffers for the time it has only fallen back a little to gather again for the spring. I mean in particular the intensity of which you were the subject and centre, and which must have at first been somewhat hampered by its own very excess. Bill's only danger is in his tendency to be *intensely* intense—which is a bit of a waste; if one *is* intense (and it's the only thing for an artist to be) one should be economically, that is carelessly and cynically so: in that way one limits the conditions and the tangles of one's problem. But don't give Bill this for a *specimen* of the way you and I are going to pull him through: we shall do much better yet—only it's past—*far* past—midnight and the deep hush of this little old huddled sleeping town suggests bed-time rather as the great question for the moment. I have come back to this admirable small corner with great joy and profit—and oh, dear Alice how earnestly you are awaited here at some not really distant hour by your affectionate old uncle,

Henry James

1. HJ's nephew William (Billy) James, his brother's second son, had just become engaged to Alice Runnells of Chicago.

To Jocelyn Persse
Ms Harvard

Lamb House, Rye
October 4*th* 1911

Dearest Jocelyn.

I have been back in England since the mid-August, yet I have, all advisedly, made you no sign. I've waited, on purpose, to do so in as fit and favouring a form only as should be worthy of both of us. You haven't been for a day out of my mind's or my heart's eye; but I returned, by a fatality, to a great many disconcerting and rather blighting influences and accidents—and I never want to approach you save when I'm as serene and steady as your poor old battered and tattered, though ever so fondly faithful, friend can nowadays ever again hope to convey to you the impression of his being. Thank goodness the last fortnight has made a great difference for the better with me—and *now*, dearest Jocelyn, I let myself celebrate it. The biggest celebration I can think of is just at last again to get into relation with *you*—as a preliminary to never getting out of it (so far as I have *been* out of it—save by mere lapses of superficial sound) so long as I may go on for the rest of my earthly course near you. I fear I mayn't at this moment be so near you—or you at least so near me—as for you to be able to dine with me all blessedly alone on Tuesday evening the 10th at the Reform Club (I shall have then to come up for two days), or if Tuesday is impossible to you would Wednesday be manageable?—I would in that case stay over for the loved sake of you. I darkly fear you may be on tour—that is out for sport—in Paris (or, more tremendously, Peebles);[1] but I greatly hope for you, as I shall all tenderly welcome [you]. Then we shall be able to settle for your coming down to me here—as I shall particularly appeal to you to do. If you are at a distance on the days I speak of that is all the greater reason why I should, on some slightly later day, have you here. That's all *now*—we shall jaw everything out so much better. Dear and beautiful to me is the prospect. Make me yourself some faithful even if undecipherable sign—and if I have to spend much "time over it" that will be nothing to the time I want now, and after this dark interregnum, to spend over *you*. Let me begin, at last, soon and well, and believe me, dearest Jocelyn, ever your old affectionate

Henry James

584

1. A country house frequented by Persse and where he was believed to have a romantic interest. He ultimately married a widow, a Mrs. Black.

To Hugh Walpole
Ms Texas

The Reform Club
October 13*th* 1911

Darling, darling little Hugh!

First, the enclosed has come to my care from one of your admirers and I pass it on.

Second, I have just been reading the *Standard*[1] at breakfast, and I am touched, I am *melted*, by the charming gallantry and magnanimity of it—my notices of *your* compositions having been so comparatively tepid. Tit *not* for Tat! Well, D.D.L.H. (it looks like "d—d" little H.,—but isn't meant for that), you do the thing handsomely when you do do it—and I seem to myself to swim in a blaze of glory—I shall wear my thrifty old hat when I next go out like a wreath of the bay imitated in fine gold. Had I known you meant to crown me I should have liked to say a thing or two for your guidance—however incorrect such proceeding would have been as from author to reviewer. It wouldn't have been—between *us*—however from Author to Reviewer but from Friend (putting it mildly) to Friend and *Maître* to *Élève*. Never mind—you will sell the edition for me and no edition of mine has ever sold yet! But I shall thank you better more face to face, more cheek by jowl—which will perhaps be on the occasion of our *Gotterdämmerung*—which (I am zealously watching it) isn't announced yet. *Now* you can tell Mrs. Yates-Thompson[2] that I adore her—and you can also add if you like that I adore *you*—which won't, I hope, diminish the value for her. Yours my damnedest little Hugh, in that posture,

Henry James

1. Walpole's review of *The Outcry* had just been published. The novel's young hero, Hugh Crimble, bears a physical resemblance to Walpole.

2. Mrs. Yates-Thompson, daughter of a publisher and wife of the former owner of the *Pall Mall Gazette*.

To Gertrude Kingston
Ms King's College

105, Pall Mall, S.W.
October 17 1911

Dear Miss Kingston.

I have received *The Other House*[1] from the country and am causing it to be left for you with this. Don't be alarmed at its apparent voluminosity, for in the first place it is full of representational and expressional indications (as *The Saloon* was) which swell it out; and, in the second, will demand much further compression (which I will disparately undertake when performance is really in question) on the terrible time-basis. Meanwhile I hold that any possible producer, or even interpreter, should read it exactly as it here stands—which is how it would easily be produced in Paris or in Germany. I can't help being struck, on looking it over again after a good while, with what I feel as its "big" theatrical value; but I am quite as conscious that it would take every inch of the beautiful *doing* that it could get—and more besides! *Every* figure in it must be beautifully done—and for Tony Bream and Rose you can imagine—! On the other hand I think it would be open to these two to cover their interpreters with glory! I don't at all hold to the term "prologue"—the thing is four straightforward Acts. I shall see Mr. Pinker in a day or two, and he will doubtless remember about the book of *The Saloon*. I go out of town towards the end of this week for four or five days—but on my return—!

Believe me yours very truly

Henry James

1. This was the play HJ outlined to Edward Compton at the time of *Guy Domville* and turned into a novel in 1896. Shortly before his 1910 illness he turned it back into a play and showed it to Herbert Trench and Granville Barker, who had asked for plays.

To Jocelyn Persse
Ms Harvard

The Reform Club
October 18*th* 1911

Dearest Jocelyn.

I am rather supposing that you will come up to town today and will find this in Park Place. Let it express to you my most affectionate welcome and my great joy that you will be able to dine with me on Friday. When we meet I will tell you better than this for what very strong reasons my attempt to "settle in" again at Lamb House with the isolated and inane autumn and winter before me ended in a dire collapse—the dreariness and the immobilization (after my long deep draughts of those matters in the past) being impossible and my necessitous flight to London again a real "blessing in disguise" and our "jaw"—and nothing else matters save that I am, dearest Jocelyn, yours all and always

Henry James

To Edith Wharton
Ms Yale

Lamb House, Rye
October 25*th* 1911

Dearest Edith.

All thanks to M. de Ségur, to the yearning niece, and to yourself, *très-chère* Madame. Poor D.M.—or poor D—mn!—has been translated (to the complete sacrifice of all her small pinch of substance or sense) by Mme Pillon, the wife of an old philosopher-friend of my brother's—twenty years ago.[1] I think we don't want two of them—and will you kindly *remercier,* with all my acknowledgments? You will see by the enclosed (isn't it sweet of dear Jacques?)[2] what IS, *auprès de moi,* the real chance of the Translator—and will find the volume itself on your table when you reach home. At least I so gave directions for it; kindly tell me if it delays. It is of course nothing but my Barrie-and-Frohman comedy, *The Outcry* of two years ago (just that now), then never acted through general collapse, simply printed, a little misleadingly—with such a running comment as

587

merely represents decent interpretation and expression. But I wince a little at your reading it after Blanche's fine hyperbole! You must indeed have had a Bacchic Tuscan time—but—oh for the details! Don't dream, however, that I *"might"* have come—I so utterly mightn't! I went to Howard for thirty-six hours—and it's deplorable (and superfluous) *comme il baisse*. A little more at this rate and *il n'en restera plus rien.* You really must come over and we'll see about it together. I go up to town tomorrow (and proceed with him, for two days, to the Wilfred, the "Clare," Sheridans'.)[3] But I spend, practically, the winter in London, most decidedly; the era of Rye hibernations is definitely closed. London, and London alone, is so excellently good for me—better than any other place in the world.——I exceedingly admire, *sachez* Madame, *Ethan Frome.* A beautiful art and tone and truth—a beautiful artful Right-downness, and yet effective cumulations. It's a "gem"—and excites great admiration here. *Nous en causerons.* I could wail over Walter—buffeted prey of the gods! But he'll "come out all right!" I calculate that this will find you at the Plantier[4]—meet you there; and beg that if it does you will assure Paul and Minnie of "my faithful and affectionate remembrance—all my sympathy and *mes voeux"*—I leave nothing, you see, to your discretion; it wouldn't be fair; if I began that I should have to leave so much—*all.* Apropos of whom I vainly watch for the *Tribun* done by Morton into Alexandrines. *Où en est* that undertaking? Oh the unutterable Theatre! I only heard that Alexander, with Oscar Wilde for a stopgap (the doddering rococo and oh so flat "fizz" now of *Lady Windermere's Fan!*) has "gone to Germany to look for a play." And Morton—whom I eternally fail to see? His *Gil Blas* etc. is nice—but not up to his best mark. He is, I hope, pushing forward his *Paris.*[5] But I shall very soon write him—and I draw breath. Make me, do, a sign from Paris—and believe me yours all affectionately

Henry James

1. Permission had been asked to translate "Daisy Miller" into French. This had been done in 1886 when it appeared with two other HJ tales translated by Mme F. Pillon.

2. Jacques-Émile Blanche.

3. Clare Sheridan, the sculptress. She had married Wilfred Sheridan.

4. The Bourget's villa at Costebelle.

5. Fullerton, having given up his job at the *Times,* had just prepared an English edition of *Gil Blas de Santillane,* the picaresque novel by Lesage first published in 1715. He also was translating Bourget's play *Le Tribun,* and he was supposed to be working on his book about Paris for Macmillan.

To Theodora Bosanquet
Ms Harvard

105 Pall Mall, S.W.
October 27*th* 1911

Dear Miss Bosanquet.

Oh if you *could* only have the real right thing to miraculously propose to me, you and Miss Bradley, when I see you on Tuesday at 4.30! For you see, by this bolting—in horror and loathing (but don't *repeat* those expressions!) from Rye for the winter—my situation suddenly becomes special and difficult; and largely through this, that having got back to work and to a very particular job,[1] the need of expressing myself, of pushing it on, on the old Remingtonese terms, grows daily stronger within me. But I haven't a seat and temple for the Remington and its priestess—*can't* have here at this club, and on the other hand can't now organize a permanent or regular and continuous footing for the London winters, which means something unfurnished and taking (*wasting, now*) time and thought. I want a small, very cheap and very clean *furnished* flat or trio of rooms etc. (like those we talked of under the King's Cross delusion—only better *and* with some, (a very few) tables and chairs and fireplaces), that I could hire for two or three—*three or four*— months to drive ahead my job in—the Remington priestess and I converging on it and meeting there morning by morning—and it being preferably nearer to her than to me; though near tubes and things for both of us![2] I must keep on *this* place for food and bed etc.—I have it by the year—till I really *have* something else—by the year—for winter purposes—to supersede it (Lamb House abides— for long summers). Your researches can have only been for the *un*furnished—but look, *think, invent!* Two or three decent little tabled and chaired and lighted rooms would do. I catch a train till Monday, probably late. But on Tuesday!

Yours ever,
Henry James

1. The writing of his autobiography.
2. Miss Bosanquet, who lived at 10 Lawrence Street, Cheyne Walk, Chelsea, when she was not at Rye, obtained two rooms immediately adjoining her flat, enabling HJ to work in London. He was not allowed to have a female typist at the Reform Club, where he retained his room, going every morning by taxi to his new work-rooms. See Theodora Bosanquet, *Henry James at Work* (1927).

To Theodora Bosanquet
Ms Harvard

Reform Club, S.W.
November 2 1911

Dear Miss Bosanquet.

In the intoxication of my relief at having resolved the Remington problem on Tuesday, I went yesterday and bought without more delay, three or four articles which I hope I shan't inconvenience you by asking you to take them gently in even if one or two—or all!—of them—have to be put into a corner of your own premises till the little rooms are ready. These articles are—so far as I recollect—first a wickerish kind of armchair, the only thing of any size and which you will perhaps let abide in your sitting-room till it can be shifted; second a long piece—or strip—of greenish felt to lie on the floor of the larger room (I had simply to *guess* at length): and third a set of washing-stand articles and waste paper basket. I shall send nothing more till the rooms are ready—when there may be two or three more wants for me to supply. I find the question of the Letters[1] to be copied or dictated baffles *instant* solution, but shall have been able to judge in two or three days. It is a bit complicated, and I may let it wait till I begin to come. I shall rather like to begin with something that goes very straight so as to get the easier back into harness. Yours very truly

Henry James

1. Family letters, and in particular letters of WJ. HJ began, however, with his own childhood, and this book became *A Small Boy and Others.*

To Edith Wharton
Ms Yale

The Reform Club
November 19*th* 1911

Dearest Edith.

There are scarce degrees or differences in my constant need of hearing from you, yet when that felicity comes it manages each time to seem pre-eminent and to have assuaged an exceptional hunger. The pleasure and relief, at any rate, three days since, were of the rarest quality—and it's always least discouraging (for the exchange of sentiments) to know that your wings are for the moment folded and your field a bit delimited. I knew you were back in Paris, as an informer passing hereby on his way thence again to N.Y. had seen you dining at the Ritz *en nombreuse compagnie,* "looking awfully handsome and stunningly dressed." And Mary Hunter *ces-jours-çi* had given me earlier and more exotic news of you, yet coloured with a great vividness of sympathy and admiration. *En voilà une* who will be "after you" *dès votre arrivée* and with whom you will really always find, I think, a good relation immensely easy and pleasant. But I feel that it takes a hard assurance to speak to you of "arriving" anywhere—as that implies starting and continuing, and before your great heroic rushes and revolutions I can only gape and sigh and sink back. It requires an association of ease—with the whole heroic question (of the "up and doing" state)—which I don't possess, to presume to suggestionise on the subject of a new advent. Great will be the glory and joy, and the rushing to and fro, *when* the wide wings are able, marvellously, to show us symptoms of spreading again—and here I am (*mainly* this winter), to thrill with the first announcement. London is better for me, during these months, than any other spot of earth, or of pavement; and even here I seem to find I can work—and *n'ai pas maintenant d'autre idée.* Apropos of which aid to life your remarks about my small latest-born are absolutely to the point. The little creature is absolutely of the irresistible sex of her most intelligent critic—for I don't pretend, like Lady Macbeth, to bring forth men-children only. You speak at your ease, *chère Madame,* of the interminable and formidable job of my producing *à mon age* another *Golden Bowl*—the most arduous and thankless task I ever set myself. However, on all that *il y aurait bien des choses à dire;* and meanwhile, I blush to say, the *Outcry* is on its way to a fifth Edition (in these few weeks) whereas it has taken the poor old G.B. eight or nine years to get even into a third. And I should have to go back and live for two continuous years at Lamb House to write it (living on dried herbs and cold water—for "staying power"—meanwhile); and that would be very bad for me, would probably indeed put an end to me altogether. My own sense is that I don't want, and oughtn't to try, to attack ever again anything *longer* (save for about seventy or eighty pages more) than *The Outcry.* That is *déjà assez difficile*—the "artistic econ-

591

omy" of that inferior little product being a much more calculated and ciphered, much more cunning and (to use your sweet expression) crafty one than that of five G.B.s. The vague verbosity of the Oxus-flood (*beau nom!*) terrifies me—*sates* me; whereas the steel structure of the other form makes every *parcelle* a weighed and related value. Moreover nobody is really doing (or, *ce me semble,* as I look about, can do) *Outcries,* while all the world is doing G.B.s—and *vous même, chère Madame, tout le premier:* which gives you really the cat out of the bag! My vanity forbids me (instead of the more sweetly consecrating it) a form in which you run me so close. *Seulement alors je compterais bâtir* a great many (a great many, *entendez-vous?*) *Outcries*—and on *données autrement* rich. About this present one hangs the inferiority, the comparative triviality, of its primal origin.[1] But pardon this flood of professional egotism. I have in any case got back to work—on something that now the more urgently occupies me as the time for me circumstantially to have done it would have been last winter when I was insuperably unfit for it, and that is extremely special, experimental and as yet occult. I apply myself to my effort every morning at a little *repaire* in the depths of Chelsea, a couple of little rooms that I have secured for quiet and concentration—to which a blest taxi whirls me from hence every morning at 10 o'clock, and where I meet my amanuensis (of the days of the composition of the G.B.)[2] to whom I *gueuler*[3] to the best of my power. In said *repaire* I propose to crouch and *me blottir* (in the English shade of the word, for so intensely revising an animal, as well), for many more weeks; so that I fear, dearest Edith, your idea of "whirling me away" will have to adapt itself to the sense worn by "away"—as it clearly so gracefully will! For there are senses in which that particle is for me just the most obnoxious little object in the language. Make your fond use of it at any rate by first coming away and away hither. I yearn for news of what is taking place over the *Tribun*[4]—so mystified am I by the fact that Alexander is announcing (for a few days hence) a dramatization of our Hichens[5] (—yours and mine, the one we back so against Lady True Benson), just at the moment I have been hoping that the version of Bourget would bring Morton, and *par la même occasion* sympathetic *you,* to just round the corner here. Your allusion to your having lent a hand in Paris reassures me, however; a reassurance confirmed by Blanche—with whom I lunched three days ago on a copious dish of little *blanchailles;* he telling me that you have "written in a love-scene." I yearn most of all then for *your* Alexandrines—or rather I yearn for them next after the passion with which I yearn for Morton's personal advent in the interest of his own is spent. Please give him my fond love. Yours and his all and always

Henry James

P.S. This was begun five days ago—and was raggedly and ruth-lessly broken off—had to be—and I didn't mark the place this Sun-day A.M. where I took it up again—on p. 6th. But I put only today's date—as I didn't put the other day's at the time.

1. *The Outcry* was originally a play.

2. *The Golden Bowl* was, in fact, dictated to Miss Bosanquet's predecessor during 1903–1904. Miss Bosanquet came to work for HJ in 1907.

3. HJ is quoting Flaubert's way of describing how he read aloud.

4. *Le Tribun* by Paul Bourget was produced in Paris on 15 March 1911.

5. Robert Hichens's novel *Bella Donna,* about an attempted murder on the Nile, had just been dramatized and was produced by George Alexander on 9 December 1911.

To Hendrik C. Andersen
Ms Barrett

Lamb House, Rye
January 2d 1912

Dearest Hendrik.

Let this take you my faithfully fond old greeting and very proper invocation and *auguries* for the dim New Year, which stands watching for us round the corner as if to fly at our throats. We must nevertheless advance whistling and with a cock of our hats—a *sufficient* game of bluff may perhaps make him respectful. I have had for some time your typed letter of November—had it a long time as you see; but perhaps pressing it to my poor old heart a little less faithfully than usual, by reason of its lacking on your part something of the weird personal touch, touch of hand and play of orthography (which means spelling, dear Hendrik) that usually commend your fine script to my fond affection. However, I am glad of your having done with the many-figured fountain the huge bare-legs and arms (and everything else bareable—or bearable), of which seemed to me, ever, to have got you in their complicated and

593

multitudinous grip very much as the Laocoön of the Capitol (or is it the Vatican?) museum is in the grip of the squeezing boa-constrictor. Make independent figures now—but make also, dear-est Hendrik, a few purchasers *apposto,* a few specimens of a new brave race of Americans who can resist the shock of such violent and expensive nudity. I won't send you any fig-leaves—I need them all myself; besides your ladies great heaving and straining* and gentlemen would split them in twain at the end of an hour. Alas, I shan't be in Paris at the end of—or in the course of—January—when am I ever in Paris now? I have utterly ceased to travel—more than from London to this place and back. I travel *back* (to town) in very few days—I am spending the winter there—that ordeal being no longer possible to me here. I have just come down to look after my small household, but am making a very short thing of it, and pray the powers I shall be able to remain in town till June. If you can come to Paris can't you come on to London? Do, dearest Hendrik, devote all your ingenuity to that question. I shan't there be able to put you up, but should give you in every other possible way the warmest welcome. I think of you all in the golden Roman air—I hang with you over your unspeakable Tiber-terrace—I sit with you in those noble chambers. And I love you, dearest Hendrik, just as much as ever, and am always your all-faithfullest old

Henry James

* Forgive that odious smirch—over "heaving and straining!"

P.S. All kindliest things to your Mother and Olivia—also to the brave Baccharisis. [1]

1. Gustave Bacaresas, a Spanish painter HJ had met in Andersen's Roman studio.

To James Jackson Putnam
Ms Countway

Lamb House, Rye
January 4th 1912

My dear Putnam.

This is a *delayed* word—partly because I have been designedly and watchfully waiting, partly by reason of the avalanche of corre-spondence that descended on me at the New Year, and with which I am still a little at a disadvantage in struggling. I meant it to have reached you on New Year's day—whereas it does not start toward you even punctually then. But it takes with it, and in it, my strong sense of owing you some faithful report of myself after so long— and after your last winter's great sympathy in particular; and also my great gladness that the report can be so bright. For I want you to know that I am quite enormously better, and so far as possible how I have come to be able to say so. It's perhaps easier for me to say now, however, why it is and *wasn't* better—I mean during those weary months of last year, when I occasionally saw you.[1] The following time has thrown some light on that—a good deal in fact: I began really to be better from the day I went back to London to *stay*—though even that was only some three months ago. I had evil times, many of them, in America, after last seeing you, and the summer conditions proved formidable to me in the extreme—I had at Nahant, e.g. in July (early) to send at short notice to Dr. Winslow there, my almost worst distresses had so come back to me. The heat, the confinement (by reason of the same), my sense of being caught in an almost fatal *trap* (I had put off my sailing to Europe from June to early in August), all *that* had brought me once more to a bad crisis, and the whole season was really but a mitigated nightmare. Things were also very unpropitious here when I first returned—the heat and drought and other *convulsions*[2] that I found poor dear old England given over to were very disconcerting and arresting, and the weeks I began by spending in this place (for I really write this from the country) saw me but little way further. I had in fact another crisis and thereupon fled to London at once, to settle and stick fast for the winter (without waiting for a later part of it, as I had tried to resign myself to doing). The big Babylon, with its great spaces for circulation, for movement, and for variety, has proved an absolute specific—the only one that was adequate for me and worthy, so to speak, of my powers and my infirmities, on the *scale* of them and proportionate to them—the contracted circle and the scant variety and the narrow circulation had comparatively done little. I have recovered myself further in consequence, during the past twelve or fourteen weeks, than I had done in any period of six or eight months before, and am in fact now really better than I have been not only since I was taken so acutely ill, (two years ago) but than I have been for at least four years. I have liabilities to relapse a little at times, but I recognize now perfectly the conditions that produce them and know how to manage, minimise and stave them off. I have got back to work, am working well, and that is an unspeakable aid and support and blessing. Speaking in a summary manner I have a *big* enough surface to expand myself nervously upon—and if I had had a bigger one at the time you were seeing me, I probably should have got forward much more continuously. It has been a matter of the *big* rhythm and the long beat, if you know what I mean—but I wish I were sitting with you again in Marlborough Street (on this basis of improvement only though!) on one of those rather melancholy winter evenings of a year ago—and just long *enough* to appeal to your comprehension and interest a little more vividly. I have at any rate worked the troubled history pretty well out for myself—in especial since that second time of my being with Joseph Collins[3] in New York—in April—after the last time of my seeing you. I had a bad crisis again there—and beyond being very kind and interested he did nothing for me at all: so that it was *then* I began to get hold of things more intimately for myself and more or less to grasp the real clue to the labyrinth. Difficult outside conditions caused it still at times to be very bewildering, as I say, but I more persistently grasped the logic of the matter and saw that the basis of my recovery was, first, the basis of all adequately and all precautionarily *feeding* (so as to *forestall* any approach to inanition); second, the basis of feeding *at the same time* as little *fatteningly* as possible; third, the basis of as much *movement,* or circulation, and multiplication of contact, and variety of vision, as much (roughly speaking) beguilement, as possible. If I stoked without movement I got too high "blood pressure" and great increase of chronic panting and heaving. If I moved (*much*) without stoking I got collapse and *bed,* in straight resumption of the effect of the Fletcherized starvation which was the *fons et origo* of all my woes and which had so nearly done me to death. If I took too much meat (as least fat-making) I distressfully and dreadfully panted and heaved: if I took too little I sooner or later fainted by the wayside and laid me down in sick despair as to die. If, *to eat enough,* I took certain other things I felt the oppression and injury of overweight—promptly and easily produced. But the worst thing of all was: first the not finding opportunity and atmosphere for the circulation and locomotion I required; and second the superstition of *fatigue,* which was more or less forced upon me from roundabout, and was very delusive and misleading and injurious (not the fatigue, but the mistake). I was only fatigued when I moved too little—I wasn't when I did so enough or too much. "Rest" was a mockery when I could stoke enough (and stoking a mockery when I couldn't be restless enough and adequately and rightly—otherwise than by heaving—work it off). I had been resting from my starvation all the years of my starvation—it was the only thing but starve that I could do. Spending most of June and July at Nahant with my extraordinarily kind old friend G. A. James,[4] a wondrous good Samaritan to me at that unholy time, I almost went mad from the desolation (I mean the narrow confines and *yet supposed extent!*) of the deadly (yet luxurious!) scene, and the sickening torrid heat that, with other hindrances, made any choice or range of circulation impossible. However, I am boring you to death (if I am not really interesting you!) and I only risk the former effect to possibly invoke the latter. It's a flood of egotism—but what are the Patient class but egotistic, especially in proportion as it's grateful? You tided me over three or four bad places during those worst months. Now everything is changed and you will after all be certainly glad to hear it, and that I am really, for a still too obese mortal, master of the situation. I hope you yourself are in good heart and hope. I hear you were in these parts in the summer, and wish I had been here to receive you. Collins spent an evening with me in the late autumn and much admired me—as an independent work of art! Soon I am hoping for Bill and his bride. But I quickly reapply the remedy of London—of the blessed miles of pavement, lamplight, shopfront, apothecary's beautiful and blue jars and numerous friends' teacups and tales! Don't think it necessary to "answer" this the least little bit. I have written to possibly strike a light for another forlorn brother—even on your professional altar, though I shall be delighted at a word of cheer from you. Yours, my dear Putnam all faithfully,

Henry James

1. This letter reveals that HJ, in consulting the eminent psychiatrist James Jackson Putnam in Boston, was exposed briefly and beneficially to early Freudian therapy. Putnam had been in touch with Freud, Ernest Jones, and Morton Prince; and he seems to have gone into James's prolonged "Fletcherizing," which had proved in the

end debilitating and demoralizing. James's own testimony in this letter, while focusing on externals, suggests that he was able to respond to the deeper psychological problems that undermined his well-being—the loss and mourning for his elder brother, the sense of aging, the deep loneliness he had come to experience in the isolation of Rye.

2. Coal and railway strikes and public discontent.

3. Dr. Joseph Collins, the fashionable New York pseudo-psychiatrist, who wrote a series of books, "The Doctor Looks at . . ." His comments on HJ as patient are in *The Doctor Looks at Biography* (1925). He prescribed, as HJ put it, "baths, massage and electrocutions."

4. George Abbot James. See letter to Josiah Royce, 30 June 1911.

To Robert Underwood Johnson
Ms American Academy-Institute

105 Pall Mall, S.W.
January 11*th* 1912

Dear R. U. Johnson.[1]

I enclose the Ballotpaper I have just received with the only name on it that means anything to me—out of the list that accompanied it. I have unfortunately never heard of the others and can obtain here no such information about them as would be a proper basis for my vote. The situation renews my lively sense of the radical defect in our constitution—our deplorable mixture and confusion of arts and interests, which demands of writers that they shall competently vote for architects, of architects that they shall do the same for musicians, of musicians that they shall do it for painters, and so on reciprocally and viciously. This absence of common ground for us to judge of each other on, to meet on and act together on, condemns us, alas, to such sterility—the last superficiality. I can estimate Owen Wister[2] only—and I do. I have an impression that Mr. Augustus Thomas[3] is a dramatist, but has his Théâtre been *published?* is what I ask myself; can we take cognizance of the *Text* on which his claims are based? That seems to me essentially to concern us—but I have never come across his works.

Yours very truly
Henry James

1. Johnson (1853–1937) was secretary of the fifty-member Academy of Arts and Letters. As customary, HJ was asked to vote on musicians and painters as well as writers eligible for membership.

2. Owen Wister was elected in 1912.

3. Augustus Thomas (1857–1934), a popular American dramatist, whose more than sixty plays depicted varied American backgrounds.

To Theodate Pope Riddle
Ms Hillstead

105, Pall Mall, S.W.
January 12*th* 1912

My dear Theodate.[1]

I return you the dreadful document,[2] pronouncing it without hesitation the most abject and impudent, the hollowest, vulgarest, and basest rubbish I could possibly conceive. Utterly empty and illiterate, without substance or sense, a mere babble of platitudinous phrases, it is beneath comment or criticism, in short beneath contempt. The *commonness* of it simply nauseates—it seems to have been given to those people to invent, richly, new kinds and degrees of commonness, to open up new oceans or vast dismal deserts of it. And that these are those for whom such lucubrations represent a series of *values,* and who spend their time and invite others to spend theirs over them, makes me wonder—well, makes me wonder at more things than I shall now undertake to tell you. I shall just simply tell you *one* of them, if you'll let me—which is the prodigy of the "effect of America" in producing a sense of proportion, a kind of perspective, a flatness of level and thinness of air, in which a person of your fine and true quality finds it natural to pass on such a tissue of trash to another. Where in such an air are criticism and comparison and education and taste and tradition, and the perception a measure and standard of—well, again of more things than I can name to you? See how you make me write—as if I were writing *at* you! But I'm not, my dear Theodate, nor expressing myself with resentment—only with a bewildered sense of strangeness through which I look at you as over the abyss of oddity of your *asking* about that thing to which I hate to accord the dignity even of sending it safely back to you! But I brush the strangeness away—as a momentary blur, and it instantly goes, and I see you again in that charming light of last summer and of all the Farmington hospitality and beauty and of the wondrous motor-days in particular, and the prodigious Hillstead to Cambridge one most of

599

all; and in the clearance I embrace you tenderly and respectfully, if you let me—as a sign of all the gratitude I've cherished for you, and all my fond hope of our renewing some such occasion here—or such a pale image of them as poor old "here" may make possible. I am spending this winter practically in London, which is doing me a world of good—in a different way from the world dear Hillstead did me but still very valuably. I saw L. a little some time ago and found her as hard as all the nails of old Jewry put up to auction. She wouldn't have sent me that document, no; but she would have sent me cold poison and then charged me Ten Pounds for it. The really nice one of that family is G. who is velvet-soft and has much more talent than the poisoner, too. I make out that you are leading a life in N.Y., and I wish indeed I could sprawl on the red cretonne. Do take in Peggy and feed her from the pink and silver, and it will all be blest to you and to *her* and all delightful to her poor old uncle and your

Affectionate old friend,
Henry James

P.S. I should so like to send my very best love to the beautiful bountiful graceful Parents.

1. HJ met Theodate Pope Riddle during his 1905 trip to the United States and saw her again during the visit of 1910–1911. She was an architect and had built Avon Old Farms at Farmington, Connecticut, where HJ enjoyed inspecting her collection of impressionist paintings.

2. The document was a report of a séance in which it was claimed William James had tried to communicate with his family.

To Edmund Gosse
Ms Leeds

The Reform Club
January 30th 1912

My dear Gosse.

How sad the situation—with your State captivity (the romance of the old scaffold and axe just tingeing it) and my very *embrouillé* condition for Thursday. I sit to Sargent all that A.M. for a charcoal drawing, and my nephew whom I go to meet this A.M. at Euston—(he arrives with his new bride from N.Y. and, as an aspiring painter will much profit I hope), is to assist at the sitting.[1] This means that we stop to luncheon afterwards—and that the whole series of hours, to 3 or 3.30, will be much compromised. I much regret it, though not in general good just now for much out-lunching—I work in far Chelsea very strenuously till 1.45—and that much interferes. May I not come one of these evenings to join the family circle in the Park? I am keeping as disengaged as possible—I will ask you for a date as soon as the immediate flurry of my care for my young and appealing relations is over. Yours all faithfully

Henry James

1. Edith Wharton commissioned John Singer Sargent to do a charcoal portrait of HJ. She was dissatisfied with the final version he sent her. (This was ultimately acquired for the Royal Collection in Windsor Castle of the recipients of the Order of Merit.) HJ's nephew Billy James, who was to be at the sitting, had just married Alice Runnells, and HJ had put Lamb House at the disposal of the couple for their honeymoon.

To Edmund Gosse
Ms Leeds

The Reform Club
February 5th 1912

My dear Gosse.

I brace myself—not (for you will frown!) to say No, but literally (and though I quake in every limb as I form the letters), to say Yes! I hate it but I will do it; I fear it but I will brave it; I curse it but I will wreathe it in smiles: all for *you*—essentially and desperately for You only.[1] I shall make up my distracted mind between two things: a shy at the subject of (as who should say) "The Browning of One's Youth"; or, quite differently, a go at "*The Ring and the Book* as a Novel" (or perhaps better "The Novel in *The Ring and the Book*"). I predominate toward the latter. I have had and still have a villainous sick cold, and am presently (9 P.M.) going dinnerless to bed; but for which and my feeling thereby a certain lack of confidence in my powers—a nervousness about these immediate next days, I should now name you an evening for the family circle—that is propose you your choice of Thursday or Friday at 9. Suppose indeed you let me do that; then if you choose—and Friday is perhaps safest—I shall know how the case stands in time to notify you promptly—I mean with all solicitude.

Will you please express to Pinero how much I am touched and gratified by his having let his decision depend in any degree on mine?

All and always yours
Henry James

1. On behalf of the Academic Committee of the Royal Society of Literature, Gosse invited HJ to speak at the celebration of the Browning centenary in May. The playwright Arthur Pinero (1855–1934) was scheduled to give a paper on Browning and the theatre, and HJ decided to speak on "The Novel in *The Ring and the Book.*" See *Notes on Novelists* (1914).

To Edith Wharton
Ms Yale

The Reform Club
March 13th 1912

Dearest Edith.

Just a word to thank you—so inadequately—for everything. Your letter of the 1st infinitely appeals to me, and the third volume of the amazing Wladimir[1] (amazing for *acharnement* over her subject) has rejoiced my heart the more that I had quite given up expecting it. The two first volumes had long ago deeply held me—but I had at last had to suppose them but a colossal fragment. Fortunately the whole thing proves less fragmentary *than* colossal, and our dear old George *ressort* more and more prodigious the nearer one gets to her. The passages you marked contribute indeed *most* to this ineffable effect—and the long letter to sweet Solange is surely one of the rarest fruits of the human intelligence, one of the great things of literature. And what a value it all gets from our memory of that wondrous day when we explored the very scene where they pigged so thrillingly together.[2] What a crew, what *mœurs*, what habits, what conditions and relations every way—and what an altogether mighty and marvellous George!—not diminished by all the greasiness and smelliness in which she made herself (and *so* many other persons!) at home. Poor gentlemanly, crucified Chop[in]!—not naturally at home in grease—but having been originally *pulled* in—and floundering there at last to extinction! *Ce qui dépasse,* however—and it makes the last word about dear old G. really—in her overwhelming *glibness,* as exemplified e.g. in her long letter to Gryzmala[3] (or whatever his name), the one to the first page or two of which your pencil-marks refer me, and in which she "posts" him, as they say at Stockbridge, as to all her *amours*. To have such a flow of remark on that subject, and everything connected with it, at her command helps somehow to make one feel that Providence laid up for the French such a store of remark, in advance and, as it were, should the worst befall, that their conduct and *mœurs*, coming *after*, had positively to justify and do honour to the whole collection of formulae, phrases and, as I say, glibnesses—so that as there were at any rate such things there for them to inevitably *say*, why not simply *do* all the things that would give them a *rapport* and a sense? The things *we*, poor disinherited race, do, we have to do so dimly and sceptically, without the sense of any such beautiful *cadres* awaiting us—and therefore poorly and going but half— or a tenth—of the way. It makes a difference when you have to invent your suggestions and glosses all after the fact: you do it so miserably compared with Providence—especially Providence aided by the French language: which by the way convinces me that Providence thinks and *really* expresses itself only in French, the language of gallantry. It will be a joy when we can next converse on these and cognate themes—I know of no such link of true interchange as a community of interest in dear old George.

I don't know what else to tell you—nor where this will find you. In what case you will be found is another matter and I scarce dare to advance to the threshold of speculation. I kind of pray that you may have been able to make yourself a system of some sort—to have arrived at some *modus vivendi*. The impossible wears on us, but we wear a little here, I think, even on the coal-strike and the mass of its attendant misery; though they produce an effect and create an atmosphere unspeakably dismal and depressing; to which the window-smashing women[4] add a darker shade. I am blackly bored when the latter are at large and at work; but somehow I am still *more* blackly bored when they are shut up in Holloway [Prison] and we are deprived of them. Mary Hunter's sister, Ethel Smyth,[5] has just been condemned to two months' hard labour there—M.H.'s depressed and *ob*sessed sense of her cold, her inanition (very little food and practically no fire) and her isolation is somehow aggravated by her thinking she really quite deserves it. A propos of whom, M.H., I am to sit to-morrow to Sargent for the third time[6] (and I surmise, and hope, she will be there—for she really helps the sitter). I have a certain amount of impression that he may sacrifice the work of the two other sittings and make a fresh start. If he does he will probably, over the known, the learnt, ground, go much straighter. *But* he may pick himself—or *me*—up, and dash along as it is.

I rejoiced in your comparatively bright evocation of Morton—as if he were engaged for the moment almost in a gay Nijinsky *pas*. *Do* be so far as possible his Lady Ripon[7] in any such performance. I hold my breath over Walter [Berry]—he might be able to bear a *mécompte*—but *I* shouldn't. But *ne parlons pas de ça*. It ravishes me to hear that Rosa, the Charleys,[8] the Bourgets, etc. "abound in their sense" more and more: Paul, above all, can never do so enough for me—what a comfort it adds to life when you feel you can absolutely count on such aboundings! Keep him at it—don't let him *faiblir*. But I hear you say *"Pas de danger qu'il faiblisse,"* and it's *du pain sur la planche!* when so much round about us fails. *You* don't fail—*you're* a store on the shelf; but then in another cupboard altogether! Yours all and always, dearest Edith,

Henry James

1. *George Sand, Sa Vie et ses œuvres*, III, *1838–1848*, by Mme Wladimir Karénine. HJ's reviews of the three volumes were published in *Notes on Novelists* (1914).
2. HJ and Mrs. Wharton had visited Nohant, George Sand's country house, when they motored in France in April 1907.
3. Albert Gryzmala, a Polish exile and a friend of Chopin.
4. The suffragettes.
5. Ethel Smyth (1858–1944), composer and conductor and feminist leader.
6. See letter to Gosse, 30 January 1912.
7. Mrs. Wharton was visiting the Marquis and Marchioness of Ripon at Coombe Court and there met Nijinsky and the members of the Russian ballet.
8. The Countess Rosa de Fitz-James and the critic Charles Du Bos (1882–1939) and his wife, Zezette.

To Edith Wharton
Ms Yale

The Reform Club
March 16*th* 1912

Dearest Edith.

Maurice[1] is indeed a sweet little flower of *snobisme,* and his *naturelle et sublime blessure* is wonderfully wide open—so that we look all the way down his throat. *Quelle engeance!*—including *sa mère aux beaux cheveux.* Why not *sa mère aux beaux seins* or *aux belles hanches* at once? However, they are made for our delectation—and what on earth should we do without them? When coal and trains and other supplies fail, as here, they are at least *toujours là.* So I thank you for these unfailing recalls to them. I wrote you two or three days ago, and this was at any rate to have been a postscript. I have sat again to Sargent with complete success,[2] and he has made an admirable drawing. He kept on with the work of the two previous séances—and brought it round, beautifully developed, and redeemed and completed. It's a regular first class living, resembling, enduring thing. Now he wants to know if: first he has your leave to have it, for safety, *photographed*, in one or two copies. Second if he shall then send it to you to Paris—or if it shall await here—in his hands—your next possible, and it is hoped probable, coming. He is all at your orders, as is your all devoted

Henry James

P.S. He will have the thing at any [rate] glazed and framed—so as to guard against rubs of the charcoal, etc.

P.S. Perhaps you will write J.S.S. a word to himself—31 Tite Street Chelsea. S.W.

1. A poem by Maurice Rostand (1891–1968), "A ma mère."
2. See letter to Gosse, 30 January 1912.

To Thomas Sergeant Perry
Ms Colby

The Reform Club
March 18th 1912

My dear Thomas.

I have two bristling letters from you and your scathing exposure of the Howells dinner[1] does me good and renews my—well, I won't say my youth but my convictions or several of them. One of the most irresistible, if not most cherished of these is that the Great Country *que vous savez* has developed the genius for vulgarity on a scale to which no other genius for anything anywhere can hold a candle. But what an awful state of things when a quiet decent honest man like W.D.H. *has* to think he can't under peril of life, do anything but become part of the horror. An old friend of mine here,

Lucy Clifford (W.K.'s widow) who was there and at the "high table" and has sent me a catalogue of the guests which I hang over in the appallment of fascination—or the fascination of appallment; and which, as she has just returned and I am to see her tonight, she will fill out with hideous detail—though indeed she appears, by a line she wrote me, to have enjoyed, rather, the weird desolation of it. I sent (though I say it who shouldn't) a quite beautiful and copious letter—and I'm sorry my fine prose, my really *very* graceful tribute, meant to be read out as an attestation of my long relation with the dear man, was simply shoved aside. As he appears not to have spoken of it to you (on the occasion of your lunching with him), I am afraid he hadn't himself even seen it. But any lapse of attention or interest is credible on the part of one who has traversed so hideous an experience.

March 21*st*

I had to break off the other day, under pressure, and, under the same pressure haven't been able to take up my pen, as we used to say, till this moment. I saw Lucy Clifford that evening, flushed with a breathless month of observation and agitation in New York (delighted with everything and everyone, and not knowing one of all these from any other), and she, in her place of pride, took a more genial view of the banquet—though finding the speeches almost incredibly fulsome and undiscriminating, all the speakers talking so extraordinarily "tall" about our friend. Fancy deliberately *stirring up* such an exhibition—pulling with a wanton hand the string to let loose the flood of shame, otherwise for the time confined! Oh objectionable "Colonel"![2] But let us banish the black vision!—Not that the vision before us here isn't black enough in its different way. We are really overdarkened by the Coal Strike, by which and its consequences a couple of million of people are out of work, a number that will be hugely swelled if it goes on much longer. But the Government is proceeding very justly, sanely and ably—don't believe anything else if you hear it said in your neighborhood. "Labour" is rising everywhere like a huge Bugaboo, and happy, or fortunate, the country that tackles him first and has it out with him to a practical issue, so far as that may be. And the Women loom monstrous beside him—they are really very wonderful here, and the end is not yet.[3] Hitherto, however, *their* question has only *bored* me

606

to extinction: strangely, it isn't interesting—I don't know, and can't say, why; *a priori* one would say it *would* be—everything else about them is. I give it up—and must give *this* up.

Ever your faithful old
Henry James

1. Perry had described the seventy-fifth birthday dinner tendered Howells in New York by publishers, friends, and admirers, for which HJ wrote an "open letter" in praise of his friend's career. See Lubbock, *The Letters of Henry James* (1920), II, 221–226, for the text of this essay-letter.

2. Colonel George Harvey, president of Harper's, the principal organizer of the dinner.

3. Britain's industrial unrest, which had begun a year earlier, abated by midsummer with defeat for the coal, transport, and dock workers. The increasing suffragette violence met resistance in Parliament. To these disturbances and to the threat of war, the Asquith government continued to react with caution.

To H. G. Wells
Ms Bodleian

The Reform Club
March 20th 1912

My dear Wells.

It has been a great sorrow—verily a shock to me—to hear from Edmund Gosse that you are not disposed to avail yourself of our invitation to Membership of the Academic Committee.[1] Is it not possible to you to reconsider—under a fond and passionate appeal—that irresponsive and unsociable attitude? On hearing of your election I felt a greater pleasure than anything in my connection with the body had yet given me, and if you maintain your refusal I shall continue, in pain and privation, to yearn for you. So I am moved to try respectfully to contend with you to some good issue on the subject. Even if you have reasons more substantial than I imagine, or *can* imagine, have them, I mean, as the matter has hitherto struck you, I find it in me to promise you, as it were, in the light of my own experience (for I too have had an experience!) that they won't seem to you *after the fact*—that is if you only *would* come in!—half as valid as they do now. The thing is a *pleasant* and a plastic, elastic, aspiring thing, greatly appealing to our good-will— by which I especially mean to yours, that of your literary and creative generation; offering us no rigour, offering us opportunities for influence, for pressure in desirable directions and asking no sacrifice worth speaking of or grudging in return. It will be what the best of us shall make it, and it is open to the best of us to make it more interesting and more amusing (if you will—"in the highest sense of the term") to ourselves, and more suggestive to others. Above all it would be so fortified by your accession that a due consideration for the prestige of current English letters surely ought to move you. You would do something for us that we lack and don't want to lack—and we would do for *you*, I think, that you would find yourself *within* still more moved than without to that critical, that ironic, that even exasperated (if I may call it) play—or reaction!—which is the mark, or one of the marks, of your genius. Don't make too much of rigours and indifferences, of consistencies and vows; I have no greater affinity with associations and academies than you—*a priori*; and yet I find myself glad to have done the simple, civil, social *easiest* thing in accepting my election— touched by the amenity and geniality of the thought that we shall probably *make something* collectively—in addition to what we may make individually. Don't think I want to harass or overbear you if I say that if these words still leave you cold I frankly don't want to let the matter go without seeing you over it. I would come up to Church Row—at any hour I might find you—after 3.30 P.M.—for the purpose, or would earnestly await you here at your own hour equally—with all the lively assurances of yours very faithfully

Henry James

1. The Academic Committee of the Royal Society of Literature. Wells had been elected a Fellow of the Society at HJ's insistence but declined the honor. The committee included at the time Barrie, Bridges, Conrad, Galsworthy, Gosse, Hardy, James, Gilbert Murray, Shaw, and Yeats.

To H. G. Wells
Ms Bodleian

105 Pall Mall, S.W.
March 25th 1912

My dear Wells.

Your letter is none the less interesting for being what, alas, I believed it might be; in spite of which interest—or in spite of which belief at least—here I am at you again! I know perfectly what you mean by your indifference to Academies and Associations, Bodies and Boards, on all this ground of ours; no one should know better, as it is precisely my own state of mind—really caring as I do for nothing in the world but lonely patient virtue, which doesn't seek that company. Nevertheless I fondly hoped that it might end for you as it did, under earnest invitation, for me—in your having said and felt all those things *and then joined*—for the general amenity and civility and unimportance of the thing, giving it the benefit of the doubt—for the sake of the good-nature. You will say that you *had* no doubt and couldn't therefore act on any; but that germ, alas, was what my letter sought to implant—in addition to its not being a question of your acting, but simply of your *not* (that is of your not refusing, but simply lifting your oar and letting yourself float on the current of acclamation). There would be no question of your being entangled or hampered, or even, I think, of your being bored; the common ground between all lovers and practitioners of our general form would be under your feet so *naturally* and not at all out of your way; and it wouldn't be you in the least who would have to take a step backward or aside, it would be *we* gravitating toward you, melting into your orbit as a mere more *direct* effect of the energy of your genius. Your plea of your being anarchic[1] and seeing your work as such isn't in the least, believe me, a reason against; for (also believe me) you are essentially wrong about that! No talent, no imagination, no application of art, as great as yours are, is able not to make much less for anarchy than for a continuity and coherency much bigger than any disintegration. There's no representation, no picture (which is your form), that isn't by its very nature preservation, association, and of a positive associational *appeal*—that is the very grammar of it; none that isn't thereby some sort of interesting or curious *order:* I utterly defy it in short not to make, all the anarchy in the world aiding, far more than it unmakes—just as I utterly defy the anarchic to express itself representationally, art aiding, talent aiding, the play of invention aiding, in short *you* aiding, without the grossest, the absurdest inconsistency. So it is that you are *in* our circle anyhow you can fix it, and with us always drawing more around (though always at a respectful and considerate distance), fascinatedly to admire and watch—all to the greater glory of the English name, and the brave, as brave as possible English array; the latter brave even with the one American blotch upon it.

Oh *patriotism!*—that mine, the mere paying guest in the house, should have its credit more at heart than its unnatural, its proud and perverse son! However, all this isn't to worry or to weary (I wish it *could!*) your ruthlessness; it's only to drop a sigh on my shattered dream that you might have come among us with as much freedom as grace. I prolong the sigh as I think how much you might have done for *our* freedom—and how little we could do against yours!

Don't answer or acknowledge this unless it may have miraculously moved you by some quarter of an inch. But then oh *do!*—though I must warn you that I shall in that case follow it up to the death!

Yours all faithfully
Henry James

1. Replying to the preceding letter, Wells wrote: "This world of ours, I mean the world of creative and representative work we do, is I am convinced best anarchic. Better the wild rush of Boomster and the Quack than the cold politeness of the established thing." In later years, Wells changed his mind and joined P.E.N., the international organization of writers, and became its president. But he continued to champion the "anarchic" world of literature.

To Edmund Gosse
Ms Leeds

The Reform Club
March 26*th* 1912

My Dear Gosse.

This is just a word, on receipt of your note, to conclude the H. G. W[ells] episode—of which absolutely nothing more will come. I wrote him last evening again, in an appealing and remonstrant way—it *interested* me to do so, and I thought there was perhaps a chance, or the fraction of one, of his response to two or three things I could still, with some point I felt, say to him. But his only response was to come into this place (Reform Club) today at luncheon time (I think he came on purpose to find me), and let me see that he is absolutely immovable. I had a good deal of talk with him—though not, his refusal once perfectly *net*, about that, and without his having answered or met in any way any one of the things my second letter (any more for that matter than any of those my first) had put to him; and my sense that he is right about himself and that he wouldn't at all do among us from the moment our whole literary side—or indeed any literary side anywhere—is a matter of such indifference to him as I felt it to be today—to an extent I hadn't been aware of. He has cut loose from literature clearly—practically altogether; he will still do a lot of writing probably—but it won't be *that*. This settles the matter, and I now agree with you settles it fortunately. He *had* decently to decline, and I think it decent of him to have felt that. My impression of him today cleared up many things. But I will tell you more about it. I won't pretend to speak of other things—to you who are at the centre of the cyclone. How interesting you will be—and how interesting everything else will be (God help all interests!) when you are next seen of yours always

Henry James

To Hendrik C. Andersen
Ms Barrett

[The Athenaeum]
April 14*th* 1912

Dearest Hendrik.

Not another day do I delay to answer (with such difficulty!) your long and interesting letter. I have waited these ten days or so just *because* of the difficulty: so little (as you may imagine or realise on thinking a little) is it a soft and simple matter to stagger out from under such an avalanche of information and announcement as you let drop on me with this terrific story of your working so in the colossal and in the void and in the air![1] Brace yourself for my telling you that (*having*, these days, scrambled a little from under the avalanche) I now, staggering to my feet again, just simply flee before the horrific mass, lest I start the remainder (what is hanging in the air) afresh to overwhelm me. I say "brace yourself," though I don't quite see why I need, having showed you in the past, so again and again, that your mania for the colossal, the swelling and the huge, the monotonously and repeatedly huge, breaks the heart of me for you, so convinced have I been all along that it means your simply burying yourself and all your products and belongings, and everything and Every One that is yours, in the most bottomless and thankless and fatal of sandbanks. There is no use or application or power of absorption or assimilation for these enormities, beloved Hendrik, anywhere on the whole surface of the practicable, or, as I should rather say, impracticable globe; and when you write to me that you are now lavishing time and money on a colossal ready-made City, I simply cover my head with my mantle and turn my face to the wall, and there, dearest Hendrik, just bitterly *weep* for you—just desperately and dismally and helplessly water that dim refuge with a salt flood. I have practically said these things to you before—though perhaps never in so dreadfully straight and sore a form as today; when this culmination of your madness, to the tune of five hundred millions of tons of weight, simply squeezes it out of me. For that, dearest boy, is the dread Delusion to warn you against—what is called in Medical Science MEGALOMANIA (look it up in the Dictionary!) in French *la folie des grandeurs*, the infatu-ated and disproportionate love and pursuit of, and attempt at, the Big, the Bigger, the Biggest, the Immensest Immensity, with all sense of proportion, application, relation and possibility madly *submerged*. What am I to say to you, gentle and dearest Hendrik, *but* these things, cruel as they may seem to you, when you write me (with so little *spelling* even—though that was always your wild grace!) that you are extemporizing a World-City from top to toe, and employing forty architects to see you through with it, etc.? How can I throw myself on your side to the extent of employing to back you a single letter of the Alphabet when you break to me anything so fantastic or out of relation to any reality of any kind in all the weary world??? The idea, my dear old friend, fills me with mere pitying dismay, the unutterable Waste of it all makes me retire into my room and lock the door to howl! Think of me as doing so, as howling for hours on end, and as not coming out till I hear from you that you have just gone straight out on to the Ripetta and chucked the total mass of your Paraphernalia, planned to that end, bravely over the parapet and well into the Tiber. As if, beloved boy, any use on all the mad earth can be found for a ready-made city, made-while-one-waits, as they say, and which is the more prepos-terous and the more delirious, the more elaborate and the more "complete" and the more magnificent you have made it. Cities are *living* organisms, that grow from within and by experience and piece by piece; they are not bought all hanging together, in *any* inspired studio anywhere whatsoever, and to attempt to plank one down on its area prepared, as even just merely projected, for use is to—well, it's to go forth into the deadly Desert and talk to the winds. Dearest Hendrik, don't ask me to *help* you so to talk—don't, don't, don't. I should be so playing to you the part of the falsest, fatallest friend. But do *this*—realise how dismally unspeakably much these cold hard, desperate words, withholding sympathy, cost your ever-affectionate, your terribly tender old friend

Henry James

1. Andersen had sent HJ his elaborate plan to create a "world city," for which he had enlisted the aid of many European notables. The plan was published in 1913 in two deluxe privately printed volumes (300 copies) titled *The World City*, designated as "a world centre of communications." It contained extensive architectural drawings of buildings and public squares, including the "Fountains of Life and of Immortality" on which Andersen had been working for some time.

To Mrs. Francis D. Millet
Ms Archives of American Art

The Reform Club
April 18th 1912

My dear old Friend.

I ask myself how I can pretend to "write" to you, to attempt to come near you with poor vain words—and yet at the same time how I can *not*; for the need to *utter*, however feebly, is insuperable for me, and this utterance can only be, in the midst of all the horrors and misery, of what is *most* present to me: the unthinkable hours that you and your children are having to live through.[1] I don't know where this will find you, but it takes with it, wherever that is, the infinite tenderness of my participation. Of the one thing that can in any degree, for you all, light up the blackness, your proud confidence that Frank was under any stress, however tragic, his magnificent manly self, asking nothing, round-about him, but giving and suggesting all, irradiating *that* beautiful genius and gallantry and humanity—of this, I say, and of each other sublime vision of him that shines for you through the darkness, we are all as deeply and helpfully possessed as you; and with the blest added sense that you have for your anguish the greatness of soul that he had for *his*, and that will keep us all, ever, so proud of both of you. I yearn over

you far more than I can tell you and am more than ever faithfully
and tenderly yours

Henry James

1. Francis D. Millet (1846–1912), the painter and illustrator, had just died in the
sinking of the Titanic. HJ had been a friend of the Millets since the 1880s. See *Letters*
III, 132.

To Jocelyn Persse
Ms Harvard

The Reform Club
April 30th 1912

Dearest Jocelyn.

If you are miraculously able to come—on the 7th—and to sit
through my twaddle,[1] to feel you beautifully there will give all the
pleasure in life, and be an immense support, to your all-affectionate
old

Henry James

1. The reading of his paper on Browning before the Royal Society of Literature.

To Edith Wharton
Ms Yale

105 Pall Mall, S.W.
May 12th 1912

Dearest Edith.

I have your beautiful letter, and am as a result of it even more
émotionné than you can probably conceive. The mere hearing from
you at all deeply moves me—oh all the past impossibilities, and the
almost equally intense present difficulties, have been but too vivid
and lurid to me. We communicate as through black darkness and
over sheer abysses, and it's all a bad time to pass; even though we
don't ever, I feel, wholly not communicate. Your beautiful envoi a
few days since of the two lemon-coloured volumes, Loti and
Lemaître, which I am so gratefully ravished to have (the eternal
readability of everything about Chateaubriand—he, of old, so admirably constructed and elaborated to be endlessly and richly un-

614

exhaustedly *exposed!*) shines with a still ampler grace than what, in it, meets the mere eye, or even the mere mind. And then your Périgord post-picture of dear old George [Sand] nosing for the human truffle—and infallibly finding it (when *il n'y en avait plus* being exactly when *il y en avait encore* in the very next jiffy!): these things, and other wandering airs, have kept the cord just vibrating even when not conveniently to be thumbed. In addition to which your good letter does thumb it—with such breadth! for the whole packed fulness of which I tenderly thank you. It might indeed have diverted you to be present at our Browning commemoration—for Pinero was by far the most salient feature of it (simple, sensuous, passionate—that is artless, audible, incredible!) and was one of the most amusing British documents we had had for many a day. He had quite exhausted the air by the time I came on—and I but panted in the void. But dear Howard and dear Percy held each a hand of me—across the width of the room—and I struggled through.[1] (My stuff is to be published in the *Quarterly*, and I will send it to you.) I seem to get the side-wind of great adventures, past, present and to come, from you, *tout de même*—not counting the chronic domestic one; which keeps my heart in my mouth. "And did you see Shelley plain?"—and did you three times go to Nohant ("coloured"), *retour d'Espagne* too?[2] all of which plunges me into yearnings and broodings ineffable, abysses of privation and resignation. It's all right for you to go—by which I mean it's all right for *me* not to; but it's all wrong for me not otherwise to participate—and I shall sit gaping, watch in hand, till I do. And you go to Salso[3] again—and you "motor in Italy"—and you're ready for anything prodigious; as such *are*, obviously, the sublimities of the sublime. It is the *grand vie*, don't deny that—for which I was so little framed, ever—and am so much less so than ever now. I hear from Mary Hunter, hoping for you at Salso—but she will be back in England for Whitsuntide by the time you get there. I don't presume to speak to you of eventualities—we are all in the lap of the gods. What are they by this time doing for Walter there?—but let me not put questions, especially as to things as to which I literally shouldn't be able to bear or survive the possibly (absit omen!) wrong answers! If you want to make the chord vibrate to a mere 2 francs 75 worth of "thumb," will you send me (excuse my voracity) the volume (*not* the Illustration one) of Bourget's play,[4] if it comes out before you leave? I like to hear of him as I do of any other bull-fight or truffles hunt; there appearing to *en être encore* of *him* too, always, even when *il n'y en a plus. Il y en aura toujours*—such as it is! I am staying on in town till about June 12th; I like my little Chelsea *repaire* so for work—and my young relatives[5] are, for that matter, to my great joy for them, still a month more in possession of Lamb House. I probably spend two or three days at Hill at Whitsuntide—but without the *attrait* that the mistress of it will have lately seen you. However, she did as she went out—and I shall grasp at that. I am really finding I can work again—and it will be all my *avenir*. My voracity for it is almost indecent—though I have to gratify that but in my still small way. What I mean is that it *goes*. Over your preventions I weep all the *larmes de mon corps*. Howard appears to have been of late extraordinarily sound and serene—and is always the dearer when he *is* so. Good-bye, dear *grande viveuse*. Keep rising above (you do it so splendidly); yet drop some day again even to your faithfully-fondest old

Henry James

1. See letter to Gosse, 5 February 1912. Howard Sturgis and Percy Lubbock were present as HJ received an ovation for his paper on Browning.

2. Mrs. Wharton had taken her increasingly disturbed husband to Madrid for Easter and on the return trip motored to Nohant to revisit scenes of George Sand's life.

3. Salsomaggiore, an Italian resort to which Edith Wharton had gone twice before in recent months for the baths, the waters, and rest. She was working on her novel *The Reef.*

4. See letter to Mrs. Wharton, 19 November 1911.

5. Billy James and his bride.

To Mrs. W. K. Clifford
Ts Lubbock

The Reform Club
May 18*th* 1912

Dearest Lucy!

Your impulse to steep me, and hold me down under water, in the Fountain of Youth, with Charles Boyd[1] muscularly to help you, is no less beautiful than the expression you have given it, by which I am more touched than I can tell you. I take it as one of your constant kindnesses—but I had, all the same, I fear, taken Filson Young's Invidious Epithet[2] (in that little compliment) as inevitable, wholly, though I believe it was mainly applied to my *voice*. My voice *was* on that Centenary itself centenarian—for reasons that couldn't be helped—for I really that day wasn't fit to speak. As for one's own sense of antiquity, my own, what is one to say?—it varies, goes and comes; at times isn't there at all and at others is quite sufficient, thank you! I cultivate not thinking about it—and yet in certain ways I like it, like the sense of having had a great deal of life. The young, on the whole, make me pretty sad—the old themselves don't. But the *pretension* to youth is a thing that makes me saddest and oldest of all; the *acceptance* of the fact that I am all the while growing older on the other hand decidedly rejuvenates me; I say "what then?" and the answer doesn't come, there doesn't seem to be any, and that quite sets me up. So I am young *enough*— and you are magnificent, simply: I get from you the sense of an inexhaustible vital freshness, and your voice is the voice (so beautiful!) of your twentieth year. Your going to America was admirably young—an act as of your twenty-fifth. Don't *be* younger than that; don't seem a year younger than you do seem; for in that case you will have quite withdrawn from my side. Keep up with me a *little*. I shall come to see you again at no distant day, but the coming week seems to have got itself pretty well encumbered, and on the 24th or 26th I go to Rye for four or five days. After that, I expect to be in town quite to the end of June. I am reading the Green Book in bits—as it were—the only way in which I *can* read (or at least disread) the contemporary novel—though I read so very few— almost none). My only way of reading—apart from that—is to imagine myself *writing* the thing before me, treating the subject—and in thereby often differing from the author and his and/or *her* way. I find G.W.[3] very brisk and alive, but I *have* to take it in pieces, or liberal sips, and so have only reached the middle. What I feel critically (and I can feel about anything of the sort but critically) is that you don't *squeeze* your material hard and tight enough, to press out of its ounces and inches what they will give. That material lies too loose in your hand—or your hand, otherwise expressed, doesn't tighten round it. That is the fault of all fictive writing now, it seems to me—that and the inordinate abuse of dialogue—though this is but one effect of the not squeezing. It's a wrong, a disastrous and unscientific economy altogether. *I* squeeze as I read you—but that, as I say, is rewriting! However, I will tell you more when I have eaten

617

all the pieces. And I shall love and stick to you always—as your old,
very old, *oldest old*

Henry James

1. Charles W. Boyd, a flamboyant journalist, associated originally with W. E. Henley's *National Observer*, later political secretary to Cecil Rhodes.
   2. Filson Young, writing in the *Pall Mall Gazette* about HJ's Browning paper, used the phrases "his mellow conversational voice," "the charm in the voice, such was the magic of this dear old man's personality," and "the voice of this charming artist." See Filson Young, *New Leaves* (1915).
   3. Mrs. Clifford's recent novel.

To Hugh Walpole
Ms Texas

The Reform Club
May 19*th* 1912

Beloved little Hugh.

Your letter greatly moves and regales me. Fully do I enter into your joy of sequestration, and your bliss of removal from this scene of heated turmoil and dusty despair, which, however, re-awaits you! Never mind; sink up to your neck into the brimming basin of nature and peace, and teach yourself—by which I mean let your grandmother teach you—that with each revolving year you will need and make more piously these precious sacrifices to Pan and the Muses. History eternally repeats itself, and I remember well how in the old London years (of *my* old London—*this* isn't that one) I used to clutch at these chances of obscure flight and at the possession, less frustrated, of my soul, my senses and my hours. So keep it up; I miss you, little as I see you even when here (for I *feel* you more than I see you); but I surrender you at whatever cost to the beneficent powers. Therefore I rejoice in the getting on of your work—how splendidly copious your flow; and am much interested in what you tell me of your readings and your literary emotions. These latter indeed—or some of them, as you express them, I don't think I fully share. At least when you ask me if I don't feel Dostoieffsky's "mad jumble, that flings things down in a heap," nearer truth and beauty than the picking and composing that you instance in Stevenson, I reply with emphasis that I feel nothing of the sort, and that the older I grow and the more I *go* the more sacred to me do picking and composing become—though I naturally don't limit myself to Stevenson's *kind* of the same. Don't let anyone persuade you—there are plenty of ignorant and fatuous duffers to try to do it—that strenuous selection and comparison are not the very essence of art, and that Form *is* [not] substance to that degree that there is absolutely no substance without it. Form alone *takes,* and holds and preserves, substance—saves it from the welter of helpless verbiage that we swim in as in a sea of tasteless tepid pudding, and that makes one ashamed of an art capable of such degradations. Tolstoi and D. are fluid pudding, though not tasteless, because the amount of their own minds and souls in solution in the broth gives it savour and flavour, thanks to the strong, rank quality of their genius and their experience. But there are all sorts of things to be said of them, and in particular that we see how great a vice is their lack of composition, their defiance of economy and architecture, directly they are emulated and imitated; *then,* as subjects of emulation, models, they quite give themselves away. There is nothing so deplorable as a work of art with a *leak* in its interest; and there is no such leak of interest as through commonness of form. Its opposite, the *found* (because the sought-for) form is the absolute citadel and tabernacle of interest. But what a lecture I am reading you—though a very imperfect one—which you have drawn upon yourself (as moreover it was quite right you should). But no matter—I shall go for you again—as soon as I find you in a lone corner.

You ask for news of those I "see"; but remember that I see but one person to ninety-five that you do. A. Bennett I've never to this day beheld[1]—and certain *American* papers of his in *Harper,* of an inordinate platitude of journalistic cheapness, have in truth rather curtailed in me any such disposition. There he writes about what I *know,* and makes me ask myself whether his writing about what I *don't* know mayn't have, after all, that same limitation of value. Lucy Clifford gallantly flourishes—on all fine human and personal lines; Jocelyn P[ersse] continues to adorn a world that is apparently so easy for him. I lately dined and went to a play with him (*Rutherford and Co.,*[2] or whatever, very helpless, but more decent than anything else that's going); and he was, as ever, sympathy and fidelity incarnate. On the whole, however, I've had very little chance to talk of you. Little May Sinclair[3] drew me to her rather desolately vast blank Albemarle Club to tea—in a dim and dumb literary circle as of pale ink-and-water; but the high tide of blankness submerged us all. *So* blank may the naiads and Ladies of the ink-and-water stream become! I've called on the little Gräfin,[4] but missed her—unconsoledly—or call it inconsolably—as yet. From the great (prose) Minstrel of the Gallery (there's Form for you!) I've had a letter—but this is an instance that I must wait to impart to you at leisure: it has *such* a harmony with—everything else! Well, dearest Hugh, love me a little better (if you *can*) for this letter, for I am ever so fondly and faithfully yours

Henry James

1. Arnold Bennett (1867–1931) author of *The Old Wives' Tale* (1908) and *Clayhanger* (1910) as well as successful plays; and a prolific journalist who contributed to English and American journals articles on the arts as well as general comment. He was one of Pinker's clients, and HJ met him in the latter's office in January 1913. See *The Journals of Arnold Bennett 1911–1921*, ed. Newman Flower (1932).
2. *Rutherford and Company*, a play by G. Sowerby.
3. May Sinclair (1865[?]–1946), a novelist.
4. Gräfin Arnim (d. 1941), the former Elizabeth Mary Beauchamp, Countess Arnim in her first marriage and later Countess Russell, whose amusing and successful novel *Elizabeth and Her German Garden* was published in 1898.

To Howard Sturgis
Ms Harvard

Lamb House, Rye
Reign of Terror[1]
ce vingt juillet, 1912

My dear, dear Howard.

This is a sort of signal of distress thrown out to you, *in the last confidence,* at the approach of the Bird o'-freedom—the whirr and wind of whose great pinions is already cold on my foredoomed brow! She is close at hand, she arrives tomorrow, and the poor old Ryebird, with the majestic Paddingtonia[2] no longer to defend him, feels his barnyard hurry and huddle, emitting desperate and incoherent sounds, while its otherwise serene air begins ominously to darken. *Bref,* the Angel ("half-angel and half-bird," as Browning so vividly prefigures her), has a *plan,* of course; which is that, struggling in her talons, as you well say, I am yet to be rapt off to Qu'acre of Tuesday in order to proceed thence that evening, as soon as we shall have hastily gulped down tea, to dine in her company with Lady Ripon at Coombe.[3] But from that plan I, in my tenderest consideration for *you*, dearest Howard, which exceeds my consideration for Lady R. (who has invited me), as the mountain exceeds the molehill, utterly dissociate myself in advance, and this is a word equally in advance to tell you so; just as I have emphatically wired to the Angel in Paris to tell *her* so—and that I absolutely refuse to make use of so large a slice of your noble hospitality for any such purpose. I will, if she insists on Lady R., go up to London from here for that (Tuesday) night, and proceed to Coombe from *there*; but I won't alight *chez vous* as at an hotel and simply give notice on arriving that I won't dine at the *table d'hôte*, but am dining (liking it so much better) at the *café* round the corner. I foresee that on Edith's arrival the battle will be engaged—and that she probably won't easily agree either to give up Lady R. (whom she appears indeed to have closed with) or go to an hotel at London for the night. In that case we shall come to you on the morrow for the day and night (by the morrow I mean Wednesday), or else not come at all, alas, if I have died fighting. I scarcely know what is before me, but I gird my loins for the worst (I am just settled here to urgent work); I shall give you further, and perhaps lurider, news; and I am *à tout évènement* yours all devotedly

Henry James

1. HJ hyperbolizes the advent of Mrs. Wharton and her motorcar.

2. Mrs. Paddington, HJ's housekeeper, was away. Mrs. Wharton visited at Lamb House from 21 to 23 July. HJ then went to London and on the 25th was motored from the Reform Club, where he stayed, to Windsor to visit Howard Sturgis at Qu'Acre. He and Mrs. Wharton remained there until the 27th, then motored to Cliveden to visit Nancy Astor. On the 28th they returned to Qu'Acre, and on the 29th drove to visit Margaret Brooke, the Ranee of Sarawak, at Ascot. There HJ met, for the first time since the 1890s, Violet Paget (Vernon Lee), "with whom," he noted, "I had a good deal of talk." (See *Letters* III, 403–404.) HJ and Mrs. Wharton returned to Cliveden from July 30 to August 2. There HJ's angina began to trouble him, and Mrs. Wharton sent him in her car, driven by Cook, back to Rye, with a stop for lunch on the way at Qu'Acre.

3. See letter to Mrs. Wharton, 13 March 1912.

Lamb House, Rye
August *9th* 1912

Beloved Howard!

The Firebird perches on my shoulder while I bend, all eagerly, to acknowledge your delightful letter—yet, luckily, not to the point of my having to deprive that beautiful record of a response as free as itself. She has been with me since last evening, and was to have remained till tomorrow, but within this afternoon the horoscope has not unnaturally shifted, and Frank Schuster and Claude Phillips[1] having been with us, from Folkestone, for a couple of hours, she moves off, as soon as we have had tea, to rejoin them there for the night—they have just dashed away in their own car— and I retreat upon my now forever inexpungable base, after wriggling out of every net cast to draw me into the onrush. She embarks tomorrow morning to all appearance—in order to arrive, at tea, at 5, with the Jacques Blanches[2] in Normandy—after which my comprehension sinks exhausted in her wake. She has held us, F.S., C.P. and I, spell-bound, this pair of hours, by her admirable talk. She never was more wound up and going, or more ready, it would appear, for new worlds to conquer. The only thing is that none at this rate will soon be left a lady who consumes worlds as you and I (*don't* even) consume apples, eating up one for her luncheon and one for her dinner. That is indeed, as your charmingly, your touchingly vivid letter so expresses, the terrible thing about (and *for*) a nature and a life in which a certain saving accommodation or gently economic bias seem able to play so small a part. She uses up everything and every one either by the extremity of strain or the extremity of neglect—by having too much to do with them (when not for *them* to do), or by being able to do nothing whatever, and passes on to scenes that blanch at her approach. She came over to us only the other day in order to help herself (and us!) through part of an embarrassing and unprovided summer, to put in a block of time that would bridge over her Season; but she has already left us in raggs (as they used to, and I inadvertently happen to, write it)* and tatters—we ground to powder, reduced to pulp, consumed utterly, and she with her summer practically still to somehow constitute. That is what fairly terrifies me for her future, possessed as I am, as to the art of life, with such intensely economic, saving, sparing, making-everyone-and-everything-go-as-far-as-possible instincts—doubtless in comparison a quite ignoble thrift. I feel as if I shouldn't know *where* I might be if I didn't somehow or other make every occasion serve—in *some* degree or other. Whereas our Firebird is like an extravagant dandy who sends thirty shirts to the wash where you and I (forgive, dear Howard, the collocation!) send one; or indeed even worse—since our Firebird dirties her days (pardon again the image!) at a rate that no laundry will stand; and in fact doesn't seem to believe in the washing, and still less in the ironing—though she does, rather inconsistently in the "mangling"!—of any of her material of life. Well, let us hope that the Divine Chemisier will always keep her supplied straight and to sufficiency with the intimate article in which he deals!—All thanks for your wishes and inquiries about my pectoral bother-ations. They will be better enough, I feel sure, when a sordid peace again reigns. All I want for that improvement is to be *let alone,* and not to feel myself far aloft in irresistible talons and under the flap of mighty wings—and about to be deposited on dizzy and alien peaks. "Take me *down*—and take me home!" you saw me having to cry that, too piteously, the other day to the inscrutable and incom-parable Cook—rescuer as well as destroyer. I am really inditing these last remarks *after* our friend's departure: the after-dinner evening has now closed about me—and the sight of poor heroic Gross[3] (who had again, for the millionth time, polished off her packing and climbed to her forward perch, but with the light of near Folkestone and fresh disintegrations in her aged eye) has already become a pathetic memory. They are all—the Firebird, Frank S., Claude P., and their respective cars to cross from Folkestone to-gether tomorrow, as I understand, Schuster and Phillips proceeding then by that means to a Strauss festival at Stuttgart. In a wonderful age—for the Firebirds, Claudes and Shoos [Schusters]—do we verily live! I have as much as I can do to live at my own very advanced one—and to that end must now get me to a belated bed; where you must take me for dreaming of you with all the devotion, dearest Howard, of your faithfullest

Henry James

* I shall recover my orthography, and other powers, only little by little.

P.S. *Please* destroy all this gross profanity!

1. See letter to Coburn, 7 December 1906.
2. See letter to Ellen Emmet Rand, 2 November 1908.
3. Mrs. Wharton's maid. Mrs. Wharton had come to Lamb House on August 8th and spent the night, proceeding on the 9th to Folkestone on her way to the Continent.

To Howard Sturgis
Ms Harvard

Lamb House, Rye
August 24*th* 1912

Dearest Howard.

I just leave you at your own door again, on condition that you don't turn round with me, but go right in and straight to bed—where I ought to be myself, at this 1.15 o'clock in the A.M. But I've *always* got something to thank you for, and I like to do it *en détail* rather than *en gros*—or rather I like to do it in both ways, neglecting no particular and yet constantly amazed at the total. Besides it *is* so much more "funny" than I can now explain to be so freshly Wilkinsonizing[1] with you, or to you, at this time of day—and still more of night! I shall, however, be able to explain a little better *why* it's funny—or *ce qui en est*—when we next fondly meet. My dear Father thought J.J.G.W. highly remarkable as a young man (when they both were, and my Father was in England—and indeed J.J. then *was* remarkable); and afterwards, always afterwards, found him very tiresome. But meanwhile he had named his third son for him, and the Wilkinsons had named their third daughter (Mary James Atwood Mathews as she is now, and most queer, and whom I saw about once in twenty years) for my Mother; and the vain *geste* had taken place. But my Father wasn't a "Swedenborgian" in the technical sense—a member of the "Church" of that name—which he never entered or had anything to do with. He was only a great reader, lover and admirer and commentator. I *think* your Aunt Sarah Shaw was a whole-hogger; but I'm not sure. I've never personally known but one—that extremely nice and touching woman James R. Lowell's wife. Wilkinson was, in his early career, a very wonderful and splendid writer—that is on several occasions and in several connections (though it all *left* him early): Get me to repeat to you an unknown and yet so fine passage from a short book of his published during the Crimean war, "War, Cholera and the Ministry

624

of Health: A Letter to Sir Benjamin Brodie—" (Dr. W. was a Homeopathic Physician) beginning: "The bulletins of the dead are issued, and the groups of sorrow are constituted. Splendid Paris bends like a Niobe, etc."—but I really think you *must* be walking home with me! Go straight back—good night, good night!

Ever your true

H.J.

P.S. If you *do* turn round again I'll throw a stone at you (I've got one here on my table as a paper-weight), quite hard. I shan't hurt or even hit you, because I *always* miss; but it will (or the fear of it perhaps will) "shoo" you off!

1. An allusion to the James family's friendship in earlier years with Dr. J. J. Garth Wilkinson (1812–1899), the British Swedenborgian, and his family.

To Logan Pearsall Smith[1]
(Telegram) *Ms Congress*

Rye

October 1, 1912

Deeply regret have just been put to bed with bad attack of shingles where apparently I must remain for some days the doctor rigid and my sick condition fatal to any decent hospitality.

Henry James

1. Logan Pearsall Smith (1865–1946) was born in the United States but spent most of his life in England. He wrote aphorisms, critical essays, and studies in the English language.

To James B. Pinker
Ms Yale

Lamb House, Rye

October 8*th* 1912

My dear Pinker.

I pull myself round, to the best of my ability, to thank you for your two letters this morning received, for, I grieve to say, my condition for practically a week past has been as prostrate a one as I gather you too, from what you say, to have been contending with;

though I earnestly hope you have been less violently floored. I was really spoiling when I last saw you (though then but dimly conscious of it) for a horrible attack of "Shingles," which broke out immediately afterwards, only leaving me margin to scramble back home and tumble into bed, where I have been till today—when I am but half out of it. Shingles, of which my conception had been vague, is really quite a horrible kind of visitation, which I hope you have never known and never may; one really suffers with the last acuteness, and I am only now beginning to emerge—with the sense heavy upon me of the miserable loss of time, ferocity of interruption, and general gratuitous irrelevance of it all. I am not yet in form for very alert or decided handling of our important matters; however, let this pass for such a well-meant stopgap as it may.

I am greatly pleased and touched by your appreciation of *A Small Boy*,[1] and of course agree with you that Scribner had better see it at once. Hadn't it been for this horrid ailment I should already have sent you the twenty-five or thirty pages more which finish the thing off, bring it to a proper pointed climax. These, however, you shall have at the very earliest date possible—the delay will not at the worst be great. Only please let Scribner understand that this valuable and effective little matter *is* to be promptly supplied. Please indeed ask him to cable on the question of the two Magazine samples—my disposition and ability to compose which, for effective serialisation, are of the most positive order. I can't but think, or at least hope, that he will view favourably the feasibility of this. I shall do it very artfully indeed.

As for the other and greater matter,[2] broken to me in his letter of four days ago, I have of course felt I had only to wait for the sign from you that you have also heard. But I don't feel that I can for a few days yet go into it very much. It is too important and demands all one's normal power of attention. At first, I mean at the very most immediate blush of the thing, I felt quite dazzled and elated—for it was not for some minutes, or even a good many, that I quite took in that what his offer involves will be the surrender of my copyright. *There* resides a quite poisonous pang; for I have never in all my course made any such surrender and have a very deep instinct of objection to it. It in fact seems strange to me that Scribner should have been moved, at this time of day, to see such a question in such a light: that of the withdrawal of one particular, and per-

626

haps "supreme" work, from the general conditions of the Big Edition, in which it must after brief delay figure. That affects me as awkward and depressing and unadvisable—though the proposal has otherwise a certain superficial "liberality" which slightly hypnotises and makes the temptation (the temptation *to* make the surrender) rather cruel in its vividness. The surrender is "for Everywhere," or in other words for this country and the Macmillan Edition as well as for America and the American. I shall have to thresh it out, the whole possibility, with a fresher spirit, after I am on my feet again and holding up my head as I should. Perhaps something of the "liberality" may be saved—at less heavy a cost. But these prodigious and remorseless masters of business! He says, as you will have observed, that he "would consider willingly any change in the form of his offer." Perhaps some possible compromise lies that way—some compromise, I mean, leaving the offer still sufficiently dazzling, or at least attractive, to make *some* sacrifice (of present time, of other intentions or preoccupations or whatever); and yet leave me with the Copyright to cling to. If you have, at your convenience, anything in this direction to suggest I shall be glad to hear of it. We must take a little time—I feel strongly the importance of my not feeling flurried or hustled; and there will be much more to say. For the moment the question of *A Small Boy* seems the pressing thing, and I hold myself already about the couple of instalments. May your wonted vigour have returned!

Yours ever
Henry James

1. HJ had sent the all-but-completed manuscript of *A Small Boy and Others* to Pinker for forwarding to Scribner.

2. Charles Scribner had written to HJ on 27 September 1912 offering "a somewhat unusual proposal": $8,000 for the world rights to his next novel—"another great novel to balance *The Golden Bowl.*" This unprecedented offer was flattering but made HJ suspicious: he had never been dealt with on such a princely scale by publishers. Nor did he discover that the offer was instigated by Edith Wharton, who after her recent visit to the modest scale of life in Lamb House had decided that HJ was in need of money. She asked Scribner to divert some of her royalties to HJ, disguised as this advance. (See Appendix II.)

To Edmund Gosse
Dictated Ts Barrett

Lamb House, Rye
October 10*th* 1912

My dear Gosse.

Your good letter of this morning helps to console and sustain. One really needs any lift one can get after this odious experience. I am emerging, but it is slow, and I feel much ravaged and bedimmed. Fortunately these days have an intrinsic beauty—of the rarest and charmingest here; and I try to fling myself on the breast of Nature (though I don't by that fling myself on my poor blisters and scars on the dew-sprinkled lawn) and forget, imperfectly, that precious hours and days tumble unrestrained into the large round, the deep dark, the ever open, hole of sacrifice. I am almost afraid my silly lessors of the Chelsea Flat *won't* apply to you for a character of me if they haven't done so by now;[1] afraid because the idea of a back-hander from you reaching them straight, would so gratify my sense of harmless sport. It was only a question of a word in case they *should* appeal; kindly don't dream of any such if they let the question rest (in spite indeed of their having intimated that they would thoroughly thresh it out).

I receive with pleasure the small Swinburne[2]—of so chaste and charming a form; the perusal of which lubricated yesterday two or three rough hours. Your composition bristles with items and authenticities even as a tight little cushion with individual pins; and, I take it, is everything that such a contribution to such a cause should be but for the not quite ample enough (for my appetite) conclusive estimate or appraisement. I know how little, far too little, to my sense, that element has figured in those pages in general; but I should have liked to see you, in spite of this, formulate and *resume* a little more the creature's character and genius, the aspect and effect of his general performance. You will say I have a morbid hankering for what a Dictionary doesn't undertake, what a Sidney Lee[3] perhaps even doesn't offer space for. I admit that I talk at my ease—so far as ease is in my line just now. Very charming and happy Lord Redesdale's[4] contribution—showing, afresh, how *everything* about such a being as S. becomes and remains interesting. Prettily does Redesdale write—and prettily will O[scar]

628

B[rowning][5] have winced; if indeed the pretty even in that form, or the wincing in any, could be conceived of him.

I have received within a day or two dear old George Meredith's *Letters*;[6] and, though I haven't been able yet very much to go into them, I catch their emanation of something so admirable and, on the whole, so baffled and so tragic. We must have more talk of them—and also of Wells's book,[7] with which however I am having extreme difficulty. I am not so much struck with its hardness as with its weakness and looseness, the utter going by the board of any real self respect of composition and expression. Interesting to me, however, your mention of his civil acceptance of your own reflections on the matter; which I should have liked to see. What lacerates me perhaps most of all in the Meredith volumes is the meanness and poorness of editing—the absence of any attempt to project the Image (of character, temper, quantity and quality of mind, general size and sort of personality) that such a subject cries aloud for; to the shame of our purblind criticism. For such a Vividness to go a-begging—and for a Will Meredith to stand there as if he were dealing with it! When one thinks of what Vividness would, in France, in such a case, have leaped to its feet in commemorative and critical response! But there is too much to say, and I am able, in this minor key, to say too little. We must be at it again. I was afraid your wife was having another stretch of the dark valley to tread—I had heard of your brother-in-law's illness. May peace somehow come! I re-greet, and regret, you all and am all faithfully yours

Henry James

1. HJ had decided to lease a flat at 21 Carlyle Mansions S.W., Cheyne Walk, in Chelsea, and had given Gosse's name as a reference to the landlord.

2. The life of Swinburne, a privately printed biographical essay, originally written for the *Dictionary of National Biography.*

3. The editor of the DNB.

4. Algernon Bertram Freeman-Mitford, 1st Baron Redesdale (1837–1916), diplomat and author, had provided Gosse with details concerning Swinburne's days at Eton. His letter is reproduced in an appendix to Gosse's *Algernon Charles Swinburne* (1917).

5. Oscar Browning (1837–1923), historian, whose reminiscences of Swinburne at Eton had been challenged by Lord Redesdale.

6. Meredith's letters in two volumes edited by his son W. H. Meredith. Further letters on Meredith are in Lubbock, *Letters of Henry James* (1920), II, 250–255.

7. The novel *Marriage* (1912).

To Edmund Gosse
Dictated Ts Congress

Lamb House, Rye
October 15*th* 1912

My dear Gosse.

Here I am at it again—for I can't not thank you for your two notes last night and this morning received. Your wife has all my tenderest sympathy in the matter of what the loss of her Brother cost her. Intimately will her feet have learnt to know these ways. So it goes on till we have no one left to lose—as I felt, with force, two summers ago, when I lost my two last Brothers within two months and became sole survivor of all my Father's house. I lay my hand very gently on our friend.

With your letter of last night came the Cornhill with the beautifully done little Swinburne chapter.[1] What a "grateful" subject, somehow, in every way, that gifted being—putting aside even, I mean, the value of his genius. He is grateful by one of those arbitrary values that dear G[eorge] M[eredith] for instance, doesn't positively command, in proportion to his intrinsic weight; and who can say quite why? Charming and vivid and authentic, at any rate, your picture of that occasion; to say nothing of your evocation, charged with so fine a Victorian melancholy, of Swinburne's time at Vichy with Leighton, Mrs. Sartoris and Richard Burton; what a felicitous and enviable image they do make together—and what prodigious discourse must even more particularly have ensued when S. and B. sat up late together after the others! Distinct to me the memory of a Sunday afternoon at Flaubert's in the winter of '75–'76, when Maupassant, still *inédit,* but always "round," regaled me with a fantastic tale, irreproducible here, of the relations between two Englishmen, each other, and their monkey![2] A picture the details of which have faded for me, but not the lurid impression. Most deliciously Victorian that too—I bend over it all so yearningly; and to the effect of my hoping "ever so" that you are in conscious possession of material for a series of just such other chapters in illustration of S., each a separate fine flower for a vivid even if loose nosegay.

I'm much interested by your echo of Haldane's[3] remarks, or whatever, about G.M. Only the difficulty is, of a truth, somehow,

that *ces messieurs*, he and Morley and Maxse and Stephen, and two
or three others, Lady Ulrica included, really never knew much more
where *they* were, on all the "aesthetic" ground, as one for convenience calls it, than the dear man himself did, or where *he* was;
so that the whole history seems a record somehow (so far as "art and
letters" are in question) of a certain absence of point on the part of
every one concerned in it. Still, it abides with us, I think, that
Meredith was an admirable spirit even if not an *entire* mind; he
throws out, to my sense, splendid great moral and ethical, what he
himself would call "spiritual," lights, and has again and again big
strong whiffs of manly tone and clear judgment. The fantastic and
the mannered in him were as nothing, I think, to the intimately
sane and straight; just as the artist was nothing to the good citizen
and the liberalised bourgeois. However, lead me not on! I thank you
ever so kindly for the authenticity of your word about these beastly
recurrences (of my disorder). I feel you floated in confidence on the
deep tide of Philip [Gosse]'s experience and wisdom. Still, I *am*
trying to keep mainly out of bed again (after forty-eight hours just
renewedly spent in it). But on these terms you'll wish me back
there—and I'm yours with no word more,

Henry James

1. Gosse's essay on Swinburne appeared in the October 1912 *Cornhill Magazine*
and was reprinted in *Portraits and Sketches* (1912).

2. Gosse replied on 16 October 1912: "The Monkey story . . . relates to a Page whom
Swinburne or Powell (they are not distinguished in the story) brought to Etretat and
who became jealous of a Monkey, which was also a member of the household, and how
after a scene (oh! what a scene!) the Page hanged the Monkey outside the master's
bedroom door, and then rushed out and drowned himself. Whereupon the master raised
a marble monument not to the Page, but to the Monkey. Is this the little horror which
you heard Maupassant relate? Or was it the completely anodyne absurdity of Swinburne's having killed and roasted his own pet monkey as a feast for Maupassant? . . .
I believe you to be the only person left who can give a first-hand report." (Charteris,
Life and Letters of Sir Edmund Gosse, 343).

3. Richard Burdon Viscount Haldane (1856–1928), lawyer, statesman, philosopher,
Lord Chancellor 1912–1915.

To Edmund Gosse
Dictated Ts Congress

Lamb House, Rye
October 17*th* 1912

My dear Gosse.

It's very well invoking a close to this raging fever of a correspondence when you have such arts for sending and keeping the temperature up! I feel in the presence of your letter last night received that the little machine thrust under one's tongue may well now register or introduce the babble of a mind "affected"; though interestingly so, let me add, since it is indeed a thrill to think that I *am* perhaps the last living depositary of Maupassant's wonderful confidence or legend. I really believe myself the last survivor of those then surrounding Gustave Flaubert. I shrink a good deal at the same time, I confess, under the burden of an honour "unto which I was not born"; or, more exactly, hadn't been properly brought up or pre-admonished and pre-inspired to. I pull myself together, I invoke fond memory, as you urge upon me, and I feel the huge responsibility of my office and privilege; but at the same time I must remind you of certain inevitable weaknesses in my position, certain essential infirmities of my relation to the precious fact (meaning by the precious fact Maupassant's having, in that night of time and that general failure of inspiring prescience, so remarkably regaled me). You will see in a moment everything that was wanting to make me the conscious recipient of a priceless treasure. You will see in fact how little I could have *any* of the right mental preparation. I didn't in the least know that M. himself was going to be so remarkable; I didn't in the least know that *I* was going to be; I didn't in the least know (and this was above all most frivolous of me) that *you* were going to be. I didn't even know that the Monkey was going to be, or even realise the peculiar degree and *nuance* of the preserved lustre awaiting *ces messieurs,* the three taken together. Guy's story (he was only known as "Guy" then) dropped into my mind but as an unrelated thing, or rather as one related, and indeed with much intensity, to the peculiarly "rum," weird, macabre and unimaginable light in which the interesting, or in other words the delirious, in English conduct and in English character, are—or were especially then—viewed in French circles sufficiently

632

self-respecting to have views on the general matter at all, or in other words among the truly refined and enquiring. "Here they are at it!"—I remember that as my main inward comment on Maupassant's vivid little history; which was thus thereby somehow more vivid to me about *him*, than about either our friends or the Monkey; as to whom, as I say, I didn't in the least foresee this present hour of arraignment!

At the same time I think I'm quite prepared to say, in fact absolutely, that of the two versions of the tale, the two quite distinct ones, to which you attribute a mystic and separate currency over there, Maupassant's story to me was essentially Version No. 1. It wasn't at all the minor, the comparatively banal anecdote. Really what has remained with me is but the note of two elements—that of the Monkey's jealousy, and that of the Monkey's death; how brought about the latter I can't at all at this time of day be sure, though I am haunted as with the vague impression that the poor beast figured as having somehow destroyed *himself*, committed suicide through the *spretae injuria formae*.[1] The third person in the fantastic complication was either a young man employed as servant (within doors) or one employed as boatman, and in either case I think English; and some thin ghost of an impression abides with me that the "jealousy" was more on the Monkey's part toward him than on his toward the Monkey; with which the circumstance that the Death I seem most (yet so dimly) to disembroil is simply and solely, or at least predominantly, that of the resentful and impassioned beast: who hovers about me as having seen the other fellow, the *jeune anglais* or whoever, installed on the scene after he was more or less lord of it, and so invade his province. You see how light and thin and confused are my data! *How* I wish I had known or guessed enough in advance to be able to oblige you better now: not a stone then would I have left unturned, not an i would I have allowed to remain undotted; no analysis or exhibition of the national character (of *either* of the national characters) so involved would I have failed to catch in the act. Yet I do so far serve you, it strikes me, as to be clear about *this*—that, whatever turn the dénouement took, whichever life was most luridly sacrificed (of those of the two humble dependants), the drama had essentially been one of the affections, the passions, the last *cocasserie*, with each member of the quartette involved! Disentangle it as you can—

I think Browning alone could really do so! Does this at any rate—the best I can do for you—throw any sufficient light? I recognise the importance, the historic bearing and value, of the most perfectly worked-out view of it. *Such* a pity, with this, that as I recover the fleeting moments from across the long years it is my then active figuration of the so tremendously *averti* young Guy's intellectual, critical, vital, experience of the subject-matter that hovers before me, rather than my comparatively detached curiosity as to the greater or less originality of *ces messieurs!*—even though with this highly original they would appear to have been. I seem moreover to mix up the occasion a little (I mean the occasion of that confidence) with another, still more dim, on which the so communicative Guy put it to me, àpropos of I scarce remember what, that though he had remained quite outside of the complexity I have been glancing at, some *jeune anglais,* in some other connection, had sought to draw him into some scarcely less fantastic or abnormal one, to the necessary determination on his part of some prompt and energetic action to the contrary: the details of which now escape me—it's all such a golden blur of old-time Flaubertism and Goncourtism! How many more strange flowers one *might* have gathered up and preserved! There was something from Goncourt one afternoon about certain Swans (they seem to run so to the stranger walks of the animal kingdom!) who figured in the background of some prodigious British existence, and of whom I seem to recollect there is some faint recall in "La Faustin"[2] (not, by the way, "*Le* Faustin," as I think the printer has betrayed you into calling it in your recent *Cornhill* paper). But the golden blur swallows up everything, everything but the slow-crawling, the too lagging, loitering amendment in my tiresome condition, out-distanced by the impatient and attached spirit of yours all faithfully

Henry James

1. Juno's scorned beauty: *Aeneid,* I.27.
2. *La Faustin,* Edmond de Goncourt's novel about a ballet dancer who sacrifices her career to please her aristocratic English lover.

To H. G. Wells
Dictated Ts Bodleian

Lamb House, Rye
October 18*th* 1912

My dear Wells.

I have been sadly silent since having to wire you (nearly three weeks ago) my poor plea of inability to embrace your so graceful offer of an occasion for my at last meeting, in accordance with my liveliest desire, the eminent Arnold Bennett;[1] sadly in fact is a mild word for it, for I have cursed and raged, I have almost irrecoverably suffered—with all of which the end is not yet. I had just been taken, when I answered your charming appeal, with a violent and vicious attack of "Shingles"—under which I have lain prostrate till this hour. I don't shake it off—and perhaps you know how fell a thing it may be. I am precariously "up" and can do a little to beguile the black inconvenience of loss of time at a most awkward season by dealing after this graceless fashion with such arrears of smashed correspondence as I may so presume to patch up; but I mayn't yet plan for the repair of other losses—I see no hope of my leaving home for many days, and haven't yet been further out of this house than to creep feebly about my garden, where a blest season has most fortunately reigned. A couple of months hence I go up to town to stay (I have taken a lease of a small unfurnished flat in Chelsea, on the river); and there for the ensuing five or six months I shall aim at inducing you to bring the kind Bennett, whom I meanwhile cordially and ruefully greet, to partake with me of some modest hospitality.

Meanwhile if I've been deprived of you on one plane I've been living with you very hard on another; you may not have forgotten that you kindly sent me *Marriage*[2] (as you always so kindly render me that valued service); which I've been able to give myself to at my less afflicted and ravaged hours. I have read you, as I always read you, and as I read no one else, with a complete abdication of all those "principles of criticism," canons of form, preconceptions of felicity, references to the idea of method or the sacred laws of composition, which I roam, which I totter, through the pages of others attended in some dim degree by the fond yet feeble theory of, but which I shake off, as I advance under your spell, with the most

635

cynical inconsistency. For under your spell I do advance—save when I pull myself up stock still in order not to break it with so much as the breath of appreciation; I live with you and in you and (almost cannibal-like) *on* you, on you H.G.W., to the sacrifice of your Marjories and your Traffords, and whoever may be of their company; not your treatment of them, at all, but, much more, their befooling of you (pass me the merely scientific expression—I mean your fine high action in view of the red herring of lively interest they trail for you at their heels) becoming thus of the essence of the spectacle for me, and nothing in it all "happening" so much as these attestations of your character and behaviour, these reactions of yours as you more or less follow them, affect me as vividly happening. I see you "behave" all along, much more than I see them even when they behave (as I'm not sure they behave *most* in *Marriage*) with whatever charged intensity or accomplished effect; so that the ground of the drama is somehow most of all in the adventure for *you*—not to say *of* you—the moral, temperamental, personal, expressional, of your setting it forth; an adventure in fine more appreciable to me than any of those you are by way of letting *them* in for. I don't say that those you let them in for don't interest me too, and don't "come off" and people the scene and lead on the attention, about as much as I can do with; but only, and always, that you beat them on their own ground and that your "story," through the five hundred pages, says more to me than theirs. You'll find this perhaps a queer rigmarole of a statement, but I ask of you to allow for it just now as the mumble, at best, of an invalid; and wait a little till I can put more of my hand on my sense. Mind you that the restriction I may seem to you to lay on my view of your work, still leaves that work more convulsed with life and more brimming with blood than any it is given me nowadays to meet. The point I have wanted to make is that I find myself absolutely unable, and still more unwilling, to approach you, or to take leave of you, in any projected light of criticism, in any judging or concluding, any comparing, in fact in any aesthetic or "literary," relation at all; and this in spite of the fact that the light of criticism is almost that in which I most fondly bask and that the amusement I consequently renounce is one of the dearest of all to me. I simply decline—that's the way the thing works—to pass you again through my cerebral oven for critical consumption: I consume you crude and whole and to the last

morsel, cannibalistically, quite, as I say; licking the platter clean of
the last possibility of a savour and remaining thus yours abjectly

Henry James

1. See letter to Walpole, 19 May 1912.
2. Wells's newly published novel.

To Edmund Gosse
Dictated Ts Congress

Lamb House, Rye
November 19*th* 1912

My dear Gosse.

I received longer ago than I quite like to give you chapter and
verse for your so-vividly interesting volume of literary *Portraits;*[1]
but you will have (or at least I earnestly beg you to have) no reproach
for my long failure of acknowledgment when I tell you that my
sorry state, under this dire physical visitation, has unintermit-
tently continued, and that the end, or any kind of real break in a
continuity of quite damnable pain, has still to be taken very much
on trust. I am now in my eighth week of the horrible experience,
which I have had to endure with remarkably little medical mitigation—really with none worth speaking of. Stricken and helpless,
therefore, I can do but little, to this communicative tune, on any
one day; which has been also the more the case as my admirable
Secretary was lately forced to be a whole fortnight absent—when I
remained indeed without resource. I avail myself for this snatch of
one of the first possible days, or rather hours, since her return. But
I read your book, with lively "reactions," within the first week of
its arrival, and if I had then only had you more within range should
have given you abundantly the benefit of my impressions, making
you more genial observations than I shall perhaps now be able
wholly to recover. I recover perfectly the great one at any rate—it is
that each of the studies has extraordinary individual life, and that
of Swinburne in particular, of course, more than any image that
will ever be projected of him. This is a most interesting and charming paper, with never a drop or a slackness from beginning to end.
I can't help wishing you had proceeded a little further *critically*—
that is, I mean, in the matter of appreciation of his essential stuff

637

and substance, the proportions of his mixture, etc.; as I should have been tempted to say to you, for instance, "Go into that a bit *now!*" when you speak of the early setting-in of his arrest of development etc. But this may very well have been out of your frame—it might indeed have taken you far; and the space remains wonderfully filled-in, the figure all-convincing. Beautiful too the Bailey, the Horne and the Creighton—this last very rich and fine and touching. I envy you your having known so well so genial a creature as Creighton, with such largeness of endowment. You have done him very handsomely and tenderly; and poor little Shorthouse not to the last point of tenderness perhaps, but no doubt as handsomely, none the less, as was conceivably possible. I won't deny to you that it was to your Andrew Lang[2] I turned most immediately and with most suspense—and with most of an effect of drawing a long breath when it was over. It is very prettily and artfully brought off—but you would of course have invited me to feel with you how little you felt you were doing it as we should, so to speak, have "really liked." Of course there were the difficulties, and of course you had to defer in a manner to some of them: but your paper is of value just in proportion as you more or less overrode them. His recent extinction, the facts of long acquaintance and camaraderie, let alone the wonder of several of his gifts and the mass of his achievement, couldn't, and still can't, in his case, not be complicating, clogging and qualifying circumstances; but what a pity, with them all, that a figure so lending itself to a certain amount of interesting *real* truthtelling, should, honestly speaking, enjoy such impunity, as regards some of its idiosyncrasies, should get off so scot-free ("Scot"-free is exactly the word!) on all the ground of its greatest hollowness, so much of its most "successful" puerility and perversity. Where I can't but feel that he *should* be brought to justice is in the matter of his whole "give-away" of the value of the wonderful chances he so continually enjoyed (enjoyed thanks to certain of his very gifts, I admit!)—give-away, I mean, by his *cultivation*, absolutely, of the puerile imagination and the fourth-rate opinion, the coming round to that of the old apple-woman at the corner as after all the good and the right as to any of the mysteries of mind or of art. His mixture of endowments and vacant holes, and "the making of the part" of each, would by themselves be matter for a really edifying critical study—for which, however, I quite recognise that the day and the occasion have already hurried heedlessly away. And I perhaps throw a disproportionate weight on the whole question—merely by reason of a late accident or two; such as my having recently read his (in two or three respects so able) Joan of Arc, or Maid of France, and turned over his just-published (I think posthumous) compendium of "English Literature," which lies on my table downstairs. The extraordinary inexpensiveness and childishness and impertinence of this latter gave to my sense the measure of a whole side of Lang, and yet which was one of the sides of his greatest flourishing. His extraordinary *voulu* Scotch provincialism crowns it and rounds it off, really making one at moments ask with what kind of an innermost intelligence such inanities and follies were compatible. The Joan of Arc is another matter of course; but even there, with all the accomplishment, all the possession of detail, the sense of reality, the vision of the truths and processes of life, the light of experience and the finer sense of history, seem to me so wanting, that in spite of the thing's being written so intensely *at* Anatole France,[3] and in spite of some of A.F.'s own (and so different!) perversities, one "kind of" feels and believes Andrew again and again bristlingly yet *bétement* wrong, and Anatole sinuously, yet oh so wisely, right!

However, all this has taken me absurdly far, and you'll wonder why I should have broken away at such a tangent. You had given me the opportunity, but it's over and I shall never speak again! I wish *you* would, all the same—since it may still somehow come in your way. Your paper as it stands is a gage of possibilities. But goodbye—I can't in this condition keep anything up; scarce even my confidence that Time, to which I have been clinging, is going, after all to help. I had from Saturday to Sunday afternoon last, it is true, the admirably kind and beneficent visit of a London friend who happens to be at the same time the great and all-knowing authority and expert on Herpes; he was so angelic as to come down and see me, for twenty-four hours, thoroughly overhaul me and leave me with the best assurance and with, what is more to the point, a remedy very probably more effective than any yet vouchsafed me. I mean Henry Head F.R.S.[4] the eminent neurologist—whose position will be known to Philip. When I do at last emerge I shall escape from these confines and come up to town for the rest of the winter. But I shall have to feel differently first, and it may not be for some time yet. It in fact can't *possibly* be soon. You shall have then, at any rate, more news—"which," à la Mrs. Gamp, I hope your own has a better show to make. Yours all, and all faithfully,

Henry James

P.S. I hope my last report on the little Etretat[5] legend—it seems (not the legend but the report) of so long ago!—gave you something of the light you desired. And how I should have liked to hear about the Colvin[6] dinner and its rich chiaroscuro. He has sent me his printed—charming, I think—speech: "the best thing he has done."

1. *Portraits and Sketches* (1912), which contained, in addition to the Swinburne essay, studies of Andrew Lang, Philip James Bailey, "Orion" Horne, Mandell Creighton, and J. H. Shorthouse, and an obituary of HJ's friend Wolcott Balestier.
2. Andrew Lang (1844–1912), British essayist and poet, and an ardent folklorist.
3. Anatole France's *Vie de Jeanne d'Arc* (1908), much criticized for romanticizing history.
4. Henry Head (1861–1940), eminent neurologist, who read and admired HJ. For the effects of his medication see letter to Mrs. Wharton, 4 December 1912.
5. Maupassant's monkey anecdote; see letter to Gosse, 17 October 1912.
6. Sidney Colvin had just retired as keeper of prints and drawings at the British Museum.

To Robert C. Witt
Ms Unknown

Lamb House, Rye
November 27*th* 1912

Dear Sir,

I am almost shocked to learn, through your appreciative note, that in imaginatively projecting, for use in *The Outcry*, such a painter as the Mantovano, I unhappily coincided with an existing name, an artistic identity, a real one, with visible examples, in the annals of the art. I had never heard (in I am afraid my disgraceful ignorance) of the painter the two specimens of whom in the National Gallery you cite; and fondly flattered myself that I had simply excogitated, for its part in my drama, a name at once plausible, that is of good Italian type, and effective, as it were, for dramatic bandying-about. It was important, you see, that with the great claim that the story makes for my artist I should have a strictly supposititious one—with no awkward existing data to cast a possibly invidious or measurable light. So *my* Mantovano was a creature

of mere (convincing) fancy—and this revelation of my not having
been as inventive as I supposed rather puts me out! But I owe it to
you none the less that I shall be able—after I have recovered from
this humiliation—to go and have a look at our N.G. interloper. I
thank you for this and am faithfully yours,

Henry James

To Hendrik C. Andersen
Dictated Ts Barrett

Lamb House, Rye
November 28*th* 1912

Dearest Hendrik.

This is only a scrap of a blessing on you, in the roundabout form
to which you see me still condemned, for your beautiful letter this
morning received, and which I have read with as much admiration
and wonder, as much appreciation and bewilderment, as you may
charitably imagine. Everything you evoke for me in it is charming
and interesting to me as being *yours,* as being part of a fond and
devoted dream, in which you are spending your life, as some Prince
in a fairy tale might spend *his* if he had been locked up in a boundless palace by some perverse wizard, and, shut out thus from the
world and its realities and complications, were able to pass his time
wandering from room to room and dashing off, on each large wall-
surface, as it came, "This is the great Temple of the Arts," or "This
is the prodigious Stadium," and "This," in the next room of the
interminable series, "is the Temple of Religions." The patience and
ingenuity, not to say the shining splendour, of your dream, touch
me more than I can say; but what I don't see is the *application* of
the vast puzzle, or the steps which, in this world of such sharp
intricate actual living facts and bristling problems and overwhelming actualities, are to convert the affair into the Reality
which is needed for giving it a Sense. You see, dearest Hendrik, I
live myself in the very intensity of reality and can only conceive of
any art-work as producing itself piece by piece and touch by touch,
in close relation to some immediate form of life that may be open
to it—I do this so much, I say, that I think of colossal aggregations
of the multiplied and the continuous and the piled up, as brilliant

castles in the air, brilliant as you will, cut off from all root-taking in this terribly crowded and smothered and overbuilt ground that stretches under the feet of the for the most part raging and would-be throat-cutting and mutually dynamiting nations. I don't, in fine, see where your vision, subject to such murderous obstruction and control and annihilating criticism, "comes in"; the very law of our difficult human sphere being that things struggle into life, even the very best of them, by slow steps and stages and rages and convulsions of experience, and utterly refuse to be taken over ready-made or *en bloc*. But here I am douching you with cold water again, when I only meant to spray on you, and on your sublime good faith and splendid imagination, a mixture, soothing and satisfying, of all the "perfumes of Araby." This is only a momentary sign of affectionate remembrance, of tender recognition *quand même*. I am fit for nothing more, for I grieve to say I am still in these accursed throes. Three days hence I shall have entered into my tenth week of them, and, frankly, I don't know what to make of that—any more than my helpless doctors do. However, they, these abominable Shingles, have been known to last three months on end, and I am perhaps but a fine three-months case. I could well dispense with the honour of being to that extent a "pathological" curiosity—which means, to simplify, medical freak or monstrous specimen. I envy you the rapid clearing off of your own indisposition. My doctor too is "dull and pleasant"—but not dull enough if that's what's wanted to cure me, like yours (for you)—nor pleasant enough to console me for this endless woe. Set down to my continued bedevilment anything in this that may have rubbed you the wrong way, and believe me yours affectionately, all

Henry James

P.S.[1] I feel how you know that I can't by that impersonal machinery dearest Hendrik, touch you, and draw you close, half as tenderly as I would on better and above all on nearer ground.

1. The postscript is in HJ's hand.

To Edith Wharton
Dictated Ts Yale

Lamb House, Rye
[December 4*th* 1912]

My dear E.W.

Your beautiful Book[1] has been my portion these several days, but as other matters, of a less ingratiating sort, have shared the fair harbourage, I fear I have left it a trifle bumped and *bousculé* in that at the best somewhat agitated basin. There it will gracefully ride the waves, however, long after every other temporarily floating object shall have sunk, as so much comparative "rot," beneath them. This is a rude figure for my sense of the entire interest and charm, the supreme validity and distinction, of *The Reef*. I am even yet, alas, in anything but a good way—so abominably does my ailment drag itself out; but it has been a real lift to read you and taste and ponder you: the experience has literally worked, at its hours, in a medicating sense that neither my local nor my London Doctor (present here in his greatness for a night and a day) shall have come within miles and miles of. Let me mention at once, and have done with it, that the advent and the effect of the intenser London Light can only be described as an anti-climax, in fact as a tragic farce, of the first water: in short one of those *mauvais tours* as far as results are concerned, that makes one wonder how a Patient ever survives *any* relation with a Doctor. My Visitor[2] was charming, intelligent, kind, all visibly a great master of the question; but he prescribed me a remedy, to begin its action directly he had left, that simply and at short notice sent me down into hell, where I lay sizzling (never such a sizzle before) for three days, and has since followed it up with another under the dire effect of which I languish even as I now write. I am of course from this day closing my mouth tight to anything received from his hand, and there will doubtless be eventually, some "explanation" of the whole monstrous muddle. I shall from this moment shake myself free of *every* form of medicine. I have really been fumbled at these nine weeks (being now in my tenth) with a futility that I can call nothing less than cruel; and my conviction or intention, is all centred on the simple idea of *escape*, escape from further torment, to take effect about a week hence, at any apparent cost: it's so impossible I should suffer less, in town, on my own hook, than I have up to this moment been suffering here—in a drawn-and-quartered fashion. So much to express both what I owe you—or *have* owed you at moments that at all lent themselves, in the way of pervading balm, and to explain at the same time how scantly I am able for the hour to make my right acknowledgment.

There are fifty things I should like to say to you about the Book, and I shall have said most of them in the long run; but there are some that eagerly rise to my lips even now and for which I want the benefit of my "first flush" of appreciation. The whole of the finest part is, I think, quite the finest thing you have done; both *more* done than even the best of your other doing, and more worth it through intrinsic value, interest and beauty.

December 9*th*

I had to break off the other day, my dear Edith, through simple extremity of woe; and the woe has continued unbroken ever since— I have been in bed and in too great suffering, too unrelieved and too continual, for me to attempt any decent form of expression. I have just got up, for one of the first times, even now, and I sit in command of this poor little situation, ostensibly, instead of simply being bossed by it though I don't at all know what it will bring. To attempt in this state to rise to any worthy reference to *The Reef* seems to me a vain thing; yet there remains with me so strongly the impression of its quality and of the unspeakably *fouillée* nature of the situation between the two principals (more gone into and with more undeviating truth than anything you have done) that I can't but babble of it a little to you even with these weak lips. It all shows, partly, what strength of subject is, and how it carries and inspires, inasmuch as I think your subject in its essence, [is] very fine and takes in no end of beautiful things to do. Each of these two figures is admirable for truth and *justesse;* the woman an exquisite thing, and with her characteristic finest, scarce differentiated notes (that is some of them) sounded with a wonder of delicacy. I'm not sure her oscillations are not beyond our notation; yet they are so held in your hand, so felt and known and shown, and everything seems so to come of itself. I suffer or worry a little from the fact that in the Prologue, as it were, we are admitted so much into the consciousness of the man, and that after the introduction of Anna

(Anna so perfectly named), we see him almost only as she sees him—which gives our attention a different sort of work to do; yet this is really I think but a triumph of your method, for he remains of an absolute consistent verity, showing himself in that way better perhaps than in any other, and without a false note imputable, not a shadow of one, to his manner of so projecting himself. The beauty of it is that it is, for all it is worth, a Drama and almost, as it seems to me, of the psychologic Racinian unity, intensity and gracility. Anna is really of Racine, and one presently begins to feel her throughout as an Eriphyle or a Bérénice: which, by the way, helps to account a little for something *qui me chiffonne* throughout; which is why the whole thing, unrelated and unreferred save in the most superficial way to its milieu and background, and to any determining or qualifying *entourage* takes place *comme cela*, and in a specified, localised way, in France—these non-French people "electing," as it were, to have their story out there. This particularly makes all sorts of unanswered questions come up about Owen; and the notorious wickedness of Paris isn't at all required to bring about the conditions of the Prologue. Oh, if you knew how plentifully we could supply them in London and, I should suppose, in New York or in Boston. But the point was, as I see it, that you couldn't really give us the sense of a Boston Eriphyle or Boston Givré, and that an exquisite instinct, "back of" your Racinian inspiration and settling the whole thing for you, whether consciously or not, absolutely prescribed a vague and elegant French colonnade or gallery, with a French river dimly gleaming through, as the harmonious *fond* you required. In the key of this, with all your reality, you have yet kept the whole thing; and, to deepen the harmony and accentuate the literary pitch, have never surpassed yourself for certain exquisite *moments*, certain images, analogies, metaphors, certain silver correspondences in your *façon de dire*: examples of which I could pluck out and numerically almost confound you with, were I not stammering this in so handicapped a way. There used to be little notes in you that were like fine benevolent finger-marks of the good George Eliot—the echo of much reading of that excellent woman, here and there, that is, sounding through. But now you are like a lost and recovered "ancient" whom *she* might have got a reading of (especially were he a Greek) and of whom in *her* texture some weaker reflection were to show. For, dearest Edith, you are stronger and firmer and finer than all of them put together; you go further and you say *mieux*, and your only drawback is not having the homeliness and the inevitability and the happy limitation and the affluent poverty, of a Country of your Own (*comme moi pour exemple!*) It makes you, this does, as you exquisitely say of somebody or something at some moment, elegiac (what penetration, what delicacy in your use there of the term!)—makes you so that, that is, for the Racinian-*sérieux*; but leaves you more in the desert (for everything else) that surrounds Apex City. But you will say that you're content with your lot; that the desert surrounding Apex City is quite enough of a dense crush for you, and that with the *colonnade* and the gallery and the dim river you will always otherwise pull through. To which I can only assent—after such an example of pulling through as *The Reef*. Clearly you have only to pull, and everything will come.

These are tepid and vain remarks, for truly I am helpless. I have had all these last days a perfect hell of an exasperation of my dire complaint, the eleventh week of which begins to-day; and have arrived at the point really—the weariness of pain is so great—of not knowing *à quel saint me vouer*. In this despair, and because "change" at any hazard and any cost, is strongly urged upon me by both my Doctors, and is a part of the regular process of *dénouement* of my accursed ill, I am in all probability trying to scramble up to London by the end of this week, even if I have to tumble, howling, out of bed and go forth in my bedclothes. I shall go in this case to Garlant's Hotel, Suffolk Street, where you have already seen me, and not to my Club, which is impossible in illness, nor to my little flat (21 Carlyle Mansions, Cheyne Walk, Chelsea. S.W.) which will not yet, or for another three or four weeks, be ready for me. The change to London may possibly do something toward breaking the spell: please pray hard that it shall. Forgive too my muddled accents and believe me, through the whole bad business, not the less faithfully yours

Henry James

1. *The Reef: A Novel* (1912).
2. Dr. Henry Head. See letter to Gosse, 19 November 1912.

To Mrs. William James
Dictated Ts Harvard

21 Carlyle Mansions, S.W.
January 5*th* 1913

Dearest Alice.

You must forgive me this form of dictation, as it is absolutely all I'm fit for just now; and these few lines are a mere stopgap, till I can rise to something better, anyhow. I have been having a very difficult struggle, all along, and the business of tumbling somehow into this place in my highly untoward state, of which I can't attempt to give you particulars, has gone on really like a rather blackish nightmare.[1] If it hadn't been for the extraordinary ability and devotion displayed by Kidd and Joan,[2] and for Miss Bosanquet's extremely helpful arts exercised here, I should have broken down half way—I don't really quite see what would have become of me. For the grip of my atrocious illness, a horrible gastric and stomachic crisis grafted upon my poor ravaged herpetic tract (herpetic being the right, the medical name for what pertains to Shingles) is really only now beginning to loosen; but of course the assault of such a real rigour of disease, so pitilessly prolonged, has left me compromised in certain old ways—from which, however, I feel I shall with patience emerge. My feeling is in fact that I *must* be reserved for some decent destiny yet to have successfully struggled with so much misery and withstood so malignant a combination of enemies. I have done the right thing to get in *here,* where I have slept yet but one night—taking, however, the measure of the real goodness of the place and situation. The servants are delighted with it, and, by an extraordinary chance, given the nature of all but the very most expensive flats, I am able to put the three up, separately; which I couldn't have done in De Vere Gardens. I have had letters from you all—a few—and heaven knows that during all the long wretched weeks they were welcome. But I can't specify now, and this is only a vague weak sign. One thing, however, take home to yourselves all—I am on a better footing here for pursuing my recovery than I have been at any moment since I began at all to get better. You see the second edition, as it were, of my illness, the aggravation of my herpetic state by this other even more damnable gastric complication, working in with it and reinforcing it, has, for intensity of suffering, proved very much the worst of the two; and when I get that well under—as I *shall* again—I shall have triumphed indeed; and shall have done it all myself; no so-called medical help having contributed a jot. What lies heavy upon me has been the interruption of profitable work at a moment when I was really and confidently getting back to it. However my first Book (of the Two) is really *done,* and I am receiving rapid proofs from New York.[3] These I have been able to attend to, in spite of everything. Have patience with me, and I shall before long write you better news. I repeat that I feel I really *have* sustained and outlived an onset that absolutely *proves* something for me and in my favour—something that now, with no end more of exercise of the withstanding faculty, I shall not inconsiderably profit by. But this is all now—it is only a sign to break my recent silence. I have, these last weeks, had all I could do to simply hold on as tight as possible—I couldn't do that and communicate with you too. Dear little Fanny Prothero has let me know of *her* writing I think three or four times, and I have much blessed her for it. This you also will have done. Don't worry about me now, for though, I have difficulties they are much slighter than they have been, and I see my way more. I worry—all this practical business has been a worry; but *out* of it too I am worrying. I embrace you all and beg each of you to have a good patience with me. Everything you have told me about your own conditions and doings has been of the deepest interest. But I could have howled, at times, for the sight and sound of you. My outlook on the River as I stand at my "drawingroom" window now is really a most blest asset. Yours, dearest Alice, ever so affectionately,

Henry James

1. The move from Lamb House to his new Chelsea flat.
2. HJ's Lamb House maidservants.
3. *A Small Boy and Others.*

648

To Charles Scribner
Dictated Ts Princeton

21 Carlyle Mansions, S.W.
January 31*st* 1913

Dear Mr. Scribner.

I am much obliged to you for your letter of January 15th, speaking of the safe arrival of my Daguerreotype[1] for frontispiece use in my Volume, and of two or three other matters—not least of these the safe arrival of the first half of my climax of Copy (making, that is, the very end) for said *Small Boy.* I greatly rejoice that this moderate addendum—or rather most accidentally delayed original Finis, can be conveniently worked in. And all my blessing goes to the happy development of the Photogravure, of which you will perhaps let me see a proof. I am going straight and very promisingly now, I think, with the progress of the Second Book,[2] which will *have*, I apprehend, to be somewhat longer than the First, embodying as it must a considerable number of Letters, or parts of Letters, of my Father's as well as my Brother's. It will only be a question, however, of a certain number more of words to a page—and I shall take care that there needn't be too many; though I regret the prospect of sacrificing even a little the so handsome page, as it strikes me, of *A Small Boy.* Let me also acknowledge with thanks what you say of the misunderstanding (of last autumn) with Mr. Pinker on the question of the Advance.[3] With my misfortune, my perversity, of a long and blighting illness, the first of which goes back to three years ago, leading in a dreadful, dragged-out period of work again and again made impossible, I was to become subject, I fear, to a rather yearning and anxious view of the question of Advances. But the prospect has so much cleared, with better health, and a kind of fierce apprehension of what I have it still grandly within me to do, that my sense of the whole case is braver and easier, and I feel that what you will have arranged with J.B.P. according to your own view won't fail to suit me very well. I only want to be without worry (I may at the same time slip in) to find myself confident of still doing, or more than ever doing—well, magnificent work. Worry, in these days, considerably blights me—though I haven't, I confess, really had much of it; and confidence hugely inspires.

I thank you kindly for sending me *Scribner*[4] with this freshness—

649

I mean straight from the fountain-head. I follow Mrs. Wharton with a devoted interest—an intimacy of view of her course of production only second to my concern about my own. I rate her ability very high, and feel there is more and more of it to come. I wish she were more *placed* in relation to her Anglo-Saxon public—she has so swallowed all Places (as Carlyle said Mirabeau had swallowed Formulas); but a wonderful inward chemistry resides at her conversion of the multitudinous into the particular—and I think her talent, in fine, incalculable. The finest parts of *The Reef* seem to me as fine, as beautifully and firmly done, as anything since the greatest felicities of George Eliot—and indeed, frankly, to have a penetration and a "hand" measurably beyond *them*. On the Scribner serial I fondly and intently hang; it seems to me to promise her a great chance, and I feel all sorts of genial confidence about it. But I inflict on you too long a letter. Believe me yours very truly

Henry James

1. The Matthew Brady daguerreotype of HJ as a boy with his father, used as frontispiece to *A Small Boy and Others* (and reproduced in *Letters* I, 8).
2. *Notes of a Son and Brother.*
3. See letter to Pinker, 8 October 1912.
4. Edith Wharton's *The Custom of the Country* was being serialized in *Scribner's Monthly.*

To Elizabeth Lee
Ms British Library

21 Carlyle Mansions, S.W.
February 10*th* 1913

Dear Miss Lee.

Alas, my knowledge of poor unpleasant little Ouida[1] was a very limited thing indeed. I met her two or three times in Florence and went once to see her—before she had fallen on her later most evil days, though there even then hung about her an air as of very precarious resources and very tarnished lustre. I had later on, here, two or three letters from her—short, very sprawling notes (which I didn't keep: they were so abusive of two or three very harmless persons), and a small painted panel, a view of a Lucca street—this an *offrande,* but of a childishly primitive "art": really a child of seven or eight might have done it. Frankly she was not sympathetic—and I scarce envy you the task of undertaking a book about her. But she was *curious*, in a common little way: she suggested somehow having come out of such a very "low-down" or even base little past, of unfathomable things, and yet being withal of a most uppish, or dauntless, little spirit of arrogance and independence. The best and most sincere thing about her I seemed to make out, was—or had been—her original genuine perception of the beauty, the distinction and quality of Italy: this almost inspired her—yet was mixed with such vulgarities and falsities too. She must have gone—and for many years—through absolute horror of growing poverty and final want—though for long too she was arrogant about her debts and obligations. The only way to treat her would be really and quite frankly, I think, as a little terrible and finally pathetic *grotesque*; but even as such she *means* nothing—is too without form and void! However, she is doubtless a challenge to the bookmaking art—if you can but get *documents*, of sorts. Old Florentincs (of the cosmopolite colony) could tell you things—and I could tell you two or three—yet either unimportant or irreproducible. But the trouble is we are all gone or going—dead or dying! I *have* the little painted panel (in the country) I think—but that would be the most irreproducible of all! Believe me yours very truly

Henry James

1. Pen-name of Marie Louise de la Ramée (1839–1908), writer of popular romantic novels. See Elizabeth Lee, *Ouida: A Memoir* (1914).

To Hugh Walpole
Ms Texas

21, Carlyle Mansions, S.W.
March 16*th* 1913

Dearest, dear Hugh.

I find I can't *not* take an interest, of the tenderest and most practical, in the material equipment of the Cobbles,[1] and I want to express it in sending down to you a very pleasant and convenient and solid old Desk, with capacious table and drawers and pigeon-holes etc. which I very fondly beg you to accept from me if you have room for it *there*. (If you haven't room for it there, or see any other adverse reason, it shall, it *must*, go to Hallam Street.) I don't want to despatch it without hearing from you as to placeability first. You will find it a very agreeable working adjunct, I think. But let me *know*—on the basis of its being a certain, a decent size of thing; not one of the very largest of its type—but large enough, probably, even for your scale of production. (There was a larger one, which I considered—but which seems to me to put a premium on the perhaps too frequent or too corpulent volume!—though I wouldn't have you thin and rare.) It would be a healing balm to me to have a little more of your news. I sent you the other day a current fiction of the same (E. Pugh) in which I had found, strange to say, a certain helpless and muddled interest. Also a *Bookman* with your "picture" in it—to say nothing of mine, by the dozen. Do you know in the least who the not entirely asinine Dixon Scott[2] is?—is he of your Tough Set or your Tender Age? He too is muddled and helpless—yet he means so well. I do hope Cornwall pans out decently. It's very splendid of you to face that stern music. I don't know how to tell you vividly enough how yearningly I pat you on the back or in fact take you to the heart. But feel it, know it, like it, and "like," for it and for ever so much more, yours, dearest Hugh, all devotedly,

Henry James

1. Walpole had acquired a cottage, The Cobbles, at Polperro in Cornwall.
2. Dixon Scott (1881–1915) had published an article on HJ in the March 1913 *Bookman*. Scott died at Gallipoli. His posthumous *Men of Letters* (1917) contains his various pieces on HJ.

To William James III
(Cable) *Ms Private*

London
March 28 1913

Immense thanks for warning taking instant prohibitive action. Please express to individuals approached my horror money absolutely returned.[1]

Uncle

1. The cable was prompted by HJ's discovering that Mrs. Wharton and others were attempting to raise a sum of money in the United States as a seventieth birthday gift for him.

21, Carlyle Mansions, S.W.
March 29*th* 1913

Dearest Bill.

How can I sufficiently thank you for the blessed notifying Cable about the dreadful project you had got wind of? I tried to do something of this yesterday afternoon by an answering cable, of which I hope you will by this time have grasped the full sense. The thing is for you to give out as strongly and emphatically as possible, to all such persons about you as may have been deplorably approached, and may be bewilderedly intending, that you have it from me, straight and strong, that the idea (all "appreciation of kindness" handsomely allowed for!) fills me with unmitigated horror, and that should it most accursedly push forward to any practical effect, every cent of the money would be instantly and ruthlessly, would be even quite resentfully, returned. A more reckless and indiscreet undertaking, with no ghost of a preliminary leave asked, no hint of a sounding taken, I cannot possibly conceive—and am still rubbing my eyes for incredulity. But you can immensely help me in Boston by the course I beseech of you—the giving out, in the strong terms, right and left, that is privately and socially, I mean, and to all it may concern, this my all but indignant, and my wholly prohibitive, protest. You will probably almost already be acting in this sense, so far as you can, as a consequence of my Cable; and please leave no stone unturned to follow it up. It occurs to me that the Perrys, perhaps even especially Lilla, who circulates the most freely, would be very good and sympathetic people to appeal to for assistance: T.S.P. himself at least will so fully understand. Possibly you may have shown them my message before sending it on, as I take for granted you will have done, to Harry; of whom I ask, for New York, the same blessed service that you will render in Boston. Between you, thus easily, you will break the back of the thing. So I don't cable Harry, as you will have passed your message on; but shall probably this afternoon send to New York a week-end cable letter—addressing it in fact to Mrs. Cadwalader Jones, the very best person I can think of for understanding and dissemination: on the assumption that the horror will have been "launched" in N.Y., naturally, at least as much as in Boston. I only want it stamped out by any violent means (not, of course, of the newspaper) that may be all necessary to really dispose of it. But this is all now. I very lately wrote you both. Tell Alice, with bestest love, that I live just now, and shall all these coming days, in deepest participation. I am doing, myself, very decently well—and having caught on to quiet work again unspeakably helps to float me. I increasingly rejoice in my propitious quarters here. Show this letter to Irving Street and let *them* send it on to Harry—if you're sure they will do so soon enough. *Je vous embrasse bien tous deux*, and am ever your fond and grateful old Uncle

Henry James

To Percy Lubbock
Dictated Ts Lubbock

21 Carlyle Mansions, S.W.
March 30*th* 1913

My very dear Percy,

Very dear as you thus are, I find I must ask of you a service that you may, all protestingly, feel to be somewhat untender, or at least difficult. The fond conspiracy[1] to raise a sum of money which shall enable my admirable friends to present me with my own expensive effigy for eventual presentation to the National Portrait Gallery has inevitably but belatedly come to my knowledge and has determined within me an overwhelming sense that an amiable submission to the scheme and acceptance of the gift are not in the least in my stiff "chords"—are in fact absolutely out of my power. It must appear very dreadful of me, I know, to be thus contumacious—as for instance who am I that I should rear up against a design so friendly, so flattering and so generous? the curse of such situations being indeed that to draw back with emphasis (and of the strongest) is to seem graceless and brutal, and that yet the objection may fail and the project triumph unless the most violent language (alternating with the sweetest supplication) *is* turned on. So behold me all tears and fires together, beseeching you to desist and at the same time declaring myself harsh adamant *unless* you do. I am hideously hateful of course—for oh I am so utterly earnest. The reasons for

654

Portrait of Henry James by John Singer Sargent, 1913, commissioned by James's friends for his seventieth birthday; now in the National Portrait Gallery, London.

which I can't countenance the project are overwhelming and insurmountable, and in asking myself how to check its further development I leap to the reflection that as you are the dear recruited secretary, or devoted treasurer, of the "movement" (heaven help us!) a word from me that reaches you will by that fact reach the others. I feel I can't write to your blest companions individually—it is too distressing and I am truly not well enough; but I also feel that you will judge best how to notify them (by trouble-saving telephone and otherwise) of the nasty character that I thus fortunately *in time* reveal. Any other course than this want of the graceful accompanied by this extreme of the obstinate is, my dear Percy, wholly impossible to me; I must beg you all to take those ugly things as my last word on the matter, and am yours gratefully, faithfully and remorselessly

Henry James

1. Percy Lubbock had been selected by a group of HJ's friends to be secretary of a subscription in England to have John Singer Sargent paint a portrait of HJ as a gift in honor of his seventieth birthday.

To Mrs. William James
Dictated Ts Harvard

21 Carlyle Mansions, S.W.
April 1st [and 16th] 1913

Dearest Alice.

Today comes blessedly your letter of the 18th written after the receipt of my cable to you in answer to your preceding one of the 6th (after you had heard from Robert Allerton of my illness). You will have been reassured further—I mean beyond my cable—by a letter I lately despatched to Bill and Alice conjointly, in which I told them of my good and continued improvement. I am going on very well, increasingly so—in spite of my having to reckon with so much chronic pectoral pain now so seated and settled, of the queer "falsely anginal" but none the less when it is bad, distressing order. It comes directly from no heart-trouble—for I haven't any—that is one element of mitigation of my consciousness of it—and it is more or less controllable by certain kinds of care: care above all as to what I eat, and above all drink (very little liquid), and care never to consent to hurry (in the *least*) or flurry or worry—care to sleep almost sitting, on a bed-rest—and care to move (walk, circulate) as much as I can while doing so very slowly and gently and *alone* (not talking at the same time). So I manage, and have got back to work, and can go about to some extent in the afternoon (to see friends) with the aid of the blest taxis of the low London tariff, the long strike in that business being over: though of course the whole thing deprives me of much sense of *margin*. I neither *ever* lunch out nor dine out—though I not infrequently dine, for change and ventilation, at the Club. *And* I shall get better, improve further still I pretty well believe—very possibly with some further control of the pectoral question: which meanwhile remains in abeyance (as regards any sharpness of it) during my hours of quietude, hours of deliberate movements only. Moreover too it is astonishing with how much pain one can with long practice learn constantly and not too defeatedly to live. Therefore, dearest Alice, don't think of this as too black a picture of my situation; it is so much brighter a one than I have thought at certain bad moments and seasons of the past that I should probably ever be able to paint. The mere power to work in such measure as I can is an infinite help to a better consciousness—and though so impaired compared to what it used to be it tends to *grow*, distinctly—which by itself proves that I have *some* firm ground under my feet. And I repeat to satiety that my conditions *here* are admirably helpful and favouring. (Now that Kidd is back from a much absence at Rye—her distracted mother having come to an end in my cottage—there is no hitch in our household order or ease, and the value of the good little apartment shines out brightly again.)

You can see, can't you? how strange and desperate it would be to "chuck" everything up, Lamb House, servants, Miss Bosanquet, *this* newly acquired and prized resource, to come over, by a formidable and expensive journey, to spend a summer in the (at best) to me torrid and (the inmost inside of 95 apart) utterly arid and vacuous Cambridge. Dearest Alice, I could come back to America (could be carried back on a stretcher) to *die*—but never, never to live. To say how the question affects me is dreadfully difficult because of its appearing so to make light of you and the children—but when I think of how little Boston and Cambridge were of old ever *my* affair, or anything but an accident, for me, of the parental life there to which I occasionally and painfully and losingly sacrificed, I have a superstitious terror of seeing them at the end of time again stretch out strange inevitable tentacles to draw me back and destroy me. And then I could never either make or afford the journey (I have no margin at all for *that* degree of effort—especially with the more and more, the eternally babyish Burgess to look after, whose powers—apart from his virtuous attachment—to take care of me is *nil,* compared with my perpetual need of taking care of *him.* He gets the wages of a good valet (here) and is incapable of any of the responsibilities.) But you will have understood too well—without my saying more—how little I can dream of any *déplacement* now—especially for the sake of a milieu in which you and Peg and Bill and Alice and Aleck would be burdened with the charge of making up *all* my life. Not one grain of it should I be able to pick up outside of you. I haven't a single other tie in America that means ten cents to me—*really* means it. You see my capital—yielding all my income, intellectual, social, associational, on the old investment of so many years—my capital is *here,* and to let it all slide would be simply to become bankrupt. Oh if you only, on the other hand, you and Peg and Aleck, *could* walk beside my bathchair down this brave Thames-side I would get back into it again (it was some three weeks ago dismissed), and half live there for the sake of your company. I have a kind of sense that you would be able to live rather pleasantly near me here—if you could once get planted. But of course I on my side understand all your present complications.

April 16th!

It's really too dismal, dearest Alice, that, breaking off the above at the hour I *had* to, I have been unable to go on with it for so many days. It's now more than a fortnight old still, though my check was owing to my having of a sudden, just as I rested my pen, to drop perversely into a less decent phase (than I reported to you at the moment of writing) and have had with some difficulty to wriggle up again, I am now none the less able to send you no too bad news. I have wriggled up a good deal, and still keep believing in my capacity to wriggle up in general.—Suffice if for the moment that I just couldn't, for the time, drive the pen myself—when I am "bad" I feel too demoralised, too debilitated, for this; and it doesn't at all do for me then to push against the grain. Don't feel, all the same, that if I resort this morning to the present help, it is because I am *not* feeling differently—for I really am in an easier way again (I mean of course specifically and "anginally" speaking) and the circumstances of the hour a good deal explain my proceeding thus. I had yesterday a Birthday, an extraordinary, prodigious, portentous, quite public Birthday, of all things in the world, and it has piled up acknowledgments and supposedly delightful complications and arrears at such a rate all round me, that in short, Miss Bosanquet being here, I today at least throw myself upon her aid for getting on correspondentially—instead of attending to my proper work, which has, however, kept going none so badly in spite of my last poor fortnight. I will tell you in a moment of my signal honours, but want to mention first that your good note written on receipt of *A Small Boy* has meanwhile come to me and by the perfect fulness of its appreciation gave me the greatest joy. There are several things I want to say to you about the shape and substance of the book—and I will yet; only now I want to get this off absolutely by today's American post, and tell you about the Honours, a little, before you wonder, in comparative darkness, over whatever there may have been in the American papers that you will perhaps have seen; though in two or three of the New York ones more possibly than in the Boston. I send you by this post a copy of yesterday's *Times* and one of the *Pall Mall Gazette*—the two or three passages in which, together, I suppose to have been more probably than not reproduced in N.Y. But I send you above all a copy of the really very beautiful Letter (expressed with singular grace and felicity and sobriety, I think, and from the hand of dear delightful Percy Lubbock), ushering in the quite wonderful array of signatures (as I can't but feel) of my testifying and "presenting" friends: a list of which you perhaps can't quite measure the very charming and distinguished and "brilliant" character without knowing your London better. What I wish I *could* send you is the huge harvest of exquisite, of splendid sheaves of flowers that converted a goodly table in this room, by the time yesterday was waning, into such a blooming garden of complimentary colour as I never dreamed I should, on my own modest premises, almost bewilderedly stare at, sniff at, all but quite "cry" at. I think I must and shall in fact compass sending you a photograph of the still more glittering tribute dropped upon me—a really splendid "golden bowl," of the highest interest and most perfect taste, which would, in the extremity of its elegance, be too proudly false a note amid my small belongings here if it didn't happen to fit, or to sit, rather, with perfect grace and comfort, on the middle of my chimney-piece, where the rather good glass and some other happy accidents of tone most fortunately consort with it. It is a very brave and artistic (exact) reproduction of a piece of old Charles II plate; the bowl or cup having handles and a particularly charming lid or cover, and standing on an ample round tray or salver; the whole being wrought in solid silver-gilt and covered over with quaint incised little figures of a (in the taste of the time) Chinese intention. In short it's a very beautiful and honourable thing indeed; and if the said American movement that Bill and Harry and I had a couple of weeks ago so flurriedly to inter-cable about, could but have proposed itself in, and resolved itself into, some such aspect as that of a not too expensive presentation object or "artistic memento," I could have faced *that* music with the very best grace I could muster. That is the only thing I *consented* to face here. Against the *giving to me* of the Portrait, presumably by Sargent, if I do succeed in being able to sit for it, I have absolutely and successfully protested. The possession, the attribution or ownership of it, I have insisted, shall be only their matter that of the subscribing friends (whose individual subscriptions were kept down, by the scheme, to the very lowest figure, most of them consisting but of a sovereign and a half-sovereign); my participation being that of the sitter alone, and not a bit of the acquisitor. And they must first catch their hare; the portrait must first come into being. Sargent, most beautifully, as a member of the Committee, tried to insist on doing it for nothing; but had to yield to the representation, of course, that if this were allowed the work would become practically *his* present altogether, and not that of the Friends. "Where," they naturally ask, "should *we* then come in?"—So he agreed, with the one condition, that, when I should have sat, he was to be free to tear the canvas straight up if he himself doesn't like the result. This is a part of the matter which will greatly appeal to Bill—appeal perhaps more than any other part; and at any rate, you see, I may perhaps after all never figure—! I tell you all this partly because I kind of want to have it clear that what I couldn't dream of accepting from Boston and New York was the crude raked-together *offrand* of a lump of money. I have had a good letter from Bill since the hour of our cables, and his mention of two or three of the names, alone, connected with the question in Boston, have made me quite gasp with dismay. It's invidious to specify, but the idea of being beholden to the rummaged pockets of Sturgis Bigelow and of Barrett Wendell,[1] for instance, would have been simply intolerable to me. If I don't feel that way about all these good people here, I can only say that somehow I *don't*—on the basis that is, of the "piece of plate." On the other hand I should thoroughly have felt so had their approach been, like the projected one we got wind of, with the crude money-lump! *And,* moreover, I haven't, you see, anything like any such number of real personal acquaintances, of individual friendly *relations,* in N.Y. and Boston as I have roundabout me here. Counting my nearest and dearest out (that is all my nearest relatives) there are not more than half a dozen persons in either city whom I should in the least care to look at as subjects of such an appeal, or to "take" anything from. The sad part of the matter of the other day is that I fear I have incurred the grave reprobation and almost resentment of the friend[2] (on this side of the world) at whose instance you heard of the attempt's being launched. That is a sorry result—though I hasten to add a "probably" but short-lived one. What is infelicitous is that she purposely kept out of the "movement" here, in order to associate herself with the American one; but now, as it happens, the American one is, thank goodness, squashed—so, though really one of the best friends I have in the world, she fails to figure in either. However, I am drenching you with this—though I shall have probably done no more than sate your just curiosity and sympathy. I am hoping now each day for a happy echo of Otis Place[3]—and supposing it, perhaps mistakenly, a little overdue. Otis Place, at any rate, has my perpetual fond thought—and the echo will happily come! I am sending Harry a copy of the Letter too—but do send him on this as well. You see there *must* be good life in me still when I can gabble so hard. The Book[4] appears to be really most handsomely received hereabouts. It is being treated in fact with the very highest consideration. I hope it is viewed a little in some such mannerly light roundabout yourselves, but I really call for no "notices" whatever. I don't in the least want 'em. What I *do* want is to personally and firmly and intimately encircle Peg and Aleck and their Mother and squeeze them as hard together as is compatible with squeezing them so tenderly! With this *tide* of gabble you will surely feel that I shall soon be at you again. And so I shall! Yours, dearest Alice, and dearest all, ever so and ever so!

Henry James

P.S. I have just heard from Alice Edgar,[5] Wilky's Alice, that she dashes out to these parts, London and Paris, for a very few weeks only (devoted mainly to Paris) and with a couple of "lady friends" (which expression, to do her justice, she doesn't use). But she writes me very sweetly and nicely, and I shall be very glad to see her and to do for her the very limited whatever that my circumstances of every kind admit of. I really want to know her—for the poor Wilky-ghost's sake.

1. William Sturgis Bigelow (1850–1926), a cousin of Mrs. Henry Adams, who had embraced Mahayana Buddhism; and Barrett Wendell, professor of English at Harvard, of whose writings (and apparently personality) HJ was critical.
2. Probably Mrs. Wharton.
3. Where Billy James and his bride were living.
4. *A Small Boy and Others.*
5. Alice Edgar (b. 1875), daughter of HJ's younger brother Garth Wilkinson (Wilky) James. She married David Alexander Edgar, a Canadian, in 1910.

To Hugh Walpole
Ms Texas

21 Carlyle Mansions, S.W.
April 11*th* 1913

Dearest Hugh.

Yes, I have been meanly and sadly silent—but I take it you always understand (so strange it would be if you didn't) that when these things happen—in the face of occasions for speech—it's because of wretched preventive physical conditions. My damnable pectoral (anginal) ailment rages at times with almost unbearable violence and that has been the case of late. Then I am simply disabled—utterly stricken—and must bow my head to the storm. I am trying to hold it up a little now. But I have sent you (my joy that you would mention a household want was of the greatest) the nearest approach to what I conceive to be a *right* little mirror that I could after much hunting find. Small and simple ones are the devil to put one's hand on—everything so big and florid. I conceive this one intended for the chimney-piece in your chamber of inspiration—and if it's too tall to stand upright it will, I think, [do] equally well (and can be easily so placed by the Village Carpenter) with its short side up—the whole reposing lengthways. So let me figure it. It's warranted a genuine old morsel—and looked so to me. Let the donor's battered old mug glimmer out of it at you in some dim benediction when the reflection of your own fresh beauty doesn't too wholly usurp the scene. And I sent you longer ago a copy of my fatuous Infant Reminiscences—which I hope will have reached you safely. It was a pleasure to me to despatch you so handsome and goodly a volume—so fair and stately a page. I do find it a joy to see one's honest prose enjoy the advantage of a brave presentment. I thank you kindly for your mention of the few of your circumjacent facts; as above all of the "real monetary success" of *Fortitude*.[1] What an abashment to my little play of the lantern of criticism over its happy constitution! But I am familiar with that irony of fate (others' fate). Very thrilling too the prospect of the Young Review and the band of brothers spewing forth Courtney[2] and his like. Hurry up with it—have fun with it too above all—before I sink to rest. You will wonder what I am coming to when I tell you I have *also* (after Pugh!) read—with difficulty—another young Fiction of the Day (yet with a shade of interest too); Gilbert Cannan's *Round the Corner.*[3] Very helpless as to the doing, but again with a certain gravity of intention—considerability of squalid *renseignement*. But, dearest boy, I am sore and spent. Good-night—your fondest, feeblest, finest old,

Henry James

1. Walpole's longest and most ambitious novel to date (his fifth) had just been published by Martin Secker and praised by John Galsworthy and Arnold Bennett. It contains a thinly disguised portrait of HJ in the character named Galleon, who says a great many things HJ had said to Walpole.
2. W. L. Courtney had given *Fortitude* a two-column review in the *Daily Telegraph*.
3. Gilbert Cannan (1884–1955), novelist and dramatist, a member of the D. H. Lawrence coterie.

To the Friends of Henry James
(A Printed Letter)

21, Carlyle Mansions
Cheyne Walk, S.W.
April 21st, 1913

Dear Friends All.[1]

Let me acknowledge with boundless pleasure the singularly generous and beautiful letter, signed by your great and dazzling array and reinforced by a correspondingly bright material gage, which reached me on my recent birthday, April 15th. It has moved me as brave gifts and benedictions can only do when they come as signal surprises. I seem to wake up to an air of breathing good-will the full sweetness of which I had never yet tasted; though I ask myself now, as a second thought, how the large kindness and hospitality in which I have so long and so consciously lived among you could fail to act itself out according to its genial nature and by some inspired application. The perfect grace with which it has embraced the just-past occasion for its happy thought affects me, I ask you to believe, with an emotion too deep for stammering words. I was drawn to London long years ago as by the sense, felt from still earlier, of all the interest and association I should find here, and I now see how my faith was to sink deeper foundations than I could presume ever to measure—how my justification was both stoutly to grow and wisely to wait. It is so wonderful indeed to me as I count up your numerous and various, your dear and distinguished friendly names, taking in all they recall and represent, that I permit myself to feel at once highly successful and extremely proud. I had never in the least understood that I was the one or signified that I was the other, but you have made a great difference. You tell me together, making one rich tone of your many voices, almost the whole story of my social experience, which I have reached the right point for living over again, with all manner of old times and places renewed, old wonderments and pleasures reappeased and recaptured—so that there is scarce one of your ranged company but makes good the particular connection, quickens the excellent relation, lights some happy train and flushes with some individual colour. I pay you my very best respects while I receive from your two hundred and fifty pair of hands, and more, the admirable, the inestimable bowl, and while I engage to sit, with every accommodation, to the so markedly indicated "one of you," my illustrious friend Sargent. With every accommodation, I say, but with this one condition that you yourselves, in your strength and goodness, remain guardians of the result of his labour—even as I remain all faithfully and gratefully yours

Henry James

P.S.—And let me say over your names.

Maria Dexter Abbott
Mildred Acheson
Jessie Allen
Edith Allendale
Laurence Alma-Tadema
Anna Alma-Tadema
Mary Arnim
Henrietta M. L. Arnold
Waldorf Astor
Nancy Astor
John Bailey
Arthur James Balfour
Maurice Baring
Granville Barker
Alice Barnard
J. M. Barrie
Constance Battersea
Max Beerbohm
Florence Bell
Arnold Bennett
A. C. Benson
Robert H. Benson
B. Berenson
Kathleen Beresford
Walter V. R. Berry
Edith Bigelow
Edward D. Boit
Charles Booth
Mary Booth
Paul Bourget

Charles W. Boyd
A. C. Bradley
A. G. Bradley
Sylvia Brooke
Rupert Brooke
Rhoda Broughton
Horatio F. Brown
J. W. Comyns Carr
John Ridgely Carter
Alice Carter
Basil Champneys
Erskine Childers
Mary Alden Childers
Mary Cholmondeley
Victoria Cholmondeley
Mary T. Clarke (*The late*)
Arthur Clay
Lucy Clifford
Margaret Clifford
Sibyl Colefax
Amy Coleridge
John Collier
Ethel Collier
Sidney Colvin
Frances Colvin
Martin Conway
Katrina Conway
Agnes Conway
C. A. Cook
F. W. Warre Cornish

Blanche Warre Cornish
Montague Crackanthorpe
Blanche A. Crackanthorpe
Crewe
Margaret Crewe
Cromer
J. W. Cross
Ariana R. W. Curtis
Nina Cust
W. E. Darwin
Louisa H. Davey
Alice Dew-Smith
Fisher Dilke
Ethel Dilke
Austin Dobson
Charles Du Bos
Zezette Du Bos
George H. Duckworth
Margaret Duckworth
Gerald Duckworth
Emma Du Maurier
Gerald Du Maurier
Maria Theresa Earle
Mary Elcho
Thomas H. Elliott
Oliver Elton
Esher
Eleanor Esher
Edith Fairchild
Filippo de Filippi
Jane H. Findlater
Mary W. Findlater
Fitzmaurice
James Fitzmaurice-Kelly
Douglas W. Freshfield
Clare Frewen
Morton Fullerton
John Galsworthy
May Gaskell

Walter Gay
Matilda Gay
W. G. von Glehn
Jane von Glehn
Louis von Glehn
May E. Gordon
Louisa Gosford
Edmund Gosse
Ellen Gosse
Philip Gosse
Teresa Gosse
Sylvia Gosse
Alice S. Green
Anstey Guthrie
Haldane of Cloan
Elizabeth C. Harcourt
Beatrice Harraden
L. A. Harrison
Alma Harrison
Anthony Hope Hawkins
W. Heinemann
George Henschel
Maurice Hewlett
Frances Horner
A. John Hugh-Smith
Mary Hunter
Lewis A. Irving
Fred. Huth Jackson
Clara Huth Jackson
Agnes Jekyll
C. F. Keary
W. P. Ker
Rudyard Kipling
E. Ray Lankester
Gaillard Lapsley
D. C. Lathbury
Ralph Latimer
Charles N. Lawrence
Louisa A. Leavitt

Sidney Lee
Marie Lee-Childe
Elizabeth Lewis
George J. G. Lewis
Mary Lovelace
A. Low
Marie Belloc Lowndes
Percy Lubbock
Alfred Lyttleton
Edith Lyttleton
Spencer Lyttleton
Maarten Maartens
Desmond MacCarthy
D. S. MacColl
Frederick Macmillan
Georgiana Macmillan
Maurice Macmillan
Helen Macmillan
Bernard Mallet
Marie Mallet
Nina Maquay
G. J. Maquay
Margaret of Sarawak
Edward Marsh
A. E. W. Mason
Elizabeth Mathew
Katharine Maxse
Mary Maxwell
Anna Lea Merritt
Alice Meynell
Milner
Violet Mond
Norman Moore
Ottoline Morrell
Eveleen Myers
I. K. Napier
Henry Newbolt
W. E. Norris
R. D. Norton

Violet Ormond
William Osler
Violet Paget
E. S. Pakenham
Alfred Parsons
Herbert Paul
Joseph Pennell
Elizabeth Robins Pennell
Jocelyn Persse
Florence Pertz
Mary J. Phillips
Jessie P. B. Phipps
Arthur Pinero
Frederick Pollock
Georgina Pollock
John Pollock
Una Pope-Hennessy
G. W. Prothero
M. F. Prothero
W. G. Rathbone
B. M. Rathbone
Elena Rathbone
Henrietta T. Reubell
J. J. Reubell
Bruce L. Richmond
W. B. Richmond
Anne Ritchie
Emily Ritchie
Elizabeth Robins
Rennell Rodd
Rosebery
Emma Louisa Rothschild
Marie de Rothschild
Mary St. Helier
Ethel Sands
Emily Sargent
John S. Sargent
T. Bailey Saunders
Owen Seaman

Anne de Sélincourt
Mildred Seymour
G. Bernard Shaw
Mary Sheridan
Wilfred Sheridan
Clare Sheridan
Edith Sichel
A. Forbes Sieveking
May Sinclair
Ernest D. Skinner
Elizabeth Smith
Reginald J. Smith
Logan Pearsall Smith
William Haynes Smith
Howard O. Sturgis
Mary Sturgis
Millicent Sutherland
Alfred Sutro
Esther Stella Sutro
Ellen Terry
H. Yates Thompson
E. A. M. Thompson
Nelly Thorpe
Mary E. Tomlinson
Henry Tonks
George Otto Trevelyan
Caroline Trevelyan

G. M. Trevelyan
Janet Trevelyan
Hilda Trevelyan
Juliet S. Trower
Margaret Vincent
H. M. Walbrook
A. B. Walkley
Donald Mackenzie Wallace
Hugh Walpole
Mary A. Ward
T. Herbert Warren
Edward Warren
Margaret Warren
Maud Warrender
Sydney Waterlow
H. G. Wells
Edith Wharton
Christopher Wheeler
Penelope Wheeler
Orlo Williams
Alice Williams
Isabel Wood
Margaret L. Woods
Virginia Woolf
George Wyndham
Filson Young

1. Copies were printed by the Chiswick Press to be sent to all who had subscribed for the Sargent portrait of HJ and for the gift of a golden bowl. HJ announced that he would offer the portrait to the National Portrait Gallery. Sargent announced that he would accept no money but would turn the sum over to the young sculptor Derwent Wood to make a bust of the novelist. HJ added certain names to the list of subscribers (including Mrs. Wharton and Walter Berry, who were on the obsolete American list, which in accordance with HJ's wishes had been abandoned).

To Howard Sturgis
Ms Harvard

105 Pall Mall, S.W.
May 12*th* or 13*th!* 1913

Dearest Howard.

Your letter is adorable; only how can I do anything toward clearing up those pale antediluvian spectres when I want so just to circle round and round you?—as I *shall,* for a little, at no distant day. (I *do* want to come down for, or toward, tea-time only—and shall presently have proposed it.) However your enquiries touch me deeply, as showing the sweetness of your interest—and there isn't really much of a muddle.

(1) Gussy Barker *was* the son of my Aunt Janet (James).[1] She, dying at his birth (I *think*) or very early indeed, had married William B., brother of "Anna Barker," Mrs. S. G. Ward; the latter the wife of the "good" Sam Ward, of Boston, and later the mother of poor dear deaf "Tom," of Bessie von Schönberg (wife of Ernst), of Lily V. Hoffmann of the old Roman days etc. My Aunt Janet's three children were, beside Gus, Bob B., who "showed some promise for sculpture" and died young (he was the eldest), and the "genial girl" of Mme. Richard's, who married (through *Lenox* meetings) George Higginson of Boston (and Lenox), eldest brother of Henry, Frank etc. She died a dozen years ago. G. H. still lives at Lenox—very, very old.

(2) There were *four* Uncles[2] (of my Father's own brothers—plus two elder half-brothers; one of these latter being Robert, father of "Bob" James, the choreographic, and of Lydia ditto, she marrying Henry Mason and becoming the mother of the "inimitable Masons," of Tours and Paris. The most surviving of these daughters of hers, of the troop of "Honorine," still lives on in Paris—the beauty, Mrs. Hayward Cutting.) The four "own" uncles were Augustus, John, Edward and Howard; this last the youngest of all my grandfather's children, very good-looking (they were *all* good-looking!) but having nothing but *that* in common with you. Howard became of an almost *épouvantable* badness, alas, later on—of about the same intensity as your goodness; and that mention of him in the Mrs. Cannon[3] picture is the sole I decided to make. But I will tell you all about your wicked namesake.

(3) "Johnny" J.,[4] of the Sillig school, the talent for music and the

early death, was the one son of my Uncle John, very early widowed this latter, but having also a daughter (alluded to as "dressing their memory"); who married Alfred Grymes, brother of Mrs. Louis von Hoffmann and of the "bad" Mrs. Sam Ward, of N.Y.—Medora. (What a mixture!) Nelly Grymes died, tragically, twenty-five years ago.

(4) My Uncle Edward never married—he was *most* particularly of Mrs. Cannon's; he died *bien jeune* and I should have liked to "put in" more about him—but feared so to be boring with trivial detail. *Now* I yearn over all I left out.

(5) Yes, my Father's two other sisters were my Van Buren and my Temple Aunts.[5] I should have *liked* to drag in the former's daughter, the intimate of our childhood, or of mine, later Mrs. Stuyvesant Morris; but forebore. Our Uncle Robert Temple was brother to (later) Lady Rose, poor dear "latest" Mary Clarke's mother.

(6) Yes, too, the enviable (though only in extreme youth) Albert was the one child of Alexander Wyckoff (whose mother had been my *maternal* grandmother's sole sister).[6]

(7) Mrs. L. was Mrs. Lidiard (Lidyard?) mother to Henry Lidiard who became father to Mrs. Spencer Lidiard, your whilom neighbour. (She had been an early intimate, I think, of my Albany grandmother—which latter adopted four nieces (daughters of a sister) in addition to her own nine children and, quartered on her, *their* (mainly) orphaned and half-orphaned ones! Those were brave days!)

(8) The beautiful barefoot feasting family my Father took me to see at Staten Island were of course (you will have divined), the Frank Shards.

(9) I speak of the "trio" of Uncles rather than the quartette because Augustus of Rhinebeck, father of Kitty Emmet, Gertrude P. and Marie Coster (also of "Willie" James, who married Julia Lowndes, sister to Mrs. Philip Schuyler, and of Mrs. Theodore Chace—of Boston, and then died young too), wasn't of the "Mrs. Cannon" company. He was the eldest of all and more detached and maritally, etc. established. Gussy Barker was his godson.

Voilà à peu près tout!

But the great thing is that we should closely embrace and converse! I won't pretend to go into the history of the way I've "felt about" you, as they say in Boston (which sounds as if they were taking manipulating liberties!)—nor of my deepening joy as you've so gallantly got better. I want to leave everything for word of mouth and feast of eye. I will come out by a kind of after-luncheon train and come [back] by a before-dinner one—and get two or three hours with you. *I intensely want to.* Of course you know in respect to our great Edith that Teddy is now definitely and legally "put away" (I mean divorced—and *incomed*—) by formal process of French law: the whole business terminated and consummated. And now I both long and shudder (though that's a rude word) to see the great author, or authoress, of the deed! But it's *you*, dearest Howard, who are the object of the utterest *Sehnsucht* of your tenderest old

Henry James

1. Sturgis had been reading *A Small Boy and Others.* "Aunt Janet" was Jeannette James (1814–1842), who married William H. Barker in 1832 and died giving birth to her fourth child, Augustus James, in 1842. Robert Barker was not her eldest but her third child; her second was Elizabeth Hazard Barker, who married George Higginson and died in 1901. "Gus" Barker was shot by Southern guerrillas during the Civil War. See *A Small Boy,* 15, 72.

2. The four uncles were Augustus (1807–1866), John Barber (1816–1856), Edward (1818–1856), and Howard (1828–1887). The half-brothers were the twins Robert (1797–1821) and William (1797–1868). Robert's daughter Lydia Lush married Henry Mason. See *A Small Boy,* 378.

3. Mrs. Cannon rented apartments to HJ's uncles "of an intimacy of comfort that the New York hotel could not yield" and also supplied them with articles of haberdashery. HJ coyly hints that in addition to the haberdashery and the fine rooms Mrs. Cannon had ladies in attendance. See *A Small Boy,* chapter 8.

4. John Vanderburgh James (1835–1858); his sister Mary Helen (1840–1881) married Charles Alfred Grymes, M.D.

5. The two other sisters of HJ's father were Catherine Margaret (1820–1854), who married Colonel Robert E. Temple, and Ellen King (1823–1849), who married Smith Thompson Van Buren.

6. For details of the collateral lines see Katherine B. Hastings, *William James of Albany* (1924), published by the New York Genealogical Society.

To Jocelyn Persse
Ms Harvard

21, Carlyle Mansions, S.W.
May 18*th* (forgive smirches—May 18*th*) 1913
My dear dear Jocelyn!

I am sitting to Sargent for my portrait—that is I began today, and have the next sitting on Thursday next 22d.[1] He *likes* one to have a friend there to talk with and to be talked to by, while he works—

for animation of the countenance etc.; and I didn't have one today and we perhaps a trifle missed it. Will you—can you, and should you care to, come for this helpful purpose the next time—on this coming Thursday aforesaid? Do if you can. The thing will then be to be at Tite Street by 11.15, say—31 Tite Street, Chelsea. I sit for about two hours—make it even 11.30 (I begin at 11). Let me kindly hear by a word—I *may*, then, "apply elsewhere." Yours, dearest Jocelyn, all and always

Henry James

1. The sitting for the 22nd mentioned in this letter took place on the 21st instead and Persse was not present. HJ's datebook shows that he sat to Sargent on May 18, 21, 25, 29, and June 1, 5, 8, 13, 15. He sat to Derwent Wood for his bust July 9–15.

To William James III
Ms Private

21 Carlyle Mansions, S.W.
May 13*th* 1913

Dearest Bill.

Too many days—at least seven, I think—have fled beyond my catching an hour out of one of them, since the arrival of your delightful baby-letter etc., of the 27th last. Also came, almost with it, a beautiful and blessed one from your mother, almost equally pervaded by the infant-girdle—so that I almost feel as if I had been lying on Alice's lap curled in a tight ball with him. He is evidently of the thrillingest interest and the most splendid promise, and even if I haven't had it, I yet seem to all the while *miss* the sight of him. Your letter is full of interesting reference, and, with your mother's, pretty well puts everything and not least Mr. R.'s[1] so kind protectingness before me. I hope indeed the Chestnut Street House has been captured, and your mother has told me of your having Chocorua *ad libitum*. But I think that what I want *most* to speak to you and Alice of, for the moment, is the question of the boy's *name*, which I can't sufficiently urge you to consider in all the good and auspicious lights.[2] Names are taken so much more seriously over here, and the sense for them is so much more developed, that I daresay I, by long association, view some of the American phenomena connected with them in what may seem to you a rather lurid light. But no matter—as long as I save you from mistakes! Of course, it is happy and delightful that your father's first grandson should be a William again—but I can't but feel sorry that you are embarking afresh on the unfortunate mere *Junior*. I have a right to speak of that appendage—I carried it about for forty years—and both you and Harry ought also to know much of it; poor dear Harry in particular, who isn't even a *real* one! Apparently, however, you don't dislike it in your own case, or you wouldn't so serenely reduce your helpless child to it. Let me nevertheless plead against it! The fact that one is completely rid of it here, where it doesn't exist, and where one finds oneself glad it doesn't, made me freshly regret the way it's multiplied, and so little avoided, the last time I was in America. The repetition of the paternal name when desired and valued, is always affected here without the tag. This comes from children's almost always having more than one—two or three or four Christian names. And this is helped by the fact that they almost always *are* Christian names, formally *given* by a charming little rite and not coming merely by the child's learning to "answer to" them like a little dog. If a child is baptized the two or three (or more) Christian names sounded over him only make the rite more weighty and more ample. I think that in such a case it can't be too ample. Most "educated" and civilized people here have so their two or three Christian names—one for common use and common signature, and the others up their sleeve for further identification or ornament, for full legal signature and *as to* the said names, usually for compliment the person or persons bearing them. When they take (as a boy) the father's *used* Christian name they use it too, but with the accompaniment of something other than the "Junior" tag, which differentiates the wearer. William your boy here, and your and your father's namesake, for instance, would be something else *William,* or William something else—the former, however, *most,* which would be so much more interesting than the tag. What I have made bold to suggest is *this:* that since you are honoring the child, his grandfather and his grandfather's grandfather, you should honor also his great-grandfather, your Dad's (and your Uncle's) father. I don't want, and wouldn't have him *at all* "William Henry," but I would quite have him "Henry William," the name of *our* father, your Dad's and mine, coming first, and being followed by your Dad's, the usable and used name, while the other remains up his sleeve. Then his common signature and his visiting card would be H. William James, as those of Charles Dickens's grandson, and Alphonse Daudet's sons are so and so Charles Dickens, and so-and-so Alphonse Daudet. (I for that matter should rejoice if *William* were to become quasi-part of our family surname itself, with whatever might be "Christianly" propitious *before* it always, *after* it *never*)—by which adopted custom not only your Dad, but the good old great grandfather (yours), who started us Jameses on this side of the world, would be duly commemorated. And don't say you don't like the initial—the initial before having all the difference in the world from the initial after—(the H. William from the William H.) and being *here*, for instance, remarkably *bien-parti*. It isn't a question of seeing "H. William" at all—but simply of signing and "carding" it. He, (the little H.W.) could, and would, be Bill or Billy Jr. or William Jr. in speech and allusion—just as the same as with the cursed "Junior." He would only thus be spoken of as *little* or *young* W. or W. the younger. That is how even *with* the "Junior" he would be spoken of—for people really don't *say* the Junior; and the signature and other marks of identity would be the same. I mean we would be rid once for all, and by the simplest, easiest process, of the Junior. When Aleck marries his first-born would thus be A. R. William James, with the easier resource for the child of becoming little Aleck, or Aleck the younger. (But that extends the question more than I meant.) The great thing is: consider well, I beseech you, what I say—*and*, get some kindly Unitarian (or even Trinitarian minister) to make a pleasant little *circumstance* in a church or in your "parlors" if you dislike the church, of the naming of the helpless one—whereby *that naming would be recorded* and the child would have an *acte-de-baptême*, a dreadful thing (*I* feel) to be without. Also the gentle minister would be delighted to do it and to partake of ice-cream and cake, or even mere tea and "scones," afterwards. Perhaps you think I make too much of a circumstance of all this—but I have been moved to: so let dear Alice help you to meditate it—while you help *her*. The only thing is that I have delivered myself so fully as to have left room for almost nothing else. I *must* mention, however, that I gave Sargent this A.M. my first sitting for the portrait—*the* portrait; and that nothing has been of such promise since that first A.M.—April 1911—that I sat to you in Mt. Vernon Street. It struck me that he could say to me—even *he*—after all his record—that in consequence of his having now stopped portraiture for these last three or four years, he had quite "lost his nerve" about it; this he said the other day when we were arranging to begin, and that he therefore felt he must reserve the faculty of destroying or not delivering the picture if he didn't succeed in pleasing himself. I seem this A.M., however, to see that this *would*n't—or won't—be the case; he got at it and *placed* it within the first half hour (more or less full face). It is an auspicious start in fact, and *looks* as if it were going to go. But I will give you news of it—and of course send a photograph if it comes rightly through. He has in this year's Academy—a deplorable show—a portrait of his own niece (Rose-Marie) which is a most exquisite and lovely image of a young girl of seventeen (of *any* young girl) that there can be in all the world—an absolutely perfect thing. I hope I may look to you for photographs of your portraits of your mother and Aleck—both of which I hear from her are so tremendously fine. Surely you will *have* them photographed, and not small, like *my* head, but big and brave and really representing the pictures. But it must be goodnight, at the crib, or rather, I suppose, the cradle-side. How lovely you all three must look there, and how I wish I were a fourth. Let Alice always *think* of me as that! Yours and hers, and *his*, all affectionately,

Henry James

1. Apparently WJ IIIs father-in-law, Mr. Runnells.

2. Billy James's first son was named William in the long line of family Williams that began with William James of Albany, who arrived in the United States in 1789. However, Billy did name his second son John.

To Bruce Richmond
Dictated Ts Lubbock

21 Carlyle Mansions, S.W.
May 23rd 1913

Dear Bruce Richmond,[1]

I hang my head for shame even while I address you in this fashion. But be reassured—what I have to tell you isn't that I can't do the bit of a Balzac,[2] but only that I must ask your indulgence for my letting you have it for a *June* appearance, rather than for any one of the now impossible Thursdays of May. Complications and obstructions have lately so much marked me for their own that I am reduced to this urgent petition; with which please understand, however, that I solemnly renew my vow. Reading Faguet's book, and reading over therewith two or three of the Monster's own—always a healthy exercise—have made me greatly want to have another go. At the same time I feel that I shamelessly strain your patience; however, I now tell you the worst. I am for the next week so pressed that I can't begin my article (which I desire to make of the best possible) till June 1st—engaging then to give it my very sharpest attention till the moment of posting it to you. I work slowly at this somewhat stricken season, and it will be sure to take me several days; though with remorse for the poor figure I have as yet made to you prodding me forward with, I trust, a proper violence. Kindly regard me then as now deeply committed, and only troubling you for one little word in acknowledgment of this: on the question, that is, of the number of columns that you allow me. You said something of this in your first letter, on which I am ashamed not to be able for the moment to put my hand, and my recollection a bit betrays me. I rather think that I shall like your maximum allowance of space. Yours all faithfully—yes, in spite of appearances, literally that—

Henry James

1. Bruce Lyttelton Richmond, editor of the *Times Literary Supplement* from 1902 to 1937.

2. HJ wrote an anonymous review of Émile Faguet's *Balzac*, which appeared in the *Times Literary Supplement*, 19 June 1913, and was reprinted in *Notes on Novelists* (1914).

To Bruce Richmond
Ts Lubbock

21 Carlyle Mansions, S.W.
Wednesday A.M.
[4] June 1913

My dear Bruce!

I have done it *tant bien que mal*—though feeling it thereby bleeds.[1] But it's a bloody trade. I don't quite see the lower numeral consort with the II at the head. Kindly notice.

H.J.

1. HJ had been asked to reduce the length of his Balzac review for the *TLS*.

To Ruth Draper
Ms N.Y. Historical

21 Carlyle Mansions, S.W.
June 15*th* 1913

Dear and admirable Ruth.[1]

How delightful to get such generously prompt news of you, both in prose and verse, and to get it so brave and beautiful. Odd as the statement may be it's a real relief to me to know thus that the situation at home was "bad enough" to justify your return—unless your subtle little mind is simply putting it so to yourself and to others to defend itself from any more convulsions on the subject. Of course you are doing good by being there—only that isn't a particular proof of anything but that it's *you*. However, your farm of the queer names[2] does just now sound like as right a place for the little fevered heroine I last saw as the transposition from those *alentours* in such a jiffy savours of the fairy-tale, and I wish you indeed a good stretch of weeks of quiet easy intercourse with your genius, out of which, the soil having been so fertilised by all you have lately seen, some fresh flower or two of character may happily spring. Mull it all over at your leisure and with the aid of a few cigarettes, and something good will surely come. I went to see your so genial and beautiful sister-in-law a few days after your flight (to exchange photographs with her, the one she gave me instead of the one I first had from you being now in the hands of the framer for the decoration of the most elegible of my poor walls). Apropos of which Sargent, dear man, the very A.M. after your last appearance here, at which he had been present, expressed simple despair at having presumed ignorantly to do you before having seen you work—and only wants the result destroyed so that he may start on you afresh altogether. But I am not destroying my copy[3] till something vivider and truer does take its place—and meantime have been sitting to him myself (for an image in oils), with a success by what everyone says that I am almost ashamed to boast of to you. He has been doing a slow and very careful portrait—I have myself greatly enjoyed the process and his company—and I judge he will really have done a fine and characteristic thing. I feel I am being hugely—and exquisitely—celebrated, dear Ruth, when on top of this I receive your slightly overgrown, but all the more luxuriant "sonnet"—a

677

brave and liberal and charming thing, whose excesses I can only blushingly acclaim. If one *is* to be glorified I rejoice in the free hand and fine brave touch you do it with. Please believe I appreciate every word of your inspiration. And I am not less happy to think that by this time you will have had a good view again of my admirable Nephew. I can't say whether I shall most want now his news of you or yours of him. I earnestly hope at any rate for the former on his part. Please greet your Mother very faithfully for me and tell her I rejoice for her in your presence with her now and all your gain of impressions and visions for her beguilement. But good night—I am sitting up for you, and am yours, dear Ruth, all affectionately

Henry James

1. The young Ruth Draper (1884–1956), who became an internationally known monologuist, had arrived in England in 1912. HJ was sufficiently impressed by her work to write a monologue for her even though she insisted she always wrote her own sketches: see *Complete Plays* (1949). She had just written to him from New York and sent him verses in homage to "the piercing vision of your kind grey eyes."
2. Draper was visiting her mother at Katonah, New York.
3. A copy of the charcoal sketch by Sargent was still hanging in Lamb House at the time of HJ's death. Sargent later did studies of Ruth Draper in two of her roles.

To Hugh Walpole
Ms Texas

Lamb House, Rye
August 21st 1913

Belovedest Hugh.

It's a proof of your poor old infatuated friend's general and particular difficulties that a couple of days, rather than a couple of hours, have elapsed, and that he has had to let them do so, since your dear letter came to bless him. But here he is with you now, though too late at night—he has had to sink to slumber awhile since dinner; and he hardly knows how to put it strongly enough that he rejoices even across this dire gulf of space in your company and conversation. You give him, it would seem, a jolly good account of yourself, and he fairly gloats over the picture. Beautiful must be your Cornish land and your Cornish sea, idyllic your Cornish setting, this flattering, this wonderful summer, and ours here doubtless may claim but a modest place beside it all. Yet as you have with you your Mother and Sister, which I am delighted to hear and whom I gratefully bless, so I can match them with my nephew and niece[1] (the former with me alas indeed but for these ten or twelve days), who are an extreme benediction to me. My niece, a charming and interesting young person and *most* conversable, stays, I hope, through the greater part of September, and I even curse that necessary limit—when she returns to America. Cultivate with me, darlingest Hugh, the natural affections, so far as you are lucky enough to have matter for them. I mean don't wait till you are eighty to do so—though indeed *I* haven't waited, but have made the most of them from far back. I like exceedingly to hear that your work has got so bravely on, and envy you that sovereign consciousness. When it's finished—well, when it's finished let some of those sweet young people the *bons amis* (yours) come to me for the small change of remark that I gathered from you the other day (you were adorable about it) they have more than once chinked in your ear as from my poor old pocket, and they will see, *you* will see, in what coin I shall have paid them. I too am working with a certain shrunken regularity—when not made to lapse and stumble by circumstances (damnably physical) beyond my control. These circumstances tend to come, on the whole (thanks to a great power of patience in my ancient organism), rather *more* within my management than for a good while back; but to live with a bad and chronic anginal demon preying on one's vitals takes a great deal of doing. However, I didn't mean to write you of that side of the picture (save that it's a large part of that same), and only glance that way to make sure of your tenderness even when I may seem to you backward and blank. It isn't to exploit your compassion—it's only to be able to feel that I am not without your fond understanding: so far as your blooming youth (*there's* the crack in the fiddle-case!) *can* fondly understand my so otherwise-conditioned age. However, there's always understanding enough when there's affection enough, and you touch me almost to tears when you tell me how I touched the springs of yours that last time in London. I remember immensely wanting to. I gather that that planned and promised visit of dear Jocelyn P.'s hasn't taken place for you (from your not naming it); it's a Jocelyn P. so whirlable into space at any incalculable moment that no want of correspondence between the bright sketch and the vague sequel is ever of a nature to surprise. And the bright sketches are so truly genial, and even the dim vaguenesses without the invidious sting. "We'll see him again, we'll see him again!" as the old Jacobite song says of bonny Prince Charlie. Perhaps I shall achieve seeing him here in the course of the autumn—and perhaps, oh beloved Hugh, *you* will achieve, for my benefit, a like—or more likely—snatch of pilgrimage. My desire is to stay on here as late into the autumn as may consort with my condition—I dream of sticking on through November even if possible: Cheyne Walk and the black-barged yellow river will be the more agreeable to me when I get back to them. I make out that you will then be in London again—I mean *by* November, though such a black gulf of time intervenes; and then of course I may look to you to come down to me for a couple of days. It will be the lowest kind of "jinks"—so halting is my pace; yet we shall somehow make it serve. Don't say to me, by the way, apropos of jinks—the "high" kind that you speak of having so wallowed in previous to leaving town—that I ever challenge you as to *why* you wallow, or splash or plunge, or dizzily and sublimely soar (into the jinks element), or whatever you may call it: as if I ever remarked on anything but the absolute inevitability of it for you at your age and with your natural curiosities, as it were, and passions. It's good healthy exercise, when it comes but in bouts and brief convulsions, and it's always a kind of thing that it's good, and considerably final, to *have* done. We must know, as much as possible, in our beautiful art, yours and mine, what we are talking about—and the only way to know is to have lived and loved and cursed and floundered and enjoyed and suffered. I think I don't regret a single "excess" of my responsive youth—I only regret, in my chilled age, certain occasions and possibilities I *didn't* embrace. Bad doctrine to impart to a young idiot or a duffer; but in place for a young friend (pressed to my heart), with a fund of nobler passion, the preserving, the defying, the dedicating, and which always has the last word; the young friend who can dip and shake off and go his straight way again when it's time. But we'll talk of all this—it's abominably late. Who is D. H. Lawrence,[2] who, you think, would interest me? Send him and his book along—by which I simply mean Inoculate me, at your convenience (don't address me the volume); so far as I can be inoculated. I always *try* to let anything of the kind "take." Last year, you remember, a couple of improbabilities (as to "taking") did worm a little into the fortress. (Gilbert Cannan was one.) I have been reading over Tolstoi's interminable *Peace and War* and am struck with the fact that I now protest as much as I admire.[3] He doesn't *do* to read over, and that exactly is the answer to those who idiotically proclaim the impunity of such formless shape, such flopping looseness and such a denial of composition, selection and style. He has a mighty fund of life, but the *waste,* and the ugliness and vice of waste, the vice of a not finer *doing,* are sickening. For me he but makes "composition" throne, by contrast, in effulgent lustre! Ever your fondest of the fond,

H.J.

1. HJ's niece Peggy and her youngest brother Aleck were staying at Lamb House.
2. D. H. Lawrence had just published *Sons and Lovers.*
3. See letter to Walpole, 19 May 1912.

To Hendrik C. Andersen
Ms Barrett

Lamb House, Rye
September 4*th* 1913

Dearest Hendrik.

If I have been silent so long it is because distress and embarrassment have kept me so; and now your letter today received makes me write, makes me unable *not* to write even with this regret at having to—having to about the matter you insist on my speaking of, I mean, and in the only sense in which, with my hand so forced, I *can.* I seem to remember that I some time ago wrote you more or less in that sense, and under your pressure—after you had sent me your plan of a "World Centre" and then again your first instalment of your pamphlet a "World Conscience"; wrote you in a manner expressive of my pain in having to pronounce on these things which I understand or enter into so little. But you appear to have forgotten the impression I tried then to give you—or I seem quite to have failed of giving it; for you urge me again as if I had said nothing— had uttered no warning. Do you think, dearest Hendrik, I *like* telling you that I don't, and can't possibly, go *with* you, that I don't, and can't possibly, understand, congratulate you on, or enter into, projects and plans so vast and vague and meaning to me simply nothing whatever? You take too much for granted, and take it too sublimely so, of the poor old friend who left you such a comparatively short time since making in all contentment, as he supposed, in a happy Roman studio, statues interesting and limited, even if alarming in scale and number, and who then at the turn of a hand finds you appeal to him and press him hard on such totally different ground altogether and as if this were what he had ever gone in for. Evidently, my dear boy, I can only give you pain that it gives *me* pain to be forced to give you, by telling you that I don't so much *understand* your very terms of "World" this and "World" the other, and can neither think myself, nor *want* to think, in any such vain and false and presumptuous, any such idle and deplorable and delirious connections—as *they seem to me*, and as nothing will suit you, rash you, but that I should definitely let you *know* they seem to me. They would so seem even if I were not old and ill and detached, and reduced to ending my life in a very restricted way—the ground on which I begged you to let me off, some time back, from a participation impossible to me, and in spite of my plea of which you again ask for what you call my *help*. You see, dear Hendrik, to be utterly and unsparingly frank, and not to drag out a statement I would so much rather not have had to make: I simply *loathe* such pretensious forms of words as "World" anything—they are to me mere monstrous sound without sense. The World is a prodigious and portentous and immeasurable affair, and I can't for a moment pretend to sit in my little corner here and "sympathise" with proposals for dealing with it. It is so far vaster in its appalling complexity than you or me, or than anything we can pretend without the imputation of absurdity and insanity to do to it, that I content myself, and inevitably *must* (so far as I can do anything at all now), with living in the realities of things, with "cultivating my garden" (morally and intellectually speaking), and with referring my questions to a Conscience (my own poor little personal), less inconceivable than that of the globe. There—see what you have made me write, and ask yourself if I enjoy distressing you as (from the immensities that you assume to the contrary) it utterly must. If it weren't that I don't want to add another word I would beseech you to return, yourself, to sound and sane Reality, to recover the proportions of things and to dread as the hugest evil of all the forces of evil the dark danger of Megalomania. For *that* way, my dear boy, Madness simply lies. Reality, Reality, the seeing of things as they *are*,

and not in the light of the loosest simplifications—come back to
that with me, and then, even now, we can talk! I say "even now,"
for it's late at night and the pen drops from the hand of your poor
old weary and sorrowing and yet always so personally and faithfully
tender old

Henry James

To Fanny Prothero
Ms Unknown

Lamb House, Rye
September 14th 1913

This, please, for the delightful young man from Texas,[1] who
shews such excellent dispositions. I only want to meet him half
way, and I hope very much he won't think I don't when I tell him
that the following indications as to five of my productions (splendid
number—I glory in the tribute of his appetite!) are all on the basis
of the Scribner's (or Macmillan's) collective and revised and pref-
aced edition of my things, and that if he is not minded somehow
to obtain access to *that* form of them, ignoring any others, he
forfeits half, or much more than half, my confidence. So I thus
amicably beseech him—! I suggest to give him as alternatives these
two slightly different lists:

1. Roderick Hudson.
2. The Portrait of a Lady.
3. The Princess Casamassima.
4. The Wings of the Dove.
5. The Golden Bowl.

1. The American.
2. The Tragic Muse.
3. The Wings of the Dove.
4. The Ambassadors.
5. The Golden Bowl.

The second list is, as it were, the more "advanced." And when it
comes to the shorter Tales the question is more difficult (for characteristic selection) and demands separate treatment. Come to me
about that, dear young man from Texas, later on—you shall have

your little tarts when you have eaten your beef and potatoes. Meanwhile receive this from your admirable friend

Henry James

1. Stark Young (1881–1963), later drama editor at the *New Republic*.

To Thomas Sergeant Perry
Ms Colby

Lamb House, Rye
September 17*th* 1913

My dear Thomas.

Will you, when you return to Boston, if you are not already there when this reaches you, be so good as to look for me into the *Harvard Memorial* Biographies—assuming that you can without difficulty put your hand on those volumes? You can do so at any rate more easily than I can here. (Such is my graceful manner of thanking you—as by the insatiable demand for new favours—for your so amiable "missive"—as we say—of August 22d—the one in which you enclose a copy of the immortal lines addressed to a youth of Slim Figure and Tall—what a glorious memory you have!) It is just merely that I should like to know in what Cavalry regiment my poor little cousin Gus Barker[1] (Class of '64, would he have been?) was when he met his death—on some skirmish, small raid or almost accidental encounter? There is a page about him in the Memorial which will say, I take it, just when and where and how—and whether he had got his officer's commission or was only a Trooper etc.? These and their like are all ghostly little facts—but I move among them a little in my divagating second volume of Reminiscences (now all but finished), and as I go over the heterogeneous pages I want to *verify*. It's only an allusion in passing, but it should be right, as all should be. Is it, e.g., right that *Sanborn,*[2] of the Concord School, was *F.B.S.* by his initials? Can you tell me *that?* and is he *living?* Or if not, what his initials were? You have in Boston *such* resources for verification! But it isn't much I want—unless you can also tell me on what day (*date*) the 54th Mass. marched out of Boston as per St. Gaudens's monument? It *was* the *54th* (Heaven forgive me)? You will know by finding Bob Shaw also

684

in the Memorials! I am disgracefully vague as to the Regiment in which my poor little brother Bob first enlisted, but *think* it was the *45th* Mass, Colonel Alfred Hartwell commanding. However, I have written to my sister-in-law, Bob's widow, at Concord, about this. She has records. And on what *day* was the attack on Fort Wagner made—and was not the first or second day (especially the first!) of the Battle of Gettysburg a Sunday? You will find one of these facts in the Memorial—and I supplicate you to confirm me as to the second (I kind of *need*, for my small context, that July 1st '63 *should* have been a Sunday.)[3] It's among ghosts, isn't it, that I invite you to walk, Thomas?—and I've no book of reference *here* but the ten volumes (from the Authors) of Hay and Nicolay's Life of dear old Lincoln, which doesn't give the days of the week! I *think* the Harvard Memorial Volumes are in the Reform Club library in town, but I don't nowadays stir from this place (while I am "in residence") and can't get at them. We have had here a summer of extraordinary cool dry beauty and are adding a most exquisite irrigated September. My dear Niece Peggy has been with me most companioningly and soothingly these two months—but sails, alas, three days hence in the Mauretania (Saturday 20th). I had also the fifteen last days of August from Harry (now repatriated)—a most able and interesting young individuality. Delightful to me, and most valuable, are William's children! Was John La Farge's early Maryland (Catholic) College the *William and Mary*?? (I have devoted several vivid pages to his early Newport etc. apparitionism.) Strange and moving indeed our survivorship of that golden haze of all the ancient history!

Yes, I see no one but us and your sister Mardj who lives on to testify. Wendell Holmes (marvelous organism!) was in London for a month this June-July—but he is formed to testify simply and solely about himself. I have found my trouble in this overflow[4] a simple glut and block of material—the vividness of all that antiquity is so compelling and beguiling to me that every item of its texture is a trap of memories and an abyss of divagation! Oh yes, and Howells and Mildred came down from London a month (or less) ago to luncheon and tea; a tremendous amount of train, in the day, for little purchased ease. But dear W.D.H. is marvelous for youth and hilarity and innocence and an optimism that is not of this world and that is fed on such *voulues* ignorances. "I have read only one book of Meredith's and *none* of Stevenson! etc."—With all his Harpering on the Novel etc. in all the years![5] But he will go on long yet by it—and I had great brief pleasure of him. Good night, good morrow—my letter-writing is always too belatedly nocturnal. All love to Lilla and to *ces demoiselles. Tell me about Mardj and how she is.*

Ever your faithful old
H.J.

1. See letter to Sturgis, 12 May 1913.
2. Franklin Benjamin Sanborn (1831–1917), Abolitionist and Thoreau's first biographer. HJ's younger brothers attended Sanborn's school in Concord.
3. The first of July 1863 fell on a Wednesday, not a Sunday, and HJ had to sacrifice his artistic need for the Sabbath. See *Notes of a Son and Brother*, 311.
4. The second volume of HJ's reminiscences.
5. Howells's editorial column in *Harper's Monthly*.

To H. G. Wells
Ms Bodleian

Lamb House, Rye
September 21st 1913

My dear Wells.

I won't take time to tell you how touched I freshly am by the constancy with which you send me these wonderful books of yours—I am too impatient to let you know *how* wonderful I find this last.[1] I bare my head before the immense ability of it —before the high intensity with which your talent keeps itself interesting and which has made me absorb the so full-bodied thing in deep and prolonged gustatory draughts. I am of my nature and by the effect of my own "preoccupations" a critical, a non-*naïf*, a questioning, worrying reader—and more than ever so at this end of time, when I jib altogether and utterly at the "fiction of the day" and find no company but yours and that, in a degree, of one or two others possible. To read a novel at all I perform afresh, to my sense, the act of writing it, that is of rehandling the subject accordingly to my own lights and over-scoring the author's form and pressure with my own vision and understanding of *the* way—this, of course I mean, when I *see* a subject in what he has done and feel its appeal to me as one: which I fear I very often don't. This produces reflections and reserves—it's the very measure of my attention and my interest; but there's nobody who makes these particular reactions less *matter* for me than you do, as they occur—who makes the whole apple-cart so run away that I don't care if I *don't* upset it and only want to stand out of its path and see it go. This is because you have so positive a process and method of your own (rare and *almost* sole performer to this tune roundabout us—in fact absolutely sole by the *force* of your exhibition) that there's an anxious joy in seeing what it does for you and with you. I find you perverse and I find you, on a whole side, unconscious, as I can only call it, but my point is that *with* this heart-breaking leak even sometimes so nearly playing the devil with the boat your talent remains so savoury and what you do so substantial. I adore a rounded objectivity, a completely and patiently achieved one, and what I mean by your perversity and your leak is that your attachment to the autobiographic form for the *kind of thing* undertaken, the whole expression of actuality, "up to date," affects me as sacrificing what I hold most dear, a precious effect of *perspective*, indispensable, by my fond measure, to beauty and authenticity. Where there needn't so much be question of that, as in your hero's rich and roaring impressionism, his expression of his own experience, intensity and avidity as a whole, you are magnificent, there your ability prodigiously triumphs and I grovel before you. This is the way to take your book, I think—with Stratton's *own* picture (I mean of himself and *his* immediate world felt and seen with such exasperated and ah such simplified impatiences), as its subject exclusively. So taken it's admirably sustained, and the life and force and wit and humour, the imagination and arrogance and genius with which you keep it up, are tremendous and all your own. I think this projection of Stratton's rage of reflection and observation and world-vision is in its vividness and humour and general bigness of attack, a most masterly thing to have done. His South Africa etc. I think really sublime, and I can do beautifully with his India and his China and America—I can do beautifully with *him* and his "ideas" altogether—he is, and they are, an immense success. Where I find myself doubting is where I gather that you yourself see your subject more particularly—and where I rather feel it escape me. That is, to put it simply—for I didn't mean to draw this out so much, and it's 2 o'clock A.M.!—the hero's prodigiously clever, foreshortened, impressionising *report* of the heroine and the relation (which last is, I take it, for you, the subject) doesn't affect me as the real vessel of truth about them; in short, with all the beauty you have put into it—and much of it, especially at the last, is admirably beautiful—I don't care a fig for the hero's report *as an account of the matter.* You didn't mean a sentimental "love story" I take it—you meant ever so much more—and your way strikes me as *not* the way to give the truth about the woman of our hour. I don't think you *get* her, or at any rate give her, and all through one hears your remarkable—your wonderful!—reporting manner and voice (up to last week, up to last night), and not, by my persuasion, hers. In those letters she writes at the last it's for me all Stratton, all masculinity and intellectual superiority (of the most real), all a more dazzling journalistic talent than I observe any woman anywhere (with all respect to the cleverness they exhibit) putting on record. It isn't in these terms of immediate—that is of her pretended *own* immediate irony and own comprehensive consciousness, that I see the woman made real at all; and by so much it is that I should be moved to take, as I say, such liberties of reconstruction. But I don't in the least *want* to take them, as I still more emphatically say—for what you *have* done has held me deliciously intent and made me feel anew with thanks to the great Author of all things what an invaluable form and inestimable art it is! Go on, go on and do it as you like, so long as you *keep* doing it; your faculty is of the highest price, your temper and your hand form one of the choicest treasures of the time; my offensive remarks are but the sign of my helpless subjugation and impotent envy, and I am yours, my dear Wells, all gratefully and faithfully

Henry James

P.S. I find I don't know where to *address* you—having heard you have left Hampstead, and not having noticed your country terms. So I am absurdly reduced to the Macmillans.

1. *The Passionate Friends,* published in September 1913.

To Joseph Conrad
Ms Barrett

Lamb House, Rye
October 13th 1913

My dear Conrad.

Will you conceive of me as approaching you as the most abject of worms, most contrite of penitents, most misrepresented—by hideous appearances—of all the baffled well-meaning and all the frustrated *fond*? If I could but *see* you for an hour all would become plain, and I should wring your heart with my true and inward history. My conditions for a long time past have been fatal to all *initiative*—through being so to all confidence (in myself); though that, I am happy to say, is coming back little by little—and hence this reaching out to you in the suppliant flat-on-my-belly, the crawling with-my-nose-in-the-dust, posture. You will say that if I had no confidence in myself for so long I might at least have had a little in you—especially after your generous signal to me by your afternoon call of some weeks, horribly many weeks, ago. You will be able to say nothing, however, that will reduce me to softer pulp than I already desire to present to you every symptom of, so don't try to be any more overwhelmingly right than I myself utterly see you: *ce serait tellement enfoncer une porte ouverte*—! Only do *this*, if you mercifully and magnanimously can: come over to luncheon with me, by an heroic effort—and believe that I shall thereby bless you to the (perhaps not very distant) end of my days. If you tell me that this is impossible through the extremity of inconvenience, I will then arrange—that is, heaven forgive me! propose or aspire to—something less onerous to you; but do let me hear from you by five bare words, that I haven't too fatally forfeited your indulgence, and that you will further consider. I attribute to you the fine facility of a motor-car (I had written c*are*, and might have left it, mightn't I?)—yet if you ask me what that has to do with the question, my reply can only be that I will recklessly procure one for the occasion myself and go over to see you at home. There are trains too, rather happily available; but, in fine, it isn't for me to teach you. The point is that if you had, so very comprehensibly, rather not come again, I *shall* place myself all at your service for the natural alternative. I do so want to see you, and to tell you, and to convince you, and to harrow you up. That is all, for tonight. I have sat up to the small hours thus to engage you; and I am, my dear Conrad, with every invocation of your generosity and of your wife's intercession for me (I bless her in advance on it), yours all-faithfully,

Henry James

To Hugh Walpole
Ms Texas

Lamb House, Rye
October 14*th* 1913

Dearest little Hugh: (*vide* the Russians in general—I have just been re-reading over Tolstoi—for the tender force of the diminutive.) It is the sweetest kind of comfort to be able to think of you as at all impending: impend therefore, impend as hard as you can, impend for all you are worth. Keep three or four early days after your return to town for coming down to me. On casting about a bit, verily—I have to *consider* so much, in my condition, in these days, as to the disposal of my times and the conservation of my so shrunken powers—I make out that something of about November *10th* would be the favourable date for me—it allows for my very final finishing of a Book,[1] which I am, under disadvantages, struggling toward; and nothing better than your so sympathetic society could accrue to me in celebration of that relief. I shall be twice as much yours, for the fleeting interval, and capable of at least trying twice as much to make you mine, when that carking care is off my mind.—And I shall feel all the deeper harmony in that you too will have then a finish[2] to commemorate. We will drink deep together—great flowing bowls from the pump—to each other's triumphs. And you will tell me much of all the elements that shall make for yours. Well can I conceive that you have found the deep peace of your refuge a benefit and a balm—though able (*I* am) to figure not less that the joy of battle in London will in due course inflate your young nostril even almost to bursting. Such is the strange rotation of our fate—that is of yours; for mine, thank God, has long since ceased to rotate, and if I accomplish an in the least safe immobility I am but too devoutly grateful. I have no fear at all but that Jocelyn found his bright account in your kind company—though when you come to the question of "subjects in common," heaven save the mark!—or of the absence of them—I have nothing to say to you but that I know (none better) what you mean. One gets on with him in a way without them, however, and says to one's self, I think, that if *he* doesn't mind, well, why should one either?[3] At any rate I am glad you were gentle with him. I am infinitely and gladly so—but the basis shrinks, and I haven't seen him these four months or so, though with the hope of getting him down before long for twenty-four hours. (My physical disabilities utterly undermine, alas, all my social initiative.) I too have read my Wells and even written him eight pages about the matter—which left him extravagantly apologetic and profoundly indifferent. Artistically, expressively of any subject but *himself,* he has gone to the dogs. But that self remains to me demonic—for life and force, cheek and impudence and a wondrous kind of vividness *quand même.* He *inveterately* goes to pieces about the middle—in this last thing the first half promised and then the collapse was gross. And he will never do anything else, and will never dream of so much as wanting to. They all seem to me money-grabbers pure and simple, naked and unashamed; and Arnold Bennett now with an indecency, verily, an obscenity, of nudity—! But good night—the hour is, as usual, absurd. Yours dearest Hugh, all affectionately,

Henry James

1. *Notes of a Son and Brother.*
2. Walpole was probably finishing his novel *The Duchess of Wrexe.*
3. It may have been of Persse that HJ once said to Hugh Walpole, "I not only love him—I *love* to love him."

To André Raffalovich
Ms Scotland

Lamb House, Rye
November 7*th* 1913

Dear André Raffalovich.[1]

I thank you again for your letter, and I thank you very kindly indeed for the volume of Beardsley's letters, by which I have been greatly touched. I knew him a little, and he was himself to my vision touching, and extremely individual; but I hated his productions and thought them extraordinarily base—and couldn't find (perhaps didn't try enough to find!) the formula that reconciled this baseness, aesthetically, with his being so perfect a case of the artistic spirit. But now the personal spirit in him, the beauty of nature, is disclosed to me by your letters as wonderful and, in the conditions and circumstances, deeply pathetic and interesting. The amenity, the intelligence, the patience and grace and play of mind and of temper—how charming and individual an exhibition! Very happy must this have made you to be able to do so much for him as you clearly did, and very right have you been to publish the letters, for which Father Gray's claim is indeed supported. The poor boy remains quite one of the few distinguished images on the roll of young English genius brutally clipped, a victim of victims, given the vivacity of his endowment. I am glad I have three or four very definite—though one of them rather disconcerting—recollections of him.

Very curious and interesting your little history of your migration to Edinburgh—on the social aspect and intimate identity of which you must, I imagine, have much gathered light to throw. The great thing is to find a possible basis and to *s'y tenir*, and I congratulate you on being in so little doubt of yours. And you are still young enough to find La Province meets your case too. It is because I am now so very far from that condition that London again (to which I return on the 20th) has become possible to me for longer periods: I am so old that I have shamelessly to simplify, and the simplified London that in the hustled and distracted years I vainly invoked, has come round to me easily now, and fortunately meets my case. I shall be glad to see you there, but I *won't*—thank you, no!—come to meat with you at Claridge's. One doesn't go to Claridge's if one simplifies. I am obliged now absolutely *never* to dine or lunch out (a bad physical ailment wholly imposes this): but I hope you will come to luncheon with *me*, since you have free range—on very different vittles from the Claridge, however, if you can stand that. I count on your having still more then to tell me, and am yours most truly

Henry James

1. André Raffalovich (1864–1934), an affluent cosmopolitan, born in Paris, who had written early about "urningism" (homosexuality). He had just sent HJ his edition of the *Last Letters of Aubrey Beardsley* (1904), with an introduction by Father John Gray.

To Logan Pearsall Smith
Ms Congress

Lamb House, Rye
November 17*th* 1913

My dear Logan.

The air may be "bleak" in the ivory tower, but it strikes me as singularly propitious, all the same, to the cultivation of—what shall I say?—the most luxuriant and elegant window-boxes. Well, I *like* to think that the sentiments of your letter (about your too brief visit here)[1] are hardy flowers, so that I may look to see them bloom again for another and a better occasion—you had here really the other day some conditions and circumstances of which I was quite ashamed. But what did come out for me was verily the pity of our being so perversely planted in this monstrous county—I mean in respect to ease of contact. We *should* have greater—to get the good of so much of our common heritage: I felt that strongly while our talk seemed to test its boundless extent; so that really you see we ought to try and make something of it. What it seems we can't make alas is a shorter space between Arundel and Rye. Kipling has sung the glorious breadth of Sussex—but damn the glorious breadth! Remember at any rate that I am to be in London (21 Carlyle Mansions, Cheyne Walk) for several months after the end of the present one, and on some near day that you are there come to luncheon with me (with a small notice given). I can't reflect with anything but complacency on your having reported to Bridges on my being so charmed both with Dolben[2] and with himself—for your report has had for its consequence a most interesting and delightful letter from him, as a murmur of response to my expression. I shall at once thank him for it, because it gives me great pleasure to be thus in communication with him. I really owe you much gratitude for having brought these things about—brought in particular, I mean, the knowledge and vision, for me, of that so very remarkable young genius and tragic (*if* tragic!) little story. I feel I should have lost something really rare by further ignorance. Apropos of which an odd coincidence of impression has, in relation to this, just taken place for me. Do you know whom I mean (and I may perhaps even say *What!*) by André Raffalovich?—with whom I had had some acquaintance, very limited, years ago, in London, but

693

have never seen nor heard from since. Out of the blue had I the other day a letter from him, at Edinburgh (where he now lives, a shining light of the Catholic church there, and a visibly intelligent and presumably altogether developed and improved person); and this was followed by a book from him, a collection—published—of the letters written him by Aubrey Beardsley in the last (dying) year or so of the latter's life. I knew Beardsley a little—and found him personally pleasing and touching, though I detested his work—which made me sick—and does still. But this volume of letters has an extraordinary pathetic charm, a beauty and amenity of spirit that are rare; and the genius (for he *had* that), the ardent Catholicism, the early death (twenty-six) and the sudden disclosure to me just after that of Bridges' book, contribute to a certain analogy of impression (which however I think Bridges wouldn't like to see noted! So don't mention it to him!) It's a case of two young Englishmen with a high imaginative and artistic endowment and ritual sensibility in common, and a common tragic abbreviation of life. I didn't mean to make too much of this, but the Beardsley letters have such singular grace, pathos and intelligence that if you care to see the volume (Longmans) I will with pleasure send it to you. Yours all faithfully

Henry James

1. HJ to Fanny Prothero, 23 October 1913: "Logan Pearsall Smith was just with me for thirty-six hours—and the tide of gossip between us rose high, he being a great master of that effect."

2. Digby Mackworth Dolben (1848–1867), educated at Eton and a Benedictine monk, was accidentally drowned in his twentieth year. His poems were edited and published with a memoir by Robert Bridges in 1915.

To Hugh Walpole
Ms Texas

21 Carlyle Mansions, S.W.
January 6*th* 1914

Darlingest and delightfullest old Hugh!

There you are—and what else is it I hinted at? but that Edinburgh should, in your writing to me, have moved you to expression and not simply to telling me that your disgust at it moved you to none.[1] Your letter this A.M. received is none other than a portion of the

694

letter that I expressed my preference for over the mere statement of a no-letter—expressed it, that is, by a personal squeeze, so to speak, of such supreme tenderness of intentions that your feeling in it a "reproach" prompts me to declare myself most reproachful then when I am exactly most—well, I'll call it single heartedly affectionate. May you never suffer from harsher usage than these sentiments of mine assault you withal. I delight in your outbreak against the singular gift for irritation possessed by the race that surrounds you—you see it's a reaction—*the* reaction—of which I invited you to give me the benefit, and now that you have given me that I thank you for it ever so kindly. I could have done even with more detail— as when you say *"Such* parties!" I want so to hear exactly what parties they are. When you refer to their "immorality on stone floors," and with prayerbooks in their hands so long as the exigencies of the situation permit of the manual retention of the sacred volumes, I do so want the picture developed and the proceedings authenticated. But I feel with you about the whole impression! it *is,* no doubt, a damnably graceless people when you're up against them as in this grim time, and one is the more exasperated by them somehow from their being in general so damnably successful and well doing. Well, *I've* been among them for the last time— never, never again!

I'm awfully amused by your "amazement" at my being struck with C. Mackenzie's novel[2]—and can only say that I have been *so* struck, and seemed to know *why,* all along, this was the case. He has a large imperfection, I think, in his remarkable inability to *select,* his need to keep putting it all down and down and down, whatever it is and however it comes, his general irresponsibility as to the reasons and connections and relations—relations to the whole and to other aspects of the story—of the things he does. But he seems to me *to do the things* with extraordinary, or at least with the most unusual, reality and truth and salience, with a singular possession of the schoolboy consciousness and character, a singular saturation with the whole sense of them and power to develop them and carry them far. He has energy and sensibility and humour and imagination in all that exhibition, I think, and he has what is so rare in all the crew in general, a sense of style and a gift for it which lapses at times in his culpable *longueurs* and promiscuities, but which frequently picks itself up with really almost admirable art and instinct. Thanks to this, some of his episodes—and he has so many—are so *done*. Isn't this so—and isn't the force and the skill of him, and the evocation of the figure and scene and sound again and again of an energy truly commendable? You will tell me later on—and it will be very interesting to talk of him; for you will have lights that I don't possess to throw. And meantime I don't think "theatrical" describes him, though he's peculiarly interesting, to my sense, as coming from the third rate theatre-nest[3] he does. However, all this will keep, and you must slate him for all he's (or isn't) worth, to me—or all you are—if you feel me too wrong. I mean to read *Carnival* if I can. I have been struck enough for that! Have patience with me, meanwhile—and believe in all my sympathy with your present ordeal. Think of me as hanging about you in it from afar—as none of your standers-off dream of the sense of and as ever, dearest boy, your all faithfullest old

H.J.

1. Walpole had just visited Edinburgh, where his father was the Anglican Bishop, and had made some critical references to Father Gray and André Raffalovich (see letters to Raffalovich, 7 November 1913, and to Smith, 17 November 1913).

2. Compton Mackenzie (1883–1972) published his first novel, *Carnival*, in 1912 and was writing *Sinister Street*. See following letter to Mackenzie.

3. Mackenzie was the son of HJ's actor friends Edward Compton and Virginia Bateman, who had produced *The American* in 1890. See *Letters* III, 306, 412–413.

To Compton Mackenzie
Ms Texas

21 Carlyle Mansions, S.W.
January 21*st* 1914

My dear "Monty Compton!"—

For that was, I think, as I first heard you named—by a worthy old actress of your father's company who, when we were rehearsing *The American* in some touring town to which I had gone for the purpose, showed me with touching elation a story-book she had provided for you on the occasion of your birthday.[1] That story-book, weighted with my blessing on it, evidently sealed your vocation—for the sharpness of my sense that you are verily a prey to the vocation was what, after reading you, I was moved to emphasise to Pinker. I am glad he let you know of this, and it gives me great pleasure that you have written to me—the only abatement of which is learning from you that you are in such prolonged exile on grounds of health. May that dizzying sun of Capri cook every peccant humour out of you. As to this untowardness I mean, frankly, to inquire of your Mother—whom I am already in communication with on the subject of going to see her to talk about you! For that, my dear young man, I feel as a need: with the force that I find and so much admire in your talent your *genesis* becomes, like the rest of it, interesting and remarkable to me; you are so rare a case of the *kind* of reaction from the theatre—and from so *much* theatre. The reaction in itself is rare—as seldom taking place; and when it does it is mostly, I think, away from the arts altogether—it is violent and utter. But your pushing straight through the door into literature and then closing it so tight behind you and putting the key in your pocket, as it were—that strikes me as unusual and brilliant! However, it isn't to go into all that that I snatch these too few minutes, but to thank you for having so much arrested my attention, as by the effect of *Carnival* and *Sinister Street*, on what I confess I am for the most part (as a consequence of some thankless experiments) none too easily beguiled by, a striking exhibition by a member of the generation to which you belong. When I wrote to Pinker I had only read *S.S.*, but I have now taken down *Carnival* in persistent short draughts—which is how I took *S.S.* and is how I take anything I take at all; and I have given myself still further up to the pleasure, quite to the emotion, of intercourse with a young talent that really moves one to hold it to an account. Yours strikes me as very living and real and sincere, making me care for it—to anxiety—care above all for what shall become of it. You ought, you know, to do only some very fine and ripe things, really solid and serious and charming ones; but your dangers are almost as many as your aspects, and as I am a mere monster of *appreciation* when I read—by which I mean of the critical passion—I would fain lay an earnest and communicative hand on you and hypnotize or otherwise bedevil you into proceeding as I feel you most *ought* to, you know. The great point is that I would so fain personally see you—that we may talk; and I do very much wish that you *had* given me a chance at one of those moments when you tell me you inclined to it, and then held off. You are so intelligent, and it's a blessing—whereby I prefigure it as a luxury to have a go at you. I am to be in town till the end of June—I *hibernate* no more at Rye; and if you were only to turn up a little before that it would be excellent. Otherwise you must indeed come to me there. I wish you all profit of all your experience, some of it lately, I fear, rather harsh, and all experience of your genius—which I also wish myself. I *think* of *Sinister Street* II,[2] and am yours most truly

Henry James

1. See letter to Walpole, 6 January 1914.
2. The second volume of *Sinister Street*, which was to follow.

To Edmund Gosse
Ms Leeds

21 Carlyle Mansions, S.W.
January 21st 1914

My dear Gosse.

Have you any recollection of once going down the river to dine with me at Greenwich long years ago?—in company with Maupassant, Du Maurier, and one or two others.[1] One of these others was Primoli,[2] who had come over from Paris with Maupassant; and on whom you made, you see, the ineffaceable impression. He wrote to me the other day to ask your address—it has lasted all these years—and you meanwhile—*infidèle*—! I have seen him since then from time to time; he is a very amiable and rather singular person— I will tell you more about him some other time. He made on dear Du Maurier, I remember, an impression that remained—though not on your sterner nature! He is a Bonaparte (exceedingly so in looks); that is his Mother was a Bonaparte Princess, and his father, I think, the offspring of the marriage of one (I *believe* they were cousins). He lives in Paris and in Rome, and if you write him a word in Rome address him M. le Comte *Joseph* P.—there is another brother. *Voilà.*——

I rejoice most heartily in your authentic word for your wife's brave state—I send my prompt blessing on it. Also I take comfort, of the greatest, in Percy L[ubbock]'s Viennese cheer. Let us indeed meet again before the year is too sensibly (or senselessly) older. I am waiting to give effect to what we talked of the other day only till I can learn that Hagberg Wright[3] is back. When I last inquired he wasn't—it was a few days since. But now—! Yours all faithfully

Henry James

1. See *Letters* III, 129.
2. Count Joseph-Napoléon Primoli (1851–1927). See *Letters* III, 475.
3. Charles T. Hagberg Wright (1862–1940), librarian of the London Library from 1893 to 1940.

To William Roughead
Ms Harvard

21 Carlyle Mansions, S.W.
January 29*th* 1914

Dear Mr. Roughead,

I devoured the tender Blandy[1] in a single feast; I thank you most kindly for having anticipated so handsomely my appetite; and I highly appreciate the terms in general, and the concluding ones in particular, in which you serve her up.[2] You tell the story with excellent art and animation, and it's quite a gem of a story in its way, History herself having put it together as with the best compositional method, a strong sense for sequences and the proper march, order and *time*. The only thing is that, as always, one wants to know *more*, more than the mere evidence supplies—and wants it even when as in this case one feels that the people concerned were after all of so dire a simplicity, so primitive a state of soul and sense, that the exhibition they make tells or expresses about all there was of them. Dear Mary must have consisted but of two or three pieces, one of which was a strong and simple carnal affinity, as it were, with the stinking little Cranstoun.[3] Yet, also, one would like to get a glimpse of how an apparently normal young woman of her class, at that period, could have viewed such a creature in such a light. The light would throw itself on the Taste, the sense of proportion, of the time. However, dear Mary was a clear barbarian, simply. *Enfin!*—as one must always wind up these matters by exhaling. I continue to have escaped a further sense of Hueffer[4] and as I think I have told you I cultivate the exquisite art of ignorance. Yet not of Blandy, Pritchard and Co.—*there*, perversely, I am all for knowledge. Do continue to feed in me that languishing need, and believe me all faithfully yours,

Henry James

1. William Roughead (1870–1952), Scottish jurist, from 1913 on sent HJ his chronicles of famous murder trials. Mary Blandy, of Henley-upon-Thames, was hanged in 1752 for poisoning her father by putting arsenic in his food. The fourteen letters HJ wrote Roughead were printed in an anthology of Roughead's writings edited by his son, W. N. Roughead, *Tales of the Criminous* (1956).

2. HJ refers here to Roughead's compliment to him, "If only she [Blandy] had been the creature of some great novelist's fancy . . . imagine her made visible for us through the exquisite medium of Mr. Henry James's incomparable art."

3. Captain the Hon. William Henry Cranstoun, the fifth son of a Scots peer, was a short ugly man, a gambler and a wastrel. Although already married, he courted Mary Blandy for her father's money; he supplied the arsenic to the love-sick girl, and ran off to France when it was clear that she would be hanged. He was never caught.

4. Ford Madox Hueffer was working on his critical study of HJ, which would be published in 1916.

To Hugh Walpole
Ms Texas

21, Carlyle Mansions, S.W.
February 5*th* 1914

Dearest Hugh.

Come to lunch on Thursday next 12th, at 1.45.

Raffalovich of Edinburgh ("immorality on stone floors!")[1] comes on Tuesday.

Come away with me tomorrow from Mrs. Colefax's[2]—I will drive you home or wherever you must go.

I have the volume (since last night), and shall attack it as soon as I finish Conrad's *Chance*.[3] I have so nearly done this that I shall probably proceed tonight, in bed, to Walpole's *Certainty*.[4]

His—"Walpole's" (I shall *have* to call you *that* if you push on so to greatness—so reflect!) all-affectionate

Henry James

1. See letter to Walpole, 6 January 1914.
2. Sybil Colefax, later Lady Colefax, whose Argyll House had become a center for her lionizing of celebrities.
3. *Chance* (1913).
4. *The Duchess of Wrexe* (1914).

To Edith Wharton
Ms Yale

21 Carlyle Mansions, S.W.
February 25*th* 1914

Dearest Edith,

The nearest I have come to receipt or possession of the interesting volumes you have so generously in mind is to have had *Bernstein's* assurance, when I met him here some time since, that *he* would give himself the delight of sending me the Proust production, which he learned from me that I hadn't seen.[1] I tried to dissuade him from this excess, but nothing would serve—he was too yearningly bent upon it, and we parted with his asseveration that I might absolutely count on this tribute both to poor Proust's charms and to my own. But *depuis lors*—! he has evidently been less *en train* than he was so good as to find *me*. So that I shall indeed be "very pleased" to receive the *Swann* and the *Vie et l'Amour*[2] from you at your entire convenience. It is indeed beautiful of you to think of these little deeds of kindness, little words of love (or is it the other way round?). What I want above all to thank you for, however, is your so brave backing in the matter of my disgarnished gums. That I am doing right is already unmistakeable. It won't make me "well"; nothing will do that, nor do I complain of the muffled miracle; but it will make me mind less being ill—in short it will make me better. As I say, it has already done so, even with my sacrifice for the present imperfect—for I am "keeping on" no less than eight pure pearls, in front seats, till I can deal with them in some less exposed and exposing conditions. Meanwhile tons of implanted and domesticated gold etc. (one's caps and crowns and bridges being *most* anathema to Des Vœux,[3] who regards them as so much installed metallic poison) have, with everything they fondly clung to, been, less visibly, eradicated; and it is enough, as I say, to have made a marked difference in my felt state. That is the point, for the time— and I spare you further details. I greatly rejoice to think that Percy [Lubbock] is with you. I understand but well the impulse that moved him—and it's so interesting to me that Vienna has sung its song. I like to hear of the limits of joys (the Vienna joy) that I haven't had. I shall perhaps even hear of those of the Algerian joy[4]—and then I shall *gloat!* Yet I want inconsistently to hurry up Coopersale. All love of course to Percy. Yours *de cœur*

Henry James

1. In an anonymous review of Proust's *Du Cote de Chez Swann* in the *Times Literary Supplement*, 4 December 1913, A. B. Walkley, the *Times* drama critic, compared this early version of Proust's later much-expanded novel with HJ's *A Small Boy and Others* and *What Maisie Knew*. On 9 February 1914 Walkley introduced HJ to the French dramatist Henri Bernstein (1876–1953), who promised to send HJ the Proust volumes, but as this letter shows it was Mrs. Wharton who ultimately supplied them. In *A Backward Glance* Mrs. Wharton says HJ "seized" upon the Proust "and devoured it in a passion of curiosity and admiration." However, HJ's letters to her tend to weaken the credibility of this reminiscence: on 2 March 1914 HJ tells her, "I shan't yet for a little fall upon Proust and Company, if you don't mind," and he adds his frequent assertion that "perusal" of current fiction had become mostly impossible to him.

George D. Painter, in the second volume of his life of Proust (1965, 252), says HJ wrote Proust "a magnificent letter, informing him that this was an extraordinary book." The letter has never been found, and word of its existence appears to be apocryphal. Lucien Daudet and Logan Pearsall Smith are two other sources for its existence, but talking to them both long ago convinced me their recollections were based on the same apocryphal evidence. Painter confirmed to me that he had heard of the letter at second hand. Further investigation suggested that the information came from Proust's celebrated domestic, Céleste Albaret, who seems to have told Mina Curtiss about this letter—but who in doing so confused HJ with the French poet Francis Jammes. It has been further conjectured that Edith Wharton may have reported HJ's talk of Proust to Walter Berry who in turn told Proust—but such a surmise assumes that HJ read Proust at this time, and given HJ's state of health and his diminished reading, this seems unlikely. Miss Bosanquet had no record of HJ's dictating a letter to Proust—and most of HJ's final letters were dictated.

2. *Vie et l'amour* by Abel Bonnard (1883–1968).
3. Dr. Des Vœux was now HJ's attending physician.
4. Mrs. Wharton had announced her impending journey to North Africa.

To Edith Wharton
Dictated Ts Yale

21, Carlyle Mansions, S.W.
February 27*th* 1914

Dear E.W. and Confrère.

Do come out from under the bed, where I am *so* sorry you have had to take refuge, and if you can't face your dinner at least try to swallow this small epistolary tit-bit.

If everything, literally everything, about Conrad and his situation were not so utterly *cocasse* the *cocasserie* of Booth Tarkington's appeal would enjoy a glittering pre-eminence;[1] but the whole thing is somehow beyond saying, at least by me in the present circumstances and even with the present admirable aid. I like so Booth's request to you that you should from the Rue de Varenne and "over your signature" testify how much you "rejoice in the man," and in the artless charm of his assurance that Mr. C. "has no part" himself in the flattering movement. However, *I* have not been invited to join in it—I am always coldly neglected in these things altogether; and it seems to me really difficult, so utterly absurd and so peculiarly more queer than I can tell you, is the whole connection anyway! Have you a personal sentiment, by which of course I mean a "realising sense," for poor dear J.C. at all? I have one myself, of a sort, a rum sort, but that is a matter of old history, going back to his having put himself in relation with me years ago, when he had written but his first book or two, and much mixed up with personal impressions since received. And even thus *I* should be hugely embarrassed! Have you read his last book, the *Chance* which has just come out, or have you it at hand? If neither of these advantages are enjoyed by you I will send you the volume at once as the most practical "leg-up" I can give you for scaling the arduous steep. This last book happens to be infinitely more practicable, more curious and readable, (in fact really rather *yieldingly* difficult and charming), than any one of the last three or four impossibilities,[2] wastes of desolation, that succeeded the two or three final good things of his earlier time. If you find yourself able to read *Chance* you may be moved to utterance, but my own sense of your case is that in your place I should be moved to none unless you find it rise in you with something of a gush. That sounds a little as if a steward with a basin might then become your recipients rather than the Tarkington stewardry with only their sheet of paper; but at any rate I wouldn't so much as trouble to answer them unless after an attempted go at the evidence I thus offer you you do feel the passion work within. I happen myself to have written a word about *Chance*,[3] but not for Booth, only for a different and more mercenary use, which I will send you in due course—that is when it comes out; for which we must wait a little. But meanwhile if Cook will but scrawl a "Send" on your behalf, on a postcard, while you are under the bed, you shall have the work—offered too quite in the hope that it may draw you forth. Forgive this scandalous wriggle out of my responsibility. I *am* glad I haven't your popularity in the

U.S.—there are *such* compensations in my obscurity. Truly there is but *us!*—I find in the document you transmit such trills and roulades and refinements of the wood-note wild as baffle all description.

I just revel in Percy's revel—please tell him; and also that the situation created by his *fugue* (not to say his *fougue*, in the Bernstein light, like mine) is almost painful here. Half London society *will* so have it that he has left Vienna for good, or in other words has come to Rue de Varenne for better; while the other half regards the affair but as a "folle équipée" which must have its hour but which will in due course blaze itself out. I side with the former version— but one takes rather, on whichever side, one's life in one's hand. What questions you thus saddle me with—between you! I stagger under them but am [none] the less your all-faithful and all artful dodger

H.J.

1. A Conrad Committee headed by the American novelist Booth Tarkington had written to Edith Wharton on 14 February 1914 asking her to take part in a *Festschrift* for Conrad to secure wider recognition for him in the United States.
2. HJ seems to be alluding here to *Nostromo* (1904), *The Secret Agent* (1907), and *Under Western Eyes* (1911).
3. HJ's article on "The Younger Generation," about to appear in the *Times Literary Supplement*, 19 March and 2 April 1914.

To Harley Granville Barker
Ms Hopkins

21 Carlyle Mansions, S.W.
March 21*st* 1914

Dear Granville Barker.

It is very kind and handsome of you to have found the great Moscow Theatre offer you the missing link of connection with the poor little old *Outcry*[1] and its author—and I heartily thank you for that considerate friendliness. But the bright vision you momentarily evoke glitters before me, I fear, but at once to fade. The thing isn't *for* that alien scene, as they would on perusal inexorably see and have to declare. It's essentially of this, our own, air and of these conditions—an Anglo-American *opportune* comedy or *pièce d'occasion* of which the very subject and basis of interest and irony relate but to England and her art-wealth and the U.S. and their art-grab and their grab-resources. No Russian audience cares—that is *would* care—whether the great picture leaves this country for another (not theirs) or not—nor for how the loss and the gain are frustrated. It is of a rosy optimism on your part to imagine they *can*. The Moscow theatre is evidently remarkable, but can't be so remarkable as that! And the very merit of the play (assuming merit!)—the way it sticks to its special and local subject and fully expresses that—would make but a difficulty, a defeat the more! Trust the fond author to have liked this amusement if he *could!* No, the one time, the one air and ground of pertinence and possibility, were those vanished ones of three years ago; actuality has gone from the charming thing (assuming charm!) and it long ago resignedly folded its wings. I mean to try to come some night to the *Dream*[2]—but though the Strand etc. isn't as far as Moscow the nocturnal adventure is on the whole apt to scare me a little in advance. However, I shall gird myself, I renew my appreciation of your gallant offer of service, and am yours and Mrs. Lillah's[3] all faithfully

Henry James

1. Granville Barker wrote to HJ on 19 March 1914 that during a visit to the Moscow Art Theatre he had mentioned *The Outcry* to the Russian directors and said he believed it to be the one theatre in the world that might do justice to the play. Barker urged HJ to send a script to Moscow.
2. Barker's recent production of *A Midsummer Night's Dream* at the Savoy.
3. The actress Lillah McCarthy (1875–1960), Barker's first wife.

To Henry Adams
Ms Mass. Historical

21 Carlyle Mansions, S.W.
March 21*st* 1914

My dear Henry.

I have your melancholy outpouring of the 7th,[1] and I know not how better to acknowledge it than by the full recognition of its unmitigated blackness. *Of course* we are lone survivors, of course the past that was our lives is at the bottom of an abyss—if the abyss *has* any bottom; of course too there's no use talking unless one particularly *wants* to. But the purpose, almost, of my printed divagations was to show you that one *can*, strange to say, still want to—or at least can behave as if one did. Behold me therefore so behaving—and apparently capable of continuing to do so. I still find my consciousness interesting—under *cultivation* of the interest. Cultivate it *with* me, dear Henry—that's what I hoped to make you do; to cultivate yours for all that it has in common with mine. *Why* mine yields an interest I don't know that I can tell you, but I don't challenge or quarrel with it—I encourage it with a ghastly grin. You see I still, in presence of life (or of what you deny to be such), have reactions—as many as possible—and the book I sent you is a proof of them. It's, I suppose, because I am that queer monster the artist, an obstinate finality, an inexhaustible sensibility. Hence the reactions—appearances, memories, many things go on playing upon it with consequences that I note and "enjoy" (grim word!) noting. It all takes doing—and I *do*. I believe I shall do yet again—it is still an act of life. But you perform them still yourself—and I don't know what keeps me from calling your letter a charming one! There we are, and it's a blessing that you understand—I admit indeed alone—Your all-faithful

Henry James

1. HJ sent *Notes of a Son and Brother* to Adams, who said the book "reduced me to a pulp." Adams wrote to his friend Mrs. Cameron: "Poor Henry James thinks it all real and actually still lives in that dreary, stuffy Newport and Cambridge with papa James and Charles Eliot Norton."

To Mrs. William James
Ms Harvard

21 Carlyle Mansions, S.W.
March 29th 1914

Dearest Alice,

This is a Saturday A.M., but several days have come and gone since there came to me your dear and beautiful letter of March 14th (considerably about my "Notes"), and though the American post closes early I must get off some word of recognition to you, however brief I have scramblingly to make it. I hoped of course you would find in the book something of what I difficultly tried to put there— and you have indeed, you have found all, and I rejoice, because it was in talk with you in that terrible winter of 1910–11 that the impulse to the whole attempt came to me. Glad you will be to know that the thing appears to be quite extraordinarily appreciated, absolutely acclaimed, here—scarcely any difficulties being felt as to "parts that are best," unless it be that the early passage and the final chapter about dear Minny seem the great, the beautiful "success" of the whole.[1] What I have been able to do for *her* after all the long years—judged by this test of expressed admiration—strikes me as a wondrous stroke of fate and beneficence of time: I seem really to have (her letters and J.G.'s and your admirable committal of them to me aiding) made her emerge and live on, endowed her with a kind dim sweet immortality that places and keeps her—and I couldn't be at all *sure* that I was doing it; I was so anxious and worried as to my really getting the effect in the right way—with tact and taste and without overstrain. I of course sent the volume to J.G., and I can't help rather wondering how he feels about what I have done in that connection—yet can't doubt, on the whole, that he feels justified of his trust. Perhaps you have seen him or he has given you some sign—I hope he hasn't been too progressively ill to have done so. I have had a most affectionate—a tender and delighted, letter from Willy Emmett, who is a very sympathetic kinsman and nature. What you tell me of Rosina's report of her mother's "upset" in presence of my chapter etc. is of course no more than I expected[2]—but I haven't felt I could communicate with Elly directly about the matter at all—over such depths of illiteracy as surround her—and have, at the same time, said to myself that she could only in the "long run" find satisfaction in the crown, so to speak, conferred upon her sister. Strange enough—almost touching—meanwhile the fatuity of her asking why the letters weren't sent to *her*. But poor Rosina ought to appreciate it all.—I am counting the weeks till Peg swims into view again—so delightful will it be to have her near and easily to commune with her, and above all to get from her all that detail of the state of the case about you all that I so constantly yearn for and that only talk can give. The one shade on the picture is my fear that she will find the poor old Uncle much more handicapped about *socially* ministering to them (two young women with large social appetites) than she is perhaps prepared to find me. And yet after all she probably does take in that I have had to cut my connections with society entirely. Complications and efforts with people floor me, anginally, *on the spot*, and my state is that of living every hour and at every minute on my guard. So I am anything but the centre of an attractive circle—I am cut down to the barest inevitabilities, and occupied really more than in any other way now in simply saving my life. However, the blest child was witness of my condition last summer, my letters have probably sufficiently reflected it since—and I am really on a *better* plane than when she was last with me. To *have* her with me is a true support and joy, and I somehow feel that with her admirable capacity to be interested in the near and the characteristic, whatever these may be, she will have lots of pleasant and informing experience and contact in spite of my inability to "take her out" or to entertain company for her at home. She knows this and she comes in all her indulgence and charity and generosity—for the sake of the sweet good she can herself do *me*. And I rejoice that she has Margaret P. with her—who will help and solidify and enrich the whole scene.[3] No. 3 will be all satisfactorily ready for them, and I have no real fear but that they will find it a true bower of ease.[4] The omens and auspices seem to me all of the best. The political atmosphere here is charged to explosion as it has never been—what is to happen no man knows; but this only makes it a more thrilling and spectacular world. The tension has never been so great—but it will, for the time at least, ease down. The dread of violence is shared all round. I am finishing this rather tiredly by night—I couldn't get it off and have alas missed a post. But all love.

Your affectionate

H.J.

1. HJ had used in *Notes of a Son and Brother* certain letters written by his long dead cousin Mary (Minny) Temple to the Boston lawyer John Chipman Gray (1839–1915). Gray, in his youth, had been one of Minny's admirers.

2. Rosina Emmet's mother, the former Ellen Temple, Minny's sister.

3. HJ's niece was to be accompanied on her journey to England by a school friend, Margaret Payson. HJ, as it turned out, disapproved of Miss Payson, whom he found to be too much like one of his early heroines.

4. HJ had rented an apartment for his niece in Carlyle Mansions.

To Arthur B. Walkley
Ms Barrett

21 Carlyle Mansions, S.W.
Monday April 6*th* 1914

My dear Walkley.[1]

The impulse to thank you for sending me the very interesting little *feuilleton* on the Moscow theatre has been strong within me these several days; but my general condition has become unfavourable to the play of the passions, and so far as these do find vent it is in a hampered and belated way. But I found in the French report something of that waft of a more living and breathing and thinking esthetic world and air than we draw any sense of in our so flat and stale medium here. The only thing is that in all this quickened question of the "theatre," as they appear to be susceptible of feeling it *là-bas*, the fond principle of the Drama itself shrinks and shrinks into so small a relativity as to become almost negligible. I am not sure that beyond a certain point scenic refinement and development are not really inimical to its—the Drama's—intrinsic life—they can in a manner live so by themselves, on some comparatively bare "scenario" grain. Whereas the poor old play, what can *it*, unaided, live by?—And yet the aid, any aid, given it tends to become, by the growing measure so much more interesting—or smothering at least—than itself. Oh shade of Sarcey[2]—! But please don't regard these crude wonderments as the faintest challenges to response. Let us wait for some charming hour again in the Car of Hospitality, which so gently shakes out, along the road, what is best in its privileged passengers. Believe me all faithfully yours

Henry James

1. Arthur Bingham Walkley (1855–1926), the drama critic of the *Times* from 1900 to 1926.

2. Francisque Sarcey (1827–1899) contributed a weekly column on the French theatre to *Le Temps* for thirty years.

To Grace Norton
Ms Harvard

21 Carlyle Mansions, S.W.
April 7*th* 1914

Dearest old Grace!

Your dear letter "about my book" should sooner have been crowned by my thanks for it and the expression of my absolute affectionate impenitence in respect of those pages about the old interest and charm, in the Cambridge scene, of Shady Hill[1]—since I feel that your gentle rectification doesn't cover the ground at all. What my remarks come to is that Shady Hill was from the date of the beginning of the war (though at the very first perhaps but in germ) the most agreeable and graceful and civilized house in a scantly civilized place, and though you wave off the soft impeachment with a magnificence of humility and chronology I defy you to break it down. Can you pretend that Elmwood, with all affectionate respect to dear J. R. L[owell], was anything *like* as equipped an interior? Mr. Lowell didn't socially *exist*, and he was in those years but a concentrated hermit. You name Mr. Longfellow with just esteem, but his *house* consisted of nobody but himself and his disagreeable children—and as for Mr. Agassiz, whom you also name, the cap (of the attractive seated life) doesn't seem to me to fit him in the smallest degree. It does, and did, for a summarized retrospect, fit Shady Hill as it fitted nothing else; for S.H. was (one) a house of *manners*, and *unique* in that; and (two) a house of ladies, with your Mother and Jane and yourself, and for a while Susan, to prove it. *There was no other such house, there were no other such ladies, at all*—therefore the thing was worth saying; it is practically all I have said, and though of course I have said it in my own foreshortened and emphasized fashion, I couldn't possibly, from the moment I spoke of you at all, have put it decently at less. But that very simple and valid proposition is the only witchcraft I have used. There *was* nothing at "Cambridge"—I entirely agree, and didn't pretend to name anything. But there was the group of you at S.H.; and S.H. on its elegant eminence of those years, hung over Cambridge and so represented what was not elsewhere represented. I surrender you the whole of the rest of the book—but I fight with my back to the wall for *that*, which is substantially what the passages to which you take exception amount to. So now there!

710

I am happy to say I sometimes see Richard [Norton], whom I exceedingly like—and yet don't see as often as I would. I can't *actively* do more than a very little in these days—but what I *can* do I still find a sort of inexplicable pleasure in, and go on tip toe lest I wake up a doubt. And then I try to emulate your admirable courage and cheer—though your long tradition of kindness to those about you (there I am at it again!) I can't keep up with. Peggy arrives a few days hence to be near me for these next months (I greatly value her being so), and she perhaps will be able to report of you as he hopes to yours, my dear Grace ever so constantly and affectionately

Henry James

1. HJ's references to Shady Hill (the Norton house) are in chapter XII of *Notes of a Son and Brother.*

To Hugh Walpole
Ms Texas

21, Carlyle Mansions S.W.
April 8*th* 1914

Belovedest little Hugh!

I am touched by your little note about the passage in the *Times* Lit. Supp.[1]—greatly touched; because I don't see quite how the passage can have given you much more pleasure than a fond ingenuity may have enabled you to extract from it. Therefore I owe your acknowledgment of my rather meagre garland for your brow not a little to your brave good-will; which, dearest Hugh, I deeply appreciate. The situation was very difficult for me—and never shall I be caught in a like again. We will some day converse further *privately* upon the fruits of your labour, but not again *coram publico.* The publicity of all those remarks, on those two dates, have had tiresome consequences in the way of inquiries from the Neglected Young as to *why* they were neglected, and as to whether they are not as good as those I *didn't* neglect—also as to whether "I only speak then of my personal friends?" I shall never speak of nobody again, and the incident—an extraordinarily accidental one—is closed. The friends of young "Mr. Beresford"[2] (who *is* young Mr. B?) want to know why I haven't raved about *him*—and the enemies of young Mr. Compton Mackenzie to know why I *have* raved, etc. etc. It's a devil's job, really—good-bye to it! (One *Mr. George* feels particularly slighted—and has sent me *The Making of an Englishman* to show me what I have lost by not giving my article the benefit of it. But it only seems to show me that I can't read it. For what do they take me? It was an insensate step!)

Well, I wish you all comfort at the Cobbles and that the contents of your packing-cases may prove sustaining and sanctifying. You affect me as distant and dim, and enshrouded in Cornish mists; still, at your age (even without your constitution) I should have also found it an adventure, I think, and have blessed the break with engagements. What suits me now, at the other end of time, is to have made myself a London without them. I hope not to have another till I next make *you* engage to come and break bread with yours, dearest Hugh, all affectionately

Henry James

1. HJ's article "The Younger Generation." He was much criticized both for certain inclusions and for certain omissions. He had devoted a few cautious paragraphs to Walpole.
2. The novelist J. D. Beresford (1873–1947).

To Jessie Allen
Dictated Ts Harvard

21, Carlyle Mansions, S.W.
May 6*th* 1914

Most gentle Friend.

Pardon my use of these cold-blooded characters, which help me to breast the high postal tide of my friends' condolences without sinking beneath the flood. I *have* in short thus to dictate—for the relief of my aged faculties, organs and members—in order to *begin* to acknowledge the 390 kind notes of condolence that bestrew my table. I am grateful none the less for yours—from the moment you allow me this help from the resources of science. Yes, it was a nasty one, or rather a nasty *three*—for she got at me thrice over before the tomahawk was stayed.[1] I naturally feel very scalped and disfigured, but you will be glad to know that I seem to be pronounced curable—to all probability, that is, when the experts have well looked into me. The damage, in other words, isn't past praying for, or rather past mending, given the magic of the modern mender's art. This at any rate is the belief I cultivate till the contrary is proved. I rejoice heartily in your return, and shall come and profit by it less obstructedly on one of these very next days. I don't see my way to *which* just yet—the 390 so shut out the view. But it shall be sooner ever so much rather than later, and I shall perhaps even bring with me my more immediate Niece. Have patience with me a wee day or two longer and believe me yours all faithfully

Henry James

1. A suffragette named Mary Wood, wearing a loose purple cloak to conceal the meat cleaver she carried, chopped three holes in the Sargent portrait of HJ at the spring exhibition of the Royal Academy. She had never heard of HJ and was simply protesting the absence of "political freedom" for women; she chose this portrait because it was attracting much attention. Sargent, with the aid of practiced restorers, was able to repair the damage.

To Rhoda Broughton
Ms Chester

Lamb House, Rye
August 10*th* 1914

Dearest Rhoda!

It is not a figure of speech but an absolute truth that even if I had not received your very welcome and sympathetic script I should be writing to you this day. I have been on the very edge of it for the last week—so had my desire to make you a sign of remembrance and participation come to a head; and verily I must—or may—almost claim that this all but "crosses" with your own. The only blot on our unanimity is that it's such an unanimity of woe. Black and hideous to me is the tragedy that gathers, and I'm sick beyond cure to have lived on to see it. You and I, the ornaments of our generation, should have been spared this wreck of our belief that through the long years we had seen civilization grow and the worst become impossible. The tide that bore us along was then all the while moving to *this* as its grand Niagara—yet what a blessing we didn't know it. It seems to me to *undo* everything, everything that was ours, in the most horrible retroactive way—but I avert my face from the monstrous scene!—you can hate it and blush for it without my help; we can each do enough of that by ourselves. The country and the season here are of a beauty of peace, and loveliness of light, and

713

summer grace, that make it inconceivable that just across the Channel, blue as *paint* today, the fields of France and Belgium are being, or about to be, given up to unthinkable massacre and misery. One is ashamed to admire, to enjoy, to take any of the normal pleasure, and the huge shining indifference of Nature strikes a chill to the heart and makes me wonder of what abysmal mystery, or villainy indeed, such a cruel smile is the expression. In the midst of it all at any rate we walked, this strange Sunday afternoon (9th), my niece Peggy, her youngest brother and I, about a mile out, across the blessed grass mostly, to see and have tea with a genial and garrulous old Irish friend (Lady Mathew, who has a house here for the summer), and came away an hour later bearing with us a substantial green volume, by an admirable eminent hand, which our hostess had just read with such a glow of satisfaction that she overflowed into easy lending. I congratulate you on having securely put it forth before this great distraction was upon us—for I am utterly pulled up in the midst of a rival effort by finding that my job won't at all consent to be done in the face of it. The picture of little private adventures simply fades away before the great public. I take great comfort in the presence of my two young companions, and above all in having caught my nephew by the coat-tail only *just* as he was blandly starting for the continent on August 1st. Poor Margaret Payson[1] is trapped somewhere in France—she *having* then started, though not for Germany, blessedly; and we remain wholly without news of her. Peggy and Aleck have four or five near maternal relatives lost in Germany—though as Americans they may fare a little less dreadfully there than if they were English. And I have numerous friends—we all have, haven't we?—inaccessible and unimaginable there; it's becoming an anguish to think of them. Nevertheless I do believe that we shall be again gathered into a blessed little Chelsea drawing-room—it will be like the reopening of the salons, so irrepressibly, after the French revolution. So only sit tight, and invoke your heroic soul, dear Rhoda, and believe me more than ever all-faithfully yours,

Henry James.

1. See letter to Mrs. WJ, 29 March 1914.

To Edith Wharton
Ms Yale

Lamb House, Rye
August 19*th* 1914

Dearest Edith.

Your letter of the 15th has come—and may this reach you as directly, though it probably won't. No I won't make it long—the less that the irrelevance of all remark, the utter extinction of everything, in face of these immensities, leaves me as "all silent and all damned" as you express that it leaves *you.* I find it the strangest state to have lived on and on for—and yet—with its wholesale annihilation, it *is* somehow life. Mary Cadwal[ader] is admirably here—interesting and vivid and helpful to the last degree, and Bessie Lodge and her boy had the heavenly beauty, this afternoon, to come down from town (by train *s'entend*) *rien que* for tea—she even sneakingly went first to the inn for luncheon—and was off again by 5.30, nobly kind and beautiful and good. (She sails in the *Olympic* with her aunt on Saturday.) Mary C. gives me a sense of the interest of your Paris which makes me understand how it must attach you—how it would attach me in your place. Infinitely thrilling and touching such a community with the so all-round incomparable nation. I feel on my side an immense community here, where the tension is proportionate to the degree to which we feel engaged—in other words up to the chin, up to the eyes, if necessary. Life goes on after a fashion, but I find it a nightmare from which there is no waking save by sleep. I *go* to sleep, as if I were dog-tired with action—yet feel like the chilled *vieillards* in the old epics, infirm and helpless at home with the women, while the plains are ringing with battle. The season here is monotonously magnificent—and we look inconceivably off across the blue channel, the lovely rim, toward the nearness of the horrors that are in perpetration just beyond. I can't begin to think of exerting any pressure upon you in relation to coming to the "enjoyment" of your tenancy—your situation so baffles and beats me that I but stare at it with a lack of lustre! At the thought of *seeing* you, however, my eye does feel itself kindle—though I dread indeed to see you at Stocks but restlessly chafe. I manage myself to try to "work"—even if I *had,* after experiment, to give up trying to make certain little

715

fantoches and their private adventure *tenir debout. They* are laid by on the shelf—the private adventure so utterly blighted by the public; but I have got hold of something else, and I find the effort of concentration to some extent an antidote. Apropos of which I thank you immensely for D'Annunzio's frenchified ode—a wondrous and magnificent thing in its kind, even if running too much—for my "taste"—to the vituperative and the execrational. The Latin Renascence mustn't be too much for and by *that*—for which its facile resources are so great. However, the thing is splendid and makes one wonder at the strangeness of the genius of Poesy—that it should be able to pour through that particular rotten little skunk! What's magnificent to me in the French themselves at this moment is their lapse of expression. I hear from Howard—flanked by Mrs. Maquay and more and more uplifted about William; and I've had some beautiful correspondence with White. Try to want *greatly* to come to him—enough greatly to do it, and then I shall want enormously to urge you. I put here in fact a huge store of urgence—all ready for you the moment you can profitably use it. The *conditions* of coming seem now steadily to improve—though a pair of American friends of ours crossed nine days ago (or upward) via Dieppe—having come *comfortably* from Paris thither and slept there—in a very tranquil, even if elongated, manner. May this not fail of you! I am your all-faithfully tender and true old

H.J.

P.S. So many, and *such* things to Walter and to Morton.

To Brander Matthews
Dictated Ts Columbia

Lamb House, Rye
August 22nd 1914

Dear Brander Matthews.[1]

My very accomplished friend A. B. Walkley of the London *Times* tells me that he is writing to you in an interesting connection, and as I took the liberty of more or less suggesting to him that he should, I want to make good my inspiration by helping on the effect of it, so far as this may be possible. Huge convulsions, of the sort we find ourselves with such appalling suddenness up to our necks in here, open strange fissures in the most familiar soil, and I judge one of these to be yawning before Walkley, as they are in fact yawning right and left before all of us. He tells me at all events that the all-else-excluding War preoccupations of *The Times* thrust upon him a kind of anguish of leisure, and has asked me whether, so far as I can appreciate the matter, there wouldn't supposedly be some good field in the American Press for the application of his talent and his name; in the way of theatrical criticism, comment, general handling of that mystery in short. I have told him that I think there well may be, but that I am too far from the scene to have much conception of his particular practical chances—and so it has been that, wanting still to be as informing to him as I can, I have recommended *you* as absolutely the authority to interrogate. I have proposed thus to be informing at your expense, you will say; but my reply to this is, with the greatest confidence, that I am enlisting you in so good a cause. A.B.W. can plead it for himself very well, no doubt—since he tells me that you and he have been for some time back in friendly communication; but he nevertheless won't say for himself what I feel I want much to say—what an admirable, delightful pen I consider that he wields, what a fine and free critical intelligence plays out from him in the theatric and dramatic connection, and from how far back I have seen here his beneficent authority grow. It has made him, with the keenness and lightness and brightness of his form, the ripeness of his wit, a blessing of the first order to us—and nothing would give me personally more pleasure than to be able to feel I had done something to pass the blessing on. He has always seemed to me the most of a master, on the literary side of the journalistic press here; and so familiar and easy and amusing and attractive a master. However, I mustn't speak as if these things were new to you, and I make no doubt that you will feel the force of the fact that the American field is open, at its discretion, to the enjoyment of him: this whatever light on actual possibilities you may be able to throw. Let me at any rate put in my plea for your kindly throwing all you can—when you shall have before you his definite inquiry—which, addressed to myself, has made me at once greatly yearn and yet feel greatly unacquainted, and thereby helpless. Condone, please, the fierce legibility of this— as expressive of the earnest emphasis of

Yours very truly,
Henry James

P.S.[2] My sense of what is *generally* happening all about us here is only unutterable—save as to this: that never has England in all her time, gone at anything with cleaner hands or a cleaner mind and slate. We hang here over the channel—we of this place, in the most wondrous ironic beauty of weather, season and sea, and when I ask myself what our sense of it all—so near, only just beyond, would be if admirable butchered Belgium and incomparable solid France had been abandoned and chucked, the idea is too mortally sickening. Everything is horrific enough, in this relation, as it is!

1. James Brander Matthews (1852–1929), professor of dramatic literature at Columbia University from 1900 to 1924 and a prolific writer on the annals of the American stage as well as of plays and fiction.
2. The postscript is in HJ's hand.

To Mrs. Thomas Sergeant Perry
Dictated Ts Colby

Lamb House, Rye
September 22*nd* 1914

My dear Lilla.

Forgive my use of this fierce legibility to speak to you in my now at best faltering accents. We eat and drink, and talk and walk and think, we sleep and wake and live and breathe only the War, and it is a bitter regimen enough and such as, frankly, I hoped I shouldn't live on, disillusioned and horror-ridden, to see the like of. Not, however, that there isn't an uplifting and thrilling side to it, as far as this country is concerned, which makes unspeakably for interest, makes one at hours forget all the dreadfulness and cling to what it means in another way. What it above all means, and has meant for me all summer, is that, looking almost straight over hence from the edge of the Channel, toward the horizon-rim just beyond the curve of which the infamous violation of Belgium has been all these weeks kept up, I haven't had to face the shame of our not having drawn the sword for the massacred and tortured Flemings, and not having left our inestimable France, after vows exchanged, to shift for herself. England all but grovelled in the dust to the Kaiser for peace up to the very latest hour, but when his last reply was simply to let loose his hordes on Belgium in silence, with no account of the act to this country or to France beyond the most fatuously arrogant

"Because I choose to, damn you!" in all recorded history, there began for us here a process of pulling ourselves together of which the end is so far from being yet that I feel it as only the most rudimentary beginning. However, I said I couldn't talk—and here I am talking, and I mustn't go on, it all takes me too far; I must only feel that all your intelligence and all your sympathy, yours and dear Thomas's, and those of every one of you, is intensely with us—and that the appalling and crowning horror of the persistent destruction of Rheims, which we just learn, isn't even wanted to give the measure of the insanity of ferocity and presumption against which Europe is making a stand. Do ask Thomas to write me a participating word: and think of me meanwhile as very achingly and shakily but still all confidently and faithfully yours,

Henry James

To Edmund Gosse
Dictated Ts Leeds

21, Carlyle Mansions, S.W.
October 15th 1914

My dear Gosse.

Forgive, please, my use of this helpful machinery for expedition of my thanks. I find it does so expedite a backward and embarrassed handling of letters that I have ceased to make an apology for it to myself; so with that pleading victim of our conditions let me associate you.

Your article for the *Edinburgh* [*Review*][1] is of an admirable interest, beautifully done, for the number of things so happily and vividly expressed in it, and attaching altogether from its emotion and its truth. How much, alas, to say on the whole portentous issue (I mean the particular one you deal with) must one feel there is—and the more the further about one looks and thinks! It makes me much want to see you again, and we must speedily arrange for that. I am probably doing on Saturday something very long out of order for me—going to spend Sunday with a friend near town; but as quickly as possible next week shall I appeal to you to come and lunch with me; in fact why not now ask you to let it be either on Tuesday or Wednesday, 20th or 21st; as suits you best, here, at 1.30? A word as to this at any time up to Tuesday A.M., and by telephone as well as any otherhow, will be sufficient.

Momentous indeed your recall, with such exactitude and authority, of the effect in France of the 1870–71 cataclysm, and interesting to me as bringing back what I seem to myself to have been then almost closely present at; so that the sense of it all again flushes for me. I remember how the death of the immense old Dumas[2] didn't in the least emerge to the naked eye, and how one vaguely heard that poor Gautier, "librarian to the Empress," had in a day found everything give way beneath him and let him go down and down! What analogies verily, I fear, with some of our present aspects and prospects! I didn't so much as know till your page told me that Jules Lemaître was killed by that stroke: awfully tragic and pathetic fact. Gautier but just survived the whole other convulsion—it had led to his death early in '73. Felicitous Sainte-Beuve, who had got out of the way, with the incomparable penetration, just the preceding year! Had I been at your elbow I should have suggested a touch or two about dear old George Sand, holding out through the darkness at Nohant, but even there giving out some lights that are caught up in her letters of the moment. Beautiful that you put the case as you do for the newer and younger Belgians, and affirm it with such emphasis for Verhaeren[3]— at present, I have been told, in this country. Immense my respect for those who succeed in going on, as you tell of Gaston Paris's[4] having done during that dreadful winter and created life and force by doing. I myself find concentration of an extreme difficulty: the proportions of things have so changed and one's poor old "values" received such a shock. I say to myself that this is all the more reason why one should recover as many of them as possible and keep hold of them in the very interest of civilisation and of the honour of our race; as to which I am certainly right—but it takes some doing! Tremendous the little fact you mention (though indeed I had taken it for granted) about the *absolute* cessation of Bourget's last "big sale" after August 1st. Very considerable his haul, fortunately—and *if* gathered in!—up to the eve of the fell hour. I have heard of him as in his native Auvergne from that time on. All I myself hear from Paris is an occasional word from Mrs. Wharton, who is full of ardent activity and ingenious devotion there—a really heroic plunge into the breach. But this is all now, save that I am sending you a volume of gathered-in (for the first time) old critical papers[5] the publication of which was arranged for in the spring, and the book then printed and seen through the press, so that there has been for me a kind of painful inevitability in its so grotesquely and false-notedly coming out now. But no—I also say to myself—nothing serious and felt and sincere, nothing "good," is anything but essentially in order today, whether economically and "attractively" so or not! Put my volume at any rate away on a high shelf—to be taken down again only in the better and straighter light that I invincibly believe in the dawning of. Let me hear however sparely about Tuesday or Wednesday and believe me all faithfully yours

Henry James

1. Gosse's article dealt with the effect on certain nineteenth-century French writers and intellectuals of the Franco-German war of 1870–1871, "the only previous catastrophe that can be compared with the present war." He reprinted it in *Inter Arma* (1916).

2. Of the writers listed by HJ, Alexandre Dumas, born in 1802, died in 1870, when the Franco-Prussian war began; Théophile Gautier, born in 1811, died in 1872; Jules Lemaître, the critic, born in 1853, had just died; and Sainte-Beuve, born in 1804, died before this war in 1869. George Sand died in 1876, when HJ was living in Paris.

3. Émile Verhaeren (1855–1916), the leading Belgian symbolist.

4. Gaston Paris (1839–1903), the foremost French medievalist.

5. HJ's *Notes on Novelists* was published the day before this letter was written.

To Edith Wharton
Ms Yale

21 Carlyle Mansions, S.W.
October 20th 1914

Very dear old Friend!

Yes, it does keep up communication a bit blessedly that Walter, who dined with me last night, brought me in your touching letter of the 15th, and that something of mine had reached you with a kind of celerity before that. I think meanwhile I must have written you something further that you *hadn't* got by the said 15th. It was a great joy to have an evening of W., who was of the richest and vividest interest[1]—though he gave my unsophisticated spirit a couple of rather dismal chills; as when putting some of the dots on the i's of what is currently meant by the state of things at Bordeaux, and even when speaking from personal observation of some of the idiosyncrasies of the Russian officer. He in fact told me some anecdotes in the course of which the Russian Army was qualified as "mushy" though I take comfort in the reflection that this proceeded probably from some German source (and sauce) that he was more or less derisively quoting, rather than from his own dark mind. His mind was in fact dark only at those two points—it diffused the brightest light for me upon everything else we talked of. He is evidently very well and interestingly occupied here for these next days; but I count on our absolutely meeting again, as he will then probably have "seen," in his magnificent way, more, for more, in the course of the week than I am able to see at all.

I had with me two days since also the dear little Walter Gays,[2] who lunched here and were full of thrilling report and picture. They are indeed an admirable little pair, and my heart goes out to them entirely. They will be able to bring you some small account of me, and they will not depart from the truth if they tell you I showed them how good I wanted them to be able to make it. They go back, I believe, before the end of this week. Yesterday I saw Henry Adams and his two young nieces,[3] the natural and the artificial; in fact I dined with them last night at their hotel, to which they had come from their stay of several weeks at the Cameron-Lindsay place in Dorsetshire—in order to sail for home today in some White Star thing of which I forget the name. Henry, alas, struck me as more changed and gone than he had been reported, though still with certain flickers and *gestes* of participation, and a surviving capacity to be very well taken care of; but his way of life, in such a condition, I mean his world-wandering, is all incomprehensible to me—it is so quite other than any I should select in his state. I have had few other private visions—though Mrs. Curtis,[4] "held" up here by various causes, and mainly by that of the fear of Italy's joining of the Allies and the consequent bombardment of Venice by the Austrians, came in to see me yesterday and told me of her being indefinitely quartered with the Charles Hunters at Hill, where are also settled upon them, apparently for all time, Rodin and his never-before-beheld and apparently most sordid and *inavouable* little wife, an incubus proceeding from an antediluvian error, and yet apparently less displeasing to the observer in general than the dreadful great man himself, of whom Mrs. C. entertains a horror and who has Loïe Fuller[5] out from town to visit him in much retirement save when she leads him forth as her companion in her car. Mrs. C., who had been lunching with Emily Sargent, further brought me in the dismal news of the death of the so distinguished little French husband of her niece, Violet Ormond's[6] daughter, the Rose-Marie whom Sargent so exquisitely painted a year ago; the said André Michel having been killed in one of these last engagements. But you of course hear nothing but the like all round you. Millicent Duchess[7] is just engaged to be married to a new young soldier—and I can think of nothing else. I don't mean than of that union, but in the way of fag-ends of the smaller matters here. I can't speak of the bigger ones—they are too, too big. Yet I did lunch the other day at 25 Grosvenor Place (where they were up for three or four days); and that in its way was big too. "Are you able to work?" I am asked. "Oh dear no, alas—are you?" "Ah yes—I have already finished half a novel." "That seems to me very wonderful: how *do* you manage?" "Well, you know, it's so preponderantly for America, where they"—*they*—"mind the War so much less." And then as I, stupefied at the account of the process, but mumbled something about my own lack of *any* recipe, came the triumphant light: "Oh but *I* shouldn't be able to do it in London, you know!" And yet after all I doubt—I think she *would* be able! But this is all just now save that I am probably investing this afternoon One Pound more of your cheque in tobacco for a considerable batch of the Belgian wounded, now at Rye, on whose behalf I have just received thence a Red Cross appeal. I am sending an equal amount from myself (the two sources kept, for your honour, separate)—as I always do when expending for you; so that you do thus double good. I told you in my last of my sending Three Pounds to the Hammersmith Refugees; and now, after to-day's tobacco, there will be Four Pounds left for me carefully to deal out for you. I am going really, I think, to try that precious solution of our friend's: I mean making it, and thinking of it as, so preponderantly for America, where they don't care, that their *belle insouciance* will infect my condition and perhaps even my style.

Walter tells me that Morton is now positively sailing for the U.S. If this catches him in time please tell him that *je l'embrasse bien* and feel with him intensely in his errand, and believe that, though the wrench, for interest, of breaking away from Paris must be *énorme*, the high benefits to him from it, and to the condition *là-bas* will admirably justify it. I *see* you from morning till night, and am

Your All Faithful
Henry James

1. Walter Berry, president of the American Chamber of Commerce in Paris, was able to move about Europe, and brought back miscellaneous war news, rumors, and gossip.

2. Walter Gay (1856–1937), American painter, and his wife, Matilda.

3. Adams's niece Mabel Hooper La Farge and one of his "nieces-in-wish," Aileen Tone.

4. Mrs. Daniel Curtis, HJ's former hostess at the Palazzo Barbaro.

5. Loïe Fuller (1862–1928), the American dancer, famous for her innovations in stage lighting and for her expertise with "serpentine" skirt dances, which greatly impressed symbolist painters and poets.

6. John Singer Sargent's sister Emily occupied an apartment in Carlyle Mansions and was on neighborly terms with HJ. Another sister, Violet, had married a Frenchman named Ormond.

7. HJ's old friend Millicent Fanny St. Clair Erskine, eldest daughter of the fourth Earl of Roslyn and widow of the fourth Duke of Sutherland. In 1914 she married Major P. D. Fitzgerald, who served on the British general staff in France and Palestine during the war. The Duchess wrote light novels and plays.

To Margaret Mary James
Ms Harvard

21 Carlyle Mansions, S.W.
23 October 1914

Dearest Peg,

I have had within two or three days two letters from you; one of the 11th, arriving on the same day as a full one from your Mother, which I answered at some length yesterday, and one this morning about the matter of Miss Maud, which I will at once attend to. I will send her, without words, a postal order for 10/6—and hope with all my heart never again to have even as much contact with her as that. I shall take good care in fact not to have any to the extent of a single syllable. I think she has a perfect fatuity of unawareness of the odious light in which she presents herself. But enough of her!

I wrote all I felt and thought on the subject of your complication at home to your Mother yesterday—as I had already pretty well done in answering your own first letter after your arrival, on which I at once delivered myself. You have my absolute sympathy, moral support and backing, and, knowing, you will now, your Mother, Harry and you, thoroughly feel this, it's a kind of relief to talk of other matters, even if these can't but consist of our huge oppressive and obsessive matter here. *That* is the only thing that exists for us—it crowds our whole sky from pole to pole. The case is very much what it was for this even before you left, save that one's whole consciousness of it *has* to be, with the increase of all the desolation wrought, heavier and sorer. But, as I said to your Mother, I can't pretend to go into particulars of the situation—these become ancient history by the time they reach you; and one can't even generalize at present with any great confidence or security. The country is facing with enormous energy the prospect of a "long" war, whatever that may mean; as to which nothing is more evident and certain than that "length" was the last thing Germany ever dreamed of or desired, ever staked her adventures upon, and consequently which she can't see imposed upon her without (by every indication and presumption) a full measure of dismay. I try not to be affected by fluctuations or the apparent and superficial from day-to-day better and worse, things now not at all measurable for the whole or the long run; I throw myself upon one or two general and I think incontrovertible truths: as that this country's power to hold on and on, with her resources as yet merely tickled on the surface, is of the grimmest—to say nothing of the same truth in respect of the Allies; while any such necessity of duration, any such doom of having to be dragged out, played no part in the enemy's original confidence. I have been finding London all this month exactly what I knew it would be, agitating and multitudinously-assaulting, but in all sorts of ways interesting and thrilling—such a reflection of the whole national consciousness; and I think of the contraction and starvation of Rye as something blessedly escaped from. Don't resent please, moreover, my reiterating what it seems they have such difficulty for taking in roundabout at home—that I haven't ceased to feel justified of your decision to return, or to draw a long breath fifty times a day over the blest fact of your absence from it all. Your being on my mind here, to speak definitely, and my feeling myself on yours, in the way that, as I am, I should be, would have been simply impossible and disastrous—in short it makes me sick to think of it. I think that that fact, and my whole judgment of the matter, should have some weight with your companions and stay their repetition of their question of what you did. I was yesterday, for a cup of tea, at the Embassy,—Mrs. Page[1] is having of course no receptions, but their attitude is so friendly to me that I like to see them; and they put it with the strongest emphasis that they hold London in these conditions no place whatever for any American not fixed here by long residence, and express the same frankly to such few of any danglers-on who still remain: there are very few of these, but they ask them, when they see them, to be so good as to go home at once. However, I think I must have put all this already in a sufficient light to you.

I try to think of any personal bits that will connect themselves for you; I think for instance of how it will sadden you to hear of the death, in action, of Violet Ormond's fine little son-in-law, that beautiful Rose-Marie's husband of only a year, Robert André-Michel; of whom Emily S[argent] told me two days ago that his father had wired to Violet here: *"Robert tué; balle au cœur; mort en héros; son lieutenant le dit."* He at least died, without any of the prolonged horrors of so many, on the spot; that he was the most accomplished and promising of the young distinguished scholars formed by the *École des Chartes;* it was a love match with that exquisite girl; and it's as lamentable as you can judge. But we hear nothing else, right and left, and all over the place; the sacrifices of life are colossal, and they of course do nothing but grow—*everyone* here that one knows (every family) has sons, brothers, husbands, parents even, fighting; those stricken are already, at this rate, as numerous as you may suppose—and my tremendously able and lucid friend Pinker, of whom you have heard me speak, told me yesterday of a quiet old lady, his neighbour in the country, who has *six* sons and every one of them in the army, as of course his own only boy is. I have heard, at second hand, of Hugh Walpole's being at Moscow, but of course haven't had a syllable of news from him directly, and probably shan't have. Desmond MacCarthy is in France, at the Front, up to his neck in Red Cross Service; Rupert Brooke at once enlisted—I am not certain in what, but was in the English force thrown into Antwerp to help the resistance (so lamentably in vain); but got away with the evacuation, and I hear is now back in this country and in camp at Deal. Karin Costello's queer marriage to Adrian Stephen[2] (which I noted for you in the *Times* that I sent) took place yesterday I believe; and it is a union, I hear, that was precipitated by her having saved his life during a boat accident which took place, I think, down at Ford; when he clumsily overturned a sailboat and got his interminable length so smothered in the impedimenta that he was rescued only by Karin's gallant and successful efforts in the water: she disengaged and kept him up, she hauled him somehow onto some perch of safety. So it's all as romantic and abnormal as you like. Fanny P[rothero] would be immersed over her head in anxiety about Mollie—who, I fear, is a very grave case, didn't the other immersion, the still bigger anxiety, those of all of us, dispute rather mercifully her attention. But I *see* nobody of your now so incredible circle—and this is all for just now—you shall have more soon again. Rye has now a houseful of Belgian wounded, as well as of the other sort, and the Red Cross invites me to renew my supplies. One's hand is eternally in one's pocket, one wonders how one will hold out. But one *must*—it mitigates so, to one's own sense, and absurd as that seems, the horror. I fear I seem to send dreadfully few newspapers; but the reason is twofold: first that there seems little in them that isn't stale and vulgar now the day after it appears; and second that we daily do up here from eight to ten of them for despatch to the British Red Cross in Paris, where Mrs. Wharton tells me they are an extreme boon, most welcome, in the very great paucity and difficulty (as to getting them) in Paris. So I make it thus my regular care that that number shall be securely enveloped, directed and postaged—and by the time this is done our forwarding energies seem spent—but still, you shan't wholly want. I can only add love to all. Ever your fond old uncle

Henry James

1. The wife of the American Ambassador to Britain, Walter Hines Page.
2. Karin Costelloe (1889–1953), daughter of Mary Pearsall Smith Costelloe, married Adrian Stephen (1883–1948), youngest son of Leslie Stephen.

To Hugh Walpole
Ms Texas

21 Carlyle Mansions, S.W.
November 21*st* 1914

Dearest Hugh.

This is a great joy—your letter of November 12th has just come, to my extreme delight, and I answer it, you see, within a very few hours. It is by far the best letter you have ever written me, and I am touched and interested by it more than I can say. Let me tell you at once that I sent you that last thing in type-copy because of an anxious calculation that such a form would help to secure its safe arrival. Your own scrap was a signal of the probable non-arrival of anything that seemed in the least to defy legibility; therefore I said to myself that what was flagrantly and blatantly legible *would* presumably reach you. At the same time the extreme spareness of your own note appeared to give me the pattern of the very little I should do well to attempt to say. It was all wretched enough—as have been the two postcards I have addressed you since, being advised that *they* would be probably the most likely-to-come-to-hand things, beggarly as they could only be. But this full free letter from you is a blissful reassurance; it has come straight and speedily (for the distance and the other conditions), and makes me feel that anything is possible.[1] Therefore may the present be no less successful. For I want you to know that the vision of your homesickness and loneliness and the "family" within your gates wrings tears of the tenderest pity from my aged eyes. You must indeed have had a regular hell of a time, and the strain on your nerves and resolutions have been of the direst. I hope the worst in that way is over—over above all with your started acquisition of the tongue, which must indeed be magnificent, and also that you have some other friends than the regular companions of your board, if not of your bed. I had better make use of this chance, however, to give you an inkling of *our* affairs, such as they are, rather than indulge in mere surmises and desires, fond and faithful though these be, about your own eventualities. London is of course under all our stress very interesting, to me deeply and infinitely moving—but on a basis and in ways that make the life we have known here fade into grey mists of insignificance. People "meet" a little, but very little, every social habit and convention has broken down, save with a few vulgarians and utter mistakers (mistakers, I mean, about the decency of things); and for myself, I confess, I find there are very few persons I care to see—only those to whom and to whose state of feeling I am really attached. Promiscuous chatter on the public situation and the gossip there anent of more or less wailing women in particular give unspeakably on my nerves. Depths of sacred silence seem to me to prescribe themselves in presence of the sanctities of action of those who, in unthinkable conditions almost, are magnificently *doing* the thing. Then right and left are all the figures of mourning—though such proud erect ones—over the blow that has come to them. *There* the women are admirable—the mothers and wives and sisters; the mothers in particular, since it's so much the younger lives, the fine seed of the future, that are offered and taken. The rate at which they are taken is appalling—but then I think of France and Russia and even of Germany herself, and the vision simply overwhelms and breaks the heart. "The German dead, the German dead!" I above all say to myself—in such hecatombs have *they* been ruthlessly piled up by those who have driven them, from behind, to their fate; and it for the moment almost makes me forget Belgium—though when I *remember* that disembowelled country my heart is at once hardened to *every* son of a Hun. Belgium we have hugely and portentously with us; if never in the world was a nation so driven forth, so on the other hand was one never so taken to another's arms. And the Dutch have been nobly hospitable! I have been going to a great hospital (St. Bart's),[2] at the request of a medical friend there, to help to give the solace of free talk to a lot of Belgian wounded and sick (so few people appear to be able to converse in the least intimately with them), and have thereby almost discovered my vocation in life to be the beguiling and drawing-out of the suffering soldier. The Belgians get worked off, convalesce, and are sent away etc.; but the British influx is steady, and I have lately been seeing more (always at Bart's) of *that* prostrate warrior, with whom I seem to get even better into relation. At his best he is admirable—*so* much may be made of him; of a freshness and brightness of soldier-stuff that I think must be unsurpassable. We only want more and more and more and more, of him; and I judge that we shall in due course get it. Immensely interesting what you say of the sublime newness of spirit of the great Russian people—of whom we are thinking here with the most confident admiration. I met a striking specimen the other day who was oddly enough in the Canadian contingent (he had been living two or three years in Canada and had volunteered there); and who was of a stature, complexion, expression, and above all of a shining candour, which made him a kind of army-corps in himself. But about individuals more immediately touching us what shall I tell you? The difficulty is that my contacts are so few and so *picked*, and that innumerable of the younger men are bearing arms. Jocelyn P[ersse] (I think I *have* told you) has joined the Royal Fusiliers (in camp as yet in Essex). Wilfred von G[lehn] exercises and drills the day long in the Artist's Corps;[3] Desmond MacCarthy is at the front in the Red Cross, Rupert Brooke was at the Siege (and surrender, alas) of Antwerp; Philip Gosse has got a commission (his father has ceased to be in the H. of L.'s);[4] in short almost everyone of anything less than my age is, or is preparing to be, in the imminent deadly breach. Little Marie Belloc[5] lunched with me the other day and bristled with the fruits of ubiquity and omniscience in a manner remarkable even for her. She struck me as being really much in the "know" (her husband and her brother minister to that); and was most interesting, was charmingly conversible. She *works* gallantly in spite of the stricken state of the worker's mind—mine is utterly blighted; book-makes and keeps the pot boiling, at the same time that she is all over the place, in a manner the most defiant of comprehension. She's the Whole Thing in petticoats. And books are being published—*some;* about as many as ought ever to be. You *shall* have my poor old *Notes* [*of a Son and Brother*]—superannuated quite now, bless you; they shall be addressed to you registered. I feel as if I were always pushing Compton M[ackenzie] into your ken—but he's to lunch with me tomorrow, Sunday, again, though it makes but the second time of my seeing him. He goes into sanitary exile (to Capri) on Monday, I believe; so be reassured. His huge II of *Sinister Street* is half a deadly failure and half an extraordinary exhibition of talent. The Oxford moiety (I like that elegant word) is of a strange platitude; but the London sequel, all about prostitutes (*exclusively*) offers a collection of these; studied *sur le vif*, which is far beyond anything done, ever, in English (naturally), and yet is not in the least an emulation of anything French—is really an original and striking performance. But I don't know what it *means*—beyond the two facts of his opportunities of observation and his ability. However, the thing affects me on the whole as a mere wide waste. Wells has published a mere flat tiresomeness (*Sir Isaac Harman's Wife*); at least I had, for the first time with anything of Wells's, simply to let it slide. The Gräfin has produced *The Pastor's Wife* (the daughter of an English Bishop married in Germany to a Pfarrer and condemned to bear nine children) which I am told is mere crude obstetrics. That lady and Wells don't seem to have brought each other luck. She came to England directly the war broke out to be naturalized—but

I believe she is back at the Châlet now, where I suppose her name (which she keeps) is less awkward for her. Poor Bobby Ross is again in hopeless litigation, against the atrocious Alfred D.[6] himself this time—but it's a deplorable squalid note in the midst of *big* bloody things. (The hearing, or whatever it's called, has but just begun; no result yet—and it *may* again be against the ravaged Ross—it's capable of being!) But good-night, dearest Hugh. I sit here writing late, in the now extraordinary London blackness of darkness and (almost) tension of stillness. The alarms we had had have as yet come to nothing. Please believe in the fond fidelity with which I think of you. Oh for the day of reparation and reunion! I hope for you that you *may* have the great and terrible experience of Ambulance service at the front. Ah how I pray you also *may* receive this benediction from your affectionate old

H.J.

1. Hugh Walpole planned to enlist, but his eyesight was too poor for military service. He was commissioned by the *Daily Mail* to cover the Russian front and also wrote for the *Saturday Review*.

2. St. Bartholomew's hospital, about which HJ wrote an account in one of his last essays, "The Long Wards," published in Edith Wharton's *Book of the Homeless* and posthumously in *Within the Rim* (1918).

3. The painter who married Jane Emmet. During the war he changed his name to *de* Glehn to avoid using the *von*.

4. Gosse had reached retirement age as Librarian of the House of Lords.

5. The novelist Marie-Belloc Lowndes (1868–1947), wife of F. S. A. Lowndes of the London *Times* and sister of Hilaire Belloc.

6. Robert Baldwin Ross (1869–1918), Oscar Wilde's executor, had been forced to bring action against Lord Alfred Douglas, who accused him of indecencies with young boys. The jury could not reach a verdict, Ross pleaded *non prosqui*, and Douglas was acquitted and discharged. Ross was ruined by the trial.

To Walter V. R. Berry
Ts Lubbock

21 Carlyle Mansions, S.W.
December 11*th* 1914

My dear Walter.

Please find enclosed the documentary proof that you didn't in the least owe me the 10 shillings you so kindly and imaginatively sent me just as you were leaving this place. They weren't due on any telegram as you fondly fancied—I *had* one from you, from the

Hague, but hadn't a penny to pay on it. So with your authority in that case to expend the neat little sum in war-relief I poured it into the lap of our so solidly seated Belgians—which is what the accompanying receipt imports.

May all be well with you now, with the sense of rest from your great adventure deep and grateful. I, even I, am beginning to rest from it, though this has taken a good deal of rallying and coming round. That has been helped by the chance of my having lately, with rather a rush, dined and lunched successively with several high in authority—the Prime Minister, Lord Chancellor, Winston Churchill, Ian Hamilton[1] etc., people I don't, in my sequestered way, often see, and finding *them* also not less in possession of the high pitch of *là-bas* which you revealed to me so luridly, and yet apparently able to glare back all right, so that I took this for a lesson and have been glaring *de mon mieux* ever since. I was present yesterday at a really moving scene—the visit, that is the *conférence,* of the really charming Boutroux (Émile)[2] at the British Academy. The lecture admirable, the audience *vibrant d'émotion,* the *entente* melting us all together. I hadn't thought to live to see the day. *Venez donc nous revoir*—but only to abide; not to pass to the more interesting. They *can't,* the brutes, love you as much as we, and especially as your all-faithful old

Henry James

P.S. I observe with dismay, just as I close this, that I never gave you, while you were here, the receipt from the same hand for the Five Pound note you so kindly gave me, for Belgian application while you were here on your way to Berlin and which I gave to the Crosby Hall Committee on your behalf. I enclose herewith their grateful recognition of it! Goodnight, and heaven reward you, again!

H.J.

1. Prime Minister Herbert Asquith (1852–1928), Lord Chancellor Viscount Haldane (1856–1928), Winston Churchill, First Lord of the Admiralty (1874–1965), and General Sir Ian Hamilton (1853–1947) Commander of the Central Force, 1914–1915.

2. Émile Boutroux (1845–1921), an outstanding nineteenth-century French philosopher.

To James B. Pinker
Ms Yale

21 Carlyle Mansions, S.W.
January 6th 1915

My dear Pinker.

Let me not delay another hour to thank you for that cheque to the amount of £27.18.9 that you report to me on from New York. Please take this for a receipt in full for it. Please also be thanked (and this I have too much delayed) for your conveyance to me of Arnold Bennett's healthy article (which I had seen and much relished, though I do myself deprecate everywhere the laying on of any rose-colour too thick), and of Wells's admirable scarification, as I hold it, of G.B.S.—in which I find myself ready to back him up to the hilt. This I should have lost if you hadn't benevolently sent it. I can neither quite live *with* Wells, nor live without him, but had I to choose between having him never or having him always the latter affliction is the one I should probably on the whole select. The huge performing frivolity of G.B.S.[1] on our actual tragic stage affects me as an indecency beyond all forgiving.

I should indeed be greatly disappointed in the President if I thought his Note[2] were really all his, and above all were really all his comprehensive scheme. I incline to believe, and much aspire to hope, that he has underneath everything a big sympathetic idea, so to speak, which this political concession (of a limited sort and to domestic conditions) needn't at all disprove. I have at any rate just heard it quoted on the best authority from [Lord] Bryce (so intensely acquainted with American phenomena) that he makes light of any uncomfortable possibilities, and *knows* Mr. Wilson to be deeply pro-English. Do, when you next have time, send me anything either of A.B.'s, or H.G.W.'s that you may imagine I shall have missed. I have had to settle down life-savingly, within a short time, to looking at almost nothing but *The Times* and *The Morning Post*; the latter for its comparative avoidance of cheap optimisms; which I hate to be too much fed with.

Yours all truly,
Henry James

P.S. I have never quite understood, but I infer from the limits of Scribner's cheque that I get nothing at all from him "down," *à la* Dent, on those *Notes.*[3]

733

1. Bernard Shaw's *Common Sense about the War* attacked British capitalism and called for "open diplomacy." It outraged many in Britain and the United States, and both Bennett and Wells took sharp issue with it.
2. President Wilson's note warning Germany about the conduct of its submarine warfare.
3. J. M. Dent and Sons gave HJ an advance against royalties for the British edition of *Notes on Novelists*.

To Henry James III
Ms Harvard

21 Carlyle Mansions, S.W.
January 16*th* 1915

Dearest Harry.

It's indeed a blessing to find myself "in touch" with you again. I do rejoice to hear that the impression of French failure of arrangement etc. has somewhat abated for you, but oh how you put your finger on the place when you say that they so strike you as wanting *in the first place* the expression of sympathy, participation, intimate fellow-feeling etc. especially from an American in whom they can't absolutely take the *état d'âme* for granted. I should very nearly say that we want and welcome the outright assurance, the dotting of the i's of participation, of the shared feeling, almost as much here too—or you'd find how we like it and bless it, especially from an American, if you were here longer. Certainly that is *my* case, feeling unutterably with them here as I myself do: *we need that sort of thing to live, to go on*, to bear up under the enormous strain, and we welcome it as balm to the awful ache and a salve to the intense sore: I should go so far as to say that it's open to the apparently but detached and unmoved, the merely considering and judging American to do even a certain *amount* of "moral" harm—in spite of the material good he may be achieving. *Faites valoir* your visions of Belgium[1] as "helpfully"—i.e. as revoltedly, to the French as possible—and remember that the absence of any allusion to *retributive* possibilities when they know you have viewed the scene itself is like a positive stab to their (and our—and *my!*) sensibility.—Alas, all I am able to send you then of the Ritchie papers today is this one little letter;[2] she has gone out of town this A.M. till Monday, and I can't get at her till next week.

I myself even am doing this afternoon an extremely un-

734

precedented sort of thing in these days, or rather years: I spend two nights at Walmer Castle, the ancient seat of the Warden of the Cinque Ports (near Deal and not far from Dover); the Prime Minister and his delightful daughter (Violet Asquith) being my hosts there, and Winston Churchill and one or two others, I gather, expected. I don't do such things easily nowadays: but I thought this, in all the present conditions, almost a matter of duty, really not to be shirked. Yet one always "hears" and "learns" on such occasions much less than one might fancy—officialdom never turns here its official side outward; only, mostly, some *other* pleasant but comparatively not at all thrilling side.—I wonder whether it would come at all within your Commissionership's purview to do anything however modest for one or other of Mrs. Wharton's extraordinarily brave and strenuous organizations—especially the one she started early in the war and has carried, with the highest ability and devotion almost (as starter and personal promoter) wholly on her own shoulders. This is her *Ouvroir*—for supplying work to women *not* receiving State aid through having sons, husbands, brother, etc. in the Army. It has been a big success, thanks to her immense labour for it, but of course is always struggling with precarious backing—though the idea is of course that it shall more or less support itself. The other is the American *Belgian Refugee Hostel*—in which she is also working hard and which owes its birth, I think, to her. Her private address is *53, rue de Varenne*—and I wish awfully you could go to see her and talk with her. She is devoted body and soul and intelligence and purse to work. The address of the *Ouvroir de Mme Wharton* is *Au Petit St. Thomas, 25 rue de l'Université*; and you will learn there about the Belgian effort—if you don't already know all about it. I think you must know from Washington days Walter Berry (14 rue St. Guillaume); who has always been immensely kind and friendly to me—and whom I hope you will have met and might even go to see (as for my sake), and I will write to him to go to see *you*. The Wharton organization must come, won't they? under the scope of your non-combattants War Relief formula. Those otherwise starving Paris *ouvrières*—! and when one thinks what wonderful little persons they mostly are. You don't tell me that your *collègues* have come back from Berlin short of its being visibly damned—! However, I'm like your French acquaintance—I don't want to hear about Berlin. But I must now

735

feed and catch my little train to Walmer. Bless you and extend you and reward you! Ever your affectionate old uncle,

Henry James

P.S. Nothing in the Syracuse Remittance way has yet come, but I dare say it will be along.

1. HJ's nephew, by now an executive at the Rockefeller Foundation, was a member of Herbert Hoover's Commission for Relief in Belgium.
2. Apparently a WJ letter for the edition Henry James III would produce after the war.

To Charles Scribner's Sons
Dictated Ts Barrett

21, Carlyle Mansions, S.W.
February 16*th* 1915

Dear Sirs.

I am much obliged to you for your letter of February 3rd and its quotations of corrections suggested to you by Prof. Burt G. Wilder in respect of several passages in my *Notes of a Son and Brother*.[1] I thank him kindly for his trouble and recognise that I was at a disadvantage, as to the small particulars he alludes to, in not having under my hand, in these alien conditions of time and place, more guidance than was afforded by my brother's letters themselves, to which my narrative refers. My Tillapenny shall certainly be Tullafinny on the next opportunity—though I am sorry it should have to, being as it is, I think, slightly the less ugly form of the two. So again there shall on the same occasion be found a *b*, instead of my *h*, in Ossabaw, as there shall be two middle *e*'s instead of my *u*, in Ogeechee. What a pity these changes, however, should make the words rather more than less resemble throat-clearing and sneezing!

I thank your correspondent particularly for setting right my mistake in using U.S.C.T. when I should have named the 55th Massachusetts; an error for which I blush, feeling it now, as Prof. Wilder says, a bad one. We must absolutely attend to it. I can only plead in attenuation that my remoteness from sources of reference and refreshments of memory laid frequent traps, no doubt, for my poor old imagination. Colonel Hallowell's first initial *shall* be N, and I am at a loss to trace the fantastic Rufus attributed to General John P. Hatch save by some sharp interference with association. I beg pardon of his shade, even though preferring Rufus to John P. and feeling quite sorry that the Official Records of the War haven't the good taste to confess to a case of it. I feel that I *have* known a General Rufus H., but it has probably been (the half-century bedims it) on this side of the world, that is in the British Army, and the confusion, the reverberation of the name, perversely thrust itself in. It shall be straightened out. Let me further, in acknowledgment of help, strain a point to meet Prof. Wilder's inquiry for the full name of G.A.J. I should have given it had I wished to make it public— therefore George Abbot James is for your and the Professor's ear only. Believe me yours very truly

Henry James

1. Scribner's had forwarded a letter from a critical reader of *Notes of a Son and Brother* who offered certain corrections to HJ's use of Irish and American place names and other imprecisions primarily relating to the Civil War.

To Burgess Noakes
Dictated Ts Harvard

21 Carlyle Mansions, S.W.
March 22nd 1915

My dear Burgess.[1]

I have delayed longer than I meant to thank you for your interesting letter of the 9th of this month—that *does* seem a good while ago. But I know Minnie has written to you (she and Joan showed me your excellent and amusing letter to them)[2] and we have sent you certain articles of refreshment which I hope you have safely received or are in the act of receiving. I shall pack off to you some more Food and Chocolate as soon as I can get again to the Stores—I judge that that is more "comforting" to you, under your wear and tear, than anything else. But remember that if there is any particular thing you want and will mention it to us even by a simple post card you shall have it at once. The jolly plucky spirit of your letters gives me the greatest pleasure, and makes me feel that you are seeing life indeed. It is an immense adventure, truly, and one in which, if things go well with you, as I so heartily hope they will,

Burgess Noakes, houseboy and later valet to James at Lamb House.

you will always be glad and proud to have played your part. Play it up to the very notch and take all the interest in it you possibly can. I like immensely your telling me how you hold out in marches, under whatever drawbacks, when longer legs have to fall out; this does you the greatest honour. What a lot you must be seeing, feeling and above all hearing—with that terrific artillery always in your ears! Notice and observe and remember all you can—we shall want to have every scrap of it from you on your return.

We go on as quietly here as all our public anxiety and suspense allow; and it helps us greatly that we believe in you all at the Front so thoroughly and are doing all we can, very great things in fact, to make you believe in *us*. I get on personally very well with such help as Minnie can render me in the small valeting way, and I think it must be a proof of my being better of those two or three old troubles, comparatively better I mean, that I manage so fairly without much aid. George[3] is coming up from Rye in a day or two, to be with us from Wednesday noon of this week (this is Monday) to Saturday evening next; and he will of course greatly miss you, as I think he has no great turn for finding his way about London alone. But we shall take good care of him and Minnie goes to meet him at the station. Make, by the way, very free use of that ointment we sent you—I hope you will find it a really good preventive; if you do we shall keep you supplied with it without interruption. We are having very decent and springlike dry days, in fact weeks, here now, and I hope the weather and the wet are all much less against you at the Front, than they were for so long. Cultivate good relations with the French whenever you come in contact with them—which must be, in one way and another, pretty often; they are a wonderfully clever and intelligent, a highly civilized people when you come to know them; though of course you see them now under the most tremendous strain and burden that ever a nation had to bear. Like them, admire them and fraternise with them as much as you can; I used to see much of them in my younger time, and I take the most enormous satisfaction in their Alliance with this country. So do all you can to contribute your mite to the success of that! But goodbye now and all good fortune to you! We shan't let you want for letters, or for anything else, if you will have a bit of patience with us; and I am yours very truly

Henry James

Oughtn't you, for your address to tell us your Brigade or Division or whatever, for locating you more easily to the postal authorities?

1. HJ's diminutive and loyal valet was now with the British Army in France.
2. Minnie and Joan were HJ's maids.
3. HJ's Lamb House gardener, George Gammon.

To Edith Wharton
Ms Yale

21, Carlyle Mansions, S.W.
March 23rd 1915

Chère Madame et Confrère.

Don't imagine for a moment that I don't feel the full horror of my having had to wait till now, when I can avail myself of this aid, to acknowledge, as the poor pale pettifogging term has it, the receipt from you of inexpressibly splendid bounties. I won't attempt to explain or expatiate—about this abject failure of utterance: the idea of "explaining" anything to *you* in these days, or of any expatiation that isn't exclusively that of your own genius upon your own adventures and impressions! I think *the* reason why I have been so baffled, in a word, is that all my powers of being anything else have gone to living upon your two magnificent letters, the one from Verdun, and the one after your second visit there; which gave me matter of experience and appropriation to which I have done the fullest honour. Your whole record is sublime, and the interest and the beauty and the terror of it all have again and again called me back to it. I have ventured to share it, for the good of the cause and the glory of the connection (mine), with two or three select others—this I candidly confess to you, one of whom was dear Howard, absolutely as dear as ever through everything, and whom I all but reduced to floods of tears, tears of understanding and sympathy. I know them at last, your incomparable pages, by heart—and thus it is really that I feel qualified to speak to you of them. With the two sublimities in question, or between them, came of course also the couple of other favours, enclosing me, pressing back upon me, my attempted contribution to your Paris labour: to which perversity I have had to bow my head. I was very sorry to be so forced, but even while cursing and gnashing my teeth I got your post office order cashed, and the money *is*, God knows, assistingly spendable here! Another pang was your mention of Jean du Breuil's death,[1] with its bearing on poor B[essie] L[odge]'s history. It can't have been sweet having to write that letter to her—any more than there can be any great other *douceur* in her life now! I didn't know him, had never seen him; but your account of the admirable manner of his end makes one feel that one would like even to have just beheld him. We are in the midst, the very midst, of histories of that sort, miserable and terrible, here too: the Neuve Chapelle business, from a strange, in the sense of being a pretty false, glamour at first flung about which we are gradually recovering, seems to have taken a hideous toll of officers, and other distressing legends (legends of mistake and confusion) are somehow overgrowing it too. But painful particulars are not what I want to give you—of anything; you are up to your neck in your own, and I had much rather pick my steps to the clear places, so far as there be any such! I continue to try and keep my own existence one, so far as I may—a place clear of the least *accablement*, I mean: apparently what it comes to is that it's "full up" with the last but one.

Wednesday 24th

I had to break this off yesterday—and it was time, apparently, with the rather dreary note I was sounding; though I don't know that I have a very larky one to go on with to-day—save so far as the taking of the big Austrian fortress, which I can neither write nor pronounce, makes one a little soar and sing. This seems really to represent something, but how much I put forth not the slightest pretension to measure. In fact I think I am not measuring anything whatever just now, and not pretending to—I find myself, much more, quite consentingly dumb in the presence of the boundless enormity; and when I wish to give myself the best possible account of this state of mind I call it the pious attitude of waiting. Verily there is much to wait for—but there I am at it again, and should blush to offer you, in the midst of what I believe to be your more grandly attuned state, such a pale apology for a living faith. Probably all that's the matter with one is one's vicious propensity to go on feeling more and more, instead of less and less—which would be so infinitely more convenient; for the former course puts one really quite out of relation to almost everybody else and causes one to circle helplessly round outer social edges like a kind of prowling pariah. However, I try to be as stupid as I can, and perhaps it was an effort in that direction that led me to lunch yesterday with Mrs. Maguire, along with Mrs. John Astor and the Gifford Pinchots,[2] both of whom I find quite "real people," and animated with a flame (oh how I hug the flame when I find it burn really clear!) of which her beautiful hair seemed to give me the note. And then there was an interesting gentleman who repeated to me his son's (an officer in the Guards) terrific account of that extraordinary battle of the "brickfields," which the British, the said Guards, I believe, almost altogether, sprang upon the enemy some months ago and which I but imperfectly grasped at the time. This worthy's (a very nice vivid veracious worthy I found him) reproduction of his young man's report of the overwhelming fury of the onset, preceded by a quarter of an hour of cannonade not intermitted for a single second, and that was exactly like the playing, all along the line, of a colossal hose of fire—this did me a kind of unholy hideous good, especially the part about the *instantaneous* rush in of the infantry on the quarter of an hour ending to the second, with the huge hose deflected for the time and spending itself during the next minutes upon the immediate near ground. It appears to have been an absolute massacre for our advance, the Germans surprised, fleeing, hiding terrified in every corner and cavity offered by the big bricky place; it overwhelmed and annihilated, to an appalling tune of numbers, while our losses were "comparatively" small and the big bricky place has never again been filched from us. I declare it quite wreathes me in smiles again—"comparatively"—to repeat it to you; so that perhaps I *shall* under the recovery of glow, be able to face the privilege just telephoned at me by Mary Hunter: that of assisting this afternoon at a vocal recital by a Belgian baritone, patronised and presided over by *Réjane*[3] and with Prince Victor Napoléon and Princess Clémentine[4] due at 5.30 sharp; which performance narrates with premeditated art, and an effect guaranteed by Réjane to drown us all in tears, the manner in which he *sang* himself out of captivity in Germany, bribing his captors by the beauty of his gift, and of one acute danger of being hung or shot for a spy to another, to get on, to go free, a little further and further, till he at last escaped altogether. He has arranged the story as a musical monologue, I believe; thirty people are to be present, and hang it if I don't go, after all, to prove to you that, like *vous autres*, I *am*, we all are, in tune and *à la hauteur.*

All the while, with this, I am not expressing my deep appreciation of your generous remarks about again placing Frederick[5] at my disposition. I am doing perfectly well in these conditions without a servant; my life is so simplified that all acuteness of need has been abated; in short I manage—and it is of course fortunate, inasmuch as the question would otherwise not be at all practically soluble. No young man of military age would I for a moment consider—and in fact there *are* none about, putting aside the physically inapt (for the Army)—and these are kept tight hold of by those who can use them. Small boys and aged men are alone available—but the matter has in short not the least importance. The thing that most assuages me continues to be dealing with the wounded in such scant measure as I may; such, e.g., as my having turned into Victoria Station, yesterday afternoon, to buy an evening paper and there been so struck with the bad lameness of a poor hobbling khaki convalescent that I inquired of him to such sympathetic effect that, by what I can make out, I must have committed myself to the support of him for the remainder of his days—a trifle on account having sealed the compact on the spot. It all helps, however—helps *me*; which is so much what I do it for. Let it help *you* by ricochet, even a little too. And if it can do the same just a trifle for W[alter] B[erry] also, *en attendant* that I do really grapple with him, the case will really be a most fortunate one.

There's another thing—but it haunts me too much, positively, for me to be able to touch on it. If this weren't so I should mention how it breaks my heart to have learnt from you that W. M. F[ullerton] hasn't done well in America and is coming back on that collapse. This is quite a hideous little pang, leaving one afresh as it does, bang up against that exquisite art in him of not bringing it off to which his treasure of experience and intelligence, of accomplishment, talent, ambition, charm, everything, so inimitably contributes. If he comes through London, as I don't see but that he must, I do hope he won't have the infamy to pass without letting me know. But when a person is capable of *such* things—! At any rate good-bye for now, and believe me less gracelessly and faithlessly than you might well your would-be so decent old

Henry James

1. Lieutenant Jean du Breuil de St. Germain, sociologist and traveler, a cavalry officer killed in action at Arras on 22 February 1915.
2. Gifford Pinchot (1865–1946), pioneer of U.S. professional forestry, head of the National Conservation Commission, and founder of the Yale School of Forestry.
3. Gabrielle Charlotte Réjane (1856–1920), a leading French comedienne between 1880 and 1915.
4. See Appendix V.
5. A servant whom Mrs. Wharton occasionally lent to HJ in the absence of Burgess Noakes.

To Brander Matthews
Ms Columbia

21, Carlyle Mansions, S.W.
March 24 1915

Dear Brander Matthews.

I am sending you back for your public use the article on Coquelin,[1] but sending it back as much "done over" as was absolutely inevitable. I have, as you will see, so very much re-expressed the sense of it as to have had to have recourse to a new text, that is a new pen and new paper, altogether; and I must ask you to be so good as to take it in this way or not to take it at all. It has been really dreadful to me to be reminded of how filthily (yes, *je maintiens le mot*) I could at one time write, how imperfectly I could leave my intention expressed. This paper, as the *Century* printed it (without so much as a proof sent me in common decency) simply bristles with those intentions baffled and abandoned; and nothing could have induced me, from the moment of owning any relation to them again, not pityingly to refather them, not decently to feed and clothe them, not, in short, to pop them into the hideous gaps that have so long and so disgracefully awaited them. The article has now, accordingly, some shadow of a right to exist—and I shall therefore even welcome its existence in your volume. I beg you to be intelligent about this, as you so easily can, and to like it very much as it now, for the first time, stands. It didn't in the least stand before—it but waggled on one leg! Kindly refer it to its former identity by some such footnote (say on the first page or somewhere) as: "The substance of this paper appeared in the *Century Magazine* for"—such and such a date, which I have no note of and the excision received from you gives me no clue to.* Let me hear of the safe arrival of my packet in spite of these desperate days and believe me yours all faithfully,

Henry James

P.S. I put my MS in a separate cover from this and register it.
* A thousand pardons—it is of course, from your hand, January 1887.

1. HJ's essay on Coquelin, which appeared in the *Century Magazine,* January 1887. Matthews was using it to introduce his four-volume series *Art and the Actor.*

To Edward Marsh
Ms Berg

21 Carlyle Mansions, S.W.
March 28*th* 1915

Dear admirable Eddie![1]

I take it very kindly indeed of you to have found thought and time to send me the publication with the five brave sonnets.[2] The circumstances (so to call the unspeakable matter) that have conduced to them, and that, taken together, seem to make a sort of huge brazen lap for their congruous beauty, have caused me to read them with an emotion that somehow precludes the critical measure, deprecates the detachment involved in that, and makes me just want—oh so exceedingly much—to be moved by them and to "like" and admire them. So I do greet them gladly, and am right consentingly struck with their happy force and truth: they seem to me to have *come,* in a fine high beauty and sincerity (though not in every line with an equal *degree* of those—which indeed is a rare case anywhere); and this evening, alone by my lamp, I have been reading them over and over to myself aloud, as if fondly to test and truly to try them; almost in fact as if to reach the far-off author, in whatever unimaginable conditions, by some miraculous, some telepathic intimation that I am in quavering communion with him. Well, they have borne the test with almost all the firm perfection, or straight inevitability, that one must find in a sonnet, and beside their poetic strength they draw a wondrous weight from his having had the *right* to produce them, as it were, and their rising out of such rare realities of experience. Splendid Rupert—to be the soldier that could beget them on the Muse! and lucky Muse, not less, who could have an affair with a soldier and yet feel herself not guilty of the least deviation! In order of felicity I think Sonnet I comes first, save for a small matter that (perhaps superfluously) troubles me and that I will presently speak of. I place next III, with its splendid first line; and then V ("In that rich earth a richer dust concealed!") and then II. I don't speak of No. IV—I think it the least fortunate (in spite of "Touched flowers and furs, and cheeks!") But the four happy ones are very noble and sound and round, to my sense, and I take off my hat to them, and to their author, in the most marked manner. There are many things one likes, simply, and then there are things one likes to like (or at least that I do); and these are of that order. My reserve on No. I bears on the last line—to the extent, I mean, of not feeling happy about that *but* before the last word. It may be fatuous, but I am wondering if this line mightn't have acquitted itself better as: "And the worst friend and foe is only death." There is an "only" in the preceding line, but the repetition is—or would be—to me not only not objectionable, but would have positive merit. My only other wince is over the "given" and "heaven" rhyme at the end of V; it has been so inordinately vulgarized that I don't think it good enough company for the rest of the sonnet, which without it I think I would have put second in order instead of the III. The kind of idea it embodies is one that always so fetches *this* poor old Anglo-maniac. But that is all—and this, my dear Eddie, is all. Don't dream of acknowledging these remarks in all your strain and stress—that you should think I could bear that would fill me with horror. The only sign I want is that if you should be able to write to Rupert, which I don't doubt you on occasion manage, you would tell him of my pleasure and my pride. If he should be at all touched by this it would infinitely touch *me*. In fact, should you care to send him on this sprawl, that would save you other trouble, and I would risk his impatience. I think of him quite inordinately, and not less so of you, my dear Eddie, and am yours all faithfully and gratefully,

Henry James

P.S. I have been again reading out V, to myself (I read them very well), and find I *don't* so much mind that blighted balance!

---

1. Edward Marsh (1872–1953), friend of poets and painters, held many important government posts which brought him into close touch with Prime Minister Asquith and Winston Churchill.

2. Rupert Brooke's "1914" sonnets, later included in Brooke's collected poems. Marsh sent a copy of this letter to Brooke in the Dardanelles Expeditionary Force; it reached him two days before his death.

To Henry James III
Ms Harvard

21 Carlyle Mansions, S.W.
April 2*d* 1915

Dearest Harry.

I have it at heart to let you know that I have given a letter to you to George M. Trevelyan,[1] who has been invited by the three Universities (Harvard, Yale and Columbia) to lecture to them on Serbia—from which he has lately returned. He is the son of Sir George (of the *American Revolution*, etc.); the great-nephew of Macaulay, the son-in-law of Mrs. Humphry Ward and the author of the admirable three-volume *Garibaldi*. He is of great ability and virtue, great general literary accomplishment etc. but perhaps of rather limited *grace*. That's his one drawback, but he will do his job well, and one likes him much as one knows him more. His father and mother have been for years very kind to me—and when he and his wife lunched with me today, on the eve of his sailing, I couldn't *but* thus sacrifice you to him, as I am sacrificing Bill and Alice while he is at Harvard. Would you mind sending this letter on to *them*—which will save me a separate statement to them (about him)? The real fact is that he will be so very much attended to through the enormous number of friends his Father and his Father's History have made in the U.S.; that he can't possibly weigh on you in the least degree—and perhaps even will scarcely be able to see you. The point is that I have *had* to testify to interest in his going by seeming to put him in relation with *les miens*; and he is really full of substance and knowledge and intelligence, though without great outward ornament.

It was such a joy to me to see the other day that you had had the straight swift run to N.Y. I go decently on. Ever your fond uncle

H.J.

1. George Macaulay Trevelyan (1876–1962), Regius professor of modern history at Cambridge (1927) and Master of Trinity (1940), author of a series on Garibaldi and other works.

747

To Margot Asquith
Ts Lubbock

21 Carlyle Mansions, S.W.
April 9*th* 1915

My dear Margot Asquith.[1]

By what felicity of divination were you inspired to send me a few days ago that wonderful diary under its lock and key?[1]—feeling so rightly certain, I mean, of the peculiar degree and particular *pang* of interest that I should find in it? I don't wonder, indeed, at your general presumption to that effect, but the mood, the moment, and the resolution itself conspired together for me, and I have absorbed every word of every page with the liveliest appreciation, and I think I may say intelligence. I have read the thing intimately, and I take off my hat to you as the Balzac of diarists. It is full of life and force and color, of a remarkable instinct for getting close to your people and things and for squeezing, in the case of the resolute portraits of certain of your eminent characters, especially the last drop of truth and sense out of them—at least as the originals affected *your* singularly searching vision. Happy, then, those who had, of this essence, the fewest secrets or crooked lives to yield up to you—for the more complicated and unimagineable some of them appear, the more you seem to me to have caught and mastered them. Then I have found myself hanging on your impression in each case with the liveliest suspense and wonder, so thrillingly does the expression keep abreast of it and really translate it. This and your extraordinary fullness of opportunity, make of the record a most valuable English document, a rare revelation of the human inwardness of political life in this country, and a picture of manners and personal characters as "creditable" on the whole (to the country) as it is frank and acute. The beauty is that you write with such authority, that you've seen so much and lived and moved so much, and that having so much chance to observe and feel and discriminate in the light of so much high pressure, you haven't been in the least afraid, but have faced and assimilated and represented for all you're worth.

I have lived, you see, wholly out of the inner circle of political life, and yet more or less in wondering sight, for years, of many of its outer appearances, and in superficial contact—though this, indeed, pretty anciently now—with various actors and figures, standing off from them on my quite different ground and neither able nor wanting to be of the craft or mystery (preferring, so to speak, my own poor, private ones, such as they have been) and yet with all sorts of unsatisfied curiosities and yearnings and imaginings in your general, your fearful direction. Well, you take me by the hand and lead me back and in, and still in, and make things beautifully up to me—*all*—my losses and misses and exclusions and privations—and do it by having taken all the right notes, apprehended all the right values and enjoyed all the right reactions—meaning by the right ones, those that must have ministered most to interest and emotion; those that I dimly made you out while getting while I flattened my nose against the shop window and you were there within, eating the tarts, shall I say, or handing them over the counter? It's today as if you had taken all the trouble for me and left me at last all the unearned increment or fine psychological gain! I have hovered about two or three of your distinguished persons a bit longingly (in the past); but you open up the abysses, or such like, that I really missed, and the torch you play over them is often luridly illuminating. I find my experience, therefore, the experience of simply reading you (you having had all t'other) veritably romantic. But I want so to go on that I deplore your apparent arrest—St. Simon is in forty volumes—why should Margot be put in one? Your own portrait is an extraordinarily patient and detached and touch-upon-touch thing; but the book itself really constitutes an image of you by its strength of feeling and living individual tone. An admirable portrait of a lady, with no end of finish and style, is thereby projected, and if I don't stop now, I shall be calling it a regular masterpiece. Please believe how truly touched I am by your confidence in your faithful, though old, friend,

Henry James

1. Emma Alice Margaret (Margot), Countess of Oxford and Asquith (1864–1945), daughter of Sir Charles Tennant, married Herbert H. Asquith in 1894. She published her autobiography in two volumes (1920–1922) and further memoirs in 1933 and 1943. Her footnote to this letter in *Margot Asquith, An Autobiography* (1922), 70–73, reads: "Out of all my diaries I have hardly been able to quote fifty pages, for on re-reading them I find they are not only full of Cabinet secrets but jerky, disjointed and dangerously frank." HJ seems to have enjoyed the frankness and the secrets, but his invocation of St. Simon and Balzac belongs to his characteristic "mere twaddle of graciousness."

To Hugh Walpole
Ms Texas

21, Carlyle Mansions, S.W.
April 10*th* 1915

Dearest Hugh.

The day I got your last excellent (pardon the pious mediocrity of this term) letter (of March 15th, the first from Petrograd), I vowed to myself that the sun should not go down on my silence—that you should have your fond acknowledgment within the few hours. But I have had to swallow my words, for everything began to conspire against me and make writing impossible, so that here I am really *with* you a bit at the end only of several days. My weight of response has meanwhile, however, lost not the value of a grain, and though your letter had been benevolently read and approved on the way, the fact that our correspondence appears to enjoy the full flavor of fortune—*absit omen!*—fills me with more joy than I can express. What you tell me of your prospects and expectations is of the liveliest interest and I don't see how, in spite of the continued absence you announce, I can do anything but give you my blessing and backing on them, from the moment that is the way you see and feel your case.[1] You have *bonnes amies* here who appear to feel it otherwise and who are rather busibodily eager to say so, but I polish them off when I meet them, as I did the other day the complacent hard-eyed critic of Onslow Square, with whom, though I owe you the burden of her acquaintance, I have, I confess, very little general patience. I have stood off this whole winter successfully enough from her tiresome little blandishments, but an appeal on the score that I was, or had been, brutally cruel, and that she was wounded to the quick, brought me to a *tête-à-tête* tea with her, on the eve of her leaving for the country in consequence of their having, through some stress of economic need, to let their house for several months. (I think the rigour is nothing more than that of their "feeling poor" in these days; which is what lots of other people, every one in fact, are feeling without the luck of her canny relief.) Frankly, her departure makes for the quieter life—though as she matters not at all, and as the quieter life itself even doesn't, why should I devote this precious space to her? It was only that I declared to her with emphasis, in dissent from *her* voluble and superfluous little opinion, that as you saw your best interests yourself in all these fearsome connections, so I in all confidence and trust could but see them with you and for you—you not being an inconsequent baby and that being the end of the matter. What it seems to remain relevant for me to say to yourself, however, on this question of your so-called invidious absence from your place[2] and your chance at this end of the line, is that as not being here does entail for you certain losses of our precious *native* experience, of the wound-up British sense of things, a most inspiring sense, "in widest commonalty spread," so your urgent *other* course, which I take you fully to recognise, can only consist in your doing very fully and thoroughly and triumphantly what you are offering yourself as an alternative and a compensation. Gather in your Russian harvest to the last possible sheaf and bring back something tremendously worth your showing—and above all your possessing. This must mean primarily, I take it, *achieve* the rare and difficult feat of acquiring the Russian tongue, so that you shall overflow with the last proficiency in it. This I take it you are quite inevitably doing through those thick associations with the Petrograd circle you enumerate to me. Master all that subject so that your mastery shall have *approvedly* borne down the scale. Return in fine reeking with an experience— that of your Sanitas enrolment or of any other that is a fine *positive* quantity—which will make us feel ours as a humdrum and familiar thing in consequence. If you can help the great Russians, glory to their name! in *their* stress and their splendid effort, nothing, to my mind, will have done you greater honour or left you a more precious and ineffaceable, because more horrific, treasure of memory. I follow you in imagination very tenderly and faithfully and fondly—I can't say fairer than that.

I wish meanwhile I had more shining lights about myself to project upon you across the continent, but really one has too little of a self in these days here to be formulated in any manner at all; one's consciousness is wholly that of the Cause, wholly the question of what becomes of it; frankly I take no interest in any other— save, that is, for two or three hours each forenoon, when I have come back to the ability to push a work of fiction[3] of sorts uphill at the rate of about an inch a day. We live immensely just now with our eyes, the most wondering and admiring and searching eyes, on your enormous companions. But we have ourselves too a vastly augmented sense of strength and of effect.

Goodnight now—with the injunction that you think of me, that you think of us all, with every sort of confidence. Everything is horrific, overwhelming; but nothing will become less so by our not doing it. Therefore the number of things we *are* doing, and doing ever so decently, is greater than can be named to you by your wearied, worried, but fast-holding-on (not least to *you,* dearest Hugh) old

H.J.

1. Walpole was now with the Red Cross ("Sanitas") in Russia and about to serve on the southern front.
2. Various persons in London had formed the opinion that Walpole was avoiding military service by prolonging his stay in Russia. Mrs. Belloc-Lowndes, in her memoirs, *The Merry Wives of Windsor* (1946) writes; "I only once saw Henry James really angry . . . in the house of a well-known London hostess, who spoke with scorn of the fact that immediately on the outbreak of the war Walpole had left his country . . . Henry James was so angry that, suddenly seizing my arm, he muttered 'Let you and me who are friends of Walpole leave this house.' " Gossip reported that some society women sent Walpole the traditional white feather of cowardice.
3. HJ had abandoned his work on *The Ivory Tower* and picked up his old notes for a ghostly novel, *The Sense of the Past.*

To Edward Marsh
Ms Berg

21 Carlyle Mansions, S.W.
April 24*th* 1915

My dear dear Eddie.

This is too horrible and heart-breaking.[1] If there was a stupid and hideous disfigurement of life and outrage to beauty left for our awful conditions to perpetrate, those things have been now supremely achieved, and no other brutal blow in the private sphere can better them for making one just stare through one's tears. One had thought of one's self as advised and stiffened as to what was possible, but one sees (or at least I feel) how sneakingly one had clung to the idea of the happy, the favouring, hazard, the dream of what still might be for the days to come. But why do I speak of my pang, as if it had a right to breathe in presence of yours?—which makes me think of you with the last tenderness of understanding. I value extraordinarily having seen him here in the happiest way (in Downing Street, etc.) two or three times before he left England, and I measure by that the treasure of your own memories and the dead weight of your own loss. What a price and a refinement of beauty and poetry it gives to those splendid sonnets—which will enrich our whole collective consciousness. We must speak further and better, but meanwhile all my impulse is to tell you to entertain the pang and taste the bitterness for all they are "worth"—to know to the fullest extent what has happened to you and not miss one of the hard ways in which it will come home. You won't have again any relation of that beauty, won't know again that mixture of the elements that made him. And he was the breathing beneficent man—and now turned to this! But there's something to keep too—his legend and his image will hold. Believe by how much I am, my dear Eddie, more than ever yours,

Henry James

1. The death of Rupert Brooke on a French hospital ship in the Aegean Sea on 23 April 1915.

To Howard Sturgis
Ms Harvard

21, Carlyle Mansions, S.W.
April 27*th* 1915

Dearest Howard.

I do indeed "understand how one's heart reaches back into the past"—that incredible past in which we once lived unimagining of these horrors and not knowing that we were fantastically happy. And I well remember how, last autumn sometime, when you told me of poor dear Ned Boit's apparent condition of that time, or of the summer—that he was reviving after a very critical state—I expressed dismay and regret that they should have tried to make him live on into a world so dreadful as ours had become and from which he was doing his best to escape. Happy he, even in his physical distress, to have closed his eyes on it at last. He had been surely a very beautiful and benignant person, a natural *grand seigneur* of purely private life (and this even though it had largely taken Iza to make him one); and my all but last impression of him—at that time at Cernitoio when you were there, threw all this into the greatest relief for me—he was so noble and tranquil, so sublime and harmonious a host. He was very kind to me too, even as he was to you

753

à la Dickens; but there was always in him to my sense something tepid and detached, something almost of fine hollow pasteboard or papier-mâché quality, out of which the passions and troubles of men didn't ring and in which they didn't reverberate—though they *ought* to have done so in that cool clear interior void, as expensively unfurnished and "hard-floored" as a modern music-room. His personal break-up, however, must have been very dreadful to him, and what refuge of silence indeed and withdrawal his extraordinary physical dignity must have had to take from it. He was in that quality of aspect and elegance, of natural aristocraticality, an extraordinary product of the thrifty old Puritan town—just as Iza had been in *her* entirely consumptional and *petite comtesse* way, though with a kind of toy-shop rattling, or tinkling, humanity that was in excess of his. They both seem to me to have been thrown back, as by the violence of our awful present, into the same sort of old-régime fabulous air into which the French Revolution must have thrown of a sudden the types of the previous age. And one wonders about those queer charming girls and their Tuscan territory, *Le Vergini delle rocce,* as D'Annunzio has the title of one of his fictions.—

Your kind report of Edith's letter is the more welcome to me as I hear from her myself not at all in these days; though quite as much on the whole as she hears from me. But her anecdote of her Abbé's enthusiasm for the Story-Book ghosts in the midst of these bristling and overwhelming ferocities and realities is fairly bewildering to me—but perhaps after all the revulsion is exactly natural, and at all events I rejoice in such a specimen of the combined urbanity of the Abbé and the grande dame.[1]—But it's even more, dearest Howard, than my belated bedtime. It gives me extraordinary pleasure to hear of your having racketted up and down the length of this island, and William not less, to such an effect of exhilaration undefiled. You could tell me nothing better of your case, and it makes me all the more affectionately yours

Henry James

1. Apparently an allusion to Mrs. Wharton's witty Faubourg St. Germain friend, Abbé Mugnier, whom she vividly describes in *A Backward Glance.*

To Clare Sheridan
Ms Private

21 Carlyle Mansions, S.W.
May 30*th* 1915

My dear, dear Clare.

I have been deeply moved and drawn to you by your beautiful letter and the infinitely touching photograph, but have had to wait till this moment to tell you so. I have been tiresomely unwell, in a manner to which I am subject, and have had to stay two or three days quite helplessly in bed—I had in fact been already reduced to this when your so interesting news came. Now I am better, but express in rather a ragged way perforce my intimate participation in your so natural sense of a violence done you.[1] I enter into that with all my heart and I wait with you, and I languish with you—for all the good it will do you; and I press the mighty little Margaret to *my* agéd breast, and tell her fifty things about her glorious Daddy—even at the risk of finding her quite *blasée* with the wonders you have already related. All this, dearest Clare, because I am really very nearly as fond of Wilfred as you are, I think—and very nearly as fond of you as Wilfred is, and very nearly as fond of Margaret as you both are together! So there I am, qualified to sit between you and hold the massive Margaret in my lap. All of which means that I utterly measure the wrench from which you are suffering and that there isn't any tender place in any part of you that some old bone of my own doesn't ache responsive to. I am incapable of telling you not to repine and rebel, because I have so, to my cost, the imagination of all things, and because I am incapable of telling you not to feel. Feel, *feel*, I say—feel for all you're worth, and even if it half kills you, for that is the only way to live, especially to live at *this* terrible pressure, and the only way to honour and celebrate these admirable beings who are our pride and our inspiration. Your account of your happiness of life and perfection of harmony with Wilfred brings tears to my eyes—not that I needed it, though,—and makes me reflect with complacency that I *knew* he was that sort to tear us from the first of my ever laying eyes on him—just as I knew you would have all the generous possibilities too;—and just as I bless you both, in fine, for being so beautiful and so brave and so exactly as one wouldn't like it the least little bit if you weren't.

Write to the blessed boy?—Won't I, rather, and at the very first of these next possible hours! "Which" I thank you no end for giving me his luminous address. I wish there were something I could send him that he would care to have or would otherwise be without—but I feel a very fifth wheel to the coach that must now be constantly rolling along his fortunes. I take an extraordinary pleasure in the memory of those hours of the early winter in that little bower off the Edgware Road where his report[s] of his first initiation held one spell-bound by their interest and their drollery. If I ever were to think of the most charmed attention I had to give, I think of Thomas Edgware's privileges, which, as far as I was concerned, might have gone on forever! But good night dearest child whom I tenderly embrace! Lift up your heart and spread wide your faith. I guarantee you that in one way and another you shall be justified of all that. I should like to be very kindly recalled to your Mother and your Father and I am your faithfully fond old

Henry James

1. Clare Frewen Sheridan (1885–1970), a sculptress, daughter of HJ's neighbors at Rye, Moreton Frewen and Clara Jerome Frewen. Her husband, Wilfred Sheridan, had left for the front. Margaret was the Sheridans' daughter, born in 1912. See letter to Mrs. Sheridan, 4 October 1915.

To Burgess Noakes
Dictated Ts Harvard

21, Carlyle Mansions, S.W.
June 13*th* 1915

My Dear Burgess.

If I haven't worried you with letters it has been because I didn't want you to have anything on your mind to answer, and because I also knew that Minnie has two or three times written to you. This, at present, isn't to press you for any sort of answer at all, but only to tell you that we hope you keep on doing well and perhaps begin to see some glimpse of your being allowed to leave for a convalescent furlough here. If that comes in sight you will of course let us know—and meantime I hope you are as happy as you can be in such rather hampered conditions. If your deafness[1] tends to diminish now that you are out of those hideous sounds we shall be very glad to hear it, and I feel convinced, at any rate, that it will gradually improve: I have seen, all winter, too many men, in hospital, slowly throw it off, even when it has been bad at first; not to have faith in your doing so. Meanwhile we go on as conveniently here as people can hope to do at this terrible time, and are thinking of getting to Rye by some sort of date in the early part of July. I have just lent the house again for a couple of weeks (from toward the end of next), to an old friend and her invalid officer son, for whom it will be a good place of convalescence; but that will probably not extend beyond a dozen days or so. Otherwise we go on, and are having a wonderful beginning of summer, with week after week of fine weather. May it do you some good even in stuffy Leicester—if it *is* stuffy, as I fear. We keep on wishing immensely that you were not so far away, and that I could get somehow to see you. If you would like to see either Minnie or me, one of us would come; though it would be probably easier for her than for me. I am not in worse health than a year ago—I am even, strange to say in decidedly better; but I have to be very careful, and anything in the nature of rushing about remains impossible to me. If you *can* manage ten words on a post card I shall, after all, be glad; and am faithfully yours,

Henry James

1. Burgess Noakes was wounded by a shell-burst and, in addition to numerous injuries, lost his hearing. He was now in a hospital at Leicester. He would remain hard of hearing for the rest of his life.

To Lilla Cabot Perry
Dictated Ts Colby

21 Carlyle Mansions, S.W.
June 17th 1915

My dear Lilla.

This is a very delightful hearing to have had from you and few days since—your letter with its lovely cheque in aid of our blest, and our quite flourishing, A.V.M.A.C.[1] I immediately took it to our Secretary, who will at once have acknowledged it straight, but I desire to express my gratitude more emotionally than he will have done. It made here £20 and a fraction, did your $100, and we are greatly touched by your bounty and rejoice in you and bless your name. It is such-like fond impulses from sympathetic souls that make us flourish, flourish so that we are effecting a considerable further reach of activity and working both for the French and the English Army. Take comfort in the conviction that it's a most admirable cause—and in the knowledge that Richard Norton, the master-spirit of it out at the Front, renews the purest legend of the *anciens preux.* Horrors encompass us, I mean above all in the limitless loss of all our most splendid young life, the England of the future; but one seems to make head against them a little in any definite deed done in mitigation of the actual woe. There are times when I feel the long aching anguish of it all scarcely to be borne—the nervous strain is so sore a thing; but one does go on, if only to feel the whole huge horror grow and grow as we get further and further into it—and if only, also, to press one's poor old ponderous, and yet so imperceptible, "moral weight" into the scale. I could wish the U.S. government were not, as in this last note, buttering so with assurances of its "friendship" the power that is perpetrating all the dastardly barbarities piled up now by Germany to her credit—the Zeppelins are all over the place even as I write, with their peculiarly unerring instinct for poor old women and young children. That, on the whole, is the heaviest strain to bear—the irrepressible amiability of Mr. Wilson in conditions that call for it so little. However, he clearly hasn't, and I don't pretend he is obliged to have, the imagination of the way that sort of sentimental sweetness comes in among us here—among the Allies all round, I mean—all at the strain of effort and sacrifice and the pitch of the heroic life as we are. And I hasten to add that if a nation has the blest fortune not to be with utter *inevitability* in our bloody welter, heaven forbid one should lift a finger to drag her. Only I seem to want to draw the line at her *fraternising* with the common foe. Your story of the Berchtolds and your children is full [of] a most illuminating Germanic psychology—they really believe that it's a sweet privilege for the British and Belgian and other civilian to be variously massacred by them, and that they do us an honour thereby that it's in shocking taste of us not to appreciate. It's the sublimity of their bloody fatuity that leaves one staring—! Nothing like it has ever been known to so-called civilization.—I thank you kindly for your statement about the seance at Hancock[2] and the communication purporting to be from William. As so often in those things, there is a glimmering appearance of a real relation to something actual—which however seems (to me) to glimmer *away* rather than to intensify as one considers it. Something of the sense of the message does indeed fit, however—if I *make* it do so; and is in fact curious and queer. What is remarkably so is the allusion to my state of health of fifty years ago (!!) for it's unmistakeably to that period and those conditions and objects—and not to any more recent. Nobody living today knows anything of that antediluvian case but the sole and single Thomas [Perry]—he is the one surviving witness. If the reference was made he being present I think thought-extraction (from *him*) would explain it. Otherwise that part is very wonderful. And the other thing, the deprecated "change" has just enough in it to seem rather to fall in—! I am really obliged to you for it. The utter historic disconnection of the young woman from the ancient time, places and facts—the abyss of the ages between and the *deadness* of the matters alluded to (save, probably, in T.'s memory), make the evocation, I confess, truly thrilling to me. At the same time, as coming from William they are extraordinary things for him to hark back to across half a century. But good night, dear Lilla—with every renewed assurance. It's very, very late—an hour for any witchery. I lately had a brave letter from Thomas, and am nevertheless so demoralized with the conditions in which we go on here—those of sympathetic and nervous depletion, I mean, that instead of telling him that I proceed to a fond answer, here I am just suggesting that he tell me all about his visit to W.D.H[owells] which you speak of his being absent on when you wrote. That is cool, but I am warmly yours and his

Henry James

1. The American Volunteer Motor Ambulance Corps, of which HJ had accepted the honorary presidency. See his war essays, *Within the Rim* (1918).
2. Hancock, New Hampshire, where the Perrys lived.

To Henry James III
Dictated Ts Harvard

21 Carlyle Mansions, S.W.
June 24th 1915

Dearest Harry.

I am writing you in this fashion even although I am writing you "intimately"; because I am not at the present moment in very good form for any free play of hand, and this machinery helps me so much when there is any question of pressure and promptitude, or above all of particular clearness. That *is* the case at present—at least I feel I ought to lose no more time.

You will wonder what these rather portentous words refer to— but don't be too much alarmed! It is only that my feeling about my situation here has under the stress of events come so much to a head that, certain particular matters further contributing, I have arranged to seek technical (legal) advice no longer hence than this afternoon as to the exact modus operandi of my becoming naturalized in this country. This state of mind probably won't at all surprise you, however; and I think I can assure you that it certainly wouldn't if you were now on the scene here with me and had the near vision of all the circumstances. My sense of how everything more and more makes for it has been gathering force ever since the war broke out, and I have thus waited nearly a whole year; but my feeling has become acute with the information that I can only go down to Lamb House now on the footing of an Alien under Police supervision—an alien friend of course, which is a very different thing from an alien enemy, but still a definite technical outsider to the whole situation here, in which my affections and my loyalty are so intensely engaged. I feel that if I take this step I shall simply rectify a position that has become inconveniently and uncomfortably false, making my civil status merely agree not only with my moral, but with my material as well, in every kind of way. Hadn't it been for the War I should certainly have gone on as I was, taking it as the simplest and easiest and even friendliest thing; but the circumstances are utterly altered now, and to feel with the country and the cause as absolutely and ardently as I feel, and not offer them my moral support with a perfect consistency (my material is too small a matter) affects me as standing off or wandering loose in a detachment of no great dignity. I have spent here all the best years of my life—they practically have *been* my life: about a twelvemonth hence I shall have been domiciled uninterruptedly in England for forty years, and there is not the least possibility, at my age, and in my state of health, of my ever returning to the U.S. or taking up any relation with it as a country. My practical relation has been to this one for ever so long, and now my "spiritual" or "sentimental" quite ideally matches it. I am telling you all this because I can't not want exceedingly to take you into my confidence about it—but again I feel pretty certain that you will understand me too well for any great number of words more to be needed. The real truth is that in a matter of this kind, under such extraordinarily special circumstances, one's own intimate feeling must speak and determine the case. Well, without haste and without rest, mine has done so, and with the prospect of what I have called the rectification, a sense of great relief, a great lapse of awkwardness, supervenes.

I think that even if by chance your so judicious mind should be disposed to suggest any reserves—I think, I say, that I should then still ask you not to launch them at me unless they should seem to you so important as to balance against my own argument and, frankly speaking, my own absolute need and passion here; which the whole experience of the past year has made quite unspeakably final. I can't imagine at all what these objections should be, however—my whole long relation to the country having been what it is. Regard my proceeding as a simple act and offering of allegiance and devotion, recognition and gratitude (for long years and innumerable relations that have meant so much to me), and it remains perfectly simple. Let me repeat that I feel sure I shouldn't in the least have come to it without this convulsion, but one is *in* the convulsion (I wouldn't be out of it either!) and one must act accordingly. I feel all the while too that the tide of American identity of consciousness with our own, about the whole matter, rises and rises, and will rise still more before it rests again—so that every day the difference of situation diminishes and the immense fund of common sentiment increases. However, I haven't really meant so much to expatiate. What I am doing this afternoon is, I think, simply to get exact information—though I am already sufficiently aware of the question to know that after my long existence here the process of naturalisation is very simple and short. I have put myself in relation with J. S. Sargent's, and the de Glehns'[1] excellent solicitor (he is also that of several other good people I know), Nelson Ward, a most sympathetic and competent person, whom I have often met at the Sargents', (and who has about him the "picturesque" association that he is, by the left-hand, great-great-grandson, or whatever, of Horatio Nelson being the not at all remote descendant of his daughter Horatia, of whom Lady Hamilton was the mamma). He will tell me definite things today—but I probably shall not instruct him to do anything at once or till I can turn round again (though I've indeed been turning round and round all these months). I shall at any rate write you again if I *have* said to him "Go ahead." My last word about the matter, at any rate, has to be that my decision is absolutely tied up with my innermost personal feeling. I think that will only make you glad, however, and I add nothing more now but that I am your all-affectionate old Uncle

Henry James

1. See letter to Walpole, 21 November 1914.

To Edmund Gosse
Ms Congress

21 Carlyle Mansions, S.W.
June 25*th* 1915

My dear Gosse.

Remarkably enough, I should be writing you this evening even if I hadn't received your interesting information about Léon Daudet, concerning whom nothing perversely base and publicly pernicious at all surprises me.[1] He is the cleverest idiot and the most pernicious talent imaginable, and I await to see if he won't somehow swing—!

But *il ne s'agit pas de ça; il s'agit* of the fact that there is a matter I should have liked to speak to you of the other day when you lunched here, yet hung fire about through its not having then absolutely come to a head. It has within these three days done so, and in brief it is *this*. The force of the public situation now at last determines me to testify to my attachment to this country, my fond domicile for nearly forty years (forty *next* year), by applying for naturalisation here: the throwing of my imponderable moral weight into the scale of her fortune is the *geste* that will best express my devotion—absolutely nothing *else* will. Therefore my mind is made up, and you are the first person save my Solicitor (whom I have had to consult) to whom the fact has been imparted. Kindly respect for the moment the privacy of it. I learned with horror just lately that if I go down into Sussex (for two or three months of Rye) I have at once to register myself there as an Alien and place myself under the observation of the Police. But that is only the *occasion* of my decision—it's not in the least the cause. The disposition itself has haunted me as Wordsworth's sounding cataract haunted *him*—"like a passion"[2]—ever since the beginning of the War. But the point, please, is this: that the process for me is really of the simplest, and *may* be very rapid, if I can obtain four honourable householders to testify to their knowledge of me as a respectable person, "speaking and writing English decently" etc. Will you give me the great pleasure of being one of them?—signing a paper to that effect? I should take it ever so kindly. And I should further take kindly your giving me if possible your sense on *this* delicate point. Should you say that our admirable friend the Prime Minister would perhaps be approachable by me as another of the signatory four?[3]—to whom, you see, great historic honour, not to say immortality, as my sponsors, will accrue. I don't like to approach him without your so qualified sense of the matter first—and he has always been so beautifully kind and charming to me. I will do nothing till I hear from you—but his signature (which my solicitor's representative, if not himself, would simply wait upon him for) would enormously accelerate the putting through of the application and the disburdening me of the Sussex "restricted area" alienship—which it distresses me to carry on my back a day longer than I need. I have in mind my other two sponsors, but if I could have from you, in addition to your own personal response, on which my hopes are so founded, your ingenious prefiguration (fed by your intimacy with him) as to how the P.M. would "take" my appeal, you would increase the obligations of yours all faithfully,

Henry James

1. Léon Daudet, son of HJ's old friend Alphonse, had become a notorious royalist in France, involved in extreme rightist activities and violence.
2. HJ is quoting from Wordsworth's "Lines Written above Tintern Abbey" (1798):
   The sounding cataract
   Haunted me like a passion: the tall rock,
   The mountain, and the deep and gloomy wood,
   Their colours and their forms, were then to me
   An appetite . . .
3. HJ's four sponsors for his naturalization were Prime Minister Asquith, Gosse, James B. Pinker, and G. W. Prothero.

To H. H. Asquith
Ms Bodleian

21 Carlyle Mansions, S.W.

June 28*th* 1915

My dear Prime Minister and Illustrious Friend.

I am venturing to trouble you with the mention of a fact of my personal situation, but I shall do so as briefly and considerately as possible. I desire to offer myself for naturalization in this country, that is, to change my status from that of American citizen to that of British subject.[1] I have assiduously and happily spent here all but forty years, the best years of my life, and I find my wish to testify at this crisis to the force of my attachment and devotion to England, and to the cause for which she is fighting, finally and completely irresistible. It brooks at least no inward denial whatever. I can only testify by laying at her feet my explicit, my material and spiritual allegiance, and throwing into the scale of her fortune my all but imponderable moral weight—"a poor thing but mine own." Hence this respectful appeal. It is necessary (as you may know) that for the purpose I speak of four honorable householders should bear witness to their kind acquaintance with me, to my apparent respectability, and to my speaking and writing English with an approach of propriety. What I presume to ask of you is whether you will do me the honour to be the pre-eminent one of that gently guaranteeing group? Edmund Gosse has benevolently consented to join it. The matter will entail on your part, as I understand, no expenditure of attention at all beyond your letting my solicitor wait upon you with a paper for your signature—the affair of a single moment; and the "going through" of my application will doubtless be proportionately expedited. You will thereby consecrate my choice and deeply touch and gratify yours all faithfully,

Henry James

1. To each of his sponsors HJ sent a memorandum, "Henry James's reasons for Naturalization July 1915": "Because of his having lived and worked in England for the best part of forty years, because of his attachment to the Country and his sympathy with it and its people, because of the long friendships and associations and interests he has formed there—these last including the acquisition of some property: all of which things have brought to a head his desire to throw his moral weight and personal allegiance, for whatever they may be worth, into the scale of the contending nations' present and future fortune."

To Julio Reuter
Ms Unknown

21 Carlyle Mansions, S.W.
July 1*st* 1915

Dear Mr. Reuter.[1]

Your inquiry, not to speak of your kindly recall of my very youthful reminiscence, much touches me, coming back from so far off; and I am only sorry not to be able to repay it in some more vivid or suggestive way. That note of the very dim recollection of our Finnish governess, in my early American childhood, is absolutely all I am possessed of:[2] you will easily imagine, under pressure, what a very remote period of history that represents, and will understand how faint and vague the whole case has become to me. It refers to the very early 'fifties, when I was a very small child indeed—since we all left America, for a long stay in Europe, when I was in my twelfth year, and the Finnish lady obscurely looms out of a time considerably antecedent to that. I mean she hadn't been with us, couldn't have been, for some three years at least before our leaving New York. I have completely forgotten her name and everything else about her, save that her stay among us was not a long one, as she was not highly proficient in the French tongue, which she proved unable, I gather, to administer to us with (quite apart from the pun!) the French finish. Nothing could have been more natural than this, and I confess I wander dimly in the whole legend of her nationality, for it faintly comes to me that she knew Russian, and also did know a certain amount of French. Her appearance on the other hand I quite definitely remember, and that she was of enormous stature, or what seemed to us then such; really a very large, powerful, mild person indeed. I don't think she could possibly have had a father with her—her isolated and unfriended condition must have been one of the grounds of her appeal to us. Also I much doubt if she could have married in America at that faraway time. You see I allude to more than sixty-five years ago, and am now myself in my seventy-third year. I haven't the least idea what became of the massive lady—we somehow *shed* everything so, everything of the antecedent kind, by our departure from New York, to which we were never to return.

Unsatisfactory as I am, please believe that I *like* to have been

765

reminded, however briefly, of a state of existence so remote from present horrors! One seeks momentary refuges, and I am in all friendly remembrance yours very truly

Henry James

1. Julio Reuter (1863–1937), of Finnish-Swedish extraction, was professor of Sanskrit and comparative Indo-European philology at the Imperial Alexander University (University of Helsinki). He had recommended HJ for the Nobel prize in 1915.
2. In the second chapter of *A Small Boy and Others* HJ alludes to one of his early teachers, "a large Russian lady in an extraordinarily short cape . . . of the same stuff as her dress, and Merovingian sidebraids that seemed to require the royal crown of Fredégonde or Brunéhaut to complete their effect."

To H. G. Wells
Ms Bodleian

21 Carlyle Mansions, S.W.
July 6*th* 1915

My dear Wells.

I was given yesterday at a club your volume *Boon, etc.*,[1] from a loose leaf in which I learn that you kindly sent it me and which yet appears to have lurked there for a considerable time undelivered. I have just been reading, to acknowledge it intelligently, a considerable number of its pages—though not all; for, to be perfectly frank, I have been in that respect beaten for the first time—or rather for the first time but one—by a book of yours: I haven't found the current of it draw me on and on this time—as unfailingly and irresistibly before (which I have repeatedly let you know). However, I shall try again—I hate to lose any scrap of you that *may* make for light or pleasure; and meanwhile I have more or less mastered your appreciation of H.J., which I have found very curious and interesting, after a fashion—though it has naturally not filled me with a fond elation. It is difficult of course for a writer to put himself *fully* in the place of another writer who finds him extraordinarily futile and void, and who is moved to publish that to the world—and I think the case isn't easier when he happens to have enjoyed the other writer enormously, from far back; because there has then grown up the habit of taking some common meeting-ground between them for granted, and the falling away of this is like the collapse of a bridge which made communication possible. But I am by nature more in dread of any fool's paradise, or at least of any bad misguidedness, than in love with the idea of a security proved, and the fact that a mind as brilliant as yours *can* resolve me into such an unmitigated mistake, can't enjoy me in anything like the degree in which I like to think I may be enjoyed, makes me greatly want to fix myself, for as long as my nerves will stand it, with such a pair of eyes. I am aware of certain things I have, and not less conscious, I believe, of various others that I am simply reduced to wish I did or could have; so I try, for possible light, to enter into the feelings of a critic for whom the deficiencies so preponderate. The difficulty about that effort, however, is that one can't keep it up—one *has* to fall back on one's sense of one's good parts—one's own sense; and I at least should have to do that, I think, even if your picture were painted with a more searching brush. For I should otherwise seem to forget what it is that my poetic and my appeal to experience rest upon. They rest upon *my* measure of fulness—fulness of life and of the projection of it, which seems to you such an emptiness of both. I don't mean to say I don't wish I could do twenty things I can't—many of which you do so livingly; but I confess I ask myself what would become in that case of some of those to which I am most addicted and by which interest seems to me most beautifully producible. I hold that interest may be, *must* be, exquisitely made and created, and that if we don't make it, we who undertake to, nobody and nothing will make it for us; though nothing is more possible, nothing may even be more certain, than that my quest of it, my constant wish to run it to earth, may entail the sacrifice of certain things that are not on the straight line of it. However, there are too many things to say, and I don't think your chapter is really inquiring enough to entitle you to expect all of them. The fine thing about the fictional form to me is that it opens such widely different windows of attention; but that is just why I like the window so to frame the play and the process![2]

Faithfully yours
Henry James

1. *Boon, The Mind of the Race, The Wild Asses of the Devil, and The Last Trump* (1915). This satirical work contained a section titled "Of Art, of Criticism, of Mr. Henry James," in which Wells mocked and parodied the novelist. See *Henry James and H. G. Wells: A Record of Their Friendship, Their Debate on the Art of Fiction, and Their Quarrel*, ed. Leon Edel and Gordon N. Ray (1958). The best-known passage of Wells's satire describes a novel by HJ "like a church lit but without a congregation to

distract you, with every light and line focused on the high altar. And on the altar, very reverently placed, intensely there, is a dead kitten, an egg-shell, a bit of string . . . Like his 'Altar of the Dead,' with nothing to the dead at all. And the elaborate copious emptiness of the whole Henry James exploit is only redeemed and made endurable by the elaborate copious wit . . ." Wells's attack seems to have been a counterattack against HJ's criticism of the Wells-Bennett school of fiction in his recent articles on "The Younger Generation." HJ had written, "they squeeze out to the utmost the plump and more or less juicy orange of a particular acquainted state and let this affirmation of energy, however directed or undirected, constitute for them the 'treatment' of the theme."

2. Wells replied on 8 July 1915: "I have set before myself a gaminesque ideal, I have a natural horror of dignity, finish and perfection, a horror a little enhanced by theory. You may take it that my sparring and punching at you is very much due to the feeling that you were 'coming over' me, and that if I was not very careful I should find myself giving way altogether to respect. There is of course a real and very fundamental difference in our innate and developed attitudes towards life and literature. To you literature like painting is an end, to me literature like architecture is a means, it has a use. Your view was, I felt, altogether too dominant in the world of criticism, and I assailed it in tones of harsh antagonism. And writing that stuff about you was the first escape I had from the obsession of this war. *Boon* is just a waste-paper basket. Some of it was written before I left my house at Sandgate, and it was while I was turning over some old papers that I came upon it, found it expressive and went on with it last December. I had rather be called a journalist than an artist, that is the essence of it, and there was no other antagonist possible than yourself. But since it was printed I have regretted a hundred times that I did not express our profound and incurable difference and contrast with a better grace. And believe me, my dear James, your very keenly appreciative reader, your warm if rebellious and resentful admirer, and for countless causes yours most gratefully and affectionately, H. G. Wells."

To H. G. Wells
Dictated Ts Bodleian

21 Carlyle Mansions, S.W.
July 10*th* 1915

My dear Wells.

I am bound to tell you that I don't think your letter makes out any sort of case for the bad manners of *Boon*, so far as your indulgence in them at the expense of your poor old H.J. is concerned—I say "your" simply because he has *been* yours, in the most liberal, continual, sacrificial, the most admiring and abounding critical way, ever since he began to know your writings: as to which you have had copious testimony. Your comparison of the book to a waste-basket strikes me as the reverse of felicitous, for what one throws into that receptacle is exactly what one *doesn't* commit to publicity and make the affirmation of one's estimate of one's contemporaries by. I should liken it much rather to the preservative portfolio or drawer in which what is withheld from the basket is savingly laid away. Nor do I feel it anywhere evident that my "view of life and literature," or what you impute to me as such, is carrying everything before it and becoming a public menace—so unaware do I seem, on the contrary, that my products constitute an example in any measurable degree followed or a cause in any degree successfully pleaded: I can't but think that if this were the case I should find it somewhat attested in their circulation—which, alas, I have reached a very advanced age in the entirely defeated hope of. But I *have* no view of life and literature, I maintain, other than that our form of the latter in especial is admirable exactly by its range and variety, its plasticity and liberality, its fairly living on the sincere and shifting experience of the individual practitioner. That is why I have always so admired your so free and strong application of it, the particular rich receptacle of intelligences and impressions emptied out with an energy of its own, that your genius constitutes; and *that* is in particular why, in my letter of two or three days since, I pronounced it curious and interesting that you should find the case I constitute myself only ridiculous and vacuous to the extent of your having to proclaim your sense of it. The curiosity and the interest, however, in this latter connection are of course for my mind those of the break of perception (perception of the vivacity of *my* variety) on the part of a talent so generally inquiring and apprehensive as yours. Of course for myself I live, live intensely and am fed by life, and my value, whatever it be, is in my own kind of expression of that. Therefore I am pulled up to wonder by the fact that for you my kind (my sort of sense of expression and sort of sense of life alike) doesn't exist; and that wonder is, I admit, a disconcerting comment on my idea of the various appreciability of our addiction to the novel and of all the personal and intellectual history, sympathy and curiosity, behind the given example of it. It is when that history and curiosity have been determined in the way most different from my own that I myself want to get at them—precisely *for* the extension of life, which is the novel's best gift. But that is another matter. Meanwhile I absolutely dissent from the claim that there are any differences whatever in the amenability to art of forms of literature aesthetically determined, and hold your distinction between a form that is (like) painting and a form that is (like) architecture for wholly null and void. There is no sense in which architecture is aesthetically "for use" that doesn't leave any other art whatever exactly as much so; and so far from that of literature being irrelevant to the literary report upon life, and to its being made as interesting as possible, I regard it as relevant in a degree that leaves everything else behind. It is art that *makes* life, makes interest, makes importance, for our consideration and application of these things, and I know of no substitute whatever for the force and beauty of its process.[1] If I were Boon I should say that any pretence of such a substitute is helpless and hopeless humbug; but I wouldn't be Boon for the world, and am only yours faithfully

Henry James

1. Lubbock, in *The Letters of Henry James* II, 488, quotes the following sentences from a letter of Wells to James dated July 13, 1915, the full text of which has not survived: "I don't clearly understand your concluding phrases—which shews no doubt how completely they define our difference. When you say 'it is art that *makes* life, makes interest, makes importance,' I can only read sense into it by assuming that you are using 'art' for every conscious human activity. I use the word for a research and attainment that is technical and special."

To Henry James III
Dictated Ts Harvard

21, Carlyle Mansions, S.W.
July 20*th* 1915

Dearest Harry.

How can I sufficiently tell you how moved to gratitude and appreciation I am by your good letter of July 9th, just received, and the ready understanding and sympathy expressed in which are such a blessing to me! I did proceed, after writing to you, in the sense I then explained—the impulse and the current were simply irresistible; and the business has so happily developed that I this morning received, with your letter, the kindest possible one from the Home Secretary, Sir John Simon, I mean in the personal and private way, telling me that he has just decreed the issue of my certificate of Naturalisation, which will at once take effect. It will have thus been beautifully expedited, have "gone through" in five or six days from the time my papers were sent in, instead of in the usual month or two. He gives me his blessing on the matter, and all is well. It will probably interest you to know that the indispensability of my step to myself has done nothing but grow since I made my application; like Martin Luther at Wittenburg "I could no other," and the relief of feeling corrected an essential falsity in my position (as determined by the War and what has happened since, also more particularly what has *not* happened) is greater than I can say. I have testified to my long attachment here in the only way I could—though I certainly shouldn't have done it, under the inspiration of our Cause, if the U.S.A. had done it a little more *for* me. Then I should have thrown myself back on that and been content with it; but as this, at the end of a year, hasn't taken place, I have had to act for myself, and I go so far as quite to think, I hope not fatuously, that I shall have set an example and shown a little something of the way. But enough—there it is!

You are very right about that other matter on which I shall consult Nelson Ward. I have a copy of the Document here, and shall speedily submit it to him. Then you shall hear from me again. You see I am still in town, which is frankly the only possible place for me just now. I have again lent Lamb House to some very good friends, E. G. Lowry and his wife—he the Diplomatic Agent of the American Government here in charge of the so-called "German Division" of the Embassy, in which he has since last September done an enormous helpful work between this country and Germany and the U.S., and is now quite fagged-out and in need of a holiday. I am helping him to one, in conditions that he and his wife greatly appreciate, and am all the more glad to do it that I have been seeing a good deal of him and extremely like and trust him. We in fact, I think, see quite eye to eye—though you mustn't give him away by bruiting this abroad. Neither must you bruit abroad too freely that the state of feeling of *all* our Embassy assemblage here leaves, by my measure, nothing to be desired; even if neither they nor I scream it from the housetops. I can't face at present at all—I mean in our actual conditions—the solitude and the mere one level walk of Rye, which it's a question of taking day after day over again: the whole thing is too difficult and depressing. (I can't do the hills.) We're having a beautifully cool summer up to now, and the London facilities make much more for my well-being. This is all, however, now. I sent you immediately the two Belgian Reports, I mean the Report itself and the much thicker illustrational appendix. I hope they will have safely reached you—I rejoiced in what you wrote me of your estimate of Bryce's Commission.

Ever your affectionate old british Uncle
Henry James

To Edmund Gosse
Ms Congress

21 Carlyle Mansions, S.W.
July 26*th* 1915

My dear Gosse.

Your good letter makes me feel that you will be interested to know that since 4.30 this afternoon I have been able to say *Civis Britannicus sum!* My Certificate of Naturalisation was received by my Solicitor this A.M., and a few hours ago I took the Oath of Allegiance, in his office, before a Commissioner. The odd thing is that nothing seems to have happened and that I don't feel a bit different; so that I see not at all how associated I have become, but that I was really too associated before for any nominal change to matter. The process has only shown me what I virtually *was*—so that it's rather disappointing in respect to acute sensation. I *haven't* any, I blush to confess!

I shall be in town like yourselves till the very end of next month—I have lent Lamb House for five weeks to some friends of the American Embassy, the E. G. Lowrys—I can't stand in these public conditions the solitude and sequestration of the country. (E. G. L., ardent for our cause, is "Attaché to the A. E. for the German Division"—and has been quartered all winter at the German Embassy.)

I thank you enormously for your confidential passage, which is most interesting and heartening; as is also this evening's news that the Boches have sunk—torpedoed—another ship; I mean another American one. That affects me as really charming! And let me mention in exchange for your confidence that a friend told me this afternoon that he had been within a few days talking with Captain McBride, one of the American naval attachés, whose competence he ranks high and to whom he had put some question relative to the naval sense of the condition of these islands. To which the reply

772

had been: "You may take it from me that England is absolutely impregnable and invincible"—and McBride repeated over— "impregnable and invincible!" Which kind of did me good.—Let me come up and sit on your terrace some near August afternoon—I can always be rung up, you know: I *like* it—and believe me yours and your wife's all faithfully,

Henry James

To Thomas Hardy
Ms Dorset

21 Carlyle Mansions, S.W.
July 28th 1915

My dear Hardy.

Your note gives me, for all its noble detachment, courage to assault you again in a sufficient measure just to say that if you *can* manage between now and the 10th to distil the liquor of your poetic genius, in no matter how mild a form, into three or four blest versicles, on Mrs. Wharton's behalf,[1] by August 10th (at which date she tells me she should receive them) you would enable me to think of you with a still more confirmed and enriched admiration, fidelity and gratitude. It is just the stray sincerities and casual felicities of your muse that that intelligent lady *is* all ready to cherish— so just gently and helpfully overflow, no matter into how tiny a cup, and believe me yours very constantly

Henry James

P.S. Let me say, to hearten you comparatively, that disgracefully void as I am of the rhyming impulse, I shall be reduced to respond to her with ponderous prose—of a sort only appreciable in the clumsy big chunk. I must hew out my block—so see how brevity breathes balmily on *you!*

---

1. Edith Wharton was editing a miscellany, *The Book of the Homeless* (1916), for the benefit of the American Hostels for Refugees and of the Children of Flanders Rescue Committee. Hardy contributed a poem, "Cry of the Homeless."

To John Singer Sargent
Ms Unknown

21 Carlyle Mansions, S.W.
July 30th 1915

My dear John.

I am delighted to hear from you that you are writing and sending to Mrs. Wharton in the good sense you mention. It will give her the greatest pleasure and count enormously for her undertaking.

Yes, I daresay many Americans *will* be shocked at my "step"; so many of them appear in these days to be shocked at everything that is not a reiterated blandishment and slobberation of Germany, with recalls of ancient "amity" and that sort of thing, by our Government. I waited long months, watch in hand, for the latter to show some sign of intermitting these amiabilities to such an enemy—the very smallest would have sufficed for me to throw myself back upon it. But it seemed never to come, and the misrepresentation of *my* attitude becoming at last to me a thing no longer to be borne, I took action myself. It would really have been *so* easy for the U.S. to have "kept" (if they had cared to!) yours all faithfully,

Henry James

To Elizabeth Gaskell Norton
Ms Harvard

21 Carlyle Mansions, S.W.
August 6th 1915

Dearest Lily.

It must have seemed to you very horrible indeed that I should leave your so interesting and touching letter of the 27th last so long unacknowledged. I have been, however, absolutely buried of late, and still utterly am, beneath an overwhelming avalanche of letters, produced by a certain recent occasion, and so have been unable to move freely in any direction whatever. Even now I can't begin to tell you half of what I feel and think about your uncle Arthur's so fine conclusive act,[1] as to which I had been practically very much informed when your letter came. But be reassured—what I think and feel is by no means all, or even very much, in the mere distressful key—so absolutely do I understand his decision and his performance and so tenderly and unreservedly do I applaud it. In fact I regard it as an act of high reason, of the finest deliberation in face of all the facts, and of the greatest wisdom and beauty. Above all it was an act of *character* and of the ripest and most "gentlemanly"; I am wholly *with* him in it, and no vulgar shock nor unintelligent regret diminishes to me for a moment the big, decent decorum of it. It has endeared him to me even more than any other impression of his long and liberal and generous life—the only sharp pang being that I couldn't have had more friendly nearness to him, and a closer participation in his ravaged life, during these latter times. I think of him with an unspeakable sympathy which has yet in it no doleful reserve or head shaking protest. In short it was all *worthy* of him, and I wish I might have been one of those who bore him in all confidence to his true rest.—As for the fine French recognition of Dick's[2] admirable coolness and gallantry, and the distinction bestowed on him for it, I delight in them intensely, and feel it a pride and a glorious privilege in any way to help him. *Do* come, after your Darwin visits to be a little near your even older and fonder friend

Henry James

1. The suicide of HJ's old friend Arthur George Sedgwick (1844–1915), brother-in-law of Charles Eliot Norton.
2. Richard Norton's ambulance work in France.

To Marie Belloc Lowndes
Ms Private

21 Carlyle Mansions, S.W.
August 17*th* 1915

My dear Marie.

It is only the deluge of benedictions that has kept me breasting it all these days to such a tune that I find the time to have gone more in panting and puffing for simple grateful life—than in really "answering" more good and beautiful words than I think ever fluttered on a poor old modest and denuded head, at such a rate and in such a compass of days, before. I still but gape, fondly and delightfully at my welcomers and well-wishers, and though I pretty well thought

I *should* like doing what I have done, I find it agrees with me still better than I have imagined. *Je vous serre bien doucement la main*—with an intended *douceur*. I mean and shall venture to invoke your presence here for a little as soon as I can have any confidence in your being back in town again. I stick fast you see—I think I *taste* my citizenship rather more on this spot—discounted as it truly was when I took it up by something forty long years so remarkably like it that I wonder anyone can tell them apart—I myself being all but unable to. I had yesterday a postcard from Hugh Walpole "in Galicia" closely about and *in* the trenches, and under fire as an intimate Red Cross ministrant, and pronouncing the last three months, in spite of his twice having but just escaped capture by the enemy—"Which I dread much more than anything else" —the very happiest of his life. He hopes to get back here in September—when I count upon his being far more interesting and informing than if he had spent this interval otherwise. I hope you keep hold (and add to your stock) of something good, and am yours affectionately ever

Henry James

To Edmund Gosse
Ms Congress

21 Carlyle Mansions, S.W.
August 25*th* 1915

My dear Gosse.

I have had a bad sick week, mostly in bed—with putting pen to paper quite out of my power: otherwise I should sooner have thanked you for the so generous spirit of that letter, and told you, with emotion, how much it has touched me. I am really more overcome than I can say by your having been able to indulge in such freedom of mind and grace of speculation, during these dark days, on behalf of my poor old rather truncated edition, in fact entirely frustrated one—which has the grotesque likeness for me of a sort of miniature Ozymandias of Egypt ("look on my *works*, ye mighty, and despair!")—round which the lone and level sands stretch further away than ever. It *is* indeed consenting to be waved aside a little into what was once blest literature to so much as answer the question you are so handsomely impelled to make—but my very statement about the matter can only be, alas, a melancholy, a blighted confusion. That Edition has been, from the point of view of profit either to the publishers or to myself, practically a complete failure; vulgarly speaking, it doesn't sell—that is, my annual report of what it does—the whole twenty-four volumes—in this country amounts to about £25 from the Macmillans; and the ditto from the Scribners in the U.S. to very little more. I am past all praying for anywhere; I remain at my age (which you know), and after my long career, utterly, insurmountably, unsaleable. And the original preparation of that collective and selective series involved really the extremity of labour—all my "earlier" things—of which the *Bostonians* would have been, if included, one—were so intimately and interestingly revised.[1] The edition is from that point of view really a monument (like Ozymandias) which has never had the least intelligent critical justice done it—or any sort of critical attention at all paid it—and the artistic problem involved in my scheme was a deep and exquisite one, and moreover was, as I held, very effectively solved. Only it took such time—*and* such taste—in other words such aesthetic light. No more commercially thankless job of the literary order was (Prefaces and all—*they* of a thanklessness!) accordingly ever achieved. The immediate inclusion of the *Bostonians* was rather deprecated by my publishers (the Scribners, who were very generally and in a high degree appreciative: I make no complaint of them at all!)—and there were reasons for which I also wanted to wait: we always meant that that work should eventually come in. Revision of it loomed peculiarly formidable and time-consuming (for intrinsic reasons), and as other things were more pressing and more promptly feasible I allowed it to stand over—with the best intentions, and also in company with a small number more of provisional omissions. But by this time it *had* stood over, disappointment had set in; the undertaking had begun to announce itself as a virtual failure, and we stopped short where we were—that is when a couple of dozen volumes were out.[2] From that moment, some seven or eight years ago, nothing whatever has been added to the series—and there is little enough appearance now that there will ever. Your good impression of the *Bostonians* greatly moves me—the thing was no success whatever on publication in the Century (where it came out), and the late R. W. Gilder, of that periodical, wrote me at the time that they had never published anything that appeared so little to interest their readers. I felt about it myself then that it was probably rather a remarkable feat of objectivity—but I never was very thoroughly happy about it, and seem to recall that I found the subject and the material, after I had got launched in it, under some illusion, less interesting and repaying than I had assumed it to be. All the same I *should* have liked to review it for the Edition—it would have come out a much truer and more curious thing (it was meant to be curious from the first); but there can be no question of that, or of the proportionate Preface to have been written with it, at present—or probably ever within my span of life. Apropos of which matters I at this moment hear from Heinemann that four or five of my books that he has have quite (entirely) ceased to sell and that he must break up the plates. Of course he must; I have nothing to say against it; and the things in question are mostly all in the Edition. But such is "success"! I should have liked to write that Preface to the *Bostonians*—which will never be written now. But think of noting now that *that* is a thing that has perished!

I am doing my best to feel better, and hope to go out this afternoon the first one for several! I am exceedingly with you all over Philip's transfer to France. We are with each other now as not yet before over everything and I am yours and your wife's more than ever,

H.J.

1. HJ actually did not include in the New York Edition any of his "American" novels and tales (with the exception of "The Jolly Corner," which had its first book appearance in the edition). The American works were edited after HJ's death by F. O. Matthiessen as *The American Novels and Stories of Henry James* (1947). It has been conjectured that HJ preferred to have the core of his edition include his "international" novels and tales and counted on issuing supplementary volumes. The edition's failure to sell froze it in its original 24 volumes, although Scribner's incongruously issued HJ's two unfinished novels as supplementary volumes. Percy Lubbock later edited a 35-volume edition that included all of HJ's fiction.

2. HJ had originally stipulated a total of 23 volumes, it will be recalled, without any thought of further volumes.

To Clare Frewen Sheridan
Ts Lubbock

21 Carlyle Mansions, S.W.
October 4*th* 1915

Dearest, dearest Clare.

I have heard twice from your kindest of Fathers, and yet this goes to you (for poor baffling personal reasons) with a dreadful belatedness. The thought of coming into your presence, and into Mrs. Sheridan's, with such wretched empty and helpless hands is in itself paralysing; and yet, even as I say that, the sense of how my whole soul is full, even to its being racked and torn, of Wilfred's belovedest image[1] and the splendour of honour and devotion in which he is all radiantly wrapped and enshrined [urges me], and I ask myself if I don't really bring you something, of a sort, in thus giving you the assurance of how absolutely I adored him! Yet who can give you anything that approaches your incomparable sense that he was yours, and you his, to the last possessed and possessing radiance of him? I can't pretend to utter to you words of "consolation"—vainest of dreams; for what is your suffering but the measure of his value, his charm and his beauty? everything we so loved him for. But I see you marked with his glory too, and so intimately associated with his noble legend, with the light of it about you, and about his children, always, and the precious privilege of making him live again whenever one approaches you; convinced as I am that you will rise, in spite of the unspeakable laceration, to the greatness of all this and feel it carry you in a state of sublime privilege. I had sight and some sound of him during an hour of that last leave, just before he went off again; and what he made me then feel, and what his face seemed to say, amid that cluster of relatives in which I was the sole outsider (of which too I was extraordinarily proud), is beyond all expression. I don't know why I presume to say such things—I mean poor things only of *mine*, to you, all stricken and shaken as you are—and then again I know how any touch of his noble humanity must be unspeakably dear to you, and that you'll go on getting the fragrance of them wherever he passed. I think with unutterable tenderness of those days of late last autumn when you were in the little house off the Edgeware Road, and the humour and gaiety and vivid sympathy of his talk (about his then beginnings and conditions) made me hang spellbound on his lips. But what memories are these not to you, and how can one speak to you at all without stirring up the deeps? Well, we are all in them *with* you, and with his mother—and may I speak of his father?—and with his children, and we cling to you and cherish you as never before. I live with you in thought every step of the long way, and as yours, dearest Clare, all devotedly and sharingly,

Henry James

1. Clare Sheridan's husband, Wilfred (see 30 May 1915), was killed in action on 9 September 1915 while leading a grenade attack into the German lines. His body was never recovered. Clare had given birth to a son three days earlier.

To Edward Marsh
Ms Berg

21 Carlyle Mansions, S.W.
October 4*th* 1915

Dearest Eddie.

I missed you yesterday, to my sorrow, through my being, thank heaven, much better—well enough to go out in the afternoon, to my great gain of further improvement. I am having a complicated moment by reason of certain multiplied human assaults (I can do so little to meet them); but I am doing the Preface[1] with some steadiness, though you must still have a little more patience with me. I foresee it may run even to something like 10,000 words—and have already done 6,000; after which of course I shall as always have to do it all over; as it is ever the second doing, for me, that is *the* doing. I feel as if I had a very ponderous and aggravating (by which I mean over-appreciating) hand; but that is part of the native curse of yours all devotedly

Henry James

P.S. I shall give you further news as the "number of words," confound it, multiplies; but probably shan't be able to see you till the deed is done. If I am *able* to keep down to 8000 I will; but that the preface should be substantial, in its weird way, is, I hold, all to the advantage of the book.

1. Marsh was Rupert Brooke's executor, and HJ had agreed to write an introduction to Brooke's letters from America. It proved to be his last piece of writing.

To Hugh Walpole
Ms Texas

Lamb House, Rye
November 13*th* 1915

Belovedest Hugh!

I take to my heart these blest Cornish words[1] from you and thank you for them as articulately as my poor old impaired state permits. It will be an immense thing to see you when your own conditions permit of it, and in that fond vision I hang on. I have been having a regular hell of a summer and autumn (that is more particularly from the end of July): through the effect of a bad—an aggravated— heart-crisis, during the first weeks of which I lost valuable time by attributing (under wrong advice) my condition to mistaken causes; but I am in the best hands now and apparently responding very well to very helpful treatment. But the past year has made me feel twenty years older, and, frankly, as if my knell had rung. Still, I cultivate, I at least attempt, a brazen front. I shall not let that mask drop till I have heard *your* thrilling story. Do intensely believe that I respond clutchingly to your every grasp of me, every touch, and would so gratefully be a re-connecting link with you here—where I don't wonder that you're bewildered. (It will be indeed, as far as I am concerned, the bewildered leading the bewildered.) I have "seen" very few people—I see as few as possible. I can't stand them, and all their promiscuous prattle, mostly; so that those who have reported of me to you must have been peculiarly vociferous. I de- plore with all my heart your plagues of boils and of insomnia; I haven't known the former, but the latter, alas, is my own actual portion. I think I shall know your rattle of the telephone as soon as ever I shall hear it. Heaven speed it, dearest Hugh, and keep me all fondestly

Yours
Henry James

1. Walpole, decorated for valor in rescuing Russian wounded, was back in England.

To Margaret Mary James
Dictated Ts Harvard

21, Carlyle Mansions, S.W.
December 1*st* 1915[1]

Dearest Pegg.

I don't lose an hour, or scarcely, in thanking you more intensely than I can say for your two letters that have just come in together, one of November 15th, and the second, smaller one, of the 19th, telling me of the note to me that you have given the young doctor; whom I shall be very glad to see if he brings me news of you, and has time, and above all, takes me as I am. I am not in these days very rewarding to visitors—so little so in fact that I am obliged to manage to have almost none at all, and haven't for a long time been able to exercise the least hospitality. The point is, however, that hearing from you does me a world of good—weeks and weeks of all this latter difficult time, ever since I have been in [Dr.] Des Vœux's hands, having somehow, and doubtless largely by my own fault, represented a sad lapse of communication with your Mother and Harry. I say by my own fault, because I doubtless might have written more—at the same time that my poor old state has made writing very difficult, and yet has, withal filled me with a kind of morbid desire to be, consolingly, in touch with you. Some ten days ago, or perhaps it was only a week, I could stand the great void of the post no longer, and cabled suppliantly to Harry to cable me back a few words that I could kind of try to go on with. This he at once blessedly did, and more will now doubtless come, though it hasn't done so yet, save indeed to this happy extent of *your* news, which is so interesting and illuminating. I learn by it for the first time what you are doing in Cincinnati, and very remarkable and valiant does it seem—if the inspiration and the reward to sustain you through those aspects of it which must sometimes, in their multiplication of bad cases, bad specimens, hopeless subjects etc., rather minister to doubt. Likewise I groan over your doom of having been fitted out with a kind of practical equivalent to M.P.[2]—similarly depressing, I fear, even though spotted with different spots. How they do grow on you, as it were; I don't mean the spots, but the spotted and the inconvertibles themselves; with the big reservoir of them, that seems to surround you, to draw upon. I can quite imagine what you mean by the panting freshness and readiness of such an American community as that, with its desire for the public good and the energy of its contribution to the same, of which you have become so brave an agent. It's all a good bit bewildering seen from here—where, however, God knows, our own bewilderments are not wanting. I shan't attempt to speak of these now—and the sign of the wondrous in yours, as it most strikes me, is such a fact as that F. Duveneck[3] is at this time of day still being "lionised"; anything there may have been to lionise him *for* goes back into such an antediluvian past. His only good work was done in his very few first years, nearly fifty of these ago—at least the long interval since has always looked like a deadly desert. I daresay, however, in fact I must often have heard, that he has flourished at Cincinnati during a large part of that time as an excellent teacher so it's doubtless all right— and it isn't of him I dreamed of writing you.

There is no good in my trying to go on without allowing to you that I am having difficult days, and weeks, and even months,—for only on that basis can I really send you any coherent news. I am having a troubled, new heart-condition, but it is being very well taken care of by Des Vœux, and I get, and evidently shall get, a good deal of relief. One feels very abject, at our pitch of life and public pain, in the midst of the huge tremendous things that press upon us, to have disqualifying personal and physical troubles; or I should, at least, if I weren't so ancient and for a long time past so *éprouvé*. My greatest *épreuve* just now, alas, by which I mean very much for all these past months, though under great present aggravation, is the fact of my almost impossibility of sleep; which has me for the moment in its clutches. Take in consideration for this letter— written in the only way I *can* write now, or shall ever, I fear, write again—that I this A.M. left my bed at 8:30, unable to stick it out longer, after not having closed my eyes the whole blessed night, from the moment I first propped myself up there on my pillows, and that this has followed upon a series of nights different only by a little. I don't tell you this for dreariness, but more, rather, to show you how I bear it than how I don't. (Des Vœux promises me im- provement as to that, but it doesn't come yet.) And the great thing I want above all to say to you is that to have heard you would like so much to come out to me moves me deeply and gratefully, and that one of these months I shall intensely and rejoicingly welcome you and clutch you and keep you. Only we must wait for that, wait for some less heavy and horrible time. The idea of your dreaming of anything of the sort in these actual conditions simply sickens and flattens me out; therefore stick to your present noble work and feel *that* your actual right mission. I shall keep afloat here successfully, I feel, with the good help I get; counting Des Vœux, that is, and also counting my admirable household, in which I venture to include Miss Bosanquet, as wonderfully helpful. I have definitely now got Burgess back—not discharged, but on indefinite and renewable leave, and with his army pay of course stopped; and I should be utterly unable to get on without him, as his service is a matter of any and every hour, and his devotion boundless and most touching.

I fear I see none of your old friends with the exception, once in a while, of Fanny P[rothero]; all social life has gone to smash; nothing exists but *the* huge enormity. George Prothero is a haggard hero of labour and courage, and she as wonderful as ever in her indefatigability. But it's all applied now to the general situation— save that she'll be intensely interested to hear about you. I rejoice unspeakably that your Mother has gone on to be with Harry, and I live in the deferred hope of a New York, in default of a Cambridge, letter from her. Let me say that what you wrote from California must really all have come—only it was difficult, all the summer long, to make the proper recognitions. Your photographs of the San Francisco house perfectly reached me, and were as interesting as possible, so that I am horrified that I didn't, and couldn't, tell you so. But this is all now—save that I am extremely glad that Aleck, bless him, wasn't able to carry out that Red Cross idea. The difficulties for Neutrals in France now are overwhelming—but the pen drops from my hand!

Your all-affectionate old Uncle
Henry James

1. This letter to WJ's daughter was HJ's last. He had a stroke the following morning and died three months later, on 28 February 1916.

2. Margaret Payson, Peggy James's friend. See letter to Mrs. WJ, 29 March 1914.

3. The painter Frank Duveneck (1848–1919), some time after the death of his wife, Elizabeth Boott, in 1888, had returned to his home city and for many years had been teaching painting at the Cincinnati Academy of Arts. See *Letters* III, 111–113, 230–231.

Appendixes

Index

Appendix I
William James on Henry James

William James to Robert Underwood Johnson
Ms Academy-Institute

Cambridge, June 17, 1905

Dear Mr. Johnson.[1]

Just back from three months in Europe, I find your letter of May 16th awaiting me, with the very flattering news of my election into the Academy of Arts and Letters. I own that this reply gives me terrible searchings of the heart.

On the one hand the lust of distinction and the craving to be yoked in one social body with so many illustrious names tempt me to say "yes." On the other, bidding me say "no," there is my life-long practice of not letting my name figure where there is not some definite work doing in which I am willing to bear a share;[2] and there is my life-long professorial habit of preaching against the world and its vanities.

I am not informed that this Academy has any very definite work cut out for it of the sort in which I could bear a useful part; and it suggests *tant soit peu* the notion of an organization for the mere purpose of distinguishing certain individuals (with their own connivance) and enabling them to say to the world at large "we are in and you are out." Ought a preacher against vanities to succumb to such a lure at the very first call? Ought he not rather to "refrain, renounce, abstain," even tho' it seem a sour and ungenial act? On the whole it seems to me that for a philosopher with my pretensions to austerity and righteousness, the only consistent course is to give up this particular vanity, and treat myself as unworthy of the honour, which I assuredly am. And I am the more encouraged to this course by the fact that my younger and shallower and vainer brother is already in the Academy, and that if I were there too, the other families represented might think the James influence too rank and strong.[3]

787

Let me go, then, I pray you, "release me and restore me to the ground." If you knew how greatly against the grain these duty-inspired lines are written, you would not deem me unfriendly or ungenial, but only a little cracked.

By the same token, I think that I ought to resign from the Institute (in which I have played so inactive a part) which act I herewith also perform.

Believe me, dear Mr. Johnson, with longing and regret, heroically yours,

Wm. James

1. Robert Underwood Johnson was the first secretary of the Academy, which had just been organized as a fifty-member body drawn out of the parent organization, the National Institute of Arts and Letters. Seven academicians were elected, and these in turn proceeded to elect, in stages, the other members. Henry James had been elected on the second ballot in February 1905; William was elected on the fourth ballot in May.

2. WJ had accepted an honorary membership in the Institut de France in 1898; he had accepted honorary degrees from Padua, Princeton, Edinburgh, and Harvard, and he would later accept degrees from Durham, Oxford, and Geneva.

3. WJ had not advanced this argument in 1898 when both he and HJ were elected to the National Institute of Arts and Letters.

Appendix II
Edith Wharton's Subsidy of *The Ivory Tower*

Edith Wharton tried three times to obtain wider recognition and large sums of money for Henry James. The first was in 1911, when she proposed James for the Nobel Prize. She enlisted Edmund Gosse and W. D. Howells, among others, in her campaign, but the prize that year went to Maurice Maeterlinck. Next, in 1912, she made a secret arrangement with Charles Scribner to pay James $8000, which she furnished, under the guise of an advance against future royalties for the novel he was writing, "The Ivory Tower." Third was her public attempt in 1913 to collect money from James's friends in the United States as a gift for his seventieth birthday. James indignantly stopped this initiative (see cable and letter to William James III, 28 and 29 March 1913).

The secret gift of 1912 is revealed in the Scribner and Wharton archives, and in a memorandum in which Charles Scribner speaks of a contract entered upon "at the suggestion of Mrs. Wharton, and upon her promise to supply money for the said payments." The letter from Scribner to James printed here shows how the novelist was deceived into taking the advance—a sum much larger than he had ever received for a promised novel. Scribner commented candidly in a letter to Mrs. Wharton: "our fell purpose was successfully accomplished. I feel rather mean and caddish and must continue so to the end of my days. Please never give me away."

Charles Scribner to Henry James
Ms Scribner

September 27, 1912

Dear Mr. James:

It was very gratifying to be able while in London to complete arrangements with Mr. Pinker for the publication of the volume of your brother's letters[1] and for the magazine articles, and to hear that we may expect the articles before the end of the year. But I do not write now about that book. What interested me even more was the information that you have in contemplation an important American novel. As the publishers of your definitive edition we want another great novel to balance the *Golden Bowl* and round off the series of books in which you have developed the theory of composition set forth in your preface.[2] In our opinion such a book would be of very great advantage to our common interests and it is most desirable that it should be produced as soon as possible. We know that such a work demands much time and all your time for a considerable period, and we have thought that under all the conditions it might be acceptable to you to receive a somewhat unusual proposal. If you can agree to begin the book soon—say within the next twelve months—and to give up your other work for it, we will pay you $8,000. for all rights in the manuscript everywhere. The payments could be made as most convenient for you; we would suggest half the amount when the book was begun and the other half on the completion of the manuscript. You will see at once that our proposal is quite different from the usual royalty and advance, and for America only, but I have tried to formulate the plan which would make possible the largest outright payment. If desired, we would agree to offer the book first to Macmillan for England and in any case that firm would have it in the collected edition.

I shall be glad to hear from you at your convenience and would consider willingly any change in the form of our offer.

It has not seemed to me necessary to make this proposal through Mr. Pinker, but as I like him and do not wish him to suspect me of any indiscretion, I am sending a copy of this to him. You will know to what extent it is desirable or necessary to act through him.

Yours sincerely
Charles Scribner

1. This became *Notes of a Son and Brother.*
2. The formulation is curious since it is not clear what series was being "rounded off." Scribner is probably thinking of the New York Edition as a whole.

James B. Pinker to Charles Scribner
Ms Princeton

15 November 1912

Dear Mr. Scribner.

. . .

I have discussed with Mr. Henry James the question of the novel, and he will be very pleased to make a contract now on the lines, more or less, suggested in your various letters. Mr. James suggests that Eight Thousand Dollars should be treated as you propose in your letter of October 28th, as an advance on account of royalty on the American and Canadian book rights, the royalty to be 20 per cent as you have paid before, and the royalty on the collected edition to be 10 percent. It might be a convenience to Mr. James to have, as you kindly suggested, half the amount when the book is begun, and the other half on completion of the Ms. Mr. James would begin the novel next year, by which time he will have finished the two family volumes that we have now arranged, and would put aside all other work until the novel were finished. Mr. James would not wish to bind himself too closely as regards length; he thinks the novel will probably be 150,000 words long, and he would undertake that it should in any case be not less than 100,000 words.

. . .

[James B. Pinker]

Charles Scribner to James B. Pinker
Ms Princeton

December 5, 1912

Dear Mr. Pinker.

. . . When I wrote to him in the first place I thought that as this was a somewhat unusual proposal, originating with us, he would not be under obligation to pay a full ten percent commission or $800 to you as agent. Please do not think that I wished to get around you or to cut you out of a commission, but I naturally wished Mr. James to get as much as possible of the money we are to pay, as there has been no work on your part . . .

Yours sincerely,
Charles Scribner

Appendix III
The Autobiographies

In three lengthy letters to his nephew, excerpted here, Henry James discusses the writing of what he first called his "Family Book." After the death of his brother, he had promised Mrs. William James that he would write a book making use of certain of William's characteristic early letters. But when he set to work, he wrote instead *A Small Boy and Others* (1913), reminiscences of his childhood and the James family background. When he informed Harry James that he had all but completed this book, his nephew seems to have assumed that he had dropped all thought of the volume of letters.

In the first letter, of 23–24 September 1912, which is twenty-eight handwritten pages, Henry James assures his nephew that he has not abandoned the original project and tells him that he is planning a second volume to contain portions of William James's correspondence. Apparently the nephew still had some misgivings, for in a second letter, of 25 November 1912, written while James was suffering from shingles, he further, and again at great length, defends his autobiographical procedure. "I wish I could persuade you to a little greater confidence . . . and I don't see what damage this can do to the future of your Dad's correspondence as a whole." Harry James's concern may have been in part related to his own plan to edit selected letters of William James. These he published in 1920 in two volumes.

The third letter, of 15–18 November 1913, after completion of *Notes of a Son and Brother* (1914), responds to criticism of certain revisions James made in his brother's letters used in that volume. He not only treated these letters as if he were revising one of his own novels, but extensively revised others (a batch from Brazil written in 1865) even though he did not use them. The nephew wrote in protest; and James's reply contains a detailed attempt to justify his artistic liberties.

To Henry James III

Ms Harvard

Lamb House, Rye
September 23–24, 1912

Dearest Harry.

... I said last night that my difficulties had in the last month very much cleared up—and *this*, without more delay, is what I meant by that: I am in possession of a *finished* Family Book No. I—or First Series or Instalment of the Same[1] (not that I dream of so *calling* it, naturally); finished, that is, as soon as Miss Bosanquet has done finally and beautifully re-copying it; which she is fast getting on with. This is, in its essence and inevitably, autobiographic—the autobiography of a very small boy, but reflecting everything imaginable and unimaginable in my whole environment, family scene and consciousness; which means of course constant reference to, and speaking for, your Dad: though I can only *most* of all, of course (as the sentient and observant organism) speak for myself. This whole record of early childhood simply *grew* so as one came to write it that one could but let it take its way—and it was a miracle to me (and is still as I go on further) how the memories revived and pressed upon me, and how they *keep* a-doing of it in the "letters" book. But this earlier thing makes a Book in itself, and I think a very charming and original and unprecedented one of its kind, and which has the merit of giving a whole introductory or initiatory Family picture as an approach to the later stage. This Book it now seems to me highly important to publish first and at once—in its chronological order, before the "letters" portion of my Record (making another and larger book in itself: indeed it will be only a mercy if I don't find myself floated onto three!) It is in fact highly *urgent* for me that the volume in question should appear as soon as possible. *It* can only go to the Scribners I feel: and *must* go to them at the earliest moment, and I earnestly hope that, as it doesn't contain a single scrap of a document or letter (save one little one from your Grandfather to the Tweedies in Italy in the early 'fifties), you will only be disposed to speed my so putting it forth. You see this making two separate (though so united) Books of it will be the only way to get the Family Bible (as I am moved to call it) realized in its *quantity*; and also that the more juvenile record couldn't, can't, with propriety, felicity or logic, come out *after* the less juvenile. The mere getting it out and clearing my foreground will make enormously for the confidence and comfort of my present work, and the reading of it by you all so soon as possible, and not least by your Mother, will, I feel, keep you in patience and renewed trust (a trust that will immensely sustain and steady me—for I feel not a little "rattled" by this sense of my having let myself in, through my reckless not dotting of more i's, for the pouring forth of so much explanatory and apologetic statement—and I haven't any margin for nervousness). I thus want you to have the First Book in your hands, as a gage and sample, as soon as possible; and after that to let me rip! My idea, my deep desire is to give the two Books titles of an *associated* sort or sense, with something in common or mutually referential—referential, that is, above all, backwardly, or from second to first (the second being meanwhile "announced," as a companion-piece on fly-leaf facing title-page of first). Any, every publisher will make a great point of a good (by which they mean of course a selling) title, and the question is difficult, and I have beaten about between the fear of the colourless and stale (of "note") on the one hand and the catchpenny-hateful on the other. The thing that suits Both and yet is separate makes the problem. I have provisionally settled on (for the forthcoming): *A Small Boy and Others* (the small boy being of course *me*). This would leave me for the second—*A Big Boy and Others.* The boy being again me, and the pre-eminent of the *Others* your Dad; but it pleases me in the first case more than in the Second. I am a mere Big Boy only in the earlier part of *that* record—I become a person of twenty-five before it is over. I have a certain license of expression, of vision, as to early age and size, I hold, in retrospect from so late in life, and I shan't let any *literality* much obstruct me if I decide as I best can. I am perfectly ready to describe myself as a Big Boy at any time up to thirty—much more up to twenty-five. If on the other hand I give up the *repetitional* title I have a very good *distinct* one then:—*Notes of a Son and Brother,* which I like; "notes," as a term, covering any and *all* the ground one can want. I *had* thought of (for the first): *Earliest Memories: Egotistic.* (And for the second): *Earliest Memories: Altruistic.* But I have decided against these—the second again there being less good than the first. I feel as I write this that you may consider I *most* probably adopt "A Small Boy and Others" for my first volume (it so perfectly *fits*); and "Notes" etc.—but with only one "a" (otherwise, on the whole it sounds as if there were two persons)—for the second. Even with that disparity in the Titles (though such identity in the subjects) I shall like extremely to announce the "Notes" on the facing-title of the "Small Boy": it seems to me so desirable the former should be the expected and implied signal (*from the start*) of the latter. This will of necessity involve their *both* being published by Scribners—it would be an enormous embarrassment if the second were not to be, and I hope you will feel that in view of the kind of book the second will be (so wholly in form and so largely in substance my own distillation and composition) your restrictive reasons as to the Scribners need no longer be the same as for a book with that first *malencontreux* title of mine. *My personal business relations with them are the best,* and they will *certainly* give me better terms for the two than I could possibly get from any one else. I have absolutely now to consider this—and feel sure that the degree and manner of my manipulation of the whole material in which your Dad's letters are employed and embedded will conjure away sufficiently any danger of a suggested connection or continuity with, or implied reference to, the fact of your reserved array of his correspondence proper. I understand perfectly your anxiety on the head of any implications of premature impingement on that big question. I enter intensely into your letter's so interesting pages on all that matter, but won't attempt to reply to them, even for fulness of agreement at the fatigued end of the present long exposition. Let me merely say that primarily—by which I mean summarily—speaking—the principle of selection of letters from the correspondence at large should be preferentially and supremely (I *did* mean "primarily") the illustration of character, personality, life etc.: *that* taking the first line, and the illustration of growth of opinions, philosophic evolution etc., the second. Also that I shall rejoice with all my heart and soul to give you all the aid and light and support in my power.

24th P.M.

There I stopped this A.M., and here I must stop again, though there are two or three things to add. One of these is that I feel upset indeed at your allusion to poor Pinker's having perhaps prevailed upon me to "give up" the Family Book! Please banish from your mind every view of my relation with him in which his having anything to say to the nature of my work itself, or to what it shall or shan't be, or may or may not consist of or how or not proceed in any degree, figures. He would never in the world presume to cross any such line, nor should I dream of allowing him to—our relations are altogether on the other side of it: on the basis of my own stuff done in my own way, where his cognizance of it only begins. I groan over the thought of the alarm and delusion into which I must indeed have bedeviled you by my inadvertance of expression, when you add that you would have been, for it, already to come straight over. Truly you must have mistrusted me and deeply must I have misled you! There is a bitterness in that—and I think how, all this year, through all the difficulties of condition, and they have again and again been extreme, though now at last, thank God, much abated, I have had but the one thought of filling the measure of your content, that of all of you, to the brim. It has been *the* thing that has kept me going! But all's well that ends well—for the end of all *will* be; and that, dearest Harry, is what I shall do still.

. . .

Yours, dearest Harry, all affectionately

Henry James

1. The plan to serialize *A Small Boy and Others* was abandoned.

To Henry James III
Ms Harvard

Lamb House, Rye
November 25*th* 1912

Dearest Harry.

. . .

What gnaws at me most of all is that the Books, First and Second, are so waiting for my power of attention to be able to play at all. The first one, of course, very much less than the second; inasmuch as the first is in Scribner's hands all but about twenty-five or thirty pages of Finis, which, however, can be got off to him within ten days after my finally shaking free of this horror.[1] As regards the other, the second, *Notes of a Son and Brother*, it is of course, as I have already, as I sometime since, assured you, not in the least as yet in the Scribner's hands at all, nor with the singlest stroke of a contract drawn about it, or possible to be for a great many weeks to come and after the publication of the other is well out of the way. (The other, containing not a single reproduced letter from anyone, is to be published at the very earliest possible date of the New Year; though the question of date will have suffered somewhat from this cruel interruption of my power of attention.) I wish I could persuade you to a little greater confidence, through all these heavy troubles of mine, in my proceeding with the utmost consideration for—well, whatever you want most to be considered; and I shall feel this confidence most, and most happily and operatively profit by it, if you won't ask me too much in advance, or at any rate now for some time to come, to formulate to you the *detail* of my use, of my conversion into part of the substance of my book, of your Dad's Letters; which will have to wait so, as to the quantity and variety etc. in which they figure, on their relation, from point to point, to the whole, and to the rest of my ingredients. In a thing intended to be intensely a work of art if there ever was one shrinks from the danger of too fixed prestatement and pre-measurement, of cutting oneself off from adjustment and plastic "handling" as one goes. What does strike me is that I may be hampered for space to use them in whatever way, by partial citation, or occasional entire quoting, beyond any such degree even as I had originally allowed for: I want so to do as much for our Father as I can and shall strain my material for some figure of *him* by quotation, evocation, description, to the last possible point. This, with everything else I have desired to "evoke," threatens to eat up space; and one thing is at any rate already quite apparent, that I have more of the Letters a good many, than I can use, individually, even in the most merely allusive and foreshortened way. But let me off—your letter in fact explicitly and mercifully does, dearest Harry—from any specified reassurances now; I am not fit to make them, and the sense of having so much to report myself is, frankly, oppressive and blighting. Don't *insist*, but trust me as far as you can; and I think that even given the utmost conceivable play, within me, of any fond devotion to my matter, the subject as a whole, that is the total fusion of the ingredients, won't suffer by it. As for the question of the Scribners' announcement of the two Parts, I am sorry it has worried you, and if my recent state had left me my wits more about me, I should have warned you by this time against taking any heed of that. It was a mere publisher's piece of precipitation and "enterprise," on the entirely uncontracted *talk* that had taken place during the time immediately after my mistake of letting them hear of the Book (the second) by the title I at first fancied. They then expressed a great desire to be able to serialise two specimen parts of that volume; and they were told that I should be perfectly willing (the pecuniary bribe being great) to prepare such a couple. This set them on advertising the fact after their own fashion and in their own terms; but they are now left with their advertisement *in that form* on their hands, and you need trouble no further about it. Any contract that will pass with me, through Pinker's care, will be a contract for the Book which I mentioned (*Notes of a Son and Brother*) to be made up exactly in such proportions, out of "Family ingredients," that seem to me good; and with the first proviso in the agreement to the effect that all property in any Letters or parts of Letters of your Dad therein embodied, shall reside wholly with your Mother, with such liberty to publish and republish whenever and wherever she shall choose. I have agreed to supply two parts for serialisation of that so-named volume in advance;[2] to be compounded exactly as I shall choose; and I don't see what damage this can do to the future of your Dad's Correspondence as a whole. The degree in which the element of his Letters shall figure in either of the parts is entirely within my discretion; and to attempt to give you pledges about that now would fill me with a sad sense rather that, for some reason, you wish me to get the minimum benefit of that blest material, rather than the blest maximum (compatible with the interests of the whole various Book) that I supposed, so fondly, to be at the bottom of your entrusting me with the Letters at all. However, let me not thus rather wearily and blightedly and difficultly talk as if I didn't feel that everything would turn out utterly for the best . . . Your all-affectionate old uncle

Henry James

1. HJ was suffering from his prolonged attack of shingles.
2. The plan to serialize *Notes of a Son and Brother* was later abandoned.

To Henry James III
Ms Harvard

Lamb House, Rye
November 15–18, 1913

Dearest Harry.

. . .

That my procedure, as applied, has been a mistake from the point of view of the independant giving to the world of your Father's correspondence as a whole I entirely agree—in the light of what you tell me of the effect on you of the *cumulative* impression you get from individual retouchings often repeated; or rather that I apprehend you at the best *must,* from the Cambridge things even, alone—in the absence of your entering into the only attitude and state of feeling that was possible to me by my mode of work, and which was one so distinct, by its whole "ethic" and aesthetic (and indeed its aesthetic, however discredited to you in fact, *was* simply its ethic) from what I should have felt my function in handling my material as an instalment merely of the great correspondence itself, just a contribution, an initial one, to the long continuity of *that.* Then the case would have been for me absolutely of the plainest— my own ethic, with no aesthetic whatever concerned in the matter, would have been the ideal of documentary exactitude, verbatim, *literatim et punctuatim*—free of all living back imaginatively, or of any of the affects of this, into one's earliest and most beguiling, and most unspeakable (for actual explainings and justifyings) contemporaneities with the writer. I should have fallen away I trust at no point, in that task, from the high standard of *rigid* editing which would have been the sole law of the matter, with no relations for the letters but their relation to their utter text, and no superstition playing over them for me but that of entire or pedantic conformity. But that wasn't in the least what I felt my job, from its very germ; my superstitions were wholly other, and playing, such as they were, at every point—the part of my matter, my *book-matter,* that the letters, with my father's, with your Uncle Wilky's and even with some of my brother Bob's and sister Alice's, as I fallaciously hoped (for these last) were to constitute, was in a related state to innumerable *other* things, the things I was to do my book *for,* which were all of the essence of the artistic ideal that hovered before me, and all tainted, as I am afraid you will call it, with that conception of an *atmosphere* which I invoked as, artistically speaking, my guiding star. By so much as atmosphere would have nothing to say—as a determinant—to any concern with the presentation of the correspondence as a whole, by so much did it have everything to say to my sense of the little backwater of the past in which my scant bundle might play its part (and in reference to this scant bundle I beg you to dissociate the Brazil series from the operation of my remark; I had been expectantly sceptical about *them* from the first, through failing to see what comment I could arrive at to accompany, or make a setting for, them; I was sceptical even in writing, or rather cabling, to you for them the other day—I then thought I might use, under stress, but a few pages of them at the most; which I couldn't explain in a cable. I was most of all sceptical in dictating them over speculatively, fourteen months ago, here, among the horrid premonitions of my illness of last autumn—I mean my so long *acute* one—and which I was thereby so unable to get into any closer quarters with composition that that quasi-mechanical Brazil dealing helped to *tromper* a little my dismal consciousness of not making head. You may say "Why in the world, if you didn't expect to use them, did you then take dictating liberties with them?"—and I will tell you later on how this came exactly from a desperation of *nervousness* in the whole connection, a positive anguish, given the way I was feeling, and which I tried with that practical futility to work off.)

It is very difficult, and even pretty painful, to try to put forward after the fact the considerations and emotions that have been intense for one in the long ferment of an artistic process; but I must nevertheless do something toward making you see a little perhaps how what strikes you as so deplorable an aberration—I mean the editing of those earliest things, other than "rigidly," had for me a sort of exquisite inevitability. From the moment of those of my weeks in Cambridge of 1911 during which I began, by a sudden turn to talk with your Mother, to dally with the idea of a "Family Book," this idea took on for me a particular light, the light which hasn't varied, through all sorts of discomfitures and difficulties and disillusionments, and in which in fact I have put the thing through. That turn of talk was the germ, it dropped the seed—once when I had been "reminiscing" over some matters of your Dad's and my old life of the time previous, far previous, to her knowing us, over some memories of our Father and Mother and the rest of us. I had moved her to exclaim with the most generous appreciation and response, "Oh Henry, why don't you *write* these things?"—with such an effect that after a bit I found myself wondering vaguely whether I *mightn't* do something of the sort. But it dated from those words of your Mother's, which gave me the impulse and determined the spirit of my vision—a spirit and a vision as far removed as possible from my mere isolated documentation of your Father's record. We talked again, and still again, of the "Family Book," and by the time I came away I felt I had somehow found my inspiration, though the idea could only be most experimental, and all at the mercy of my putting it, perhaps defeatedly, to the proof. It was such a very special and delicate and discriminated thing to do, and only governable by proprieties and considerations all of its own, as I should evidently, in the struggle with it, more and more find. This is what I did find above all in coming at last to work these Cambridge letters into the whole harmony of my text—the general purpose of which was to be a reflection of all the amenity and felicity of our young life of that time at the highest pitch that was consistent with perfect truth—to show us all at our best for characteristic expression and colour and variety and everything that would be charming. And when I laid hands upon the letters to use as so many touches and tones in the picture I frankly confess I seemed to see them in a better, or at all events in another light, here and there, than those rough and rather illiterate copies I had from you showed at their face value. I found myself again in such close relation with your Father, such a revival of relation as I hadn't known since his death, and which was a passion of tenderness for doing the best thing by him that the material allowed, and which I seemed to feel him in the room and at my elbow asking me for as I worked and as he listened. It was as if he had said to me on seeing me lay my hands on the weak little relics of our common youth, "Oh but you're not going to give me away, to hand me over, in my raggedness and my poor accidents, quite unhelped, unfriended, you're going to do the very best for me you *can*, aren't you, and since you appear to be making such claims for me you're going to let me seem to justify them as much as I possibly may?" And it was as if I kept spiritually replying to this that he might indeed trust me to handle him with the last tact and devotion—that is do with him everything I seemed to feel him *like*, for being kept up to the amenity pitch. These were small things, the very smallest, they appeared to me all along to be, tiny amendments in order of words, degrees of emphasis etc., to the end that he should be more easily and engagingly readable and thereby more tasted and liked—from the moment there was no excess of these *soins* and no violence done to his real identity. Everything the letters meant affected me so, in all the business, as of *our* old world only, mine and his alone together, with every item of it intimately known and remembered by me, that I daresay I did instinctively regard it at last as all *my* truth, to do what I would with. In point of fact I don't think I did very much that matters *unfortunately*, because for a reason that I will presently tell you I can't compare my text in the printer's hands—that is my copies—with the originals. At the same time I have no doubt that if you do make the comparison, in detail, yourself, I shall strike you as having been much more excessive—as to changes—than I intended. I imagine that if none of them can be very grave you may find they are, in their slightness, pretty frequent. This I couldn't judge of or keep account as I went, and I am perfectly willing therefore that my effect on the pages embodied shall be pronounced a mistake—that I quite inevitably, by my irrepressible "aesthetic," lost the right reckoning, the measure of my *quantity* of amendment, and that this makes my course practically an aberration. Yet I think I am none the less right as to the passages hanging better together so with my own text, and "melting" so with my own atmosphere, than if my superstition had been, as I said above, of the opposite and the absolutely hands-off kind. And the case is really that if it had been for me, from the first, of that hands-off kind, by a foreseen necessity, that consideration would have begun, *could* only have begun, further back and warned me from *any* sort of reproduction. *That* really will have been my mistake, I feel—there it will have begun; in thinking that with so literary, so compositional, an obsession as my whole bookmaking impulse is governed by, any mere merciless transcript might have been possible to me. I have to the last point the instinct and the sense for fusions and interrelations, for framing and encircling (as I think I have already called it) every part of my stuff in every other—and that makes a danger when the frame and circle play over too much upon the image. Never again shall I stray from my proper work—the one in which that danger is the reverse of one and becomes a rightness and a beauty. But strange is the "irony of fate" that has made the very intensity of my tenderness on your Dad's behalf a stumbling-block and an offense—for the sad thing is I think you're right in being offended. I could only dictate my transcript in all the rest of my condition, with emotion and imagination, and those things misled and betrayed me . . .

. . .

I may mention however that your exception that particularly caught my eye—to "poor old Abraham" for "poor old Abe"—was a case for change that I remember feeling wholly irresistible. Never, *never*, under our Father's roof did we talk of Abe, either *tout court* or as "Abe Lincoln"—it wasn't *conceivable:* Abraham Lincoln he was for us, when he wasn't either Lincoln or Mr. Lincoln (the Western note and the popularization of "Abe" were quite away from us *then*): and the form of the name in your Dad's letter made me *reflect:* how off, how *far* off in his queer other company than ours, I must at the time have felt him to be. You will say that this was just a reason for leaving it so—and so in a sense it was. But I could *hear* him say Abraham and couldn't hear him say Abe, and the former came back to me as sincere, also graver and tenderer and more like ourselves, among whom I couldn't image any "Abe" ejaculation under the shock of his death as possible. I can't help thinking this one of many such things (as motives of my small changes) as to which my long backward perspective is as right—as it takes one far to follow—as it surely is again in respect to some remark on your sheets of comment about our talking in "jolly." My recollection of that time is that we never talked in anything *else;* we had known in our time abroad nothing *but* jolly—we should have had nothing at all if we hadn't had it; and I remember no moment and no influence for our foreswearing it. Surely all our colloquy with T. S. Perry for instance bristled with it—and at one time half our whole colloquy was with *him.* William Hunt and John La Farge overflowed with it—and in short I can only say that, letters in hand, I must have found myself affectionately missing it. However, I am not pretending to pick up any particular challenge to my appearance of wantonness—I should be able to justify myself (*when* able) only out of such abysses of association, and the stirring up of these, for vindication, is simply a strain that stirs up tears.

. . .

Yours, dearest Harry, all affectionately,

Henry James

Appendix IV
"A Curse Not Less Explicit Than Shakespeare's Own"

In his tale "The Aspern Papers," Henry James told the world of his conviction that private letters should be burned. His own burning of forty years' accumulation of letters and manuscripts is described in this volume (see letter to Mrs. J. T. Fields, 2 January 1910). He felt happy about this "gigantic bonfire" even though he knew he was burning letters received from others, not those he himself had written.

Early in 1914 Harry James, his nephew and executor, asked him about his papers. In a letter almost as long as a short story, dealing with many other matters—his health, his personal affairs, his work and family matters—he incorporated a passage asking his nephew to act as "a check and a frustrator" of posthumous publication of his correspondence. He had once said that it was a writer's own responsibility to clear "the approaches" to his privacy. He recognized that the rest was a matter for vigilance by his heirs. James had seen during his long life what happened to the papers of other famous men, and he had often reviewed, with interest and sympathy, published volumes of literary remains.

In the excerpt given here, James's pronouncing of Shakespeare's curse on future publishers of his letters refers to the well-known lines on Shakespeare's tomb at Stratford-on-Avon:

> Blest be ye man yt spares these stones
> And curst be he yt moves my bones.

This is the only passage in James's letter to his nephew dealing with his private papers. He did not include the promised directive in his will. Immediately after his death, Mrs. William James began seeking an editor to publish a selection from his letters (as described in the Introduction to *Letters* I).

Henry James III, during the next quarter of a century, tended to follow his uncle's directive. He considered Percy Lubbock's edition sufficient for all purposes. He refused requests for publication of certain of James's letters unless they contained material of distinct literary interest, and he stipulated that the archive he gave to Harvard should be available only to postdoctoral researchers.

To Henry James III
Ms Harvard

21 Carlyle Mansions S.W.
7 April 1914

Dearest Harry.

. . .

I am greatly touched, dear Harry, by your interest in the other question you speak of—that of my own "literary remains" and my liability to the invading chronicler. It has often occupied my mind—though never yet to the effect of my trying to provide against it (and, much less, to provide *for* it) by some anticipatory clause. My sole wish is to frustrate as utterly as possible the post-mortem exploiter—which, I know, is but so imperfectly possible. Still, one can do something, and I have long thought of launching, by a provision in my will, a curse not less explicit than Shakespeare's own on any such as try to move my bones. Your question determines me definitely to advert to the matter in my will—that is to declare my utter and absolute abhorrence of any attempted biography or the giving to the world by "the family," or by any person for whom my disapproval has any sanctity, of any part or parts of my private correspondence. One can discredit and dishonour such enterprises even if one can't prevent them, and as you are my sole and exclusive literary heir and executor you will doubtless be able to serve in some degree as a check and a frustrator. If I am myself able to live on and work a while longer I probably *shall* perpetrate a certain number more passages of retrospect and reminiscence—though quite disconnectedly from these two recent volumes, which are complete in themselves and of which the original intention is now a performed and discharged thing; that of producing some picture of the medium and atmosphere in which your Dad and I drew breath and grew up together during the far-off juvenile years previous to the time at which his earlier Letters begin. I wanted to give above all *his* young background, and now there it *is,* given. Anything more I do in the memorizing line will be an evocation of *Choses Vues* (Victor Hugo's formula is so good!) in my own later connections altogether—though I confess that something of the appeal of the period from 1869 to the beginning of my life in London (the rest of *that* making a history by itself altogether) *does* a good deal hang about me.

. . .

[Henry James]

Appendix V
The Deathbed Dictation

It has long been known that Henry James, after his first and second strokes in December 1915, called for his typist, Theodora Bosanquet, and told her to take dictation. The familiar Remington machine was brought into James's bedroom. He was in a semidelirious state but was capable of mobilizing for the work he unconsciously intended. The doctors felt that the routine forms of his dictation might relieve anxieties and enable him to rest more easily. James first called for Miss Bosanquet on December 8, six days after the onset of his final illness. On that day he dictated the first portion quite clearly. Three days later, on Saturday the 11th, during a day of much mental confusion, he dictated a second passage. On the next day, December 12th, before lunch he dictated a passage about motoring, apparently some recollection of his trips with Edith Wharton. "After luncheon," Miss Bosanquet's diary records, "he wanted me again and dictated, perfectly clearly and coherently, two letters from Napoleon Bonaparte to one of his married sisters—I suspect they weren't original composition but subconscious memory—one letter about the decoration of the Louvre and the other about some great opportunity being offered them which they mustn't fall below the level of. After he finished the second letter, he seemed quite satisfied not to do any more and fell into a peaceful sleep."

Actually the first letter was the one to which James affixed the name Napoléone—with an "e" ending (he dictated always certain spellings), the Emperor's original Corsican name. The second letter, written in the Imperial style, carried his own name and seems to have been intended for his brother William and his sister-in-law Alice.

We have no record of the dates of the final fragments, which were set down on succeeding days whenever James called for his typist. When she was not there, his niece Peggy filled in, writing in longhand. But he dictated only a few sentences or even phrases; some-

808

times he was inaudible. By the end of December he ceased to dictate. Occasionally Mrs. William James observed his hand moving across his bedcover as if he were writing. He died at the end of February.

The text reproduced here is from the copy I took of the original document in the autumn of 1937 when Henry James III gave me access to the James papers, then in the basement of the Widener Library. At some later time, James's nephew decided that the original should be destroyed, since it showed his uncle's mind in a state of disintegration. He did not know that my copy existed. I printed it twenty years after his death in the *Times Literary Supplement*, 2 May 1968, and in the June 1968 *Atlantic Monthly*, and I gave an account of it in the final volume of my life of Henry James. By the time I published it, portions of the dictation had been read by Miss Bosanquet over the BBC in a program devoted to James, and allusions were on occasion encountered to James's "Napoleonic fragment." As long ago as 1927, when Pelham Edgar of the University of Toronto published his pioneering book *Henry James: Man and Author*, the existence of the dictation was known, for Edgar wrote that it contained a letter "couched in the genuine Imperial style, succinct and dictatorial, with comment in the most highly developed Jamesian manner on the complexities of the Napoleonic problem."

Following is the text of Henry James's final dictation:

[8 December 1915]
I find the business of coming round about as important and glorious as any circumstance I have had occasion to record, by which I mean that I find them as damnable and as boring. It is not much better to discover within one's carcase new resources for application than to discover the absence of them; their being new doesn't somehow add at all to their interest but makes them stale and flat, as if one had long ago exhausted them. Such is my sketchy state of mind, but I feel sure I shall discover plenty of fresh worlds to conquer, even if I am to be cheated of the amusement of them.

[11 December 1915]
Wondrous enough certainly to have a finger in such a concert and to feel ourselves touch the large old phrase into the right amplitude. It had shrunken and we add to its line—all we can scarce say how,

save that we couldn't have left it. We simply shift the sweet nursling of genius from one maternal breast to the other and the trick is played, the false note averted. Astounding little stepchild of God's astounding young stepmother!

. . . on this occasion moreover that having been difficult to keep step, we hear of the march of history, what is remaining to that essence of tragedy the limp? We scarce avoid rolling, with all these famished and frustrate women in the wayside dust . . . mere patchwork transcription becomes of itself the high brave art. We [word missing—the typist apparently could not make out what he said] five miles off at the renewed affronts that we see coming for the great, and that we know they will accept. The fault is that they had found themselves too easily great, and the effect of that, definitely, had been, within them, the want of long provision for it. It wasn't why *they* [were] to have been so thrust into the limelight and the uproar, but why they [were] to have known as by inspiration the trade most smothered in experience. They go about shivering in the absence of the holy protocol as in the—they dodder sketchily about—as in the betrayal of the lack of early advantages; and it is upon *that* they seem most to depend to give them distinction—it is upon that, and upon the *crânerie* and the *rouerie* that they seem most to depend for the grand air of gallantry. They pluck in their terror handfuls of plumes from the imperial eagle, and with no greater credit in consequence than that they face, keeping their equipoise, the awful bloody beak that he turns round upon them. We see the beak sufficiently directed in that vindictive intention, during these days of cold grey Switzerland weather, on the huddled and hustled campaigns of the first omens of defeat. Everyone looks haggard and our only wonder is that they still succeed in "looking" at all. It renews for us the assurance of the part played by that element in the famous assurance [divinity] that doth hedge a king.

[12 December 1915]

We squeeze together into some motorcar or other and we so talk and talk that what comes of it.—Yes, that is the turn of public affairs. Next statement is for all the world as if we had brought it on and had given our push and our touch to great events. The Bonapartes have a kind of bronze distinction that extends to their finger-tips and is a great source of charm in the women. Therefore they don't have to swagger after the fact; fortune has placed them too high and anything less would be trivial. You can believe anything of the Queen of Naples or of the Princess Caroline Murat. There have been great families of tricksters and conjurors; so why not this one, and so pleasant withal? Our admirable father keeps up the pitch. He is the dearest of men. I should have liked above all things seeing our sister pulling her head through the crown; one has that confident—and I should have had it most on the day when most would have been asked. But we jog on very well. Up to the point of the staircase where the officers do stand it couldn't be better, though I wonder at the *souffle* which so often enables me to pass. We are back from [word lost] but we breathe at least together and I am, devotedly yours

[12 December 1915, P.M.]
Dear and most esteemed brother and sister,
    I call your attention to the precious enclosed transcripts of plans and designs for the decoration of certain apartments of the palaces, here, of the Louvre and the Tuileries, which you will find addressed in detail to artists and workmen who are to take them in hand. I commit them to your earnest care till the questions relating to this important work are fully settled. When that is the case I shall require of you further zeal and further taste. For the present the course is definitely marked out, and I beg you to let me know from stage to stage definitely how the scheme promises, and what results it may be held to inspire. It is, you will see, of a great scope, a majesty unsurpassed by any work of the kind yet undertaken in France. Please understand I regard these plans as fully developed and as having had my last consideration and look forward to no patchings nor perversions, and with no question of modifications either economic or aesthetic. This will be the case with all further projects of your affectionate

Napoléone

My dear brother and sister,
    I offer you great opportunities in the exchange for the exercise of great zeal. Your position as residents of our young but so highly considered Republic at one of the most interesting minor capitals is a piece of luck which may be turned to account in the measure

of your acuteness and experience. A brilliant fortune may come to crown it and your personal merit will not diminish that harmony. But you must rise to each occasion—the one I now offer you is of no common cast, and please remember that any failure to push your advantage to the utmost will be severely judged. I have displayed you as persons of great taste and great judgment. Don't leave me a sorry figure in consequence but present me rather as your very fond but not infatuated relation able and ready to back you up, your faithful brother and brother-in-law

Henry James

[Undated]

across the border
all the pieces

Individual souls, great . . . of [word lost] on which great perfections are If one does . . . in the fulfilment with the neat and pure and perfect—to the success or as he or she moves through life, following admiration unfailing [word lost] in the highway—Problems are very sordid.

One of the earliest of the consumers of the great globe in the interest of the attraction exercised by the great R.L.S. [Robert Louis Stevenson] of those days, comes in, afterwards, a visitor at Vailima and [word lost] there and pious antiquities to his domestic annals.

These final and faded remarks all have some interest and some character—but this should be extracted by a highly competent person only—some such, whom I don't presume to name, will furnish such last offices. In fact I do without names not wish to exaggerate the defect of their absence. Invoke more than one kind presence, several could help, and many would—but it all better too much left than too much done. I never dreamed of such duties as laid upon me. This sore throaty condition is the last I ever invoked for the purpose.

Appendix VI
Holdings of Henry James's Letters

No census of Henry James's letters has been made; it would be a considerable task. Published letters are listed in Edel and Laurence, *A Bibliography of Henry James* (1957), in the Soho Bibliographies.

The list given here includes libraries with substantial holdings of James letters, but also some institutions where a few miscellaneous letters are to be found. Where there are more than fifty letters an approximate number is given. The list is extensive but not exhaustive. It does not include private holdings; some indication of the existing letters in private hands is given below.

Abernethy Library of American Literature, Middlebury College, Middlebury, Vermont: miscellaneous.

American Academy–Institute of Arts and Letters, New York: letters from HJ and WJ relating to membership in the Institute and the Academy.

Archives of American Art, Washington: Francis B. Millet family, Walter Gay.

George Arents Research Library, Syracuse, New York: miscellaneous.

Bancroft Library, University of California, Berkeley: Bruce Porter Collection (Peggy James married Bruce Porter): 158 typescripts of letters, the originals of which are in other collections. Gelett Burgess, Hamlin Garland, Julie Heyneman.

C. Waller Barrett Collection, University of Virginia; Hamilton Aïdé, Hendrik C. Andersen (77—of which inaccurate typescripts exist in the Library of Congress and the British Library), Grace Carter, Theodore E. Child, Sir John Clark, Alvin Langdon Coburn, W. Morton Fullerton, Edmund Gosse, Alice Stopford Green, Violet Hunt, André Raffalovich, Mrs. Humphry Ward (60), Joseph Conrad, Daniel Curtis.

University of Basel, Switzerland: the Clara and Clare Benedict papers.

The Henry W. and Albert A. Berg Collection of English and American Literature, New York Public Library, Astor, Lenox and Tilden Foundations: a few letters to the Stephen family, Sir Edward Marsh, Lady Gregory, miscellaneous.

Biblioteca Marucelliana, Florence: miscellaneous.

Bodleian Library, Oxford: H. G. Wells; Sydney Lee, A. C. Benson; Lord Bryce, miscellaneous.

Boston Public Library: miscellaneous.

British Library, formerly British Museum: William Archer, Matilda Betham-Edwards, Edmund Gosse, Macmillan and Company archive (131), W. Barclay Squire, miscellaneous.

Brotherton Collection Library, The University, Leeds, U.K.: Edmund Gosse papers (334), Clement Shorter.

Brown University, John Hay Library, Providence, Rhode Island: John Hay papers (52); Whitelaw Reid.

Cheshire Records Office, Chester, Cheshire, U.K.: Rhoda Broughton (67).

Colby College Library, Waterville, Maine: Thomas Sergeant Perry (125), Gosse, Violet Paget (Vernon Lee), miscellaneous. (Some of the letters to Perry printed in the Harlow biography of Perry are not in this collection. See Duke University.)

Columbia University, Butler Library: Margaret Brooke, Cora Crane, Emma Lazarus, Brander Matthews, miscellaneous.

Library of Congress: Gosse, George Harvey, Manton Marble papers, Joseph Pennell, Logan Pearsall Smith, Henry White papers, Owen Wister, Sarah Butler Wister, miscellaneous.

Cornell University Library: miscellaneous.

Dartmouth University, Baker Library: Daniel and Ariana Curtis (96).

Duke University Library, Durham, North Carolina: microfilm of some of the letters to T. S. Perry not at Colby; copies of Gosse letters; miscellaneous.

East Sussex Records Office, U.K.: miscellaneous.

Edward L. Doheny Memorial Library, St. John's Seminary, Camarillo, California: miscellaneous.

Gardner Museum, Fenway Court, Boston: Isabella Stewart Gardner (100).

Glasgow, University Library, U.K.: James McNeill Whistler.

Hillstead Museum, Farmington, Connecticut: Theodate Pope Riddle.

Harvard University, Houghton Library: The collections in the Houghton Library constitute the fundamental archive. The James family papers were presented to Harvard by Henry James III, who was executor for both his father, William James, and his uncle Henry. The initial gift included 448 of the novelist's letters to various members of the family, 295 to WJ, and 815 to other correspondents. It also included 487 letters to James from family and friends. The novelist kept very few others after burning his papers. Among those preserved were 25 letters from Robert Louis Stevenson, 15 from Turgenev, 7 from Henry Adams, 34 from Howells, 13 from C. E. Norton, 90 from Paul Bourget, and 41 from George du Maurier. In many instances James preserved a single letter from a correspondent. Some of these were among the papers of his sister Alice, to whom he had given them as autographs. To this collection Henry James III added gifts of letters from HJ to Frances P. Morse, Theodora Sedgwick, Elizabeth and Francis Boott, and Mrs. Cadwalader Jones. Other correspondents later gave their letters to the archive, and still other letters were obtained by purchase or gift. The James archive was enlarged when the Houghton Library obtained the Houghton Mifflin papers and the papers of other New England figures, as for instance the Lowell and Norton papers, which include HJ's letters to Grace Norton.

Percy Lubbock presented to the Houghton Library some of the transcripts of letters he had gathered while editing the two volumes published in 1920. His Italian villa was occupied by German troops during the Second World War, and his copies of letters before 1881 were destroyed. Those remaining cover 1881 to 1894, 1900 to 1908, and 1911 to 1915. The originals of many of these are in other collections; but in some cases Lubbock's transcripts—made for him by Miss Bosanquet—provide the only text available. Thus more than 60 letters to Mrs. W. K. Clifford and 23 letters to Alice Dew-Smith exist at present only in Lubbock, as well as the very few extant letters to Jonathan Sturges.

A breakdown of the most important Houghton Library holograph holdings follows: Jessie Allen (181), Anna Balestier, Elizabeth Boott (83), Francis Boott (52), Theodora Bosanquet (68), Witter Bynner, Joseph Conrad, Augustin F. Daly, Alphonse Daudet, the Emmet cousins, W. Morton Fullerton (60) (other Fullerton letters are in the Princeton and Barrett collections), the Godkins (53), Oliver Wendell Holmes, Jr., W. J. Hoppin, Houghton Mifflin (64), W. D.

Howells (131), Ford Madox Hueffer (Ford), Mrs. George Hunter, George Abbot James (59), Rudyard Kipling, Gaillard Lapsley, James Russell Lowell, Manton Marble, Urbain Mengin, C. C. Hoyer Millar and family, Burgess Noakes, Charles Eliot Norton (57), Elizabeth Norton, Grace Norton (126), Jocelyn Persse (78), Sir George and Fanny Prothero (144), Henrietta Reubell (106), Anne Thackeray Ritchie, William Rothenstein, William Roughead, Horace Scudder, Howard Sturgis (101), the J. J. Garth Wilkinson papers. Family letters were augmented by the letters to Henry James III and Margaret Mary James. The letters to William (Billy) James are privately held.

Hove, Sussex, Central Library: Viscount and Lady Wolseley (91).

Henry E. Huntington Library, San Marino, California: Edward Warren (134), Mrs. J. T. Fields, Hamlin Garland, miscellaneous.

Imperial College Library, London: T. H. Huxley, Lord Playfair, miscellaneous.

Johns Hopkins University, Milton S. Eisenhower Library: miscellaneous.

Joseph Regenstein Library, University of Chicago: Robert Herrick, miscellaneous.

King's College Library, Cambridge: miscellaneous.

Louvenjoul Collection, Chantilly, France: a single letter to Gustave Flaubert.

Massachusetts Historical Society, Boston: Henry Adams, Mrs. Henry Adams, miscellaneous.

Mellon Gallery, Washington: Elizabeth Cameron.

Pierpont Morgan Library, New York: Dr. William Wilberforce Baldwin (74), W. E. Henley, miscellaneous.

New York Historical Society: John La Farge, Margaret Perry La Farge, Ruth Draper.

New York Public Library, Manuscript Division: Church papers (*The Galaxy*), Elizabeth Jordan, Gilder family papers, miscellaneous.

Pennsylvania State University, Pattee Library: miscellaneous.

Pennsylvania, University of, Philadelphia: miscellaneous.

Public Library of the Literary and Philosophical Society, Edinburgh: miscellaneous.

Princeton University, Firestone Library: W. Morton Fullerton, Scribner archive (correspondence concerning the New York Edition), miscellaneous.

Rochester, University of, Rush Rhees Library: miscellaneous.
Rutgers University Library, New Brunswick, New Jersey: miscellaneous.
Scotland, The National Library: Lord Rosebery, Blackwood papers, Graham Balfour, André Raffalovich, George M. Smith, miscellaneous.
Texas, University of, at Austin, Humanities Research Center: Elizabeth Robins (143), Sir Hugh Walpole (75), Lady Bell (69), Compton Mackenzie, Mr. and Mrs. Waldo Story, miscellaneous.
Tate Gallery, London: Charleston papers.
Trinity College, Cambridge: Lord Houghton.
University of Newcastle upon Tyne Library, England: Sir George Otto Trevelyan and Lady Trevelyan.
Watkinson Library, Hartford, Connecticut: miscellaneous.
Yale University, Beinecke Rare Book and Manuscript Library: Robert Louis Stevenson; W. E. Norris; Edith Wharton (177); Sir Sidney and Lady Colvin (54); F. A. Duneka; D. A. Munro; James B. Pinker (379).

Letters from HJ to the following correspondents were seen in private collections, which may subsequently have changed hands or been presented to institutions: George Alexander, Sir Lawrence Alma-Tadema, Paul and Minnie Bourget (63), Henry Brewster, Edward Lee Childe, Katherine De Kay Bronson (59), Mme Alphonse Daudet, Mary Anderson (Mrs. Antonio de Navarro), Herbert Dunster, Gertrude Elliott (Lady Forbes-Robertson), Sir George Henschel, Dana Horton, Mrs. Charles Hunter (61), Edward Holton James, Robert Underwood Johnson, Elizabeth Lady Lewis, Antonio de Navarro, Angelina Milman, F. W. H. Myers, Edith Contessa Rucellai, Ethel Sands, Mrs. Mahlon Sands, Emily Sargent, Arthur Sedgwick, Clare Sheridan, Clement Shorter, Sir Sidney Waterlow, Mary Weld. The Robertson James papers were made available by the late Mary James Vaux; they are now owned by her son, Henry James Vaux.

Index

825

Ward, Mrs. Humphry—*Cont.*
115, 185–187, 242–243,
413–416
Ward, Nelson, 761, 771
Ward, Sam and Medora, 670
Ward, Samuel G. and Mrs.,
260–261, 669
Warren, Alice Bartlett, 260
Warren, Edward P., 3, 63, 114,
153, 168; letters to, 56, 98–99,
276–278, 355–356
Waterlow, Alice (Pollock), 437
Waterlow, Sydney, 436–437; let-
ter to, 570–571
Weld, Mary, 4, 180; letter to, 267
Wells, H. G., xxxi, 179, 440, 610,
773; *The Time Machine,*
132–133; *Mankind in the Mak-
ing,* 303–304, 378n; *Twelve
Stories and a Dream,* 304n;
Kipps, 377–379, 383, 399; *A
Modern Utopia,* 377–379, 383;
Anticipations, 378n; *The Future
in America,* 420–421, 425; *Marriage,* 629n, 635–636; *The Passionate Friends,* 687n; *Sir Isaac
Harman's Wife,* 730; *Boon, The
Mind of the Race, The Wild
Asses of the Devil, and the
Last Trump,* 766–770; letters
to, 85–87, 132–133, 303–305,
377–380, 420–422, 561–562,
607–610, 635–637, 686–688,
766–770
Wendell, Barrett, 20–21, 661
West, Rebecca, xiv
Wharton, Edith, xxi–xxix, xxx,
104, 180, 222, 237–238, 325,
335, 363, 388, 401, 432–433,
435, 441, 473, 506, 525, 526,
545, 550, 558–559, 563, 569,
581–582, 600n, 620–623, 626n,
671, 720, 727, 735, 754, 773,
774, 789–790, 808; *The House
of Mirth,* xxii, 346, 373–374,
387; *The Fruit of the Tree,*

xxviii, 461–462, 476; "The Line
of Least Resistance," 170n; *The
Valley of Decision,* 235, 237;
Crucial Instances, 237n; *The
Touchstone,* 237n; "The Moving
Finger," 238n; *A Backward
Glance,* 441n, 701n, 754n;
Ethan Frome, 588; *The Reef,*
615n, 643–646, 650; *The Custom of the Country,* 649n; *The
Book of the Homeless,* 729n,
773n; letters to, 170–171,
234–236, 333–335, 340–343,
346–348, 373–377, 384–387,
399–400, 455–459, 461–463,
475–477, 485–488, 494–495,
509–510, 518–519, 521–522,
527–528, 529–531, 537–540,
545–546, 554–555, 557–558,
572–574, 587–588, 590–593,
602–605, 614–616, 643–646,
701–704, 715–716, 721–724,
740–744
Wharton, Edward (Teddy), xxiii,
376, 401, 433, 441, 494n, 519,
550, 563, 573, 615n, 671; letter
to, 455–459
Whistler, James Abbott McNeill:
letters to, 41, 43, 199
White, Mr. and Mrs. Henry, 76,
574
White, Dr. J. William, 335, 338
Whitman, Walt, xxvii
Wiggin, Kate Douglas, 222
Wilde, Oscar, xv, xxiii, 9n, 12n,
25–26; *Lady Windermere's Fan,*
588
Wilkins, Mary Eleanor, 223, 260
Wilkinson, J. J. Garth, 624–625
Wilson, Edmund, xiv, xv, xvi
Wilson, Woodrow, 733, 758
Wister, Owen, 336, 338, 342, 598;
The Virginian, 232–234; letter
to, 232–234, 261
Wister, Sarah Butler, 341, 347;
letter to, 258–262, 335–336